Fodor's
ESSENTIAL
COSTA RICA

D0911429

Welcome to Costa Rica

Little did we realize that the emergence of a novel coronavirus in early 2020 would abruptly bring almost all travel to a halt. Although our Fodor's writers around the world have continued working to bring you the best of the destinations they cover, we still anticipate that more than the usual number of businesses will close permanently in the coming months, perhaps with little advance notice. We don't expect things to return to "normal" for some time. As you plan your upcoming travels to Costa Rica, please confirm that places are still open and let us know when we need to make updates by writing to us at this address: editors@fodors.com.

TOP REASONS TO GO

★ **Active Volcanoes:** Five imposing behemoths exude, fume, seethe, and smolder.

★ **Beaches:** From pristine secluded hideaways to palm-fringed resort strands.

★ **Coffee:** A plantation tour shows you what makes the country tick.

★ **Eco-friendly Hotels:** Wilderness lodges set the standard for green tourism with style.

★ **Outdoor Adventure:** Ziplining, canopy tours, hiking, and surfing are all top-notch.

★ **Wildlife Galore:** Monkeys, sloths, and turtles abound, and the birding is superb.

Contents

Fodor's Features

MAPS

EXPERIENCE COSTA RICA

18 ULTIMATE EXPERIENCES

Costa Rica offers terrific experiences that should be on every traveler's list. Here are Fodor's top picks for a memorable trip.

1 Discover Tropical Paradise at Manuel Antonio National Park

Costa Rica's most famous national park is also its smallest, logging in at a scant 3 square miles on the Central Pacific coast. You'll find some of the country's best beaches here, as well as lodging of all shapes and sizes and terrific dining. *(Ch. 9)*

2 Catch a Glimpse of Rare Birds

Costa Rica is one of the world's premier birding destinations, with hundreds of resident and migratory species like hummingbirds, toucans, and macaws. *(Ch. 10)*

3 Strike a Yoga Pose

Costa Rica is the land of *pura vida* (literally, "pure life"), and yoga retreats around the country offer a nirvana-like experience. *(Ch. 7, 8)*

4 Stand in Awe of Volcán Arenal

Local seismologists refer to Arenal as "resting," but it remains one of the country's five active volcanoes. Its last major eruption took place in 2010. *(Ch. 6)*

5 Go White-Water Rafting

From family-friendly floats to wild multiday adventures, Costa Rica's long, May–November rainy season creates great white-water experiences for rafters and kayakers. *(Ch. 5)*

6 Float with Butterflies

Costa Rica counts 1,500 butterfly species—the most famous is the blue morpho, with its neon wings. Several enclosed, netted gardens around the country showcase these insects. *(Ch. 5)*

7 Gobble Gallo Pinto

Take yesterday's leftover rice, add some black beans, onion, and chopped red pepper. Top with a dollop of sour cream or Salsa Lizano, and you have *gallo pinto*, or "spotted rooster." *(Ch. 4)*

8 Scuba and Snorkel Coral Reefs

Two oceans and 1,465 km (910 miles) of coastline make Costa Rica a popular diving and snorkeling destination. Try the North Pacific's Gulf of Papagayo. *(Ch. 7)*

9 Get Wild in Corcovado National Park

Costa Rica's largest national park is also its most biologically diverse, with tapirs, sloths, jaguars, peccaries, and all four of the country's monkey species. *(Ch. 10)*

10 Soak in a Hot Spring

Ranging from luxurious resorts to roadside rivers, Costa Rica has a collection of hot-springs complexes dotting the area around La Fortuna, thanks to the presence of the Arenal Volcano. *(Ch. 6)*

11 Look into a Smoldering Volcano

The Poás Volcano, about an hour outside San José, lets visitors gaze into a seething cauldron and sulfurous lake. Visit early in the morning for the best views. *(Ch. 5)*

12 Go Surfing on the Nicoya Peninsula

Costa Rica has no shortage of beaches, but nothing tops the Nicoya Peninsula on the north Pacific coast. From hippie beach towns to all-inclusive resorts, there's a place for every skill level. *(Ch. 8)*

13 Witness a Sea Turtle Hatching

Remote Tortuguero, on the north Caribbean coast, is Costa Rica's most famous spot to take in the amazing spectacle of turtle nesting. *(Ch. 11)*

14 Learn About the Origins of Coffee

A handful of coffee estates—Britt, Doka, Don Juan, and Monteverde—offer informative half-day tours and let you see it all, from picking to brewing. *(Ch. 5)*

15 Get Cultured at the Teatro Nacional

San José's Teatro Nacional was built in 1897 as a venue for international operas. Today, the ornate theater offers tours, concerts, plays, and performances. *(Ch. 4)*

16 Get a Bird's-Eye View of the Rain Forest

Costa Rica has hundreds of ziplines, hanging bridges, and even gondolas that take you on a thrilling ride through the forest canopy. *(Ch. 6)*

17 Stay at an Ecolodge

Costa Rica's premier ecolodges offer secluded comfort surrounded by nature. Cabo Matapalo's Lapa Ríos is one of the best. *(Ch. 10)*

18 Celebrate Carnaval on the Caribbean Coast

For a week in October, the Afro-Caribbean port city of Limón is awash in colorful parades and dances. *(Ch. 11)*

WHAT'S WHERE

1 San José. The capital city is increasingly trendy, with great restaurants and nightlife, in addition to fascinating museums dedicated to gold and jade. Almost everyone passes through on their way to the beach or the mountains.

2 The Central Valley. You likely won't linger long in the Central Valley, as it lacks big-name attractions. But there are day-trip possibilities from San José, including exploring mountain villages, rafting through whitewater rapids, and seeing volcanoes.

3 Arenal, Monteverde, and the Northern Lowlands. After zipping along cables through Monteverde Cloud Forest, windsurfing on Lake Arenal, or taking in the Arenal Volcano, reward yourself with a dip in Tabacón Hot Springs.

4 Guanacaste. If you came for beaches, this area is for you. Each has a unique personality: Tamarindo's nightlife is legendary; Avellanas's swells challenge surfers; and the Papagayo Peninsula's all-inclusive resorts provide every creature comfort.

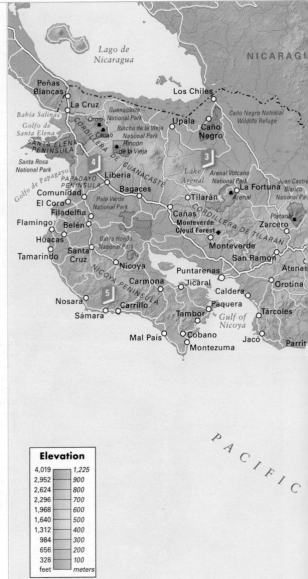

Elevation	
4,019	1,225
2,952	900
2,624	800
2,296	700
1,968	600
1,640	500
1,312	400
984	300
656	200
328	100
feet	meters

5 The Nicoya Peninsula. Still beachy, the southern peninsula gets rave reviews for its lodgings, smaller and more intimate than those farther north up the coast. Nature lovers flock to Nosara, and the twin towns of Malpaís and Santa Teresa have both surfers' digs and luxury villas.

6 Manuel Antonio and the Central Pacific Coast. The area's not just for spring breakers, although it does include funky surf towns like Jacó. The national park, on a peninsula jutting into the ocean, has the easiest wildlife viewing on the planet.

7 The Osa Peninsula and the South Pacific. Rustic lodges in the Osa Peninsula sit on the edge of the country's wildest region, consisting almost entirely of Corcovado National Park. Hikes reveal toucans and scarlet macaws.

8 Tortuguero and the Caribbean Coast. Come here for the spirited music, the tasty Afro-Caribbean-style food, and the turtle-watching at Tortuguero National Park.

18

Best Beaches in Costa Rica

PLAYA SÁMARA
A horseshoe-shape cove with an entrance protected by a coral reef keeps Sámara one of Costa Rica's rare, easily swimmable beaches. A friendly town, not too developed but still with many family-friendly activities, anchors the area. *(Ch. 8)*

PLAYA DOMINICAL
Friendly Dominical, a fun surfers' town with a palm-lined beach, is the picture of "laid back." It's one of the few beaches staffed by lifeguards, and there are world-class wildlife refuges nearby. *(Ch. 10)*

PLAYA PAVONES
An end-of-the-world vibe awaits you at this rocky, black-sand beach near the Panamanian border. It's a favorite for surfers but nonsurfers can enjoy its isolation and lush rain forest. *(Ch. 10)*

PLAYA TORTUGUERO
Nobody comes to rainy Tortuguero to sunbathe. Four sea turtle species nest here, providing a different type of nightlife than Costa Rica's hipper beaches: watching hatchlings scurry toward the sea. *(Ch. 11)*

PLAYA MONTEZUMA
Known for its bohemian town and gray-sand beaches, Costa Rica's onetime "hippie" capital today offers plenty of grown-up offerings among the backpackers' digs and quirky New Age-y shops and restaurants. *(Ch. 8)*

PLAYA UVITA
Some snazzy new dining and lodging options and a growing number of resident expats make Playa Uvita one of Costa Rica's up-and-coming beaches. Uvita anchors the north end of Ballena National Marine Park, a sanctuary for humpback whales and bottlenose dolphins. *(Ch. 10)*

PUNTA UVA
Outside the party center of Puerto Viejo de Talamanca, the dark-sand Punta Uva, or "grape point" (named for its signature sea-grape trees) is the prettiest beach on the South Caribbean coast. There's more rain here than other areas—but that keeps prices lower than on the Pacific and tempers mega-development. *(Ch. 11)*

MANUEL ANTONIO
Costa Rica's powerhouse beach is actually a string of palm-lined strands that go by the collective name Manuel Antonio. A lively tourist scene and a national park of the same name, home to an array of monkeys, birds, and sloths, make this Costa Rica's top tourist attraction. *(Ch. 9)*

PLAYA JUNQUILLAL
Junquillal (pronounced *hoon-key-YAHL*) on the Nicoya Peninsula is a bit more difficult to access than beaches north and south, but the locals and expats who call it home are happy to keep things that way. Though primarily the province of surfers, everyone can love the scenic beach. *(Ch. 7)*

PLAYA HERMOSA
The name of this north Pacific coast playa translates to "beautiful beach"—and it really is. Terrific sunsets and great lodging and dining make it a top choice. What's more, Hermosa's calm waters are an exception to most other Costa Rica beaches: You can actually swim here. *(Ch. 7)*

Best Ecolodges in Costa Rica

THE HARMONY HOTEL, NOSARA

Green goes chic at this holistic retreat on the north Pacific coast. The majority of guests come to Harmony for the yoga—one complimentary class is included in your stay—and the spa treatments. *(Ch. 8)*

PLAYA NICUESA RAINFOREST LODGE, GOLFITO

One of the country's top green lodgings, Playa Nicuesa's commitment to sustainability shines, from the use of fallen wood and recycled materials in construction to the bounty of land and sea served up family-style at dinner. *(Ch. 10)*

DANTICA LODGE & GALLERY, SAN GERARDO DE DOTA

Small, luxurious white stucco houses decorated in tropical colors are scattered around Dantica's forested grounds, where you have ample opportunity for hiking and a very good chance of spotting a resplendent quetzal. *(Ch. 10)*

ARENAL OBSERVATORY LODGE, ARENAL

You cannot stay closer than this to a volcano summit—you're less than 3.2 km (2 miles) away—although, admittedly, northern Costa Rica's Volcán Arenal has settled into a less-active phase these days. With the best views of the volcano around, Arenal Observatory Lodge sits amid an 870-acre private reserve perfect for nature walks. Plus, the folks here take active steps to protect the environment and participate in local community projects. *(Ch. 6)*

FINCA ROSA BLANCA COFFEE PLANTATION RESORT, HEREDIA

One of the Central Valley's most sumptuous lodgings is on a hilltop amid a working organic coffee plantation. Although you are in the San José metro area, the capital seems far away; the only reminder is the restaurant's spectacular view of the city lights below. The Gaudí-esque main building and neighboring structures have spacious rooms decorated with local art. *(Ch. 5)*

HOTEL SÍ COMO NO, MANUEL ANTONIO

"Sustainability" is the watchword at Sí Como No, a hip and trendy green hotel with environmentally friendly practices at its core. In addition to its nine buildings on the forested hillside grounds, Sí Como No operates its own Greentique Nature Reserve, a great opportunity to observe wildlife. *(Ch. 9)*

LA CAROLINA LODGE, VOLCÁN TENORIO

Costa Rica's remote lodges do amazing things with no electricity or Wi-Fi. You can help with chores at this proudly off-the-grid working farm—if the spirit so moves you—or pamper yourself after a forest walk or horse ride with a massage or yoga session. Swap travel stories over a sumptuous family-style dinner, and wind up your evening with a soak in the fire-heated hot tub. *(Ch. 6)*

RANCHO NATURALISTA, TURRIALBA

A perfect perch for accessing Costa Rica's premier bird-watching location on the fringes of the Central Valley southeast of Turrialba, Rancho Naturalista has upscale rustic rooms and resident birding guides available during the high season. Hiking and horseback riding will also keep you occupied. *(Ch. 5)*

TORTUGA LODGE, TORTUGUERO

A riverside lodge known for its nature packages, Tortuga sets itself apart in location and service. Packages include charter flights to Tortuguero, where guides take you on nocturnal turtle-watching excursions. *(Ch. 11)*

LAPA RÍOS, CORCOVADO NATIONAL PARK

Costa Rica's original green lodging pioneered the concept of the sustainability tour. You'll leave feeling educated about ways you can help conserve nature. The screened, open-air bungalows sit amid a private 1,000-acre reserve. *(Ch. 10)*

What to Eat and Drink in Costa Rica

Arroz con pollo

GALLO PINTO
Costa Rica's signature dish translates to "spotted rooster." It's so typical of the country there's a saying: "Más tico que el gallo pinto" (More Costa Rican than gallo pinto). You'll find this mix of rice, black beans, chopped bell peppers, and cilantro all over the country—even at McDonald's.

TRES LECHES
This sweet, decadent sponge cake gets soaked in a sauce made with three different types of milk: condensed, evaporated, and sweet cream. Though it sounds like the cake would be soggy, successful takes are actually quite light. Some variations substitute whole milk for the cream to cut the sweetness.

ARROZ CON POLLO
Comfort food at its finest, this chicken-and-rice dish is a staple in any Tico home, although you'll see Latin America–wide variations. Even finicky eaters enjoy the shredded chicken, with sautéed and chopped veggies like celery, corn, bell peppers, cilantro, and carrots over rice.

Gallo pinto

CASADO
Fortify yourself with a midday *casado* at a small mom-and-pop restaurant. "Casado" means "married," and the plate "marries" meat, vegetables, rice, and plantains.

IMPERIAL
Far and away, the most popular locally brewed beer is this pale lager. The same brewery—jointly Costa Rican and Dutch owned—also makes Pilsen and Bavaria.

SALSA LIZANO
It's the quintessential Costa Rican condiment, and no self-respecting home or restaurant does without it. It started as a response to Lea & Perrins' 1920 introduction of Worcestershire sauce to Costa Rica. "I can do better," insisted a local man, and Salsa Lizano was born.

FRUTAS
Sure, you know bananas and pineapples, two of Costa Rica's top agricultural exports. But you'll also encounter the egg-shape *maracuyá* (similar to passion fruit) and *guanábana* (soursop).

CAFÉ
Café is coffee, the country's signature product. Here's the kicker: Quality coffee goes for export, leaving an inferior bean behind. Your best bet for a good cup is an upscale restaurant.

ENSALADA DE PALMITO
The cylindrical, ivory-color vegetable comes from the inner stem of coconut and peach palms; you'll equate its flavor with artichokes. A particularly Costa Rican treat, especially popular around Easter, is palmito salad.

SOPA NEGRA
This filling black-bean soup with a poached egg is thick enough to spoon onto a tortilla. Most cooks garnish it to add some visual pizzazz to an otherwise unattractive-looking dish—though there's nothing ho-hum about the flavor.

RONDÓN
Afro-Caribbean immigrants brought this hearty soup to the Caribbean coast. They called it "run down"—made with whatever ingredients the cook could run down. Expect fresh fish, lobster, or crab, with plantains, cassava, and yams.

RICE AND BEANS
This is not gallo pinto. It's a Caribbean dish (its name always in English) with rice and beans steeped in fresh coconut milk.

Costa Rica Today

GOVERNMENT

Costa Rica is a democratic republic whose structure will be familiar to any citizen of the United States. The 1949 constitution divides the government into independent executive, legislative, and judicial branches. All citizens are guaranteed equality before the law, the right to own property, freedom of speech, and freedom of religion. The country is justifiably proud of its long-established tradition of democracy, with free elections and peaceful transitions of power.

The country is famous for lacking an army, which was abolished when the constitution was ratified. The country's stable government and economy have made this possible, even as its neighbors were embroiled in civil war in the 1970s and 1980s. Costa Rica does maintain a small national guard.

ECONOMY

Costa Rica has diversified its economy beyond traditional agriculture, and tourism brings in more money than its three major cash crops: coffee, bananas, and pineapples. High-tech companies such as Intel, Hewlett-Packard, and Motorola; Internet purveyor Amazon; and pharmaceutical companies like Procter & Gamble and GlaxoSmithKline operate plants and service centers in Costa Rica, providing well-paid jobs for educated professionals. The U.S. chains and big-box stores have arrived, too—most notably Walmart, which operates 12 supercenters here.

Costa Rica has staked hopes on international free-trade agreements in recent years, most notably with Mexico (1995), Canada (2002), the United States (2008), the European Union (2010), and China (2011). Opponents of the treaties are wary of how much benefit they provide for the country, however.

The economy historically bedevils Costa Rica and never more so than in the wake of the worldwide COVID-19 pandemic. Costa Rica received high marks for keeping numbers of cases and deaths far lower than jurisdictions with comparable populations. Like every other country, though, it wonders what the long-term economic impact will be.

TOURISM

In good times, some 3.1 million international visitors inject a much-needed $3.9 billion into Costa Rica's economy. The COVID-19 pandemic meant a several-month shutdown of all ports of entry and abruptly threw those numbers into reverse. As the tourism industry slowly recovers from the crisis, it hopes to reestablish Costa Rica as one of the hemisphere's great travel destinations. When things return to "normal," the industry will return to its classic, spirited debates on how to reconcile ecotourism and sustainable development with resort construction, adventure tourism, and extreme sports. Tourism's various sub-sectors here do not always see eye to eye.

RELIGION

Because it was a Spanish colony, Costa Rica continues to have a close relationship with the Catholic Church. Catholicism was made the country's official religion in the constitution. Because of this, priests are the only type of clergy authorized to perform civil marriages. (Others require the assistance of a legal official.)

More than 70% of Costa Ricans consider themselves Catholics. But even among this group, most people do not have a strong identification with the church or with its teachings. The live-and-let-live attitude of most Costa Ricans does not mesh well with religious doctrine.

That's also probably why the evangelical churches that have made huge inroads in neighboring countries are not as prevalent here.

Every village has a church on its main square—always hopping once a year, when the town's patron saint is honored. These are times for food, music, and dancing in the streets. If the celebrations lack much religious fervor—well, that's Costa Rica for you.

SPORTS

Like everyone else on this soccer-mad isthmus, Costa Ricans take their game seriously, and passions bubble over when it comes to their beloved national team.

On the national level, the big local rivalry is between LD Alajuelense (*La Liga,* or "the League") and Deportivo Saprissa (*El Monstruo Morado,* or "the Purple Monster"). They have won the Costa Rican championship 29 and 34 times, respectively, which makes the rivalry particularly intense. You can tell how important the sport is when you fly into the country. As your plane flies across the Central Valley, you'll notice that every village, no matter how small, has a soccer field.

CASH CROPS

If nearby Honduras was the original Banana Republic, 19th-century Costa Rica was a Coffee Republic. Coffee remains inexorably entwined with the country, with economists paying close attention to world prices and kids in rural areas still taking class time off to help with the harvest.

The irony is that it's hard to get a decent cup of the stuff here. True to economic realities of developing countries, the high-quality product gets exported, with the inferior coffee staying behind for the local market. (The same is true of bananas, Costa Rica's other signature agricultural product.) The best places to get a cup of high-quality Costa Rican coffee are upscale restaurants and hotels. Owners understand foreign tastes and have export-quality coffee on hand. Gift shops sell the superior product as well.

The Central Valley is where you'll find many of the coffee plantations. You'll recognize them immediately by the rows of brilliant green plants covered in red berries. Because many of these plants are sensitive to light, they are often shaded by tall trees or even by canopies of fabric. Tours of the plantations are a great way to get to know the local cash crop.

In recent years, the producers of coffee have focused on quality rather than quantity. That's why bananas are now the top agricultural export, followed by pineapples. Both grow in sunny lowland areas, which are abundant on both the Atlantic and Pacific coasts. These crops are treated with just as much care as coffee. You're likely to see bunches of bananas wrapped in plastic bags—while still on the tree. This prevents blemishes that make them less appealing to foreign consumers.

Ecotourism in Costa Rica

DEFINING ECOTOURISM

Ecotourism has become the buzzword of Costa Rica's travel industry. From the original concept revolving around travel to enjoy nature, it has morphed into everything from hiking through the rain forest to rumbling over hillsides in all-terrain vehicles. We'll go with the oft-stated definition that ecotourism is "environmentally responsible travel." Costa Rica does itself proud in the domain of adventure tourism and extreme sports, but those activities sometimes conflict with that lofty ecotourism goal. That is not to say that adventure sports can't be part of a green vacation. It all depends what impact they have on the environment and the local community.

GOING GREEN

Over the past decade, the concept of ecotourism has made a strong impression on the average traveler. Many people now realize that mass tourism can be damaging to environmentally sensitive places like Costa Rica but that much can be done to alleviate the negative effects. At the same time, "ecotourism" has become a marketing term used to attract customers who have the best intentions.

In addition to giving travelers the chance to observe and learn about wildlife, ecotourism should accomplish three things: refrain from damaging the environment, strengthen conservation efforts, and improve the lives of local people.

The last part might seem a bit beside the point, but environmentalists point out that much of the deforestation in Costa Rica and other countries is by poor people trying to eke out a living through subsistence farming. Providing them with other ways to make a living is the best way to prevent this.

WHAT CAN YOU DO?

Make sure the hotel you choose is eco-friendly. A great place to start is the Costa Rican Tourism Board (⊕ *www.turismo-sostenible.co.cr*). It has a rating system for hotels and lodges called the Certification for Sustainable Tourism. The New York–based Rainforest Alliance (⊕ *www.rainforest-alliance.org*) has a convenient searchable database of sustainable lodges. The International Ecotourism Society (⊕ *www.ecotourism.org*) also has a database of tour companies, hotels, and other travel services that are committed to sustainable practices.

Use locally owned lodges, car-rental agencies, or tour companies. Eat in local restaurants, shop in local markets, and attend local events. Enrich your experience and support the community by hiring local guides.

Make sure your tour company follows sustainable policies, including contributing to conservation efforts, hiring and training locals for most jobs, educating visitors about the local ecology and culture, and taking steps to mitigate negative impacts on the environment.

Don't be overly aggressive if you bargain for souvenirs, and don't shortchange local people on payments or tips for services.

Stray from the beaten path—by visiting areas where few tourists go, you can avoid adding to the stress on hot spots.

Support conservation by paying entrance fees to parks and protected sites. You can go a few steps further by making donations to local or international conservation groups such as Conservation International, the Rainforest Alliance, and the World Wide Fund for Nature.

Costa Rica Outdoor Adventures

Ziplining and Canopy Tours

Costa Rica gave the world the so-called canopy tour, a series of ziplines that let you glide through the treetops, attached to a secure harness. Although billed as a way to get up close and personal with nature, your focus and attention will likely be on the ride rather than spotting that elusive resplendent quetzal. No matter. Ziplining has become one of Costa Rica's signature activities for visitors. The term "canopy tour" has expanded to include hanging bridges and elevated trams where you walk or ride through the forest canopy. The latter two really are more effective ways to view all the nature the treetops have to offer.

Ziplines are a fast-paced, thrilling experience. You're attached to a zipline with a safety harness, and then you "fly" at about 15–40 mph from one tree platform to the next. (You may be anywhere from 60 to 300 feet above the forest floor.) Tree-to-tree ziplines date from the 19th century and have been a bona fide activity for visitors to Costa Rica since the mid-1990s when the first tour opened in Monteverde. These tours are tremendous fun, but you won't see any animals. An average fitness level—and above-average level of intrepidness—are all you need. Be brutally frank in assessing your desire and ability to do this, and remember that once you start, there's no turning back.

Bridges and trams are canopy tours in a literal sense, where you walk along suspension bridges, ride along in a tram, or are hoisted up to a platform to get a closer look at birds, monkeys, and sloths. They're also called hanging-bridges tours, sky walks, or platform tours. If seeing nature at a more leisurely pace is your goal, opt for these, especially the bridge excursions. Early mornings are the best time for animal sightings—at 50–250 feet above ground, the views are stupendous.

BEST CANOPY TOURS

El Santuario Canopy Adventure Tour, Manuel Antonio National Park. The mile-plus cable in the system here is Costa Rica's longest single zipline.

Original Canopy Tour, Limón. A branch of Costa Rica's first zipline tour is the highlight of a nature-themed park near the Caribbean coast.

Osa Canopy Tour, Uvita. One of the South Pacific's few such operations combines ziplines with rappelling stations and a Tarzan swing.

Rainforest Adventures, Braulio Carrillo National Park. These folks pioneered the concept of guided gondola rides through the canopy.

Rincón de la Vieja Canopy, Rincón de la Vieja National Park. Combine ziplines with horseback riding and sulfur springs on the summit of northern Costa Rica's best-known volcano.

Selvatura, Monteverde Cloud Forest. Some of the longest ziplines in the country are here. There is also an extensive bridge system that lets you walk through the canopy at your own pace.

Sportfishing

Adventurous anglers flock to Costa Rica to test their will—and patience—against an assortment of feisty fresh- and saltwater fish. Just remember: catch-and-release is usually expected, so the pleasure's all in the pursuit. With so many options, the hardest decision is where to go. Inshore fishing in the country's rivers and lakes yields roosterfish, snapper, barracuda, jacks, and snook. Fly-fishing aficionados love the extra-large tarpon and snook because of their sheer size and fight. The country's coasts swarm with a multitude of bigger game, including the majestic billfish—the marlin and the sailfish. There are many top-notch fishing outfitters up and down both coasts and around rivers and lakes, so planning a fishing trip is easy. Charter boats range from 22 feet to 60 feet in length. With a good captain, a boat in the 22- to 26-foot range for up to three anglers can cost from $500 to $900 a day. A 28- to 32-foot boat fits four and costs from $800 to $1,500 per day. A boat for six people costs $1,400 to $2,000 and measures between 36 and 47 feet. A 60-foot boat for up to 10 anglers costs about $3,000 a day. A good charter boat company employs experienced captains and offers good equipment, bait, and food and beverages.

You're guaranteed a few good catches no matter what the season, as demonstrated by the cadre of sportsmen who circle the coasts year-round chasing that perfect catch. If your heart is set on an area or a type of fish, do your research ahead of time and plan accordingly. Costa Rica teems with a constant supply of fish, some of which might seem unique to North Americans.

Northern Lowlands: Lake Arenal and Caño Negro are great freshwater spots to snag extra-large tarpon, snook, and the ugly-but-fascinating guapote bass. Start your fishing journey in nearby La Fortuna.

Guanacaste: Tamarindo is the main departure point for anglers looking to find big game, including tuna, roosterfish, and marlin. Boats also leave from Playas del Coco, Ocotal, Tambor, and Flamingo Beach, which are best fished May through August. All are close to the well-stocked northern Papagayo Gulf.

Central Pacific coast: If you're hunting sailfish and marlin between December and April, head to the Central Pacific coast

around Los Sueños and Quepos, where up to 10 sailfish are caught per boat.

South Pacific: Puerto Jiménez, Golfito, and Zancudo are less developed than the other Pacific regions and are famous for their excellent inshore fishing for snapper and roosterfish, though offshore big game is also good in the area, especially November through January.

Caribbean coast: Barra del Colorado is a popular sportfishing hub and a great departure point for freshwater fishing on the Caribbean side of the country. Fly fishers looking for the ultimate challenge head to the San Juan River for its legendary tarpon. The Colorado River lures anglers with jack, tuna, snook, tarpon, and dorado. Transportation and tours can be arranged by the hotels listed in Tortuguero or Puerto Viejo de Sarapiquí.

Scuba Diving and Snorkeling

For snorkelers and scuba divers, Costa Rica is synonymous with swarms of fish and stretches of coral that hug the country's 1,291 km (802 miles) of coastline. Submerge yourself in crystalline waters and enter another world, with bull sharks, brain coral, and toothy green eels. The variety and abundance of marine life are awe-inspiring.

Beach towns on both coasts are riddled with diving schools and equipment-rental shops. Look for outfitters that are PADI (Professional Association of Diving Instructors) trained or give PADI certifications. If you're a first-timer and plan to go diving just once, taking a basic half-day class isn't difficult, and it will allow you to dive up to 40 feet with an instructor. A three- or four-day certification course gets you a lifetime license and allows you to dive up to 130 feet and without a guide.

The Pacific tends to be clearer than the Caribbean, and the fish are bigger and more abundant. Northern waters are generally best May through July, after winds die down and the water turns bluer and warmer. The southern Osa Peninsula is popular during the dry season, from January to April. The Caribbean, known for its diverse coral and small fish, is good for beginners because it has less surge. The best months are September and October, when the ocean is as calm and flat as a swimming pool. April and May also offer decent conditions, but steer clear during the rest of the year, when rain and strong waves cloud the water.

Cahuita. Mounds of coral and a barrier reef (dubbed Long Shoal) run from Cahuita to Punta Mona, along 25 km (15 miles) of Caribbean coastline. Arches, tunnels, and canyons in the reef form a playground for small fish, crabs, and lobsters. Even though sediment and wastewater have damaged much of the coral, the healthy sections are dense, colorful, and delightfully shaped. Gentle pools right off the beach allow for some of the country's best snorkeling.

Golfo de Papagayo (Papagayo Gulf). This northern gulf has Costa Rica's highest concentration of snorkel and dive shops. Calm, protected waters make it the best place for beginner divers on the Pacific.

Isla de Caño (Caño Island). With visibility of 20 to 80 feet, strong currents, and very changeable conditions, Caño is best suited for advanced divers. The huge schools of large fish and potential shark sightings are the attractions here. Novice snorkelers can frolic in the Coral Garden, a shallow area on the north side of this biological reserve.

Isla del Coco (Cocos Island). One of the world's premier sites for advanced divers lies 295 nautical miles and a 36-hour sail from Puntarenas. Visibility is good all year, and hammerhead and white-tipped reef sharks are the main attractions.

Isla Murciélago (Bat Island). Located inside Santa Rosa National Park, this cluster of rocks is good for advanced divers and famous for its fearsome bull sharks.

Isla Santa Catalina (Santa Catalina Island). Known for sightings of golden cownose rays and giant mantas, these big rocks near Playa Flamingo have spots for beginner and advanced divers. Snorkelers should head to shallower waters, near the beach.

Bird-Watching

Even if you've never seen yourself as a bird-watcher, Costa Rica will get you hooked. Waking you before dawn, calling to you throughout the day, and serenading you through tropical nights, birds are impossible to ignore here. Luckily, Costa Rica has a wealth of world-class ornithologists and local bird guides who can answer all your questions. Every licensed naturalist guide also has some birding expertise, so many tours you take in the country will include some bird-watching.

The sheer variety and abundance of birds here make bird-watching a daily pastime—with less than 0.03% of the planet's surface, Costa Rica counts some 900 bird species, more than the United States and Canada combined. You don't have to stray far from your hotel or even need binoculars to spot, for instance, a kaleidoscopic-colored keel-billed toucan (the bird of Froot Loops cereal fame). But armed with a pair of binoculars and a birding guide, the sky is literally the limit for the numbers of birds you can see.

Catching sight of a brilliantly colored bird is exciting; being able to identify it after a couple of encounters is even more thrilling. For kids, spotting birds makes a great game. With their sharp young eyes, they're usually very good at it—plus it's wildly educational. About 10% of Costa Rica's birds are endemic, so this is a mecca for bird-watchers intent on compiling an impressive life list.

The best time to bird is November to May, when local species are joined by winter migrants. Breeding season, which varies by species throughout the year, is the easiest time to spot birds, as males put on displays for females, followed by frequent flights to gather nesting material and then food for the chicks. Also keep your eye on fruit-bearing trees that attract hungry birds.

The most sought-after bird is the aptly named resplendent quetzal, sporting brilliant blue, green, and red plumage and long tail feathers. The best places to spot it are **Los Quetzales National Park** in the **Cerro de la Muerte** highlands, the **San Gerardo de Dota** valley, and the **Monteverde Cloud Forest Reserve.** Another bird high on many bird-watchers' lists is the scarlet macaw, the largest of the parrot family here. You'll see pairs performing aerial ballets and munching in beach almond trees in **Corcovado National Park,** along the Osa Peninsula's coastline, and around **Carara National Park** in the Central Pacific region. The **Tempisque River** delta's salty waters, at the north end of the Gulf of Nicoya, are famous for a wealth of water birds, notably wood storks, glossy ibis, and roseate spoonbills. Farther north, in **Palo Verde** and **Caño Negro National Parks,** look for the rarest and largest of wading birds, the jabiru. The network of jungle-edged natural canals in **Tortuguero National Park,** in the northern Caribbean, is home to a host of herons, including

the spectacular rufescent tiger heron and the multihued agami heron. More than 50 species of hummingbirds hover around every part of the country. Look for them around feeders at lodges in the **Cerro de la Muerte** area, Monteverde, and the Turrialba region.

Sea Turtle-Watching

Five species of sea turtle visit Costa Rican shores: olive ridley, green sea turtle, loggerhead, hawksbill, and leatherback. The gentle giants, which can weigh up to 1,000 pounds, spend most of their time at sea but come ashore by the thousands for two or three nights to lay their eggs. There are just seven places in the world where these mass nesting events, called arribadas, happen. This includes both of Costa Rica's coasts, with the most turtles coming to the Nicoya Peninsula on the Pacific coast and Tortuguero on the Caribbean coast.

Head to the Nicoya Peninsula on the Pacific coast during the rainy season. In September, October, and November, at least once a month and sometimes twice, more than 100,000 olive ridley sea turtles come to Ostional National Wildlife Refuge north of Nosara, filling the beach over the course of three or four days with more than 100 million eggs in one of the largest arribadas in the world. Around sixty days later, in a flurry of flying sand, the tiny hatchlings emerge from their shells, dig their way to the surface, and make their cumbersome and perilous journey to the sea. After many years and thousands of miles at sea, olive ridleys will return to the exact beach where they are born when it is their time to nest.

On the east coast in Tortuguero, you are likely to see different types of turtles' mass nesting events. There is a good chance of seeing leatherbacks nesting on the shore from March to July, green sea turtles from June to October, and hawksbills from July to October. While the numbers aren't quite as grandiose as in Ostional—leatherback sea turtle numbers continue to decline, and scientists estimate that there may be as few as 32,000 nesting females left in the world—they're still a sight to behold. ■TIP➜ **Book a turtle watching tour ahead of your trip, noting that a responsible guide never allows animal interactions. Below is a handy guide of where to spot turtles around the country and where to stay.**

Ostional. See turtles at Ostional National Wildlife Refuge ☎ 506/682–0470 and stay at Luna Azul ☎ 506/2682–1400 ⊕ hotellunaazul.com (Ch. 8)

Tortuguero. See turtles at the Sea Turtle Conservancy ☎ 5062767–1576 and stay at Tortuga Lodge ☎ 800/672–8704 ⊕ tortugalodge.com (Ch. 11)

Montezuma. See turtles at ASVO ☎ 506/2222–3612 and stay at Ylang Ylang Beach Resort ☎ 888/795–8494 ⊕ ylangylangbeachresort.com (Ch. 8)

Sámara. See turtles at the Camaronal National Wildlife Foundation ☎ 506/2659–8190 and stay at Villas Kalimba ☎ 506/2656–0929 ⊕ villaskalimba.com (Ch. 8)

Playa Hermosa. See turtles at Playa Hermosa/Punta Mala National Wildlife Refuge (inquire at hotel about tour) and stay at DoceLunas ☎ 506/2643–2211 ⊕ docelunas.com (Ch. 9)

Cabo Matapalo. See turtles at Osa Conservation ☎ 5068719–8582 and stay at Bosque del Cabo ☎ 5062735–5206 ⊕ bosquedelcabo.com (Ch. 10)

Puerto Viejo de Talamanca. See turtles at Gandoca Manzanillo National Wildlife Refuge with ATEC Eco-Tours

☎ 506/2750–0398 and stay at Cariblue Beach & Jungle Resort ☎ 506/2750–0035 ⊕ cariblue.com (Ch. 11)

Surfing

Costa Rica's big surfing community, consistent waves, and not-too-crowded beaches make surfing accessible to anyone who is curious enough to paddle into the lineup; surf schools and board rentals are plentiful.

At many of Costa Rica's top surf spots, a wide range of ages and skills can be found bobbing together in the water. With the right board—ideally a foam longboard for first timers—and good instruction, just about anybody can stand up and ride. Trained instructors can adapt lessons to different levels, ages, and body types. If you want to get a head start before your vacation, practice pop-ups at home (YouTube has dozens of tutorials) or swim laps at your local pool to get in shape before your first wipeout.

With warm water, offshore winds, and friendly locals, you really can't find a better place to learn the sport. Costa Ricans are known for their pura vida attitude, and this usually translates into a welcoming vibe in the water. Just steer clear of the hotshots until you know local protocol.

On the Pacific, waves are consistent from December through April. As you move southward, the breaks are best from May to November. On the Caribbean side, conditions are best January through April.

Dominical, Pacific Coast. A long set of fast, powerful breaks that are great for advanced levels. When waves get too big, head south to Dominicalito.

Esteríllos, Pacific Coast. Divided into three beaches, this wide stretch of coast is uncrowded to the point of desolation. The surf and currents can be tough for beginners, and Este and Centro have waves much like Hermosa. Oeste has softer waves.

Jacó, Pacific Coast. Unless the surf gets too big, the consistent beach breaks produce forgiving waves that are good for beginner to intermediate surfers.

Malpaís, Pacific Coast. A variety of beach breaks plus a point break that's good when waves are pumping.

Manuel Antonio, Pacific Coast. Playitas, at the national park's north end, is perhaps the most consistent spot here. It's only good at high tide, about three hours per day, and usually flat September through December.

Pavones, Pacific Coast. This advanced and fickle spot is said to be one of the world's longest lefts, lasting nearly three minutes.

Playa Cocles, Caribbean Coast. Plenty of beach breaks and good for all levels, but beware of riptides.

Playa Guiones, Pacific Coast. If not the best surf in the vicinity of Nosara, it's the best beach break for beginners and longboarders, with plenty of long rights and lefts.

Playa Hermosa, Pacific Coast. A steep beach break just south of Jacó with some of the country's best barrels and surfers. Waves can get big, mean, hollow, and thunderously heavy.

Salsa Brava, Caribbean Coast. When it's on, this is arguably Costa Rica's best and most powerful wave, breaking right over a shallow coral reef.

Sámara, Pacific Coast. Protected, mellow beach breaks great for beginners, yet close to advanced spots like Playa Camaronal.

Tamarindo, Pacific Coast. Surfer's paradise for all levels, with famous breaks like Ollie's Point, Playa Avellanas, and Playa Negra (south), and Witch's Rock (north). Solid waves are formed at a point break called Pico Pequeño and at the river mouth called El Estero at the beach's north end.

Weddings and Honeymoons

Ever dreamed of getting married on a sandy beach shaded by palm trees? Many people who envision such a scene immediately think of the Caribbean. But Costa Rica is fast becoming a favored destination for tropical nuptials.

Compared with the complicated procedures in many other destinations, getting married in Costa Rica is easy. There are no residency restrictions or blood-test requirements. At least a month in advance, couples who are over 18 should provide their local wedding planner with a copy of their birth certificates and passports so they can be submitted to the local authorities. With Costa Rica legalizing same-sex marriage in 2020, all couples, gay and straight, may tie the knot here.

Any previous marriage complicates things a bit. The couple needs to provide documentation that the marriage was terminated. Divorce papers or death certificate of a previous spouse must be translated into Spanish and notarized.

THE BIG DAY

Judges, attorneys, and Catholic priests have legal authority to certify a marriage in Costa Rica. (Most foreign couples avoid the latter because a Catholic wedding requires months of preparation.) The official ceremony is simple, but couples are free to add their own vows or anything else they would like. The officiant will register the marriage with the civil registry and the couple's embassy.

At the wedding, the couple needs to have at least two witnesses who are not family members. Many couples choose their best man and maid of honor. If necessary, the wedding planner can provide witnesses.

The license itself takes three months to issue and is sent to the couple's home address. For an extra fee, couples can ask for the process to be expedited. Virtually all Western countries recognize the legality of a Costa Rican marriage.

BEAUTIFUL BACKDROPS

Although Costa Rica offers no shortage of impressive backdrops for a ceremony, the Central Pacific coast sees the most tourist weddings and honeymoons. May and June are the most popular months for foreigners, but many people choose January or February because you are virtually guaranteed sunny skies. (Costa Ricans favor December weddings.) Manuel Antonio's Makanda by the Sea, La Mariposa, Sí Como No, and Punta Leona's Villa Caletas are among the many lodgings here with events staff well versed in planning ceremonies and tending to the legalities.

There are many details to attend to: flowers, music, and photography. Most large hotels have on-staff wedding planners to walk you through the process. Couples can also hire their own wedding planner, which is often less expensive. Either way, wedding planners have a wide range of services available, and couples can pick and choose.

HONEYMOONS

As far as honeymoons go, no place in Costa Rica is inappropriate. Although honeymoons on the beach, especially along the Northern Pacific and Central Pacific coasts, are popular, many couples opt for treks to the mountains or the rain forests. Dozens of newlyweds choose offbeat adventures, such as spotting sea turtles along the Caribbean coast or swimming with pilot whales off the Osa Peninsula.

The People of Costa Rica

Unlike many of its neighbors, Costa Rica never had a dominant indigenous population. When Christopher Columbus arrived in the early 16th century, he didn't encounter empires like those in present-day Mexico and Peru. Instead, a small contingent of indigenous Caribs rowed out in canoes to meet his ship. The heavy gold bands the indigenous peoples wore led to Columbus mistakenly calling the land Costa Rica, or "Rich Coast."

On the mainland, the Spanish encountered disparate peoples like the Chorotega, Bribri, Cabécar, and Boruca peoples. Archaeological evidence shows that they had lived in the region for thousands of years. But that would change with breathtaking speed. European diseases felled many of their members, and the brutality of slavery imposed by the colonial power drove most of those remaining into the mountains.

Some of these peoples still exist, although in relatively small communities. Several thousand Bribri, Kekoldi, and other peoples live in villages scattered around Talamanca, a mountainous region close to the border of Panama. Although many traditions have been lost over the years, some have managed to retain their own languages and religions. If you're interested in seeing the local culture, tour companies in the coastal communities of Limón and Puerto Viejo de Talamanca can arrange visits to these villages.

That isn't to say that there's no local culture. More than 90% of the country's residents are descendants of the Spanish. But few people express any pride in their Spanish heritage. Perhaps that is because Spain had little interest in Costa Rica, the smallest and poorest of its Central American colonies. Instead, the people here created a unique culture that mixes parts of Europe, Latin America, and the Caribbean. There's a strong emphasis on education, and the 97% literacy rate is by far the highest in the region. There's a laid-back attitude toward life, typified by the common greeting of *pura vida,* which translates literally as "pure life" but means something between "no worries" and "don't sweat the small stuff."

It sounds like a cliché, but Costa Ricans are an incredibly welcoming people. Anyone who has visited other Central American countries will be surprised at how Ticos seem genuinely happy to greet newcomers. If you ever find yourself lost in a town or village, you may find locals willing to not only point you in the right direction but walk you all the way to your destination. A trip to Costa Rica will supply you with memories of beaches, nature, and adventure, but we wager you'll also remember the friendly people here.

Kids and Families

With so much to keep them interested and occupied, Costa Rica is a blast with kids. The activities here are things the whole family can do together: discovering a waterfall in a rain forest, snorkeling with sea turtles, or white-water rafting down a roaring river. There are also activities for kids that will allow parents time to stroll hand in hand down a deserted beach.

CHOOSING A DESTINATION
Basing yourself in one place for several days is a great idea. Climbing into the car every day or two not only makes the kids miserable but means that the best part of the day is spent traveling. (Kids who are prone to carsickness won't do well on the winding, twisting roads, like the road to Monteverde Cloud Forest.) The good news is that there are many destinations where you could stay for a week and still not do and see everything.

Headed to the beach? Remember that for families, not all beaches are created equal. Choose a destination with a range of activities. Manuel Antonio, on the Central Pacific coast, is your best bet. The proximity to the national park is the main selling point, but you're also close to other nature preserves. As for activities, there's everything from snorkeling and surfing lessons to kayaking excursions to zipline adventures. And the range of kid-friendly restaurants is unmatched anywhere in the country. On the Nicoya Peninsula, Playas del Coco and Playa Tamarindo have a decent amount of activities for the small fry.

Santa Elena, the closest town to Monteverde Cloud Forest Biological Reserve, is another great base. There are several nature preserves in the area, and they offer both day and night hikes. If skies are cloudy—as they often are—there are indoor attractions like the display of slithering snakes. The town is compact and walkable, and has many eateries with children's menus. La Fortuna, the gateway to the Lake Arenal area, has activities from waterfall hikes to canopy tours. The town itself isn't attractive, so you'll want to choose a place nearby.

Believe it or not, the San José area is not a bad base. Activities like white-water rafting are nearby, and on rainy days you can visit the city's excellent museums dedicated to gold and jade. The hotels in the surrounding countryside are often a long drive from good restaurants. We prefer the hotels in the city, as dozens of restaurants line the pedestrian-only streets.

KID-FRIENDLY ACTIVITIES
You can't beat the beach in Costa Rica. Unfortunately, few have lifeguards; take warning signs about rip currents very seriously. Snorkeling and surfing lessons are great for older kids, but stick with a licensed company rather than that enthusiastic young person who approaches you on the beach.

Canopy tours are good for kids of all ages. Ask the staff about how long a tour will take, because once you set out on a hike over a series of hanging bridges, you have no choice but to continue on to the end. Ziplines are appropriate for older teens, who should always be accompanied by an adult.

For the smallest of the small fry, the butterfly enclosures and hummingbird gardens that you find near many resort areas are wonderful diversions. Indoor activities, like the display of frogs at Santa Elena, fascinate youngsters. And don't avoid the easier hikes in the national parks. Seeing animals in the wild is likely to start a lifelong love of animals.

What to Watch and Read

AFTER EARTH
In a post-apocalyptic world, Will and Jaden Smith are a dad and son whose spaceship crash-lands on 31st-century Earth—with humanity long since departed for another planet. As they struggle to return home, the steaming, gurgling, bubbling landscape around Arenal Volcano is the backdrop.

THE BLUE BUTTERFLY
Entomologist William Hurt accompanies a terminally ill 10-year-old boy from Montreal to Costa Rica in this 2004 film. His goal? Fulfill the boy's final wish to see the country's wondrous blue morpho butterfly. See if you can spot the lush scenery of Puerto Viejo de Talamanca on the south Caribbean coast.

CARNIVAL IN COSTA RICA
In this 1947 movie, a young man and woman return to Costa Rica after time abroad to discover their families have arranged for them to marry. The problem is that they're in love with other people. Technicolor filming was done in Hollywood; on-location footage of San José's carnival celebration and coffee harvest was patched in.

THE ENDLESS SUMMER II
Credit this documentary by Bruce Brown for putting Costa Rica on the map in surfing circles. His original *Endless Summer* (1966) did not visit here, but three decades later, this sequel coincided with the launch of Costa Rica's tourism boom. The film follows two surfers around the world. First stop? Costa Rica.

DOWN TO EARTH WITH ZAC EFRON
One episode of this 2020 Netflix series brings Efron and wellness expert Darin Olien to Costa Rica. Ziplines, beaches, animal-rescue centers, and community-based tourism lead them to conclude the country holds a key to sustainable living—and is a lot of fun to boot.

JURASSIC PARK
Contrary to popular belief, movies in the *Jurassic Park* franchise were not filmed in Costa Rica. Yes, author Michael Crichton based his fictional Isla Nublar on the real-life Isla del Coco, some 350 miles southwest of Costa Rica, but director Steven Spielberg found Hawaii simpler to reach for the films.

MONKEYS ARE MADE OF CHOCOLATE: EXOTIC AND UNSEEN COSTA RICA BY JACK EWING
Onetime cattle rancher Jack Ewing let nature reclaim his deforested land near Dominical in the 1980s, resulting in Hacienda Barú, one of Costa Rica's best nature reserves. In 32 essays—arguably the quintessential modern nature guide to the country—Ewing paints a picture of Costa Rica's flora and fauna, with humans as guests who inhabit the land.

PURA VIDA (LOVE HAS NO BOUNDARIES) BY SARA ALVA
You'll hear the expression ¡Pura vida! a lot during your Costa Rica trip. Literally translated as "pure life," it serves as a greeting, a farewell, and an all-around expression of approval. Most important, it describes a uniquely Costa Rican enjoyment of life. Tourist Simon, on vacation with his family, finds a holiday romance with Costa Rican Juan in this breezy 100-page novella by Sara Alva.

RADICAL SABBATICAL BY GLEN TIBALDEO AND LAURA BERGER
A husband and wife duo write about taking the expat plunge with wit and style. You can dive into and out of the book's 42 fun short- to medium-length chapters at will, in any sequence. If you find yourself saying "Let's move here!" during your vacation, give this book a read first.

Chapter 2

TRAVEL SMART

Updated by
Jeffrey Van Fleet

★ **CAPITAL**
San José

✹ **POPULATION**
5.1 million

🗨 **LANGUAGE**
Spanish

$ **CURRENCY**
Costa Rican colón

☎ **AREA CODE**
506

⚠ **EMERGENCIES**
911; U.S. Embassy in San José: 506/2519–2000

🚗 **DRIVING**
On the right side

⚡ **ELECTRICITY**
120 volts/60 cycles; plugs are U.S. standard two- and three-prong

🕐 **TIME**
Two hours behind New York during U.S. daylight saving; one hour behind otherwise

🌐 **WEB RESOURCES**
www.visitcostarica.com,
www.ticotimes.net,
www.therealcostarica.com

Know Before You Go

When should you go to Costa Rica? Does the country use addresses? What if you need medical attention during your vacation? You may have some important questions before your trip to Costa Rica. We've got the answers and a few tips to help you make the most of your visit.

YOU CAN'T SEE THE WHOLE COUNTRY IN ONE TRIP

No matter how small Costa Rica looks on a map—it's the size of Vermont and New Hampshire combined—your best-laid plans to see the entire country will never materialize. Choose two or three destinations to see in two weeks.

THE RAINY SEASON IS A GREAT TIME TO VISIT

Don't let the May-through-November wet season stop you from visiting Costa Rica. You can also think of it as the "green season." Crowds are smaller, prices are lower, and the countryside is lush and verdant. For most of those months, you'll have showers for a couple of hours in the afternoon, and you plan your activities around that. Nature activities go on rain or shine, though, and many outfitters provide ponchos and boots.

IT CAN GET COLD, ESPECIALLY IN THE CLOUD FOREST

Much of your time spent in Costa Rica won't require warm clothing, but make sure to pack layers and a sweater, especially if you're visiting the Cloud Forest. The forest is aptly named and full of mist. It can get quite chilly, and not just in the mornings and late at night.

EXPECT TO STAY AT SMALL LODGINGS

All-inclusives exist, but they have never been the focus of tourism here. Although you will see Hilton, Hampton, Marriott, Radisson, Four Seasons, and Best Westerns here, Costa Rica remains the province of smaller, independently owned lodgings with local touches, where the owners will give you nearby dining and sightseeing recommendations, or where you can exchange such information with your fellow travelers over breakfast.

COSTA RICA DOES NOT USE ADDRESSES AS WE KNOW THEM

Looking for street names? If they exist, nobody here knows or uses them. Costa Rica relies instead on a charming, exasperating system of expressing locations in reference to a landmark. Think in units of 100 meters, which denote how far it is to the next cross street. Historically, the reference point was the church, always in the center of town ("200 meters north and 50 meters west of the church," for example), but these days, that landmark could be anything: a bakery, a gas station, a Taco Bell. Just keep asking.

RESEARCH SPORTS OUTFITTERS

Costa Rica lets you—take a deep breath—raft, hike, zipline, swim, surf, kayak, rappel, bike, climb, sail, spelunk, hang glide, bungee jump, snorkel, balloon, dive, fish, trek, and skydive. Be brutally frank with yourself about your capabilities, and evaluate the outfitter carefully. No government body here sets standards for any of these activities, so remember that you're not at a giant outdoor amusement park. This is real nature with all its accompanying forces.

PRICES ARE GENERALLY FIXED

Bargaining is not the sport here that it is in other countries. Souvenir prices are fixed and fair, certainly at brick-and-mortar establishments, and attempts to haggle down the amount might come across as rude. It never hurts to ask for a discount (*descuento*). Merchants are charged high credit-card fees, and you might get a small price break if you pay in cash, with local currency (the *colón*). Do feel free to bargain, say, for produce in an outdoor farmers' market or if you want to negotiate hiring a taxi for a day.

YOU HAVE TO TAKE THE CAR RENTAL COMPANY'S INSURANCE

Insurance in Costa Rica is a government monopoly. At a minimum, you must take the third-party insurance the rental agency offers. Your own back-home car insurance does not exempt you, and neither does any coverage your credit card provides. Don't be fooled by online offers for car rental that will cost you "Only $10 a day!" as such rates are impossible. Ask what is included when you get a price quote. Some agencies tell you everything up front while others advertise only the base rate.

KEEP CALM AND DOWNLOAD WAZE

Speaking of driving, when you get out on the road, be extremely cautious. A mountainous spine bisects the country, and even on the beaten tourist track you can encounter some of Costa Rica's legendarily rough roads. Consider downloading a navigation app like Waze, which seems to work best here, and slow down. If you're really worried, you can cut down on driving by taking domestic flights.

STAY CONNECTED WITH WHATSAPP

To avoid massive roaming charges, consider a prepaid local SIM card for your unlocked phone, from one of Costa Rica's three cell companies—Kölbi, Claro, or Tigo. (Kölbi has counters in the arrivals area of both international airports, in San José and Liberia.) Better yet, download the free messaging app, Whatsapp, and hunt out a Wi-Fi hotspot to make phone calls and send messages.

DON'T FORGET THE DEPARTURE TAX

Costa Rica levies a $29 airport departure tax, payable in dollars or the equivalent in colones. Nearly all airlines bundle the tax into ticket prices; charter flights often do not. If not already included, you pay the tax at the airport upon departure. Paying with a MasterCard or Visa credit card means the transaction will be processed as a cash advance and incur additional fees. A few hotels will collect the tax for you as well.

EVERYONE CAN GET MARRIED HERE

Costa Rica's 2020 legalization of same-sex marriage means both gay and straight couples can say a tropical "I do." The Supreme Court here has ruled that the country must implement marriage equality, making it the first Central American nation to do so. You need to be at least 18 and supply your wedding planner—as a foreigner, you should use one to navigate logistics—with copies of your and your witnesses' passports and birth certificates. (Witnesses cannot be related to you.) Some big lodgings have a planner on staff, with those in LGBTQ-friendly Manuel Antonio on the central Pacific coast taking the lead serving the new market.

THE HEALTH CARE IS SOME OF THE BEST IN CENTRAL AMERICA

Many medications are available at the pharmacy without prescriptions, such as birth control and high blood pressure medication, though you'll need a prescription for antibiotics, narcotics, or psychotropic medicines. It generally costs a fraction of what you'd pay in the United States.

LEARN THE PHRASE "PURA VIDA"

You can't go wrong by saying an amiable *pura vida*, which serves as "hello," "good-bye," "thanks," "cool," and so on. The phrase has become synonymous with the country and its way of life.

SOME NATIONAL PARKS ARE CLOSED ONCE A WEEK

Make sure to plan your trips to the national parks around weekly closures. Manuel Antonio, one of the most popular national parks in Costa Rica, is closed on Monday.

COSTA RICANS PREFER FORMAL SPANISH

If you're going to speak Spanish in Costa Rica, err on the side of formality. For example, use *con mucho gusto* (with much pleasure) instead of the typical *de nada* for "you're welcome." And note that it's considered impolite to ask about marital status and family.

Getting Here

Air

If you are visiting several regions of the country, flying into San José, in the center of Costa Rica, is your best option. Flying into Liberia, in northwest Costa Rica, makes more sense if you are planning to spend your vacation entirely in the North Pacific. Fares are usually lower to San José than to Liberia. San José also has many more flights each day, making it easier if you miss a flight or have some other unexpected mishap.

Rarely does an international flight arrive in San José early enough to make a domestic connection, particularly in the rainy season, as the weather is typically difficult for flying small planes in the afternoon. You'll likely end up spending your first night in or near San José, leaving for your domestic destination the next morning.

It's rare, but afternoon and evening storms during the May-to-November rainy season occasionally cause flights coming into San José to be rerouted to Panama City, where you may be forced to spend the night. October, with its frequent evening fog, tends to be the worst month for reroutes. ■ TIP➜ **In the rainy season, try to book a flight with the earliest arrival time available.**

Once you're in Costa Rica, a few airlines recommend that you call them about three days before your return flight to reconfirm. Most explicitly say it's not necessary. It's always a good idea to check the day before you are scheduled to depart to make sure your flight time hasn't changed.

AIRPORTS

Costa Rica has two international airports. Aeropuerto Internacional Juan Santamaría (SJO) is the country's main airport, about 17 km (10 miles) northwest of downtown San José, just outside the city of Alajuela. The drive takes about 30 minutes. Domestic airline SANSA operates from here in its own terminal. The country's other international airport is Aeropuerto Internacional Daniel Oduber Quirós (LIR), a small airport near the city of Liberia in the North Pacific. It's about 13 km (8 miles) west of the city.

The small Aeropuerto Tobías Bolaños, in the Pavas district on San José's west side, serves a few local charter airlines.

Other places where planes land in Costa Rica aren't exactly airports. They're more like carports with landing strips, and airline representatives arrive a few minutes before a plane is due to land or take off. (A few of these actually do have a tiny terminal building.)

Most international flights arrive in the evening and depart early in the morning. Prepare yourself for long waits at immigration and customs. When you're departing the country, prepare for security checkpoints at both airports. Liquids and gels of more than 3 ounces are not permitted. Carry-on bags are sometimes searched again at the gates for flights to the United States. Get to the airport three hours before your flight.

GROUND TRANSPORTATION

At Aeropuerto Internacional Juan Santamaría, you exit the terminal into a fume-filled parking area flanked by hordes of taxis and tour vans. If you're with a tour, you need only look for a tour company representative with a sign that bears your name. If you need a taxi, a uniformed agent will escort you to one of the orange Taxi Aeropuerto cabs (no other taxis are allowed in the arrivals area). The metered fare to most areas of San José is $25 to $40.

Transportation at Aeropuerto Internacional Daniel Oduber Quirós is also a mix of taxis and tour vans. The big Pacific-coast resorts provide transportation, but always check with your lodging for recommendations on the best way to arrive.

FLIGHTS

From North America to San José: American flies from Miami, Dallas, New York (JFK), and Charlotte, and, from November to April, from Phoenix; United flies from Houston (IAH) and Newark, and, from December to April, from Chicago O'Hare and Washington Dulles (IAD); Delta flies from Atlanta and Los Angeles; Alaska flies from Los Angeles; Spirit flies from Fort Lauderdale and Orlando; JetBlue flies from Orlando, Fort Lauderdale, and New York (JFK); Southwest flies from Baltimore, Fort Lauderdale, and Houston Hobby (HOU); Air Canada Rouge, the leisure division of Air Canada, flies from Toronto and, from December through April, from Montreal; WestJet flies from Toronto; Avianca offers connections from several U.S. airports through its hubs in San Salvador, El Salvador, or Bogotá, Colombia. Mexico's AeroMéxico, Interjet, and Volaris do the same via their hubs in Mexico City, and Panama's Copa also offers connections through its hub in Panama City.

From New York or Los Angeles, nonstop flights to San José are 5½ hours. San José is 2½ hours from Miami, 3½ hours from Houston, and 4 hours from Charlotte and Dallas. In general, nonstop flights aren't that much more expensive. Ticket prices from hubs such as New York, Los Angeles, and Miami hover between $500 and $600, although the range varies widely.

From North America to Liberia: American flies from Dallas, Charlotte, New York (JFK), and Miami, with the smaller American Eagle taking a few of the Miami flights; Delta flies from Atlanta,

and, from December through April, from Los Angeles and Minneapolis; United flies from Houston, and, from December through April, from Chicago, Denver, and Newark; JetBlue flies from New York (JFK), and, from December through April, from Boston; Alaska flies from Los Angeles; Southwest flies from Baltimore and Houston Hobby (HOU); Air Canada Rouge flies from Toronto, and, from December through April, from Montreal; and WestJet flies from Toronto, and, from December through April, from Calgary. Copa connects its U.S. gateways to Liberia via its hub in Panama City.

Avianca and Copa connect San José with other Central American cities.

Given Costa Rica's often-difficult driving conditions, domestic flights are a desirable and practical option. The informality of domestic air service—"airports" other than Liberia and San José usually consist of only an airstrip with no central building at which to buy tickets—means you should purchase your domestic airplane tickets in advance. You can also buy them at travel agencies once you're in the country. We recommend grabbing a seat as soon as you know your itinerary, especially during the December–April high season.

SANSA is the largest domestic commercial airline, and it flies to 14 destinations around the country from San José. You can buy tickets online, over the phone, and at most travel agencies in Costa Rica. The tiny, domestic passenger planes in Costa Rica require that you pack light. SANSA imposes a luggage weight limit of 30 pounds. Extra luggage is sometimes allowed, but costs $1 to $3 per pound and will go standby. Skyway flies from San José to nine destinations in Costa Rica, as well as Bocas del Toro, Panama. Green Airways connects San José with Quepos and Tambor. The three domestic airlines cannot store extra

Getting Here

baggage, but hotels and lodges *may* be able to store your luggage—ask ahead and bring a smaller bag for your domestic travels. None has interline ticketing or baggage transfers with the international airlines serving Costa Rica.

Charter flights within Costa Rica are not as expensive as you might think, and can be a good deal if you are traveling in a group. The price per person will be only slightly more than taking a regularly scheduled domestic flight, and you can set your own departure time. The country has dozens of airstrips that are accessible only by charter plane. Charter planes are most often booked through tour operators, travel agents, or remote lodges. Most charter planes are smaller than domestic commercial planes.

■TIP➜ **Don't book a domestic flight for the day you arrive in or leave Costa Rica; connections are extremely tight, and you'll be at the mercy of the weather.**

Bus

Tica Bus has daily service to Panama and Nicaragua, with connections to Honduras, El Salvador, Guatemala, and far southern Mexico. Transnica serves Nicaragua and Honduras. Central Line offers service to Nicaragua. We recommend Tica Bus—it's more established and serves more destinations—but Transnica and Central Line are acceptable, too. All three companies have comfortable, air-conditioned coaches with videos and onboard toilets, and help with border procedures.

All Costa Rican towns are connected by regular bus service that's reliable, comprehensive, and inexpensive. Buses between major cities are modern, but in rural areas you may get a converted U.S. school bus without air-conditioning.

On longer routes, buses stop midway at modest restaurants. Near their destinations many buses turn into large taxis, dropping passengers off one by one along the way. To save time, take a *directo* (express) bus, which still might make a few stops. Be prepared for bus-company employees and bus drivers to speak only Spanish.

The main inconvenience of long-distance buses is the time spent getting there. For example, a bus from San José to the Osa Peninsula is nine hours or more, whereas the flight is one hour. Shorter distances reduce the difference—the bus to Quepos is 3½ hours, while the flight is 30 minutes. There is no central bus station in San José; buses leave from a variety of departure points, depending on the region they serve. You frequently have to return to San José to travel between outlying regions.

■TIP➜ **Avoid putting your belongings in the overhead bin. If you must, keep your eye on them.** If anyone—even someone who looks like a bus employee—offers to put your things in the luggage compartment, politely decline. If you have to put your luggage underneath the bus, get off quickly when you arrive to retrieve it.

Buses usually depart and arrive on time; they may even leave a few minutes early if they are full. Tickets are sold at bus stations and on the buses themselves; reservations aren't accepted, and you must pay in person with cash. Be sure to have loose change and small bills handy; employees won't have change for a 10,000-colón bill. Buses to popular beach and mountain destinations often sell out on weekends and holidays. It's difficult to get tickets to San José on Sunday afternoon. Some companies won't sell you a round-trip ticket from the departure point; if that's the case, make sure the first thing you do on arrival at your destination is to buy a return ticket. Sometimes tickets include seat numbers, which are usually printed on the tops of the seats or above the windows. Smoking is not permitted.

Two private bus companies, Gray Line and Interbus, travel to the most popular tourist destinations in modern, air-conditioned vans. Vehicles for both companies seat 10 to 20 people. (Interbus can also supply coaches for large groups.) Costs from San José range from $45 to $105 one way, but can take hours off your trip. Reservations must always be made at least 24 hours in advance. Be sure to double-check information on the websites—published prices do change and routes may be discontinued. Costa Rica Shuttle offers minivan service that's great if you're traveling in a group. Rates range from $65 to $465 for up to five people.

Car

Hiring a car with a driver makes the most sense for sightseeing in and around San José. You can also usually hire a taxi driver to ferry you around; most will stick to the meter, which will tick at a rate of about $25 for each hour the driver spends waiting for you. At $130 to $150 per day plus the driver's food, hiring a driver for areas outside the San José area costs almost the same as renting a four-wheel-drive vehicle, but is more expensive for multiday trips because you also have to pay for the driver's lodging. Some drivers are also knowledgeable guides; others just drive. Unless they're driving large passenger vans for established companies, it's doubtful that drivers have any special training or licensing.

Hotels can usually direct you to trusted drivers. Alamo provides professional car-and-driver services for a minimum

of three days. On top of the rental fee, you pay $80 for the driver, plus food and lodging.

GASOLINE

You'll usually find 24-hour stations (*gasolineras*) only in San José or along the Pan-American Highway. Most other stations are open 7 to 7, although some are open until midnight. Regular unleaded gasoline is called *regular,* and high-octane unleaded, required in most modern vehicles, is called *súper.* Gas is sold by the liter. Prices are fixed by the government and do not vary from station to station.

Try to fill your tank in cities—gas is more expensive (and more likely to be dirtier) at informal fill-up places in rural areas, where gas stations can be few and far between. Major credit cards are widely accepted. There are no self-service gas stations in Costa Rica. It is not customary to tip attendants. If you want a *factura* (receipt), ask for it.

PARKING

On-street parking is scarce in downtown San José. Where you find a free spot, you'll also find *guachimanes* ("watchmen," informal, usually self-appointed guards). They won't actually get involved if someone tries something with your car, but it's best to give them a couple of dollars (1,000 colones) anyway. It's illegal to park in zones marked by yellow curb paint, or in front of garage doors or driveways, usually marked *no estacionar* (no parking). Downtown parking laws are strictly enforced; the fine for illegal parking may be as high as $90. In places like Alajuela, and Heredia, you'll find signs with a large E in a red circle, and the words *con boleto* (with a ticket). These tickets can be bought for ½-hour (250 colones), one-hour (500 colones), or two-hour (1,000 colones) increments. San José has abandoned this ticket system in favor of an online app.

Getting Here

Safer and ubiquitous are the public lots (*parqueos*), which average about $2 per hour. Most are open late, especially near hopping nightspots or theaters, but check beforehand. Never leave anything inside the car.

Outside San José and the surrounding communities, parking rules are far more lax. Guarded hotel or restaurant parking lots are the rule, with few public lots.

RENTAL CARS

When you reserve a car, ask about cancellation penalties, taxes, drop-off charges (if you're planning to pick up the car in one city and leave it in another), insurance, and surcharges (for being under or over a certain age, for additional drivers, or for driving beyond a specific distance). All these things can add substantially to your costs. Request such extras as car seats and GPS devices when you book.

■ TIP→ **If you're visiting only one or two major areas, taking a shuttle van or a domestic flight is cheaper and more convenient than driving.** Renting is a good choice if you're destination hopping, staying at a hotel outside town, or going well off the beaten path. Car trips to northern Guanacaste from San José can take an entire day, so flying is a better option if you don't have a lot of time. Flying is definitely better than driving for visiting the South Pacific.

A standard vehicle is fine for most destinations, but a *doble-tracción* (four-wheel-drive vehicle) is often essential to reach the remote parts of the country, especially during the rainy season. Even in the dry season, a 4WD vehicle is necessary to reach Monteverde and some off-the-beaten-path destinations on the North and South Pacific coasts. The biggest 4WD vehicles can cost twice as much as an economy car, but compact 4WDs are more reasonable.

Japanese and Korean cars are all the rage in Costa Rica, and that's what your rental vehicle will be too. Most cars in Costa Rica have manual transmission.
■ TIP→ **Specify when making a reservation if you want automatic transmission; it usually costs around $10 more per day.**

Costa Rica has around 30 car-rental firms. Most local firms are affiliated with international chains and offer the same guarantees and services. Tricolor, a local company, gets high marks from visitors. Renting in or near San José is by far the easiest way to go. Around a dozen rental offices line San José's Paseo Colón. It's getting easier to rent outside San José, particularly on the Pacific coast. Several rental companies have branches in Liberia, Quepos, Manuel Antonio, Jacó, Tamarindo, and La Fortuna. In most other places across the country, it's either impossible or very difficult and expensive to rent a car.

Rental cars may not be driven across borders to Nicaragua and Panama. For a $50 fee, Alamo will let you drop off a Costa Rican rental car at the Nicaraguan border at Peñas Blancas and provide you with a Nicaraguan rental on the other side. Another $50 fee applies when returning to Costa Rica. Transfers must be scheduled in advance.

High-season rates in San José begin at $60 per day and $260 per week for an economy car with air-conditioning, manual transmission, and unlimited mileage, along with obligatory insurance. Rates fluctuate considerably according to demand, season, and company. (Although July and August are technically "low season" here, most rental agencies levy high-season rates during those months.) Rates for a 4WD vehicle during high season are $100 per day and $500 to $600 per week. Companies often require a $1,500 deposit, payable by credit card. Some levy a larger amount. Debit cards and cash are not accepted for deposits.

Cars picked up at or returned to San José's Aeropuerto Internacional Juan Santamaría or Liberia's Aeropuerto Internacional Daniel Oduber Quirós incur a 13% surcharge. Check cars thoroughly for damage before you sign the contract. Even tough-looking 4WD vehicles should be coddled. ■TIP→ **Repair charges levied by rental companies for damage—no matter how minor—are outrageous even by U.S. or European standards.** One-way service surcharges are $50 to $150, depending on the drop-off point. To avoid a hefty refueling fee, fill the tank just before you return the car.

It's wise to opt for full insurance coverage. Auto insurance in Costa Rica is a government monopoly. At a minimum, you are required to purchase a collision-damage waiver as well as third-party liability insurance through the rental agency to cover damages to other persons and vehicles. Your own credit-card coverage does not exempt you from this charge. Some rental agencies include such costs in your quoted rates. Many do not, however, and we hear numerous tales of clients shocked at the final tally when they pick up the car. Always ask what is included when you reserve. A few websites trumpet rental vehicles here for as little as $10 per day. Such rates are impossible all-in; you'll always end up paying much, much more.

International driving permits (IDPs), which translate your license into 10 languages, are not necessary in Costa Rica. Your own driver's license is good for a maximum of 90 days. You must carry your passport, or a copy of it with the entry stamp, to prove when you entered the country.

ROAD CONDITIONS
Many travelers shy away from renting a car in Costa Rica. Indeed, this is not an ideal place to drive. In San José, traffic is bad and car theft is rampant (look for guarded lots or hotels with parking). Roads in rural areas are often unpaved or potholed—and tires usually aren't covered by the basic insurance. Ticos have a reputation as reckless drivers—with one of the highest accident rates in the world. Although driving can be a challenge, it's a great way to explore certain regions, especially the North Pacific, the Northern Lowlands, and the Caribbean coast (apart from roadless Tortuguero). Keep in mind that winding roads and poor conditions make most trips longer than you'd normally expect.

The winding Pan-American Highway south of the capital is notorious for long snakes of traffic stuck behind slow-moving trucks. Look out for potholes, even in the smoothest sections of the best roads. Also watch for unmarked speed bumps where you'd least expect them, particularly on main thoroughfares in rural areas. During the rainy season, roads are in much worse shape. Check with your destination before setting out; roads, especially in Limón Province, are prone to washouts and landslides.

San José and the metro area are terribly congested during weekday rush hours (7 to 9 am and 4 to 6 pm). Try to avoid returning to the city on Sunday evening, when traffic from the beaches can be backed up for miles. Frequent fender benders tie up traffic. Keep your windows rolled up in the center of the city, because thieves may reach into your car at stoplights and snatch purses, jewelry, and valuables.

Getting Here

Signposting off main highways is notoriously bad but improving. Distances are given in kilometers (1 km = 0.6 miles). Watch carefully for *No Hay Paso* (Do Not Enter) signs; one-way streets are common, and it's not unusual for a two-way street to suddenly become one way. Single-lane bridges are common in rural areas. A *Ceda el Paso* (Yield) sign facing you means just that: let oncoming traffic proceed before you enter the bridge.

Highways are numbered on signs and maps, but few people use or even know the numbering system. Asking for directions to "Highway 27" will probably be met with a blank stare. Everyone calls it the "Carretera a Caldera" (highway to Caldera, on the Pacific coast) instead. Your best bet is to download the Waze app to navigate. Outside San José you may run into long stretches of unpaved road. Look out for potholes, landslides during the rainy season, and cattle on the roads. Driving at night outside cities and towns is not recommended, because roads are poorly lighted and many don't have painted lines. The sun sets here around 5:30 pm all year long with little variation. Make a point to arrive at your destination before then.

ROADSIDE EMERGENCIES

Costa Rica has no highway emergency service organization. In Costa Rica, 911 is the nationwide number for accidents and all emergencies. Traffic Police (*tránsitos*) are scattered around the country, but Costa Ricans are very good about stopping for people with car trouble. Whatever happens, don't move the car after an accident, even if a monstrous traffic jam ensues. Call 911 first if the accident is serious (nearly everyone has a mobile phone), then call the emergency number of your car-rental agency.

RULES OF THE ROAD

■ TIP➜ **Obey traffic laws religiously, even if Costa Ricans don't.** Fines are frightfully high—a speeding ticket could set you back $500—and evidence exists that transit police target foreigners. Don't plan on skipping the country with an unpaid traffic fine. Your rental agency will get the ticket and bill it to your credit card after your return home.

Driving is on the right side of the road in Costa Rica. The highway speed limit is usually 90 kph (54 mph), which drops to 60 kph (36 mph) in residential areas. In towns, limits range from 30 to 50 kph (18 to 31 mph). Speed limits are enforced in all regions of the country. *Alto* means "stop" and again, *Ceda el Paso* means "yield." Right turns on red are permitted except where signs indicate otherwise, but in San José this is usually not possible because of one-way streets and pedestrian crossings.

Local drunk driving laws are strict. You'll get nailed with a $540 fine if you're caught driving in a "predrunk" state (blood alcohol levels of 0.05% to 0.075%). If your level is higher than that, the car will be confiscated, your license will be taken away, and you risk jail time. Police officers who stop drivers for speeding and drunk driving are sometimes looking for payment on the spot—essentially a bribe. Asking for a ticket instead of paying the bribe discourages corruption and does not compromise your safety. You can generally pay the ticket at your car-rental company, which will pay it on your behalf.

Seat-belt use is mandatory ($170 fine). Car seats are required for children ages four and under; older children must use a booster seat until age 12 ($250 fine). Children over 12 are allowed in the front seat. Drivers are prohibited from texting or using handheld cell phones ($490 fine). Although drivers here appear to park anywhere, parking tickets can set you back up to $90.

 Cruise

Costa Rica is a popular cruise destination on many Panama Canal and Western Caribbean itineraries during a season that runs August through May. Most large cruises stop in the country only once. Smaller ships, including those of Windstar Cruises (capacity 148 guests), Variety Cruises (49 guests), and highly recommended, conservation-minded Lindblad Expeditions (100 guests) offer Costa Rica–focused cruises along the Pacific coast that may include calls in neighboring Panama or Nicaragua.

 Taxi

Taxis are cheap and your best bet for getting around San José. Just about every driver is friendly and eager to use a few English words to tell you about a cousin or sister in New Jersey; however, cabbies truly conversant in English are scarce. Tipping is not expected, but it's a good idea when you've had some extra help, especially with your bags. Taxis are not shared with strangers here; the ride is for you and your party only.

Cabs are red, usually with a yellow light on top. To hail one, extend your hand and wave it at about hip height. If it's available, the driver will often flick his headlights before pulling over. The city is dotted with *paradas de taxi,* taxi queues where you stand the best chance of grabbing one. Taxis generally congregate around the central park in most other cities and towns. Your hotel can usually call you a reputable taxi or private car service, and when you're out to dinner or on the town, ask the manager to call you a cab—it's much easier than hailing one on the street, and safer, too.

■TIP➜ **Taxi drivers are notorious for "not having change." If it's just a few hundred colones, you may as well round up. If it's a lot, ask to go to a store or gas station where you can make change.** To avoid this situation, never use a 10,000-colón bill in a taxi, and avoid paying with 5,000-colón bills unless you've run up almost that much in fares. Drivers will round the fare up to the nearest 100 colones.

Outside the capital area, drivers often use their odometers to creatively calculate fares. Manuel Antonio drivers are notorious for overcharging. It's illegal, but taxis charge up to double for hotel pickups or fares that take them out of the province (such as San José to Alajuela). Ask the manager at your hotel about the going rate. Try to avoid taking an unofficial taxi (*pirata*), although it's sometimes the only option. It's better to ask your hotel for recommendations.

The ride service Uber operates in Costa Rica with service primarily in San José and the metro area. The legality of its status here is unsettled. Until Uber and the authorities work out their differences, you use its services at some risk.

Essentials

⊕ Customs and Duties

When shopping in Costa Rica, keep receipts for all purchases. Be ready to show customs (*aduanas*) officials what you've bought. Pack purchases together in an easily accessible place. The only orchids you can take home are packaged in a tube and come with an export permit.

Visitors entering Costa Rica may bring in 500 grams of tobacco, 5 liters of wine or spirits, 2 kilograms of sweets and chocolates, and the equivalent of $500 worth of merchandise. You can also bring one camera and one video camera, six rolls of film, binoculars, and electrical items for personal use only, including laptops and other electronics. Make sure you have personalized prescriptions for any medication you are taking. Customs officials at San José's international airport rarely examine tourists' luggage by hand, although all incoming bags are x-rayed. If you enter by land, they'll probably look through your bags. Officers at the airport generally speak English and are generally your best (only, really) option for resolving any problem. It usually takes about 30 minutes to clear immigration and customs when arriving in Costa Rica.

🍴 Dining

Dining options around Costa Rica run the spectrum from elegant and formal to beachy and casual. San José and popular tourist centers, especially Manuel Antonio, offer a wide variety of cuisine types. Farther off the beaten track, expect hearty, filling local cuisine. Increasingly common as you move away from San José are the conical thatch roofs of the round, open *rancho* restaurants that serve a combination of traditional staples with simple international fare.

By law, smoking is prohibited in all restaurants and bars.

Every town has at least one *soda*—that's Costa Rican Spanish for a small, family-run restaurant frequented by locals. Don't expect anything as fancy as a menu. A board usually lists specials of the day. The lunchtime *casado* (literally, "married")—a "marriage" of chicken, pork, or beef with rice, beans, cabbage salad, and natural fruit drink—sets you back about $3. No one will bring you a bill; just pay the cashier when you're finished. Having a meal at the local soda always provides a good opportunity to practice your Spanish.

MEALS AND MEALTIMES

In San José and surrounding cities, most sodas are open daily 7 am to early evening, though some close Sunday. Other restaurants are usually open 11 am to 9 pm, and in resort areas some restaurants may stay open later. Normal dining hours in Costa Rica are noon to 3 and 6 to 9. *Desayuno* (breakfast) is served at most sodas and hotels. The traditional breakfast is *gallo pinto*, which includes eggs, plantains, and fried cheese; hotel breakfasts vary widely and generally offer lighter international options in addition to the local stick-to-your-ribs plate. *Almuerzo* (lunch) is the biggest meal of the day for Costa Ricans, and savvy travelers know that lunch specials are often a great bargain. *Cena* (dinner or supper) runs the gamut.

Except for those in hotels, many restaurants close between Christmas and New Year's Day and during Holy Week (Palm Sunday to Easter Sunday). Unless otherwise noted, the restaurants listed in this guide are open daily for lunch and dinner. Credit cards are not accepted at many rural restaurants. Always ask before you order to find out if your credit card will be accepted. Visa and MasterCard are the most commonly accepted cards; American Express and Diners Club are less widely accepted. Discover card is increasingly accepted. ■TIP→ **Remember that 23% is added to all menu prices: 13% for tax and 10% for tip.** Legally, menus are required to show after-tax, after-tip prices in colones; in practice, many tourist-oriented places do not. Because a gratuity (*propina*) is included, there's no need to tip, but if your service is good, it's nice to add a little money to the obligatory 10%.

RESERVATIONS AND DRESS
Costa Ricans generally dress more formally than North Americans. For dinner at an upscale restaurant, long pants and closed-toe shoes are standard for men except in beach locations, and women tend to wear high heels and dressy clothes that show off their figures. Shorts, flip-flops, and tank tops are not acceptable, except at inexpensive restaurants in beach towns.

VEGETARIAN OPTIONS
Vegetarians sticking to lower-budget establishments won't go hungry, but may develop a love-hate relationship with rice, beans, and fried cheese. A simple *sin carne* (no meat) request is often interpreted as "no beef," so specify *solo vegetales* (only vegetables), and for good measure, *nada de cerdo, pollo, o pescado* (no pork, chicken, or fish). More cosmopolitan restaurants are more conscious of vegetarians—upscale Asian restaurants often offer vegetarian options.

WINES, BEER, AND SPIRITS
The ubiquitous sodas generally don't have liquor licenses, but getting a drink in any other eatery isn't usually a problem. This is not a wine-drinking culture; the fruit of the vine you do find likely will come from Chile or Argentina. Don't let Holy Thursday and Good Friday catch you off guard; both are legally dry days.

In general, restaurant prices for imported alcohol—which includes just about everything except local beer, rum, and *guaro,* the local sugarcane firewater—may be more than what you'd like to pay.

News reports have surfaced in recent years of methanol-tainted alcohol. ⚠ **Drink distilled spirits only in reputable hotels and upscale establishments.**

Health
COVID-19
A novel coronavirus brought all travel to a virtual standstill in the first half of 2020. Although the illness is mild in most people, some experience severe and even life-threatening complications. Once travel started up again, albeit slowly and cautiously, travelers were asked to be particularly careful about hygiene and to avoid any unnecessary travel, especially if they are sick.

Older adults, particularly those over 65, have a greater chance of experiencing severe complications from COVID-19. The same is true for people with compromised immune systems or those living with some medical conditions, including diabetes, asthma, heart disease, cancer, HIV/AIDS, kidney disease, and liver disease.

Starting two weeks before a trip, anyone planning to travel should be on the lookout for some of the following symptoms: cough, fever, chills, trouble breathing, muscle pain, sore throat, and new loss of smell or taste. If you experience any of these symptoms, you should not travel at all.

And to protect yourself during travel, do your best to avoid contact with people showing symptoms. Wash your hands often with soap and water. Limit your

Essentials

time in public places, and, when you are out and about, wear a cloth face mask that covers your nose and mouth. Indeed, a mask may be required in some places, such as on an airplane or in a confined space like a theater, where you share the space with a lot of people.

You may wish to bring extra supplies, such as disinfecting wipes, hand sanitizer (12-ounce bottles were allowed in carry-on luggage at this writing), and a first-aid kit with a thermometer.

Given how abruptly travel was curtailed in March 2020, it is wise to consider protecting yourself by purchasing a travel insurance policy that will reimburse you for any costs related to COVID-19 related cancellations. Not all travel insurance policies protect against pandemic-related cancellations, so always read the fine print.

SPECIFIC ISSUES IN COSTA RICA

Costa Rica is one of several Latin American countries where transmission of the mosquito-borne Zika virus has been identified. Because risks to fetal development during any trimester of pregnancy have been reported, the CDC recommends that pregnant women avoid travel to Costa Rica. If travel is necessary, take strict steps to avoid mosquito bites.

The CDC marked Costa Rica as an area infested by the *Aedes aegypti* (dengue-carrier) mosquito, but not as an epidemic region. The highest-risk area is the Caribbean, especially in the rainy season. The mosquito-borne chikungunya virus began appearing in Costa Rica in 2015. In areas with Zika, chikungunya, and dengue, use mosquito nets, wear clothing that covers your whole body, and use *repelente* (insect repellent) and *espirales* (mosquito coils), sold in supermarkets, pharmacies, and, sometimes, small country stores. ■ TIP→ **Repellents made**

with DEET or picaridin are most effective. Perfume and aftershave can actually attract mosquitoes.

It's unlikely that you will contract chikungunya or dengue, but if you start suffering from high fever, the shakes, or joint pain, make sure you ask to be tested for these diseases at a local clinic. Your embassy can provide you with a list of recommended doctors and dentists. Such symptoms in the weeks following your return should also spark concern.

Poisonous snakes, scorpions, and other pests pose a small threat in Costa Rica.

Water is generally safe to drink, especially around San José, but the quality can vary; to be safe, drink bottled water. In rural areas you run a mild risk of encountering drinking water, fresh fruit, and vegetables contaminated by fecal matter, which in most cases causes a bit of traveler's diarrhea but can cause leptospirosis (which can be treated by antibiotics if detected early). Stay on the safe side by avoiding uncooked food, unpasteurized milk, and ice—ask for drinks *sin hielo* (without ice). Ceviche, raw fish cured in lemon juice—a favorite appetizer, especially at seaside resorts—is generally safe to eat.

Mild cases of diarrhea may respond to Imodium (known generically as loperamide) or Pepto-Bismol, both of which can be purchased over the counter. Drink plenty of purified water or tea; chamomile (*manzanilla* in Spanish) is a good folk remedy. In severe cases, rehydrate yourself with a salt-sugar solution (½ teaspoon salt and 4 tablespoons sugar per quart of water).

Heatstroke and dehydration are real dangers, especially for hikers, so drink lots of water. Take at least 1 liter per person for every hour you plan to be on the trail. Sunburn is the most common traveler's health problem. Use sunscreen with SPF 30 or higher. Most pharmacies and supermarkets carry sunscreen in a wide range of SPFs, though it is relatively pricey.

The greatest danger to your person actually lies off Costa Rica's popular beaches: riptides are common wherever there are waves, and tourists run into serious difficulties in them every year. If you see waves, ask the locals where it's safe to swim; and if you're uncertain, don't go in deeper than your waist. If you get caught in a rip current, swim parallel to the beach until you're free of it, and then swim back to shore. ■TIP➡ **Avoid swimming where a town's main river opens up to the sea. Septic tanks aren't common.** Do not fly within 24 hours of scuba diving.

OVER-THE-COUNTER REMEDIES
Farmacia is Spanish for pharmacy, and the names for common drugs like *aspirina, ibúprofen,* and *acetaminofina* (Tylenol or Panadol) are basically the same as they are in English. Some drugs for which you need a prescription back home are sold over the counter in Costa Rica. Pharmacies throughout the country are generally open from 8 to 8. Some pharmacies in San José stay open 24 hours.

Government facilities—the so-called Caja hospitals (short for Caja Costarricense de Seguro Social, or Costa Rican Social Security System)—and clinics are of acceptable quality, but notoriously overburdened. Private hospitals are more accustomed to serving foreigners.

Immunizations
No specific immunizations or vaccinations are required for visits to Costa Rica from the United States. The U.S. Centers for Disease Control and Prevention recommends that all travelers to Costa Rica

be up to date on routine immunizations, namely seasonal influenza, tetanus, diphtheria, and pertussis (whooping cough). (Measles reappeared in Costa Rica in 2019, imported by an unvaccinated visitor. The country had been measles-free for many years.) The CDC also suggests being immunized against typhoid and hepatitis A, especially if you're headed off the beaten path or staying a few weeks. The agency no longer recommends malaria prophylaxis for travel to Costa Rica for most visitors, except for a couple of small pockets near the Nicaraguan border. The CDC does suggest taking precautions to avoid mosquito bites. You must have the yellow fever vaccination if arriving directly from certain countries in South America and Africa.

Lodging
Costa Rica excels in its selection of boutique hotels, tasteful bungalows, and bed-and-breakfasts, which offer a high degree of personalized service. Because they're generally small, you may have to book one or two months ahead, and up to six months in the high season, especially around Christmas or Easter. Reserving through an association or agency can significantly reduce the time you spend scanning the Internet, but you can often get a better deal and negotiate longer-stay or low-season discounts directly with the hotel.

Nature lodges in the South Pacific may be less expensive than they initially appear, as the nightly rate usually includes three hearty meals and sometimes even guided hikes. Internet access isn't a given, even if a place has a website. Many have an eco-friendly approach (even to luxury), so air-conditioning might not be included. Consider how isolated you want to be; some lodges are miles from neighbors and have few rainy-day diversions. The voluntary "green leaf" rating system evaluates eco-friendly lodgings. A listing can be found at 🌐 *www.turismo-sostenible.co.cr*.

The lodgings we list are Costa Rica's cream of the crop in each price category. When pricing accommodations, always ask what's included and what costs extra. Keep in mind that prices don't include 16.4% service and tax. Smoking is prohibited in all hotels, both in rooms and public areas. *Our local writers vet every hotel to recommend the best overnights in each price category, from budget to expensive. Unless otherwise specified, you can expect private bath, phone, and TV in your room. Hotel reviews have been shortened. For full information, visit Fodors.com.*

APARTMENT AND HOUSE RENTALS

Rental houses are common all over Costa Rica, particularly in the Pacific coast destinations of Manuel Antonio, Tamarindo, Ocotal, and Jacó. Homes can accommodate whole families, often for less money and at a higher comfort level than a hotel. Properties are often owned by foreigners, most of them based in the United States, with property managers in Costa Rica.

Resort communities with villa-style lodgings are also growing. Escape Villas Costa Rica lists rentals in Manuel Antonio, Dominical, Jacó, Playa Flamingo, Tamarindo, Nosara, Sámara, Arenal, Puerto Viejo de Talamanca, and the Central Valley. Villas & Apartments Abroad has a good selection of rentals on the North and Central Pacific coasts. For the southern Nicoya Peninsula and Playa Hermosa on the North Pacific coast, check Costa Rica Beach Rentals.

BED-AND-BREAKFASTS

A number of quintessential bed-and-breakfasts—small and homey—are clustered in the Central Valley, generally offering hearty breakfasts and friendly inside information for $60 to $120 per night. You'll also find them scattered through the rest of the country, mixed in with other self-titled bed-and-breakfasts that range from small cabins in the mountains to luxurious boutique-hotel-style digs in the North Pacific region. The service Airbnb brokers many lodgings and homestay experiences in Costa Rica.

HOME EXCHANGES

With a direct home exchange, you stay in someone else's home while they stay in yours. Some outfits also deal with vacation homes, so you're not actually staying in someone's full-time residence, just their vacant weekend place.

Home exchanges are an excellent way to immerse yourself in the true Costa Rica, particularly if you've been here before. Drawbacks include restricted options and dates. Many companies list home exchanges, but we've found Home Exchange, which lists a handful of jazzy houses around Costa Rica, to be the most reliable.

$ Money

In general, Costa Rica is cheaper than North America or Europe, but travelers looking for dirt-cheap developing-nation deals may find it's more expensive than they bargained for—and prices are rising as more foreigners visit.

The tourism industry quotes prices in dollars. You may certainly pay for hotels and tours in local currency, but they will be priced at that day's equivalent colón exchange rate.

Food in modest restaurants and public transportation are inexpensive. A 2-km (1-mile) taxi ride costs about $2. Although they are springing up at a healthy rate, don't count on using an ATM outside San José.

CURRENCY AND EXCHANGE

Costa Rica's currency is the *colón* (pronounced *koh-LOHN*; the plural is *colones*). Prices are shown with a "¢" sign in front of the number. At this writing, the colón is about 570 to the U.S. dollar and 620 to the euro. Coins come in denominations of 5, 10, 25, 50, 100, and 500 colones. Be careful not to mix up the very similar 100- and 500-colón coins. Bills come in denominations of 1,000 (red), 2,000 (blue), 5,000 (yellow), 10,000 (green), 20,000 (orange), and 50,000 (purple) colones. As you'd expect, prices have a lot of zeroes. If you want to approximate a colón price in dollars, lop off the last two digits and divide by 6. You'll be pretty close (3,000 colones = a little more than $5). Avoid using larger-denomination bills in taxis, on buses, or in small stores. Many tourist-oriented businesses accept U.S. dollars, although the exchange rate might not be favorable to you. Make sure your dollars are in good condition—no tears or writing—and don't use or accept anything larger than a $20. Many counterfeit $50 and $100 bills circulate here and almost no one will accept them for payment.

Assuming you can find them at all, Costa Rican colones are sold abroad at terrible rates, so wait until you arrive in Costa Rica to get local currency. U.S. dollars are still the easiest to exchange, but euros can be exchanged for colones at just about any Banco Nacional office and at the San José and Escazú branches of other banks. Private banks—Scotiabank and BAC San José—are the best places to change U.S. dollars and traveler's checks. The arrivals area of the international airports in San José and Liberia both have ATMs and are your best bet for getting cash after you land. There is a branch of the BAC San José upstairs in the check-in area of Juan Santamaría airport where you can exchange money when you arrive or depart—it's a much better deal than the Global Exchange counter in the baggage-claim area or at the departure gates. Airport taxi and van drivers accept U.S. dollars. Outdoor money changers are rarely seen on the street, but avoid them if they approach; you will most certainly get a bad deal, and you risk robbery by pulling out wads of cash.

■ TIP➔ **Even if a currency-exchange booth has a sign promising no commission, rest assured that there's some kind of huge, hidden fee. (Oh … that's right. The sign didn't say no fee). And as for rates, you're almost always better off getting foreign currency at an ATM or exchanging money at a bank.**

⊙ Passport

U.S. citizens need only a passport to enter Costa Rica and a return plane ticket home or to another country for stays of up to 90 days. Make sure it's up to date. We've received much conflicting information, even within officialdom, about how long your passport must be valid—the official answer is "for the duration of your trip," but government officials, passport officers, and airline check-in agents frequently interpret the rules differently. ⚠ **To be on the safe side, make sure your passport is valid for at least six months.**

Essentials

➕ Safety

Violent crime is not a serious problem in Costa Rica, but thieves can easily prey on tourists, so be alert. The government has created a Tourism Police unit whose more than 250 officers can be seen on bikes or motorcycles patrolling areas in Guanacaste, San José, and the Arenal area.

For many English-speaking tourists, standing out like a sore thumb can't be avoided. But there are some precautions you can take, including not bringing anything you can't stand to lose, not flashing your expensive jewelry or watches, and using your hotel's safe for valuables.

■ In cities, don't carry expensive cameras or lots of cash.

■ Wear backpacks on your front; thieves can slit your backpack and run away with its contents before you notice.

■ Don't wear a waist pack, because thieves can cut the strap.

■ Distribute your cash and any valuables (including credit cards and passport) between a deep front pocket, an inside jacket or vest pocket, and a hidden money belt. (If you use a money belt, have some small bills handy so you don't have to reach for it in public.)

■ Keep your hand on your wallet if you are in a crowd or on a bus.

■ Don't let your purse dangle from your shoulder; always hold on to it with your hand for added security.

■ Keep car windows rolled up and car doors locked at all times in cities.

■ Park in designated lots—car theft is common—or if that's not possible, accept the offer of the *guachimán* (a term adopted from English, pronounced "watchie man")—men or boys who watch your car while you're gone. Give them the equivalent of a dollar an hour when you return.

■ Never leave valuables in a car, even in an attended parking lot.

■ Padlock your luggage.

■ Talk with locals or your hotel staff about any areas you should avoid. Never leave a drink unattended in a club or bar: scams involving date-rape drugs have been reported, targeting both men and women.

■ Never leave your belongings unattended, including at the beach or in a tent.

■ If someone does try to rob you, immediately surrender your possessions and don't try to be a hero.

Scams do occur in San José. A distraction artist might squirt you with something, or spill something on you, then try to clean you off while his partner steals your backpack. Pickpockets and bag slashers work buses and crowds. Beware of anyone who seems overly friendly, aggressively helpful, or disrespectful of your personal space. Be particularly vigilant around San José's Coca-Cola bus terminal, one of the dicier areas but a central transportation hub.

A few tourists have been hit with the slashed-tire scam: someone punctures the tires of your rental car (often right at the airport, when you arrive) and then comes to your "aid" when you pull off to the side of the road and robs you. Forget about the rims: always drive to the nearest open gas station or service center if you get a flat.

Costa Rica remains a *mostly* safe destination for solo travelers, but a few high-profile cases of violence against visitors in recent years have rattled everyone here. Striking a proper balance—being guarded without refusing all contact with people—can be done, but also can be difficult. Ask at your hotel which neighborhoods to avoid at night. If you want to fend off persistent admirers, you can politely say, *Por favor, necesito un tiempo a solas* (I'd like some time on my own, please). Stronger is *Por favor, no me moleste* (Please, stop bothering me).

$ Taxes

The airport departure tax for tourists is $31. Most airlines include the tax in the ticket price. A few do not, which will require you to pay the tax upon departure in cash (dollars or colones) or with a Visa or MasterCard. All Costa Rican businesses charge a 13% sales tax, called the IVA. It is included in the shelf price you see. There is no additional hotel tax. You'll pay only the IVA, usually on top of the posted rates. Restaurants add the 13% IVA tax and 10% service fee to meals. By law, menu prices are supposed to reflect the final price you pay in local currency; many tourist-oriented dining spots ignore the requirement. Tourists are not refunded for taxes paid in Costa Rica.

Tipping

Costa Rica doesn't have a tipping culture, but positive reinforcement goes a long way to fostering a culture of good service; good intentions are usually there, but execution can be hit or miss. Tip only for good service. ■TIP→ **Tipping in colones is best. Never tip with U.S. coins, because there's no way for locals to exchange them.**

Tipping	
Bellhop	$1–$5 or 500 colones per bag, depending on the level of the hotel
Hotel Concierge	$5 or more, if he or she performs a service for you
Hotel Doorman	$1–$2 if he helps you get a cab
Hotel Maid	$1–$3 or 500–1,500 colones per day (either daily or at the end of your stay, in cash)
Hotel Room-Service Waiter	$1–$2 or 500–1,000 colones per delivery, even if a service charge has been added
Tour Guide	$10 or 5,000 colones per group member per day
Hired Driver	10% of the rental
Waiter	10%–15%, with 15% being the norm at high-end restaurants; nothing additional if a service charge is added to the bill
Bartender	$1 per drink
Restroom Attendant	$1
Coat-check	$1–$2 per item checked unless there is a fee, then nothing
Taxi Driver	200–300 colones if they've helped you navigate a complicated set of directions, or 500 colones if they've helped you with luggage; otherwise nothing

Essentials

Visa

A visa is not required for U.S. citizens for stays less than 90 days, but you must have a return ticket.

Visitor Information

The official tourism board, the Instituto Costarricense de Turismo (ICT), has an office on Avenida Central in San José and a small desk in the baggage claim area at Juan Santamaría airport. The airport counter contains a few brochures but is staffed only sporadically. Visitor information is provided by the Costa Rica Tourism Board in the United States.

ONLINE TRAVEL TOOLS

The REAL Costa Rica slips in a bit of attitude with its information, and is a bit lax on updating, but scores high marks for overall accuracy. Scope out detailed maps, driving distances, and pictorial guides to the locations of hotels and businesses in some communities at CostaRicaMap.com. The Association of Residents of Costa Rica online forums are some of the region's most active and informed, with topics ranging from business and pleasure trips to the real-estate market, with loads of information if you're interested in moving to the country. *The Tico Times* publishes news about Costa Rica, much of it of interest to visitors.

When to Go

HIGH SEASON $$$$

The sunniest, driest season in most of the country occurs from mid-December through April, with Christmas and Easter bracketing the busiest tourist season. March and April are sweltering in lowland areas, with temperatures in the arid North Pacific frequently exceeding 90°F.

LOW SEASON $

Afternoon showers kick in by May and last through November, with a brief drier season in June and July. Rain or not, North American and European summer vacations do increase the influx of visitors from June through August. Rains become heavy in September and October.

VALUE SEASON $$

The transition periods between rainy and dry seasons and back again make a marvelous time to visit Costa Rica. Visitor numbers are smaller and the threat of rain is minimal.

What to Pack for Costa Rica

FRAMELESS BACKPACK OR DUFFEL BAG

Even if you're planning to stay only in luxury resorts, odds are that at least once you'll have to haul your stuff a distance from the shuttle drop-off or the airport. Consider, too, that domestic airlines have tight weight restrictions—at this writing 11 to 13 kilograms, or 25 to 30 pounds—and not all buses have luggage compartments. Frameless backpacks and duffel bags can be squeezed into tight spaces and are less conspicuous than fancier luggage.

COMFORTABLE, HAND-WASHABLE CLOTHING

T-shirts and shorts are acceptable near the beach and in tourist areas; long-sleeve shirts and pants protect your skin from ferocious sun and, in coastal regions, mosquitoes. Leave your jeans behind—they take forever to dry.

WATERPROOF, LIGHTWEIGHT JACKET

A lightweight jacket and sweater will be welcome on cool nights, early mornings, and trips up volcanoes; you'll need even warmer clothes for trips to Chirripó National Park or Cerro de la Muerte and overnight stays in San Gerardo de Dota or on the slopes of Poás Volcano.

ONE WRINKLE-FREE NICE OUTFIT

While daytime activities require your active gear, you'll still want to go to a nice dinner or a bar when you're in Costa Rica, too. You likely won't need anything too fancy. By "nice," we mean a casual wrinkle-free dress or pants.

YOUR OWN TOILETRIES

It's sometimes tough to find tampons, so bring your own and, since septic systems here generally cannot handle them, refrain from flushing them down the toilet. For almost all toiletries, including contact lens supplies, a pharmacy is your best bet once you arrive. Don't forget sunblock, and expect to sweat it off and reapply regularly in the high humidity.

PACKING CHECKLIST FOR COSTA RICA

- Quick-drying synthetic-fiber shirts and socks

- Hiking boots or shoes that can get muddy and wet

- Waterproof sport sandals (especially for the Osa Peninsula)

- Knee-high socks for rubber boots that are supplied at many lodges

- A pair of lightweight pants

- Waterproof, lightweight jacket, windbreaker, or poncho

- Day pack for hikes

- Sweater for cool nights and early mornings

- Swimsuit

- Insect repellent with DEET

- Flashlight with spare batteries

- Sunscreen with a minimum SPF 30

- Large, portable water bottle

- Hat and/or bandannas

- Binoculars (with carrying strap)

- Imodium and Pepto-Bismol

- Swiss Army knife

- Zip-style plastic bags

- Toilet paper (rarely provided in public bathrooms) and toiletries

- One wrinkle-free, nice outfit

- Frameless backpack or duffel bag

Helpful Phrases in Costa Rica

BASICS

Hello	Hola	**oh**-lah
Yes/no	Sí/no	see/no
Please	Por favor	pore fah-**vore**
May I?	¿Me permite?	may pair-**mee**-tay
Thank you	Gracias	**Grah**-see-as
You're welcome	De nada	day **nah**-dah
I'm sorry	Lo siento	lo see-**en**-toh
Good morning!	¡Buenos días!	**bway**-nohs **dee**-ahs
Good evening!	¡Buenas tardes! (after 2pm)	**bway**-nahs-**tar**-dess
	¡Buenas noches! (after 8pm)	**bway**-nahs **no**-chess
Good-bye!	¡Adiós!/¡Hasta luego!	ah-dee-**ohss/ah** -stah **lwe**-go
Mr./Mrs.	Señor/Señora	sen-**yor**/ sen-**yohr**-ah
Miss	Señorita	sen-yo-**ree**-tah
Pleased to meet you	Mucho gusto	**moo**-cho **goose**-toh
How are you?	¿Que tal?	keh-tal

NUMBERS

one	un, uno	oon, **oo**-no
two	dos	dos
three	tres	tress
four	cuatro	**kwah**-tro
five	cinco	**sink**-oh
six	seis	saice
seven	siete	see-**et**-eh
eight	ocho	**o**-cho
nine	nueve	new-**eh**-vey
ten	diez	dee-**es**
eleven	once	**ohn**-seh
twelve	doce	**doh**-seh
thirteen	trece	**treh**-seh
fourteen	catorce	ka-**tohr**-seh
fifteen	quince	**keen**-seh
sixteen	dieciséis	dee-es-ee-**saice**
seventeen	diecisiete	dee-**es**-ee-see-**et**-eh
eighteen	dieciocho	dee-**es**-ee-**o**-cho
nineteen	diecinueve	dee-**es**-ee-new-**ev**-eh
twenty	veinte	**vain**-teh
twenty-one	veintiuno	**vain**-te-**oo**-noh
thirty	treinta	**train**-tah
forty	cuarenta	kwah-**ren**-tah
fifty	cincuenta	seen-**kwen**-tah
sixty	sesenta	sess-**en**-tah
seventy	setenta	set-**en**-tah
eighty	ochenta	oh-**chen**-tah
ninety	noventa	no-**ven**-tah
one hundred	cien	see-**en**
one thousand	mil	meel
one million	un millón	oon meel-**yohn**

COLORS

black	negro	**neh**-groh
blue	azul	ah-**sool**
brown	marrón	mah-**ron**
green	verde	**ver**-deh
orange	naranja	na-**rahn**-hah
red	rojo	**roh**-hoh
white	blanco	**blahn**-koh
yellow	amarillo	ah-mah-**ree**-yoh

DAYS OF THE WEEK

Sunday	domingo	doe-**meen**-goh
Monday	lunes	**loo**-ness
Tuesday	martes	**mahr**-tess
Wednesday	miércoles	me-**air**-koh-less
Thursday	jueves	hoo-**ev**-ess
Friday	viernes	vee-**air**-ness
Saturday	sábado	**sah**-bah-doh

MONTHS

January	enero	eh-**neh**-roh
February	febrero	feh-**breh**-roh
March	marzo	**mahr**-soh
April	abril	ah-**breel**
May	mayo	**my**-oh
June	junio	**hoo**-nee-oh
July	julio	**hoo**-lee-yoh
August	agosto	ah-**ghost**-toh
September	septiembre	sep-tee-**em**-breh
October	octubre	oak-**too**-breh
November	noviembre	no-vee-**em**-breh
December	diciembre	dee-see-**em**-breh

USEFUL WORDS AND PHRASES

Do you speak English?	¿Habla usted inglés?	ah-blah oos-**ted** in-**glehs**
I don't speak Spanish.	No hablo español	no **ah**-bloh es-pahn-**yol**
I don't understand.	No entiendo	no en-tee-**en**-doh
I understand.	Entiendo	en-tee-**en**-doh
I don't know.	No sé	no **seh**
I'm American.	Soy americano (americana)	soy ah-meh-ree-**kah**-no (ah-meh-ree-**kah**-nah)
What's your name?	¿Cómo se llama ?	koh-mo seh **yah**-mah
My name is . . .	Me llamo . . .	may **yah**-moh
What time is it?	¿Qué hora es?	keh **o**-rah es
How?	¿Cómo?	**koh**-mo
When?	¿Cuándo?	**kwahn**-doh
Yesterday	Ayer	ah-**yehr**
Today	hoy	oy
Tomorrow	mañana	mahn-**yah**-nah
Tonight	Esta noche	es-tah **no**-cheh
What?	¿Qué?	keh
What is it?	¿Qué es esto?	keh es **es**-toh

Why?	¿Por qué?	pore **keh**
Who?	¿Quién?	kee-**yen**
Where is . . .	¿Dónde está . . .	**dohn**-deh es-**tah**
. . . the train station?	la estación del tren?	la es-tah-see-**on** del trehn
. . . the subway station?	estación de metro	la es-ta-see-**on** del **meh**-tro
. . . the bus stop?	la parada del autobus?	la pah-**rah**-dah del ow-toh-**boos**
. . . the terminal? (airport)	el aeropuerto	el air-oh-**pwar**-toh
. . . the post office?	la oficina de correos?	la oh-fee-**see**- nah deh koh-**rreh**-os
. . . the bank?	el banco?	el **bahn**-koh
. . . the hotel?	el hotel?	el oh-**tel**
. . . the museum?	el museo?	el moo-**seh**-oh
. . . the hospital?	el hospital?	el ohss-pee-**tal**
. . . the elevator?	el ascensor?	el ah-sen-**sohr**
Where are the restrooms?	el baño?	el **bahn**-yoh
Here/there	Aquí/allí	ah-**key**/ah-**yee**
Open/closed	Abierto/cerrado	ah-bee-**er**-toh/ ser-**ah**-doh
Left/right	Izquierda/derecha	iss-key-**eh**-dah/ dare-**eh**-chah
Is it near?	¿Está cerca?	es-**tah sehr**-kah
Is it far?	¿Está lejos?	es-**tah leh**-hoss
I'd like . . .	Quisiera . . .	kee-see-**ehr**-ah
. . . a room	un cuarto/una habitación	oon **kwahr**-toh/**oo**-nah ah-bee-tah-see-**on**
. . . the key	la llave	lah **yah**-veh
. . . a newspaper	un periódico	oon pehr-ee-**oh**-dee-koh
. . . a stamp	un sello de correo	oon **seh**-yo deh korr-**eh**-oh
I'd like to buy . . .	Quisiera comprar . . .	kee-see-**ehr**-ah kohm-**prahr**
. . . soap	jabón	hah-**bohn**
. . . suntan lotion	crema solar	**kreh**-mah soh-**lar**
. . . envelopes	sobres	**so**-brehs
. . . writing paper	papel	pah-**pel**
. . . a postcard	una tarjeta postal	**oon**-ah tar-**het**-ah post-**ahl**
. . . a ticket	un billete (travel)	oon bee-**yee**-teh
	una entrada (concert etc.)	oona en-**trah**-dah
How much is it?	¿Cuánto cuesta?	**kwahn**-toh **kwes**-tah
It's expensive/ cheap	Es caro/barato	es **kah**-roh/ bah-**rah**-toh
A little/a lot	Un poquito/mucho	oon poh-**kee**-toh/ **moo**-choh
More/less	Más/menos	mahss/**men**-ohss
Enough/too (much)	Suficiente/	soo-fee-see-**en**-teh/
I am ill/sick	Estoy enfermo(a)	es-**toy** en-**fehr**-moh(mah)
Call a doctor	Llame a un medico	**ya**-meh ah oon **med**-ee-koh

| Help! | Socorro | soh-**koh**-roh |
| Stop! | Pare | **pah**-reh |

DINING OUT

I'd like to reserve a table . . .	Quisiera reservar una mesa . . .	kee-**syeh**-rah rreh-sehr-**bahr** oo-nah **meh**-sah . . .
. . . for two people.	para dos personas.	**pah**-rah dohs pehr-**soh**-nahs
. . . for this evening.	para esta noche.	**pah**-rah **ehs**-tah **noh**-cheh
. . . for 8 PM	para las ocho de la noche.	**pah**-rah lahs **oh**-choh deh lah **noh**-cheh
A bottle of . . .	Una botella de . . .	oo-nah bo-**teh**-yah deh
A cup of . . .	Una taza de . . .	oo-nah **tah**-sah deh
A glass of . . .	Un vaso (water, soda, etc.) de...	oon **vah**-so deh
	Una copa (wine, spirits, etc.) de...	oona **coh**-pah deh
Bill/check	La cuenta	lah **kwen**-tah
Bread	El pan	el pahn
Breakfast	El desayuno	el deh-sah-**yoon**-oh
Butter	La mantequilla	lah man-teh-**kee**-yah
Coffee	Café	kah-**feh**
Dinner	La cena	lah **seh**-nah
Fork	El tenedor	el ten-eh-**dor**
I don't eat meat	No como carne	noh koh-moh **kahr**-neh
I cannot eat . . .	No puedo comer . . .	noh **pweh**-doh koh-**mehr**
I'd like to order . . .	Quiero pedir . . .	**kee**-yehr-oh peh-**deer**
I'd like . . .	Me gustaría . . .	Meh goo-stah-**ee**-ah
I'm hungry/thirsty	Tengo hambre/sed	**Tehn**-goh hahm-breh/seth
Is service/the tip included?	¿Está incluida la propina?	es-**tah** in-cloo-ee-dah lah pro-**pee**-nah
Knife	El cuchillo	el koo-**chee**-yo
Lunch	La comida	lah koh-**mee**-dah
Menu	La carta, el menú	lah **cart**-ah, el meh-**noo**
Napkin	La servilleta	lah sehr-vee-**yet**-ah
Pepper	La pimienta	lah pee-mee-**en**-tah
Plate	plato	
Please give me . . .	Por favor déme . . .	pore fah-**vor** deh-meh
Salt	La sal	lah sahl
Spoon	Una cuchara	oo-nah koo-**chah**-rah
Sugar	El ázucar	el ah-**su**-kar
Tea	té	teh
Water	agua	**ah**-gwah
Wine	vino	**vee**-noh

Tours

Bicycle

Costa Rica is mountainous and rough around the edges. It's a rare bird who attempts a road-biking tour here. But the payoff for the ungroomed, tire-munching terrain is uncrowded, wildly beautiful off-road routes. Most bike-tour operators want to make sure you're in moderately good shape and do some biking at home. Operators generally provide top-notch equipment, including bikes and helmets, but welcome serious mountain bikers who bring their own ride. Operators usually meet you at the airport and take care of all logistics.

Useful topographical maps (not biking maps per se) are generally provided as part of the tour, and include unpaved roads. If you're striking out on your own, these maps can usually be found at downtown San José's Lehmann bookstore for about $5. Some basic Spanish is highly recommended if you're going to do it yourself.

■ TIP➔ **Check with individual airlines about bike-packing requirements.** Cardboard bike boxes can be found at bike shops for about $15; more secure options start at $40. International travelers often can substitute a bike for a piece of checked luggage at no charge (if the box conforms to regular baggage dimensions), but U.S. airlines will sometimes charge a $100 to $200 handling fee each way.

Bike Arenal
BICYCLE TOURS | Biking packages in the Arenal area and around the country are suitable for all skill levels, with short and long ride options for each day. ☎ 2479–9020, 866/465–4114 in North America ⊕ www.bikearenal.com ☒ From $80 for ½-day tour.

Coast to Coast Adventures
BICYCLE TOURS | Multiday cycling tours are available for a variety of skill levels, some easier than the jaunts other outfitters do. ☎ 4001–2342 in Costa Rica ⊕ www.coasttocoastadventures.com ☒ From $1,150 for 8-day tour.

✪ Bird-Watching

You will get more out of your time in Costa Rica by taking a tour rather than trying to find birds on your own. Bring your own binoculars, but don't worry about a spotting scope; if you go with a company that specializes in birding tours, your guide will have one. Expect to see about 300 species during a weeklong tour. Many U.S. travel companies subcontract with Costa Rican tour operators. By arranging your tour directly with local companies, you save money.

Birdwatching Costa Rica
SPECIAL-INTEREST | Comprehensive multiday birding tours are offered by this company, with eight options in various regions of Costa Rica as well as tours customized to your own requirements. You can opt for a single-day excursion as well. ☎ 2771–4582 in Costa Rica ⊕ www.birdwatchingcostarica.com ☒ From $194 per person for 1-day tour.

✪ Diving

Costa Rica's remote Cocos Island—one of the world's best dive spots—can be visited only on multiday scuba safaris, but Guanacaste, the South Pacific, and, to a lesser extent, the Caribbean offer some respectable underwater adventures. Also in the south lies Caño Island, a good alternative to Cocos Island, particularly in the rainy season, when dive sites closer to shore are clouded by river runoff.

Aggressor Adventures

ADVENTURE TOURS | The *Okeanos Aggressor I* and *II* visit Cocos Island several times throughout the year on multiday diving excursions. ☎ *800/348–2628 in North America* ⊕ *www.aggressor.com* ✉ *From $5,199 per person in 10-night packages.*

Bill Beard's Costa Rica

ADVENTURE TOURS | This Gulf of Papagayo outfitter pioneered Costa Rican diving tours and offers several Pacific-coast options. ☎ *877/853–0538 in North America, 2479–7089 in Costa Rica* ⊕ *www.billbeardcostarica.com* ✉ *From $95 for ½-day dive.*

Sirenas Diving Costa Rica

ADVENTURE TOURS | Based in Playa Hermosa, Sirenas Diving has trips to all the dive sites in Guanacaste and the North Pacific coast, as well as the complete range of PADI courses. ☎ *8721–8055 in Costa Rica* ⊕ *www.sirenasdivingcostarica.com* ✉ *From $125.*

Undersea Hunter

ADVENTURE TOURS | The *Argo* and *Sea Hunter* make 10-day, nine-night excursions several times a year to Cocos Island, with six full days of diving. ☎ *2228–6613, 800/203–2120 in North America* ⊕ *www.underseahunter.com* ✉ *From $4,445.*

🚶 Fishing

If fishing is your primary objective in Costa Rica, you are best off booking a package. During peak season you may not even be able to find a hotel room in the hot fishing spots, let alone one of the top boats and skippers. The major fish populations move along the Pacific coast through the year, and tarpon and snook fishing on the Caribbean is subject to the vagaries of seasonal wind and weather but viable year-round.

Costa Rica Outdoors

SPECIAL-INTEREST | San José–based Costa Rica Outdoors is one of the best bets for full service and honest advice about where to go and works with the widest range of operators around the country. ☎ *800/308–3394 in North America* ⊕ *www.costaricaoutdoors.com* ✉ *4-night packages from $950.*

J. P. Sportfishing Tours

SPECIAL-INTEREST | This longtime operator is the place to get hooked up for fishing in Quepos and the Central Pacific coast. Experienced skippers are fluent in English and, depending on the season, offer the chance to catch marlin, dorado, Pacific sailfish, snapper, yellowfin, or roosterfish. You'll need to obtain your own fishing license. ☎ *2777–1613, 866/620–4188 in North America* ⊕ *www.jpsportfishing.com* ✉ *From $885 for 1–4 anglers for ½ day.*

Kingfisher Sportfishing

SPECIAL-INTEREST | Anglers in the know recommend Kingfisher Sportfishing in Playa Carrillo, Guanacaste. Trips to suit experienced anglers and novices of all ages are available. ☎ *2656–0091 in Costa Rica* ⊕ *www.costaricabillfishing.com* ✉ *From $800 for 2–4 anglers for ½ day.*

Río Colorado Lodge

SPECIAL-INTEREST | This is the best known of the fishing lodges in Barra del Colorado, north of Tortuguero on the northern Caribbean coast, specializing in tarpon, snook, and light-tackle game fish. Accommodations are in an air-conditioned lodge with good amenities. ☎ *2232–4063, 800/243–9777 in North America* ⊕ *www.riocoloradolodge.com* ✉ *From $2,248 for 6 days, 5 nights, with 3 full days of fishing.*

Tours

The Zancudo Lodge

SPECIAL-INTEREST | Near Golfito on the South Pacific coast, this lodge mixes sportfishing with upscale accommodations and a variety of other activities. ☎ 2776–0008, 800/854–8791 in North America ⊕ www.zancudolodge.com ✉ From $3,595 for 3 days' fishing, accommodations, and meals.

 ## Golf

Putting on a green against a dramatic Pacific backdrop isn't the first image that springs to mind for Costa Rican vacations, but the increase in luxury resorts and upscale tourism has created a respectable, albeit small, golfing circuit in the Central Valley and along the Pacific coast. Most packages maximize links time with side excursions to explore the country's natural riches.

Costa Rica Golf Adventures

SPECIAL-INTEREST | Multiday golf tours include accommodations at four- and five-star lodgings and a choice of six courses, including some of Central America's finest. ☎ 888/536–8510 in North America, 2293–9785 in Costa Rica ⊕ www.golfcr. com ✉ From $609 (3 days of golf, including lodging).

Spanish-Language Programs

Thousands of people travel to Costa Rica every year to study Spanish. Dozens of schools in and around San José offer professional instruction and homestays, and there are several smaller schools outside the capital. Bundling a homestay with a local family into the course is always a way to increase your proficiency.

Conversa

SPECIAL-INTEREST | This school in Santa Ana, in the west Central Valley, offers hourly classes as well as "Intense" (4 hours a day) and "Super Intense" (5½ hours per day) programs ranging from a week to a month (with further add-on weeks available). ☎ 4001–2497, 888/669–1664 in North America ⊕ www.conversa. com ✉ From $840 for 1 wk.

CPI Spanish Immersion School

SPECIAL-INTEREST | You can sign up for four or five hours per day of study at CPI's schools in Heredia, Monteverde, and Playa Flamingo. ☎ 2265–6306, 877/373–3116 ⊕ www.cpi-edu.com ✉ From $460 (1 wk).

Escuela d'Amore

SPECIAL-INTEREST | In beautiful Manuel Antonio, this is one of Costa Rica's prime places to combine language study and beach time. ☎ 2777–1143, 800/261–3203 in North America ⊕ www.edcostarica. com ✉ From $845 (2 wks).

ILISA

SPECIAL-INTEREST | Cultural-immersion classes are based in San Pedro, San José's preeminent east-side suburb. ☎ 2280–0700, 727/230–0563 in North America ⊕ www.ilisa.com ✉ From $440 (1 wk).

Institute for Central American Development Studies (ICADS)

SPECIAL-INTEREST | Language programs here include optional academic seminars in English about Central America's political, social, and economic conditions. ☎ 2225–0508 ⊕ www.icads.org ✉ From $1,990 (4 wks).

Surfing

Most Costa Rican travel agencies have packages that ferry both veterans and newcomers between the country's famed bicoastal breaks.

Del Mar Adventures

SPECIAL-INTEREST | Based in Nosara and with a branch at Playa Hermosa on the Central Pacific coast, this company offers a variety of surf lessons, including women-only classes. ☎ 8385–8535 in Costa Rica, 855/833–5627 in North America ⊕ www.delmarsurfcamp.com ✉ Lessons from $90.

◉ Volunteer Programs

In recent years more and more Costa Ricans have realized the need to preserve their country's precious biodiversity. Both Ticos and far-flung environmentalists have founded volunteer and educational concerns to this end.

Volunteer opportunities span a range of diverse interests. You can tag sea turtles as part of a research project, build trails in a national park, or volunteer at an orphanage. Many of the organizations require at least rudimentary Spanish. Beach cleanups, recycling, and some wildlife projects don't require proficiency in Spanish.

Costa Rican Humanitarian Foundation
(*Fundación Humanitaria*)

SPECIAL-INTEREST | Volunteer opportunities include working with indigenous communities, women, children, community-based clinics, and education centers. ☎ 8390–4192 in Costa Rica, 310/402–2377 in North America ⊕ www.crhf.org ✉ Donation to foundation, plus $40/day for homestay.

Institute for Central American Development Studies (*ICADS*)

SPECIAL-INTEREST | The Institute delves into development and social justice in a variety of volunteer programs that let you work with schools and disadvantaged communities. ☎ 2225–0508 in Costa Rica ⊕ www.icads.org ✉ From $1,990 (4 wks).

Talamancan Association of Eco-Tourism and Conservation (*ATEC*)

SPECIAL-INTEREST | As well as designing short group and individual outings centered on Costa Rican wildlife and indigenous culture, ATEC keeps an updated list of up to 30 Caribbean-based organizations that welcome volunteers. A two-month commitment is required. ☎ 2750–0398 in Costa Rica ⊕ www. ateccr.org.

Great Itineraries

Great Itineraries in Costa Rica

Costa Rica looks disarmingly small on the map. This country the size of Vermont and New Hampshire combined *should* be easy to take in, right? Arrive here and you'll see that a mountainous spine transects the country and dirt roads make driving downright abysmal. Ambitious plans to see the entire country never materialize. Rather than rushing around—and rushing is something you can't easily do here—pick and choose a couple of destinations and get to know them well.

LAY OF THE LAND

San José and the Central Valley. Costa Rica's congested capital sits smack-dab in the center of the country. Because it's the country's transportation hub, you'll likely pass through, even if only on your first and last days here. Coming to Costa Rica on business? You'll probably get to know the city well. San José gives way to bustling suburbs, then smaller towns, then pastoral countryside ringing the capital in a mountain valley (elevation 3,000–5,000 feet). Take in the valley as day trips from the city or base yourself out here. San José's Aeropuerto Internacional Juan Santamaría sits in the Central Valley, too.

The North. Transportation is straightforward in the vast, mostly flat northern one-third of the country that makes up the Northern Lowlands. This area has two of Costa Rica's biggest attractions, Arenal Volcano and Monteverde Cloud Forest. Roads are decent here, with the exception of the notoriously awful route to Monteverde—and, even here, paving is on the drawing board. You'd think a highway, north to south, would line the northern Pacific coast, making it easy to bop among this region's famed beaches

and down through the Nicoya Peninsula. However, you frequently have to head back inland to get to the next strand of sand down the coast. If this area is your sole destination, book your flights to Liberia's Aeropuerto Internacional Daniel Oduber Quirós, rather than down to San José.

Manuel Antonio and the Central Pacific Coast. A spiffy highway puts San José an hour or two from the beaches along this section of the coast. That's great for the tourism industry here, but you should book space for holidays and high-season weekends in advance: Costa Ricans love to take minibreaks to this region, too.

The Osa Peninsula and the South Pacific. The south is rarely first-timer's territory—even most Costa Ricans have never ventured to the southern third of their country, a land of remote beaches, mountains, and wilderness ecolodges. Transportation is improving to and within this splendid region, but can still be a chore. Sample it, though, and you might count yourself among the growing number of fans.

Tortuguero and the Caribbean Coast. Once you get over the hump of the mountains north of San José, a good road puts you directly en route to the sultry, tropical southern Caribbean coast, still largely the province of European visitors and less known in American circles. The northern Caribbean coast near Tortuguero National Park is a different story entirely: no roads exist up here, making boat or plane your only travel options.

TIMING

Costa Rican Tourist Board surveys show that U.S. visitors spend an average of nine days on a trip here. That's ample occasion to take in destinations in a couple of regions, and it accounts for time to get from one place to the other. (Depending on the places you choose,

that last part can be more of a chore than you may realize.) Rather than packing too much in, keep repeating that most Costa Rican of expressions, *si Dios lo quiere*: "If God is willing," you'll get back here to partake of what you didn't see the first time around.

ITINERARIES

We proffer five possible itineraries, each taking in a small slice of the country and showcasing some of the crowd-pleasing destinations for which Costa Rica is known. The San José, Central Valley, and Tortuguero itinerary leans more toward the "leave the driving to them" end of the spectrum; the Osa Peninsula itinerary incorporates domestic air travel. If you have time, these itineraries can be combined or broken apart and reassembled to suit your needs. If you are doing the driving, remember the sun sets here around 5:30 pm all year long, give or take about 15 minutes. Always plan to arrive at your destination before dark.

PEAK SEASON: DECEMBER TO APRIL

The Christmas-to-Easter period essentially defines Costa Rica's high season. With little rain and temperatures in the 80s and higher, the country makes an ideal escape for North Americans and Europeans fleeing those frigid winters.

Great Itineraries

Best of Costa Rica: 7-Day Itinerary

Volcanoes and beaches are two of the things Costa Rica does best, so the classic first-timer's itinerary to Costa Rica takes in two of its most popular destinations: the impressive Arenal Volcano and the beaches of the Central Pacific coast's lovely Manuel Antonio.

DAY 1: SAN JOSÉ

Arrive in **San José's Aeropuerto Internacional Juan Santamaría** (most arrivals are in the evening) and head straight to one of the small hotels north of the city in the **Central Valley.** The airport lies northwest of the capital, so staying in San José requires a bit of backtracking. The **Hampton Inn** just across from the airport lets you ease into your Costa Rican experience in familiar surroundings; the **Xandari Resort & Spa** offers a far more local, and pricier, first night here. Brace yourself for lines at immigration if you arrive in the evening along with several other large flights from North America. Try to get a seat near the front of the plane, and don't dawdle when disembarking.

DAY 2: POÁS VOLCANO AND ARENAL
(45 minutes by paved road from airport to Poás Volcano; 2½ hours by paved road from airport to La Fortuna)

If you have the time, set out early for **Poás Volcano,** where you can peer over the edge of the crater. It makes an interesting start to your first full day in Costa Rica. Fortify yourself with the fruits, jellies, and chocolates sold by vendors on the road up to the summit. Otherwise, get going to the Arenal area right away. Set out on the scenic drive—turn north at San Ramón—to **La Fortuna,** which sits at the foot of **Arenal Volcano**

and is its hub. Bear in mind that portions of the route twist and turn and fog over by noon. Drop your luggage at one of many fantastic hotels, and partake of the myriad activities here. Take a zipline or hanging-bridges tour through the forest canopy north of the volcano with amazing views of the mountain itself. Follow up with a visit to one of many hot-springs complexes in the area as the sun sets behind Volcán Arenal. They all line the road that runs west from La Fortuna around the north side of the volcano.

Shuttle vans have hotel-to-hotel service, usually from the Hampton Inn to many Arenal-area hotels. We like **Nayara Gardens** with its terrific views of the volcano.

DAY 3: CAÑO NEGRO WILDLIFE REFUGE
(90 minutes by paved road from La Fortuna)

Spend the day in the **Caño Negro Wildlife Refuge,** a lowland forest reserve replete with waterfowl near the Nicaraguan border. Book your trip the night before; tour operators in La Fortuna keep evening hours for exactly that reason. All transport is included, and it's far easier than trying to visit the refuge on your own.

DAY 4: SCENIC DRIVE TO THE CENTRAL PACIFIC
(4–4½ hours by paved road from La Fortuna)

Today's a traveling day—a chance to really see the country's famous landscape. Four hours' drive from Arenal takes you to fabled **Manuel Antonio** on the Central Pacific coast. Beyond-beautiful hotels are the norm here, and you have your choice of seaside luxury—we like the **Arenas del Mar Beachfront and Nature Resort**—or tree-shrouded lodges like **Villas Nicolás.**

Hotel-to-hotel shuttle-van services can get you from Arenal to Manuel Antonio.

If you drive instead, start out as early as possible. You'll pass again through the mountainous stretch between La Fortuna and San Ramón—that's the way you came—to get back to the main highway heading east. Exit at **Atenas,** a pleasant town that makes a good lunch stop. South of Atenas, hook up with the Pacific Highway—follow the signs directing you to Caldera. The Jacó exit takes you on the fairly good road to Manuel Antonio.

DAY 5: MANUEL ANTONIO NATIONAL PARK
(10–20 minutes from most area lodgings)

Manuel Antonio is Costa Rica's most famous national park for a reason: it has beaches, lush rain forest, mangrove swamps, and rocky coves with abundant marine life. You can—and should—spend an entire day exploring the park, home to capuchin monkeys, sloths, agoutis, and 200 species of birds. It's also one of two locales in the country where you'll see squirrel monkeys. Almost all Manuel Antonio hotels have transport to the park. If yours doesn't, taxis are plentiful and cheap. Don't forget: the park is closed on Monday.

DAY 6: BEACHES
(10–20 minutes from most area lodgings)

Days 1 through 5 were on-the-go days. Reward yourself today with lots of relaxation. One of Costa Rica's most popular strands of sand, **Playa Espadilla** hums with activity on weekends and holidays. Alas, riptides can make swimming risky here. Within the national park, **Playa Manuel Antonio** and **Playa Espadilla Sur** offer more seclusion, but no real facilities. Manuel Antonio and its neighboring town, **Quepos,** have the best selection of restaurants of any beach community in the country.

DAY 7: SAN JOSÉ
(2–2½ hours by paved road from Manuel Antonio)

An easy morning drive back to San José gives you time to spend the afternoon in the city. Visit the **Teatro Nacional** and the **Museo de Oro Precolombino,** and save time for late-afternoon shopping. An evening meal caps off your trip before you turn in early to get ready for tomorrow morning's departure. We recommend that you check in three hours before your flight.

Great Itineraries

Day Trips from Playa Hermosa: 6-Day Itinerary

The province of Guanacaste and the Nicoya Peninsula are known as Costa Rica's "fun in the sun" destination. Kids and adults alike enjoy the region's huge variety of land- and water-based activities.

DAYS 1 AND 2: PLAYA HERMOSA
(30 minutes by paved road from Liberia airport)

Most arrivals to **Liberia's Aeropuerto Internacional Daniel Oduber Quirós,** Costa Rica's second international airport, are in the early afternoon. You can't go wrong with any North Pacific beach, but we like **Playa Hermosa** for its location about 30 minutes from the airport—it's convenient as a base for visiting area attractions. The smaller lodgings here make the perfect antidote to the megaresorts that are not too far away. They can arrange to have transport waiting at the airport, with advance notice. The **Hotel Playa Hermosa Bosque del Mar** hugs the beach itself. The big all-inclusives up here have their own minivans to whisk you in air-conditioned comfort from airport to resort. Otherwise, the airport contains the full selection of car-rental counters.

Start Day 2 off lazing on the beach. Morning is a great time of day to hit the beach in this part of Costa Rica—the breezes are refreshingly cool and the sun hasn't started to beat down yet. After lunch, explore Playa Hermosa's "metropolis," the small town of **Playas del Coco.** Quite frankly, Coco is our least favorite beach up here. But we like the town for its little souvenir shops, restaurants, and culture.

Taxis are the easiest way to travel between Playa Hermosa and Coco, about 10 minutes away. Have your hotel call one, and flag one down on the street in town when it's time to return.

DAY 3: RINCÓN DE LA VIEJA VOLCANO
(1½-hour drive from Playa Hermosa, the last 45 minutes by dirt and stone road)

The top of **Rincón de la Vieja Volcano,** with its steaming, bubbling, oozing fumaroles, lies about 90 minutes from Hermosa. Lather on the sunscreen and head for the **Hacienda Guachipelín**—tours are open to nonhotel guests, too—and its volcano-viewing hikes, canopy tours, rappelling, horseback riding, mountain biking, and river tubing. Cap off the day with a spa treatment, complete with thermal mud bath.

If you don't have a rental car, book a private driver for the day, which can usually be arranged through your hotel. The region has seen an increase in tour operators who can take you to area attractions, too, which your hotel can arrange.

If you are driving yourself, you may wish to spend the night up here and not trek back down to the coast the same day. Hacienda Guachipelín itself is a solid lodging value.

DAY 4: GOLF OR DIVING
(30 minutes by paved road from Playa Hermosa to Papagayo Golf & Country Club; 10 minutes by paved road from Playa Hermosa to Playas del Coco)

Golf is big up here. The 18-hole **Vista Ridge Golf & Country Club** is just southeast of Playas del Coco. The other popular, slightly pricey, sport here is scuba diving. Dive operators are based in nearby Playas del Coco—we like **Rich Coast Diving**—or Playa Panamá. A daylong diving course won't certify you, but gives you a taste of the deep. A taxi can transport you to and from the golf course, and dive operators will pick you up from and return you to your hotel.

PACIFIC OCEAN

Rincón de la Vieja Volcano

Hacienda Guachipelín

Aeropuerto Internacional Daniel Oduber Quirós

Liberia

Playa Panamá
Playa Hermosa

Playas del Coco

Papagayo Golf & Country Club

Río Corobicí

Cañas

Palo Verde National Park

DAY 5: PALO VERDE NATIONAL PARK

(1½ hours by paved road from Playa Hermosa to Palo Verde, the last 45 minutes by dirt road)

Start with a morning guided tour at **Palo Verde National Park,** one of the last remaining dry tropical forests in Central America. The **Organization for Tropical Studies,** which operates the biological station here, has terrific guides. Spend the afternoon observing nature in a more relaxed fashion with a float (easy Class I and II rapids) down the nearby Río Corobicí. The aptly named **Safaris Corobicí,** near Cañas on the Pan-American Highway, specializes in the floating trips. This excursion is a bit roundabout, so this is the day your own vehicle would come in handiest. But you can also hire a private driver or get a tour operator to fix you up (arranged through your hotel). Bring water to drink: it gets hot here.

DAY 6: DEPARTURE

(30 minutes by paved road from Playa Hermosa)

Grab a last dip in the ocean this morning, because your flight departs from Liberia in the early afternoon. The airport terminal is modern and spacious, but you should still allow yourself plenty of time for check-in.

Tips

■ A car is ideal for this itinerary, yet many area attractions and tour operators provide transport to and from area lodging if you aren't too far afield.

■ All-inclusive resorts do a good job of organizing local excursions with local operators, so if you're staying at one, take advantage of them.

■ Getting from beach to beach often requires travel back inland. There is no real (i.e., navigable) coastal road.

■ If ever there were a case for an off-season vacation, this is it. This driest, hottest part of the country gets very dry and hot from January through April. We prefer the region during the low season after April.

Great Itineraries

Discovering San José, the Central Valley, and Tortuguero: 7-Day Itinerary

It's entirely possible to take in a mix of urban, suburban, and remote Costa Rica without having to rent a car with this let-someone-else-do-the-driving itinerary. Tortuguero, on the Caribbean coast, is accessible only by boat.

DAY 1: ARRIVAL

Following your evening arrival in **San José,** head to one of the many in-town lodgings. **Hotel Grano de Oro,** west of downtown, or the **Gran Hotel Costa Rica,** downtown, are good options. Your hotel can arrange for transport with advance notice. The big players have their own hotel shuttle vans, but smaller lodgings can arrange for a taxi. Otherwise, grab one of the official orange airport cabs at the customs exit. Plan on spending $30 for a taxi ride into the city.

DAY 2: SAN JOSÉ

A full day in the city gives you time to spend the morning visiting the **Teatro Nacional** and the **Museo de Oro Precolombino**—they're on the same block. Duck into the **Museo del Jade** in the afternoon, especially if it's raining, or partake of some late-afternoon crafts shopping. An evening meal at one of San José's fine restaurants caps off the day. Asian restaurant **Tin Jo** is one of the country's top dining experiences.

DAY 3: DAY TOURS TO THE CENTRAL VALLEY

San José's location makes it the perfect place from which to fan out to the Central Valley's many sights. The list of things to see and do in the valley is impressive: learn all about coffee at the installations of **Café Britt,** near Heredia, or the **Doka Estate,** near Alajuela; peer over the rim into bubbling cauldrons of the **Poás** or **Irazú** volcanoes; wander among fluttering butterflies at the **Butterfly Farm** in Alajuela; step back into history in the **Orosi Valley**; or shop for crafts in **Sarchí,** the country's signature artisan town. Hitting all the attractions in one day is next to impossible, of course—Café Britt lies 30 minutes from the capital, but plan on up to an hour to reach the others. San José's several tour operators offer half- or full-day excursions that incorporate various Central Valley attractions, or can tailor one that fits your interests. Plan to be picked up from your hotel between 7 and 8 in the morning and return after midday for a half-day tour, or around 5 for a daylong excursion.

DAYS 4 AND 5: TORTUGUERO
(2 hours by paved road plus 2–2½ hours by boat from San José)

An early-morning pickup at your San José hotel and you are off to one of Costa Rica's most remote destinations. Once you traverse **Braulio Carrillo National Park** north of the capital, you switch from van to boat at a put-in point in the Caribbean lowlands. The final stretch to **Tortuguero** takes place by boat; this is a roadless part of Costa Rica. Arrive at your lodge by midafternoon. Rest and get cleaned up for a sumptuous dinner.

Although you can do Tortuguero on your own, most visitors opt for an all-inclusive tour. **Pachira Lodge,** along the main canal, or the more secluded **Evergreen Lodge** are good options.

The knock at the door comes early in the morning of Day 5 as you are roused out of bed to go on a prebreakfast bird-watching excursion in **Tortuguero National Park.** (Remember: there are no roads, so transport is by boat.) The day entails a guided hike in the national park

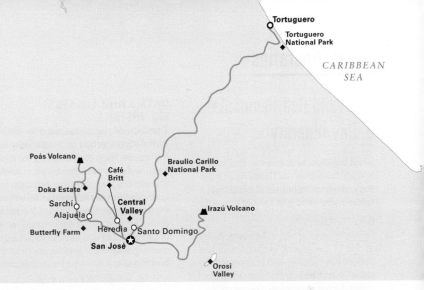

Tortuguero

Tortuguero National Park

CARIBBEAN SEA

Poás Volcano ▲

Café Britt

Braulio Carillo National Park ◆

Doka Estate ◆

Sarchí ○

Central Valley

Alajuela ○

Irazú Volcano ▲

Butterfly Farm ◆

Heredia ○   Santo Domingo

San José ✪

Orosi Valley

and a stroll through the tiny village of the same name. Evenings give way to turtle-watching during the nesting season (July through October).

Tortuguero is the rainiest spot in Costa Rica, and the rains spread evenly throughout the year. Plan to get wet (it's half the fun). Most of the lodges here provide ponchos and rain boots.

DAY 6: BACK TO SAN JOSÉ
(60–90 minutes by boat plus 2 hours by paved road from Tortuguero)

Day 6 is your fourth day in reverse. After a hearty breakfast at your lodge, you board the launches back to civilization. The boat travels faster than it did on the way up here. You transfer to a waiting van at the put-in point and head back to your city hotel, arriving in the afternoon. Tortuguero lodges do offer two-day/one-night excursions, but go for the extra day if your schedule permits.

DAY 7: DEPARTURE
(30–45 minutes from San José)

Most international flights depart Aero-puerto Internacional Juan Santamaría in the morning. Recommended check-in time is always three hours in advance of departure.

Tips

■ Tortuguero has no roads. Forget the car; someone else has to take care of your transportation needs.

■ A few San José hotels might allow you to leave your things while you're touring outside the city, a particular boon when you're headed to Tortuguero. Space inside the small boats is limited.

■ July through October is prime turtle-nesting season in Tortuguero.

■ If you have more money than time, the Tortuguero lodges can arrange for you to fly to and from San José on domestic airline SANSA.

Great Itineraries

The Wild Osa Peninsula: 8-Day Itinerary

Most travelers who make it this far south already have a trip to Costa Rica under their belts, but feel free to break that rule. All you need is a spirit of adventure.

DAY 1: ARRIVAL

Following your arrival in **San José,** head to one of the several lodgings near the airport. We recommend staying out here rather than heading into San José itself, about 30 minutes away; you need to be back at the airport the next morning for your flight to the Osa Peninsula, and you'll appreciate the extra time. You cannot get closer to the airport than the **Hampton Inn,** just across the highway. Wherever you stay, your hotel can arrange for transport with advance notice, whether its own shuttle vans or sending a taxi for you. Otherwise, grab one of the official orange airport cabs as you exit customs.

DAY 2: SAN JOSÉ TO PUERTO JIMÉNEZ TO CABO MATAPALO

(1 hour by air to Puerto Jiménez and 1 hour by gravel road)

You're back at the airport for your hour-long flight to Puerto Jiménez on domestic airlines SANSA or Skyway. Check-in is a leisurely affair, but you should arrive at the airport at least 45 minutes before departure. Arrival at the airstrip in Puerto Jiménez, Osa's "metropolis," is even more low-key. Our recommended lodgings in Cabo Matapalo, 21 km (14 miles) south, can arrange for transfers. Each has its own style: **Lapa Ríos** rates as one of the world's premier ecolodges; **El Remanso** is quiet and intimate; **Bosque del Cabo** draws an engaging, sociable clientele.

DAYS 3 AND 4: NATURE EXCURSIONS

The Cabo Matapalo lodges offer their own nature-themed activities. They range from quiet hikes to snorkeling to horseback riding to more strenuous rappelling and climbing. Highly regarded local tour operator **Everyday Adventures** takes you on excursions that skew toward the adrenaline-rush end of the spectrum. The end of the day puts you back at your lodge, chatting with other guests well into the evening about what you saw that day.

DAY 5: CABO MATAPALO TO CARATE

(1 hour by road)

Carate is literally Osa's end of the road. The lodges here can arrange for an overland transfer from Cabo Matapalo or all the way from Puerto Jiménez if you're skipping Matapalo entirely. Accommodations here have their own personalities, too: **Finca Exótica** caters to nature lovers, **Luna Lodge** is for the yoga or wellness devotee. A trip to the beach rounds out your day. Alas, as is the case elsewhere in Costa Rica, riptides are dangerous here.

DAY 6: CORCOVADO NATIONAL PARK

(45-minute hike to La Leona park entrance from Carate; half day or full day of hiking in park)

If you've come this far, Costa Rica's famed **Corcovado National Park** should be on your agenda. The lodges here can arrange for guided walks to the park—it's the only way to approach Corcovado from this direction. You must enter Corcovado accompanied by a guide, and you must pay your entry fee in advance. Accommodation inside the park—advance reservations are mandatory—is rustic. Any overnights would necessitate adding extra days onto this itinerary. No

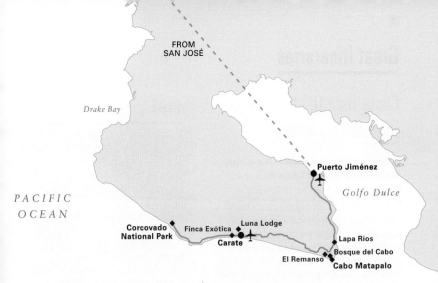

FROM
SAN JOSÉ

Drake Bay

PACIFIC
OCEAN

Puerto Jiménez

Golfo Dulce

Corcovado
National Park   Finca Exótica   Luna Lodge
                        Carate

Lapa Ríos
Bosque del Cabo
El Remanso   Cabo Matapalo

one ever tires of repeating the platitudes about Corcovado, most often citing *National Geographic*'s description of the park as "the most biologically intense place on earth in terms of biodiversity."

DAYS 7 AND 8: CARATE TO PUERTO JIMÉNEZ TO SAN JOSÉ
(2 hours by road and 1 hour by air to San José)

The lodges here can arrange for an overland transfer back to Puerto Jiménez, or you can take the *colectivo,* the public transport here. Carate does have its own tiny airstrip with charter planes making the quick jaunt back to Puerto Jiménez. If timing does not coincide with SANSA or Skyway's schedules, a night in Puerto Jiménez gives you a dose of civilization again in the style of a tropical frontier town. You can catch a flight back to San José the next morning, from where you can depart for other destinations in Costa Rica.

Tips

■ Opt for morning flights during the rainy season.

■ Same-day international-to-domestic and domestic-to-international air connections are risky; both SANSA and Skyway advise against them.

■ Domestic airlines limit your luggage to anywhere from 15 to 30 pounds, depending on your fare. Pack lightly, or make advance arrangements with your hotel.

■ September and October are the wettest months of the rainy season and Osa roads occasionally become impassable.

■ Lodges and tour operators here can take care of your advance fee payment to enter Corcovado National Park. Visitor numbers are limited; make arrangements far in advance.

Great Itineraries

Costa Rica Off the Beaten Path: 9-Day Itinerary

Avoid the crowds in lesser-known, but up-and-coming, destinations.

DAY 1: ARRIVAL

Following your evening arrival at Juan Santamaría International Airport, head into San José. The airport lies northwest of the capital, and because you'll be heading east out of the city the next morning, this gets you well on your way there. The west-side **Hotel Grano de Oro** or the downtown **Gran Hotel Costa Rica** are tried-and-true favorites and make for wonderful ways to ease into your Costa Rican experience.

DAY 2: SAN JOSÉ TO CARTAGO TO THE OROSI VALLEY
(1 hour by road)

Allow yourself a leisurely breakfast at your hotel and avoid San José's morning rush hour. Get going by 10 and you'll be fine. A half-hour drive takes you to Cartago and its two must-see sights: tradition holds that the **Basílica de Nuestra Señora de los Ángeles** was the site of a 17th-century apparition of the Virgin Mary; and Magmática fills you in on all you wanted to know about earthquakes and lets you shake and rattle in a simulated tremor. A leisurely drive east takes you to Paraíso. Just before Paraíso lies the **Jardín Botánico Lankester,** a must for orchid lovers. Turn south at the center of town and descend steeply into the Orosi Valley. Spend the night at the rustic, but smart, **Hotel Quelitales** or the sumptuous **La Casona del Cafetal.**

DAY 3: OROSI VALLEY

A loop road lets you easily navigate the entire valley. **Ujarrás** houses the ruins of Costa Rica's first church. The town of Orosi itself contains the **Church of San José de Orosi,** the country's oldest house of worship still in use. Whether you stay there or not, **La Casona del Cafetal** is one of Costa Rica's most famous lunch stops. Expect a long wait on weekends.

DAY 4: OROSI VALLEY TO SAN GERARDO DE DOTA
(2 hours by road)

For optimal driving conditions, get an early start today. Head back toward Paraíso and Cartago, then south on the Pan-American Highway. You'll pass over the ominously named Cerro de la Muerte (Hill of Death). You'll be fine, but the high-elevation stretch of highway fogs over by noon. At Km 80, turn off to San Gerardo de Dota and navigate the steep descent carefully. You'll welcome the sight of the **Savegre Hotel** or **Dantica Cloud Forest Lodge,** both wonderful places to spend a couple of nights.

DAY 5: SAN GERARDO DE DOTA

San Gerardo means bird-watching. The activity generally requires some hiking here. The two lodges we suggest both have top-notch on-site guides. If you're not a birder, don't forget that this is one of Costa Rica's premier trout-fishing and horseback-riding destinations.

DAY 6: SAN GERARDO DE DOTA TO COSTA BALLENA

(2 hours by road)

Another early start today and it's back up the road and back down the Pan-American Highway. The highway descends to the hub city of San Isidro de El General, a good refueling stop. An hour-long descent to the coast takes you to the beach town of Dominical. Your reward for the rugged highway conditions you've endured so far is the so-called Costanera, a modern highway that hugs the Pacific Ocean. Head south along the coast.

DAYS 7 AND 8: COSTA BALLENA AND BALLENA NATIONAL MARINE PARK

A couple of days of exploring this stretch of coast between Dominical and Ojochal allow you to experience up-and-coming Costa Rica. **El Castillo Boutique Luxury Hotel** and **Kura** offer some amazing luxury down here, but **Río Tico Safari Lodge** provides comfort at affordable prices. Ballena National Marine Park, the region's original sine qua non, provides whale- and dolphin-watching tours, along with terrific sunsets and sections with swimming—a treat hard to come by at many of the country's beaches.

DAY 9: COSTA BALLENA TO SAN JOSÉ

(3–4 hours by road)

You need not return to San José the same way you came. At Dominical, the Costanera continues northwest to Quepos and Jacó, from where you can catch the tolled Carretera a Caldera (Highway 27) back to the capital with much better road conditions.

Contacts

Visitor Information

Association of Residents of Costa Rica. (*ARCR*). ⊕ *www.arcr.net.* **CostaRicaMap.com.** ⊕ *www.costaricamap.com.* **Instituto Costarricense de Turismo.** (*ICT*). ☏ *2299–5800* ⊕ *www.visitcostarica.com.* **The REAL Costa Rica.** ⊕ *www.therealcostarica.com.* **The Tico Times.** ⊕ *www.ticotimes.net.*

Embassy

United States Embassy. (*Embajada de los Estados Unidos*). ✉ *C. 120 and Avda. 0, Pavas* ☏ *2519–2000* ⊕ *cr.usembassy.gov.*

✈ Air

AIRPORT INFORMATION Aeropuerto Internacional Daniel Oduber Quirós. (*LIR*). ☏ *2666–9600 in Costa Rica.* **Aeropuerto Internacional Juan Santamaría.** (*SJO*). ☏ *2437–2400* ⊕ *www.sjoairport.com.*

DOMESTIC AND CHARTER AIRLINES Aerobell Air Charter. ✉ *Pavas* ☏ *4000–2030 in Costa Rica* ⊕ *www.aerobell.com.* **Green Airways.** ☏ *4070–0771*, *888/828–8471* ⊕ *www.costaricagreenair.com.* **SANSA.** ☏ *2290–4100 in Costa Rica,* *877/767–2672 in North America* ⊕ *www.flysansa.com.* **Skyway.** ☏ *4010–0244*, *877/841–8330* ⊕ *www.skywaycr.com.*

Bus

Central Line. ✉ *Avda. 7, C. 10, Barrio La Merced* ☏ *2221–9115* ⊕ *www.transportescentralline.com.* **Tica Bus.** ✉ *Avda. 3, C. 26, 200 m north and 100 m west of Torre Mercedes, Paseo Colón* ☏ *2296–9788* ⊕ *www.ticabus.com.* **TransNica.** ✉ *C. 22, Avdas. 3–5, San José* ☏ *8408–0000* ⊕ *www.transnica.com.*

SHUTTLE-VAN SERVICES Costa Rica Shuttle. ☏ *4000–1040*, *800/849–9403 in North America* ⊕ *www.costaricashuttle.com.* **Gray Line.** ☏ *2220–2126*, *800/719–3905 in North America* ⊕ *www.2020.graylinecostarica.com.* **Interbus.** ☏ *4100–0888* ⊕ *www.interbusonline.com.*

Car

LOCAL AGENCIES Economy. ☏ *877/326–7368 in North America, 2299–2000 in Costa Rica* ⊕ *www.economyrentacar.com.* **Tricolor.** ☏ *800/949–0234 in North America, 2440–3333 in Costa Rica* ⊕ *www.tricolorcarrental.com.* **Vamos.** ☏ *4000–0557 in Costa Rica, 800/601–8806 in North America* ⊕ *www.vamosrentacar.com.*

MAJOR AGENCIES Alamo. ☏ *2242–7733 in Costa Rica, 844/354–6962 in North America* ⊕ *www.alamocostarica.com.* **Avis.** ☏ *2293–2222 in Costa Rica, 800/633–3469 in North America* ⊕ *www.avis.cr.* **Budget.** ☏ *2436–2018 in Costa Rica, 800/218–7992 in North America* ⊕ *www.budget.co.cr.*

🛏 Lodging

Airbnb. ⊕ *www.airbnb.com.* **Costa Rica Beach Rentals.** ☏ *8340–3842*, *973/917–8046 in North America* ⊕ *www.costarica-beachrentals.com.* **Escape Villas Costa Rica.** ☏ *6078–4297*, *888/818–2097 in North America* ⊕ *www.villascostarica.com.* **Home Exchange.** ☏ *No phone* ⊕ *www.homeexchange.com.* **Villas & Apartments Abroad.** ✉ *385 Fifth Ave., Suite 1008, New York* ☏ *212/213–6435 in North America* ⊕ *www.vaanyc.com.*

Chapter 3

BIODIVERSITY

Updated by
Jeffrey Van Fleet

Costa Rica's forests hold an array of flora and fauna so vast and diverse that scientists haven't even named thousands of the species found here. The country covers less than 0.03% of Earth's surface, yet it contains nearly 5% of the planet's plant and animal species. Costa Rica has at least 9,000 plant species, including more than 1,200 types of orchids, some 2,000 kinds of butterflies, and 876 bird species.

Costa Rica acts as a natural land bridge between North and South America, so there is a lot of intercontinental exchange. But the country's flora and fauna add up to more than what has passed between the continents. Costa Rica's biological diversity is the result of its tropical location, its varied topography, and the many microclimates resulting from the combination of mountains, valleys, and lowlands. The isthmus also acts as a hospitable haven to many species that couldn't complete the journey from one hemisphere to the other. The rain forests of Costa Rica's Caribbean and southwestern lowlands are the northernmost home of such southern species as the crab-eating raccoon. The tropical dry forests of the northern Pacific slope are the southern limit for such North American species as the Virginia opossum. And then there are the dozens of northern bird species that spend their winter holidays here.

Research and planning go a long way in a place like Costa Rica. A short trip around the country can put you in one landscape after another, each with its own array of plants and animals, from the false bird of paradise and guanacaste tree to the three-toed sloth and the holy grail of birds, the resplendent quetzal. The country's renowned national park system holds examples of all of its major ecosystems, including cloud forests, mangroves and wetlands, rain forests, and tropical dry forests, and some of its most impressive sights. In terms of activities, there's more interesting stuff to do here than could possibly ever fit into one vacation. But keep in mind that somewhere around three-fourths of the country has been urbanized or converted to agriculture, so if you want to see the spectacular nature that we describe in this book, you need to know where to go.

In addition to this section on biodiversity, you'll find regional planning information and a list of our favorite ecolodges at the front of the book.

Did You Know?

For some time, the Monte-verde Cloud Forest had been under serious threat from homesteading. In 1972, scientist George Powell and longtime resident Wilford Guindon established Reserva Biológica Bosque Nuboso Monteverde (Monteverde Cloud Forest Biological Reserve). In 2007, Costa Ricans voted it one of Costa Rica's Seven Wonders.

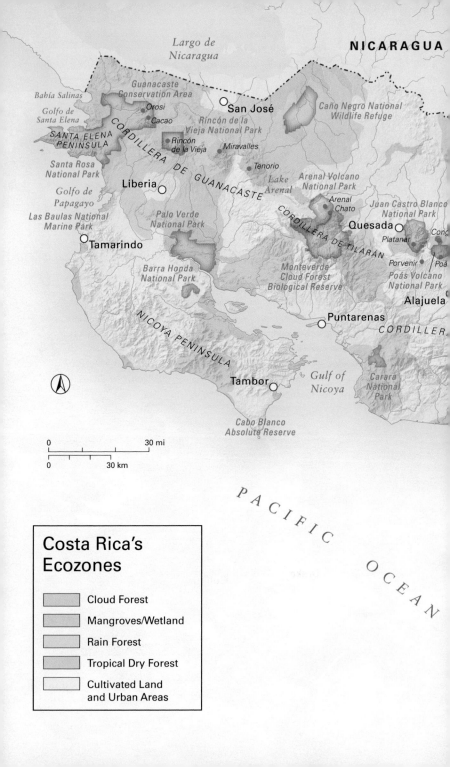

Largo de
Nicaragua

NICARAGUA

Bahía Salinas

Guanacaste
Conservation Area

Orosi

Cacao

○ San José

Caño Negro National
Wildlife Refuge

Golfo de
Santa Elena

Rincón de la
Vieja National Park

SANTA ELENA
PENINSULA

Rincón
de la Vieja

Miravalles

Santa Rosa
National Park

Tenorio

Lake
Arenal

Arenal Volcano
National Park

Arenal
Chato

Juan Castro Blanco
National Park

Liberia ○

Golfo de
Papagayo

Palo Verde
National Park

Quesada ○

Cong

Las Baulas National
Marine Park

Platanar

Tamarindo

Porvenir

Poá

Barra Honda
National Park

Poás Volcano
National Park

Monteverde
Cloud Forest
Biological Reserve

Alajuela

Puntarenas ○

CORDILLER...

Carara
National
Park

Tambor ○

Gulf of
Nicoya

Cabo Blanco
Absolute Reserve

PACIFIC

OCEAN

0   30 mi

0   30 km

Costa Rica's
Ecozones

Cloud Forest

Mangroves/Wetland

Rain Forest

Tropical Dry Forest

Cultivated Land
and Urban Areas

RAIN FOREST

Warm and wet, Costa Rica's rain forest is the quintessential dripping, squawking, chirping, buzzing jungle. In this sultry landscape of green on green, birds flap and screech overhead and twigs snap under the steps of unseen creatures. All the ingredients for life—water, sunlight, and more water—drench these areas.

DID YOU KNOW?

Despite the apparent vibrancy of life found in Manuel Antonio, one of the most popular rain forests in Costa Rica, it has no biological bridges to other forests and is threatened by encroaching development.

The amount of rain in a rain forest is stunning. The enormous swath of forest in the Caribbean lowlands averages more than 13 feet of rain a year. Corcovado National Park, on the Osa Peninsula, can get 18 feet. September and October, Costa Rica's rainiest months, can mean difficult travel to these areas. The rest of the year, you should still count on getting rained on, but not washed out.

The soaring canopy soaks up the lion's share of sunlight, seriously depriving the plants below. Underneath the highest trees are several distinct layers of growth. The understory is made up of smaller and younger trees,

shaded but also protected from harsh winds and rainfall. Shrubby species and even younger trees stand farther below, and small plants, fungus, dead trees, and fallen leaves cover the constantly decomposing forest floor.

Light rarely passes through these layers and layers of growth. At the forest floor, plants lie poised, in a stasis of sorts, waiting for one of the giants above to fall and open a patch of sky. When this does happen, an incredible spectacle occurs as the waiting plants unveil an arsenal of evolutionary tricks. Vines twist out, looking for other trees to pull themselves up along, shoots explode from hidden bulbs, and ferns and lianas battle for height and access to the sun.

But as competitive as the jungle sounds, it is essentially a series of ecosystems based on interdependence and cooperation. Trees depend on the animals that eat their fruit to disperse their seeds. Fungi feed off the nutrients produced by the decomposing forest floor. From death comes life—an abundance of life.

Costa Rica's rain forests have suffered from incursions by agriculture, logging, and cattle farming, but they're still home to the majority of the nation's biodiversity, with more species per square mile than anywhere else.

ADVENTURE HIGHLIGHTS

- Novice bird-watchers can enroll in La Selva's Birding 101 class. It's taught by some of the finest naturalists in the country.

- Join the folks at Brisas del Nara, 32 km (20 miles) outside Manuel Antonio, for an all-day horse-back-riding excursion through the protected Cerro Nara mountain zone. It ends with a swim in a natural pool with a 350-foot waterfall.

- Stray way off the beaten path on a multi-day hike through Corcovado National Park with tropical biologist Mike Boston from Osa Aventura.

TOP DESTINATIONS

Most of Costa Rica's rain forest can be found across the Caribbean lowlands and on the South Pacific coast.

CORCOVADO NATIONAL PARK

At the other end of the spectrum is Corcovado National Park, the remote, untamed jewel of Costa Rica's biodiversity crown. Covering one-third of the Osa Peninsula, Corcovado National Park holds about one-quarter of all tree species in Costa Rica and at least 140 identified species of mammals. Covering 445 square km (172 square miles), the park includes Central America's largest tract of lowland Pacific rain forest, including some old-growth areas. Corcovado is home to the largest concentration of jaguars left in the country, and the biggest population of scarlet macaws. There are at least 116 species of amphibians and reptiles, and about 370 bird species. Ranger stations and campsites are available for the more adventurous, and luxurious ecolodges surround the park for those who don't like to rough it. (⇨ See Chapter 10.)

LA SELVA

If anybody knows anything about the rain forest, it is the researchers at La Selva biological station, situated in the midst of 3,900 acres of protected forest

Squirrel monkey; danmike, Fodors.com member

in northern Costa Rica. The station, run by the Organization for Tropical Studies, was founded by famed biologist Leslie Holdridge in 1954 and is one of the most important sites worldwide for research on tropical rain forests. The research station can sleep up to 80 people in dormitory-style rooms and two-room family cabins, and feed as many as 100 in the dining hall. More than 50 km (31 miles) of trails provide access to a variety of ecosystems. (⇨ See Chapter 11.)

MANUEL ANTONIO NATIONAL PARK

For a tame, up-close glimpse of the rain forest and some of its more photogenic inhabitants, Manuel Antonio National Park is a favorite. Located on the Central Pacific coast, Manuel Antonio is one of Costa Rica's most visited—and smallest—national parks. Capuchin monkeys are used to humans to the point of practically ignoring them, unless a snack is poking out from an unattended backpack. The highly endangered squirrel monkeys are less bold, but can be seen at the park or from nearby hotels. Sloths are a common sight along the trail, as are a host of exotic birds and other creatures. (⇨ See Chapter 9.)

A green and black poison frog, La Selva

EXPERIENCING A RAIN FOREST

Kayaking in Drake Bay

There are a variety of ways to explore and experience the rain forest, which is only fitting given the diversity of the rain-forest ecosystem.

CANOPY TOURS

Canopy tours are a wonderful way to get a bird's-eye—or sloth's—view of the rain forest. Suspension bridges and ziplines, originally used for canopy research, offer a fantastic glimpse into the upper reaches of the forest. If you're not very mobile or don't feel like walking, go on a rain-forest tram; it's a small, slow-moving gondola that carries passengers gently through the jungle canopy.

HIKING

Hiking or walking through any one of Costa Rica's numerous national parks is an easy way to fully experience the vibrancy of the life found there. And we can't say this too many times: guided hikes are the way to go for anyone who hopes to catch a glimpse of the more exotic and hard-to-find species or better understand the complexity of the surrounding ecosystems.

MOUNTAIN BIKING

During the dry season, some parks open up trails for mountain bikers. But once the rains begin, a bike trip can turn into a long slog through the mud. Before you rent a bike, ask about the conditions of the trails.

RAFTING

Gentle, slow-moving rivers beg to be explored by canoe or kayak. It's a wonderful way to experience the deep calm of the jungle, and stealthy enough to increase your chances of seeing wildlife. If you're more of a thrill seeker, choose from any of the white-water rafting tours that pass through rain forests.

FLORA

To enter into a Costa Rican rain forest is to be overwhelmed by the diversity and intensity of life. Just 2½ acres contain almost 100 species of trees, and many of the more than 1,000 species of orchids are nested in their branches.

FALSE BIRD OF PARADISE

No avid photographer will return from Costa Rica without snapping a few shots of a heliconia, one of the most vibrant families of plants in the rain forest. This genus of flowering plant, containing between 100 and 200 species, includes the false bird of paradise (*Heliconia rostrata*), a dangling, impossibly colorful flower of alternating bulbous protrusions, colored red and tipped with green and yellow. Its vibrant colors and nectar make it a favorite for hummingbirds.

False bird of paradise

GUARIA MORADA

Almost every tree here plays host to lichens, woody vines called lianas, and rootless epiphytes, including the national flower, *guaria morada* (*Guarianthe skinneri*). Because this is an orchid species, you'll find it in several different shapes and colors: the flowers can be from pure white to deep magenta, and the base of its lip can range from yellow to white. There can be anywhere from four to 14 flowers per stem.

Guaria morada

SILK COTTON TREE

The silk cotton tree (*Ceiba pentandra*), known locally as *ceiba*, is one of the most easily recognizable of the rain-forest giants. Growing nearly 200 feet tall, it can be identified close to the ground by its tall, winding, and narrow roots, which act as buttresses to support the enormous trunk.

The silk cotton tree

STRANGLER FIG

Aptly called *matapalo* in Spanish, meaning "tree killer," the strangler fig begins its life as an epiphyte, living high in the branches of another tree. Over several years, it grows dangling roots to the forest floor that capture nutrients from the soil, thicken, and slowly meld onto the host tree. Eventually—it might take as long as 100 years—the strangler completely engulfs its host. In time the "strangled" tree decomposes and disintegrates, leaving the strangler fig—replete with branches, leaves, flowers, and fruit—standing hollow but victorious.

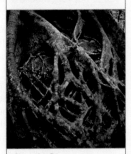
Strangler fig

FAUNA

Keep an eye out for three-wattled bellbirds, chestnut-mandibled toucans, or the secretive Baird's tapir. A host of wildcats include the ocelot, jaguarundi, puma, margay, and rarely seen jaguar.

Harpy eagle

HARPY EAGLE

The endangered harpy eagle, nearly extinct from Costa Rica, is the country's largest and most powerful raptor. It's named for the Greek spirits that carried the dead to the underworld of Hades and who are said to have the faces of humans but the bodies of eagles. Harpy eagles are huge—females are more than 2 feet in length and have a 6-foot wingspan. They hunt above the canopy, searching for large mammals or, occasionally, for large birds like the macaw.

MORPHO BUTTERFLY

The bright blue morpho butterfly bounces through the jungle like a small piece of sky on a string. The entire life cycle, from egg to death, is approximately 137 days, and adult butterflies live for only about a month. Once they emerge from the cocoon, morphos have few predators, thanks to the poisonous compounds that they retain from feeding habits back in their caterpillar days. In fact, the hairy brown tufts on the morpho caterpillar have been known to irritate human skin.

Blue morpho

SCARLET MACAWS

Every bit the pirate's crimson parrot, these large and noisy birds mate for life, travel in pairs or large groups, and can often be found gathered in almond trees in low-elevation forests of the central and southern Pacific coast. Their cousin, the critically endangered great green macaw, travels across the Caribbean lowlands, following the ripening of the mountain almond.

Scarlet macaw

THREE-TOED OR TWO-TOED SLOTH

Though difficult for us to spot, the barely moving three-toed sloth and two-toed sloth are principal meals for the harpy eagle. This animal's fur is a small self-sustaining ecosystem unto itself: because the forest is so wet and the sloth so inert, two species of blue-green algae thrive on its fur and provide it with needed camouflage. Nonparasitic insects also live here, feeding off the algae and keeping the growth under control.

■TIP➜ **The vibrantly colored red-eyed tree frog, like the white tent bat, sometimes rests on the underside of large jungle leaves. If you're lucky, your guide may be able to coax one out for you to see.**

Three-toed sloth

VOLCANOES

As part of the Pacific Ring of Fire, the country has three volcanic mountain ranges: Guanacaste, Central, and Tilarán. There are around 300 volcanic points in Costa Rica, but only five have formed volcanoes that have erupted in recent memory: Turrialba, Irazú, Poás, Rincón de la Vieja, and Arenal.

Arenal, the crown jewel of volcanoes here, has settled into a less active phase these days. The others have, conversely, experienced more activity, necessitating occasional safety closures of their namesake national parks, with the Turrialba volcano simply becoming too dangerous to visit.

Costa Rica's volcanoes are the result of friction between two enormous tectonic plates—the Cocos plate and the Caribbean plate. As these plates rub against each other, the friction partially melts rock. Although everyone uses the term "lava," pyroclastic flow, or hot gas and rock,

more accurately describes the product spewed from the volcanoes here. The flow is forced toward the surface, leaking through cracks or weak spots in the crust along with volcanic gas. In Rincón de la Vieja, gas escapes through craters high on the volcano, as well as seeping up through the surrounding ground, creating bubbling mud pits, hot springs, and fumaroles.

The volcanic mountain ranges divide the country's Pacific and Caribbean slopes and are responsible for the differences in climate between each side. Rain-laden trade winds blowing westward can't pass over these ranges without shedding their precipitation and rising. This creates Guanacaste's rain shadow: the dry plains and tropical dry forest that lie leeward, or west of the mountains. The mountains block the rain-producing weather system and cast a "shadow" of dryness.

Costa Rica's volcanic lakes occur when there is no natural drainage from a crater. The chemicals, minerals, and gases from below the earth's crust infuse the water and vibrantly color it. Irazú's lake is neon green; the baby-blue lagoon in Poás is extremely acidic and gives off toxic sulfur clouds and massive amounts of carbon dioxide.

ADVENTURE HIGHLIGHTS

■ A hike through lush cloud forest will take you to the five magnificent waterfalls at La Paz Waterfall Gardens near Poás Volcano National Park.

■ Anglers love the guapote, tilapia, and machaca pulled from Lake Arenal.

■ The Arenal area is the jumping-off point for Class II–IV white-water rafting trips on the Blancas, Arenal, Toro, and San Carlos rivers.

■ Take the tough hike to La Fortuna Waterfall, near Arenal. Swimming under the waterfall is a slice of paradise.

TOP DESTINATIONS

Costa Rica's volcanoes are often the centerpieces of large national parks.

ARENAL VOLCANO

At 5,512 feet, Arenal Volcano, rising on the northwestern plains of San Carlos, is every bit an awesome sight. Tall and perfectly conical, its sides are scarred by a history of violent eruptions and textured by decades of pyroclastic flow. Located at the northern end of the Tilarán Mountain Range, northwest of the capital, it is Costa Rica's best-known volcano. Arenal has settled into a less active phase these days. It's likely temporary: research suggests that Arenal has a 400-year cycle of major eruptions, and the activity since the 1968 explosion is small in comparison with what it's capable of. (⇨ *See Chapter 6.*)

POÁS VOLCANO

Poás Volcano is Costa Rica's most visited national park, in part because it is the closest active volcano to the capital of San José and the Aeropuerto Internacional Juan Santamaría. Located in the Cordillera Volcánica Central Mountain Range, Poás is topped by three craters, the tallest reaching 8,885 feet above sea level. Only the main cone has shown any volcanic eruptions in the last 200 years. You can get a good look

Gaudy leaf frog; Marco13, Fodors.com member

at the crater from the viewing deck. (⇨ *See Chapter 5.*)

Note: Costa Rica's hot spot (literally) these days is the Turrialba Volcano, which occasionally spews ash over the metro area and periodically closes the international airport. Authorities currently prohibit entry to the national park.

RINCÓN DE LA VIEJA

A mass of slopes, craters, and biodiversity that bridges the Continental Divide, Rincón de la Vieja is in Costa Rica's arid northwest. It's not the classic conical volcano, but rather a ridge made of a series of craters that include bare, rocky bowls with brilliantly colored lakes, and velvety cones covered in rain forest. Scientists believe Rincón de la Vieja was born of simultaneous volcanic activity at nine different eruption points. The Rincón de la Vieja National Park covers nearly 35,000 acres and is a wonderland of volcanic activity that includes bubbling mud pits, hot springs, and geysers, as well as refreshing lagoons and spectacular waterfalls. (⇨ *See Chapter 7.*)

On the Road to Arenal; piper35w, Fodors.com member

EXPERIENCING THE VOLCANOES

Horseback riding in Arenal

The Guatuso people believed that the fire god lived inside the Arenal Volcano—and in 1968, the gods were not happy. After 500 years of dormancy, Arenal erupted savagely, burying three small villages and killing 87 people. Today, thousands live at its base in the thriving town of La Fortuna, which is literally in Arenal's shadow.

HIKING

Volcano tourism is a major draw for international visitors, but given the dangers at the active sites, activities at the top are limited. The parks have hiking trails. For your safety, we recommend hiking with a guide, especially at Arenal. The volcano has settled into a less active phase these days, but it's still one of those you-never-know situations, and a knowledgeable guide knows where not to tread. At Poás and Irazú, you can go right up to the summit and peer inside.

HORSEBACK RIDING

All of Costa Rica's active volcanoes are the centerpieces of national parks. Arenal and Poás have good horseback-riding trails and many outfitters, especially in Arenal. For safety's sake and the well-being of the animals, stick with the operators we recommend.

GEOTHERMAL WONDERS

Volcanic activity is not limited to a volcano's peak. The underground heat that fuels these giants also results in hot springs, bubbling mud pits, and geysers, among other geological wonders. Minerals from the dormant Tenorio Volcano create a fascinating effect in one of the rivers running down its side, the Río Celeste, giving it a baby-blue tint.

FLORA

The habitat and ecology of these geologic giants is influenced mostly by their surrounding ecological zones and elevation. Conditions around the crater of an active volcano are intensely harsh, but some tougher species do manage to survive.

FERN

Contrary to popular stereotypes, ferns don't necessarily grow in shady, moist environments. The tongue fern (*Elaphoglossum lingua*) extends long, rubbery tongue-shape leaves and has evolved to grow around volcanic rock and hardened ash. You'll find it around the top of the Poás Volcano. Farther down, you'll find other types of ferns adapted to friendlier conditions.

Ferns

MYRTLE

Myrtle (*Myrtaceae*) and other low-lying shrubs survive this environment thanks to their slow growth rate. Myrtle, poor man's umbrella (*Gunnera insignis*), *papelillo* (*Senecio oerstedianus*), and other shrubs and ferns cover the higher bluffs around Irazú's crater. Mistletoe (*Psittacanthus*) can be found near the major volcanoes in the Central Valley. These flowering plants are interesting because they attach to trees by haustoria, special structures that penetrate the host plant and absorb its water and nutrients. When the mistletoe dies, it leaves a mark on the tree, a woodrose or *rosa de palo*.

Myrtle

OAK

Forests in Costa Rica's higher mountain areas share some plant species with cloud forests. However, the plants here have adapted to live in cold temperatures and, if the volcano is active, in compacted ash. Surrounding the Botos Lagoon, on the south side of the principal Poás crater, is high-elevation cloud forest of oak (*Quercus costaricensis* and *Q. copeyensis*), small cedar (*Brunellia costaricensis*), and flowering cypress (*Escallonia poasana*)—trees that are typically crowded with epiphytes, bromeliads, and mosses.

Great roble oak

WILD BALSAM

Wild balsam, oak, and poor man's umbrella carpet the inactive cones around Rincón de la Vieja. Tropical dry-forest species grow farther down. Look for the guanacaste tree (*Enterolobium cyclocarpum*), Spanish cedar (*Cedrela odorata*), oak (*Quercus oocarpa*), and the country's largest wild population of the guardia morada orchid, Costa Rica's national flower.

Wild balsam aka Touch-me-not balsam

FAUNA

Like the flora around a volcano, the wildlife diversity of this region is dictated by the ecology around the mountain. Also, the more humans there are, the fewer animals you'll see.

Fiery-throated hummingbird

FIERY-THROATED HUMMINGBIRD

Birds are one of the most populous types of creatures to live on the flanks of Poás and many more of Costa Rica's volcanoes. The fiery-throated hummingbird, the summer tanager, the sooty robin, and the emerald toucanet are among the 79 bird species that have been recorded at Poás. The fiery-throated hummingbird is recognizable by its forecrown, throat, and breast colors, as well as its bluish hump and blue-black tail.

NINE-BANDED ARMADILLO

Irazú is home to smaller creatures such as the nine-banded armadillo, the eastern cottontail, and the little spotted cat. The nine-banded armadillo has a long snout and fantastic sense of smell. It can hold its breath for up to six minutes. This helps it keep dirt out of its nostrils while digging. Under stressful conditions, a female armadillo can prolong her pregnancy for up to three years by delaying the implantation of the fertilized egg into the uterus wall.

Nine-banded armadillo

NORTH AMERICAN PORCUPINE

The much drier region of Rincón de la Vieja has a distinctly different—and broader—set of animal inhabitants, including the North American porcupine and the agouti (a large, short-legged relative of the guinea pig). Pumas, ocelots, raccoons, and three species of monkeys (the howler, the white-faced capuchin, and the Central American spider monkey) are among the larger mammals. More than 300 bird species have been recorded there, including the collared aracari, the bare-necked umbrella bird, and the three-wattled bellbird.

North American porcupine

PUMA

In the Barva region, pumas (also called mountain lions and cougars) and even jaguars still stalk the more remote forests, searching for the tapir or an unlucky spider monkey. The puma is an excellent climber and can jump to branches 16 feet off the ground, essentially giving monkeys nowhere to hide. Pumas have never been hunted for their pelts, but are suffering from habitat destruction. In Costa Rica, they are rarely found outside protected areas.

Puma

CLOUD FOREST

The four mountain ranges that make up Costa Rica's own piece of the Continental Divide split the country into its Caribbean and Pacific regions. At these higher altitudes, temperatures cool, clouds settle, and rainfall increases. The forests found here are shrouded in mist and rich in biodiversity. Welcome to Costa Rica's famed cloud forests.

DID YOU KNOW?

Monteverde is one of the best places in the country for canopy tours. Another unique excursion here is a guided nocturnal nature hike. Much of the wildlife only comes out after dusk.

Like their lowland rain-forest cousins, cloud forests are packed with plant and animal species, thanks largely to their water-drenched conditions. There's an average of 16 feet of rainfall a year, but that number doubles when you factor in the amount of moisture gleaned from the clouds and fog that drift through every day. As in rain forests, giant hardwoods reaching as high as almost 200 feet set the ceiling for this ecology zone, while a variety of smaller trees, ferns, shrubs, and other plants fill the understories. Epiphytes flourish here, as do mosses, lichens, and liverwort. These plants cling to passing moisture and capture

it like sponges. As a result, cloud forests are constantly soaking wet, even when there is no rain.

Because conditions in a cloud forest can be harsh, many of the tougher and more adaptable rain-forest species make their home here. The relentless, heavy cloud cover can block sunlight even from the highest reaches of the forest, and deeper inside, light is rare. Photosynthesis and growth are slower, so the plants tend to be smaller with thicker trunks and stems. These unique conditions also produce an unusually high number of endemic and rare species.

The Monteverde Cloud Forest Biological Reserve, one of the world's most famous protected cloud forests, shelters innumerable life-forms. There are more than 100 mammal species; 400 bird species, including at least 30 species of hummingbird; 500-plus species of butterfly; and more than 2,500 plant species, including 420 types of orchid. Monteverde, in particular, lets you groove to a different style of Costa Rican nightlife: the big reserve and several smaller adjoining ones offer guided nocturnal walks. There are only a handful of protected cloud forests here and worldwide, and this type of ecozone is increasingly threatened by human encroachment.

ADVENTURE HIGHLIGHTS

■ Leave the car at home and travel on horseback to or from the Arenal Volcano area and Monteverde Cloud Forest. Contact Desafío Adventures, the only guides we recommend for this journey.

■ The good folks at the Savegre Hotel will give you an education on one of their daylong natural-history hikes around San Gerardo de Dota cloud forest.

■ Selvatura, right next to Monteverde, is the only canopy tour in the area with a zipline built entirely inside the cloud forest.

TOP DESTINATIONS

Regardless of which cloud forest you visit, bring a raincoat and go with a guide if you want to see wildlife. You'll marvel at their ability to spot a sloth at a hundred paces.

BRAULIO CARRILLO NATIONAL PARK

Descending from the Cordillera Volcánica Central Mountain Range, Braulio Carrillo National Park is an awesome, intimidating, and rugged landscape of dense cloud forest that stretches toward the rain forests of the Caribbean lowlands. The enormous park encompasses 117,580 acres of untamed jungle and is less than an hour's drive from San José. The country's principal eastbound highway cuts a path straight through it. Elusive (and endangered) jaguars and pumas are among the many animal species here, and scenic viewpoints are plentiful along the highway. A handful of trails, including the easy-to-access loop trails at the Quebrada González station, can be taken a short distance into the park's interior. (⇨ *See Chapter 11.*)

MONTEVERDE CLOUD FOREST BIOLOGICAL RESERVE

Costa Rica's most famous cloud forest reserve is packed with an astonishing variety of life: 2,500 plant species, 400

Braulio Carrillo National Park

species of bird, 500 types of butterfly, and more than 100 different mammals—many of them bats—have been cataloged so far. The reserve reaches 5,032 feet above sea level, spans the Tilarán Mountain Range, and encompasses 9,885 acres of cloud forest and rain forest. There are 13 km (8 miles) of well-marked trails, zipline tours, and suspended bridges for canopy viewing, as well as bird tours, guided night walks, and a field research station with an amphibian aquarium. Allow a generous slice of time for leisurely hiking; longer hikes are made possible by some strategically placed overnight refuges along the way. (⇨ *See Chapter 6.*)

SAN GERARDO DE DOTA

One of Costa Rica's premier nature destinations, San Gerardo de Dota is a damp, epiphyte-laden forest of giant oak trees and an astonishing number of resplendent quetzals. Outdoors enthusiasts may never want to leave these parts—some of the country's best hiking is in this valley, and it's popular with bird-watchers. It's also great for horseback riding and trout fly-fishing. (⇨ *See Chapter 10.*)

Banded anteater; maddytem, Fodors.com member

EXPERIENCING A CLOUD FOREST

Gearing up for the Tarzan swing at the end of the zipline tour at Selvatura

You may need to get down and dirty—well, more like wet and muddy—to experience a cloud forest's natural wonders, but then, that's half the fun.

BIRD-WATCHING

Bird-watching is rewarding in the cloud forest, where some of the most vibrant and peculiar of nature's winged creatures can be found. Rise early, enjoy some locally grown coffee, and check the aguacatillo trees for quetzals. If you opt to go without a guide, bring along waterproof binoculars and a good guidebook (we recommend *The Birds of Costa Rica,* by Richard Garrigues and Robert Dean) for spotting and identifying birds.

CANOPY TOURS

Canopy tours and suspended bridges run right through the upper reaches of the cloud forest—an ecosystem in its own right. Spot birds, monkeys, and exotic orchids from a viewpoint that was once nearly impossible to reach. Get even closer to butterflies, amphibians, snakes, and insects at various exhibits in the parks' research centers.

FISHING

If freshwater fishing in spectacular surroundings is right up your alley, check out the Savegre River, in the San Gerardo de Dota Valley. It's been stocked with rainbow trout since the 1950s.

HIKING

Well-guided hikes through this eerie landscape, draped with moss and vines, make it easier to spot the less obvious features of this complex ecosystem. Compared with the barren tropical dry forest and colorful rain forest, cloud forests don't easily offer up their secrets. Binoculars and a good guide will go a long way toward making your hike and wildlife spotting richer experiences.

FLORA

A typical 2½ acres of cloud forest might be home to nearly 100 species of trees. Contrast that with a mere 30 in the richest forests of North America.

EPIPHYTES

Epiphytes thrive in cloud and rain forests, thanks to all the moisture and nutrients in the air. The *stanhopea* orchid is interesting because of its clever pollination tricks. The blossoms' sweet smell attracts bees, but the flower's waxy surface is slippery so they slide down inside. As they slowly work their way out, they brush up against the flower's column and collect pollen. This pollen is then transferred to the sticky stigma of other flowers.

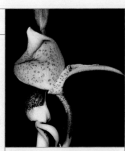

Epiphyte stanhopea

Bromeliads, another family of flowering plants, compete with epiphytes for space on the branches and trunks of the forest's trees. The spiraling leaves form caches for water, falling plant material, and insect excretions. These are mineral-rich little ponds for insects and amphibians, and drinking and bathing water for birds and other animals.

Poor man's umbrella

POOR MAN'S UMBRELLA

If you're caught in the rain, take cover under a poor man's umbrella (*Gunnera insignis* and *G. talamancana*), whose broad and sturdy leaves sometimes grow large enough to shelter an entire family. These shrubby plants love the dark, moist interior of the cloud forest.

ROBLE TREE

Majestic roble, or oak—principally the white oak (*Quercus copeyensis*) and black oak (*Q. costaricensis*)— is the dominant tree of Costa Rica's cloud forests and grows to 200 feet. The deciduous hardwood *cedro dulce,* or Spanish cedar (*Cedrela odorata*), is also a giant at 147 feet. These two are joined by evergreens like the *jaúl,* or alder, and the *aguacatillo,* a name meaning "little avocado" that's given to a variety of trees from the *lauracea* family.

White oak tree

STAR ORCHID

The star orchid (*Epidendrum radicans*) is one of the few orchids that is not an epiphyte. It grows on land and mimics in color and shape other nectar-filled flowers in order to attract butterflies who unwittingly become pollinators.

Star orchid

FAUNA

The resplendent quetzal, the blue-crowned motmot, the orange-bellied trogon, and the emerald toucanet are just some of the hundreds of species that can be logged in a cloud forest.

Collared trogon

COLLARED TROGON

The collared trogon and the orange-bellied trogon are in the same family as the quetzal. They all share square black-and-white tail plumage and bright orange or yellow chest feathers. The collared trogon perches very quietly and is easy to miss. Luckily, it doesn't fly far, so its flight is easy to follow.

GLASS FROGS

One of the more bizarre amphibians is the tiny, transparent glass frog of the *Centrolenellu* genus, whose internal organs can be seen through its skin. It lives in trees and bushes and can often be heard at night near the rivers and streams. Cloud forests have fewer amphibian species than rain forests, but amphibian populations worldwide have plummeted in recent decades. No one knows the cause yet. Some blame acid rain and pesticides; others believe it is yet another sign of coming ecological disaster.

Glass frogs

HOWLER MONKEYS

One of the largest New World monkeys, howlers are named for their loud, barking roar that can be heard for miles. If you want to spot a howler, be sure to scan the treetops; their diet consists mainly of canopy leaves, and they rarely leave the protection of the trees. Other cloud-forest mammals include the white-faced capuchin monkey, white-nosed coatis, porcupines, red brocket deer, and Alston's singing mouse.

Howler monkey

RESPLENDENT QUETZAL

Perhaps the most famed resident of Costa Rica's cloud forests is the illustrious resplendent quetzal. Every year, bird-watchers come to Costa Rica hoping to spot the green, red, and turquoise plumage of this elusive trogon. Considered a sacred creature by the Maya and the namesake of Guatemala's currency, the quetzal spends much of its time perched in its favorite tree, the aguacatillo.

Resplendent quetzal

TROPICAL DRY FOREST

The most endangered biome in the world, these seasonal forests swing between two climate extremes—from drenching wet to bone-dry. To survive, plants undergo a drastic physical transformation: forests burst into life during the rainy months, and are brown, leafless, and seemingly dead during the dry season.

For about half the year, northwestern Costa Rica is almost as wet as the rest of the country. The weather blows in from the Pacific, and you can expect rain most days. During the dry season, from January to April, weather patterns change, winds shift, and the land becomes parched.

Tall deciduous hardwoods are the giants in this ecology zone, with spindly branches creating a seasonal canopy as high as 100 feet. A thorny and rambling understory of smaller trees and bushes thrives thanks to the plentiful light permitted once the canopy leaves fall to the forest floor. The challenges of the dry months have forced plants to specialize. The hardwoods are solitary and

diffuse, their seeds spread far and wide by animals and insects. Some even flower progressively through the dry season, depending on the plant species and the particular bees and birds that have evolved to pollinate them.

If you can take the heat, the dry season is perfect for bird- and animal-watching since the lack of foliage makes wildlife spotting easy. (Water, sunscreen, and wide-brimmed hats are musts.) Keep your eyes peeled for monkeys, parrots, lizards, coyotes, rabbits, snakes, and even jaguars.

There was once one great, uninterrupted swath of dry forest that began in southern Mexico, rolled across Mesoamerica, and ended in northwest Costa Rica. Today, less than 2% of the Central American tropical dry forest remains, the majority of it in Costa Rica. But even here, the forest is fractured into biologically isolated islands, thanks to decades of logging and agriculture. The Guanacaste Conservation Area has managed to corral off large chunks of land for preservation, and private and government efforts are under way to create biological corridors between isolated dry forests so that animals and plants can roam farther and deepen their gene pools, which is critical to their survival.

TOP DESTINATIONS

Most of Costa Rica's remaining tropical dry forests are located in the northwest of the country, not too far from the Nicaragua border.

GUANACASTE CONSERVATION AREA

Santa Rosa is part of the larger Guanacaste Conservation Area, which is composed of some tropical dry forest and former farmland that's being regenerated to its natural state. The park is intended to serve as a much-needed biological corridor from Santa Rosa up to the cloud forests of the Orosi and Cacao volcanoes, to the east. Park infrastructure is generally lacking, though three biological stations offer some accommodations to student groups and researchers. (⇨ *See Chapter 7.*)

PALO VERDE NATIONAL PARK

Farther south, Palo Verde National Park skirts the northeastern side of the Río Tempisque, straddling some of the country's most spectacular wetlands and tropical dry forest. Thanks to these two very different ecology zones, Palo Verde is packed with very diverse bird, plant, and animal species—bird-watchers love this park. The Organization for Tropical Studies has a biological station at Palo Verde and offers tours

Hummingbird nesting; reedjoella, Fodors.com member

Canopy tour at Rincón de la Vieja National Park

and accommodations. Park guards also maintain a ranger station with rustic overnight accommodations. (⇨ *See Chapter 8.*)

RINCÓN DE LA VIEJA NATIONAL PARK

More tropical dry forest can be found inside the Rincón de la Vieja National Park, ringing the base of the two volcanoes of this protected area—the dormant Santa María and the active Rincón de la Vieja. The park hosts some 300 bird species as well as cougars, kinkajous, and the shy, elusive jaguar. A handful of lodges inside the park and the proximity to the city of Liberia make Rincón an easy destination to visit. (⇨ *See Chapter 7.*)

SANTA ROSA NATIONAL PARK

The largest piece of tropical dry forest under government protection in Central America spreads out over Santa Rosa National Park, about 35 km (22 miles) north of Guanacaste's capital, Liberia. The park, which covers 380 square km (146 square miles), also includes two beaches and coastal mangrove forest. Thanks to trails and equipped campsites, you can venture deep into the park. During the dry season, visibility is excellent and chances are good that you'll spot wildlife. (⇨ *See Chapter 7.*)

EXPERIENCING A TROPICAL DRY FOREST

Rincón de la Vieja National Park

Many of Costa Rica's roads are rough at best, and tropical forests are often remote. We recommend renting a four-wheel-drive vehicle for getting around.

BIKING
Some parks allow biking, but again, this is certainly something you don't want to do during the rains. Contact the park that you'll be visiting ahead of time for trail and rental information.

BIRD- AND WILDLIFE-WATCHING
Most people come to these areas for bird-watching and wildlife spotting, but it's best done during the dry season, when all the foliage drops from the trees. Bring a good bird or wildlife guide, binoculars, lots of water (we can't stress this enough), and plenty of patience. It's a good idea to find a watering hole and just hunker down and let the animals come to you. If you don't want to explore the forest alone,

tours can be arranged through hotels, ranger stations, and private research centers inside the parks. In terms of bird and wildlife guides, we recommend *The Birds of Costa Rica* by Richard Garrigues and Robert Dean and *The Mammals of Costa Rica* by Mark Wainwright. If you'd like to know more about plants, pick up *Tropical Plants of Costa Rica* by Willow Zuchowski.

HIKING
The best way to experience these endangered woods is to strap on your hiking boots, grab a hat and lots of water, and get out and walk. Most of the dry forests are protected lands and found in Guanacaste's national parks. Some have road access, making it possible to drive through the park, but most are accessible only by hiking trails. During the rainy season, roads become mud pits and hiking trails are almost impassable.

FLORA

Among other types of flora, tropical dry forests are filled with deciduous hardwoods, such as mahogany (*Swietenia macrophylla*), black laurel (*Cordia gerascanthus*), ronrón (*Astronium graveolens*), and cocobolo (*Dalbergia retusa*). Much of the wood is highly prized for furniture and houses, so many of these trees are facing extinction outside national parks and protected areas.

Cornizuelo

CORNIZUELO

The spiky *cornizuelo* (*Acacia collinsii*) is an intriguing resident of the lower levels because of its symbiotic relationship with ants. This small evergreen tree puts out large thorns that serve as a home for a certain ant species. In exchange for food and shelter, the ants provide the tree protection from other leaf-munching insects or vines. Sometimes the ants will even cut down encroaching vegetation on the forest floor, allowing the tree to thrive.

FRANGIPANI TREE

The frangipani tree (*Plumeria rubra*) can grow up to 26 feet and has meaty pink, white, or yellow blossoms. The flowers are most fragrant at night to lure sphinx moths. Unfortunately for the moth, the blooms don't produce nectar. The plant simply dupes their pollinators into hopping from bloom to bloom and tree to tree in a fruitless search for food.

Frangipani; plumboy, Fodors.com member

GUANACASTE

Perhaps the most striking and easy-to-spot resident of Costa Rica's tropical dry forest is the *Guanacaste* (*Enterolobium cyclocarpum*), an imposing tree with an enormous, spherical canopy that seems straight out of the African savanna. The guanacaste is the northwest province's namesake and Costa Rica's national tree. It is most easily identified standing alone in pastures: Without the competition of the forest, it sends massive branches out low from its trunk, creating an arching crown of foliage close to the ground. The ear-shape seedpods are also a distinct marker; the hard seeds inside are popular with local artisan jewelers.

Guanacaste

GUMBO-LIMBO

Costa Ricans call the gumbo-limbo tree (*Bursera simaruba*) *indio desnudo* (naked Indian) because of its red, peeling bark. This tree is also found in Florida, and the wood has historically been used for making carousel horses in the United States.

Gumbo-limbo

FAUNA

Tropical dry forests are literally crawling with life. Bark scorpions, giant cockroaches, and tarantulas scuttle along the forest floor, and the buzz from wasps and cicadas gives the air an almost electric feel. A careful eye may be able to pick out walking sticks frozen still among the twigs. The jaguar, and one of its favorite prey, the endangered tapir, also stalk these forests.

Black-headed trogon

BLACK-HEADED TROGON

With an open canopy for much of the year, and plentiful ground rodents and reptiles, these forests are great hunting grounds for birds of prey like the roadside hawk and the spectacled owl. The white-throated magpie jay travels in noisy mobs, while the scissor-tailed flycatcher migrates from as far north as the southern United States. The rufous-naped wren builds its nest in the spiky acacia trees. The black-headed trogon, with its bright yellow breast, and the elegant trogon both nest exclusively in Costa Rica's tropical dry forest.

COYOTE

Nearly unique to the dry tropical forest is the coyote, which feeds on rodents, lizards, and an assortment of small mammals, as well as sea turtle eggs (when near the beach) and other improvised meals. Like the Virginia opossum and the white-tailed deer, the coyote is believed to have traveled south from North America through the once-interconnected tropical dry forest of Mesoamerica.

Coyote

NEOTROPICAL RATTLESNAKE

The venomous neotropical rattlesnake and the exquisite painted wood turtle are among the reptiles that exclusively call this region home. Salvin's spiny pocket mouse, the eastern cottontail rabbit, and both spotted and hooded skunks are unique to Costa Rica's dry forests.

Neotropical rattlesnake

WHITE-FACED CAPUCHIN

Monkeys are common all over Costa Rica, and the dry forests are home to three species: the howler monkeys, with their leathery black faces and deep barking call, are the loudest of the forest's mammals; the white-faced capuchin travel in playful packs; and the endangered spider monkey requires large, undisturbed tracts of forest for a healthy population to survive. This last group is in steep decline—another indicator of the overall health of this ecoregion.

White-faced capuchin

3

Biodiversity TROPICAL DRY FOREST

WETLANDS AND MANGROVES

Wetlands are any low-lying areas that are perpetually saturated with water. Their complex ecosystems support a variety of living things—both endemic species unique to the area and visitors who travel halfway around the hemisphere to get here. Here, land species have evolved to live much of their lives in water.

One common type of wetland in Costa Rica is a flood-plain, created when a river or stream regularly overflows its banks, either because of heavy rains or ocean tides. Thanks to huge deposits of sediment that are left as the floodwaters recede, the ground is extremely fertile and plants thrive, as do the animals that feed here.

Mangroves are a unique type of wetland and cover a scant 1% of the country. They are found at the edges of tidal areas along both coasts, such as ocean inlets, estuaries, and canals where saltwater mixes with fresh. Mangrove forests are made up of a small variety of

plants—principally mangrove trees—but attract a huge variety of animals.

Costa Rica's seven species of mangrove trees are able to survive in this stressful habitat because they have developed the ability to cope with constant flooding, tolerate a lack of oxygen, and thrive in a mix of salt and fresh water thanks to uniquely adapted roots and leaves. The nutrient-rich sediment and mud that build up around these trees and between their prop roots create habitat for plankton, algae, crabs, oysters, and shrimp. These, in turn, attract larger and larger animals that come to feed, giving mangrove forests a remarkable level of biodiversity.

What they lack in number, mangroves make up for in biological impact. These thick coastal forests are protective barriers for inland ecosystems; they dissipate the force of storm winds and sudden surges in tides or floods triggered by coastal storms or tsunamis. Working in the opposite direction, a fully functioning mangrove prevents erosion of the coastline.

Sadly, coastal development is a big threat to mangroves. It is illegal to clear mangrove forests, but enforcement is weak.

ADVENTURE HIGHLIGHTS

■ Witness the spectacle of nesting turtles at Tortuguero National Park. Turtle-watching excursions require a certified guide and take place only between February and November.

■ Anglers can hook mackerel, tarpon, snook, calba, and snapper in the canals and along the coast of Tortuguero and Barra Colorado.

■ Take a kayaking tour through the mangrove estuary of Isla Damas, near Manuel Antonio. You'll probably see monkeys, crocodiles, and numerous birds.

TOP DESTINATIONS

The Ramsar Convention on Wetlands is an intergovernmental treaty to provide a framework for the conservation of the world's wetlands. There are 11 Ramsar wetlands in Costa Rica: all are impressive, but we've listed only our top three.

CAÑO NEGRO NATIONAL WILDLIFE REFUGE

One Ramsar wetland is found in the Caño Negro National Wildlife Refuge, in the more remote northern plains close to the border with Nicaragua. Caño Negro has a seasonal lake that can cover as many as 1,975 acres and grow as deep as 10 feet. The lake is actually a pool created by the Frio River that dries up to nearly nothing between February and May. The park also has marshes, semipermanently flooded old-growth forest, and other wetland habitats. (⇨ *See Chapter 6.*)

PALO VERDE NATIONAL PARK

Within the Palo Verde National Park is perhaps Costa Rica's best-known wetland—a system that includes permanent shallow freshwater lagoons, marshes, mangroves, and woodlands that are seasonally flooded by the Tempisque River. A good portion of this 45,511-acre park is covered by tropical dry forest. In fact, this park has 12 different habitats, creating one of the most

Alpha howler monkey; Liz Stuart, Fodors.com member

Tortuguero; StupFD, Fodors.com

diverse collections of life in the country. At least 55 aquatic plants and 150 tree species have been identified here, and the largest number of aquatic and wading birds in all of Mesoamerica can be found in Palo Verde wetlands. A total of 279 bird species have been recorded within Palo Verde, so little surprise that it's listed by the Ramsar Convention as a wetland of international importance. The Organization for Tropical Studies maintains a research station at the park with limited accommodations but great views of the marshes, as well as extremely knowledgeable guides. (⇨ *See Chapter 8.*)

TORTUGUERO NATIONAL PARK

Ninety-nine percent of mangrove forests are found on Costa Rica's Pacific coast. But the best place to see some of the remaining 1% on the Caribbean side is Tortuguero National Park. Like Palo Verde, Tortuguero is home to a wide variety of life—11 distinct habitats in total, including extensive wetlands and mangrove forests. Beach-nesting turtles (*tortugas*) are the main attraction, but the park is included in the Ramsar list of internationally important wetlands. Many species can be spotted along Tortuguero's famous canals. (⇨ *See Chapter 11.*)

EXPERIENCING THE WETLANDS AND MANGROVES

Paddling through Tortuguero at dawn; Thornton Cohen, Fodors.com member

Wildlife viewing in general can be very rewarding in these areas because a wide variety of creatures come together and share the habitat.

BIRD-WATCHING
The most populous and diverse of the creatures that live in and depend on wetlands and mangroves are birds, so bring some binoculars and your field guide, and prepare to check off some species. For good photos, take a long lens and tripod, and get an early start; midday sun reflecting off the ubiquitous water can make your photos washed out or create some challenging reflections.

BOATING
The best way to see Costa Rica's remaining mangrove forests is by boat; we recommend using a kayak or canoe. These vessels allow you to slip along canals and protected coastlines in near silence, increasing your chance

of creeping up on many of the more impressive creatures that call this habitat home. A guided boat tour is also recommended—a good naturalist or biologist, or even a knowledgeable local, will know where creatures habitually hang out and will be able to distinguish between thick branches and a knotted boa at the top of a shoreside tree.

FISHING
Canals that are not part of protected areas can be ripe for fishing—another, tastier way to get a close-up look at some of the local fauna. Make sure to ask about what's biting, as well as local fishing regulations.

VIEWING PLATFORMS
Hiking can be more difficult in these areas because wetlands are by definition largely underwater. But some areas have elevated platforms that make for great up-close viewing of the interior parts of marshes and shallow lagoons.

FLORA

Wetland and mangrove plants share an ability to live in soggy conditions. However, not all wetland plants are able to survive brackish water in the way coastal mangrove flora can.

BLACK MANGROVE

The black mangrove can grow as tall as 40 feet and has adapted to survive in its habitat by excreting salt through special glands in its leaves. It grows on the banks above the high-tide line and has evolved to breathe through small roots it sends up vertically in case of flooding.

Black mangrove

RED MANGROVE

Costa Rica has seven species of mangrove trees, including red mangrove (*Rhizophora mangle*), black mangrove (*Avicennia germinans*), white mangrove (*Laguncularia racemosa*), and the rarer tea mangrove (*Pelliciera rhizophorae*). Red mangrove is easily identified by its tall arching prop roots that give it a firm foothold against wind and waves. The tidal land is also unstable, so all mangroves need a lot of root just to keep upright. As a result, many have more living matter underwater than aboveground. They also depend on their prop roots for extra nutrients and oxygen; the red mangrove filters salt at its roots.

Red mangrove

THORNY SENSITIVE PLANT

Aquatic grasses and herbs grow along the shallower edges of swamps and marshlands where they can take root underwater and still reach the air above. The curious *dormilona,* or thorny sensitive plant (*Mimosa pigra*), is another invasive wetland shrub and can be identified by the way its fernlike leaves wilt shyly to the touch, only to straighten out a little later.

Thorny sensitive plant

WATER HYACINTH

The succulent floating water hyacinth (*Eichornia crassipes*) is recognizable by its lavender-pink flowers that are sometimes bundled at 8–15 per single stalk. The stems rise from a bed of thick floating green leaves, whereas the plant's feathery roots hang free in the still fresh water. The water hyacinth is prolific and invasive; they've even been known to clog the canals of Tortuguero.

Water hyacinth

FAUNA

Though the diversity of plant life in mangrove swamps and wetlands is small compared with other ecozones, this habitat attracts an extremely wide variety of fauna.

BLACK-BELLIED WHISTLING DUCK

Bird-watchers love the wide-open wetlands and marshes, with flocks of thousands of migrating and resident species. In these tropical floodplains pink-tinged roseate spoonbills will be found stalking the shallow water alongside the majestic great egret and the bizarre and endangered jabiru stork. Keep an eye out for the black-bellied whistling duck, which actually perches and nests in trees. These migrant ducks can also be found in some southern U.S. states.

Black-bellied whistling duck

BLACK-CROWNED NIGHT HERON

Mangroves are critical nesting habitats for a number of birds, including the endangered mangrove humming-bird, the yellow-billed continga, the Amazon kingfisher, and the black-crowned night heron. Interestingly, black-crowned night herons don't distinguish between their own young and those from other nests, so they willingly brood strange chicks.

Black-crowned night heron

CRAB-EATING RACCOON

Bigger creatures are attracted to these mangroves precisely because of the veritable buffet of sea snacks. The crab-eating raccoon will prowl the canopy of the mangrove forests as well as the floor, feeding on crabs and mollusks. The endangered American crocodile and the spectacled caiman can be found lurking in still waters or sunning themselves on the banks of mangrove habitat.

Crab-eating raccoon

RAINBOW PARROTFISH

Rainbow parrotfish, in addition to many other fish species, spend time as juveniles in mangrove areas, feeding in the relative safety of the roots until they're big enough to venture out into more open water. Parrotfish have a few unusual abilities: they are hermaphroditic and can change sex in response to population density; at night they wrap themselves in a protective mucus cocoon; and they eat algae off the coral and excrete a fine white sand. One parrotfish can create up to 200 pounds of sand per year, which ultimately washes ashore. Think about it the next time you're lying on the beach.

Rainbow parrotfish

3

Biodiversity WETLANDS AND MANGROVES

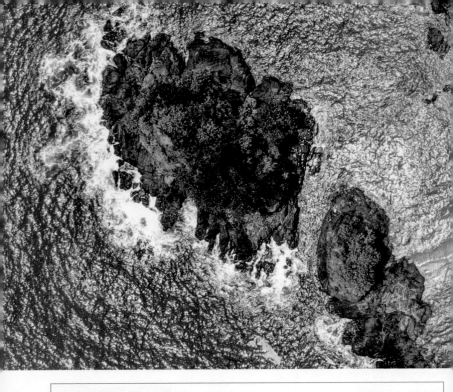

SHORELINE

Costa Rica has a whopping 1,290-km-long (799-mile-long) coastline that varies from expansive beaches to tranquil bays, muddy estuaries, and rocky outcroppings. They're backed by mangrove, transitional, and tropical rain and dry forests.

Few visitors who come to the Costa Rican shore think of it as an ecosystem in its own right. But venture beyond the tanned bodies and the accompanying party scene and you'll be rewarded with a panorama of life that rivals that of any rain forest. Each of Costa Rica's coastal environments, as well as the currents and the wind, has its own distinct impact on the ecology of the beach.

By law, all of Costa Rica's beaches are public, but beaches near population centers get strewn with trash quite quickly. It's one of the great ironies of Costa Rica that a country renowned for its environmental achievements

litters with such laissez-faire. Limited access tends to make for more scenic beaches. If you're worried about pollution, keep an eye out for Blue Flag beaches (marked on our maps with blue flags), an ecological rating system that evaluates water quality—both ocean and drinking water—trash cleanup, waste management, security, signposting, and environmental education. Blue Flags are awarded to communities rather than to individual hotels, which feeds a sense of cooperation. In 2002, the competition was opened to inland communities.

Costa Rica's sand beaches come in different shades and textures: pulverized black volcanic rock (Playa Negra), crushed white shells (Playa Conchal), finely ground white coral and quartz (Playa Carrillo), and gray rock sediment (many stretches along both coasts). These strips of sand may seem devoid of life, but they're actually ecological hotbeds, where mammals, birds, and amphibians live, feed, or reproduce. The hardiest of creatures can be found in the tidal pools that form on rockier beaches; keep an eye out for colorful fish, starfish, and sea urchins, all of which endure pounding waves, powerful tides, broiling sun, and predator attacks from the air, land, or sea.

■ From October 15 to February 15, Playa Grande sees lumbering, huge leatherback turtles come ashore to nest. Sixty days later, the hatchlings will scramble toward the water.

■ Gentle, consistent waves and a couple of good surfing schools make Sámara, on the north Pacific coast, a good choice for first-timers hoping to catch a wave.

■ Snorkeling is phenomenal near Cahuita's coral reef and at Punta Uva on the Caribbean coast. Look for colorful blue parrotfish, angelfish, sponges, and seaweeds.

TOP DESTINATIONS

Costa Rica's beach scenes are wildly diverse, so a little planning can go a long way.

BALLENA NATIONAL MARINE PARK

This unique park is along one of the more remote stretches of coastline, on the southern end of the Central Pacific region, and encompasses several beaches. Parque Nacional Marino Ballena (*ballena* is Spanish for "whale") gets its name from the humpback whales who feed here, and for a peculiar sandbar formation at Playa Uvita that goes straight out toward the ocean before splitting and curving in two directions, much like a whale's tail. (⇨ *See Chapter 10.*)

THE CARIBBEAN

This coast has an entirely different feel from the Pacific. North of Limón, there are miles of undeveloped, protected beaches where green sea turtles come from July to October to lay eggs. There have also been sightings of the logger-head, hawksbill, and leatherback turtles. The currents here are strong, so don't plan on swimming.

To the south of Limón, beaches are bordered by dense green vegetation all year long, and the quality of the sand can change dramatically as you

Montezuma, Justin Hubbell, Fodors.com member

wander from cove to cove. Some of the country's healthiest living coral reefs are offshore, so snorkeling is worthwhile. Beaches of note are Cahuita's Playa Negra and Playa Blanca, and Puerto Viejo de Talamanca's Punta Uva. (⇨ *See Chapter 11.*)

MANUEL ANTONIO NATIONAL PARK

On the northern end of the Pacific coast, Manuel Antonio National Park shelters some of the country's more precious beaches. A series of half-moon bays with sparkling sands are fronted by transitional forest—a combination of flora and fauna from the tropical dry forests farther north and the tropical rain forests that stretch south. Wildlife is abundant at Manuel Antonio, and the towering jungle at the beach's edge can give the area a wild and paradisiacal feel. (⇨ *See Chapter 9.*)

THE NICOYA PENINSULA

A succession of incredible beaches are scattered along this region of the Pacific coast, from Playa Panama in the north all the way south to Montezuma, including Avellanas, Guiones, and Sámara. Ostional, just north of Guiones, offers something none of the others can: the turtle *arribada* (mass nesting times).(⇨ *See Chapter 8.*)

Playa Uvita; Toronto Jeff, Fodors.com member

EXPERIENCING THE SHORELINE

Nesting olive ridley turtles at Ostional Wildlife Refuge

Costa Rica's beaches have tons of activities. If you like getting wet, the ocean is bathwater-warm and there are watersports outfitters just about everywhere. There are also plenty of hammocks and cafés.

HORSEBACK RIDING
Horseback riding on the beach is great fun, but you can't do it everywhere. Many of the most popular beaches have outlawed it for health reasons, especially if it's where a lot of people swim.

SURFING
Costa Rica is a world-class surfing destination, and the Pacific coast in particular has enough surf spots to satisfy both pros and novices. You can arrange lessons in most beach towns. Surfing is an activity that involves a lot of floating, so it allows for plenty of wildlife-watching: keep a weather eye for jumping fish, stingrays, dolphins, and squads of brown pelicans.

TURTLE TOURS
Witnessing the nesting ritual of Costa Rica's visiting sea turtles is a truly unforgettable experience. Various organizations oversee the nesting beaches and arrange tours. The onslaught of mother sea turtles is most intense throughout the night, so setting out just before dawn is the best way to see and take pictures of the phenomenon in progress at first light.

■ TIP→ Take great care at beaches that drop off steeply as you enter the water. This is an indicator not only of large waves that crash straight onto the shore but also of strong currents.

FLORA

The plants along the coast play an important role in maintaining the dunes and preventing erosion in the face of heavy winds and other forces.

COCONUT PALMS

Coconut palm trees are the most distinctive plants in any tropical setting. No postcard photo of a white-sand beach would be complete without at least one palm tilting precariously over the shore. Palm trees (from the *Arecaceae* family) require a lot of sunlight and, thanks to their strong root system, will often grow at nearly horizontal angles to escape the shade of beachside forests. The coconut palm is also the proud parent of the world's largest seed—the delicious coconut—which can float long distances across the ocean, washing up on a foreign shore and sprouting a new tree from the sand.

Coconut palms

MANGROVE

Mangrove swamps are rich, murky forests that thrive in brackish waters up and down Costa Rica's coasts. They grow in what's known as the intertidal zone, the part of the coast that's above sea level at low tide and submerged at high tide. Mangrove trees (*rhizophora*) are just one of the species that live in these coastal swamps—you can recognize them by their stilt roots, the long tendril-like roots that allow the tree to breathe even when it's partially submerged. These forests are vibrant and complex ecosystems in their own right.

Mangrove tree

MANZANILLO DE PLAYA

Steer clear of the poisonous manchineel, or *manzanillo de playa* (*Hippomane mancinella*), the most toxic tree in Costa Rica. Its fruit and bark secrete a white latex that's highly irritating to the touch and poisonous—even fatal—if ingested. Don't burn it either, because the smoke can also cause allergic reactions. The tree can be identified by its small yellowish apples and bright green leaves. It's found along the north Pacific coast, stretches of the Nicoya Peninsula, the Central Pacific's Manuel Antonio National Park, and on the Osa Peninsula.

Manzanillo de playa

SEA GRAPE

Sea grape (*Coccoloba uvifera*) and similar types of shrubby, ground-hugging vegetation grow closer to the water, around the edges of the beach. These plants play a part in keeping the beach stable and preventing erosion.

Sea grape

FAUNA

Beaches are tough environments where few animals actually make their home. But as we all know, you don't have to live on the beach to enjoy it.

Brown pelican

BROWN PELICAN

Brown pelicans fly in tight formation, dropping low over the sea and running parallel with the swells in search of shoals of fish. Browns are unique in that they're the only pelican species that plunge from the air to catch their food. After a successful dive, they have to guard against gulls, who will actually try to pluck the freshly caught fish from their pouch.

IGUANAS

A common sight on Costa Rica's sandy shores are iguanas. The green iguana (*Iguana iguana*) and the black spiny-tailed iguana, or black iguana (*Ctenosaura similis*), are often found sunning themselves on rocks or a few feet from the shade (and protection) of trees. Interestingly, the green iguana has been known to lay eggs and share nests with American crocodiles and spectacled caimans.

Iguanas

OLIVE RIDLEY TURTLE

At 75 to 100 pounds, the olive ridley (*Lepidochelys olivacea*) is the smallest of the five marine turtles that nest in Costa Rica. During mass nesting times (arribada), anywhere from tens to hundreds of thousands of females drag themselves ashore, gasping audibly, to lay their eggs. Between dusk and dawn, the prehistoric creatures crawl over the beach, sometimes even over one another, on their way between the ocean and their nests. People who are lucky enough to witness the event never forget it. Costa Rica's shores are also visited by the green turtle, the hawksbill, the loggerhead, and the leatherback turtle.

Olive ridley turtle

PAINTED GHOST CRAB

These intriguingly named crabs are called "ghosts" because they move so quickly that they seem to disappear. They're also one of the few creatures that actually live full-time on the beach. Sun beats down, wind is strong, danger lurks everywhere, and there's little to no cover, but painted ghost crabs (*Ocypode gaudichaudii*) survive all this by burrowing deep under the sand where the temperature and humidity are more constant and there's protection from surface threats like the black iguana.

Painted ghost crab

Did You Know?

Two types of iguana can be spotted sunning themselves along Costa Rica's coastline, the green iguana and the black iguana.

Chapter 4

SAN JOSÉ

4

Updated by
Jeffrey Van Fleet

⊙ **Sights**
★★★☆☆

🍴 **Restaurants**
★★★★★

🛏 **Hotels**
★★★★★

👜 **Shopping**
★★★★☆

🍸 **Nightlife**
★★★★★

WELCOME TO SAN JOSÉ

TOP REASONS TO GO

★ **Eating out:** Instead of relying on mostly rice and beans and chicken like the rest of Costa Rica, San José's diverse restaurants offer a welcome change of pace.

★ **Gold and jade museums:** For a sense of indigenous Costa Rica, frequently forgotten during the nation's march to modernity, the country's two best museums are must-sees.

★ **Historic Barrios Amón and Otoya:** These northern neighborhoods abutting and sometimes overlapping downtown have tree-lined streets and century-old houses turned into trendy hotels and restaurants.

★ **Location, location, location:** From the capital's pivotal position, you can be riding river rapids or taking a coffee tour atop a giant volcano in an hour or less.

★ **Shopping:** San José is the best place to stock up on both essentials and souvenirs. Look for leather-and-wood rocking chairs, ceramics, textiles, and, of course, wonderful coffee.

The metropolitan area holds around 2.2 million residents, but the city proper is small, with some 340,000 people living in its 44 square km (17 square miles). Most sights are concentrated in three downtown neighborhoods—La Soledad, La Merced, and El Carmen—named for their anchor churches. Borders are fuzzy: one *barrio* (neighborhood) flows into the next, districts overlap, and the city itself melts into its suburbs with nary a sign to denote where one community ends and another begins.

1 **Downtown.** This area holds San José's historic and commercial districts and many top attractions: the Museo del Jade (Jade Museum), Museo del Oro Precolombino (Pre-Columbian Gold Museum), Mercado Central (Central Market), and Teatro Nacional (National Theater).

2 **West of Downtown.** The mostly residential neighborhoods here are anchored by large Parque Metropolitano La Sabana (La Sabana Park) and the Museo de Arte Costarricense (Museum of Costa Rican Art).

3 **North of Downtown.** Historic barrios Amón and Otoya and the Museo de los Niños (Children's Museum) are a few of the attractions to the north.

4 **East of Downtown.** Several good restaurants and hotels and the Universidad de Costa Rica (University of Costa Rica) are ensconced in and on the way to the San Pedro suburb.

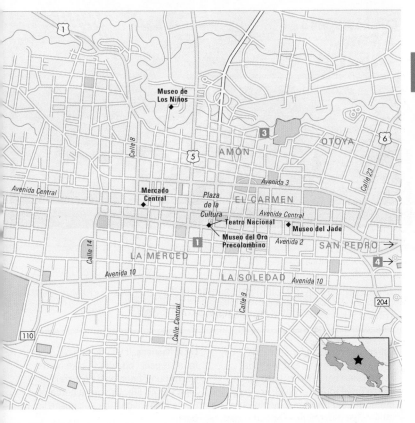

SOUVENIR SHOPPING IN SAN JOSÉ

Handwoven baskets

San José's shops and markets can be crowded, but they're great fun for the savvy shopper and a great way to explore. The city's bustling downtown is compact enough to make it easy to visit a few markets in a day, or even an afternoon.

Coffee. The most authentic modern-day Costa Rica souvenir, and the most appreciated back home. Load up on whole bean (*grano entero*), or if you prefer ground (*molido*), buy the *puro* (otherwise it might have added sugar). Café Britt is the most famous brand ($5/lb).

Coffee brewers. The original Costa Rican coffeemaker is called a *chorreador*. It's a simple wooden stand that's fitted with cloth socklike filters. Finely ground coffee is dumped in the sock, and hot water is filtered into the mug beneath. Unadorned ones in sleek cherrywood cost around $15. Don't forget extra filters ($1).

Local libations. If you don't have room for a six-pack, be sure to take home the Imperial beer label on a stein or T-shirt (both $5). Or snag a bottle of Costa Rica's signature sugarcane liquor, *guaro*.

Mayan ocarinas. Calling the ocarina two-faced would be an insult, but only because you wouldn't be giving it nearly enough credit. The Mayan resonant vessel flutes ($10–$20) depict more than a half-dozen animal faces when flipped around and were often given as gifts to travelers by the Chorotega indigenous group in northwestern Guanacaste.

Hammocks. Swinging in one of these is the official *pura vida* posture. Structured hammocks with wooden dowels on the ends ($50 and up) are optimal, but dowel-less, cocoonlike hammocks ($35 and up) are infinitely more packable. Get a chair hammock ($25) if you have limited space back home.

Oxcarts. From the Sarchí region, the oxcart has become Costa Rica's most iconic craftsman artifact. Full-size ones can run several hundred dollars, and dealers can arrange to have them shipped. There's also a coffee table–size version ($35) or, better yet, an oxcart napkin holder ($5).

Boruca ceremonial masks. The Boruca people, one of the country's last active indigenous groups, don these masks in their annual end-of-the-year festival, Dansa de los Diablitos (Dance of the Devils). Cheaper imitations abound, but Galería Namu has the best—and most authentic—selection ($120–$150).

Machetes. Knives and machetes are commonly used in the country's rural jungle areas and happily sold in leather slings to travelers ($15). Also, knives ($5–$10) and other items, like frogs and butterflies made out of colored resin, might not be considered traditional but represent the Rastafarian side of the country.

Boruca ceremonial mask

A coffee vendor bags Costa Rica's top souvenir.

Jewelry. Go for oversize wooden hoop earrings ($10), wire-wrought gold and silver baubles ($10), or plaster-molded earrings adorned with toucans, frogs, and pineapples ($5). Jewelry made from carved-out coco shells is popular, too.

Tropical woods and papers. Sleek mango-wood vases ($15), inlaid rosewood cutting boards ($15), and hand-painted rum-wood mugs ($10) are among the many elegant woodworks here. There are also scratch-and-sniff writing materials that would make Willy Wonka proud, with banana, mango, lemon, and coffee-scented stationery sets ($7).

Folkloric dresses and shirts. While they're often only pulled out on national holidays like Independence Day, a flounced dress ($15 and up) or pinafore ($10) might be just the gift you're looking for. Ranchero-style shirts ($15) and straw hats ($8) are also options.

San José is the center of all that is Costa Rica, and to Ticos in the countryside at least, it glitters every bit as much as New York City. True to developing-country patterns, everything—politics, business, art, cuisine, nightlife, and culture—converges here in the capital. It may not be the center of your trip to Costa Rica—those rain forests and volcanoes have your name written on them. But the city is worth a day or two of exploring, as a way to ease into Costa Rica at the start of a visit or to wrap things up with a well-deserved dose of civilization following your adventures to more remote parts of the country.

San José is—dare we say it—hip these days. Hands down, it has Costa Rica's best dining and nightlife scene, with the eastside neighborhoods of Barrios Escalante and La California leading the way as the new places to be. Amid the noise and traffic—and make no mistake: San José still serves up those annoyances in abundance—shady parks, well-maintained museums, lively plazas, great hotels, cool shops, and fun tours do exist. Further, the city makes a great base for day trips: from downtown it's a mere 30- to 40-minute drive to the tranquil countryside and myriad outdoor activities of the surrounding Central Valley.

You'd never know San José is as old as it is—given the complete absence of colonial architecture—but settlers founded the city in 1737. After independence in 1821, San José cemented its position as the new nation's capital. Revenues from the coffee and banana industries financed the construction of stately homes, theaters, and a trolley system (later abandoned and now visible only in old sepia photographs). As recently as the mid-1900s, San José was no larger than the present-day downtown area; old-timers remember the vast coffee and cane plantations that extended beyond its borders. The city began to mushroom only after World War II, when old buildings were razed to make room for concrete monstrosities. The sprawl eventually connected the capital with nearby cities. Today, the city spells out its new slogan, ¡SJO VIVE! ("San José lives!"), in colorful eight-foot letters in the Central Park, near the National Theater, and in front of the post office. Caught up in that new spirit, Costa Ricans visiting the capital like to have their pictures taken in front of those signs. You might enjoy that, too.

San José has attracted people from all over Costa Rica, yet it remains, in many ways, a collection of distinct neighborhoods where residents maintain friendly small-town ways. For you, this might mean the driver you're following will decide to abruptly stop his vehicle to buy a lottery ticket or chat with a friend on the street. Or it might mean you have to navigate a maze of fruit-vendor stands on a crowded sidewalk. But this is part of what keeps San José a big small town.

Planning

When to Go

HIGH SEASON: MID-DECEMBER TO APRIL

San José's 3,800-foot altitude keeps temperatures pleasant and springlike year-round. The capital's status as a business-travel destination means lodging rates rarely vary throughout the year. The dry season literally blows in with a change in wind patterns that makes December and January brisk but sunny. February warms up; by March and April, the heat and dust pick up considerably.

LOW SEASON: MAY TO MID-NOVEMBER

The wet season moves in gradually, with manageable brief afternoon showers from May through July. August becomes wetter. September and October might mean constant rain for days at a time, and navigating a traffic-clogged city in a torrential rush-hour downpour is not fun.

SHOULDER SEASON: MID-NOVEMBER TO MID-DECEMBER

Rains wind down by mid-November and you'll even experience a bit of a nip in the air—it's still the tropics, though—as the city decks itself out for the holidays. The big influx of tourists won't arrive until just before the end of the year, so this is the time to enjoy the capital at its best.

Planning Your Time

SAN JOSÉ IN A DAY

If you have only a day to spend in San José, the must-see stops are the Teatro Nacional (National Theater) and the Museo del Oro Precolombino (Pre-Columbian Gold Museum). It's easy to accomplish this because they sit on the same block.

With more time, take in the Museo del Jade (Jade Museum) and Museo Nacional (National Museum). The Museo de los Niños (Children's Museum) is a kid pleaser. It's in a dicey part of the barrio El Carmen, more north of downtown than actually in downtown; take a taxi.

DAY TRIPS FROM THE CAPITAL

The capital sits smack-dab in the middle of the country in the fertile Central Valley. Although a day trip to either coast would be grueling—despite Costa Rica's small size, it takes longer than you think to get from place to place—you can easily pop out to the Central Valley's major sights and be back in the city in time for dinner. Several of these attractions provide pickup service in San José, some for a nominal additional cost. Alternatively, tour operators include many of these attractions on their itineraries.

DESTINATION	FROM SAN JOSÉ (BY CAR)
Basílica de Nuestra Señora de los Ángeles	30 mins southeast
Café Britt	30 mins north
Carara National Park	2 hrs southwest
Doka Coffee Estate	1 hr west
Guayabo National Monument	2 hrs southeast, 4WD necessary
Irazú Volcano	1 hr east
Jardín Botánico Lankester	45 mins southeast
La Paz Waterfall Gardens	2 hrs north
Orosi Valley	1 hr southeast
Poás Volcano	1 hr northwest
Rainforest Adventures	1 hr north
River Rafting	2–2½ hrs southeast or north
Sarchí	1 hr northwest
Tortuga Island	3 hrs west
Zoo Ave	45 mins west

BYPASS SAN JOSÉ?

San José isn't necessarily the Costa Rica you came to see. Those beaches and rain forests beckon, after all. If that is, indeed, the case, you can avoid the city altogether.

The international airport actually lies just outside the city of Alajuela, about 30 minutes northwest of the capital. Look for lodgings in Alajuela, San Antonio de Belén, Escazú, or Santa Ana—all within striking distance of the airport. Or head west. ⇨ For information about lodgings near Aeropuerto Internacional Juan Santamaría, see Chapter 5.

Few international flights arrive in the morning, but they do exist, especially via Miami. Get here early and you can head out of town immediately.

If your vacation takes you only to northwest Costa Rica (including the North Pacific beaches), don't fly into San José at all. Use Aeropuerto Internacional Daniel Oduber Quirós outside the northwestern hub city of Liberia. Search for airport code LIR instead of SJO.

Getting Here and Around

AIR

Aeropuerto Internacional Juan Santamaría, 16 km (10 miles) northwest of downtown, receives international flights and those of domestic airlines SANSA and Skyway.

BUS

San José has no central bus terminal. The city's public bus stations are all in sketchy neighborhoods. Always take a taxi to and from them. Bag-snatching is common inside the so-called Coca-Cola terminal, a onetime Coke bottling plant converted into a bus station. Watch your things carefully. Even better: use air-conditioned minivan shuttles operated by Grayline and Interbus instead of buses to travel between the capital and key tourist destinations.

City buses are cheap (¢100–¢150) and easy to use. For Paseo Colón and La Sabana, take buses marked "Sabana–Cementerio" from stops at Avenida 2 between Calles 5 and 7 or Avenida 3 next to the post office. For Los Yoses and San Pedro, take the various "San Pedro" buses from Avenida Central between Calles 9 and 11.

BUS TERMINALS Gran Terminal del Caribe. ⊠ C. Ctl., Avda. 13, Barrio Tournón ☎ 2222–0610. **Terminal Coca-Cola.** ⊠ Avda. 1, C. 16, Barrio La Merced. **Terminal Empresarios Unidos.** ⊠ C. 16, Avda. 12, Barrio La Merced ☎ 2221–6600 ⊕ www.eupsacr.com. **Terminal MEPE.** ⊠ C. 12, Avda. 9, Barrio La Merced ☎ 2257–8129 ⊕ www.mepecr.com. **Terminal 7-10.** ⊠ C. 10, Avda. 7, across from former Cine

Líbano, Barrio La Merced ☎ *2519–9743* ⊕ *www.terminal7-10.com.* **Terminal Tracopa.** ✉ *C. 5, Avda. 20, Barrio El Pacífico* ☎ *2221–4214* ⊕ *www.tracopacr.com.*

SHUTTLE COMPANIES Grayline. ☎ *2220–2126, 800/719–3905 in North America* ⊕ *www.2020.graylinecostarica.com.* **Interbus.** ☎ *4100–0888* ⊕ *www.interbusonline.com.*

CAR

Paved roads fan out from Paseo Colón west to Escazú and northwest to the airport and Heredia. For the North Pacific coast, Guanacaste, and on to Nicaragua, take the Pan-American Highway north (CA1). The Carretera a Caldera (Highway 27) takes you to Escazú, Santa Ana, and beyond to the Central Pacific coast. Calle 3 runs north into the highway to Guápiles, Limón, and the Atlantic coast through Braulio Carrillo National Park, with a turnoff to Sarapiquí. Follow Avenida Central or 2 east through San Pedro to enter the Pan-American Highway south (CA2), which has a turnoff for Cartago, Volcán Irazú, and Turrialba before it heads toward the South Pacific coast and Panama.

Avoid driving in the city if you can help it. Streets are narrow, rush hour (7 to 9 am and 5 to 7 pm) traffic is horrible, and drivers can be reckless. What's more, San José and neighboring San Pedro enforce rigid weekday driving restrictions (6 am to 7 pm) for all private vehicles, including your rental car. The last digit of your license plate determines your no-driving day: Monday (1 and 2), Tuesday (3 and 4), Wednesday (5 and 6), Thursday (7 and 8), and Friday (9 and 0).

Street parking is difficult to find and requires payment by a locally available app. Park your vehicle instead in a guarded lot and plan to pay $2 per hour. Leave nothing of value inside the car.

Driving is forbidden on 44 blocks in the center city—sections of Avenidas Central and 4, and Calles 2, 3, 8, 9, and 17—which have been turned into pleasant pedestrian-only thoroughfares. More of these *bulevares* are on the drawing board. Thank China and the European Union for much of the funding.

TAXI

You can hail cabs on the street or call for one. Licensed cabs are red with a gold triangle on the front doors. A 3-km (2-mile) ride costs around $3; tipping isn't customary. By law cabbies must use *marías* (meters) within the metropolitan area; the meter starts at about $1.15. Any taxi can take you to the airport. Taxi Aeropuerto—whose vehicles are orange—is the only authorized taxi service from the airport into San José. Expect to pay $25 to $40 depending on your destination in the city. Cab drivers hate it if you slam the door; close the door gently.

The ride service Uber operates in San José and surrounding suburbs, albeit without proper government permits. Until Uber and the authorities work out their differences, you use the service at some risk.

TAXIS Alfaro. ☎ *2221–8466.* **Coopetaxi.** ☎ *2235–9966.* **San Jorge.** ☎ *2221–3434.* **Taxi Aeropuerto.** ☎ *2221–6865* ⊕ *www.taxiaeropuerto.com.*

Health and Safety

San José is safer than other Latin American capitals. Violent crime is rare; the greatest threat you're likely to face is petty theft. Standard big-city precautions apply.

Use only licensed red taxis with yellow triangles on the front doors. The license plate of an official taxi begins with TSJ (Taxi San José).

Park in guarded, well-lighted lots ($2 an hour). If you must park on the street, make sure informal *guachimen* (watchmen) are present. Usually this is someone with a big stick who will expect payment of about $2 per hour. Never leave anything valuable in your parked vehicle.

MEDICAL ASSISTANCE Clínica Bíblica. ✉ *Avda. 14, Cs. Ctl.–1, Barrio El Pacífico* ☎ *2522–1000* ⊕ *www.clinicabiblica.com.* **Hospital La Católica.** ✉ *C. Esquivel Bonilla, Guadalupe* ☎ *2246–3000* ⊕ *www.hospitallacatolica.com.*

Money Matters

San José state banks—Banco Nacional, Banco de Costa Rica, Bancrédito, Banco Popular—come complete with horrendous lines. The private BAC San José and Scotiabank are better bets. Bypass that process entirely and get cash with your ATM card instead. Cash machines inside a bank, during the day while a guard keeps watch, are your safest bet.

BANKS/ATMS BAC San José. ✉ *Avda. 2, Cs. Ctl.–1, Barrio El Carmen* ☎ *2295–9797* ⊕ *www.baccredomatic.com.* **Banco Nacional.** ✉ *Avda. 1, Cs. 2–4, Barrio La Merced* ☎ *2212–2000* ⊕ *www.bncr. fi.cr.* **Scotiabank.** ✉ *C. 5, Avdas. Ctl.–2, behind Teatro Nacional, Barrio La Soledad* ☎ *2521–5680* ⊕ *www.scotiabankcr.com.*

Sights

In San José some streets have names, but no one seems to know or use them. Streets in the center of the capital are laid out in a grid, with *avenidas* (avenues) running east and west, and *calles* (streets) north and south. Odd-number avenues increase in number north of Avenida Central; even-number avenues to the south. Streets east of Calle Central have odd numbers; those to the west are even. Locals rarely use the numbers, however.

Costa Ricans rely instead on a charming and exasperating system of designating addresses by the distance from landmarks, as in "100 meters north and

50 meters west of the school." Another quirk: "100 meters" always refers to one city block, regardless of how long it actually is. Likewise, "200 meters" is two blocks, and so on.

Historically, the reference point was the church, but these days it might be a bar, a Taco Bell, or even a quirky landmark: the eastern suburb of San Pedro uses the *higuerón*, a prominent fig tree. The city has embarked on an ambitious project to name all its streets once and for all. Even after it's completed, it's improbable that anybody will know or use the names. Your best bet is to follow the time-honored practice of *ir y preguntar* (keep walking and keep asking).

Tours

★ Art City Tour

SPECIAL-INTEREST | The city sponsors a monthly evening showcase of its cultural venues from February through November. Several museums and galleries around town participate. You won't be able to hit them all in the four-hour 5–9 pm timeframe, but grab one of the free shuttles and check out a few of them. ✉ *San José* ⊕ *www.gamcultural.com.*

Barrio Bird Walking Tours

GUIDED TOURS | Despite the name, the specialty of this company is not birding but rather two-hour walking tours of the city, with a focus on sights, art, and food. ☎ *6280–6169* ⊕ *www.toursanjosecostarica.com* 🎫 *From $32.*

Carpe Chepe

WALKING TOURS | Among a variety of city tours, these enthusiastic folks operate a popular Friday- and Saturday-evening Pub Crawl excursion ($30) and a Central Market tour ($48) weekday afternoons. Local hotel pickup and dropoff can be arranged for an added fee. ☎ *8347–6198* ⊕ *www. carpechepe.com* 🎫 *from $30.*

Gray Line Costa Rica

GUIDED TOURS | This respected international company operates city sightseeing tours, as well as excursions to the surrounding Central Valley. ✉ *San José* ☎ *2220–2106 in Costa Rica, 800/719–3905 in North America* ⊕ *www.2020. graylinecostarica.com* 💲 *From $74.*

San José Free Walking Tour

WALKING TOURS | As the name promises, the 2½-hour walk is free and covers downtown sights. The 9 am walk departs from in front of the Aurola Holiday Inn on the north side of Parque Morazán, but advance reservations are required. The cheery guides do a good job. They rely on tips: be generous. ☎ *8721–9443* ⊕ *www. facebook.com/sanjosefreewalkingtour.*

★ San José Urban Adventures

GUIDED TOURS | Partake in a selection of fun half-day or evening walking tours with these knowledgeable folks. Barrio Bites & Sites and the Art of Craft Beer are especially popular. ☎ *4000–5730, 888/927–2128 in North America* ⊕ *www. sanjoseurbanadventures.com* 💲 *from $38.*

Restaurants

Costa Rica's capital beckons with the country's most varied and cosmopolitan restaurant scene. Italian, Spanish, Asian, French, Middle Eastern, Peruvian— they're all here, along with upscale Costa Rican cuisine.

Wherever you eat in San José, be it a small *soda* (snack bar) or a sophisticated restaurant, dress is casual. Meals tend to be taken earlier than in other Latin American countries; few restaurants serve past 9 or 10 pm. Local cafés usually open for breakfast at 7 and remain open until 7 or 8 in the evening. Restaurants serving international cuisine are usually open from 11 am to 9 pm. Some downtown eateries that serve mainly San José office workers limit evening hours and close

entirely on Sunday. Restaurants that do open on Sunday do a brisk business: it's the traditional family day out (and the maid's day off). Remember: All restaurants are no-smoking. ⚠ **Watch your things, no matter where you dine. Even at the best restaurants, thieves occasionally target purses slung over chair arms or placed under chairs.**

WHAT IT COSTS in U.S. Dollars			
$	$$	$$$	$$$$
RESTAURANTS			
under $10	$10–$15	$16–$25	over $25

Hotels

San José may be a big city, but it truly shines in its selection of small to medium-size inns. They're all locally owned, and their friendly, attentive staff will make you feel as if you're staying in an oasis in the middle of Costa Rica's noisy, congested capital.

San José has plenty of chains, including Best Western, Holiday Inn, Radisson, Quality Inn, Meliá, and Barceló (the last two are Spanish). But it also has historic houses with traditional architecture that have been converted into small lodgings.

The historic houses are usually without concierge or pool and are found mainly in Barrios Amón and Otoya, and in the eastern suburb of San Pedro. The city also has a lower tier of lodgings with the simplicity (and prices) beloved of backpackers. Most smaller hotels don't have air-conditioning, but it rarely gets hot enough at this altitude to warrant it.

Many lodgings operate at near-full occupancy in high season (December–April), but the capital's status as a business-travel destination means the lodging rates remain constant year-round. Reconfirm all reservations 24 hours in advance. If you're flying out early in the morning and prefer to stay near the airport, consider booking a hotel near Alajuela or San Antonio de Belén in the Central Valley. (⇨ See Chapter 5.)

Hotel reviews have been shortened. For full information, visit Fodors.com.

WHAT IT COSTS in U.S. Dollars			
$	$$	$$$	$$$$
HOTELS			
under $75	$75–$150	$151–$250	over $250

Nightlife

No one can accuse San José of having too few watering holes; finding ones welcoming to visitors is a bit more of a challenge. Downtown, hotels and the couple of places we recommend are good bets for a quiet drink. The rest of the center city can get boozy and brawly at night. Be careful. Barrios Amón and Otoya, north of downtown, have little in the way of nightlife; even hotel bars are rare.

East of downtown, Barrios Escalante and La California house the places to see and be seen these days. Some of the city's trendiest nightspots have sprung up here in these two neighborhoods that connect central San José with the eastern suburb of San Pedro. The young and the restless hang out in the student-oriented places around the University of Costa Rica in San Pedro. Most rock loudly each night. Finding the few quiet university bars and cafés where you can carry on a real conversation takes some hunting.

Other nightlife has migrated to the Central Valley suburbs of Escazú and Heredia. *(See Chapter 5.)* Both are about 20- to 30-minute taxi rides southwest and north, respectively, from downtown San José.

Take taxis to and from when you're out at night; it's always the safest option after dark. Most places will be happy to call you a cab—or, if there's a guard, they can hail you one—when it's time to call it a night. Remember that all venues are no-smoking.

Performing Arts

The best source for theater, dance, film, and arts information is the "Viva" entertainment section of the Spanish-language daily *La Nación*. The paper also publishes the "Tiempo Libre" section each Friday, highlighting what's going on over the weekend. *GAM Cultural,* a free monthly flyer found in many upscale hotels and restaurants, publishes features about what's going on around town. Listings in both publications are in Spanish but are easy to decipher. The website of the English-language *The Tico Times* (⊕ www.ticotimes.net) lists many events of interest to visitors and the expat community.

Unfortunately, arts offerings in the city are nearly nonexistent during the high-season weeks from mid-December through early February. That's holiday and school vacation time.

Dubbing of movies is rare; films are screened in their original language, usually English, and subtitled in Spanish. Children's movies, however, *are* dubbed (*doblada*), although a multiplex cinema may offer some *hablada en inglés,* or screenings in English. Plan to pay $6 for a ticket. Don't expect anything too avant-garde in most theaters; month-old Hollywood releases are the norm. Following trends seen elsewhere, theaters have fled downtown for the suburban malls.

More than a dozen theater groups (many of which perform slapstick comedies) hold forth in smaller theaters around town. If your Spanish is up to it, call for a reservation. The curtain rises at 8 pm, Friday through Sunday, with some companies staging performances on Thursday night, too. If your Spanish isn't quite theater-ready, there are plenty of dance and musical performances.

Shopping

Although it might seem more "authentic" to buy your souvenirs at their source, you can find everything in the city—a real bonus if you're pressed for time. If the capital has any real tourist shopping district, it's found loosely in the cluster of streets around Parque Morazán, just north of downtown, an area bounded roughly by Avenidas 1 and 7 and Calles 5 and 9. Stroll and search, because many other businesses congregate in the area as well.

The northeastern suburb of Moravia has a cluster of high-quality crafts and artisan shops—for good reason very popular with tour groups—in the three blocks heading north from the Colegio María Inmaculada high school. The street is two blocks behind the city's church.

Prices in shops are fixed and fair. You might be able to bargain at the Calle Nacional de Artesanía y Pintura, but bargaining isn't the sport it is in other countries. Haggling, even if not ill-intended, will come off as rude. Your best bet for getting a deal is to simply suggest you'll come back later and walk away. If the vendors really want to lower the price, they will.

Visitor Information

The ubiquitous "Tourist Information" signs you see around downtown are really private travel agencies looking to sell you tours rather than provide unbiased information. The Instituto Costarricense de Turismo, the official tourist office, operates an office on Avenida Central and a booth in the arrivals area of the international airport. The staff here are

not allowed to make specific recommendations, so answers to questions often come across as vague and lackadaisical.

VISITOR INFORMATION Instituto Costarricense de Turismo. (*ICT*) ⊠ *Avda. Ctl., Cs. 1–3* ☎ *2222–1090* ⊕ *www.visitcostarica. com.*

Downtown

It's a trend seen the world over: businesses and residents flee city centers for the space, blissful quiet, and lower-priced real estate of the 'burbs. Although Costa Rica's capital is experiencing this phenomenon, downtown still remains the city's historic and vibrant (if noisy and congested) heart. Government offices have largely stayed put here, as have most attractions. It's impossible to sightsee without finding yourself downtown.

Boundaries are fuzzy. For example, the subneighborhoods of El Carmen, La Merced, and La Soledad are anchored in downtown but sprawl outward from the center city. And, in an effort to seem trendier, several establishments in downtown's northern fringes prefer to say that they're in the more fashionable barrios of Amón or Otoya.

The city has only three must-see sights—the Teatro Nacional, the Museo del Oro Precolombino (Pre-Columbian Gold Museum), and the Museo del Jade (Jade Museum)—and they are simply fabulous. All sit within a three-block walk of each other and could fill a day if that's all the time you have in the capital.

Sights

Catedral Metropolitana (*Metropolitan Cathedral*)
RELIGIOUS SITE | Built in 1871 and completely refurbished in the late 1990s to repair earthquake damage, the neoclassical cathedral, topped by a corrugated tin dome, isn't terribly interesting

outside. But inside are patterned floor tiles, stained-glass windows depicting various saints and apostles, and framed polychrome bas-reliefs illustrating the Stations of the Cross. A magnificent 1891 Belgian pipe organ fills the church with music.

The interior of the small Capilla del Santísimo (Chapel of the Host) on the cathedral's north side evokes ornate old Catholicism, much more so than the main sanctuary itself. A marble statue of Pope John Paul II stands guard over the garden on the building's north side. Masses are held throughout the day on Sunday starting at 7 am, with one in English each Saturday at 4 pm. Although not part of the cathedral complex, a small statue of Holocaust victim Anne Frank graces the pedestrian mall on the building's south side. It was donated by the Embassy of the Netherlands. ⊠ *C. Ctl., Avdas. 2–4* ☎ *2221–3820.*

Centro Nacional de la Cultura (*National Cultural Center*)
ARTS VENUE | Rather than tear it down, the Ministry of Culture converted the sloped-surface, double-block 1853 Fábrica Nacional de Licores (National Liquor Factory) into a 150,000-square-foot cultural center, with government offices, two theaters, and a museum. The Teatro FANAL and Teatro 1887 are two of the capital's foremost performing-arts venues. Both spaces were used for storage and testing in the original factory complex. ⊠ *C. 13, Avdas. 3–5* ☎ *2257–5524* ⊕ *www.mcj.go.cr* ⊠ *Tours free.*

Correos de Costa Rica (*Central Post Office*)
BUILDING | The handsome carved exterior of the post office, dating from 1917, is hard to miss among the bland buildings surrounding it. The lobby is not as interesting as the exterior, but it and the small pedestrian plaza in front are a perpetual hive of activity. ⊠ *C. 2, Avdas. 1–3* ☎ *2202–2900* ⊕ *correos.go.cr* ☾ *Closed Sun.*

Estatua de John Lennon (*Statue of John Lennon*)
MEMORIAL | A whimsical statue of John Lennon sits on a small, slightly out-of-the-way plaza across from La Soledad church. Sculptor José Ramón Villa's work marks the spot where, in 1966, Costa Ricans smashed Beatles records in protest of Lennon's statement that the iconic pop group was "more popular than Jesus." The official name of the statue is *Imagine All the People Living Life in Peace*, evoking the lyrics of Lennon's song "Imagine." After more than five decades, bygones are apparently bygones: residents and tourists alike enjoy having their photos taken sitting with the casually seated figure. ⊠ *C. 9, Avda. 4.*

Mercado Central (*Central Market*)
MARKET | This block-long melting pot is a warren of dark, narrow passages flanked by stalls packed with spices (some purported to have medicinal value), fish, fruit, flowers, pets, and wood and leather crafts. The 1880 structure is a kinder, gentler introduction to a Central American market; there are no pigs or chickens or their accompanying smells to be found here. A few stands selling tourist souvenirs congregate near the entrances, but this is primarily a place where the average Costa Rican comes to shop. There are dozens of cheap restaurants and snack stalls, including the country's first ice-cream vendor. Be warned: the concentration of shoppers makes this a hot spot for pickpockets, purse snatchers, and backpack slitters. Enter and exit at the southeast corner of the building (Avenida Central at Calle 6). The green-and-white *salida* signs direct you to other exits, but they spill onto slightly less-safe streets. Use the image of the Sacred Heart of Jesus, the market's patron and protector, near the center of the building, as your guide; it faces that safer corner by which you should exit. (We doubt it was planned that way.) ⊠ *Bordered by Avdas. Ctl.–1 and Cs. 6–8* ☾ *Closed Sun.*

The Museo del Oro Precolombino has the largest collection of pre-Columbian gold jewelry in Central America.

Museo de Arte y Diseño Contemporáneo
(*Museum of Contemporary Art and Design*)

MUSEUM | This wonderfully minimalist space is perfect as the country's premier modern-art venue. The MADC, as it's known around town, hosts changing exhibits by artists and designers from all over Latin America. While the museum holds a permanent collection, space constraints mean that even that must rotate. You will probably not recognize the artists here, but names such as Miguel Hernández and Florencia Urbina tower over the field of contemporary art in Costa Rica. You can arrange for a guided visit with a couple of days' notice. The museum occupies part of a government-office complex in the Centro Nacional de la Cultura (CENAC). ⊠ *Centro Nacional de la Cultura, C. 15, Avdas. 3–5* 🕾 *2257–9370* ⊕ *www. madc.cr* 🖃 *$4* 🕙 *Closed Sun. and Mon.*

★ **Museo del Jade** (*Jade Museum*)
MUSEUM | San José's starkly modern Jade Museum displays the world's largest collection of the green gemstone. The holdings log in at 5,000-plus pieces, and are, in a word, amazing. Nearly all the items on display were produced in pre-Columbian times, and most of the jade (pronounced *HAH-day* in Spanish) dates from 300 BC to AD 700. A series of drawings explains how this extremely hard stone was cut using string saws with quartz-and-sand abrasive. Jade was sometimes used in jewelry designs, but it was most often carved into oblong pendants. The museum also has other pre-Columbian artifacts, such as polychrome vases and three-legged *metates* (small stone tables for grinding corn), as well as a gallery of modern art. Also included on display is a startling exhibition of ceramic fertility symbols. While the collection is undeniably fabulous, the pieces may begin to look the same after a time. Let your own tastes and interests guide you in how much time you spend here. ⊠ *Avda. Ctl., C. 13* 🕾 *2521–6610* ⊕ *www.museodeljadeins.com* 🖃 *$16.*

★ **Museo del Oro Precolombino** (*Pre-Columbian Gold Museum*)
MUSEUM | This dazzling modern museum in a three-story underground structure beneath the stark plaza north of the Teatro Nacional contains Central America's largest collection of pre-Columbian gold jewelry—20,000 troy ounces in more than 1,600 individual pieces—all owned by the Banco Central (the country's central bank) and displayed attractively in bilingual exhibits. Many pieces are in the form of frogs and eagles, two animals perceived by the region's early cultures to have great spiritual significance. A spiffy illumination system makes the pieces sparkle. All that glitters here is not gold: most spectacular are the various shaman figurines, which represent the human connection to animal deities. One of the halls houses the Museo Numismática (Coin Museum), a repository of historic coins and bills and other objects used as legal tender throughout the country's history. Rotating art exhibitions happen on another level. ⊠ *C. 5, Avdas. Ctl.–2* ✦ *Eastern end of Plaza de la Cultura* ☎ *2243–4202* ⊕ *www. museosdelbancocentral.org* 🎟 *$13, includes Museo Numismática.*

Museo Nacional (*National Museum*)
MILITARY SITE | In the mango-color Bellavista Fortress, which dates from 1870, the museum gives you a quick and insightful lesson (in English and Spanish) on Costa Rican culture from pre-Columbian times to the present. Cases display pre-Columbian artifacts, period dress, colonial furniture, religious art, and photographs. Some of the country's foremost ethnographers and anthropologists are on the museum's staff. Nearly 1,000 pre-Columbian Costa Rican stone and ceramic objects dating from about AD 1000 are on display here. The artifacts were taken from the country in the late 19th century by businessman Minor Keith during the construction of the Atlantic Railroad and were repatriated from the Brooklyn

Museum in 2012. Outside are a veranda and a pleasant, manicured courtyard garden. A former army headquarters, this now-tranquil building saw fierce fighting during a 1931 army mutiny and the 1948 revolution, as the bullet holes pocking its turrets attest. But it was also here that three-time president José Figueres abolished the country's military in 1949. ⊠ *Bellavista Fortress, C. 15, Avdas. Ctl.–2* ✦ *Eastern end of Plaza de la Democracia* ☎ *2211–5700* ⊕ *www.museocostarica. go.cr* 🎟 *$11* ⊘ *Closed Mon.*

Parque Central (*Central Park*)
PLAZA | At the city's nucleus, the tree-shaded Central Park is more plaza than park. A life-size bronze statue of a street sweeper (*El Barrendero*) cleans up some bronze litter; look also for *Armonía* (*Harmony*), a sculpture of three street musicians. In the center of the one-square-block park is a spiderlike gazebo donated by onetime Nicaraguan dictator Anastasio Somoza. ⊠ *Bordered by Avdas. 2–4 and Cs. 2–Ctl.*

Parque España
CITY PARK | This shady little park is a favorite spot for locals and visitors alike. A bronze statue of Costa Rica's Spanish founder, Juan Vázquez de Coronado, overlooks an elevated fountain on its southwest corner; the opposite corner has a lovely tiled guardhouse. A bust of Queen Isabella of Castile stares at the yellow compound to the east of the park, the Centro Nacional de la Cultura. The bright yellow colonial-style

building to the east of the modern INS building is the 1912 Casa Amarilla, home of Costa Rica's Foreign Ministry. The massive ceiba tree in front, planted by John F. Kennedy and the presidents of all the Central American nations in 1963, gives you an idea of how quickly things grow in the tropics. A garden around the corner on Calle 13 contains a 6-foot-wide section of the Berlin Wall donated by Germany's Foreign Ministry after reunification. Ask the guard to let you into the garden if you want a closer look. As with all San José parks, safety declines markedly after dark. Be on your way out before 5 pm. ⊠ *Bordered by Avdas. 7–3 and Cs. 11–17.*

Parque Nacional (*National Park*)

MEMORIAL | A bronze monument commemorating Central America's battles against North American invader William Walker in 1856 forms the centerpiece of the large, leafy park. Five Amazons, representing the five nations of the isthmus, attack Walker, who shields his face from the onslaught. Costa Rica maintains the lead and shelters a veiled Nicaragua, the country most devastated by the war. Guatemala, Honduras, and El Salvador might dispute this version of events, but this is how Costa Rica chose to commission the work by French sculptor Louis Carrier Belleuse, a student of Rodin, in 1895. Bas-relief murals on the monument's pedestal depict key battles in the war against the Americans. As with all San José parks, you should avoid the space after dark. ⊠ *Bordered by Avdas. 1–3 and Cs. 15–19.*

Plaza de la Democracia

PLAZA | President Óscar Arias built this terraced space west of the Museo Nacional to mark 100 years of democracy and to receive dignitaries during a 1989 hemispheric summit. The view west toward the dark green Cerros de Escazú is nice in the morning and fabulous at sunset. Jewelry, T-shirts, and crafts from Costa Rica, Guatemala, and South America are sold in a string of stalls along the western edge. ⊠ *Bordered by Avdas. Ctl.–2 and Cs. 13–15.*

★ Teatro Nacional

ARTS VENUE | The National Theater is Costa Rica at its most enchanting. Chagrined that touring prima donna Adelina Patti bypassed San José in 1890 for lack of a suitable venue, wealthy coffee merchants raised import taxes and hired Belgian architects to design this building, lavish with cast iron and Italian marble. The soft coppers, golds, and whites highlight the theater's exterior nightly from 6 pm to 5 am.

The sumptuous neo-baroque interior is of interest, too. Given the provenance of the building funds, it's not surprising that frescoes on the stairway inside depict coffee and banana production. Note Italian painter Aleardo Villa's famous ceiling mural *Alegoría del Café y Banano* (*Allegory of Coffee and Bananas*), a joyful harvest scene that appeared on Costa Rica's old 5-colón note. You can see the theater's interior by attending one of the performances that take place several nights a week; intermission gives you a chance to nose around. Stop at the *boletería* (box office), just off the lobby, and see what strikes your fancy. Ticket prices are a fraction of what you'd pay at a similar stateside venue. Don't worry if you left your tuxedo or evening gown back home; as long as you don't show up for a performance wearing shorts, jeans, or a T-shirt, no one will care.

For a fee you can also move beyond the lobby for a guided tour in Spanish and English; offered hourly on the hour from 9 until 4 daily. If you're downtown on a Tuesday from March through November, take in one of the Teatro al Mediodía (Theater at Midday) performances that begin at 12:10 pm. It might be a chamber-music recital or a one-act play in Spanish. ⊠ *Plaza de la Cultura, C. 3, Avda. 2* ☎ *2010–1100* ⊕ *www.teatronacional.go.cr* ⤳ *$11.*

Downtown San José

TO AIRPORT

MÉXICO

TOURNÓN

Parque México

Río Torres

AMÓN

EL CARMEN

Morazár Park

COCA-COLA

LA MERCED

Plaza de la Cultura

Paseo Colón

Avenida Central

Parque de la Merced

Central Park

LA SOLEDAD

SANTA LUCÍA

DOLOROSA

BOLÍVAR

PACIFICO

0   300 yards
0   300 m

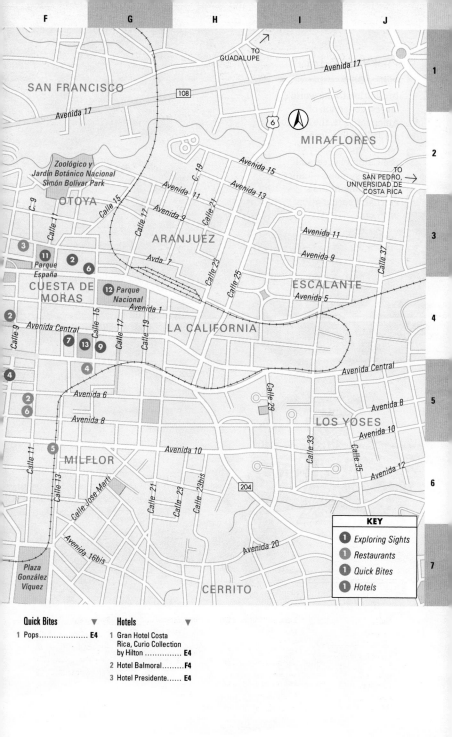

F   **G**   **H**   **I**   **J**

TO
GUADALUPE

Avenida 17

SAN FRANCISCO

108

Avenida 17

MIRAFLORES

Zoológico y
Jardín Botánico Nacional
Simón Bolívar Park

Avenida 15

TO
SAN PEDRO,
UNIVERSIDAD DE
COSTA RICA

OTOYA

C. 19

Avenida 11

Avenida 13

Calle 15

Calle 17

Avenida 9

Calle 21

Avenida 11

ARANJUEZ

Avenida 9

Calle 37

Avda. 7

Parque
España

Calle 23

Calle 25

ESCALANTE

CUESTA DE
MORAS

Parque
Nacional

Avenida 5

Avenida 1

LA CALIFORNIA

Calle 9

Avenida Central

Calle 15

Calle 17

Calle 19

Avenida Central

Avenida 6

Calle 29

Avenida 8

LOS YOSES

Avenida 8

Avenida 10

Calle 33

Calle 35

MILFLOR

Avenida 10

Avenida 12

Calle 11

Calle 13

Calle José Martí

Calle 21

Calle 23

Calle 23bis

204

Avenida 16bis

Avenida 20

Plaza
González
Víquez

CERRITO

KEY

❶ Exploring Sights
❶ Restaurants
❶ Quick Bites
❶ Hotels

Quick Bites ▼

1 Pops.................... **E4**

Hotels ▼

1 Gran Hotel Costa
Rica, Curio Collection
by Hilton **E4**

2 Hotel Balmoral......... **F4**

3 Hotel Presidente...... **E4**

🍴 Restaurants

Alma de Café

$ | **COSTA RICAN** | Duck into the Teatro Nacional's sumptuous café, off the theater lobby, to sit at a marble table and sip a hazelnut mocha beneath frescoed ceilings. The frescoes are part of an allegory celebrating the 1897 opening of the theater. **Known for:** coffee (with option to add ice cream and alcohol); cake and sandwiches; artistic surroundings. [$] *Average main: $8* ✉ *Teatro Nacional, C.3, Avda. 2* ☎ *2010–1110* 🌐 *www.teatronacional.go.cr/Cafeteria* ⏰ *Closed Sun. May–Nov.*

Don Wang

$$ | **CHINESE** | In a country where "Chinese cuisine" usually means simply white rice and vegetables, Don Wang's authenticity is a treat. Cantonese cuisine is the mainstay, and Don Wang is known for its immensely popular dim sum, called *desayuno chino* (literally "Chinese breakfast") here. **Known for:** all-day dim sum; friendly service; authentic Cantonese and Szechuan flavors. [$] *Average main: $14* ✉ *C. 11, Avdas. 6–8* ☎ *2223–5925* 💳 *No credit cards.*

La Criollita

$ | **COSTA RICAN** | Kick off your day with a breakfast platter here: the *americano* (U.S.-style) or the *tico* (Costa Rican), with eggs, fried plantains, and *natilla* (sour cream). Mornings or afternoons are the perfect time to snag one of the precious tables in the back garden, an unexpected refuge from noise and traffic. **Known for:** crowded lunch spot; bargain prices; coffee and dessert. [$] *Average main: $9* ✉ *Avda. 7, Cs. 7–9* ☎ *2256–6511.*

Nuestra Tierra

$ | **COSTA RICAN** | The generous homemade meals at this ranch-style restaurant are delicious, and the incredibly friendly waitstaff, who epitomize Costa Rican hospitality and dress in folkloric clothing, prepare your coffee filtered through the traditional cloth chorreador. The place keeps late hours, just in case those late-night *gallo pinto* (Costa Rican–style rice and beans) pangs hit. **Known for:** típico setting; lots of tourists; generous portions. [$] *Average main: $9* ✉ *Avdas. 2–4, C. 13* ☎ *2258–6500.*

Did You Know?

What's an old theater without its resident ghost? Patrons have claimed to see figures moving in the Teatro Nacional's second-floor paintings. Sightings were common during the theater's early days, although none have been reported in years.

Shakti

$$ | **VEGETARIAN** | The baskets of fruit and vegetables at the entrance and the wall of herbal teas, health-food books, and fresh herbs for sale by the register signal that you're in a vegetarian-friendly joint. The bright and airy macrobiotic restaurant serves homemade bread, soy burgers, pita sandwiches (veggie or chicken), fruit shakes, and a hearty *plato del día* that comes with soup, green salad, and a beverage. **Known for:** vegetarian oasis; local ingredients; monster salads. [$] *Average main: $10* ✉ *Avda. 8, Cs. 11–13* ☎ *2222–4475* ⏰ *Closed Sun. No dinner.*

★ Tin Jo

$$$ | **ASIAN** | The colorful dining rooms of this converted house evoke Japan, India, China, Indonesia, and Thailand. Start with a powerful Singapore sling (brandy and fruit juices) before trying such treats as Thai shrimp and pineapple curry in coconut milk, Chinese mu shu stir-fry with crepes, Indian samosas, and sushi rolls. **Known for:** one of Costa Rica's best restaurants; impeccable service; vegetarian options. [$] *Average main: $19* ✉ *C. 11, Avdas. 6–8* ☎ *2221–7605* 🌐 *www.tinjo.com.*

San José's ornate Correos de Costa Rica building houses a stamp museum on the second floor.

Coffee and Quick Bites

Pops

$ | **COSTA RICAN** | To sample the crème de la crème of locally made ice cream, head to Pops. After a long walk on crowded sidewalks, it may be just what the doctor ordered. **Known for:** mango ice cream; good spot for a quick break; a Costa Rica institution. [$] *Average main: $2* ✉ *C. 3, Avda. Ctl.* ☎ *2222–2336* 🌐 *www.pops.co.cr* 💳 *No credit cards.*

Hotels

Staying in the downtown area allows you to travel around the city as most Ticos do: on foot. Stroll the parks, museums, and shops, and then retire to one of the many character-filled small or historic hotels.

★ Gran Hotel Costa Rica, Curio Collection by Hilton

$$$ | **HOTEL** | You cannot get more centrally located than this grande dame of San José lodgings, the first choice among travelers who want to be where the action is. **Pros:** central location; impeccable service; modern amenities. **Cons:** modern rooms don't reflect building's history; sometimes congested traffic to get here; some rooms look into interior skylight rather than outdoors. [$] *Rooms from: $219* ✉ *Avda. 2, C. 3* ☎ *2103–9000, 800/446–8667 in North America* 🌐 *www.hilton.com* 🛏 *79 rooms* 🍴 *Free Breakfast.*

Hotel Balmoral

$$ | **HOTEL** | You'll find all the standard amenities of a medium-price business-class hotel here, but leisure travelers also enjoy using the Balmoral as their San José base. **Pros:** central location; good restaurant; close to downtown sights. **Cons:** some street noise; many rooms do not face the outside; restaurant service can be slow at times. [$] *Rooms from: $145* ✉ *C. 7, Avdas. Ctl.–1* ☎ *2222–5022, 800/691–4865 in North America* 🌐 *www.balmoral.co.cr* 🛏 *112 rooms* 🍴 *Free Breakfast.*

Hotel Presidente
$$ | **HOTEL** | A largely American clientele looking for all the downtown hubbub enjoys the medium-price business-class accommodations here. **Pros:** close to downtown sights; eco-friendly; rooftop patio. **Cons:** some street noise; some rooms have thin walls; a few dated furnishings in some rooms. [$] *Rooms from: $118* ✉ *Avda. Ctl., C. 7* ☎ *2010–0000, 877/540–1790 in North America* 🌐 *www.hotel-presidente.com* 🛏 *92 rooms* 🍴 *Free Breakfast.*

Nightlife

Azotea Calle 7
BARS/PUBS | Downtown's most elegant nightspot perches in a garden on the rooftop of the Hotel Presidente and offers terrific views and inventive cocktails. ✉ *Hotel Presidente, Avda. Ctl., C. 7, Barrio La Soledad* ☎ *2010–0000* 🌐 *www.hotel-presidente.com.*

Club Teatro
CABARET | RuPaul has nothing on the performers at San José's largest LGBTQ+ venue. The drag shows here aren't just any drag shows; they include gymnastics and trapeze, too. The venue is safe, but the neighborhood is dicey. Take a taxi to and from here. ✉ *Avda. 16, C. 2, Barrio El Pacífico* ☎ *2256–1003* 🌐 *www.facebook.com/el.teatro.cr.*

La Avispa
DANCE CLUBS | An LGBTQ+ crowd frequents La Avispa, which has two dance floors with videos and karaoke, as well as a quieter upstairs bar with pool tables. The last Friday of each month is ladies' night. The neighborhood between downtown and the bar is sketchy; take a taxi. ✉ *C. 1, Avda. 8* ☎ *2223–5343* 🌐 *www.laavispa.com.*

Be Aware

A few gems really do populate the downtown area, but several bars there double as prostitute pickup joints or are just boozy places where patrons go to pick fights. If you're downtown at night, drink at your hotel or one of the places we recommend, and never wander directly south or west of Parque Central on foot.

Performing Arts

Centro Nacional de la Cultura
MUSIC | There are frequent dance performances and concerts in the Teatro FANAL and Teatro 1887, both in the Centro Nacional de la Cultura. ✉ *C. 13, Avdas. 3–5, Barrio Otoya* ☎ *2257–5524* 🌐 *www.mcj.go.cr.*

Teatro Nacional (*National Theater*)
CONCERTS | This neo-baroque theater is the home of the excellent National Symphony Orchestra, which performs on several Friday evenings and Sunday mornings between March and November. The theater also hosts visiting musical groups and dance companies. Tickets are $5–$50—far less than you'd pay for a comparable production back home. ✉ *Plaza de la Cultura, Barrio La Soledad* ☎ *2010–1100* 🌐 *www.teatronacional.go.cr.*

Teatro Popular Melico Salazar
MUSIC | San José's second-most-popular theater has a full calendar of music and dance shows, as well as a few offbeat productions. There is something on several nights a week; tickets are $5–$25. ✉ *Avda. 2, Cs. Ctl.–2, Barrio La Merced* ☎ *2295–6000* 🌐 *www.teatromelico.go.cr.*

Shopping

CRAFTS

⭐ Chietón Morén

CRAFTS | A nonprofit association assembles the works of 220 artisans from Costa Rica's eight original indigenous communities in this attractively arranged setting on the pedestrian mall south of the Museo Nacional. While the place bills itself as "part museum," all works are for sale at prices fair to the creators and fair to you. (The name translates as "fair deal" in Costa Rica's indigenous Boruca language.) You'll find a good selection of ceramics, jewelry, weavings, and paintings here. ⊠ *C. 17, Avdas. 2–4* ☎ *2221–0145* ⊕ *www.chietonmoren.org* ☉ *Closed Sun. May–Nov.*

⭐ Galería Namu

CRAFTS | Downtown San José's must-stop shop is Galería Namu, which sells the best indigenous crafts in town. Its inventory brims with colorful creations by the Guaymí, Boruca, Bribri, Chorotega, Huetar, and Maleku peoples—all Costa Rican indigenous groups. Such crafts used to be the exclusive domain of male artisans, but a growing number of works by women are on display here these days. You can also find exquisitely carved ivory-nut tagua figurines, dolls, and baskets made by the Wounan people from Panama's Darién region and Tuno textiles and Lenca pottery from Honduras. Take note of carved balsa masks, woven cotton blankets, and hand-painted ceramics.

The store looks expensive—and indeed, the sky's the limit in terms of prices—but if your budget is not so flush, say so: the good folks here can help you find something in the $20–$25 range that will make a cherished souvenir. As a bonus you'll get an information sheet describing your work's creator and art style. Namu has a reputation for fair prices for customers, and for fair pay to artists and artisans. ⊠ *Avda. 7, Cs. 5–7* ☎ *2256–3412* ⊕ *www.galerianamu.com.*

MUSIC

Universal

MUSIC STORES | In addition to selling everything else imaginable, downtown department store Universal stocks a good selection of Latin CDs in its first-floor music department. ⊠ *Avda. Ctl., Cs. Ctl.–1* ☎ *6105–2222* ⊕ *www.tiendauniversal.com.*

SOUVENIRS

La Traviata

GIFTS/SOUVENIRS | The small shop off the lobby of the National Theater has a terrific selection of thespian-themed postcards, tote bags, and glassware. You can access the shop without an admission ticket to a theater production. In addition to being open Monday through Saturday during the day, the shop is also open before evening performances and during intermission. ⊠ *Teatro Nacional, Plaza de la Cultura* ☎ *2010–1100* ⊕ *www.teatronacional.go.cr.*

Mercado Central

GIFTS/SOUVENIRS | This maze of passageways is where the average Costa Rican comes to stock up on day-to-day necessities, but a few stalls of interest to tourists congregate near the southeast entrance. ⊠ *Bordered by Avdas. Ctl.–1 and Cs. 6–8.*

Museo del Jade (*Jade Museum*)

GIFTS/SOUVENIRS | The small shop in the Jade Museum sells replicas of many of the pieces in the museum collection. The shop is accessible only if you've paid the $16 museum admission. ⊠ *Avda. Ctl., C. 13* ☎ *2287–6034* ⊕ *www.museodeljadeins.com.*

Museo del Oro Precolombino (*Pre-Columbian Gold Museum*)

GIFTS/SOUVENIRS | The shop at the entrance of the Museo del Oro Precolombino (Gold Museum) offers a great selection of pre-Columbian-themed jewelry, art, exclusively designed T-shirts, coin key chains, notebooks, and mouse pads. You can access the shop without paying the museum admission. ✉ *C. 5, Avdas. Ctl.–2* ☎ *2243–4202* ⊕ *www. museosdelbancocentral.org.*

Tienda Eñe

GIFTS/SOUVENIRS | The big red *Ñ* on the window marks this cute little boutique with goods all made by Costa Rican artists and designers. Look for prints, bags, jewelry, and a big selection of mugs. ✉ *Avda. 7, C. 11a, Barrio Amón* ☎ *2222–7681.*

West of Downtown

Paseo Colón, one of San José's major boulevards, heads due west from downtown and leads to vast La Sabana Park, the city's largest parcel of green space. La Sabana anchors the even vaster west side of the city. A block or two off its exhaust-ridden avenues are quiet residential streets, and you'll find the U.S., Canadian, and British embassies here.

Sights

Museo de Arte Costarricense

MUSEUM | Located in La Sabana Park, which was once Costa Rica's international airport, this—the country's foremost art museum—was once its terminal and control tower. A splendid collection of 19th- and 20th-century Costa Rican art, labeled in Spanish and English, is housed in 12 exhibition halls. Be sure to visit the top-floor Salón Dorado to see the stucco, bronze-plate bas-relief mural depicting Costa Rican history, created by French sculptor Louis Feron. Guided tours are offered Tuesday through Friday from 10 to 3. Wander into the sculpture garden in back and take in Jorge Jiménez's 22-foot-tall *Imagen Cósmica*, which depicts pre-Columbian traditions. ✉ *Parque La Sabana, C. 42, Paseo Colón, Paseo Colón* ☎ *4060–2300* ⊕ *www.mac.go.cr* ✎ *Free.*

Parque La Sabana

ARTS VENUE | FAMILY | Though it isn't centrally located, the 180-acre La Sabana ("the savannah") comes the closest of San José's green spaces to achieving the same function and spirit as New York's Central Park. La Sabana was once San José's airport, and the whitewashed Museo de Arte Costarricense, just south of the Cortes statue, served as its terminal and control tower.

The round Gimnasio Nacional (National Gymnasium) sits at the park's southeast corner and hosts sporting events and the occasional concert. The Estadio Nacional, a sleek, futuristic-looking 40,000-seat stadium—a controversial gift from the government of China, which decided to use its own construction workers rather than employ locals—looms over the park's northwest corner. It hosts soccer matches primarily, but Paul McCartney, Elton John, Shakira, and Lady Gaga have all performed in the stadium. In between are acres of space for soccer, basketball, tennis, swimming, jogging, picnicking, and kite flying. The park hums with activity on weekends. The stadium grounds are fine, but avoid walking through the rest of the park after the sun goes down. ✉ *Bordered by Cs. 42–68, Avda. de las Américas, and Carretera a Caldera, Paseo Colón.*

Restaurants

★ Grano de Oro Restaurant

$$$ | ECLECTIC | The Hotel Grano de Oro houses one of San José's premier dining destinations: a splendid restaurant wrapped around a lovely indoor patio and bromeliad-filled garden. The garden area is a perfect spot for lunch on a warm day—choose from among a variety of light sandwiches and salads, or opt for dinner in the elegant indoor dining area for dishes like breaded sea bass with orange sauce and macadamia nuts or *cerdo en salsa tamarindo* (roasted pork in tamarind sauce). **Known for:** elegant

hotel setting; yummy desserts; impressive wine selection. $ *Average main: $23* ⊠ *C. 30, Avdas. 2–4, Paseo Colón* ☎ 2255–3322 ⊕ *www.hotelgranodeoro. com* ⊟ *No credit cards.*

L'Olivo

$$$ | **ITALIAN** | The vaulted ceilings and a vineyard mural on one wall evoke old Italy at this restaurant serving homemade pastas—spinach cannelloni and linguine with clam sauce are popular dishes. An extensive wine list rounds out the offerings, and service is attentive—the chef makes the rounds to ensure that you're satisfied. **Known for:** small dining area; lively atmosphere; reservations recommended. $ *Average main: $16* ⊠ *Paseo Colón* ✛ *300 m north and 50 m east of ICE Bldg.* ☎ 2220–0453 ⊕ *www. apartotelcristina.com* ⊟ *No credit cards* ⊘ *Closed Sun.*

Lubnan

$$ | **MIDDLE EASTERN** | The Lebanese owners at one of San José's few Middle Eastern restaurants serve a wide variety of dishes from their native region, but if you can't decide, the meze platter serves two people and gives you a little bit of everything. Try the juicy shish kebab *de cordero* (of lamb) or, if you're feeling especially adventurous, the raw ground-meat *kebbe naye* (with wheat meal) and *kafta naye* (without wheat meal). **Known for:** yummy kebabs; hip bar in back; belly-dancing show on Thursday night. $ *Average main: $12* ⊠ *Cs. 22–24, Paseo Colón* ☎ 2257–6071 ⊘ *Closed Mon. No dinner Sun.*

Machu Picchu

$$ | **PERUVIAN** | A few travel posters are the only props that evoke Peru, but no matter: the Peruvian food is anything but plain, and the seafood is excellent. The *especial de mariscos* (special seafood platter), big enough for two, presents you with shrimp, conch, and squid cooked four ways. **Known for:** extra-spicy Peruvian hot sauce; authentic Peruvian-style ceviche; smooth pisco sours. $ *Average*

main: $12 ⊠ *C. 32, Paseo Colón* ✛ *130 m north of KFC* ☎ 2222–7384 ⊕ *www. facebook.com/restaurante.machu.picchu* ⊘ *No dinner Sun.*

Park Café

$$$ | **ECLECTIC** | Set within an antiques shop, the internationally inspired all-tapas menu includes Thai-style tuna salad, red-snapper couscous, and other tasty dishes. The colonial-style house is only about a decade old, but attention to architectural detail and antique furnishings make you think the building was transplanted from Antigua or Granada. **Known for:** inventive menu; reservations recommended; no kids allowed. $ *Average main: $24* ⊠ *Sabana Norte* ✛ *100 m north of Rosti Pollos* ☎ 2290–6324 ⊕ *parkcafecostarica.blogspot.com* ⊘ *Closed Sun.–Mon. and Sept.–Oct. No lunch Tues.*

Soda Tapia

$ | **COSTA RICAN** | Don't expect anything fancy at this extremely popular restaurant, but food here is cheap and filling. The ubiquitous gallo pinto for breakfast and *casados* (meat, fish, or poultry, accompanied by rice, cabbage salad, and dessert) for lunch are on the menu, along with a variety of sandwiches and burgers. **Known for:** late-night, early-morning hangout; cheap eats; filling lunch specials. $ *Average main: $9* ⊠ *C. 42, Avdas. 2–4, Sabana Este* ☎ 2222–8401 ⊟ *No credit cards.*

Hotels

San José's vast west side contains only a smattering of lodgings, but among them are two of the city's best, Hotel Grano de Oro and the Park Inn by Radisson.

★ Hotel Grano de Oro

$$$ | **HOTEL** | Two wooden houses have been converted into one of the city's most charming inns, decorated throughout with old photos of the capital and paintings by local artists; head up to your room for the old coffee-plantation feel for

West of Downtown San José

URUCA CENTRO

Autopista General Cañas

Calle 60

Avenida 13

CASTRO

Calle 56

Calle 50

Avenida 13

Calle 30

Avenida 9

108

Av. de las Américas

Calle 40

Avenida 5

Calle 30A

PITAHAYA

Avenida 3

Avenida 1

Parque La Sabana

Paseo Colón

Hungría Libre

Calle 40

Calle 36

Calle 34

Calle 30

Calle 28

27

Autopista Próspero Fernández

TOVAR

SABANA SUR

Avenida 10

transversal 24

Calle 58

Calle 54

Calle 50

Avenida 14

Calle 36

MORENOS

Avenida 16

Calle 42

Diagonal 16

Av. 18

| 0 | | 300 yards |
| 0 | | 300 m |

Sights ▼
1 Museo de Arte Costarricense **C4**
2 Parque La Sabana **B4**

Restaurants ▼
1 Grano de Oro Restaurant........ **E5**
2 L' Olivo................. **B2**
3 Lubnan **F5**
4 Machu Picchu **E4**
5 Park Café **B3**
6 Soda Tapia............. **I5**

Hotels ▼
1 Hotel Grano de Oro.................. **E5**
2 Park Inn by Radisson **E5**
3 Suites Cristina......... **B2**

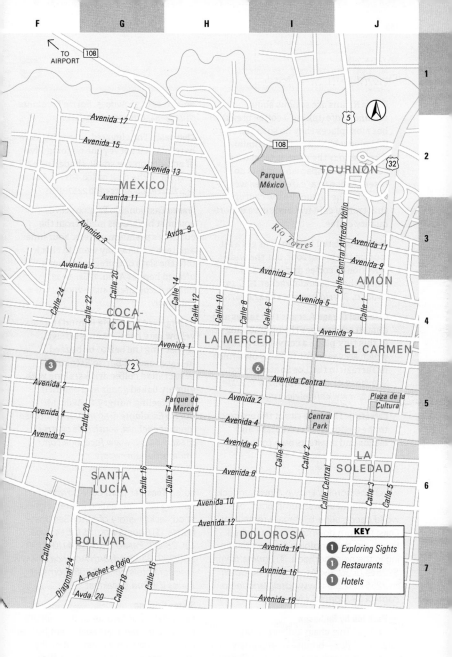

San José's Cafés

Costa Ricans are serious about *tomando café* (taking a coffee break), but most places they do so in the city feel pretty basic and institutional. A *cafetería* is the generic term for a coffee shop in Spanish and has no resemblance to a "cafeteria" as we know it. The venues below capture that trendy café feel and serve export-quality coffee.

Café del Barista The rain does get a bit loud on the metal roof, but the wide selection of coffee drinks here is worth the occasional racket. ✉ *C. 19, Avda. 11, Barrio Aranjuez* ☎ *2221–4712.*

Café Miel Garage A scant two tables and a small counter are the only seating at this tiny place, a converted garage, which serves coffee from its own *finca* in Tarrazú in the Los Santos region. ✉ *Avda. 9, C. 13, Barrio Otoya* ☎ *2221–0897* 🌐 *www.cafemielgarage.com.*

Cafeoteca This café sits at the entrance to the trendy Kalú restaurant and blends and roasts its own coffee on-site. ✉ *C. 31, Avda. 5, Barrio Escalante* ☎ *2253–8426* 🌐 *www.kalu.co.cr.*

Club Unión The elevated, glassed-in café here lets you survey the ongoing hive of activity on the small, shaded plaza in front of the post office. ✉ *C. 2, Avdas. 1–3, Barrio La Merced* ☎ *2257–1555.*

Franco Fashionable Franco serves gourmet beverages made from the country's premium coffees. Your inner amateur barista may want to check into the slate of coffee workshops offered here. ✉ *Avda. 7, Cs. 31–33, Barrio Escalante* ☎ *4082–7006* 🌐 *www.franco.cr.*

Underground Brew Café Behind the yellow gate here—there's no sign, so just ring the bell to be buzzed in—are some of Barrio Escalante's best-crafted coffee drinks, along with yummy baked goods and panini if you're feeling hungry. ✉ *Avda. 1A, Barrio Escalante* ✣ *50 m east of Intensa language school, south side of street* ☎ *8884–6817* 🌐 *www.facebook.com/undergroundbrewcafe.*

which the hotel is known. **Pros:** sundeck with beautiful views; sumptuous, old-world decor; superb, elegant restaurant. **Cons:** far from downtown sights; need taxi to get here; nothing else worth seeing in the neighborhood. [$] *Rooms from: $225* ✉ *C. 30, Avdas. 2–4, Paseo Colón* ☎ *2255–3322* 🌐 *www.hotelgranodeoro.com* 🛏 *39 rooms* 🍴 *No meals.*

★ Park Inn by Radisson
$$ | **HOTEL** | This chain lodging incorporates local flair—bright, fresh primary colors and a rotating selection of Costa Rican art throughout—while providing business amenities in a clean, modern hotel. **Pros:** impeccable service; friendly staff; local style despite being a chain hotel. **Cons:** far from downtown sights; nothing else interesting in the neighborhood; lacks history of other San José hotels. [$] *Rooms from: $125* ✉ *Avda. 6, Cs. 28–30, Paseo Colón* ☎ *4110–1100, 800/333–3333 in North America* 🌐 *www.radissonhotels.com* 🛏 *108 rooms, 9 suites* 🍴 *Free Breakfast.*

Suites Cristina
$$ | **HOTEL** | Our favorite of the capital's many *apartotels* (part apartment house, part hotel) sits on a quiet, out-of-the-way street north of La Sabana Park. **Pros:** friendly staff; quiet street; terrific rates for what is offered. **Cons:** far from downtown sights and center of town; some rooms have no TV; some noise

on rare nights when there's an event at the nearby stadium. $ *Rooms from: $78* ✉ *Sabana Norte ✤ 300 m north of ICE Bldg.* ☎ *2220–0453, 773/253–5965 in North America* ⊕ *www.apartotelcristina. com* ⇨ *50 suites* ⦿ *Free Breakfast.*

Nightlife

La Bodeguita del Medio

BARS/PUBS | The mojitos flow and the chips and guacamole keep coming at this west-side restaurant that showcases live (usually Cuban) music most evenings after 9. ✉ *Avda. 4, C. 40, Paseo Colón ✤ 200 m south of Banco de Costa Rica* ☎ *2255–8383.*

 Performing Arts

Sala Garbo

FILM | This theater shows arty films, often in languages other than English, with Spanish subtitles. ✉ *Avda. 2, C. 28, Paseo Colón* ☎ *6351–1799* ⊕ *www. salagarbo.com.*

Shopping

Hotel Grano de Oro

CRAFTS | The small gift shop at the Hotel Grano de Oro has an impressive selection of carvings and jewelry on hand. ✉ *C. 30, Avdas. 2–4, Paseo Colón* ☎ *2255–3322* ⊕ *www.hotelgranodeoro. com.*

North and East of Downtown

Immediately northeast of downtown lie Barrio Amón and Barrio Otoya. Both neighborhoods are repositories of historic houses that have escaped the wrecking ball; many now serve as hotels, restaurants, galleries, and offices—a few are even private residences. Where these barrios begin and end depends on who's doing the talking. Locales on the fringes of the city center prefer to be associated with these "good neighborhoods" rather than with downtown. Barrio Escalante, to the east, has quickly become San José's hippest neighborhood, with an ever-increasing number of restaurants and bars.

The sprawling suburb of San Pedro begins several blocks east of downtown San José. It's home to the University of Costa Rica and all the intellect and cheap eats and nightlife that a student could desire. But away from the heart of the university, San Pedro is awash with malls, fast-food restaurants, and car dealerships—although it manages to mix in such stately districts as Los Yoses for good measure. To get to San Pedro, take a $3 taxi ride from downtown and get off in front of Banco Nacional, just beyond the rotunda with the fountain at its center.

Sights

Jardín de Mariposas Spyrogyra (*Spyrogyra Butterfly Garden*)

ZOO | FAMILY | Spending an hour at this magical butterfly garden is entertaining and educational for nature lovers of all ages. Self-guided tours enlighten you on butterfly ecology and let you see the winged creatures close up. After an 18-minute video introduction, you're free to wander screened-in gardens along a numbered trail. Some 30 species of colorful butterflies flutter about, accompanied by six types of hummingbirds. Try to come when it's sunny, as butterflies are most active then. A small, moderately priced café borders the garden and serves sandwiches and tico fare. The place is difficult to find if you're driving, so keep your eyes peeled. ✉ *Barrio Tournón ✤ 50 m east and 150 m south of main entrance to El Pueblo shopping center* ☎ *2222–2937* ⊕ *www.butterfly-gardencr.com* ⌨ *$7.*

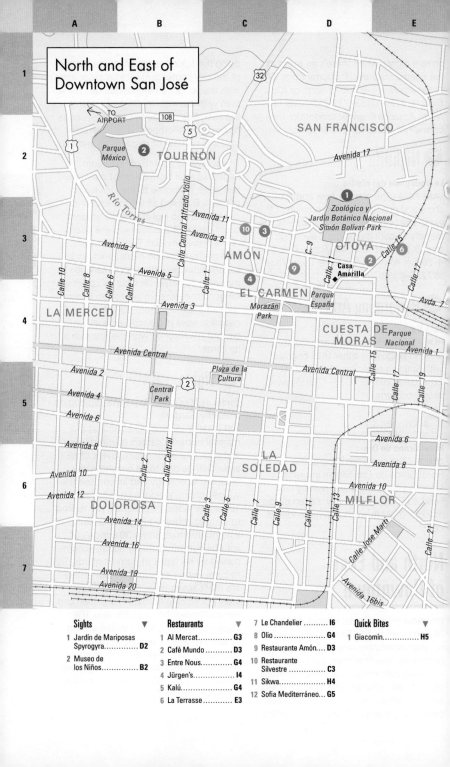

North and East of Downtown San José

A **B** **C** **D** **E**

TO AIRPORT
108
5
SAN FRANCISCO
Parque México
2 TOURNÓN
Avenida 17
Río Torres
Calle Central Alfredo Volio
Avenida 11
Avenida 9
10 **3**
1
Zoológico y Jardín Botánico Nacional Simón Bolívar Park
OTOYA
Calle 15
6
Avenida 7
AMÓN
C. 9
2
Calle 17
Avenida 5
Calle 10
Calle 8
Calle 6
Calle 4
9
Calle 11
Casa Amarilla
4
EL CARMEN
Calle 1
Avenida 3
Morazán Park
Parque España
Avda. 7
LA MERCED
CUESTA DE MORAS
Parque Nacional
Avenida Central
Avenida 1
Avenida 2
Plaza de la Cultura
Avenida Central
Calle 15
Calle 17
Calle 19
Avenida 4
Central Park
2
Avenida 6
Avenida 6
Avenida 8
Calle 2
Calle Central
Avenida 8
LA SOLEDAD
Avenida 10
Avenida 10
MILFLOR
Avenida 12
DOLOROSA
Calle 3
Calle 5
Calle 7
Calle 9
Calle 11
Calle 13
Avenida 14
Avenida 16
Calle José Martí
Calle 21
Avenida 18
Avenida 20
Avenida 16bis

Sights ▼	Restaurants ▼	7 Le Chandelier **I6**	Quick Bites ▼
1 Jardín de Mariposas Spyrogyra............. **D2**	1 Al Mercat............. **G3**	8 Olio **G4**	1 Giacomín.............. **H5**
2 Museo de los Niños.............. **B2**	2 Café Mundo **D3**	9 Restaurante Amón.... **D3**	
	3 Entre Nous............ **G4**	10 Restaurante Silvestre **C3**	
	4 Jürgen's................ **I4**	11 Sikwa.................. **H4**	
	5 Kalú.................... **G4**	12 Sofia Mediterráneo... **G5**	
	6 La Terrasse **E3**		

Are You Ready for Some Fútbol?

Sports mean one thing in San José: soccer. Very young boys (and a slowly increasing number of girls) kick around a ball—or some other object if no ball is available—in street pickup games, and they grow into fans passionate about their local team. But everyone puts aside regional differences when the reputation of Costa Rica's national team is on the line, as it is during the World Cup.

Consult the Spanish-language daily *La Nación* or ask at your hotel for details on upcoming games—you simply show up at the stadium box office. Prices range from $6 to $15. *Sombra numerado* (shaded seats) are the most expensive.

Professional soccer matches are usually played on Sunday morning or Wednesday night in either of two San José stadiums. The Estadio Ricardo Saprissa (next to the Clínica Integrada de Tibás) is home to Saprissa, the capital's beloved hometown team, in the northern suburb of Tibás; the Chinese-built Estadio Nacional sits at the northwest corner of La Sabana Park and hosts visiting national teams who come to take on La Sele, Costa Rica's own national squad.

Museo de los Niños (*Children's Museum*)
MILITARY SITE | FAMILY | Three halls of this museum are filled with eye-catching seasonal exhibits for kids, ranging in subject from local ecology to outer space. The exhibits are labeled in Spanish only, but most are interactive, so language shouldn't be much of a problem. The museum's most popular resident is the Egyptian exhibit's sarcophagus; the mummy draws oohs and aahs. Located in a former prison, big kids may want to check it out just to marvel at the castle-like architecture and the old cells that have been preserved in an admittedly gruesome exhibit about life behind bars. The complex that houses the museum is called the Centro Costarricense de Ciencia y Cultura (Costa Rican Center of Science and Culture), and that will be the sign that greets you on the front of the building. Though just a short distance from downtown, a walk here takes you through a dodgy neighborhood. Always take a taxi to and from. ✉ *Centro Costarricense de Ciencia y Cultura, north end of C. 4, Barrio Tournón* ☎ *2105–0523* 🌐 *www.museocr.org* 🎫 *$4* 🕒 *Closed Mon.*

🍴 Restaurants

★ Al Mercat
$$$ | COSTA RICAN | Located in the heart of Barrio Escalante, this hip eatery takes its name ("at the market" in Catalan) very seriously—with its always changing, always creative, and always delicious menu that reimagines what Costa Rican cuisine can be. Chef Jose González sources all the products that go into the dishes here himself, with 60 percent coming from his own farm just north of the city and the rest coming from San José's weekly farmers' market (and therefore other Costa Rican farms). **Known for:** simple yet impressive Costan Rican cuisine at its most creative and locally sourced; rotating menu with options like veggie ceviche and a chicharron burger; airy, casual atmosphere with lots of greenery. [$] *Average main: $24* ✉ *Avda. 13, Cs. 25–31, Barrio Escalante* ✥ *200 m north and 150 m east of Sta. Teresita Church* ☎ *2221–0783* 🌐 *www.almercat.com* 🕒 *Closed Mon. No dinner Sun.–Wed.*

Café Mundo

$$ | **CAFÉ** | The upstairs café at this corner restaurant serves meals on a porch, on a garden patio, or in two dining rooms. Try the soup of the day and fresh-baked bread to start; main courses include shrimp in a vegetable cream sauce or *lomito en salsa de vino tinto* (tenderloin in a red-wine sauce). **Known for:** popular LGBTQ hangout; delicious chocolate cake; place to see and be seen. $ *Average main: $14* ⊠ *C. 15, Avdas. 9–11, Barrio Otoya* ☎ *2222–6190* ⊗ *Closed Sun. No lunch Sat.*

Entre Nous

$ | **ECLECTIC** | It's the crepes—salty or sweet—that draw the crowds here. It's a bright, cheery place with a covered terrace to stop for dessert after an evening out in Barrio Escalante. **Known for:** to-die-for Grand Marnier crepes; sampler platters, great for a group; attentive service. $ *Average main: $8* ⊠ *Avda. 7, Cs. 29–31, Barrio Escalante* ☎ *4034–8030* ⊕ *www. entrenouscreperie.com.*

★ Jürgen's

$$$ | **ECLECTIC** | A common haunt for *políticos,* Jürgen's attracts San José's elites, and you'll feel pretty elite too when you dine at this contemporary restaurant with leather and wood accents. The inventive menu, with delicacies such as medallions of roasted duck and tuna fillet encrusted with sesame seeds, sets this place apart from the city's more traditional venues. **Known for:** haunt for "who's who" of San José society; impeccable service; sleek, modern furnishings. $ *Average main: $24* ⊠ *Blvd. Dent, Barrio Dent* ♦ *250 m north of Grupo Q* ☎ *2224–2455* ⊕ *www. hotelboutiquejade.com* ⊗ *Closed Sun. No lunch Sat.*

★ Kalú

$$$ | **ECLECTIC** | At one of the capital's trendiest dining spots, the panini and pastas are the standouts, but Kalú's menu incorporates Costa Rican, Thai, and American elements, too. For one of those Americanized touches, try the *hambuguesa Kalú,* with portobello mushrooms, mozzarella cheese, and hummus. **Known for:** pleasant garden setting; inventive menu; adjoining art gallery for browsing while you wait. $ *Average main: $23* ⊠ *C. 31, Avda. 5, Barrio Escalante* ☎ *2253–8426* ⊕ *www.kalu. co.cr* ⊗ *Closed Mon. No dinner Sun.*

La Terrasse

$$$$ | **FRENCH** | Dining here (by advance reservation only) feels as though you're a guest in a private home, and indeed, the restaurant is located in a converted house that dates back to the 1920s. Main-course offerings at this cozy restaurant rotate, but might include a *blanquette de veau* (veal ragout) or a *daube provençale* (a hearty wine-marinated beef stew). **Known for:** carefully prepared French food; impeccable service; strict reservation policy. $ *Average main: $40* ⊠ *C. 15, Avda. 9, Barrio Otoya* ♦ *50 m north of Café Mundo* ☎ *8939–8470* ⊕ *restaurantlaterrasse.blogspot.com* ▤ *No credit cards* ⊗ *Closed Mon. No dinner Sun., no lunch Sat.*

★ Le Chandelier

$$$$ | **FRENCH** | Formal service and traditional sauce-heavy French dishes are part of the experience at this elegant dining room with wicker chairs, tile floors, and original paintings. Start off with saffron ravioli stuffed with ricotta cheese and walnuts, and opt for a unique main course like corvina in a *pejibaye* (peach palm) sauce or hearts of palm and veal chops glazed in a sweet port-wine sauce. **Known for:** duck à l'orange; impeccable, formal service; San José's most elegant restaurant. $ *Average main: $32* ⊠ *C. 49, San Pedro* ♦ *50 m west and 100 m south of ICE Bldg.* ☎ *2225–3980* ⊕ *www.lechandelier. cr* ⊗ *Closed Sun. No lunch Sat.*

Olio

$$ | **MEDITERRANEAN** | Although this century-old redbrick house with stained-glass windows serves the full contingent of Mediterranean cuisine, it's best for drinks and Spanish-style tapas. The pub atmosphere draws everybody from tie-clad business executives to university students, and there are umbrella-covered tables on the sidewalk to enjoy warm evenings. **Known for:** friendly, efficient service; good pizza selection; sceney atmosphere. [$] *Average main: $12* ✉ *C. 33, Avda. 3, Barrio Escalante* ☎ *2281–0541* 🌐 *www.facebook.com/Restaurante.olio* 🕓 *Closed Sun. No lunch Sat.*

Restaurante Amón

$ | **COSTA RICAN** | Reasonable prices and a hearty breakfast of gallo pinto, scrambled eggs, bread, and coffee at this artsy restaurant will fortify you for a morning of sightseeing. The bargain $7 lunch special consists of the standard casado—choose from fish, chicken, beef, or pork—accompanied by rice, beans, vegetable, salad, and dessert. **Known for:** typical Costa Rican flavors; minimalist setting; rotating art exhibits. [$] *Average main: $6* ✉ *C. 7, Avdas. 7–9, Barrio Amón* ☎ *2221–2960* 🕓 *Closed weekends. No dinner.*

★ **Restaurante Silvestre**

$$$$ | **COSTA RICAN** | Chef Santiago Fernandez is at the helm of this ambitious and wildly successful exploration of upscale contemporary Costa Rican cuisine. The regularly changing menus use local and organic ingredients (along with fish and meat procured through responsible means) to take diners on a journey into some of the most creative (and delicious) food Costa Rica has to offer. **Known for:** gorgeous setting in a renovated mansion with a plant-filled indoor terrace; prix-fixe menus of sustainable fine dining, including wine pairings; hip downstairs bar. [$] *Average main: $28* ✉ *Avda. 11, C. 3A, #955, Barrio Amón* ☎ *2221–2465* 🌐 *www.restaurantesilvestre.com* 🕓 *Closed Sun. and Mon.*

Sikwa

$$ | **COSTA RICAN** | The indigenous cultures of Costa Rica don't get too much attention from tourists, but this small, intimate restaurant in Barrio Escalante is trying to change that. By incorporating recipes derived from the history and culture of the eight surviving indigenous ethnic groups, Sikwa has deliciously (and respectfully) bridged the gap between the country's past and present. **Known for:** unique dining experience blending history and storytelling; traditional indigenous dishes like peach palm soup and escarole tomato sauce with white corn and pork; small space best for smaller groups. [$] *Average main: $13* ✉ *Casa Batsú, Avda. 1, C. 33, Barrio Escalante* ✣ *125 m. east of Fresh Market* ☎ *7093–1662* 🕓 *Closed Mon. No dinner Sun.*

Sofia Mediterráneo

$$ | **MEDITERRANEAN** | Natives of Istanbul, the chef and owner rely on authentic recipes for excellent red peppers stuffed with spicy beef and rice, eggplant-tomato salad, and other Mediterranean treats. You'll find a good selection of vegetarian salads, too. **Known for:** to-die-for baklava; potent Turkish coffee; sceney atmosphere. [$] *Average main: $14* ✉ *C. 33, Avda. 3, Barrio Escalante* ☎ *2224–5050* 🕓 *No lunch Mon.*

Have Some Sauce 🍴

Any self-respecting tico home or restaurant keeps a bottle of Salsa Lizano, one of the country's signature food products, on hand. Its tang brightens up meat, vegetable, and rice dishes. Bottles of the stuff make great souvenirs, and you can buy them at **Más X Menos** (pronounced Más *por* Menos) supermarkets throughout the country. The main San José branch is at Avenida Central, between Calles 11 and 13.

Coffee and Quick Bites

Giacomín

$ | **BAKERY** | We have to admit that Costa Rican baked goods tend toward the dry-as-dust end of the spectrum. But Italian-style bakery Giacomín, near the University of Costa Rica, is an exception—a touch of liqueur added to the batter makes all the difference. **Known for:** Italian-style pastries; espresso bar; upstairs balcony. [$] *Average main: $5* ✉ *Los Yoses* ✢ *Next to Automercado supermarket* ☎ *4001–7478* 🌐 *www.giacomincr.com* 💳 *No credit cards.*

Hotels

Just north of downtown, old homes converted into small lodgings populate Barrios Amón and Otoya, two of the capital's most historic neighborhoods. The small properties 10 minutes by cab east of downtown, toward the university, offer personalized service and lots of peace and quiet. Plenty of restaurants and bars are within easy reach.

Hotel Aranjuez

$ | **HOTEL** | Several 1940s-era houses with extensive gardens and lively common areas—visitors swap travel advice here—make up this family-run lodging. **Pros:** good budget value; great place to meet other budget travelers; excellent complimentary breakfast. **Cons:** a few rooms share bath; far from sights; can be hard to find space in high season. [$] *Rooms from: $54* ✉ *C. 19, Avdas. 11–13, Barrio Aranjuez* ☎ *2256–1825* 🌐 *www.hotelaranjuez.com* 🛏 *35 rooms* 🍴 *Free Breakfast.*

★ **Hotel Boutique Jade**

$$ | **HOTEL** | The European owners of this small east-side lodging have instilled a standard for attentive service in their staff and the result is a devoted return clientele, mostly from Europe. **Pros:** friendly service; quiet street; close to lots of east-side shopping. **Cons:** can be difficult to find; far from sights; a few of the rooms look a bit dated. [$] *Rooms from: $102* ✉ *Blvd. Dent, Barrio Dent* ✢ *250 m north of Grupo Q Hyundai dealership* ☎ *2224–2455* 🌐 *www.hotelboutiquejade.com* 🛏 *29 rooms* 🍴 *Free Breakfast.*

Hotel Dunn Inn

$$ | **B&B/INN** | Adjoining 1926 and 1933 houses fuse to create the cozy Barrio Amón experience at bargain prices. **Pros:** good value; friendly staff; many online specials. **Cons:** difficult to get reservations; interior rooms catch noise from lobby and bar; sits at bottom of steep street. [$] *Rooms from: $84* ✉ *Avda. 11, C. 5, Barrio Amón* ☎ *2222–3232, 800/545–4801 in North America* 🌐 *www.hoteldunninn.com* 🛏 *28 rooms* 🍴 *Free Breakfast.*

Hotel Santo Tomás

$ | **B&B/INN** | The front of this century-old former coffee-plantation house is along a busy street, but close the front door behind you and you'll find an oasis of quiet in the center of the city. **Pros:** good value; friendly staff; central location. **Cons:** difficult parking; safe, but borders a sketchy neighborhood; small rooms. [$] *Rooms from: $65* ✉ *Avda. 7, Cs. 3–5, Barrio Amón* ☎ *2255–0448* 🌐 *www.hotel-santotomas.com* 🛏 *30 rooms* 🍴 *Free Breakfast.*

Kap's Place

$ | **B&B/INN** | The owners of this multi-building lodging are committed to maintaining a family atmosphere, and you'll be guaranteed peace and quiet during your stay here. **Pros:** good budget value; quiet atmosphere; good place to meet other budget travelers. **Cons:** far from sights; small rooms; you can pay with a credit card if you stay in the main building, but not in one of the annexes. [$] *Rooms from: $65* ✉ *C. 19, Avdas. 11–13, Barrio Aranjuez* ✢ *200 m west and 50 m north of Shell station* ☎ *2221–1169* 🌐 *www.kapsplace.com* 🛏 *23 rooms* 🍴 *Free Breakfast.*

In markets, you'll find friendly artists and artisans.

Nightlife

Café Mundo

CAFES—NIGHTLIFE | The highly recommended restaurant Café Mundo is a quiet spot for a drink or bite to eat and is frequented by LGBTQ and bohemian crowds. ⊠ *C. 15, Avda. 9, Barrio Otoya* ☎ *2222–6190.*

Costa Rica Beer Factory

BREWPUBS/BEER GARDENS | One of Costa Rica's budding brewpubs serves up four of its own craft beers and one seasonally rotating one, as well as possibly the country's best selection of international brews, plus burgers and appetizers. Weekend nights get crowded. ⊠ *C. 33, Avda. 7, Barrio Escalante* ☎ *8447–9732* ⊕ *www.costaricabeerfactory.com.*

Craic Irish Pub

BARS/PUBS | Craic's certainly looks Gaelic and has several beers on tap—some are Irish, some are not—and the pub grub here is pretty American. The overflow at this popular place spills into the outdoor garden on warm nights. ⊠ *C. 25, Barrio La California* ⊹ *100 m south of Nicaraguan embassy* ☎ *2221–9320.*

El Observatorio

BARS/PUBS | El Observatorio strikes an unusual balance between casual and formal: it's the kind of place where an over-30 crowd in ties goes to watch a soccer game. Something is on here every night except Sunday: usually a selection of stand-up comedy, live music, or karaoke. ⊠ *C. 23, Barrio La California* ⊹ *Across from Cine Magaly* ☎ *2223–0725* ⊕ *www. elobservatorio.tv.*

Mercado La California

BREWPUBS/BEER GARDENS | You find food stands (tacos, pizzas, and sandwiches) and a bar kiosk (beer, wine, or mixed drinks) all to your liking at this sprawling place—part bar, part food court, part night market. Order and grab a seat. That's the system at this always-hopping spot. ⊠ *C. 21, Avda. 1, Barrio La California* ⊕ *www.facebook.com/ mercadolacalifornia.*

Merecumbé

DANCE CLUBS | Many Costa Ricans learn to merengue, rumba, mambo, cha-cha, and swing (called *cumbia* elsewhere) at a young age. Play catch-up at dance school Merecumbé, which has 16 branches around Costa Rica. With a few days' notice you can arrange a private lesson with an English-speaking instructor. An hour or two is all you need to grasp the fundamentals of merengue and *bolero* (what Costa Ricans call the rumba), both of which are easy to master and work with the pop music you're likely to hear back home. ⊠ *100 m south and 25 m west of Banco Popular, San Pedro* ☎ *2224–3531* ⊕ *www.facebook.com/ merecumbe.sanpedro.*

Mil948

BARS/PUBS | At this cozy cocktail lounge, once the house of iconic president José María Figueres, the mixologists will whip up any of your favorite drinks or acquaint you with inventive new ones. The name is a mashup of "1948" in Spanish, the year Figueres came to power in a brief civil war. ⊠ *Avda. Ctl, Cs. 29–33, Barrio Escalante* ⊕ *across from KFC* ☎ *2234– 8186* ⊕ *www.mil948.com.*

Olio

CAFES—NIGHTLIFE | Fill up on Spanish-style tapas at the Mediterranean bar and restaurant Olio. It draws a mix of professionals and older college students. ⊠ *C. 33, Avda. 3, Barrio Escalante* ☎ *2281–0541* ⊕ *www.facebook.com/Restaurante.olio.*

Ram Luna

MUSIC CLUBS | In the far, far southern suburbs, 9 miles south of downtown San José, Ram Luna is most famous for the views—the lights of the Central Valley sparkle at your feet—and the music. Make reservations if you plan to be here for Wednesday or Thursday evening's folklore show—a bilingual emcee fills you in on the cultural background of what you're enjoying—or Friday evening's dancing to live music. Gray Line Costa Rica offers evening tours out here.

Transportation, dinner, and tour guide are included in the $72 price. ⊠ *Aserrí* ⊕ *15 km (9 miles) south of San José between Aserrí and Tabarca* ☎ *2230–3022* ⊕ *www. restauranteramluna.com.*

Stiefel Pub

BARS/PUBS | Craft beer is taking hold in Costa Rica, and Stiefel has 10 microbrews on tap to the accompaniment of a lively pub atmosphere. ⊠ *Avda. 7, Barrio Amón* ⊕ *50 m east of INS building* ☎ *8850–2119* ⊕ *www.facebook.com/ stiefelpub.*

Performing Arts

Eugene O'Neill Theater

MUSIC | This theater has chamber concerts and plays most weekend evenings. The cultural center is a great place to meet North American expatriates. ⊠ *Centro Cultural Costarricense–Norteamericano, Avda. 1, C. 37, Barrio Dent* ☎ *2207–7549* ⊕ *www.centrocultural.cr.*

Teatro La Aduana

THEATER | You'll find frequent dance and stage performances at this theater, and it is home to the Compañía Nacional de Teatro (National Theater Company). ⊠ *C. 25, Avda. 3, Barrio La California* ☎ *2257– 8305* ⊕ *www.mcj.go.cr.*

Shopping

BOOKS AND MAGAZINES

Librería Internacional

BOOKS/STATIONERY | The city's largest bookstore evokes that Barnes & Noble ambience, though on a much smaller scale. It stocks English translations of Latin American literature, as well as myriad coffee-table books on Costa Rica. There are 23 other smaller branches around San José and the Central Valley. ⊠ *Plaza Antares, Rotonda La Bandera, Barrio Dent* ☎ *2253–9553* ⊕ *www.libreriainternacional.com.*

CRAFTS

Kiosco

CRAFTS | Ensconced inside Barrio Escalante's trendy Kalú restaurant, the equally trendy Kiosco proffers a good selection of locally made woodwork, fabrics, and ceramics. ⊠ *Kalú, C. 31, Avda. 5, Barrio Escalante* ☎ *2253–8426.*

Mi Pueblo Verde

CRAFTS | This is a standout among the Moravia shops for its fine carvings made from native *cocobolo* and *guápinol* wood. Check out the unusual salad bowls. ⊠ *San Vicente de Moravia* ✛ *50 m north of Colegio María Inmaculada* ☎ *2235–5742.*

FARMERS' MARKET

Feria Verde

FOOD/CANDY | It's a tad out of the way, but just up the street from the Hotel Aranjuez is the city's best Saturday-morning farmers' market. Stock up on organic fruits and veggies and take in the local scene. For something tropical, try some coconut water—you'll get a coconut whacked in half by a machete, and you can sip the water through a straw. Things get under way at 7 am and wind down at 12:30. ⊠ *North end of C. 19, Barrio Aranjuez* ✛ *150 m north of Hotel Aranjuez, then downhill to left.*

SOUVENIRS

Artesanías Zurquí

CERAMICS/GLASSWARE | You'll find a well-rounded selection of ceramics, wood, and leather at Artesanías Zurquí. ⊠ *San Vicente de Moravia* ✛ *50 m north of Colegio María Inmaculada* ☎ *2240–5342.*

Mundo de Recuerdos

GIFTS/SOUVENIRS | If you can't find it at Mundo de Recuerdos, it probably doesn't exist. Here's the largest of the Moravia shops with simply everything—at least of standard souvenir fare—you could ask for under one roof. ⊠ *San Vicente de Moravia* ✛ *Across from Colegio María Inmaculada* ☎ *2240–8990.*

Chapter 5

THE CENTRAL VALLEY

Updated by
Jeffrey Van Fleet

👁 Sights	🍴 Restaurants	🏨 Hotels	🛍 Shopping	🍸 Nightlife
★★★★★	★★★★☆	★★★★★	★★★☆☆	★★★★☆

WELCOME TO THE CENTRAL VALLEY

TOP REASONS TO GO

★ **Avian adventures:** Flock to Tapantí National Park to see emerald toucanets, resplendent quetzals (if you're lucky), and nearly every species of Costa Rican hummingbird. Rancho Naturalista is the bird lover's hotel of choice.

★ **Coffee:** Get up close and personal with harvesting and processing on coffee tours at two of the valley's many plantations: Café Britt and Doka Estate.

★ **Poás Volcano:** Peer right down into the witches' cauldron that is the Poás Volcano.

★ **The Orosi Valley:** Spectacular views and quiet, bucolic towns make this area a great day trip or overnight from San José.

★ **Rafting the Pacuare River:** Brave the rapids as you descend through tropical forest on one of the best white-water rivers in Central America.

The Central Valley is something of a misnomer, and its Spanish name, the *meseta central* (central plateau) isn't entirely accurate either. The two contiguous mountain ranges that run the length of the country—the Cordillera Central range (which includes Poás, Barva, Irazú, and Turrialba volcanoes) to the north and the Cordillera de Talamanca to the south—don't quite line up in the middle, leaving a trough between them. The "valley" floor is about 3,000 to 5,000 feet above sea level. In the valley, your view toward the coasts is obstructed by the two mountain ranges. But from a hillside hotel, your view of San José and the valley can be spectacular.

1 Escazú. Posh town with a growing number of shops and restaurants.

2 Santa Ana. Explore the wildlife refuge and traditional church in quaint Santa Ana.

3 Grecia. Home to the area's best farmers' market and a unique metal church.

4 Sarchí. This relaxing town is known for its crafts and oxcarts.

5 Carara National Park. Spot monkeys and toucans in the biologically diverse park.

6 San Antonio de Belén. Convenient departure town for trips to the western Central Valley and more.

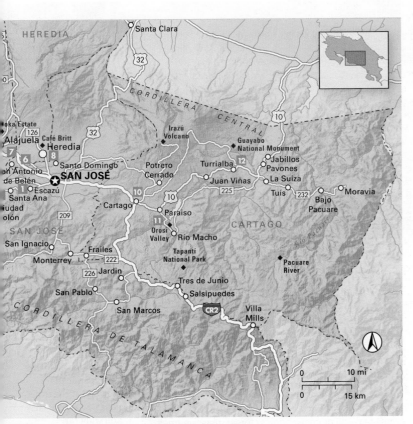

7 Alajuela. Costa Rica's second most populated city is a 30-minute ride from San José.

8 Heredia. An important coffee center and buzzing city with university life and old colonial structures.

9 Poás Volcano National Park. Peer into the crater of Costa Rica's most famous volcano here.

10 Cartago. Costa Rica's oldest city and colonial capital is home to the country's national shrine.

11 The Orosi Valley. This pastoral land is the cradle of Costa Rican history.

12 Turrialba. Near the bustling market town are its namesake volcano and the archaeological ruins of Guayabo.

CARARA NATIONAL PARK

Carara National Park

One of the last remnants of an ecological transition zone between Costa Rica's drier northwest and more humid southwest, Carara National Park holds a tremendous collection of plants and animals.

Squeezed into its 47 square km (18 square miles) is a mixed habitat of evergreen and deciduous forest, river, lagoon, and marshland. Much of the park's terrain is blanketed with dramatic primary forest, massive trees laden with vines and epiphytes. This is a birder's and plant lover's haven. The sparse undergrowth makes terrestrial wildlife and ground birds easier to see. The most famous denizens—aside from the crocodiles in the adjoining Río Tárcoles—are the park's colorful and noisy scarlet macaws, which always travel in pairs. An oxbow lake (a U-shaped body of water that was once part of a river) adds an extra wildlife dimension, attracting turtles and waterfowl—and the crocodiles that dine on them. Bring lots of drinking water; this park can get very hot and humid. *(For more information, see the review in this chapter.)*

BEST TIME TO GO

Dry season, January to April, is the best time to visit. The trails get muddy during the rainy season and usually close in the wettest months. This small park can feel crowded at the trailheads, so arrive early and walk far.

FUN FACT

The crowning glory of Carara is the successful conservation program that has doubled its scarlet macaw population. You can't miss these long-tailed, noisy parrots—look for streaks of blue and red in the sky.

BEST WAYS TO EXPLORE

BIRD-WATCHING

With more than 400 species recorded here, Carara is on every bird-watcher's must-visit list. It's an especially good place to see elusive ground birds, such as antpittas (a small ground-dwelling bird that eats ants), early in the morning and late in the afternoon. Around the lake and in the marshy areas, you may also spot roseate spoonbills, northern jacanas, and stately boat-billed herons. The park's most famous fliers are the scarlet macaws. Once almost absent from the area, a decades-long conservation program has revitalized the local population.

HIKING

The best and really only way to explore this park is on foot. Trails are well marked and maintained but the ground is often muddy—this is rain forest, after all. The shortest—and most popular—loop trail can be done in only 15 minutes. But if you venture farther afield, you'll quickly be on your own. The longer trail that connects with the Quebrada Bonita loop takes about 90 minutes to hike. There is also a short wheelchair-accessible route that starts at the main entrance. It goes deep enough into the forest to give visitors a sense of its drama and diversity.

WILDLIFE-WATCHING

Carara is famous for an amazing variety of wildlife, given its relatively small area. Keep alert (and quiet) while walking and you'll have a good chance of spotting lizards, coatimundis (a member of the raccoon family), and sloths. You're almost guaranteed to see white-faced monkeys and, with luck, howler and spider monkeys, too. You may even see a nine-banded armadillo.

Visitors spot wildlife in Carara National Park.

TOP REASONS TO GO

BIRDS

With a varied habitat that attracts both forest and water birds, Carara is a treasure trove for birders. Even if you're not a birder, you'll get a thrill hearing the raucous crowing of beautiful scarlet macaws as they soar over the forest canopy.

THE JUNGLE

The forest here is simply magnificent. Even if you don't spot a single bird or animal, you will experience the true meaning of jungle. Carara has one of the most diverse collections of trees in the country. Breathe deeply, be alert to the symphony of forest sounds, and bask in a totally natural world.

WILDLIFE

For most visitors, wildlife is the park's main attraction. You can count on seeing monkeys and lots of lizards as you walk the trails. Although they are a little harder to spot, look for anteaters, sloths, and armadillos.

POÁS VOLCANO

Poás Volcano

Towering north of Alajuela, the verdant Poás Volcano is covered with a quilt of farms and topped by a dark green shawl of cloud forest.

That pastoral scene disappears once you get to the 8,885-foot summit, and you gaze into the steaming, bubbling crater with smoking fumaroles and a gurgling, gray-turquoise sulfurous lake. You'll swear you're peering over the edge of a giant witches' cauldron. That basin, 2 km (1 mile) in diameter and nearly 1,000 feet deep, is thought to be the largest active volcanic crater in the world.

Poás is one of Costa Rica's five active volcanoes—it has erupted 40 times since the early 1800s—and is one of those rare places that permit you to see volcanic energy this close with minimal risk. Authorities closely monitor Poás's activity following several eruptions in March 2006, the first significant increase in activity since 1994. The most recent activity took place in late 2018 and produced clouds of smoke. Access is normally open, but park officials close the route up here when there is evidence of any activity they deem "irregular."

BEST TIME TO GO

The peak is frequently shrouded in mist, and you might see little beyond the lip of the crater. Be patient and wait awhile, especially if some wind is blowing—the clouds can disappear quickly. Aim to get here before 10 am. The earlier you arrive, the better the visibility.

FUN FACT

Forgot your umbrella? Duck under a *sombrilla de pobre* (poor man's umbrella) plant. These giant leaves can grow to diameters of 3 to 5 feet.

BEST WAYS TO EXPLORE

BIRD-WATCHING

Although birding can be a little frustrating here because of cloud and mist, more than 330 bird species call Poás home. One of the most comical birds you'll see in Costa Rica is usually spotted foraging in plain sight on the ground: the big-footed finch, whose oversize feet give it a clownish walk. Its cousin, the yellow-thighed finch, is easy to recognize by its bright yellow, er … thighs. Arrive early and bird around the gate before the park opens, and stop along the road to the visitor center wherever you see a likely birding area. In the underbrush you may find spotted wood quail or the elusive buffy-crowned wood-partridge. The trees along the road are a favorite haunt of both black-and-yellow and long-tailed silky flycatchers.

HIKING

From the summit, two trails head into the forest. The second trail, on the right just before the crater, winds through a thick mesh of shrubs and dwarf trees to the eerie but beautiful Botos Lake (Laguna Botos), which occupies an extinct crater. It takes 30 minutes to walk here and back, but you'll be huffing and puffing if you're not used to this altitude.

VOLCANIC TIPS

A paved road leads all the way from Alajuela to Poás's summit. No one is allowed to venture into the crater or walk along its edge. ■TIP→ **Take periodic breaks from viewing: step back at least every 10 minutes, so that the sulfur fumes don't overcome you. Be sure to bring a sweater or a jacket—it can be surprisingly chilly and wet up here.**

Peer into Poás Volcano from the park's overlook.

TOP REASONS TO GO

A+ FACILITIES
You're on your own in many Costa Rican national parks, most of which are lacking in facilities, but this wheelchair-accessible park is a pleasant exception, with an attractive visitor center containing exhibits, a cafeteria, gift shop, and restrooms.

BUBBLES AND ASH
"Up close and personal with nature" takes on a whole new meaning here. Costa Rica forms part of the Pacific Rim's so-called Ring of Fire, and a visit to the volcano's summit gives you a close-up view of a region of the earth that is still in formation.

LOCATION, LOCATION, LOCATION
Poás's proximity to San José and the western Central Valley makes it an easy half-day trip.

MORE THAN A VOLCANO
The park is not just about its namesake volcano. A few kilometers of hiking trails let you take in the cloud forest's flora.

IRAZÚ VOLCANO

Irazú Volcano

The word *Irazú* is likely a corruption of Iztaru, a long-ago indigenous community whose name translated as "hill of thunder." The name is apt.

Volcán Irazú, as it's known in Spanish, is considered active, but the gases and steam that billow from fumaroles on the northwestern slope are rarely visible from the peak above the crater lookouts. The mountain's first recorded eruption took place in 1723; the most recent was a series of eruptions that lasted from 1963 to 1965. Boulders and mud rained down on the countryside, damming rivers and causing serious floods, and the volcano dumped up to 20 inches of ash on sections of the Central Valley.

When conditions are clear, you can see the chartreuse lake inside the Cráter Principal. The stark moonscape of the summit contrasts markedly with the lush vegetation of Irazú's lower slopes, home to porcupines, armadillos, coyotes, and mountain hares. Listen for the low-pitched, throaty song of the *yigüirro*, or clay-color thrush, Costa Rica's national bird. Its call is most pronounced just before the start of the rainy season. *(For more information, see the review in this chapter.)*

BEST TIME TO GO

Early morning, especially in the January–April dry season, affords the best views, both of the craters and the surrounding countryside. Clouds move in by late morning. Wear warm, waterproof clothing if you get here that early.

FUN FACT

Irazú has dumped a lot of ash over the centuries. The most recent eruptive period began on the day John F. Kennedy arrived in Costa Rica in 1963. The "ash storm" that ensued lasted on and off for two years.

BEST WAYS TO EXPLORE

BIRD-WATCHING

The road to Irazú provides some of the best roadside birding opportunities in the country, especially on a weekday when there isn't a constant parade of cars and buses heading up to the crater. Some of the most fruitful areas are on either side of the bridges you'll pass over. Reliable bird species that inhabit these roadsides are acorn and hairy woodpeckers; the brilliant flame-throated warbler; buzzing around blossoms, the fiery-throated green violetear; and (aptly named) volcano hummingbirds. Once past the main entrance, there are also plenty of opportunities to stop and bird-watch roadside. Look for volcano juncos on the ground and slaty flowerpiercers visiting flowering shrubs.

HIKING

Even before you get to the main entrance, check out the park's Prusia Sector, which has hiking trails that pass through majestic oak and pine forests and picnic areas. They're popular with Tico families on weekends, so if you want the woods to yourself, come on a weekday. Trails in the park are well marked; avoid heading down any paths marked with *"paso restringido"* (passage restricted) signs.

VOLCANIC TIPS

A paved road leads all the way to the summit, where a small coffee shop sells hot beverages, and a persistent pair of coatis cruise the picnic tables for handouts. (Please resist the urge to feed them!) The road to the top climbs past vegetable fields, pastures, and native oak forests. You pass through the villages of Potrero Cerrado and San Juan de Chicuá before reaching the summit's bleak but beautiful main crater.

TOP REASONS TO GO

EASY TO GET TO
Irazú's proximity to San José and the entire eastern Central Valley makes it an easy half-day or day trip. Public transportation from the capital, frequently a cumbersome option to most of the country's national parks, is straightforward.

THE VIEW
How many places in the world let you peer directly into the crater of an active volcano? Costa Rica offers you two: here at Irazú and at Poás Volcano. Poás's steaming cauldron is spookier, but Irazú's crater lake with colors that change according to the light is nonetheless impressive.

MORE VIEWS
"On a clear day, you can see forever," goes the old song from the musical of the same name. Irazú is one of the few places in Costa Rica that lets you glimpse both the Pacific and Atlantic (Caribbean) oceans at once. "Clear" is the key term here: clouds frequently obscure the view. Early morning gives you your best shot.

Irazú's crater lake changes color with the light.

San José sits in an almost-mile-high mountain valley ringed by volcanoes whose ash has fertilized the soil and turned the region into Costa Rica's historic breadbasket. This will always be the land that coffee built, and the small cities of the Central Valley exhibit a tidiness and prosperity you don't see in the rest of the country. The valley is chock-full of activities and is Costa Rica at its most *típico*, giving you the best sense of what makes the country tick.

You can't find a more ideal climate than out here in the valley. When people refer to Costa Rica's proverbial "eternal spring," they're talking about this part of the country, which lacks the oppressive seasonal heat and rain of other regions. It's no wonder the Central Valley has drawn a growing number of North American and European retirees.

There's no shortage of terrific lodgings out here—everything from family-run boutique hotels to the big international chains are yours for the night. It used to be that everyone stayed in San José and took in the various attractions in the Central Valley on day trips. With the good selection of quality accommodations out here, why not base yourself in the Central Valley, and make San José your day trip instead?

MAJOR REGIONS

The communities immediately **West of San José** are the capital's booming, upscale suburbs. Things turn more pastoral the farther west you go, and you'll find one of the country's best craft communities, Sarchí, and pleasant countryside lodges near Atenas, a thriving agricultural center and quintessential Costa Rican town. Heading farther west toward the Central Pacific coast, Carara National Park is home to an impressive collection of plants and animals.

Coffee farms and small valley towns dominate the area **North of San José.** Their beautiful hotels attract visitors on their first and last nights in the country. Coffee plantations Café Britt and Doka Estate are both here, as is the international airport, near Alajuela. North of Alajuela, Poás Volcano's turquoise crater lake and steaming main crater make it many visitors' favorite volcano stop.

The less visited eastern Central Valley (**East of San José**) holds Cartago, older than San José, with a couple of historic attractions. Irazú is Costa Rica's tallest volcano. On a clear day you can see both the Atlantic and Pacific oceans from its peak. The nearby Orosi Valley is an often overlooked beauty. The drive into the valley is simply gorgeous, and a tranquil way to spend a day. Birding destination Tapantí National Park is at the southern edge of the valley. Rafting trips on the Pacuare and Reventazón are based in bustling, growing Turrialba. The nearby Guayabo National Monument, ruins of a city deserted in AD 1400, is Costa Rica's only significant archaeological site.

Planning

When to Go

HIGH SEASON: MID-DECEMBER TO APRIL

The Central Valley's elevation keeps temperatures pleasant and springlike year-round, slightly warmer to the west and slightly cooler to the east. Turrialba and the Orosi Valley represent a transition zone between the valley and the Caribbean slope; expect warmer temperatures there. December and January kick off the dry season with sunny days and brisk nights. February, March, and April warm up considerably. Most hotels here keep rates constant throughout the year; a few follow high-season/low-season fluctuations.

LOW SEASON: MAY TO MID-NOVEMBER

The rainy season moves in gradually with afternoon showers from May through July. August becomes wetter, and September and October can mean prolonged downpours. The valley's western sector—Alajuela, San Antonio de Belén, Escazú, and Santa Ana—always catches a tad less rain than its eastern counterpart.

SHOULDER SEASON: MID-NOVEMBER TO MID-DECEMBER

Rains start to wind down by mid-November, and the month before December holidays is a terrific time to enjoy the Central Valley at its most lush and green, and before the big influx of tourists arrives. As an added bonus, the coffee harvest is under way in earnest in this part of the country, too—always a bustling, fascinating spectacle.

Planning Your Time

You could spend an entire week here without getting bored, but if you have only a week or two in Costa Rica, we recommend a maximum of two days before heading to rain forests and beaches in other parts of the country. Spending a day after you arrive, then another day or two before you fly out gives you a taste of the region, breaks up the travel time, and makes your last day interesting, rather than spent in transit back to San José. The drive between just about any two points in the Central Valley is two hours or usually less, so it's ideal for short trips. Tour operators in and around San José offer daylong excursions that mix and match the valley's sights—perhaps a volcano visit in the morning and a coffee tour in the afternoon.

Getting Here and Around

AIR

Although Aeropuerto Internacional Juan Santamaría (SJO) is billed as San José's airport, it sits just outside the city of Alajuela in the near northwestern part of the valley. You can get taxis from the airport to any point in the Central Valley for $10–$120. Some hotels arrange pickup.

BUS

Many visitors never consider taking a local bus to get around, but doing so puts you in close contact with locals—an experience you miss out on if you travel by taxi or tour bus. It's also cheap. Always opt for a taxi at night or when you're in a hurry.

CAR

All points in the western Central Valley can be reached by car. For San Antonio de Belén, Heredia, Alajuela, and points north of San José, turn right at the west end of Paseo Colón onto the Pan-American Highway (Autopista General Cañas). The eastern Central Valley is accessible from San José by driving east on Avenida 2, then Central, through San Pedro, then following signs from the intersection to Cartago. To get to the Orosi Valley, head straight through Cartago, turn right at the Basílica de Nuestra Señora de los Angeles, and follow the signs to Paraíso. The road through Cartago and Paraíso continues east to Turrialba. Driving from one side of the valley to the other means you need to get across San José. There's no efficient way to bypass the capital.

The best way to get around the Central Valley is by car. Most of the car-rental agencies in San José have offices at or near the airport in Alajuela. They will deliver vehicles to many area hotels, but not those in Turrialba and the Orosi Valley.

TAXI

All Central Valley towns have taxis, which usually wait for fares along their central parks. The rideshare service Uber operates, albeit without proper permits, in a few of the larger suburbs—Escazú, Santa Ana, Alajuela, Heredia, and Cartago—in the Central Valley. Until Uber and the government reconcile their differences, you use the service at some risk.

Restaurants

Growing Escazú has become as metropolitan as San José and has the restaurant selection to prove it. Elsewhere, as befits this cradle of the country's tradition, typical Costa Rican cuisine still reigns.

Hotels

Most international flights come into Costa Rica in the evening and head out early in the morning, meaning you likely have to stay your first and last nights in or near San José, and the Central Valley can be considered "near." For getting away from it all and still being close to the country's main airport, the lodgings around San José make splendid alternatives to staying in the city itself. It may pain you to tear yourself away from that beach villa or rain-forest lodge, but you can still come back to something distinctive here on your last night in Costa Rica. Small mom-and-pop places, sprawling coffee plantations, nature lodges, and hilltop villas with expansive views are some of your options. The large chains are here as well, but the real gems are the boutique hotels, many of which are family-run places and have unique designs that take advantage of exceptional countryside locations. Subtropical gardens are the norm, rather than the exception. The Central Valley's climate is often a great surprise to first-time visitors—it's usually cool enough at night to go without air-conditioning, so don't be surprised if many hotels don't have it. *Hotel reviews have been shortened. For full information, visit Fodors.com.*

WHAT IT COSTS in U.S. Dollars			
$	$$	$$$	$$$$
RESTAURANTS			
under $10	$10–$15	$16–$25	over $25
HOTELS			
under $75	$75–$150	$151–$250	over $250

Escazú

5 km (3 miles) southwest of San José.

Costa Rica's wealthiest community and the Central Valley's most prestigious address, Escazú (pronounced *es-cah-SOO*) nevertheless mixes glamour with tradition, BMWs with oxcarts, trendy malls with farmers' markets, Louis Vuitton with burlap produce sacks. As you exit the highway and crest the first gentle hill, you might think you made a wrong turn and ended up in Southern California, but farther up you return to small-town Central America. Narrow roads wind their way up the steep slopes, past postage-stamp coffee fields and lengths of shoulder-to-shoulder, modest houses with tidy gardens and the occasional oxcart parked in the yard. Unfortunately, the area's stream of new developments and high-rises has steadily chipped away at the rural landscape—each year you have to climb higher to find the kind of scene that captured the attention of many a Costa Rican painter in the early 20th century. In their place are plenty of fancy homes and condos, especially in the San Rafael neighborhood. Escazú's historic church faces a small plaza, surrounded in part by weathered adobe buildings. The town center is several blocks north of the busy road to Santa Ana, which is lined with a growing selection of restaurants, bars, and shops.

During colonial days, Escazú was dubbed the "City of Witches" because many native healers lived in the area. Locals say that Escazú is still Costa Rica's most haunted community, home to witches who will tell your fortune or concoct a love potion for a small fee, but you'd be hard-pressed to spot them in the town's busy commercial district. Try a soccer field instead: the city's soccer team is christened Las Brujas (the Witches). You'll see a huge number of witch-on-a-broomstick decals affixed to vehicles here, too; it's the city's official symbol.

GETTING HERE AND AROUND

To drive to Escazú from San José, turn left at the western end of Paseo Colón, which ends at the Parque La Sabana. Take the first right onto the Caldera Highway, and get off the highway at the second exit. The off-ramp curves right, then sharply left; follow it about 1 km (½ mile), sticking to the main road, to El Cruce at the bottom of the hill (marked by the large Physiomed orthopedic clinic). Continue through the traffic light for San Rafael addresses; turn right for the old road to Santa Ana. The trip takes about 20 minutes, much longer during rush hour. A steady stream of buses for Escazú runs from several stops near, but not inside, the Terminal Coca-Cola in San José (Avenidas 1–3, Calles 14–16), with service from 5 am to 11 pm. ⚠ **Be careful: the Coca-Cola neighborhood is a dicey part of downtown San José.**

TAXIS Coopetico. ☎ 2224–7979.

ESSENTIALS

BANKS/ATMS BAC San José. ✉ 200 m south of El Cruce, San Rafael ☎ 309/2295–9797 ⊕ www.bac.net. **Banco de Costa Rica ATM.** ✉ 125 m west of Municipalidad. **Banco Nacional.** ✉ Southwest side of Parque Central ☎ 2228–0009 ⊕ www.bncr.fi.cr.

MEDICAL ASSISTANCE Hospital CIMA. ✉ 12 km (7½ miles) west of downtown San José, next to PriceSmart, just off hwy. to Santa Ana ☎ 2208–1500,

855/782–6253 in North America 🌐 *www.hospitalcima.com.*

PHARMACY Farmacia San Miguel. ✉ *North side of Parque Central* ☎ *2228–2339.*

POST OFFICE Correos. ✉ *100 m north of church* 🌐 *correos.go.cr.*

👁 Sights

Butterfly Kingdom

ZOO | FAMILY | Butterflies are the "livestock" at this working farm in the heart of Escazú, where caterpillars are raised and then exported in chrysalis form. A two-hour tour of the operation takes you through the stages of a butterfly's life. The highlight is the garden where fluttering butterflies surround you. Sunny days fuel the most activity among them; they are quieter if the day is overcast. (The latter conditions make for easier photos.) Bilingual tours in English and Spanish are included in the admission price. ✉ *Bello Horizonte, 1 km (½ mile) south and 100 m west of Distribuidora Santa Bárbara* ☎ *2288–6667* 🌐 *www.butterflykingdom.net* 🎟 *$5.*

Iglesia San Miguel Arcángel (*Church of St. Michael the Archangel*)

RELIGIOUS SITE | According to tradition, ghosts and witches work their spells, good and bad, over Escazú. The founders of this haunted town fittingly chose the archangel Michael, reputed to have driven Satan from heaven, as their patron saint. The original church on this site dates from 1796, but earthquakes took their toll, as they have on so many historic sites throughout Costa Rica. A complete reconstruction was done in 1962, remaining as true as possible to the original design, but up to current earthquake building codes. The results are still impressive six decades later. A statue of St. Michael watches from the left side of the main altar. ✉ *Parque Central* ☎ *2228–0635.*

🍴 Restaurants

Barbecue Los Anonos

$$ | BARBECUE | FAMILY | Costa Ricans flock here to enjoy Los Anonos' family-friendly grill fest. Your best bet is the grilled meat, and there is plenty to choose from, including imported U.S. beef and less expensive Costa Rican cuts. **Known for:** hearty grilled steaks; family-friendly service; reasonably priced weekday lunch specials. [$] *Average main: $14* ✉ *400 m west of Los Anonos Bridge* ☎ *2228–0180* 🌐 *www.restaurantelosanonos.com* 🕑 *No dinner Mon.*

Búlali

$$ | CAFÉ | The name means "honey" in Costa Rica's indigenous Bribri language, and that—rather than refined sugar—provides the added sweetness to the baked goods here. Croissants, quinoa pancakes, and omelets make for filling breakfasts while light beef, chicken, and veggie fare with salads round out the lunch offerings. **Known for:** plenty of gluten-free offerings, a rarity in Costa Rica; fruit and honey smoothies; mouth-watering baked goods. [$] *Average main: $14* ✉ *Avda. Escazú, Autopista Próspero Fernández* ☎ *2519–9090* 🌐 *www.bulaliartesanal.com.*

Gallo Rojo

$$ | ASIAN | An upscale tour of the street food of east and southeast Asia focuses primarily on the owner's mother's native Taiwan, with flavors from Japan, Korea, Vietnam, Thailand, and Singapore mixed in for good measure. The wealth of riches includes *gua bao* (a Taiwanese steamed meat or chicken sandwich), *gyoza* (Japanese-style pork and ginger rolls), pad thai, and Singapore noodles. **Known for:** gastronomic tour of Asia; friendly staff; several gluten-free options. [$] *Average main: $10* ✉ *Escazú* ✥ *100 m east, 300 m north of Centro Comercial El Paco* ☎ *2289–5254* 🌐 *www.gallorojocr.com* 🕑 *Closed Mon.*

★ La Divina Comida

$$$$ | PERUVIAN | The country's top Peruvian restaurant uses fresh local ingredients to recreate Peru's greatest hits, served with style. A variety of ceviches accompany favorites such as aji chicken risotto, grilled octopus in balsamic vinaigrette, or *lomito saltado* (beef tenderloin in tomato sauce). **Known for:** attention to detail; impeccable service; sceney vibe. $ *Average main: $26 ⊠ Avda. Escazú, Autopista Próspero Fernández* ☎ 2208–8899 ⊕ www.ladivinacomidacr.com.

Le Monastère

$$$$ | FRENCH | This monastery-themed formal restaurant high in the hills has a great view of the Central Valley. The dining room is dressed up in antiques, with tables set for a five-course meal, and the classic French dishes are outstanding. **Known for:** impressive French menu; elegant surroundings; other more casual dining options on-site, too. $ *Average main: $29 ⊠ 1½ km (1 mile) southwest of the Paco Shopping Center in San Rafael de Escazú; take old road west to Santa Ana, turn left at Paco and follow signs, always bearing right* ☎ 2228–8515 ⊕ www.lemonasterecr.com ⊗ Closed Sun. No lunch.*

Plaza España

$$$ | SPANISH | Generous portions of Spanish tapas and entrées draw diners to this whitewashed adobe house up the hill near San Antonio de Escazú. Presentation isn't the strong suit here: straight-up good food is, as are reasonable prices. **Known for:** reasonably priced Spanish; friendly, informal setting; mouthwatering sangrias. $ *Average main: $16 ⊠ Del Cruce del Barrio El Carmen, San Antonio de Escazú* ☎ 2228–1850 ⊗ Closed Mon. and Tues. No dinner Sun.*

★ Taj Mahal

$$$ | INDIAN | This burst of northern Indian flavor is a surprising treat. Richly swathed in warm fuchsias, red ochers, and golds, the mansion's dining area sprawls through a handful of small, intimate rooms and out to a gazebo in the tree-covered backyard. **Known for:** great tandoori menu; impressive vegetarian offerings in a mostly meat-devouring country; pleasant, helpful waitstaff. $ *Average main: $20 ⊠ 1 km (½ mile) west of Paco mall on old road to Santa Ana* ☎ 2228–0980 ⊕ www.thetajmahalrestaurant.com.

Hotels

Casa de las Tías

$$ | B&B/INN | The full range of city services is at your doorstep here, but you're blissfully apart from them at this tranquil bed-and-breakfast at the quiet end of a short road. **Pros:** tranquil, without sacrificing convenience; service goes the extra mile; excellent breakfast. **Cons:** walls could be a little thicker; slightly dated feel; no kids under 10. $ *Rooms from: $85 ⊠ 100 m south and 150 m east of El Cruce; turn east just south of Restaurante Carpe Diem* ☎ 2289–5517 ⊕ www.casadelastias.com ⟿ 5 units ❀❀ Free Breakfast.*

Costa Verde Inn

$ | B&B/INN | When they need to make a city run, many beach-living expats head straight for this quiet B&B on the outskirts of Escazú, and it's a good example to follow. **Pros:** inviting public areas; excellent value; friendly staff. **Cons:** large student groups in summer; can be difficult to find; pool is for plungers, not swimmers. $ *Rooms from: $74 ⊠ Escazú ✛ 300 m south of southeast corner of second cemetery (the farthest west)* ☎ 2289–9509, 800/773–5013 ⊕ www.costaverdeinn.com ⟿ 19 rooms ❀❀ Free Breakfast.*

Posada El Quijote

$$ | B&B/INN | Perched on a hill in Escazú's Bello Horizonte neighborhood, with a great view of the city, this B&B strikes the right balance between a small inn and a tasteful private residence. **Pros:**

Costa Rica's oxcarts are folkloric symbols and a common canvas for local artisans.

peaceful, friendly place to spend first or last night; excellent staff; stupendous views. **Cons:** need a car to get around; can be difficult to find; standard rooms not quite as nice. $ *Rooms from: $85* ✉ *1st street west of Anonos Bridge, 1 km (½ mile) up hill, Bello Horizonte* ☎ *2289–8401* ⊕ *www.quijote.cr* ↩ *8 units* ¶◯ *Free Breakfast.*

Nightlife

Escazú is the Central Valley's hot spot for nightlife—many San José residents head here for the restaurants, bars, and dance clubs that cater to a young, smartphone-toting crowd. You can't miss the bright lights as you swing into town off the toll highway.

Henry's Beach Cafe

CAFES—NIGHTLIFE | A popular watering hole with the under-30 set, this spot has televised sports by day, varied music by night, and an island theme of beach paintings and surfboards. Costa Ricans refer to this style of bar as an "American bar," which is fairly accurate. ✉ *Plaza San Rafael, 200 m north of Centro Comercial Paco* ☎ *2289–6239* ⊕ *www.henrysbeachcafe.com.*

Jazz Café Escazú

MUSIC CLUBS | Music fans chill out here. The boxy club hosts an eclectic live-music lineup. ✉ *First exit after tollbooths, next to Confort Suizo, across hwy. from Hospital Cima* ☎ *2288–4740* ⊕ *www. jazzcafecostarica.com.*

La Cava Lounge

BARS/PUBS | The cellar tavern beneath Le Monastère restaurant is a great place to stop for a drink before dinner, or stay on and while the evening away. You can dance to live music on Thursday through Saturday nights. ✉ *1½ km (1 mile) southwest of Paco Shopping Center in San Rafael de Escazú. Take old road west to Santa Ana, turn left at Paco, and follow signs, always bearing right* ☎ *2228–8515* ⊕ *www.lemonasterecr.com.*

Pocket

BARS/PUBS | A great cocktail selection with very smooth gin-tonics is yours at this unassuming place in downtown Escazú. Occasional live music is on the schedule, too. ⊠ *Escazú* ✛ *175 m south of Musmanni bakery* ☎ *2289–3432* ⊕ *www.pocketcr.com.*

Tintos y Blancos

WINE BARS—NIGHTLIFE | Although part of the enormous Multiplaza mall, sophisticated wine bar Tintos y Blancos ("reds and whites," as in wine colors) has its own entrance in back. It offers a quality selection of libations, primarily Chilean and Argentine wines, with several French and Italian to round out the choices. ⊠ *Multiplaza mall, C. Multiplaza* ☎ *2201–5937* ⊕ *www.tintosyblancos.com.*

🛍 Shopping

Escazú's Saturday-morning farmers' market makes a terrific place to stock up on fresh fruit and vegetables if you're preparing a do-it-yourself lunch or just want to snack. Vendors start lining the street on the south side of the church around dawn, and things begin to wind down by late morning. If you get the shopping bug and absolutely must visit a mall while on vacation, Escazú is the place to do it. Multiplaza, on the south side of the toll highway, approximately 5 km (3 miles) west of San José, is Costa Rica's most luxurious mall.

★ Biesanz Woodworks

CRAFTS | Expat artist Barry Biesanz creates unique, world-class items from Costa Rican hardwoods, which are turned (a form of woodworking) on-site. Local artisans also ply their trade here. It's difficult to find, so take a taxi or call for directions from your hotel. ⊠ *Bello Horizonte, 800 m south of Escuela Bello Horizonte* ☎ *2289–4337* ⊕ *www.biesanz. com.*

Congo

CRAFTS | Congo offers a good selection of wood carvings and ceramic bowls and vases made by local artisans. It's a small four-store chain. ⊠ *Avda. Escazú, Autopista Próspero Fernández* ☎ *2201–8017* ⊕ *www.costaricacongo.com.*

Multiplaza

SHOPPING CENTERS/MALLS | Costa Rica's most upscale mall—think Kenneth Cole, Giorgio Armani, Oscar de la Renta, and many of their Costa Rican counterparts—looms over the highway with its 194 stores between Escazú and Santa Ana. ⊠ *Caldera Hwy., between Escazú and Santa Ana* ☎ *4001–7999* ⊕ *www. multiplaza.com.*

🏃 Activities

HIKING

High in the hills above Escazú is the tiny community of **San Antonio de Escazú,** famous for its annual oxcart festival held the second Sunday of March. The view from here—of nearby San José and distant volcanoes—is impressive by both day and night. If you head higher than San Antonio de Escazú, brace yourself for seemingly vertical roads that wind up into the mountains toward **Pico Blanco,** the highest point in the Escazú Cordillera, which is a half-day hike to ascend. You can also hike **San Miguel,** one peak east. We recommend you go with an outfitter—far safer than hiking on your own.

Aventuras Picotours

HIKING/WALKING | The owner of Aventuras Picotours was the first Costa Rican to reach the summit of Everest; he can lead you on a variety of far less daunting daylong hikes in the hills above town. ⊠ *From Church of San Antonio de Escazú, 300 m east, 1,800 m south, and 50 m east* ☎ *8880–2676* ⊕ *www.picotours.com* 🎫 *Tours from $59.*

Santa Ana

17 km (10 miles) southwest of San José.

Santa Ana's tranquil town center, with its rugged stone church, has changed little through the years, even though condos and shopping malls now spread out in all directions. The church, which was built between 1870 and 1880, has a Spanish-tile roof, carved wooden doors, and two pre-Columbian stone spheres flanking its entrance. Its rustic interior—bare wooden pillars and beams and black iron lamps—seems appropriate for an area with a tradition of ranching. Because it's warmer and drier than the towns to the east, Santa Ana is one of the few Central Valley towns that doesn't have a good climate for coffee. (It is Costa Rica's onion capital, however.) Though development encroaches every year—Santa Ana is well on its way to becoming another Escazú—you can still find pastures and patches of forest around the area; it isn't unusual to see men on horseback here.

GETTING HERE AND AROUND

From San José, turn left at the western end of Paseo Colón, which ends at the Parque La Sabana. Take the first right, and get on the highway. Get off at the sixth exit; bear left at the flashing red lights, winding past roadside stands selling ceramics and vegetables before hitting the town center, about 2 km (1 mile) from the highway. The trip takes about 25 minutes if there's little traffic. Blue buses to Santa Ana leave from inside San José's Terminal Coca-Cola every 8-10 minutes during the day. ⚠ **Be careful: the Coca-Cola area is a dodgy part of downtown San José.** To get to places along the toll highway or Piedades, take buses marked "Pista" or "Multiplaza." Those marked "Calle Vieja" leave every 15 minutes and pass through Escazú on the old road to Santa Ana. Buses run from 5 am to 11 pm.

ESSENTIALS

BANKS/ATMS Banco de Costa Rica. ✉ *Northwest corner of central park* ☎ *2203–4281* 🌐 *www.bancobcr.com.* **Banco Nacional.** ✉ *100 m south of church* ☎ *2282–2479* 🌐 *www.bncr.fi.cr.*

MEDICAL ASSISTANCE Clínica Bíblica. ✉ *Autopista Próspero Fernández* ☎ *2522–1000* 🌐 *www.clinicabiblica.com.* **Farmacia Sucre.** ✉ *25 m south of church* ☎ *2282–1296.*

POST OFFICE Correos. ✉ *Next to Municipalidad* 🌐 *correos.go.cr.*

👁 Sights

Refugio Animal

ZOO | **FAMILY** | This former "herpetology refuge" between Santa Ana and Escazú has opened its doors to more than just snakes: macaws, monkeys, and crocodiles reside here, too. As with all such facilities around Costa Rica, the ultimate goal is to release animals back into the wild. But for many, their fragile condition means they will live out their days here. ✉ *Santa Ana* ✣ *2 km (1 mile) east of Santa Ana on old road to Escazú* ☎ *2282–4614* 🌐 *www.refugioanimalcr.com* 🎫 *$20* 🕒 *Closed Mon.*

🍴 Restaurants

Andiamo Là

$$$ | **ITALIAN** | One of the Central Valley's trendiest restaurants stands out with its daily fish and meat specials, including starter carpaccios of salmon, octopus, and beef. The sea bass and jumbo shrimp combination plate comes with a sauce of chopped fresh tomatoes, white wine, and garlic. **Known for:** delicious homemade pastas; terrific-value lunch specials; polished, friendly service. [$] *Average main: $21* ✉ *Next to Más X Menos supermarket* ☎ *2282–7879* 🌐 *www.andiamola.com* 🕒 *No dinner Sun.*

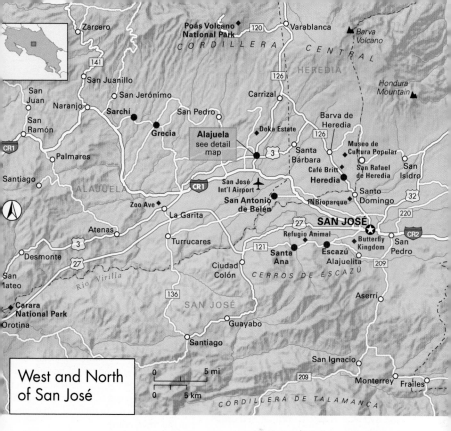

West and North
of San José

Bacchus

$$$ | ECLECTIC | Take a Peruvian chef who trained in France and an Italian owner, and the result is this solid member of the local dining scene. Duck breast in a port sauce, baked mushroom-and-polenta ragout, and a variety of pizzas are among the delights to be found on the menu. **Known for:** impressive French and Italian menu; extensive wine list; elegant setting with modern art and garden terrace. $ *Average main: $19* ⊠ *200 m east and 100 m north of church* ☎ *2282–5441* ⊘ *Closed Mon.*

 Hotels

Hotel Alta

$$$ | HOTEL | The view from this hotel perched on a hillside above Santa Ana is impressive, but so is the building itself with its blend of colonial and modern

style—think archways, hardwoods, and leather. **Pros:** classy service; panoramic views; excellent value for the price. **Cons:** lower-floor rooms lose out on the view; little to do within walking distance; best to have a car to stay here. $ *Rooms from: $180* ⊠ *2½ km (1½ miles) west of Paco shopping center, on old road between Santa Ana and Escazú, Alto de las Palomas* ☎ *2103–4990, 888/388–2582 in North America* ⊕ *www.thealtahotel. com* ⇨ *23 rooms* ⦿ *Free Breakfast.*

★ Hotel Villa Los Candiles

$$ | HOTEL | You'd never expect to find such a quiet, homey oasis smack-dab in the middle of a suburban business neighborhood, but here it is. **Pros:** attentive staff; suites have kitchenettes; pet-friendly. **Cons:** can be difficult to find; hot water sometimes takes time to heat up; middle of busy commercial area.

[$] *Rooms from: $95* ✉ *350 m east, 25 m south of Más X Menos supermarket* ☎ *2282–8280* 🌐 *www.hotelvillaloscandiles.com* 💳 *No credit cards* 🛏 *28 rooms* 🍴 *Free Breakfast.*

Nightlife

As metro-area development marches west, a few nightspots have set up shop out here, too.

Costa Rica's Craft Brewing Company
BREWPUBS/BEER GARDENS | One of the pioneers of the country's nascent microbrewery industry has set up shop west of Santa Ana, serving two year-round ales and several seasonal ones. They make a nice change from the ubiquitous Imperial beer. ✉ *Santa Ana* ✥ *200 m south of Parques del Sol* ☎ *2249–4277* 🌐 *www.facebook.com/lacraftcr.*

Latitud 9
GATHERING PLACES | This stylish bar serves good cocktails in a sleek, modern setting with indoor and outdoor seating. DJs take over after 9 on weekend nights. ✉ *City Place* ✥ *200 m north of Red Cross* ☎ *4035–3111* 🌐 *www.facebook.com/latitud9lounge.*

MAD Burger & Beer
BARS/PUBS | These folks make some of the country's best burgers, served to the accompaniment of a good selection of beer and other drinks. ✉ *Santa Ana Town Center* ✥ *100 m east of Red Cross* ☎ *4700–1888* 🌐 *www.facebook.com/madbarcr.*

Tap House
BARS/PUBS | This low-key, mostly local place serves up 30 types of beer—domestic and imported—with the requisite selection of chicken wings, nachos, and other appetizers. ✉ *City Place* ✥ *200 m north of Red Cross* ☎ *2100–8447* 🌐 *www.facebook.com/TapHouseCR.*

Shopping

Cerámica Las Palomas
CERAMICS/GLASSWARE | Large glazed pots with ornate decorations that range from traditional patterns to modern motifs are the specialties here. Flowerpots and lamps are also common works, and the staff will happily show you the production process, from raw clay to art. ✉ *Old road to Santa Ana, opposite Hotel Alta* ☎ *2282–7001* 🌐 *www.ceramicalaspalomas.webs.com.*

Grecia

26 km (16 miles) northwest of Alajuela, 46 km (29 miles) northwest of San José.

The quiet farming community of Grecia—the name means "Greece" in Spanish—is reputed to be Costa Rica's cleanest town, and some enthusiastic civic boosters extend that superlative to all of Latin America, but the reason most people stop here is to admire its unusual church. A growing number of expats now call the town home.

GETTING HERE AND AROUND

From San José continue west on the highway past the airport—the turnoff is on the right—or head into Alajuela and turn left just before the Alajuela cemetery. Buses leave Calle 20 in San José for Grecia every 30 minutes from 5:30 am to 10 pm. From Alajuela, buses to Grecia/Ciudad Quesada pick up on the southern edge of town (Calle 4 and Avenida 10).

ESSENTIALS

BANKS/ATMS BAC San José. ✉ *100 m north of central park* ☎ *2295–9696* 🌐 *www.bac.net.* **Banco Nacional.** ✉ *Northwest corner of central park* ☎ *2444–0690* 🌐 *www.bncr.fi.cr.*

Sights

Church of Our Lady of Mercy (*Iglesia de Nuestra Señora de las Mercedes*)
RELIGIOUS SITE | This brick-red Gothic-style church is made of prefabricated iron. It's one of two buildings in the country made from steel frames and iron sheets imported from Belgium in the late 19th century (the other is the metal schoolhouse next to San José's Parque Morazán), when some prominent Costa Ricans decided that metal structures would better withstand the periodic earthquakes that had taken their toll on so much of the country's architecture. The frames were shipped from Antwerp to Limón, then transported by train to Alajuela—from which the metal walls of the church were carried by oxcarts. Locals refer to the building as simply the "Iglesia Metálica" (Metal Church). The splendid 1886 German pipe organ, regarded as Costa Rica's finest, is worth a look inside. ⊠ *Avda. 1, Cs. 1–3* ☎ *2494–1616.*

Shopping

★ **Feria del Agricultor**
OUTDOOR/FLEA/GREEN MARKETS | Grecia's covered weekend farmers' market is one of Costa Rica's liveliest and best. It runs Friday afternoon and evening until 9—fairy lights sparkle during the evening hours—and starts up again at 5 the next morning, winding down around noon. Fresh produce is yours for the buying and, if you time it right, homemade tortillas and cinnamon rolls too. ⊠ *Grecia* ✛ *200 m west of Tribunales de Justicia* ☎ *2494–7360.*

Sarchí

8 km (5 miles) west of Grecia, 53 km (33 miles) (1½ hrs) northwest of San José.

Tranquil Sarchí is Costa Rica's premier center for crafts and carpentry. People drive here from all over the country to shop for furniture, and tour buses regularly descend upon the souvenir shops outside town. The area's most famous products are its brightly painted oxcarts—replicas of those traditionally used to transport coffee. Sarchí, as Costa Rica's consummate day-trip destination, has developed little acceptable lodging of its own. There are plenty of places to stay, however, in the nearby communities (San Ramón, Atenas, and Alajuela).

GETTING HERE AND AROUND
To get to Sarchí from San José, take the highway well past the airport to the turnoff for Naranjo; then veer right just as you enter Naranjo. Direct buses to Sarchí depart from Alajuela (Calle 8, Avenidas 1–3) every 30 minutes from 6 am to 9 pm; the ride takes 90 minutes.

ESSENTIALS
BANK/ATM Banco Nacional. ⊠ *South side of soccer field* ☎ *2454–3044* ⊕ *www.bncr.fi.cr.*

POST OFFICE Correos. ⊠ *South side of soccer field* ⊕ *correos.go.cr.*

Sights

Else Kientzler Botanical Garden (*Jardín Botánico Else Kientzler*)
GARDEN | FAMILY | Some 2,000 plant species, tropical and subtropical, flourish on 17 acres here, and all are well-labeled. The German owner named the facility, affiliated with an ornamental-plant exporter, after his late plant-loving mother. About half of the garden's pathways are wheelchair accessible. When the tropical fruit trees are in season, visitors are permitted to pick and eat the fruit. Kids enjoy the maze and playground. ⊠ *400 m north of soccer field* ☎ *2454–2070* ⊕ *www.elsegarden.com* ☞ *$6.*

★ **La Carreta**
LOCAL INTEREST | The world's largest oxcart, constructed and brightly painted by longtime local factory Souvenirs Costa Rica and enshrined in the *Guinness Book*

of World Records can be found in Sarchí's central park. The work—locals refer to it as simply La Carreta (the Oxcart)—logs in at 45 feet and weighs 2 tons. Since no other country is attached to oxcarts quite like Costa Rica, we doubt that record will be broken anytime soon. Oxcarts were used by 19th-century coffee farmers to transport the all-important cash crop to the port of Puntarenas on the Pacific coast. Artisans began painting the carts in the early 1900s. Debate continues as to why: The kaleidoscopic designs may have symbolized the points of the compass, or may have echoed the land-scape's tropical colors. In any case, the oxcart has become the national symbol. ⊠ *Center of Sarchí, central park.*

Mariposas Sarchí

ZOO | FAMILY | This small butterfly garden makes a nice break from Sarchí's ubiquitous shopping. Your admission price includes the services of a knowledgeable guide who will fill you in on all the butterfly trivia, both fun and scientific. ⊠ *Sarchí ✛ 150 m west of northwest corner of Parque Central* ☎ *8622–9027* ⊕ *www. facebook.com/sarchimariposas* 🖃 *$5.*

Souvenirs Costa Rica (*Taller Eloy Alfaro e Hijos*)

FACTORY | Costa Rica's only real remaining oxcart factory was founded in 1920, and its carpentry methods have changed little since then. The guiding spirit of founder Eloy Alfaro lives on here, but the business and tradition have passed onto subsequent generations of his family. The two-story wooden building housing the wood shop is surrounded by trees and flowers—mostly orchids—and all the machinery on the ground floor is powered by a waterwheel at the back of the shop. Carts are painted in the back, and although the factory's main products are genuine oxcarts—which sell for up to $2,500—there are also some smaller mementos that can easily be shipped home. A cavernous restaurant serves food, buffet-style. ⊠ *Sarchí ✛ 200*

m north of soccer field ☎ *2454–4131* ⊕ *www.souvenirscostarica.com.*

 Restaurants

Restaurante La Finca

$ | COSTA RICAN | This is a good place to stop for lunch when you need a break from shopping, with a variety of steaks, spicy chorizos, *arroz con pollo* (rice and chicken), and soups—we recommend the maize soup—on the menu. You might not expect it in this mix, but the pizza is pretty good, too. **Known for:** hearty tico food; nice variety of pizza; popular with tour groups. 🖺 *Average main: $9* ⊠ *Down road at turnoff next to Plaza de Artesanía* ☎ *2454–1602* ⊕ *www.restaurantelafin-casarchi.com* ☾ *No dinner.*

Shopping

Sarchí is the best place in Costa Rica to buy miniature oxcarts, the larger of which are designed to serve as patio bars or end tables and can be broken down for easy transportation or shipped to your home. Another popular item is a locally produced rocking chair with a leather seat and back.

★ Chaverrí Oxcart Factory (*Fábrica de Carretas*)

CRAFTS | In the nicest of the many stores south of town, you can wander through the workshops and see the artisans in action. Despite the name, offerings extend well beyond oxcarts, and Chaverrí is a good place to buy wooden crafts of all kinds. Chaverrí also runs a restaurant next door, Las Carretas, which serves a variety of local food all day until 6 pm and has a good lunch buffet. ⊠ *Main Rd., 2 km (1 mile) south of Sarchí* ☎ *2454–4411* ⊕ *www.carretaschaverri.com.*

Plaza de la Artesanía

SHOPPING CENTERS/MALLS | Sarchí's answer to a shopping mall gathers a dozen artisan and souvenir shops under one roof. Expect to find oxcarts, the town's

En Route

Zarcero The central park of this small, tidy town 15 km (9 miles) north of Sarchí on the road to Ciudad Quesada looks as if it were designed by Dr. Seuss. Evangelista Blanco, a local landscape artist, modeled cypress topiaries in fanciful animal shapes— motorcycle-riding monkeys, a lightbulb-eyed elephant—that enliven the park in front of the town church. (An NPR feature on Zarcero once dubbed Blanco "Señor Scissorhands.") Soft lighting illuminates the park in the evening. The church interior is covered with elaborate pastel stencil work and detailed religious paintings by the late Misael Solís, a well-known local artist. Sample some cheese if you're in town, too; Zarcero-made cheese is one of Costa Rica's favorites, and it's available in a few shops on the west side of the central park. The town is frequently included as a short stop on many organized tours heading to the northern region of the country. ⊠ *Zarcero.*

signature symbol, and everything else imaginable. If you can't find it here, it probably doesn't exist in Costa Rica. ⊠ *2 km (1 mile) south of Sarchí, Sarchí Sur.*

Carara National Park

43 km (27 miles) southwest of Atenas, 85 km (53 miles) southwest of San José.

In the wilderness of Carara National Park and surroundings, you might encounter white-faced capuchin monkeys in the trees or crocodiles lounging on a riverbank. The region is extremely biologically diverse, making it an excellent destination for bird-watchers and other wildlife enthusiasts.

GETTING HERE AND AROUND

Take Highway 27 west of San José beyond Orotina and follow the signs to Jacó and Quepos. The reserve is on the left after you cross Río Tárcoles. From San José, you can hop on a bus to Jacó, Quepos, or Manuel Antonio, and ask to be dropped off near the park entrance, about a two-hour drive. An organized tour is far easier. Jacó is the nearest town and the most logical base for trips into the park. Local travel agencies and tour operators arrange transportation to and guides through the park.

⚠ **Cars parked at the trailhead have been broken into. If you don't see a ranger on duty at the Sendero Laguna Meandrica trailhead, avoid leaving anything of value in your vehicle. You may be able to leave your belongings at the main ranger station (several miles south of the trailhead), where you can also buy drinks and souvenirs and use the restroom. Otherwise, visit the park as a day trip from a nearby hotel.**

TOURS

Horizontes

ECOTOURISM | The country's premier nature-tour operator can arrange visits to Carara National Park as a day trip from San José or as part of a longer tour. ☎ *4052–5850, 888/786–8748 in North America* ⊕ *www.horizontes.com* ⊠ *From $45.*

Jaguar Riders

SPECIAL-INTEREST | This Jacó-based tour operator can arrange guided ATV tours through the forests of Carara National Park. ⊠ *Avda. Pastor Díaz, next to Pancho Villa restaurant, Jacó* ☎ *2643–0180* ⊕ *www.jaguariders.com* ⊠ *From $69.*

Sights

Carara National Park (*Parque Nacional Carara*)

NATURE PRESERVE | Sparse undergrowth here makes wildlife easier to see than in most other parks, although proximity to major population centers means that tour buses arrive regularly in high season, prompting some animals to head deeper into the forest. Come very early or late in the day to avoid the crowds. Bird-watchers can call the day before to arrange admission before the park opens. If you're lucky, you may glimpse armadillos, basilisk lizards, coatis, and any of several monkey species, as well as birds such as blue-crowned motmots, chestnut-mandibled toucans, and trogons. A network of trails takes 15 minutes to four hours to navigate. (Many of the trails are wheelchair accessible.) The park has guides, but you must arrange their services in advance. Camping is not permitted. *For more information, see the highlighted listing in this chapter.* ✉ *East of Costanera, just south of bridge over Río Tárcoles, Orotina* ☎ *2637–1080, 1192 national park hotline* 🎫 *$10.*

San Antonio de Belén

17 km (10 miles) northwest of San José.

San Antonio de Belén has little to offer visitors but its rural charm and proximity to the international airport. The latter led developers to build several of the San José area's biggest hotels here. The country's sole Church of Jesus Christ of Latter-day Saints temple is also found here, open only to visitors of the faith. The town is a convenient departure point for trips to the western Central Valley, Pacific coast, and northern region. If you stay at any of the big hotel chains here, you likely won't even see the town, just the busy highway between San José and Alajuela.

GETTING HERE AND AROUND

From San José, turn right at the west end of Paseo Colón onto the Pan-American Highway (Carretera General Cañas). The San Antonio de Belén exit is at an overpass 6 km (4 miles) west of the Heredia exit, by the Real Cariari Mall. Turn left at the first intersection, cross over the highway, and continue 1 km (½ mile) to the forced right turn, driving 1½ km (1 mile) to the center of town. San Antonio is only 10 minutes from the airport.

ESSENTIALS

BANK/ATM Banco de Costa Rica. ✉ *50 m north of rear of church, San Antonio* ☎ *2239–1149* 🌐 *www.bancobcr.com.*

MEDICAL ASSISTANCE Farmacia Sucre. ✉ *North side of church, San Antonio* ☎ *2293–9160.*

POST OFFICE Correos. ✉ *3 blocks west and 25 m north of church, San Antonio* 🌐 *correos.go.cr.*

TAXIS Taxi Belén. ☎ *2293–3300.*

Hotels

Costa Rica Marriott Hacienda Belén

$$$$ | **HOTEL** | **FAMILY** | The stately Marriott offers comprehensive luxury close to the airport, and, despite being a U.S. chain, has many distinctively Costa Rican touches. **Pros:** excellent service; lavish grounds; close to airport. **Cons:** tendency to nickel-and-dime guests; tricky car access from highway; far from all sights. [$] *Rooms from: $305* ✉ *Nearly 1 km (½ mile) west of Bridgestone/Firestone, off Autopista General Cañas, San Antonio* ☎ *2298–0000, 800/535–4028 in North America* 🌐 *www.marriott.com* 🛏 *300 rooms* 🍴 *No meals.*

El Rodeo Estancia

$$ | **HOTEL** | This quiet hotel bills itself as a "country hotel," though this is more in image than fact—El Rodeo's proximity to the airport and major business parks is the real draw. **Pros:** proximity to airport; spacious rooms; popular steak house restaurant. **Cons:** generic feel; cat on premises, so not a place to go if you dislike felines. [$] *Rooms from: $85* ✉ *Road to Santa Ana, 2 km (1 mile) east of Parque Central, San Antonio* ☎ *2293–3909* 🌐 *www.elrodeohotel.com* 🛏 *29 rooms* 🍴 *Free Breakfast.*

Alajuela

20 km (13 miles) northwest of San José.

Because of its proximity to the international airport (5–10 minutes away), many travelers spend their first or last night in or near Alajuela (pronounced *ah-lah-WHAY-lah*), but the beauty of the surrounding countryside persuades some to stay longer. Alajuela is Costa Rica's second-most-populated city, and a mere 30-minute bus ride from the capital, but it has a decidedly provincial air compared with San José. Architecturally, it differs little from the bulk of Costa Rican towns: it's a grid of low-rise structures painted in dull pastel colors. A slightly lower elevation keeps Alajuela a couple of degrees warmer than the capital.

GETTING HERE AND AROUND

To reach Alajuela, head west on the highway past the San Antonio de Belén turnoff and turn right at the airport (watch for the overhead signs). Buses travel between San José (Avenida 2, Calles 12–14, opposite north side of Parque La Merced), the airport, and Alajuela, and run every five minutes from 4:40 am to 10:30 pm. The bus stop in Alajuela is 400 meters west, 25 meters north of the central park (Calle 3 and Avenida 1). Buses leave San José for Zoo Ave from La Merced church (Calle 14 and Avenida 4) daily on the hour from 8 am to noon, returning on the hour from 10 am to 3 pm.

TAXIS Cootaxa. ☎ *2443–3030.*

ESSENTIALS

BANKS/ATMS BAC San José. ✉ *100 m north of cathedral* ☎ *2295–9797* 🌐 *www.bac.net.* **Banco de Costa Rica.** ✉ *50 m west of southwest corner of central park* ☎ *2440–9039* 🌐 *www.bancobcr.com.* **Banco Nacional.** ✉ *West side of central park* ☎ *2441–0373* 🌐 *www.bncr.fi.cr.*

HOSPITAL Hospital San Rafael. ✉ *1 km (½ mile) northeast of airport, on main road to Alajuela* ☎ *2436–1001.*

MEDICAL ASSISTANCE Farmacia Chavarría. ✉ *C. 4, Avdas. 1–Ctl.* ☎ *2441–1231.*

POST OFFICE Correos. ✉ *Avda. 5, C. 1* 🌐 *correos.go.cr.*

👁 Sights

Alajuela Cathedral (*Catedral de Alajuela*)
RELIGIOUS SITE | The large neoclassical Alajuela Cathedral has columns topped by interesting capitals decorated with local agricultural motifs, and a striking red metal dome. Construction was completed in 1863. The interior is spacious but rather plain, except for the ornate cupola above the altar. ✉ *C. Ctl., Avdas. 1–Ctl.* ☎ *2443–2928.*

★ **Doka Estate**
FARM/RANCH | The Central Valley is coffee country. Consider devoting an hour of your vacation to learning about the crop's production. Doka Estate, a working coffee plantation for more than 70 years, offers a comprehensive tour that takes you through the fields, shows you how the fruit is processed and the beans are dried, and lets you sample the local brew. The best time to take this tour is during the October-to-February picking season. Transportation can be arranged from San José, Alajuela, Heredia, Escazú, or San Antonio de Belén. Various add-on packages include breakfast and/or lunch. Doka features on many organized area tours in combination with various other Central Valley attractions. ✉ *10 km (6 miles) north of Alajuela's Tribunales de Justicia,*

Sabanilla ✥ Turn left at San Isidro and continue 6 km (4 miles), follow signs ☎ 2449–5152, 888/946–3652 in North America 🌐 www.dokaestate.com 🎟 $25.

Museo Juan Santamaría (*Juan Santamaría Museum*)
JAIL | The heroic deeds of Juan Santamaría are celebrated in this museum housed in the old jail, on the north side of Parque Central. It's worth a quick look if you have the time; Santamaría's story is an interesting one. A pleasant café inside is a great place to stop for a coffee. ✉ *Avda. 3, Cs. Ctl.–2* ☎ *2441–4775* 🌐 *www.museojuansantamaria.go.cr* 🎟 *Free* 🕒 *Closed Mon.*

Parque Central
CITY PARK | Royal palms and massive mango trees fill Alajuela's central park—residents frequently refer to the park as the Parque de los Mangos—which also has a lovely fountain imported from Glasgow and concrete benches where locals gather to chat. The futuristic gazebo at the center of the park is a bit of an eyesore. Surrounding the plaza is an odd mix of charming old buildings and sterile concrete boxes. ✉ *C. Ctl., Avdas. 1–Ctl.*

Zoo Ave
ZOO | **FAMILY** | Spread over lush grounds, the zoo has a collection of large cages holding toucans, hawks, parrots, and free-ranging macaws as part of a breeding project for rare and endangered birds, all of which are destined for eventual release. It has 115 bird species, including such rare ones as the quetzal, fiery-billed aracari, several types of eagles, and even ostriches. An impressive mural at the back of the facility shows Costa Rica's 850 bird species painted to scale. Wingless animals include crocodiles, caimans, a boa constrictor, turtles, monkeys, wildcats, and other interesting critters. A botanical garden rounds out the offerings here. Unfortunately, exhibits are labeled in Spanish only. ✉ *La Garita de Alajuela* ✥ *Head west from Alajuela center past cemetery, turn left after stone church in Barrio San José, continue for 2 km (1 mile); or head west on Pan-American Hwy. to Atenas exit, then turn right* ☎ *2433–8989* 🌐 *www.rescateanimalzooave.org* 🎟 *$20.*

🍴 Restaurants

Bar y Restaurante El Mirador
$$ | **ECLECTIC** | Perched on a ridge several miles north of town, El Mirador has a sweeping view of the Central Valley that is impressive by day but more beautiful at dusk and after dark. Get a window table in the dining room, or one on the adjacent porch if it isn't too cool. **Known for:** stunning views of Central Valley; lomito (tenderloin) in variety of sauces; friendly service. [$] *Average main: $13* ✉ *Road to Poás, 5 km (3 miles) north of Tribunales de Justicia* ☎ *2441–9347.*

Jalapeños Central
$$ | **MEXICAN** | Tasty, hearty, filling Tex-Mex food and a gregarious owner make this basic downtown joint a great place for lunch or dinner. Everybody seems to know everybody else here—this is a favorite hangout among the area's expat community—and you'll be welcome, too. **Known for:** great fajitas; friendly service; fun dining atmosphere. [$] *Average main: $13* ✉ *150 m north of cathedral* ☎ *2430–4027.*

🛏 Hotels

Buena Vista Hotel
$$ | **HOTEL** | **FAMILY** | Perched high above Alajuela, this hotel's superb staff make up for the somewhat dated, uninspired interior, and it does have the "good view" it is named for, although most rooms overlook the lawns or pool area. **Pros:** excellent service; family-friendly; great views from some rooms. **Cons:** mediocre restaurant; farther from the airport than other options; best to have a car to stay here. [$] *Rooms from: $130* ✉ *Road to Poás, 6 km (4 miles) north of Alajuela's Tribunales de Justicia*

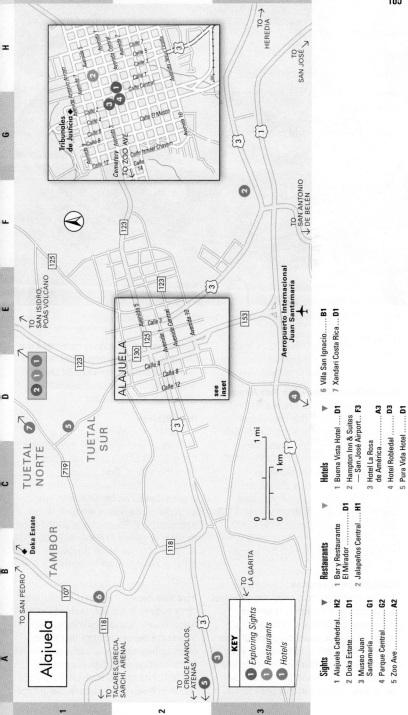

Alajuela

TO TACARES, GRECIA, SARCHÍ, ARENAL

TO SAN PEDRO

TAMBOR

◆ Doka Estate

TUETAL NORTE

TUETAL SUR

TO SAN ISIDRO POÁS VOLCANO

ALAJUELA

see inset

Avenida 5
Avenida 3
Avenida Central
Avenida 10

Calle 4
Calle 8
Calle 12

Aeropuerto Internacional Juan Santamaría

TO SAN ANTONIO DE BELÉN

TO HEREDIA

TO SAN JOSÉ

TO LA GARITA

Tribunales de Justicia ◆

Cemetery
TO ZOO AVE

Calle 7
Calle 5
Calle 3
Calle 1
Calle Central
Calle 2
Calle 4
Calle 6
Calle 8
Calle 12

Avenida Antonio Arroyo
Avenida 5
Avenida 7
Avenida Central
Avenida 3
Avenida José María Zeledón
Avenida 1
Avenida 3
Avenida 10

Calle El Mesón
Calle Ismael Chavern
Calle 14

KEY

1 Exploring Sights
1 Restaurants
1 Hotels

0   1 km
0   1 mi

Sights

1 Alajuela Cathedral.... **H2**
2 Doka Estate............. **D1**
3 Museo Juan
Santamaría............. **G1**
4 Parque Central......... **G2**
5 Zoo Ave.................. **A2**

Restaurants

1 Bar y Restaurante
El Mirador **D1**
2 Jalapeños Central.... **H1**

Hotels

1 Buena Vista Hotel **D1**
2 Hampton Inn & Suites
— San José Airport.. **F3**
3 Hotel La Rosa
de América............. **A3**
4 Hotel Robledal **D3**
5 Pura Vida Hotel **D1**
6 Villa San Ignacio...... **B1**
7 Xandari Costa Rica ... **D1**

Alajuela Cathedral's painted domed cupola was rebuilt after the 1991 earthquake.

☎ 2442–8605, 855/877–3732 in North America ⊕ www.hotelbuenavistacr.com ⇨ 22 rooms ❖ Free Breakfast.

Hampton Inn & Suites – San José Airport

$$ | **HOTEL** | A longtime favorite for first- and last-night stays, this chain hotel lets you ease into and out of Costa Rica in familiar surroundings. **Pros:** airport proximity; U.S. amenities; friendly staff. **Cons:** some noise from planes in the evening; sameness of a chain hotel; as with all airport hotels, your stay here may be very short. $ *Rooms from:* $129 ✉ Blvd. del Aeropuerto ☎ 2436–0000, 877/461–1402 in North America ⊕ www. hamptoninn.hilton.com ⇨ 100 rooms ❖ Free Breakfast.

Hotel La Rosa de América

$$ | **HOTEL** | **FAMILY** | This small hotel tucked off the road to La Garita is a simple and relaxed place to unwind, with its owners adding a welcoming energy and a personalized touch to the place. **Pros:** great for families; helpful owners; close to a number of restaurants. **Cons:** lacks flair of other options in this price range;

best to have a car to stay here; far from all sights. $ *Rooms from:* $98 ✉ 1 km (½ mile) east of Zoo Ave ☎ 2433–2741 ⊕ www.larosadeamerica.com ⇨ 16 rooms ❖ Free Breakfast.

Hotel Robledal

$$ | **HOTEL** | A *robledal* is an oak grove in Spanish, and ample oak trees shade the grounds of this quiet oasis not far from the airport. **Pros:** attentive service; good Costa Rican restaurant; free airport shuttle. **Cons:** can be difficult to find; a couple of the rooms are dark; small bathrooms. $ *Rooms from:* $105 ✉ 400 m west of Iglesia El Roble ☎ 2438–3937, 812/962–4386 in North America ⊕ www. hotelrobledal.com ⇨ 15 rooms ❖ Free Breakfast.

Pura Vida Hotel

$$ | **B&B/INN** | Extremely well-informed, helpful owners and proximity to the airport (15 minutes) make this a good place to begin and end a trip, and thanks to its location on a ridge north of town, several of its rooms have views of Poás Volcano. **Pros:** owners active in the local

community; stellar breakfast; attentive service. **Cons:** large dogs may turn off those with less-than-fuzzy feelings for animals; stairs to climb; best to have a car to stay here. $ *Rooms from: $120* ✉ *Tuetal, 2 km (1 mile) north of Tribunales de Justicia; veer left at Y intersection* ☎ *2430–2929* ⊕ *www.puravidahotel.com* ☞ *6 units* ❙❍❙ *Free Breakfast.*

Villa San Ignacio

$$ | **B&B/INN** | **FAMILY** | The friendly Villa San Ignacio, with its classy Spanish-style architecture, proves that affordable does not have to equal generic. **Pros:** spirited environment; great for first or last night; excellent service. **Cons:** roadside rooms can be noisy, opt for garden rooms; pet friendly; can be difficult to find. $ *Rooms from: $95* ✉ *2½ km (1½ miles) northwest of the Princesa Marina* ☎ *2433–6316* ⊕ *www.villasanignacio.com* ☞ *16 rooms* ❙❍❙ *Free Breakfast.*

★ Xandari Costa Rica

$$$$ | **HOTEL** | The tranquil and colorful Xandari is a strikingly original inn and spa, tailor-made for honeymooners and romantic getaways. **Pros:** ideal setting for romance; guilt-free gourmet delights; eco-friendly, including on-site nature reserve. **Cons:** some noise from other rooms; should have car to stay here; far from any sights. $ *Rooms from: $281* ✉ *5 km (3 miles) north of Tribunales de Justicia* ⊕ *Turn left after small bridge, follow signs* ☎ *2443–2020, 866/363–3212 in North America* ⊕ *www.xandari.com* ☞ *24 villas* ❙❍❙ *Free Breakfast.*

🛍 Shopping

City Mall

SHOPPING CENTERS/MALLS | Central America's largest shopping mall weighs in at 330 stores and is most notable for its indoor snow-themed amusement park. ✉ *Radial Francisco J. Orlich* ☎ *4200–5100* ⊕ *www.citymall.net.*

Goodlight Books

BOOKS/STATIONERY | One of Costa Rica's largest used-book stores stocks around 9,000 volumes, and a huge number of those are in English. It's also a great place to hang out for coffee and baked goods. ✉ *100 m north and 300 m west of La Agonía church* ☎ *2430–4083.*

Heredia

4 km (3 miles) north of Santo Domingo, 11 km (6 miles) northwest of San José.

The lively city of Heredia, capital of the important coffee province of the same name, contains a couple of the country's best-preserved colonial structures, along with a contrasting, youthful buzz provided by the National University (UNA) and century-old *colegios* (high schools) scattered around the town. Heredia is nicknamed the City of Flowers (La Ciudad de Flores, in Spanish), which refers less to the flowers that decorate the city than to a leading founding family named Flores. Flores also refers to beautiful women, for which Heredia is known. (On the topic of names, remember that "h" is always silent in Spanish; pronounce the small city's name *air-AY-dee-ah.*) Founded in 1706, the city bears witness to how difficult preservation can be in an earthquake-prone country; most of its colonial structures have been destroyed by tremors and the tropical climate, not to mention modernization. Still, the city and neighboring towns retain a certain historic flavor, with old adobe buildings scattered amid the concrete structures. Nearby Barva is also notable for its colonial central square and venerable adobe structures. From Heredia, scenic mountain roads climb northeast, passing through the pleasant, high-altitude coffee towns of San Rafael and San Isidro, each anchored by a notable, tico-style Gothic church and a pleasant central park.

The verdant Central Valley is Costa Rica's breadbasket.

GETTING HERE AND AROUND

The narrow routes from San José to Heredia are notoriously clogged at almost all times; avoid them during rush hours if possible—and realize that you may encounter traffic jams at other times of the day, too. Turn right at the west end of Paseo Colón. Follow the Pan-American Highway 2 km (1 mile); take the second exit, just before the highway heads onto an overpass and just after the Hotel Irazú (on the right). To get to the center of Heredia, follow that road for 5½ km (3½ miles), being careful to note which direction traffic in the alternative middle lane is traveling, then turn left at the Universidad Nacional.

Buses run between San José (300 meters east of Hospital San Juan de Dios) and Heredia every 5 to 10 minutes daily, between 5 am and 10 pm. The steady stream of buses leaving from Calle 1, Avenidas 7–9 every three to five minutes, passing through Santo Domingo, is sometimes a better bet during rush hour—particularly the *directo* buses

that start after 3:30 pm (these buses also run from midnight to 3:30 am on the hour). Better still, hop aboard the new, modern train, departing San José from the vintage Atlantic Station, on the north side of the Parque Nacional, and arriving in downtown Heredia 30 minutes later. Trains run every half hour on weekdays from 5:30 to 8 am, then 3:30 to 7:30 pm—geared more toward the needs of workaday commuters than tourists—and the fare is about $0.95. If you're without a car, a taxi is the best way to get to Café Britt or Barva.

ESSENTIALS

BANKS/ATMS BAC San José. ⊠ *Paseo de las Flores* ☎ *2295–9797* ⊕ *www. bac.net.* **Banco Nacional.** ⊠ *25 m south of southwest corner of Parque Central* ☎ *2277–6900* ⊕ *www.bncr.fi.cr.*

PHARMACY Farmacia Chavarria. ⊠ *South side of Parque Central* ☎ *2263–4668* ⊕ *www.facebook.com/ farmaciachavarriaexpress.*

POST OFFICE Correos. ✉ *Avda. Ctl., Cs. Ctl.–2, northwest corner of Parque Central* ⊕ *correos.go.cr.*

Sights

★ Café Britt
FARM/RANCH | The producer of Costa Rica's most popular export-quality coffee gives a lively Classic Coffee Tour highlighting the history of Costa Rica's coffee cultivation through a theatrical presentation that is admittedly a bit hokey. Your "tour guides" are professional actors, and pretty good ones at that, so if you don't mind the song and dance, it's fun. (You might even be called upon to participate.) During the 1½-hour tour, you'll take a short walk through the coffee farm and processing plant, and learn how professional coffee tasters distinguish a fine cup of java. A two-hour Coffee Lovers tour delves into the process at a more expert level. You can also stop in at its Coffee Bar and Factory Store. Although both tours are devoted entirely to the production and history of Costa Rica's most famous agricultural product, Britt is also a purveyor of fine chocolates, cocoas, cookies, macadamia nuts, and coffee liqueurs; you'll see its products for sale in souvenir shops around the country and at the airport as you leave. The coffee tour is often a half-day inclusion on many Central Valley tours operated by San José tour companies. ✉ *Heredia* ✛ *From Heredia, take road to Barva, follow signs* ☎ *2277–1600, 800/462–7488 in North America* ⊕ *www.coffeetour.com* ✑ *From $26.*

Costa Rica Meadery
WINERY/DISTILLERY | Costa Rica's climate sadly doesn't allow for wine grapes to flourish, but crafty brewers have discovered perhaps the next best thing: mead, which is created by fermenting honey with water. This farm is the first and currently only meadery in the country, with the mead's honey coming directly from the farm's nearby beehives and other local beekeepers. The meads are flavored with a variety of tropical fruits and flowers, including passion fruit and hibiscus. Book ahead to enjoy one- or two-hour tours of the farm, hives, and production facility, all ending with a tasting. You can also just visit the tasting room for a half-hour tasting, accompanied by honey and cheeses (advanced reservations are still required). They occasionally host dinners too. The meadery proudly practices environmentally sound, socially equitable, and econonically viable sustainability. ✉ *The Ark Herb Farm, Calle La Sabaneta, Santa Bárbara de Heredia* ✛ *800 m north of Escuela Rosales* ☎ *8718–4094* ⊕ *www.costaricameadery.com* ✑ *Tour $25.*

Fortín (*Little Fort*)
BUILDING | On the north side of the Parque Central in its own little park stands a strange tower. Built as a military post in the 1870s. It never did see action and now serves as the symbol of the province, one of the few military monuments in this country without an army. The tower is closed to the public. The old brick building next to the Fortín is the Palacio Municipal (Town Hall). ✉ *C. Ctl., Avda. Ctl.*

Iglesia de la Inmaculada Concepción
(*Church of the Immaculate Conception*)
RELIGIOUS SITE | On the east side of the park stands this impressive neoclassical church that locals refer to as simply "La Inmaculada." It was built between 1797 and 1804 to replace an adobe temple dating from the early 1700s and is one of the few structures in Costa Rica remaining from the colonial era. The flat-fronted, whitewashed church has thick stone walls, small windows, and squat buttresses, which have kept it intact through two centuries of earthquakes and tremors. The serene, white interior has two rows of stately, gold-trimmed Ionic columns marching down a long aisle, past 20 lovely stained-glass windows constructed in France. The

church is flanked by tidy side gardens, where you can stroll among sculpted trees along concrete paths incised with a floral pattern. The church's soft exterior illumination brightens up the park nightly from 6 pm until midnight. ⊠ *Eastern side of Parque Central* ☎ *2237–0779.*

Mercado Nuevo (*New Market*)
MARKET | Three blocks southeast of the Parque Central is Heredia's covered New Market—that's how everybody refers to it here—officially the Mercado Central, which holds dozens of *sodas* (simple restaurants) along with the usual food stands and vendors supplying the day-to-day needs of the average Costa Rican. While generally safe, the crowded conditions here do invite the occasional pickpocket. Watch your possessions. ⊠ *C. Ctl., Avda. 6.*

Museo de Cultura Popular (*Museum of Popular Culture*)
MUSEUM | At the edge of a middle-class neighborhood between Heredia and Barva, this museum is housed in a farmhouse with a large veranda built in 1885 using an adobe-like technique called *bahareque.* Run by the National University, the museum is furnished with antiques and surrounded by a garden and a small coffee farm. Just walking around the museum is instructive, but calling ahead to reserve a hands-on cultural tour (such as one on tortilla making) really makes it worth the trip. An open-air restaurant serves bread baked in a clay oven, and fresh tortillas and tamales. The museum is officially open only on Sunday, but can be visited other days of the week by prior arrangement. ⊠ *Heredia* ✛ *From Musmanni bakery in Santa Lucía de Barva, go 100 m north, then turn right for 1 km (½ mile); follow signs* ☎ *2260–1619* ⊕ *www.museo.una. ac.cr* 🎟 *$2* ⊘ *Closed Mon.–Sat.*

★ **Parque Central**
CITY PARK | Heredia is centered on tree-studded Parque Central, which gets our vote for the country's loveliest and liveliest central park, surrounded by some notable buildings spanning more than 250 years of history. The park has a large, round, cast-iron fountain imported from England in 1879 and a Victorian bandstand where the municipal band plays on Sunday morning and Thursday night. Families, couples, and old-timers sit on park benches, shaded by fig and towering palm trees, often inhabited by noisy and colorful flocks of crimson-fronted parakeets. Drop into Pops, a national ice-cream chain, at the south side of the park and pick up a cone, then take a seat on a park bench and watch the passing parade. ⊠ *C. Ctl., Avda. Ctl.*

San Rafael de Heredia
TOWN | This quiet, tidy coffee town 2 km (1 mile) northeast of Heredia has a large church notable for its stained-glass windows and bright interior. The road north from the church winds its way up Barva Volcano, ending atop the Monte de la Cruz lookout point. ⊠ *San Rafael de Heredia.*

★ **Toucan Rescue Ranch**
ZOO | One of Costa Rica's many animal-rescue facilities, Toucan Rescue Ranch is a great place to see wildlife. There are more than just toucans—the good-hearted folks here care for many sloths and owls, too. The ultimate goal is to return the animals to the wild; the frail condition of some means that this will be their permanent home. The general 2½-hour walk focuses on observing the facility's work with toucans and sloths. Tickets must be purchased in advance on the facility's website. ⊠ *San Josecito* ☎ *2268–4041* ⊕ *www.toucanrescueranch.org* 🎟 *From $62* ⊘ *Closed Sun.*

Continued on page 196

Picking coffee beans from plant

COFFEE, THE GOLDEN BEAN

Tour a working coffee plantation and learn about the product that catapulted Costa Rica onto the world's economic stage, built the country's infrastructure, and created a middle class unlike any other in Central America.

Costa Rica B.C. (before coffee) was a poor, forgotten little colony with scant infrastructure and no real means of making money. Coffee production changed all of that and transformed the country into one of the wealthier and most stable in Central America. Coffee remains Costa Rica's bread and butter—the industry employs one-fourth of Costa Rica's population full- or part-time—and coffee plantations are sprinkled throughout the Central Valley and Northern Lowlands. All cultivate fine Arabica beans (by government decree, the inferior Robusta variety is not grown here). Visit one and learn what makes the country tick.

By Jeffrey Van Fleet

HISTORY IN A CUP

Coffee plantations near Poás Volcano, Central Valley

The country's first leaders saw this new crop as a tool with which to engineer a better life for their people. After gaining independence, new laws were created to allow average Costa Ricans to become coffee-growing landowners. These farmers formed the foundation of a middle-class majority that has long distinguished the country from the rest of Latin America. Costa Rica's infrastructure, institutional organizations, and means of production quickly blossomed—young entrepreneurs established small import-export houses, growers banded together to promote a better infrastructure, and everyone plowed their profits into improving the country's primitive road system.

SOCIAL TRANSFORMATION

As the coffee business became more profitable, prominent families were sending their children abroad to study, and doctors, lawyers and other skilled professionals in search of jobs began arriving by the boat-

DRINKING THE GOOD STUFF

Here's the kicker for you, dear coffee-loving visitor: it's tough to find a decent cup in Costa Rica. True to the realities of developing-country economics, the good stuff goes for export, leaving a poorer quality bean behind for the local market. Add to that that the typical household here makes coffee with heaps of sugar. Your best bet for a good cup is an upscale hotel or restaurant, which is attuned to foreign tastes and does use export-quality product. The decorative foil bags you see in souvenir shops and supermarkets are also export-quality and make terrific souvenirs.

COFFEE TIMELINE

Local workers harvesting coffee beans in 1800s

1720	Coffee arrives in New World.
1791	Coffee plants introduced to Costa Rica.
1820	First coffee exports go to Panama.
1830	Legislation paves way for coffee profits to finance government projects.
1860	Costa Rican coffee first exported to United States.
1890	Atlantic Railroad opens, allowing for easier port access.

Enjoying a cup of coffee in Montezuma, Nicoya Peninsula

load. Returning students and well-educated immigrants brought a new world view that contributed to the formation of Costa Rica's liberal ideology.

MODERN TIMES

Development gobbled up land in the Central Valley by the last half of the 20th century, and coffee production began to spread to other areas of the country. A worldwide slump in coffee prices in the 1990s forced many producers out of the business. Prices have risen since 2002, and the government looks to smooth out any fluctuations with added-value eco-certification standards and innovative marketing.

Today, some 70% of the country's *número uno* agricultural crop comes from small family properties of under 25 acres owned by 250,000 farmers. They seasonally employ more than four times that number of people, and kids in rural areas still take class time off to help with the harvest.

CAFÉ CHEAT SHEET

café solo: black

con azúcar: with sugar

con crema: with cream

con leche: with milk

descafeinado: decaffeinated (not easy to find here)

grano entero: whole beans

grano molido: ground

tostado claro or tueste claro: light roast

tostado oscuro or tueste oscuro: dark roast

Oxcarts built in the early 1900s to transport coffee

1897	Coffee barons construct San José's ornate Teatro Nacional.
1992	Costa Rica adopts new environmental laws for coffee industry.
1997	Tourism displaces coffee as Costa Rica's top industry.
Today	Costa Rica turns to eco-certification and fair-trade marketing of coffee.

COSTA RICA'S BEAN COUNTRY

Coffee plantations from Cervantes to Orosi Central Valley

Monteverde

Puerto Viejo de Sarapiquí

La Virgen

Cariari

Tilarán

Monteverde Coffee Tour

La Fortuna

San Miguel

Bagaces

Don Juan Coffee Tour

Ciudad Quesada

Cinchona

Guápile

Santa Elena

CORDILLERA DE TILARÁN

San Ramón

Doka Coffee Estate

GUANACASTE

Atenas

Café Britt

TRES RÍOS

Santa Cruz

Nicoya

Isla Chira

VALLE OCCIDENTAL

Alajuela

Tamarindo

Puntarenas

Orotina

SAN JOSÉ

Cartago

OR

Nosara

Carmona

Ojical

Caldera

TARRAZÚ

Or

Sámara

Punta Islita

Paquera

Tárcoles

VALLE CENTRAL

San Marcos

San Gerar de Dota

Carrillo

Tambor

Cobano

Jacó

Parrita

Mal País

Montezuma

Quepos

0 — 30 miles
0 — 45 km

Cabo Blanco

Dominic

Costa Rica possesses all the factors necessary—moderately high altitude, mineral-rich volcanic soil, adequate rainfall but distinct rainy and dry seasons—to be a major coffee player. Costa Rican growers cultivate only Arabica coffee beans. The industry eliminated the inferior Robusta variety in 1989 and hasn't looked back. The Costa Rican Coffee Institute certifies eight regional coffee varieties.

The coffee-growing cycle begins in April or May, when rains make the dark-green bushes explode in a flurry of white blossoms. By November, the fruit starts to ripen, turning from green to red. The busy harvest begins as farmers race to get picked "cherries" to beneficios (processing mills), where beans are removed, washed, machine-dried, and packed in burlap sacks either for export or to be roasted for local consumption.

Coffee plantations, Central Valley

❶ Aficionados wax poetic about the beans that come from **Tarrazú,** the high-altitude Los Santos Region in the Southern Pacific. It has good body, high acidity, and a chocolaty flavor.

❷ Coffee grown in **Tres Ríos,** east of San José, has high acidity, good body, and a nice aroma.

❸ Altitude of the **Valle Central** (around San José, Heredia and Alajuela) affects the size and hardness of the coffee bean and can influence certain components, particularly the acidity. This is an important characteristic of Arabica coffee.

❹ **Valle Occidental,** in the prosperous western Central Valley, gives you hints of apricots and peaches.

Arabica coffee beans

Coffee beans · Coffee bean pickers · Hand picking Coffee beans

Coffee plant

PLANTATIONS WITH TOURS

Wonder where your cup of morning coffee originates? The following purveyors give informative tours of their facilities and acquaint you with the life and times of the country's favorite beverage.

Tours guide you through the plant-to-crop process in English or Spanish, taking you from picking to drying to roasting to packing to brewing.

Reservations are essential. Plan on spending a half-day for any of these outings. The whole package will set you back about $30 per person.

CAFÉ BRITT Barva, Heredia Café Britt incorporates a small theater production into its informative tour, presenting the history of Costa Rican coffee in song and dance.

COOPEDOTA SANTA MARIA Santa Maria de Dota A tour here acquaints you with the standard bean-to-bag experience, as well as the cooperative's pioneering environmental practices.

DOKA COFFEE ESTATE San Luis de Sabanilla, Alajuela Doka Coffee Estate offers a comprehensive tour through the entire growing and drying process and lets you sample the local brew.

DON JUAN COFFEE TOUR Monteverde A personalized excursion with a small group is the hallmark of this tour to a coffee plantation a few miles outside the town of Santa Elena.

MONTEVERDE COFFEE TOUR Monteverde Monteverde Coffee offers you some hands-on experience. Depending on the time of year, you can help with picking, drying, roasting, or packing.

❺ Tasters describe **Orosi** coffee, from the southeastern Central Valley, as "floral."

❻ The lower altitudes of nearby **Turrialba** give its product a medium body.

❼ The high-altitude **Brunca** region, near San Vito in southern Costa Rica, produces coffee with excellent aroma, good body, and moderate acidity.

❽ **Guanacaste** is a diverse region that includes Monteverde and the central Nicoya Peninsula. Here they produce a medium-body coffee.

Restaurants

Bromelias del Río

$$ | COSTA RICAN | This simple garden dining spot in the far northern Central Valley makes a great breakfast stop if you're on your way to the Caribbean. Fortify yourself with the *tradicional* (gallo pinto, eggs, bread, and coffee) or *americano* (ham, eggs, bacon, toast, and juice) breakfasts. **Known for:** hearty, filling breakfasts; good value; coffee drinks. $ *Average main: $11* ⊠ *San Isidro de Heredia* ✣ *North side of Parque Central* ☎ *2268–8445* ⊕ *www.facebook.com/cafeteriayrestaurantebromeliasdelrio* ⊗ *No dinner.*

L'Antica Roma

$$ | ITALIAN | More than 40 versions of pizza baked in a wood-burning oven are the main event at this popular upscale Italian eatery. Every pizza comes with a trio of condiments to spice it up to your taste: homemade hot chili or a garlicky sauce, and grated cheese. **Known for:** impressive pizza variety; quality homemade pastas; pleasant outdoor patio for evening dining. $ *Average main: $12* ⊠ *C. 7, Avda. 7, across from Hotel Valladolid* ☎ *2262–9073.*

Hotels

★ Finca Rosa Blanca Coffee Plantation Resort

$$$ | B&B/INN | Set amid fields of green coffee, this exclusive, hilltop B&B hideaway has a much-deserved reputation as one of the country's sumptuous splurges. **Pros:** eco-consciousness; indulgence with style; service par excellence. **Cons:** some units short on closet and drawer space; expensive restaurant; hard to find if you are driving your own car. $ *Rooms from: $250* ⊠ *800 m north of Café Britt Distribution Center, Santa Bárbara de Heredia* ☎ *2269–9392, 305/395–3042 in North America* ⊕ *www.fincarosablanca.com* ⇆ *14 suites* ⊗ *Free Breakfast.*

Hotel Hojarascas

$ | HOTEL | The entrance here resembles any other storefront downtown, and you could pass right by without noticing this quiet, family-run gem. **Pros:** good value for what is offered; attentive owner; great service. **Cons:** can hear a bit of noise from the hallway; access can be difficult in your own vehicle because of street congestion; difficult parking. $ *Rooms from: $72* ⊠ *Avda. 8, Cs. 4–6* ☎ *2261–3649* ⊕ *www.hotelhojarascas.com* ⇆ *15 units* ⊗ *Free Breakfast.*

Hotel Valladolid

$$ | HOTEL | The classiest hotel in downtown Heredia, this four-story narrow building attracts business travelers and visiting professors at the nearby National University, although guests are just as likely to be vacationers. **Pros:** central location; friendly staff; extensive buffet breakfast with homemade tortillas. **Cons:** limited parking; a few rooms show their age; on slightly steep hill if walking. $ *Rooms from: $87* ⊠ *C. 7, Avda. 7* ☎ *2260–2905* ⊕ *www.hotelvalladolid.net* ⇆ *12 rooms* ⊗ *Free Breakfast.*

⬣ Shopping

Feria

OUTDOOR/FLEA/GREEN MARKETS | On Saturday morning starting at 5, Heredia's open-air *feria*, a lively farmers' market, stretches for almost a kilometer (½ mile) along Avenida 14. Things start to wind down around noon. ⊠ *Avda. 14.*

Paseo de Las Flores

SHOPPING CENTERS/MALLS | This airy, pleasant, and huge shopping mall with 320 stores is on the main road south of town. It has a branch of almost every international fashion boutique, as well as a multiplex cinema and a wide choice of cafés and restaurants. ⊠ *2 km (1 mile) south of town on hwy. to San José* ☎ *2261–9898* ⊕ *www.paseodelasflores.com.*

En Route

Barva de Heredia About 3 km (2 miles) due north of Heredia, this colonial town is famous for mask-making and for its **Parque Central**, still with the original adobe buildings with Spanish-tile roofs on three sides, and a white-stucco church to the east. The park is filled with whimsical sculptures, including a park bench shaped like an entire seated family, and bizarre masks and clown's heads decorating garbage receptacles. An amphitheater and stage stand ready for the annual mask festival held every August. (A less pleasant part of the August festival is the tradition of smacking one's fellow townspeople with cow or pig bladders—perhaps *not* a good time to visit.) The stout, handsome church with terra-cotta bas-relief flourishes dates from the late 18th century and has a lovely grotto shrine to the Virgin Mary in the church garden. On a clear day you can see verdant Volcán Barva towering to the north. ⊠ *3 km (2 miles) north of Heredia, Barva.*

Sibö Chocolate

FOOD/CANDY | Get to know a bean of another kind during a private tasting at the workshop of the country's best artisanal chocolate makers. It starts with an informative talk about the historical and cultural significance of the cacao bean, includes a demonstration of tempering chocolate by hand, and ends, of course, with a sampling of exquisite chocolates made from 100% organic cacao. Tasters can also stay for an elegant lunch on Sibö's pretty terrace. Reserve 48 hours in advance. ⊠ *Heredia ✛ Turnoff for San Isidro de Heredia, 1½ km (1 mile) off hwy. to Braulio Carrillo National Park* ☎ *2268–1335* ⊕ *www.sibuchocolate.com.*

Poás Volcano National Park

37 km (23 miles) (45 mins) north of Alajuela, 57 km (35 miles) (1 hr) north of San José.

Arenal may be Costa Rica's most famous volcano, but you can peer right into the crater here at Poás—from the vantage point of an observation platform. That gives it an edge in the "cool volcano visit" department.

GETTING HERE AND AROUND

From the Pan-American Highway north of Alajuela, follow the signs for Poás. The road is in relatively good condition. One public bus departs daily at 8 am from San José (Avenida 2, Calles 12–14) and returns at 2 pm. Taxis from San José are around $100 (and around $50 from Alajuela). A slew of tours from San José take in the volcano and combine the morning excursion with an afternoon at La Paz Waterfall Gardens, or with tours of Café Britt near Heredia or the Doka Estate near Alajuela.

 Sights

La Paz Waterfall Gardens

BODY OF WATER | **FAMILY** | Five magnificent waterfalls are the main attractions at these gardens on the eastern edge of Volcán Poás National Park, but they are complemented by the beauty of the surrounding cloud forest, an abundance of hummingbirds and other avian species, and the country's biggest butterfly garden. A concrete trail leads down from the visitor center to the multilevel, screened

La Paz Waterfall Gardens attracts 24 different species of hummingbirds and has a huge butterfly garden.

butterfly observatory and continues to gardens where hummingbird feeders attract swarms of these multicolor creatures. Other exhibits are devoted to frogs and snakes. The trail then enters the cloud forest, where it leads to a series of metal stairways that let you descend into a steep gorge to viewing platforms near each of the waterfalls. A free shuttle will transport you from the trail exit back to the main building if you prefer to avoid the hike uphill. Several alternative paths lead from the main trail through the cloud forest and along the river's quieter upper stretch, providing options for hours of exploration—it takes about two hours to hike the entire complex. (Enter before 3 pm to give yourself adequate time.) The complex's Jungle Cat exhibit serves as a rescue center for felines (jaguars, ocelots, and pumas). The visitor center has a gift shop and open-air cafeteria with a great view. The gardens are a stop on many daylong tours from San José that take in the Poás Volcano or area coffee tours. The complex is especially busy on weekends. ⊠ *6 km (4 miles) north of Vara Blanca, Poás Volcán National Park* 🕾 *2482–2720, 954/727–3997 in North America* ⊕ *www.waterfallgardens.com* 🎫 *From $48.*

★ Poás Volcano National Park (*Parque Nacional Volcán Poás*)

NATIONAL/STATE PARK | This is widely regarded as Costa Rica's coolest volcano experience. An observation platform lets you peer right inside what is thought to be the largest active volcanic crater in the world. The ride up here is disarming: pleasant farms and lush green cloud forest line the volcano's slopes; friendly fruit and jam vendors along the road beckon you to stop and sample their wares. Only when you get to the bubbling, gurgling, smoking summit do you leave those pastoral scenes behind and stare into the crater.

It's wise to step away from the crater and its fumes for fresh air at least once every 10 minutes, and a good place to take that break is the park's bustling visitor center—the country's best—with complete park information, a cafeteria, and a gift shop. The volcano features prominently on many itineraries of area tour operators. Increased volcanic activity in recent years, notably during 2019, forces periodic closure of the park. Check conditions before heading up here on your own. *For more information, see the highlighted listing in this chapter.* ✉ *Poás Volcán National Park* ✣ *From Alajuela, drive north through town and follow signs* ☎ *2482–2424, 1192 national park hotline* 🎫 *$15.*

Restaurants

Freddo Fresas

$$ | **COSTA RICAN** | *Fresas* means "strawberries," and they're the star at this rustic wooden place on the way to the volcano. They end up on your corn pancakes, in juices, as desserts, or as sides to the variety of típico dishes here. **Known for:** tortillas aliñadas (huge corn tortillas with cheese and cream); piping hot coffee; strawberry everything. [$] *Average main: $10* ✉ *Poás Volcán National Park* ✣ *200 m north of Fraijanes cemetery* ☎ *2482–2800* 🌐 *www.facebook.com/freddofresas* 🕒 *No dinner.*

Restaurante Chubascos

$$ | **COSTA RICAN** | Dine amid tall pines and colorful flowers on the upper slopes of Poás Volcano. There's a small menu of traditional Tico dishes that includes platters of *gallos* (homemade tortillas with meat, cheese, or potato filling) as well as delicious daily specials. **Known for:** terrific Tico cooking; refreshing fruit drinks; pleasant countryside setting. [$] *Average main: $11* ✉ *1 km (½ mile) north of Laguna de Fraijanes, Poás Volcán National Park* ☎ *2482–2280* 🌐 *www.facebook.com/chubascos.co.cr* 🕒 *Closed Tues. No dinner.*

Hotels

Peace Lodge

$$$$ | **HOTEL** | These rooms overlooking the misty forests of La Paz Waterfall Gardens seem like something out of the *Lord of the Rings,* with their curved, clay-stucco walls, hardwood floors, stone fireplaces, four-poster beds made of varnished logs, and grotto-like bathrooms with private waterfalls. **Pros:** many activities, plus admission to the Waterfall Gardens, included in rates; whimsical furnishings; excellent river trail. **Cons:** pricey; popular with tour groups; all but the top floors can be a bit noisy because of creaky stairs. [$] *Rooms from: $400* ✉ *6 km (4 miles) north of Vara Blanca, Poás Volcán National Park* ☎ *2482–2720, 954/727–3997 in North America* 🌐 *www.waterfallgardens.com* 🛏 *18 units* 🍴 *No meals.*

★ **Poás Volcano Lodge**

$$$ | **B&B/INN** | Stylish luxury prevails here: king-size beds, outdoor whirlpool tubs, and luxurious fabrics grace the rooms and many have balconies overlooking the volcano. **Pros:** close to volcano; coffeemakers and electric teakettles in rooms; great breakfasts. **Cons:** hotel is often fully booked; a bit pricey; best to have a car to say here. [$] *Rooms from: $190* ✉ *4 km (2½ miles) east of Churrasco restaurant, on road to Vara Blanca, Poás Volcán National Park* ☎ *2482–2194* 🌐 *www.poasvolcanolodge.com* 🛏 *12 rooms* 🍴 *Free Breakfast.*

Shopping

Volcán Poás National Park Visitor Center

GIFTS/SOUVENIRS | The park's visitor center has a well-stocked shop that sells nature-themed T-shirts, cards, and posters. A portion of the profits goes to support conservation projects. ✉ *Poás Volcán National Park* ☎ *2482–2424.*

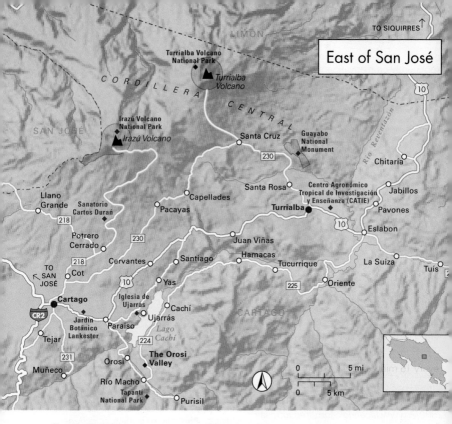

Cartago

22 km (14 miles) southeast of San José.

Although most of its structures from the colonial era are gone, Cartago still has some attractive restored buildings, most of them erected after the devastating 1910 earthquake. The city served as the country's first capital until 1823, when the seat of government was moved to the emerging economic center of San José. Today, Cartago is a bustling market town, 900 feet higher in elevation and a few degrees cooler than San José. Most visitors see Cartago on their way to or from the Orosi Valley or Turrialba, and there is little reason (or place) to stay the night. The Orosi Valley, a short drive away, has better lodging choices. A couple of interesting sights warrant a half day if you're out this way, however.

GETTING HERE AND AROUND

For the 25-minute drive from San José, drive east on Avenida 2 through San Pedro and Curridabat to the toll highway entrance, where you have three road options—take the middle one marked Cartago. Shortly before Cartago, a Y intersection marks the beginning of the route up Irazú, with traffic to Cartago veering right.

Buses between San José and Cartago leave every 10 minutes daily (Avenida 10 and Calle 5, 400 meters south of the Teatro Nacional) from 5 am to 6 pm; after 6 the buses leave from Avenida 2 between Calles 1–3, in front of the National Theater. Cartago buses to San José pick up 300 meters west of the Municipal Museum of Cartago (formerly called the Comandancia), from 4:35 am to 11 pm. Buses to Orosi leave Cartago

Bulls dressed in their finest for an oxcart parade in Cartago

every 15 minutes from 5:15 to 7:30 am, then every 30 minutes until 7 pm, with a bus at 8 and 9 pm, 100 meters east, 25 meters south of the southeast corner of Las Ruinas.

TAXIS Taxis El Carmen. ☎ 2551–4646.

ESSENTIALS

BANKS/ATMS BAC San José. ⊠ 100 m south of Ruinas ☎ 2295–9797 ⊕ www. bac.net. **Banco Nacional.** ⊠ Southeast corner of Las Ruinas ☎ 2550–1400 ⊕ www. bncr.fi.cr.

HOSPITAL Hospital Dr. Max Peralta. ⊠ 200 m south, 150 m west of Las Ruinas ☎ 2550–1999. **Hospital Universal.** ⊠ 400 m south of Las Ruinas ☎ 4052–5700 ⊕ www.hospitaluniversal.com.

PHARMACY Farmacia Fischel. ⊠ 300 m west of Basílica de Nuestra Señora de los Angeles ☎ 2552–2430.

POST OFFICE Correos. ⊠ Avda. 2, Cs. 15–17.

◉ Sights

Basílica de Nuestra Señora de los Angeles
(*Our Lady of the Angels Basilica*)
RELIGIOUS SITE | Cartago's major tourist sight is a hodgepodge of architectural styles from Byzantine to baroque, with a dash of Gothic thrown in. The interior of this 1926 basilica is striking, with a colorful tile floor, intricately painted, faux-finish wood columns, and lots of stained glass. Tradition holds that an apparition of the Virgin Mary in the form of a dark stone occurred here in 1635. This "Black Virgin" (La Negrita) is Costa Rica's patron saint, and she sits high above the main altar. To the left as you face the altar is a room decorated with amulets given in dedication to the Virgin for her intercession in everything from triumphs over disease to triumphs on the soccer field. ⊠ C. 16, Avdas. 2–4, 7 blocks east of central square ☎ 2551–0465 ⊕ www.santuarionacional.org.

Cartago's Basilica de Nuestra Señora de los Angeles is the focus of the annual pilgrimage to celebrate the appearance of La Negrita, the Black Virgin.

Irazú Volcano National Park (*Parque Nacional Volcán Irazú*)
VOLCANO | Costa Rica's highest volcano, at 11,260 feet, is one of the most popular with visitors, since you can walk right down into the crater. Its presence is a mixed blessing: the ash fertilizes the Central Valley soil, but the volcano has caused considerable destruction through the centuries. ⚠ **Do not leave anything of value in your car while you visit the volcano. There have been a lot of thefts in the parking lot here, even though it is supposed to be guarded.** Most San José and area tour operators include the volcano among their excursions, and this is the easiest way to visit. *For more information, see the highlighted listing in this chapter.* ✉ *Irazú Volcano National Park* ☎ *2200–5025, 1192 national park hotline* 💲 *$15.*

Las Ruinas
ARCHAEOLOGICAL SITE | Churches in one form or another stood at the site of the present-day central park from 1575 to 1841; they kept being knocked down by earthquakes and reconstructed again

and again. After a major earthquake in 1841, the citizens of Cartago began work on a new, Romanesque cathedral. But a devastating earthquake in 1910 ended that project, too. Is there a connection between building churches on this spot and the occurrence of earthquakes? No one knows, but townspeople have decided not to tempt fate any longer. Among the many legends attributed to the ruins is the gruesome story of the priest who, after falling in love with his sister-in-law, was murdered by his brother. Folks here say his headless ghost still haunts the grounds at night. ✉ *Avda. 2, Cs. 1–2* 💲 *Free.*

Sanatorio Carlos Durán (*Carlos Durán Sanatorium*)
HOSPITAL—SIGHT | These ruins of a former sanatorium were featured on the Syfy TV series *Ghost Hunters International* and have acquired cult status among visitors interested in paranormal phenomena. The complex sits just off the highway on the way to the Irazú Volcano and functioned as Costa Rica's hospital for

tuberculosis patients from 1918 to 1973. The institution bears the name of its physician-founder, who also served as the country's president in the late 19th century. The attendant who takes your admission can provide some information, but you're essentially on a self-guided visit here. Most of the alleged spectral sightings are of the nuns who cared for the patients, with a few visitors claiming to see images in their photos they didn't notice when they were snapping pictures. Other visitors don't see anything but claim to hear what they assume are the nuns' voices. We can't promise you'll spot any ghosts, but don't let that spoil the intrigue. Your greatest risk here is likely natural, rather than supernatural: the outdoor walkways get slippery on rainy days. Tread carefully. ✣ *Prusia de Cartago, 18 km southeast of Irazú volcano, 8 km north of Cartago* ☎ *2240–3016 in San José* 🎟 *$3.*

🍴 Restaurants

Although you can find decent pasta and pizza, haute cuisine just doesn't exist here. Cartago does give you a fine opportunity to eat some *comida típica* (typical food). On just about any street downtown you'll find a soda, and the women in the kitchen will serve you the same style of food they cook at home for their own families. One rule of thumb: the busier, the better—the locals know where to eat well.

La Puerta del Sol

$$ | COSTA RICAN | A cut above the usual soda, this large, long-established restaurant across from the basilica has been feeding pilgrims for seven decades. Along with hearty portions of seafood, grilled meats, and typical casados, the restaurant has a popular bar and terrace. **Known for:** ample servings; decent dining in a town that generally lacks it; good view of the basilica. [$] *Average main: $10* ✉ *North side of basilica plaza* ☎ *2551–0615* 🌐 *www.facebook.com/restaurantlapuertadelsol.*

Restaurant 1910

$$ | COSTA RICAN | The menu here at this upscale countryside spot is predominantly Costa Rican, with such traditional specialties as *trucha* (trout) and rice with chicken, along with some more sophisticated dishes, like *corvina* (sea bass) fillet with a coconut-liqueur sauce. The Sunday típico buffet is a great introduction to Costa Rican cooking. **Known for:** variety of trout dishes; pleasant rural setting; vintage photo exhibit. [$] *Average main: $11* ✉ *Road to Parque Nacional Volcán Irazú, 300 m north of Cot–Pacayas turnoff, Irazú Volcano National Park* ☎ *2536–6063* 💳 *No credit cards* 🕒 *No dinner Sun.*

🚴 Activities

CYCLING

The hills around Cartago make fertile training ground for Costa Rica's small but passionate Olympic cycling team.

San José Urban Adventures

BICYCLE TOURS | A six-hour tour, beginning and ending in San José, takes you by train to Cartago, followed by a cycling jaunt around town. ☎ *2208–3838* 🌐 *www.sanjoseurbanadventures.com.*

The Orosi Valley

45 km (28 miles) southeast of San José.

If you have a day to spend near San José, this idyllic valley makes a classic day trip, passing through coffee plantations shaded by poró trees—their flame-color flowers make a stunning sight during the dry season—oceans of chayote-squash vines, and small towns backed by verdant landscapes, with countless breathtaking views. It's a popular weekend drive for Costa Ricans, but still relatively off the beaten tourist path. The region is one of the few areas in Costa Rica that has remnants (ruins and churches) of the 17th-century Spanish colonial era. Paraíso, the valley's not-so-interesting metropolis, is your first point of access. Heading counterclockwise around the loop road are the area's real gems: Orosi, Tapantí National Park, Cachí, and Ujarrás.

GETTING HERE AND AROUND

A good road makes a loop around the valley, and it's easy to take in all the sights along the circle if you have your own vehicle, or if you go on a guided tour—it's a staple of most San José tour operators' offerings. Buses to the town of Orosi leave Cartago every 15 minutes from 5:15 to 7:30 am, then every 30 minutes until 7 pm, with a bus at 8 and 9 pm, 100 meters east and 25 meters south of the southeast corner of Las Ruinas. Public transportation around the valley is tricky: buses travel clockwise and counterclockwise, but neither route completes the circle.

ESSENTIALS

BANKS/ATMS Banco Nacional. ⊠ *200 m south of soccer field, Orosi* ☎ *2533–1390* ⊕ *www.bncr.fi.cr.*

PHARMACIES Farmacia Candelaria. ⊠ *North side of Restaurante Coto, across from soccer field, Orosi* ☎ *2533–1919.*

POST OFFICE Correos. ⊠ *100 m north of Municipalidad, Paraíso* ⊕ *correos.go.cr.*

Sights

Iglesia de San José de Orosi (*Church of San José de Orosi*)
RELIGIOUS SITE | The town of Orosi, in the heart of the valley, has but one major sight: this beautifully restored 1743 church, the country's oldest house of worship still in use, and one of the few structures in Costa Rica remaining from the colonial era. Set in a garden, against a green mountainside, it has a classic Spanish colonial whitewashed facade and bell tower, with a roof made of cane overlaid with terra-cotta barrel tiles. Inside are an antique wooden altar and

ancient paintings of the Stations of the Cross and the Virgin of Guadalupe, all brought to Costa Rica from Guatemala. The religious-art museum next door has a small but exquisite collection of furniture and artifacts from the original Franciscan monastery here. A huge modern church sits beside the historic one, but happily, it's just far enough away not to spoil photos of the picturesque original church. ⊠ *West side of soccer field, Orosi* ☎ *2533–3051* ⓦ *Museum $1* ⊙ *Closed Mon.*

Iglesia de Ujarrás (*Church of Ujarrás*)
RELIGIOUS SITE | The ruins of Costa Rica's first church lie past the Cachí dam near the small hamlet of Ujarrás (*oo-hah-RRASS*). An unlikely Spanish victory over a superior force of invading British pirates was attributed to a stop here to ask for the protection of the Virgin Mary, and a church was constructed in thanksgiving to honor the Virgin of Ujarrás. The entire village was abandoned in 1833 after a series of earthquakes and floods wreaked havoc in the lowest point of the Orosi Valley, and the inhabitants resettled at the site that would become the present-day town of Paraíso. Today the impressive, often-photographed limestone ruins sit in a beautifully maintained park with lawns, flower gardens, and a pretty picnic area. A final, scenic 6-km (4-mile) winding drive to Paraíso from Ujarrás completes the road that loops the valley. Visitors fill the site on weekends, but on weekdays you'll likely have the place to yourself. ⊠ *In a small park, 1 km (½ mile) from Restaurante Típico Ujarrás, Orosi* ☎ *2574–8366* ⓦ *Free.*

Jardín Botánico Lankester
GARDEN | The lush gardens of Lankester Botanical Garden, operated by the University of Costa Rica, house one of the world's foremost orchid collections, with more than 1,100 native and introduced species. Bromeliads, heliconias, and aroids also abound in the 7-acre garden, along with 80 species of trees, including

Iglesia de San José de Orosi is the county's oldest church that is still in use.

rare palms. A Japanese garden has a graceful bridge and a teahouse. ✉ *4 km (2½ miles) east of Cartago at west entrance to Paraíso, Cartago* ☎ *2511–7939* 🌐 *www.jbl.ucr.ac.cr* 🎟 *$10.*

Tapantí National Park (*Parque Nacional Tapantí*)
NATIONAL/STATE PARK | Stretching all the way to the Talamanca Mountains, this reserve encompasses 47 square km (18 square miles) of largely pristine, remote cloud forest, a refuge for more than 400 bird species, including the emerald toucanet, violaceous trogon, and many of the country's hummingbirds. The rangers' office and visitor center are on the right just after the park entrance. You can leave your vehicle at a parking area 1½ km (1 mile) up the road. From here loop trails head off into the woods on both sides. Get an early start—you can enter on foot before 8 am, as long as you pay as you leave. The park clouds over markedly by afternoon and, with between 250 and 300 inches of rain annually, it's renowned as the country's wettest national park. Be prepared with a poncho or sturdy umbrella. ✉ *14 km (8 miles) south of Orosi, Orosi* ☎ *2206–5615* 🎟 *$10.*

🍴 Restaurants

Bar y Restaurante Coto
$$ | **COSTA RICAN** | A local institution since 1952, this large rancho restaurant and bar is famous for its huge meat platters—we're talking 1 to 1½ kilos (2¼ to 3½ pounds) of meat—with all the típico side dishes. Or you can dine more daintily on sautéed trout. **Known for:** enormous meat platters; good seafood dishes; pleasant view of Orosi church. [$] *Average main: $14* ✉ *Northeast corner of soccer field, Orosi* ☎ *2533–3032* 💳 *No credit cards.*

La Casona del Cafetal
$$ | **COSTA RICAN** | The valley's most scenic and famous lunch stop sits on a coffee plantation overlooking the Cachí Reservoir. It's firmly on the beaten path, which means frequent visits from tour groups. **Known for:** popular weekend lunch buffet; yummy coffee desserts; solid menu of

típico food. $ *Average main: $13* ✉ *2 km (1 mile) south of Cachí Dam, Orosi* ☎ *2577–1414* ⊕ *www.lacasonadelcafetal. com* ◔ *No dinner.*

Hotels

★ Hotel Quelitales

$$$ | **B&B/INN** | For quiet, get-away-from-it-all seclusion, this eco-friendly lodging can't be beat. **Pros:** quiet seclusion; great views; careful attention to sustainability and environment. **Cons:** rough final road to get here; best to have a car; steep walk to a couple of bungalows. $ *Rooms from: $165* ✉ *3 km (2 miles) east of Cachí, Orosi* ☎ *2577–2222* ⊕ *www. hotelquelitales.com* ⬎ *9 bungalows* ⦿ *Free Breakfast.*

La Casona del Cafetal

$$ | **B&B/INN** | This sophisticated lodging offers dark-wood queen or king rooms in units scattered around a coffee plantation. **Pros:** amenities such as flat-screen TV and Wi-Fi, which are uncommon in these parts; attentive service; quiet seclusion. **Cons:** all units, especially standard rooms, are a bit dark; best to have a car to stay here; restaurant gets very busy on weekends. $ *Rooms from: $130* ✉ *2 km (1 mile) south of Cachí Dam, Orosi* ☎ *2577–1414* ⊕ *www.lacasonadelcafetal. com* ⬎ *7 rooms* ⦿ *Free Breakfast.*

Orosi Lodge

$ | **B&B/INN** | Run by a young German couple who have built a warm rapport with the community, the little lodge blends in with Orosi's pretty, old-town architecture: whitewashed walls are trimmed in blue, ceilings are high, and natural wood is used throughout. **Pros:** affordable and pleasant; views from second-floor rooms; charming decor. **Cons:** no restaurant, just a café; hearty breakfasts; reception sometimes closes early. $ *Rooms from: $65* ✉ *350 m south, 100 m west of soccer field, Orosi* ☎ *2533–3578* ⊕ *www. orosilodge.com* ⬎ *8 units* ⦿ *No meals.*

Shopping

Casa del Soñador (*House of the Dreamer*)
CRAFTS | Stop in at this unique artisan shop, a picturesque wood cottage embellished with monumental carvings by local wood sculptor Macedonio Quesada, the creator of the House of the Dreamer. Though Macedonio died years ago, his sons Miguel and Hermes continue the tradition, carving interesting, often comical little statues out of coffee roots, which they sell for only $10 to $15. ✉ *2 km (1 mile) south of Cachí Dam, Orosi* ☎ *2577–1812.*

Turrialba

58 km (36 miles) east of San José.

The well-to-do agricultural center of Turrialba is a bustling town, with a youthful vibe from the nearby university, a colorful open-air market, and a tree-shaded central park filled with an intriguing collection of large-scale animal sculptures. The region's moist cheese, made in nearby Santa Cruz, is famous all over Costa Rica. As you begin the descent to Turrialba town, the temperature rises markedly and sugarcane alternates with fields of neat rows of coffee bushes. Turrialba also makes a product you might have heard of: Rawlings makes all the baseballs used in the major leagues. (The plant does not offer tours.) Thanks to some spectacular scenery, patches of rain forest in the surrounding countryside, and a handful of upscale nature lodges, ecotourism is increasingly the focus of the town's efforts. Significant numbers of kayakers and rafters also flock here to run the Pacuare and Reventazón rivers. And looming above the town is Volcán Turrialba. Recent eruptions of ash, along with a heavily damaged road, prevent visitors from going to the top or even getting near the base. Although volcanic activity keeps you away from the behemoth for safety reasons, don't let that scare you off from visiting other area attractions.

GETTING HERE AND AROUND

There are two ways to reach this area from San José, both of which pass through spectacular landscapes. The more direct route, accessible by heading east through Cartago, continues east through Paraíso, where you turn left at the northeast corner of the central park to pick up the road to Turrialba. Marked by signs, this road leads north to Guayabo National Monument. For the second route, turn off the road between Cartago and the summit of Irazú near the town of Cot, heading toward Pacayas. That narrow route twists along the slopes of Irazú and Turrialba volcanoes, with some stunning scenery—stately pollarded trees lining the road, riotous patches of tropical flowers, and metal-girder bridges across crashing streams.

Direct buses between San José and Turrialba leave hourly from 8 to 8 (slower buses run as early as 5:15 am and as late as 10 pm) from Calle 13, Avenida 6, just west of the downtown court buildings. Direct buses depart from the Turrialba terminal (at the entrance to Turrialba) for San José on the hour from 5 to 5, on the half hour to Cartago, and every two hours to Siquirres.

TAXIS Asocut. ☎ 2556–7070.

ESSENTIALS

BANKS/ATMS Banco de Costa Rica. ⊠ Avda. 0, C. 1 ☎ 2556–0472. **Banco Nacional.** ⊠ C. 1, Avda. Ctl. ☎ 2556–1211 ⊕ www. bncr.fi.cr.

HOSPITAL Hospital Dr. William Allen. ⊠ Avda. 2, 100 m west of C. 4 ☎ 2558–1300.

PHARMACY Farmacia San Buenaventura. ⊠ 50 m south of east side of central park ☎ 2556–0379.

Sights

Guayabo National Monument (*Monumento Nacional Guayabo*)
ARCHAEOLOGICAL SITE | On the slopes of Turrialba Volcano lies Costa Rica's

only true archaeological site. The city was abandoned in AD 1400, probably because of disease or war. Starting from the round, thatch-roof reception center, guided tours will take you through the rain forest to a lookout from which you can see the layout of the excavated circular buildings. Only the raised foundations survive, since the conical houses themselves were built of wood. As you descend into the ruins, notice the well-engineered surface and covered aqueducts leading to a trough of drinking water, which still functions today.

Guayabo has been recognized by the American Society of Civil Engineers as a feat of Latin American civil engineering second only to Machu Picchu. The hillside jungle is captivating, and the trip is further enhanced by bird-watching possibilities: 200 species have been recorded. ⊠ *Turrialba* ✛ *Drive through center of Turrialba to girdered bridge; take road signed Guayabo National Monument northeast for total of 16 km (10 miles), about 25–30 mins driving; watch for signed left turnoff, which will take you final 3 km (2 miles) to monument. If you've taken scenic Irazú foothills route to Turrialba, the Santa Cruz route—11 km (7 miles) (about 35 mins driving)—is an option. Turn left on rough road from Santa Cruz; climb 5 km (3 miles), past the Escuela de Guayabo; turn right at the sign for the monument; the road descends 6 km (4 miles) to the site* ☎ 2559–1220, 8534–1063 *to reserve a guide, 1192 national park hotline* ☞ *From $5.*

Turrialba Volcano National Park (*Parque Nacional Volcán Turrialba*)
VOLCANO | Although you've never been able to drive up to its summit as you can at Poás and Irazú, Volcán Turrialba is an impressive sight from a distance, albeit with some major precautions. The volcano has been increasingly active since early 2010. A series of explosions from 2015 well into 2020 have spewed out steam and ash to far reaches of the country and temporarily closed Juan Santamaría

Off the Beaten Path

Centro Agronómico Tropical de Investigación y Enseñanza A good place for bird-watchers and garden enthusiasts, the Tropical Agricultural Research and Higher Education Center—better known by its Spanish acronym, CATIE—is one of the leading tropical research centers in Latin America, with headquarters here and affiliates in nine other countries. You might catch sight of the yellow-winged northern jacana or the purple gallinule in the lagoon near the main building. The 10-square-km (4-square-mile) property includes landscaped grounds, seed-conservation chambers, greenhouses, orchards, experimental agricultural projects, a large swath of rain forest, labs and offices, and lodging for students and teachers. The most popular attraction is the **Botanical Garden Tour,** a two-hour guided walk to taste, smell, and touch tropical fruits, along with cacao, coffee, and other medicinal and stimulant plants. A favorite stop is the "miracle fruit" tree, whose berries magically make anything sour taste sweet. Reservations are required for guided tours. ✉ *3 km (2 miles) outside Turrialba, on road to Siquirres* ☎ *2558–2000* 🌐 *www.catie.ac.cr* 🎟 *From $15.*

International Airport. (Volcanic ash can corrode airplane engines.) Sulfur dioxide fumes emanate from the volcano, a phenomenon that has taken its toll on plant and animal life in the immediate vicinity. ⚠ **If you suffer from a heart or respiratory condition or are pregnant, stay away.** The area beyond the Volcán Turrialba Lodge (*see Activities*) remains closed off to residents and visitors at this writing. ✉ *20 km (12 miles) east of Cot.*

🍴 Restaurants

La Garza Bar y Restaurante

$ | **COSTA RICAN** | With weathered, blondwood tables and chairs, and big windows with a view out onto the central park, La Garza is a popular meeting spot with a little more atmosphere than most of the eateries in town in spite of its extremely plain interior. The menu runs the gamut from hamburgers to chicken and has a good seafood selection. **Known for:** decent burgers; nice outdoor view, even if plain interior; late-night eats. [$] *Average main: $9* ✉ *Northwest corner of central park* ☎ *2556–1073.*

Restaurante La Feria

$$ | **COSTA RICAN** | A permanent exhibition of local art and the expertise of the owner make this a worthwhile stop. This pleasant family-style restaurant has the usual midscale Costa Rican fare, ranging from fast food to filet mignon. **Known for:** beef tenderloin in mushroom and wine sauce; good menu of Costa Rican favorites; reasonably priced lunch specials. [$] *Average main: $14* ✉ *Across from Enersol gas station at western entrance to town* ☎ *2556–5550* 💳 *No credit cards* 🕒 *No dinner Tues.*

🛏 Hotels

★ **Casa Turire**

$$$ | **B&B/INN** | Lush gardens and manicured lawns surround this gorgeous, hacienda-style luxury hotel overlooking a scenic lake. **Pros:** beautiful grounds; attention to sustainable tourism; luxurious suites. **Cons:** small, one-room spa; standard-room bathrooms could use a little upgrading; can be difficult to find. [$] *Rooms from: $155* ✉ *8 km (5 miles) south on Carretera a la Suiza from*

"For a fun ride, try rafting the Pacuare River in October or November when the water is high." —Photo by Linda137, Fodors.com member

Turrialba ☎ *2531–1111* 🌐 *www.hotelcasaturire.com* 🛏 *16 rooms* 🍴 *Free Breakfast.*

Guayabo Lodge

$$ | **B&B/INN** | If fresh mountain air appeals to you, this upscale mountain retreat has comfortable rooms, a first-class restaurant, and spacious, glassed-in sitting areas to enjoy unbeatable volcano and valley views by day and blazing fireplaces by night. **Pros:** cozy and comfortable; high sustainability consciousness; great views. **Cons:** weather can be wet and cool; clouds can obscure the view; can be difficult to get through by phone. [$] *Rooms from: $105* ✉ *2 km (1 mile) west of Santa Cruz de Turrialba* ☎ *2538–8400* 🌐 *www.guayabolodge.co.cr* 🛏 *26 rooms* 🍴 *Free Breakfast.*

Hotel Villa Florencia

$$ | **HOTEL** | **FAMILY** | This country inn a few miles outside of Turrialba offers peace and quiet, a rural feel, and friendly owners and staff. **Pros:** warm, helpful staff; family-friendly; quiet surroundings. **Cons:** some rooms have dated furnishings; best to have car to stay here; can be difficult to find. [$] *Rooms from: $145* ✉ *La Susanita de Turrialba, 800 m west* ☎ *2557–3536* 🌐 *www.villaflorencia.com* 🛏 *9 rooms* 🍴 *Free Breakfast.*

★ **Rancho Naturalista**

$$$$ | **B&B/INN** | Unparalleled bird-watching within a 160-acre private nature reserve with more than 450 recorded species, plus first-class food and comfortable lodging are the reasons nature lovers from all over the world stay here. **Pros:** birder's paradise; warm atmosphere; gourmet meals included. **Cons:** some rooms are a little dated; not a convenient base for day trips; rough final stretch of road to get here. [$] *Rooms from: $400* ✉ *20 km (12 miles) southeast of Turrialba, 1½ km (1 mile) south of Tuís, then up rough road* ☎ *8994–8994, 2100–1855 for reservations* 🌐 *www.ranchonaturalista.net* 💳 *No credit cards* 🛏 *15 rooms* 🍴 *All meals.*

Turrialtico Lodge

$$ | **B&B/INN** | Dramatically positioned on a hill overlooking the valley east of Turrialba, this Costa Rican–owned rustic wood

lodge is a good budget option. **Pros:** rich views at budget prices; coffeemakers in rooms; good opportunity to mingle with Ticos. **Cons:** thin walls in main lodge; less service-oriented than other area options; need a car to stay here. $ *Rooms from: $77* ⊠ *8 km (5 miles) east of Turrialba on road to Siquirres* ☎ *2538–1111* ⊕ *www. turrialtico.com* ⊃ *19 units* ⦿ *Free Breakfast.*

Activities

Costa Rica Ríos

WHITE-WATER RAFTING | Specializing in weeklong rafting, kayaking, and canoeing excursions on the Pacuare and Pejibaye rivers, this outfitter has rafter-to-guide ratios of no more than 5:1. ⊠ *50 m north of central park* ☎ *2556–8664, 888/434–0776 in North America* ⊕ *www. costaricarios.com* ⛵ *Excursions from $1,899/week.*

Ecoaventuras

TOUR—SPORTS | All the best activities—horseback riding, mountain biking, kayaking, and rafting—are covered with this adventure company's one- to three-day excursions with pickup from San José area hotels. ⊠ *750 m south of bus terminal* ☎ *2556–7171* ⊕ *www.ecoaventuras. co.cr* ⛵ *From $95.*

Explornatura

TOUR—SPORTS | This downtown company organizes kayaking, horseback riding, mountain biking, and rafting tours, including a family-friendly Class II rafting trip with lots of thrills but fewer chances of spills. ⊠ *40 m west of Hotel Wagelia* ☎ *2556–0111, 866/571–2443 in North America* ⊕ *www.explornatura.com* ⛵ *From $85.*

Ríos Tropicales

WHITE-WATER RAFTING | Long-established outfitter Ríos Tropicales begins and ends its Pacuare and Reventazón white-water excursions in San José with the option to overnight on the Pacuare. Rafter-to-guide ratios don't exceed 5:1. ⊠ *50 m north of Centro Colón, Paseo Colón* ☎ *2233–6455, 866/722–8273 in North America* ⊕ *www.riostropicales.com* ⛵ *From $96.*

Volcán Turrialba Lodge

HIKING/WALKING | Although ascending to the summit of the Turrialba Volcano is not permitted, the lodge can arrange for guided walks and horseback tours of the area, all at a safe distance from the volcano. The lodge itself offers only very rustic accommodation. ⊠ *Turrialba* ⊹ *20 km (12 miles) east of Cot, turn right at Pacayas on road to Volcán Turrialba, 4 km (2½ miles) on dirt road; or from Turrialba side, follow signs in La Pastora for national al park, 14 km (8½ miles) along patchy paved road; 4WD advised because last 3 km (2 miles) is on rough road* ☎ *2273–4335* ⊕ *www.facebook.com/turrialbalodge* ⛵ *From $55.*

Chapter 6

ARENAL, MONTEVERDE, AND THE NORTHERN LOWLANDS

Updated by
Rachel White

 Sights
★★★★★

🍴 Restaurants
★★★☆☆

🛏 Hotels
★★★★☆

🛍 Shopping
★★☆☆☆

🍸 Nightlife
★☆☆☆☆

WELCOME TO ARENAL, MONTEVERDE, AND THE NORTHERN LOWLANDS

TOP REASONS TO GO

★ **Soak in a volcano-heated hot spring:** For four decades Arenal was one of the world's most active volcanoes, but it has been in a state of slumber since 2010. It still provides a majestic backdrop for the steamy thermal waters nearby.

★ **Hike to a waterfall:** The reward for a tough hike down to La Fortuna Waterfall is a magnificent waterfall, plummeting nearly 250 feet into a freshwater pool.

★ **Float on a cloud:** Explore Monteverde's misty world on treetop walkways or on exhilarating ziplines up to 328 feet off the ground.

★ **Watch wildlife:** Birds, monkeys, turtles, caiman, and sloths abound in the 25,000-acre Caño Negro National Wildlife Refuge.

★ **Set sail:** Lake Arenal is one of the top windsurfing and kitesurfing spots in the world; winds can reach 50 to 60 mph mid-November through April.

The rich, lush terrain of the Zona Norte (Northern Zone), as it is known locally, runs from the base of the Cordillera Central in the south to the Río San Juan, on the border with Nicaragua in the north. Most visitors begin their visit to Costa Rica in San José, and then head north to La Fortuna. This adventure hub is a base for exploring the Arenal Volcano, La Fortuna Waterfall, and Caño Negro National Wildlife Refuge, and for sportfishing, windsurfing, and kitesurfing at Lake Arenal and rafting on the Sarapiquí River.

1 Arenal and La Fortuna. A three-hour drive northwest of San José brings you to Arenal Volcano, one of the top 10 most visited attractions in Costa Rica. Book the right hotel, such as Arenal Kioro, and you can wake up to views of the 5,300 ft-tall dome from your window. Although the volcano is in a passive stage, you might see a few plumes of smoke during your visit. La Fortuna is the closest town to the volcano; nearby diversions include include hot springs, hanging bridges, white-water rafting, ziplines, waterfalls, and rain forest tours.

2 Nuevo Arenal. About an hour away from Arenal Volcano, the "nuevo" or "new" town of Arenal is popular for windsurfers who come to visit Lake Arenal. It also makes a good base for exploring the area, offering a few truly memorable restaurants and hotels.

3 Monteverde Cloud Forest and Santa Elena. Home to the rainiest of cloud forests, the Monteverde Cloud Forest area is also the canopy-tour capital of Costa Rica. Hanging bridges, treetop tram tours, and ziplines abound. As if that's not enough, horseback riding, coffee tours, and nature hikes are also available. Santa Elena, the closest town to Monteverde Cloud Forest, is the best base for a trip here.

4 Tenorio Volcano and the Río Celeste. Located about an hour north of Arenal in a verdant national park, the lesser known but magnificent Tenorio Volcano is surrounded by great hiking trails, a waterfall, hot springs, and Costa Rica's most striking blue river, the Río Celeste.

5 Caño Negro National Wildlife Refuge. In the far northern lowlands, this rain forest reserve and wetland, reminiscent of a small Florida Everglades, is a great place for fishing, bird-watching, and communing with nature. Boat tours are a popular way to take in all the flora and fauna of the area. It's about 90 minutes driving from La Fortuna.

ARENAL VOLCANO

Arenal Volcano

Rising to a height of roughly 5,000 feet, Arenal Volcano, Costa Rica's youngest volcano, dominates the region's landscape.

Volcanologists estimate Arenal's age at around 7,000 years, and it was dormant for nearly 500 years until 1968. On July 29, 1968, an earthquake shook the area, and 12 hours later Arenal blew.

Until October 2010, Arenal was in a constant state of activity—thunderous, rumbling eruptions occurred sometimes as frequently as once per hour. Tourists flocked here for the nightly show of rocks spewing skyward. Experts believe the volcano could now remain in a "resting" state for up to 800 years. After heavy rainfall, puffs of steam occasionally rise from the crater, making for an impressive photo of plumes over its cone. Sleeping or not, the lack of lava hasn't dissuaded travelers from seeing the magnificent mound or even hiking its flanks, which offer views of Lake Arenal in the distance. It still remains among the most visited attractions in the country. *(For more information, see the review in this chapter.)*

BEST TIME TO GO

Despite its size, viewing Arenal Volcano can be hit or miss anytime of year. January through April, especially in the early morning, usually means fewer clouds to obscure daytime views.

FUN FACT

It's no wonder Arenal Volcano is so photogenic—the conical supermodel has the third-most-picture-perfect crater in the world. Take aim quickly if you want to get a good shot, as cloud cover makes this natural attraction camera shy.

BEST WAYS TO EXPLORE

BIRD-WATCHING

If you decide to hike Los Tucanes trail, chances are you'll see at least one of the five species of toucan that have been recorded here: chestnut-billed and keel-billed toucans, the yellow-eared and emerald toucanet, and the collared aracari. You'll never look at a box of Froot Loops the same way after seeing the real thing. Hummingbirds also abound on the volcano's slopes. Look for anything tiny and purple.

HIKING

For intrepid hikers, Las Heliconias trail ($15), which starts at the national park's reception center, wends through secondary forest and passes by the cooled lava flow from the 1968 eruption. Outside the park, Los Tucanes trail ($10) also leads to the lava fields, but it's more of an uphill hike, beginning near the entrance to the Arenal Observatory Lodge. There's also a steep and arduous four-hour hike up to Cerro Chatto ($10), a dormant volcano with a lopsided, extinct crater partially filled with water, creating a pretty lake. The Los Miradores trail is completely paved and handicap accessible. It leads you through 1.3 km (0.8 miles) of forest to views of Lake Arenal, then takes you right to its shores. Arenal Observatory Lodge has a day pass ($32) including 11 km (7 miles) of trails, lunch, and use of swimming pools.

VOLCANIC TIPS

Two words: "from afar." Under no circumstances should you hike the volcano's trails on your own. In rainy season, some trails like Cerro Chatto are extremely muddy and treacherous. Pre-2010, lava rocks and volcanic gas occasionally killed trekkers who got too close to the action. The tour operators we recommend know where the danger lies and take appropriate precautions.

Waterfalls, streams, and lush rain forest surround Arenal.

TOP REASONS TO GO

ALL BUDGETS WELCOME

Travelers on tight budgets are being priced out of the market in some regions of Costa Rica. Not so here. You'll find everything from backpackers' digs to luxury hotels in the area around Arenal.

A PERFECT VOLCANO

Arenal's perfect cone, hiking trails, and thermal activity that heats neighboring hot springs keep the volcano at the top of the "must see" list despite the fact that its dormant phase may last another 800 years.

SPORTS AND ADVENTURE

It might have been the volcano that put Arenal on the map, but it's the area's recreational activities that keep travelers coming back. From ziplines and hanging bridges to waterfalls and raging rivers, Arenal has more attractions than any other destination in the country.

CAÑO NEGRO NATIONAL WILDLIFE REFUGE

Caño Negro National Wildlife Refuge

Think of a smaller version of Florida's Everglades and you'll have a good picture of the Refugio Nacional de Vida Silvestre Caño Negro.

This lowland rain-forest reserve in the far northern reaches of Costa Rica near the Nicaraguan border covers 98 square km (38 square miles). It looks remote on the map but is easily visited on an organized day tour, especially from La Fortuna. Caño Negro is the core of a UNESCO biosphere called Agua y Paz (Water and Peace), which encompasses more than 2 million acres of wildlife habitat in Costa Rica and Nicaragua.

Caño Negro has suffered severe deforestation over the years, but most of the length of the Río Frío, its principal river, is still lined with trees. The park's vast lake, which floods after seasonal rains, is an excellent place to watch waterfowl. The reserve is home to more than 350 migratory and resident bird species and 310 types of plants. On land, pumas, tapirs, ocelots, cougars, and the always-elusive jaguar are among the more than 160 mammal species that thrive here—consider yourself fortunate if you spot a jaguar.

BEST TIME TO GO

It gets *hot* here, with March and April brutally so, but the January–March dry season is the best time to spot the reserve's migratory bird population. Opportunities abound the rest of the year, too, though. No matter what season, bring sunscreen, a hat, and bug spray.

FUN FACT

In addition to other bird species, the reserve is the best place to spot the Nicaraguan grackle. This New World blackbird is found only in Nicaragua and northern Costa Rica.

BEST WAYS TO EXPLORE

BIRD-WATCHING

This is the best place in the country to see waterbirds. Just sit back in your tour boat and survey the passing parade. You're sure to see anhingas spreading their wings to dry; both glossy and white ibis recognizable by their long curved beaks; roseate spoonbills, often mistaken for flamingos; and the jabiru, king of the storks. Herons and kingfishers lurk on the banks, ready to spear fish, while jacanas, with their huge feet, forage in the water lettuce, looking as though they are actually walking on water. Above the water, watch for gray-color snail kites, which, true to their name, are hunting for snails.

BOAT TOURS

In the dry season you can ride horses, but a visit here chiefly entails a wildlife-spotting boat tour. You could drive up here on your own—roads to the area are in good shape until you approach Los Chiles; then it's 19 km (12 miles) on a gravel road to the park entrance in Caño Negro Town. Once here, you'd need to arrange for boat transportation. You can book the most reputable guides directly through Natural Lodge Caño Negro. Visiting with a tour company out of La Fortuna—it's a two-hour ride each way—is the most common way to see the park, but keep in mind that most Fortuna-based companies tour the perimeter of the reserve rather than the park interior in order to avoid the $5 entrance fee.

CAIMAN TOURS

Famous for its caimans, Caño Negro boasts a sizable population. They're smaller than crocodiles, though—at most, 8 feet long—and relatively unthreatening, because they're too small to eat large mammals (such as humans). It's a thrill to see them sunning on a bank.

Hiking Caño Negro Trail

6

Arenal, Monteverde, and the Northern Lowlands CAÑO NEGRO NATIONAL WILDLIFE REFUGE

TOP REASONS TO GO

BIRD-WATCHING

The reserve is one of Costa Rica's lesser-sung bird-watching and wildlife-viewing destinations. Caño Negro is growing in popularity, but, for now, a visit here still feels special.

FISHING

It's not all about wildlife viewing here: Caño Negro is also one of Costa Rica's prime freshwater fishing destinations, with tarpon, snook, and garfish yours for catch-and-release bragging rights during the September–March season (fishing is prohibited April–July, and the garfish ban is March–August). The two lodges inside the reserve can hook you up.

GREAT TOURS

It's easy to get here from the Arenal area, with tour operators organizing day tours from La Fortuna. If time allows, stay overnight in Caño Negro and reserve a tour through one of the lodges. When selecting a company, make sure the tour actually enters the reserve.

The vast expanse that locals call the Zona Norte (Northern Zone) packs in a larger variety of activities than any other part of the country. You'll find almost everything in this region that Costa Rica has to offer, from volcanoes to rain forests to waterfalls. Everything except beaches, of course.

Spend any amount of time here and you can partake of—take a deep breath—horseback riding, canoeing, kayaking, rafting, rappelling, windsurfing, kite-surfing, wildlife viewing, bird-watching, bungee jumping, shopping, cloud- and rain-forest hiking, swimming, hot-springs soaking, and volcano (albeit now dormant) viewing. The zipline canopy tour deserves special mention. The activity was invented in Costa Rica and has spread to all corners of the planet, while zipping along cables from platform to platform high in the trees has become Costa Rica's signature adventure activity.

The myriad activities make this, and especially Monteverde, Costa Rica's most kid-friendly region. Young children will "oooooh" (and "eeewwww") at various area animal exhibits devoted to bats, frogs, butterflies, hummingbirds, and snakes. Guided nature hikes abound; shorter treks can be entertaining and cater to younger ones' shorter attention spans. Most sure-footed and confi-dent teenagers can participate in adult activities such as white-water rafting and canopy tours.

A few operators around here will tell you that kids older than eight can participate in canopy tours. Even if their brochures

show children happily zipping from platform to platform, the gondola-like trams and hanging bridges are far safer ways for preteens to see the rain-forest canopy.

Most nature- and adventure-themed excursions go on rain or shine, so don't feel you have to avoid a rainy-season visit here. (While rare, thunder and lightning *do* cancel such activities.) During the wet months, it's almost a given that you'll get a bit damp on your canopy tour, hike, or horseback ride, and most tour operators provide ponchos. But to avoid a thorough soaking, plan activities for the morning. Rains usually begin around 2 pm, like clockwork, from July through December, although they can be more prolonged in September and October. The clearest time of day is normally before 8 am.

MAJOR REGIONS

About 3½ hours from San José, the **Arenal Volcano** area is one of Costa Rica's biggest attractions. Whether you come here from San José or Liberia, prepare yourself for some spectacular scenery and curvy roads. Although the roads are well paved, they are quite narrow in places with steep drops and sharp turns. Any discomfort passengers might occa-sionally experience is more than made up for by the swaths of misty rain forest and dramatic expanses of the Cordillera Central.

Monteverde Cloud Forest is 167 km (104 miles, 3½ hrs) northwest of San José and 110 km (67 miles, 4 hrs) southwest of La Fortuna, and **Santa Elena** is 6 km (4 miles, 30 mins) north of Monteverde and 35 km (22 miles, 2 hrs) southeast of Tilarán.

Northwest of Monteverde is **Tenorio Volcano National Park and the Río Celeste,** home to an azure river and a dazzling waterfall that proves to be the most underrated attraction in Costa Rica. Also largely undiscovered, but with great bird-watching and wildlife, is **Caño Negro National Wildlife Refuge** in the far north reaches of the area.

Planning

When to Go

HIGH SEASON: MID-DECEMBER TO APRIL

Climate is difficult to pinpoint in this vast region. The Northern Lowlands link the rainier Caribbean in the east to drier Guanacaste in the west. Precipitation generally decreases from east to west. Monteverde is cool, damp, and breezy much of the time, with high winds in January and February. Elsewhere, rain can occur outside the official wet season since the area's low elevation frequently hosts battles between competing weather fronts. Visibility changes daily (and hourly), so your chances of seeing the Arenal volcano crater are more or less the same year-round, though you may have more luck from February to April, the hottest and driest time of the year.

LOW SEASON: JUNE TO MID-NOVEMBER

Throughout the entire region, the warm and humid rainy season normally lasts from June to December. Many places

in Arenal and Monteverde are beginning to impose high-season rates in July and August to correspond with prime North American and European vacation times.

We frequently overhear comments such as "I didn't know it would be so rainy in the rain forest." You heard it here first: that's why they call it the rain forest! During the rainy season it's not unusual for it to rain for several days straight, and even during the dry season, brief showers will come up without notice. Be sure to bring a poncho or rain jacket and waterproof footwear.

SHOULDER SEASON: MAY TO JUNE

The wet season just starts to kick in by May, but rarely to a degree that will interfere with your travels. A little precipitation provides a welcome clearing and freshening of the air in the countryside.

Planning Your Time

Although not centrally located, the Northern Lowlands can be easily tacked onto stays in other regions of Costa Rica. Fairly decent—decent for Costa Rica, that is—transportation links the region to San José, the Central Valley, and the North Pacific. (Monteverde is the exception, isolated and approached only by rugged roads from all directions, although there are plans to pave one access route.)

A week is more than enough time to experience a great deal of this area—especially if you're longing to get out and get moving. Give yourself four days in La Fortuna and the surrounding Arenal area, a great base for exploring the region. Devote the rest of your week to the Monteverde Cloud Forest. If your stay here is limited to two or three days, make La Fortuna–Arenal your base. Don't miss the inactive volcano, a day at the hot springs, or a trip to Caño Negro National Wildlife Refuge.

Most tour operators who have hikes end the day at one of the various thermal springs in the area. The most popular are Baldi, Ecotermales, Springs Resort, and Tabacón, all with cascading pools at varying temperatures and day packages that include lunch or dinner. With waterslides, buffet lines, and busloads of tourists, the larger hot springs can feel a bit like the Disneyland of relaxation. If you plan on spending a good amount of time soaking in the hot springs, opt for staying at a hotel with on-site thermal pools.
■ TIP→ **There are free public hot springs past the yellow gate next to Tabacón.**

"Half-day" tours to Caño Negro actually take most of a day, from around 7:30 am to 4 pm, and you'll spend about two hours each way in a bus or van.

Getting Here and Around

AIR
Nature Air and SANSA have daily flights from their own airport in San José to La Fortuna (FTN). It's located directly next to the international airport, with a fleet of puddle jumpers and a fast and easy check-in of only 30 minutes before boarding. Most travelers to this region fly into San José's Aeropuerto Internacional Juan Santamaría or Liberia's Daniel Oduber Airport and rent a car. Monteverde and Arenal are equidistant from both. Base your choice of airport on which other areas in Costa Rica you plan to visit in addition to this one.

BUS
Buses in this region are typically large, clean, and fairly comfortable, but often crowded Friday through Sunday. Don't expect air-conditioning. Service tends toward the agonizingly slow: even supposedly express buses marked *directo* often make numerous stops. Terminal 7-10 in San José serves most of the major towns in this chapter.

CAR
Road access to the northwest is by way of the paved two-lane Pan-American Highway, which starts from the west end of Paseo Colón in San José and runs northwest to Peñas Blancas at the Nicaraguan border. Turn north at Naranjo for La Fortuna; at Lagarto for Monteverde; and at Cañas for Tilarán. This region manages to mix some of the country's smoothest highways with some of its most horrendous roads. The various roads to Monteverde are legendary in the latter regard—but the final destination makes it worth the trip. Four-wheel-drive vehicles are best on the frequently potholed roads. If you don't want to pay for 4WD, at least rent a car with high clearance (many rental agencies insist you take a 4WD vehicle if you mention Monteverde as part of your itinerary). You'll encounter frequent one-lane bridges; if the triangular *Ceda el Paso* sign faces you, yield to oncoming traffic. Driving in this region can be slow going if you get behind a large truck transporting sugarcane. As the north is prime sugar country, that's quite likely.

It is possible to rent a car in La Fortuna, but for a far better selection, most visitors pick up their rental vehicles in San José or Liberia. Considering downloading the Waze app to help guide you with directions.

Health and Safety

This region is Costa Rica's capital of adventure tourism—it gave birth to the zipline canopy tour—so any risks up here are far more likely to be natural than criminal. Before you set out rafting, ziplining, rappelling, or bungee jumping, be brutally frank with yourself about your abilities, your physical condition, and your fear levels: it's almost impossible to turn back on many excursions once you've started. Even an activity as innocuous as hiking or horseback riding poses a certain amount of risk, and you should never go alone. Nature here is not an amusement park.

Remember also that there is little government oversight of adventure tourism here. Pay close attention during any safety briefings and orientation. Don't be afraid to ask questions, and don't be afraid to walk away if something seems off to you. Look for zipline tours with built-in brake systems, double cables, and chest harnesses in addition to the normal waist harness. Many companies include GoPro helmet mounts so you can document your canopy adventure hands-free. If you have travel insurance, make sure it covers action sports or adrenaline activities—most standard packages do not cover injuries related to kayaking, horseback riding, ziplining, kitesurfing, or other such sports.

Money Matters

Outside the centers of Monteverde, La Fortuna, Nuevo Arenal, San Carlos, and Tilarán, ATMs are still few and far between. Stock up on cash when you get a chance.

Restaurants

The north is the country's breadbasket, and the hotels and restaurants out here make use of the bounty to whip up the best in *típico* Costa Rican cuisine. Don't be afraid to ask for tap water; it is safe to drink in all but the most rural areas. Service is generally slow but well worth the wait at most restaurants. Your final bill will include a 13% sales tax and a 10%–12% service charge, though we suggest you tip a little extra.

Hotels

A few sumptuous resorts hold court in northern Costa Rica, but this region is largely the province of smaller,

nature-themed lodgings that invite you to partake of all their eco-activities, and offer good value. Due to the comfortable inland temperatures, most hotels do not have air-conditioning. Also, it's not uncommon for some hotels to request that toilet paper be disposed of in a bin rather than flushed down the toilet, due to local plumbing challenges. Hotel rooms are taxed at the national rate of 13%. *Hotel reviews have been shortened. For full information, visit Fodors. com.*

WHAT IT COSTS in U.S. Dollars			
$	$$	$$$	$$$$
RESTAURANTS			
under $10	$10–$15	$16–$25	over $25
HOTELS			
under $75	$75–$150	$151–$250	over $250

Arenal and La Fortuna

50 km (30 miles, 45 mins) northwest of Ciudad Quesada, 17 km (11 miles) east of Arenal Volcano, 190 km (118 miles, 3½ hrs by car, 25 mins by plane) northwest of San José.

As they say, "Location, location, location." Who would think that a small town sitting at the foot of massive Arenal Volcano would attract visitors from around the world? Nobody comes to La Fortuna—an ever-expanding mass of hotels, tour operators, souvenir shops, and *sodas* (small, family-run restaurants)—to see the town alone. Instead, thousands of tourists flock here each year to use it as a hub for visiting the natural wonders that surround it. The volcano, as well as waterfalls, vast nature preserves, great rafting rivers, and an astonishing array of birds are to be found within an hour or less of your hotel. La Fortuna is also the

Canyoneering and waterfall rappelling near the currently inactive Arenal Volcano

best place to arrange trips to the Caño Negro National Wildlife Refuge.

Many people who settled the Northern Lowlands came to the then-isolated region in the 1940s and '50s from other parts of the country to take part in government-sponsored homesteading programs. Thanks to its rich volcanic soil, the agricultural region became one of the most productive in Central America. After the 1968 eruption of Arenal Volcano, La Fortuna was transformed from a tiny, dusty farm town to one of Costa Rica's tourism powerhouses, where visitors converged to see the volcano in action.

As of 2010, the volcano went into a resting phase, which means it is still "active" below the surface, but it's doubtful you'll see more than a puff of steam. Viewing the volcano's peak can be hit or miss, especially during the rainy season (May through November). One minute Arenal Volcano looms menacingly over the village; the next minute clouds shroud its cone. Early morning (and sometimes late afternoon), especially in the dry season, is the best time to catch a longer glimpse.

GETTING HERE AND AROUND
Choose from two routes from San José: for a slightly longer but better road, leave the Pan-American Highway at Naranjo, continuing north to Zarcero and Ciudad Quesada. Head northwest at Ciudad Quesada to La Fortuna; or for a curvier but shorter route, continue beyond Naranjo on the Pan-American Highway, turning north at San Ramón, arriving at La Fortuna about 90 minutes after the turnoff. (Opt for the first route if you are prone to motion sickness.) Either route passes through a mountainous section that begins to fog over by afternoon. Get as early a start as possible. SANSA flies daily to La Fortuna (FTN); flights land at an airstrip at the hamlet of El Tanque, 7 km (4 miles) east of town. Van transport ($10 one way) meets each flight to take you into La Fortuna.

Gray Line has daily shuttle bus service between San José, La Fortuna, and Arenal ($50), and Monteverde ($49).

Interbus also connects San José with La Fortuna ($52) and Monteverde ($49) daily, with connections from here to a few of the North Pacific beaches. Public buses depart five times daily from San José's Terminal Atlántico Norte. Travel time is four hours. Although billed as an express route, the bus makes many stops.

Desafío Adventures provides a fast, popular, three-hour transfer between Monteverde and La Fortuna via taxi, boat, then another taxi, for $32 each way. It also offers private transfers from San José to La Fortuna for $165 one way. Shared shuttles departing San José daily at 1 pm and 5 pm cost $55 per person.

Taxis in and around La Fortuna are relatively affordable and will take you anywhere; a taxi to the Tabacón resort should run about $18. Get a cab at the stand on the east side of Parque Central.

The string of properties on the highway between La Fortuna and the Tabacón resort has led to a noticeable increase in traffic. It is hardly the proverbial urban jungle, and it is one of the country's prettiest stretches of road, but you should drive with caution. Cars dart in and out of driveways. Visitors congregate along the side of the road (likely sloth-spotting), and drivers gaze up at the volcano that looms over the highway. Keep your eyes on the road.

BUS CONTACTS Interbus. ✉ *1 block south of Catholic church, in front Hotel Fas* ☎ *4100–0888 reservations, 2479–7074 La Fortuna office* ⊕ *www.interbusonline. com.*

RENTAL CARS Alamo. ✉ *100 m west of church, La Fortuna* ☎ *2479–9090* ⊕ *www. alamocostarica.com.* **Mapache.** ✉ *800 m west of church, La Fortuna* ☎ *2586–6300* ⊕ *www.mapache.com.*

ESSENTIALS

BANKS/ATMS BAC San José. ✉ *75 m north of gas station, La Fortuna.* **Banco de Costa Rica.** ✉ *East of Parque Central, in front of the school, La Fortuna* ☎ *2479– 9113.* **Banco Nacional.** ✉ *Central Plaza, 100 m east of Catholic church, La Fortuna* ☎ *2479–9355.*

MEDICAL CLINIC Clínica La Fortuna CCSS. ✉ *300 m east of Parque Central, La Fortuna* ☎ *2479–8565.*

PHARMACY Farmacia Fishel. ✉ *On main road, 25 m east of public park, La Fortuna* ☎ *2479–9778.*

POST OFFICE Correos. ✉ *Across from north side of church, La Fortuna* ☎ *2479–8070.*

 Sights

Arenal Volcano National Park (*Parque Nacional Volcán Arenal*)

NATIONAL/STATE PARK | Although the volcano is in a resting phase, you might see an occasional plume of smoke. It is still worth visiting the network of three easy trails leading to old lava flows, secondary rain forest, and a lookout point. (You are still limited in how close you can get, since no one can predict when Arenal will roar to life again.) The park is home to more than 200 species of birds, as well as monkeys, sloths, coatis, deer, and anteaters. A top trail within the park is Heliconias (0.61 km [0.38 mile]), which has a lookout point and connects to Las Coladas Trail (2 km [1 mile]). You'll see hardened lava streams from 1992 and a 200-year-old ceiba tree on El Ceibo loop (2.3 km [1.43 miles]) toward the edge of the park. Los Miradores Trail (1.29 km [0.8 mile]) takes you on a paved trail to Lake Arenal. Outside the national park is the noteworthy Cerro Chatto, an inactive volcano which you can hike from a trailhead near La Fortuna Waterfall or from the Arenal Observatory Lodge. Both trailheads start on private land so expect to pay an entrance fee of up to $10. The challenging, steep, and often muddy Cerro Chatto Trail takes about three to four hours to reach the crater lake. Old lava flows are also visible on the popular Los

Tucanes Trail that begins near the Arenal Observatory Lodge. Guides are available for hire at the neighboring tour office, Arenal 1968. Bring plenty of water. ⊠ *1½ km (1 mile) from police station, on road to Arenal Observatory Lodge, La Fortuna* ☎ *2460–0620 regional office, 2200–4192 park administration* 💲 *$15 cash only.*

Church of San Juan Bosco

RELIGIOUS SITE | The town's squat, pale, concrete church, unremarkable on its own, just might win Costa Rica's most-photographed-house-of-worship award. The view of the church from across the central park, with the volcano in the background, makes a great photo of the sacred and the menacing. ⊠ *West side of Parque Central, La Fortuna.*

Eco Termales

HOT SPRINGS | Open hours at these family-owned hot springs are divided into two intervals per day (10 to 4 and 5 to 10), with only 100 guests permitted entry per segment. This means the six pools and restaurant never get too crowded. Temperatures range from 37° to 41°C (98.6° to 105.8°F), and there is one chilly waterfall to cool you off. Admission includes towel and locker. This is a great alternative to the overcrowded Baldi Hot Springs across the road or the mammoth Tabacón Hot Springs. ⊠ *3½ km (2 miles) east of Catholic church, across from Baldi, diagonal from Volcán Look Disco Club, La Fortuna* ☎ *2479–8787* ⊕ *www. ecotermalesfortuna.cr* 💲 *From $40.*

Ecocentro Danaus (*Danaus Ecocenter*)

NATURE PRESERVE | **FAMILY** | A small ecotourism project outside town exhibits 60 species of medicinal plants, abundant animal life—including sloths and caimans—and butterfly and orchid gardens. This is a great place to see Costa Rica's famed red poison dart frogs up close. Seven guided tours are offered daily from 8 am to 3:30 pm. A two-hour guided evening tour begins at 5:45 and should be reserved in advance. The center can arrange your transportation, too. ⊠ *2 km (1 mile) south of La Fortuna, 600 m above road to Agua Azul, La Fortuna* ☎ *2479–7019, 506/8588–9314 WhatsApp* 💲 *From $19.*

★ La Fortuna Waterfall (*Cataratas de la Fortuna*)

BODY OF WATER | A strenuous walk down 500 steps (allow 25 to 40 minutes) is worth the effort to swim in the pool under the waterfall. Wear sturdy shoes or water sandals with traction, and bring snacks and water. You can get to the trailhead from La Fortuna by walking, by horseback, or by taking a taxi (approximately $10). Arranging a tour with an agency in La Fortuna is the easiest option. There are restrooms, free parking, a restaurant, and gift shop. ⊠ *Yellow entrance sign off main road toward volcano, 7 km (4 miles) south of La Fortuna, La Fortuna* ☎ *2479–9515* ⊕ *www. cataratalafortuna.com* 💲 *$15.*

Lake Arenal

BODY OF WATER | Costa Rica's largest inland body of water, shimmering Lake Arenal, all 85 square km (33 square miles) of it, lies between rolling green hills and a picture-perfect volcano. Many visitors are surprised to learn it's a man-made lake, created in 1973 when a giant dam was built to provide hydroelectric power for the country. A natural depression was flooded, and a lake was born. Depending on the season, the depth varies between 100 and 200 feet, with rainbow bass and machaca fish lurking below the surface. When water levels drop, you can see ruins of a cemetery and church jutting from the lake. The almost constant winds from the Caribbean make this area a windsurfing and kiteboarding mecca. Outfitters in La Fortuna, Nuevo Arenal, and Tilarán run fishing, windsurfing, and kiteboarding trips on the lake. Desafío, an operator based in La Fortuna and Monteverde, has a half-day horseback trip between the two towns, with great views of the lake. For the best lake views, reserve a hotel

Off the Beaten Path

Venado Caves In 1945 a farmer in the mountain hamlet of Venado fell into a hole, and thus discovered Cavernas de Venado, subterranean limestone chambers extending about 2½ km (1½ miles). If you're not claustrophobic, willing to get wet, and don't mind bats or spiders (think carefully) this could be the ticket for you. Rubber boots, flashlights, and helmets are provided. Bring insect repellent and knee pads but leave your phone at the hotel—it will get wet. If you want to capture the adventure, consider hiring their on-site photographer to follow you through the 10 caves. Lunch is an option here; it must be reserved in advance. Most La Fortuna–based tour companies run trips to Venado Caves for about $90. ⊠ *45 mins north of La Fortuna and 20 mins southeast of San Rafael, La Fortuna* ☎ *2478–8008* ⊕ *www.cavernasdelvenadocr.com* ⊠ *From $50.*

in Nuevo Arenal. ⊠ *15 km (9 miles) south-west of La Fortuna, La Fortuna.*

Místico Arenal Hanging Bridges

BRIDGE/TUNNEL | A series of trails and bridges form a loop through the primary rain forest of a 250-acre private reserve, providing great bird-watching and volcano viewing. Sixteen fixed and hanging bridges allow you to see the forest at different levels. There are self-guided tours, but if you want to spot animals in addition to the breathtaking views, we recommend a guide. Trails are open rain or shine, and there are things to do in both types of weather, including horseback-riding tours that start at 9 am and 1 pm. Shuttle service from La Fortuna and area lodgings can be arranged. ⊠ *2½ km (1½ miles) east of Lake Arenal dam on paved road, La Fortuna* ☎ *2479–8282* ⊕ *www.mistico-park.com* ⊠ *From $26.*

The Spa at Tabacón

HOT SPRINGS | Grab a robe and settle into the jungle Jacuzzi while spa valets serve you healthy smoothies. Treatments like the chocolate body wrap and the couples' two-hour massage in private jungle bungalows utilize locally made products and end with champagne and fresh fruit. For a full day of pampering, request the spa package ($160), which includes access to the thermal baths, lunch or dinner, and credit for $100 in spa services. ⊠ *13 km (8 miles) northwest of La Fortuna on hwy. toward Nuevo Arenal, across from Tabacón Resort, La Fortuna* ☎ *2479–2028* ⊕ *www.tabacon.com* ⊠ *From $60 (free for Tabacón guests).*

🍴 Restaurants

Chipotle's

$$ | MEXICAN | Fresh bold flavors, local products, first-class service, and marvelous murals elevate this basic roadside restaurant to a delightful dining experience. The chef and owner trained in Mexico, so you can taste the authenticity in the tacos and the mezcal in the margaritas. **Known for:** fresh guacamole and homemade chips; tacos every which way; churros. $ *Average main: $10* ⊠ *Plaza Arenal, 500 meters west of parque de la Fortuna de San Carlos, La Fortuna* ☎ *2479–9700.*

Don Rufino

$$$ | ECLECTIC | The L-shape bar fronting the main street is a popular expat and tourist hangout. The user-friendly menu is marked with symbols of chili peppers for spicy dishes, a tomato for vegetarian dishes, and a check mark for those that are highly recommended, like the chicken seasoned with chocolate, coffee, and tarragon or forest lasagna made with wild mushrooms, caramelized onions, and ricotta cheese. **Known for:** organic, local meats; friendly service and clientele; occasional live music. $ *Average main: $17 ⊠ Across from gas station, La Fortuna ☎ 2479–9997 ⊕ donrufino.com.*

La Choza de Laurel

$$ | COSTA RICAN | The aroma of rotisserie chicken, porterhouse steak, and fresh fish bathed in garlic attracts passersby to this open-air restaurant a short walk from the center of town. Wooden picnic tables and a cigar shop storefront replicate an old Costa Rican village, adding a cultural touch to your meal. **Known for:** banana splits served in a pineapple; Choza plate with chicken; black bean soup with homemade tortillas. $ *Average main: $12 ⊠ 400 m northwest of church, La Fortuna ☎ 2479–7063 ⊕ lachozadelaurel.com/en.*

★ Que Rico

$$$ | ITALIAN | This lovely Italian-inspired restaurant adds touches of romance with wooden tables draped with red-and-white linens and soft music and candles. The menu is long, with options ranging from local ceviche to tamarind chicken, but the Italian specialties are best: the brick-oven Volcán pizza with ham, mushrooms, bacon, and pepperoni is a local favorite. **Known for:** beef carpaccio; Baci Peruguna pastries stuffed with Nutella and caramelized onions; wine-pairing recommendations. $ *Average main: $20 ⊠ 6½ km (4 miles) west of church, La Fortuna ☎ 2479–1020 ⊕ www.quericoarenal.com.*

Rain Forest Café

$ | COSTA RICAN | Reasonable prices and excellent quality have made this café a traveler's favorite, with meals ranging from *churrasco* (grilled meat) and empanadas to salads and sandwiches.

There's typical Costa Rican *casado* (chicken, beef, or fish served with rice, beans, plantains, and salad) along with tempting desserts like chocolate pie, carrot cake, flan, and a variety of pastries. **Known for:** homemade tortillas; local coffee; Crazy Monkey smoothie made with banana, milk, cinnamon, and coffee. $ *Average main: $8 ⊠ In front of Hotel Las Colinas, 125 m south of park, La Fortuna ☎ 2479–7239.*

Soda y Pizzería La Parada

$$ | COSTA RICAN | La Fortuna's only late-night eatery (open until midnight) does a brisk business serving pizza, pasta, nachos, burgers, and grilled fish. There's a buffet, if you'd rather just point and choose. **Known for:** quick, cheap food; surprisingly impressive wine selection; busy atmosphere. $ *Average main: $11 ⊠ Across from Parque Central and regional bus stop, La Fortuna ☎ 2479–9098 ⊕ www.restaurantelaparada.com.*

 Hotels

★ Amor Arenal

$$$$ | RESORT | Perched canyonside with views of the forest and the volcano beyond, these spacious, modern cabins of stone and wood below soaring ceilings and massive windows are cozy and comfortable. **Pros:** many amenities as well as on-site trails; delectable farm-to-table buffet breakfast; close to town but it feels like you're in the middle of the forest. **Cons:** long walks to casitas (resort provides golf cart rides 24 hours); no kids allowed; bathrooms lack privacy. $ *Rooms from: $400 ⊠ West of Centro De La Fortuna 7 Km on Ruta 142, La Fortuna ☎ 2479–7070 ⊕ amorarenal.com ⤴ 31 casitas ⦿ Free Breakfast.*

Arenal Kioro Suites & Spa

$$$$ | RESORT | This is one of the closest properties to the volcano, with rooms boasting hydro-massage Jacuzzis, sitting areas, jaw-dropping views, Juliet balconies, and nearly 700 square feet of

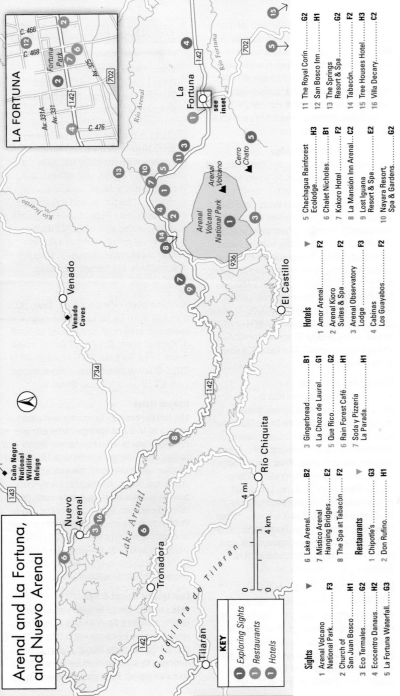

227

6

Arenal, Monteverde, and the Northern Lowlands

ARENAL AND LA FORTUNA

Sights ▶

1 Arenal Volcano National Park.........**F3**
2 Church of San Juan Bosco.........**H1**
3 Eco Termales.........**G2**
4 Ecocentro Danaus.........**H2**
5 La Fortuna Waterfall.........**G3**
6 Lake Arenal.........**B2**
7 Místico Arenal Hanging Bridges.........**E2**
8 The Spa at Tabacón.........**H1**

Restaurants ▶

1 Chipotle's.........**G3**
2 Don Rufino.........**H1**
3 Gingerbread.........**B1**
4 La Choza de Laurel.........**G1**
5 Que Rico.........**G2**
7 Rain Forest Café.........**H1**
7 Soda y Pizzería La Parada.........**H1**

Hotels ▶

1 Amor Arenal.........**F2**
2 Arenal Kioro Suites & Spa.........**B1**
3 Arenal Observatory Lodge.........**F2**
4 Cabinas Los Guayabos.........**C2**
5 Chachagua Rainforest Ecolodge.........**H3**
6 Chalet Nicholas.........**B1**
7 Kokoro Hotel.........**F2**
8 La Mansión Inn Arenal...**C2**
9 Lost Iguana Resort & Spa.........**F3**
10 Nayara Resort, Spa & Gardens.........**E2**
11 The Royal Corin.........**G2**
12 San Bosco Inn.........**H1**
13 The Springs Resort & Spa.........**G2**
14 Tabacón.........**F2**
15 Tree Houses Hotel.........**H3**
16 Villa Decary.........**C2**

space. **Pros:** plentiful breakfast; all rooms face the volcano; enormous rooms. **Cons:** dim rooms; no bottled water or ceiling fans in rooms; steep walkways. [$] *Rooms from: $366* ✉ *10 km (6 miles) northeast of La Fortuna, before Tabacón, Arenal Volcano National Park* ☎ *2479–1700* 🌐 *www.hotelarenalkioro.com* 🛏 *53 rooms* 🍴 *Free Breakfast.*

★ Arenal Observatory Lodge

$$$ | **HOTEL** | These cozy, comfortable, and simple rooms allow you to sleep as close as anyone should to a volcano—it's a mere 2¾ km (1¾ miles) away, and stellar views and outdoor activities are what the place is all about. **Pros:** best volcano views; secluded location; rate includes breakfast, taxes, and guided hike. **Cons:** rough road to get here; isolated location; patchy Wi-Fi. [$] *Rooms from: $159* ✉ *5 km (3 miles) from national park entrance, La Fortuna* ☎ *2479–1070 lodge, 2290–7011 in San José, 877/804–7732 in U.S. and Canada* 🌐 *www.arenalobservatorylodge.com* 🛏 *48 rooms* 🍴 *Free Breakfast.*

Cabinas Los Guayabos

$ | **HOTEL** | As one of the low-priced options with a volcano view, these orange adobe cabins are basic but clean with big windows and private patios, which are great for viewing wildlife and, on clear days, Arenal. **Pros:** good budget value; friendly owners; great volcano views. **Cons:** rustic rooms; breakfast not included; Wi-Fi at reception only. [$] *Rooms from: $72* ✉ *9 km (5½ miles) west of La Fortuna, La Fortuna* ☎ *2479–1444* 🌐 *www.cabinaslosguayabos.com* 💳 *No credit cards* 🛏 *9 cabins* 🍴 *No meals.*

Chachagua Rainforest Ecolodge

$$$ | **HOTEL** | At this working ranch with a brook running through it you can see *caballeros* (cowboys) at work, take a horseback ride into the rain forest, and look for toucans from your room or the deck of your bungalow. **Pros:** children under 11 stay free; free use of fishing and bike gear; nice pool area. **Cons:** 30 minutes from La Fortuna; Wi-Fi signal in reception area only; rough road to hotel. [$] *Rooms from: $219* ✉ *12 km (7 miles) south of La Fortuna, La Fortuna* ☎ *4000–2026* 🌐 *www.chachaguarainforesthotel.com* 🛏 *19 units* 🍴 *Free Breakfast.*

En Route

Viento Fresco Waterfalls On the road from Monteverde, just south of Tilarán, this private farm boasts five cascading waterfalls and swimming holes. The largest plunges 328 feet into a freshwater pool. Note that it's not great for anyone with moblilty issues or for children. The site also offers hiking trails, a dairy farm, several caves, changing facilities, and a restaurant serving Costa Rican fare. Horseback riding is also available. ✉ *Tilarán* ✢ *11 km (6 miles) south of Tilarán near San Miguel* ☎ *2695–3434* 🎟 *$15 waterfalls; $55 horseback riding.*

Kokoro Hotel

$$ | **HOTEL** | **FAMILY** | Spacious and clean rooms at this hot-springs hotel are like mini log cabins with hardwood floors and sugarcane ceilings—numbers 16, 17, and 18 even offer views of the volcano. **Pros:** small spa offers massages; lovely pool; private hot springs; tour desk with good rates. **Cons:** dim lighting in rooms; Wi-Fi in common areas only; hot springs open at 4 pm. [$] *Rooms from: $110* ✉ *500 m west of Quebrada la Palma, La Fortuna* ☎ *2479–1222* 🌐 *kokoroarenal.net* 🛏 *29 rooms* 🍴 *Free Breakfast.*

Lost Iguana Resort & Spa

$$$$ | **HOTEL** | Despite the relative isolation, travelers flock to this rain-forest resort largely because each hillside room has a huge picture window and door opening to an individual balcony with volcano views. **Pros:** good breakfast;

The perfect way to end the day: a nice soak in the hot springs in Arenal Volcano National Park

great volcano views in rain-forest setting; plenty of wildlife; nice spa and gym. **Cons:** removed from sights; small pool; poor lighting in rooms; Wi-Fi in reception area only. [$] *Rooms from: $260* ✉ *Off Hwy. 142, 20 km (12 miles) west of La Fortuna, La Fortuna* ☎ *2479–1557* 🌐 *www.lostiguanacr.com* 🛏 *42 rooms* 🍴 *Free Breakfast.*

★ Nayara Resort, Spa & Gardens
$$$$ | **RESORT** | Scattered over expansive grounds are freestanding casitas, all tastefully decorated with dark-wood furnishings and equipped with luxurious touches like indoor-outdoor showers, four-post canopy beds, plasma TVs, and whirlpool tubs. **Pros:** luxurious rooms; attentive staff; early check-in can be arranged; excellent breakfast. **Cons:** hotel books up early; villas lack volcano views; need to use golf carts to get around sprawling grounds. [$] *Rooms from: $475* ✉ *7 km (4½ miles) west of La Fortuna, Arenal Volcano National Park* ☎ *2479–1600, 888/332–2961 in North America* 🌐 *www.arenalnayara.com* 🛏 *66 units* 🍴 *Free Breakfast.*

The Royal Corín
$$$$ | **RESORT** | This hotel has a volcano view along with luxury perks like a swim-up bar, five-star cuisine, a swanky lobby, and an impressive spa. **Pros:** on-site hot springs; pleasant hotel-style surroundings; excellent showers. **Cons:** some street noise; poor lighting in the rooms; not a lot of local flavor. [$] *Rooms from: $290* ✉ *4 km (2½ miles) west of La Fortuna, La Fortuna* ☎ *2479–2201, 800/742–1399 in North America* 🌐 *www.royalcorin.com* 🛏 *54 rooms* 🍴 *Free Breakfast.*

San Bosco Inn
$$ | **HOTEL** | In downtown La Fortuna, this inn has clean, bright rooms linked by a long veranda lined with benches and potted plants, and added perks like a large pool and in-room Wi-Fi. **Pros:** gated property; good value; close to center of town; use of spa at sister property Volcano Lodge. **Cons:** some rooms get street noise; boxy design; no bar or restaurant. [$] *Rooms from: $88* ✉ *220 m north of*

gas station, La Fortuna ☎ *2479–9050, 800/393–0902 in North America* 🌐 *www.hotelsanbosco.com* 🛏 *33 rooms* 🍴 *Free Breakfast.*

The Springs Resort & Spa
$$$$ | **RESORT** | **FAMILY** | With its own adventure park, hot-springs complex, and activities for all ages, this resort caters to both hotel guests and the outside public with day passes to its massive grounds. **Pros:** stupendous volcano views; hot springs rich in minerals; excellent sushi bar. **Cons:** property has a theme-park feel; rooms are pricey; Wi-Fi signal weak in some areas. [$] *Rooms from: $615* ✉ *9 km (5½ miles) west of La Fortuna, then 4 km (2½ miles) north, La Fortuna* ☎ *2401–3300, 954/727–8333 in North America* 🌐 *www.thespringscostarica.com* 🛏 *47 units* 🍴 *No meals.*

Tabacón
$$$$ | **RESORT** | At one of Central America's most relaxing and romantic resorts, it's the hot springs and lovely spa, coupled with attractive rooms (the suites are some of the country's finest) that customarily draw happy guests inland from the ocean. **Pros:** elegant hotel; luxurious hot springs; great volcano views; good restaurant. **Cons:** hot springs can get crowded; two-night minimum stay. [$] *Rooms from: $295* ✉ *13 km (8 miles) northwest of La Fortuna on Hwy. 142, La Fortuna* ☎ *2479–2000, 2519–1999 in San José, 855/822–2266 in North America* 🌐 *www.tabacon.com* 🛏 *102 rooms* 🍴 *Free Breakfast.*

Tree Houses Hotel
$$ | **B&B/INN** | Whether whiling away the mornings on the porch amid the toucans, trekking to the river, or spotting nocturnal creatures on night hikes, nature lovers will be enthralled with the stilted cabins of this 10-acre property in the trees. **Pros:** lots of wildlife including sloths, monkeys, birds; unique perspective from the treetops without sacrificing A/C; complimentary perks like morning coffee delivery to your porch and guided hikes. **Cons:** some road noise; remote location 25 minutes from major attractions; limited Wi-Fi and cell signal. [$] *Rooms from: $124* ✉ *300 meters north of the cemetery, Ciudad Quesada* ☎ *2475–6507* 🌐 *www.treehouseshotelcostarica.com* 🛏 *7 tree houses* 🍴 *Free Breakfast.*

Nightlife

People in La Fortuna tend to turn in early, though there are a couple of spots for night owls.

Kazan
BARS/PUBS | Although La Fortuna is not known for its happening nightlife, this central bar is where locals and tourists alike gather to watch the game over a cold beer. They have two-for-one cocktails from 5 to 7, free Wi-Fi, and a kitchen serving late-night quick bites. ✉ *North of park, below Arenal Fitness Center, La Fortuna* ☎ *2479–7561* 🌐 *www.facebook.com/KazanCR.*

Lava Lounge
BARS/PUBS | This La Fortuna hot spot has local and imported beers plus plenty of cocktails to get you in the mood for live music every Wednesday and Saturday from 7 to 10. An unorthodox happy hour is from 9 to 11 am, and you're likely to have desperate-looking dogs under foot, telepathically begging you to take them home. Lava Lounge owner Scott Alan runs a dog rescue at this pooch-friendly establishment. Donations to the cause are always appreciated. ✉ *25 m west of Catholic church, La Fortuna* ☎ *2479–7365* 🌐 *www.lavaloungecostarica.com.*

Activities

TOUR OPERATORS

★ **Desafío Adventure Company**
HIKING/WALKING | Expert Desafío guides can take you rafting, horseback riding, hiking, rappelling—you name the adventure. Desafío pioneered rafting trips in this region, and has day trips on the

Sarapiquí River (Class III–IV) for experienced rafters ($95) and half-day rafting on the Balsa River (Class II–III) for less experienced paddlers ($75). Kayaking outings on Lake Arenal ($65) are ideal for beginners. If you're in the mood for something different, Desafío has half-day stand-up-paddling excursions on the lake ($65), and the popular Mambo Combo tour that combines waterfall rappelling and white-water rafting ($165).

If you're interested in getting up to Monteverde from the Arenal–La Fortuna area without taking the grinding four-hour drive, there's an alternative: Desafío Adventures has a five-hour guided horseback trip ($85). Alternatively, you can travel by mountain bike for the same price. ⊠ *Behind church, La Fortuna* ☎ *2479–0020, 855/818–0020 in North America* ⊕ *www.desafiocostarica.com* ✉ *From $65.*

Jacamar Naturalist Tours

TOUR—SPORTS | The variety of tours here ranges from bird walks and sunset lake cruises to white-water rafting and safari float trips. There are boat trips on Lake Arenal and Caño Negro Lagoon in the morning. ⊠ *Across from Parque Central, south side of Catholic church, La Fortuna* ☎ *2479–9767, 800/719–6377 in North America* ⊕ *www.arenaltours.com* ✉ *From $63.*

Sunset Tours

TOUR—SPORTS | One of the country's best tour operators pioneered excursions to the Caño Negro National Wildlife Refuge and Venado Caverns. (Note, though, that like most La Fortuna tour operators, its tours do not actually enter Caño Negro itself.) They also offer tours to La Fortuna Waterfall, the volcano, Lake Arenal, and nearby rivers. ⊠ *Across from south side of church, La Fortuna* ☎ *2479–9585, 2479–9800* ✉ *From $45.*

CANOPY TOURS
Ecoglide Arenal Park

TOUR—SPORTS | Unlike most zipline companies, Ecoglide adds an element of safety with their double cables and allows guests to request starting times outside of their regular tour schedule. There are 12 standard ziplines and a Tarzan swing at platform No. 8. For those who want to film while they fly, Ecoglide rents helmets with front camera mounting systems. As with all zipline tours in Costa Rica, reservations should be made in advance. Set tours start at 8, 10, noon, and 3. ⊠ *3 km (2 miles) west of La Fortuna, La Fortuna* ☎ *2479–7120* ⊕ *www.arenalecoglide.com* ✉ *$75.*

★ Sky Adventures Arenal Park

TOUR—SPORTS | This adventure park on the outskirts of Arenal Volcano operates two other parks on Lake Arenal and in Monteverde. Alpine-style gondolas transport you to the site, from which you can descend via 3 km (2 miles) of ziplines, hike through the cloud forest along a series of suspended bridges, or go back the way you came, on the tram. You'll pass from rain forest into cloud forest, and can fly above the treetops on Costa Rica's highest zipline. Adrenaline-seekers might opt for biking, canyoning, or tubing back to base camp. You can mix and match tours for a full-day adventure, too. ⊠ *26 km (16 miles) west of La Fortuna, El Castillo* ☎ *2479–4100, 844/486–6759 in North America* ⊕ *www.skyadventures.travel* ✉ *From $35.*

HORSEBACK RIDING
★ Eponicity

HORSEBACK RIDING | A ride to a waterfall is the beginning of the offerings from Eponicity. From family retreats to corporate coaching, their equine therapy in the rain forest is guided by the principle of natural horsemanship. ⊠ *La Fortuna* ☎ *2478–0023* ⊕ *eponicity.com.*

RAFTING AND KAYAKING

Canoa Aventura

BIRD WATCHING | Canoeing trips with ample wildlife viewing on the Río Peñas Blancas are a specialty, as are daylong canoe tours of the Caño Blanco Wildlife Refuge. The three-hour Caño Negro tour takes place on the Río Frío near the Nicaraguan border, where you're sure to see birds, monkeys, caimans, iguanas, and bats. Tours are appropriate for beginners, with a selection of easy floats if you're not feeling too adventurous, and instruction is provided, but the folks here can tailor excursions if you're more experienced. ⊠ *1 km (½ mile) west of the church, La Fortuna* ☎ *2479–8200* ⊕ *www. canoa-aventura.com* ⊠ *From $57.*

Flow Trips

KAYAKING | Local guides lead rafting excursions on the Sarapiquí River (Classes II, III, and IV), as well as kayaking trips on Lake Arenal and the Peñas Blancas River. ⊠ *1 km (½ mile) west of La Fortuna, La Fortuna* ☎ *2479–0075* ⊕ *www.flowtrips. com* ⊠ *From $70.*

RAPPELLING

Pure Trek Canyoning

CLIMBING/MOUNTAINEERING | Rappel down three waterfalls and one rock wall ranging in height from 39 to 164 feet. Two guides lead small groups—10 is the maximum size—on a four-hour tour ($101) that departs at 7 am or noon to a private farm near La Fortuna, with plenty of wildlife-watching opportunities along the way. There is a bit of hiking between waterfalls and long periods of waiting for others in your group, so patience and proper shoes are a must. The excursion includes transportation, all rappelling gear, and a light lunch. ⊠ *7 km (4½ miles) west of town center, La Fortuna* ☎ *2479–1313, 866/569–5723 in North America* ⊕ *www.puretrekcanyoning.com* ⊠ *$101.*

Cau

Four-wheel-ATV a[...]
popular in Monteverd[...]
but not recommended. The[...]
disturb vegetation and the ecos[...]
tem, not to mention that the noise often frightens wildlife.

Nuevo Arenal

40 km (25 miles, 1 hr) west of La Fortuna.

Much of the original town of Arenal, at one of the lowest points near Lake Arenal, was destroyed by the volcano's 1968 eruption, and the rest was destroyed in 1973, when Lake Arenal flooded the region. This new (*nuevo*) town was created about 30 km (19 miles) away from the site of the old. It is about halfway between La Fortuna and Tilarán, making it a good stop for a break, and an even better base, with a few truly lovely lodgings and restaurants nearby.

GETTING HERE AND AROUND

The route from La Fortuna to Nuevo Arenal around the north shore of Lake Arenal has been greatly improved over the years. Watch out for the raccoonlike coatimundis (*pizotes* in Spanish) that scurry along the road. Longtime human feeding has diminished their ability to search for food on their own, and the cookies and potato chips they're frequently fed make matters worse. Don't contribute to the problem. Public buses run twice daily from La Fortuna to Nuevo Arenal and five times daily from Tilarán. On the main road, at the entrance of town, there's a small shopping area with a pharmacy, post office, and a gas station across the street. The small town has three grocery stores including Super Compro on the main road.

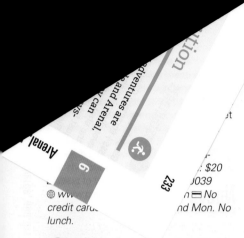

… : $20 … 039 … 🌐 ww … n 💳 No credit car… nd Mon. No lunch.

Hotels

Chalet Nicholas

$$ | **B&B/INN** | This rain-forest B&B has old-fashioned charm with three chalet-style bedrooms looking out onto the mystic lake and volcano. **Pros:** attentive owners; great breakfasts; terrific value; birders' paradise. **Cons:** dogs on-site, so not a place if you dislike canines; need a car to stay here; no children under 10. [$] *Rooms from: $75* ✉ *3 km (2 miles) west of Nuevo Arenal* ☎ *2694–4041* 🌐 *www.chaletnicholas.com* 🛏 *3 rooms* 🍴 *Free Breakfast.*

La Mansión Inn Arenal

$$$ | **HOTEL** | Nicely decorated cottages are scattered around 25 acres on Arenal's northeast shore at the point where the volcano begins to disappear from sight, but the lake views (and the sunsets) remain as spectacular as ever. **Pros:** luxurious furnishings; stupendous lake views from private terraces; great pool area. **Cons:** far from sights; need a car to stay here; very slippery path after rain. [$] *Rooms from: $200* ✉ *Hwy. 142, 34 km (21 miles) west of La Fortuna* ☎ *2692–8018, 877/660–3830 in North America* 🌐 *www.lamansionarenal.com* 🛏 *18 units* 🍴 *Free Breakfast.*

…la Decary

… **B&B/INN** | There's much to recom-…end at this hillside property, including …he large picture windows and balconies overlooking Lake Arenal and the attentive service from the owners. **Pros:** attentive owners; great breakfasts; yoga classes offered. **Cons:** need a car to stay here; minimal road noise; Wi-Fi reaches only lower-level rooms and common areas. [$] *Rooms from: $129* ✉ *2 km (1 mile) east of Nuevo Arenal* ☎ *2694–4330, 800/556–0505 in North America* 🌐 *www.villadecary.com* 🛏 *8 units* 🍴 *Free Breakfast.*

Monteverde Cloud Forest and Santa Elena

Monteverde is 167 km (104 miles, 3½ hrs) northwest of San José and 110 km (67 miles, 4 hrs) southwest of La Fortuna, Santa Elena is 6 km (4 miles, 30 mins) north of Monteverde and 35 km (22 miles, 2 hrs) southeast of Tilarán.

Monteverde is a rain forest, but you won't be in the tropics—rather in the cool, gray, misty world of the cloud forest. Almost 900 species of epiphytes, including 450 orchids, thrive here; most tree trunks are covered with mosses, bromeliads, ferns, and other plants. Monteverde spans the Continental Divide, extending from about 4,920 feet on the Pacific slope and 4,430 feet on the Atlantic slope up to the highest peaks of the Tilarán Mountains at around 6,070 feet. Make Santa Elena your base of operations when visiting this area.

The area's first residents were a handful of Costa Rican families fleeing the rough-and-tumble life of nearby gold-mining fields during the 1940s. They were joined in the early 1950s by Quakers, conscientious objectors from Alabama fleeing conscription into the Korean War.

Continued on page 240

Zip lining is an exhilarating experience.

CANOPY TOURS

Costa Rica invented the concept of the canopy tour, and the idea has spread across the globe. Zip lining through the treetops is a once-in-a-lifetime experience, and exploring the jungle canopy is the best way to see the most eye-catching animals.

A canopy tour is an umbrella term describing excursions that take you to the jungle's ceiling. The experience is distinctly Costa Rican and is one of the country's signature activities for visitors. There are two types of tours: one gives you a chance to see animals (from bridges and platforms), and the other lets you swing through the trees on zip lines. We know of around 80 tours nationwide but recommend only about a third of that number. *You'll find tour information in most chapters of this book.*

By Jeffrey Van Fleet

WHAT EXACTLY IS A CANOPY TOUR?

Canopy zip line tour at Rain Forest Adventures

WHAT TO EXPECT

Plan on a half-day for your canopy tour, including transportation to and from your hotel and a safety briefing for zip line excursions. Most zip line tours begin at fixed times and reservations are always required, or at least advised. A tour over hanging-bridges is far more leisurely and can be done at your own pace. The latest craze on zip line tours is an optional Tarzan swing, a freefall drop similar to bungee jumping but with swinging instead of bouncing. Several outfitters also offer rappelling as part of the package. The occasional mega-complex, such as Monteverde's Selvatura, offers both types of tours. For most, it's one or the other.

BRIDGES AND TRAMS

These are canopy tours in a literal sense, where you walk along suspension bridges, ride along in a tram, or are hoisted up to a platform to get a closer look at birds, monkeys, and sloths. They're also called hanging-bridges tours, sky walks, or platform tours. If seeing nature at a more leisurely pace is your goal, opt for these, especially the bridge excursions. Early mornings are the best time for animal sightings—at 50–250 feet above ground, the views are stupendous.

ZIP LINES

This type of tour is a fast-paced, thrilling experience. You're attached to a zip line with a safety harness, and then you "fly" at about 15–40 miles per hour from one tree platform to the next. (You may be anywhere from 60–300 feet above the forest floor.) Tree-to-tree zip lines date from the 19th century and have been a bona fide activity for visitors to Costa Rica since the mid-1990s when the first tour opened in Monteverde. These tours are tremendous fun, but you won't see any animals. An average fitness level—and above-average level of intrepidness—are all you need.

TOP CANOPY TOURS BY REGION

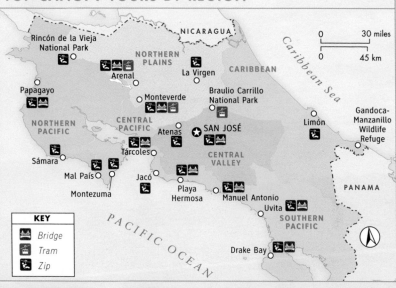

TOUR OPERATER	LOCATION	TYPE		
Místico Arenal Park	Arenal		Bridge	
Sky Adventures	Arenal	Zip	Bridge	Tram
Canopy Safari	Manuel Antonio	Zip	Bridge	
Canopy Mal Pais	Malpaís	Zip		
Montezuma Waterfall Canopy Tour	Montezuma	Zip		
Ecoglide Arenal Park	Arenal	Zip		
Hotel Villa Lapas	Tárcoles	Zip	Bridge	
Hacienda Guachipelín	Rincón de La Vieja National Park	Zip	Bridge	
Original Canopy Tour	Monteverde	Zip		
Original Canopy Tour	Drake Bay	Zip	Bridge	
Original Canopy tour	Veragua, Limón	Zip		
Rain Forest Adventures	Braulio Carrillo National Park	Zip	Bridge	Tram
Rain Forest Adventures	Jacó	Zip	Bridge	Tram
Las Pavas Zip Line	Rincón de la Vieja National Park	Zip		
Selvatura	Monteverde	Zip	Bridge	
Tití Canopy Tour	Manuel Antonio	Zip		
Sky Adventures	Monteverde	Zip	Bridge	Tram
Wing Nuts Canopy Tour	Sámara	Zip		
Witch's Rock Canopy Tour	Papagayo	Zip	Bridge	
Osa Canopy Tour	Uvita	Zip	Bridge	
El Santuario Canopy Adventure Tour	Manuel Antonio	Zip	Bridge	

SAFETY FIRST

(top left) Kids enjoy zip lining. (bottom left) Brown-Throated Three-Toed Sloth. (right) Sky Tram, Rainforest Canopy Tour, Arenal

PLAYING IT SAFE

Flying through the air, while undeniably cool, is also inherently dangerous. Before you strap into a harness, be certain that the safety standards are first rate. There's virtually no government oversight of the activity in Costa Rica. Here is a list of questions you should ask before you book:

1. How long has the company been in business?

2. Are they insured?

3. Are cables, harnesses, and other equipment manufacturer-certified?

4. Is there a second safety line that connects you to the zip line in case the main pulley gives way?

5. What's the price? Plan on paying $50 to $80— a low price could indicate a second-rate operation.

6. Are participants clipped to the zip line while on the platform? (They should be.)

KEEP IN MIND

■ Listen closely to the guides' pre-tour safety briefing and obey their instructions.

■ Never argue with the guide when s/he is making a decision to preserve your safety.

■ Don't attempt to take photos in flight.

■ Gauge your abilities frankly. Remember, once you start, there's no turning back.

■ If anything seems "off" or makes you uncomfortable, walk away.

A number of things drew them to Costa Rica: just a few years earlier it had abolished its military, and the Monteverde area offered good grazing. The cloud forest that lay above the dairy farms soon attracted the attention of ecologists. Educators and artisans followed, giving Monteverde and its "metropolis," the village of Santa Elena, a certain mystique. These days, Monteverde looks quite a bit different than it did when the first wave of Quakers arrived. New hotels have sprouted up everywhere, traffic grips the center of town, and there's a small shopping center outside of town on the way to the mountain. A glut of rented all-terrain vehicles (ATVs) contributes to the increasing din that disrupts Monteverde's legendary peace and quiet, and the paving of one access route will no doubt increase visitor numbers. Some define these moves as progress while others lament the gradual chipping away at what makes one of Costa Rica's most special areas so special. Reminiscent of a ski town in summer, Monteverde still lets you get away from it all, but you'll have to work harder at it than you used to. In any case, you'll not lack for things to do if seeing nature is a primary reason for your visit. The only way to see the area's reserves, including the Monteverde Cloud Forest, is to hike them.

Note that a casual reference to "Monteverde" generally indicates this entire area, but officially the term applies only to the original Quaker settlement, which is by the dairy-processing plant just down the mountain from the reserve entrance. If you follow road signs exclusively, you'll end up outside the town of Santa Elena, halfway to the reserve.

It takes a little effort to get here, and it can get crowded during high season, but this exceptionally well-protected reserve affords visitors one of the country's best opportunities to view abundant—and stunning—wildlife and colorful high-elevation flora.

Did You Know?

Monteverde's Quakers, or more officially, the Society of Friends, no longer constitute the majority here these days, but their imprint on the community remains strong. Their meetinghouse at Escuela de los Amigos, just south of the Cheese Factory on the road to the reserve, welcomes visitors at meetings of worship, 10:30 am Sunday and 9 am Wednesday. Most of the time is spent in quiet reflection.

GETTING HERE AND AROUND

Monteverde's isolation is coming to an end with the paving of one access route. The completion of "Highway" 606—remember that Costa Ricans rarely use or know highway numbers—via Sardinal has made the area more accessible than ever. Whether that's good or bad depends on your point of view. (Other roads in and out still mean negotiating some of the country's legendarily rough roads.) Your own vehicle gives you the greatest flexibility, but a burgeoning number of shuttle-van services connect Monteverde with San José and other tourist destinations throughout the country.

Buses from San José leave twice daily from the Terminal 7-10 (at Calle 10 and Avenida 7), at 6:30 am and 2:30 pm, stopping in the center of Santa Elena and at various locations on the way up the mountain as far as the Cheese Factory. Buses from Santa Elena leave for San José at 6:30 am and 2:30 pm daily. Taxis from Santa Elena are $10 to $13. Buses from Tilarán to Santa Elena leave once a day, at 12:30 pm. Desafío Adventure Company offers shared transportation from San José to Monteverde for $52 one way. The San José–Monteverde public bus route is notorious for theft; watch your bags, and never let your passport and money out of your sight—or off your person. Never take advice from the "guides" who meet incoming buses in Monteverde and La Fortuna. They claim to want to help you find accommodations and tours, when in reality they receive kickbacks for sending tourists to less-than-desirable hotels or to unqualified "tour guides."

If you can handle the curvy roads, a windy track leads from Tilarán via Cabeceras to Santa Elena, near the Monteverde Cloud Forest Biological Reserve, doing away with the need to cut across to the Pan-American Highway. You need a 4WD vehicle, and you should inquire locally about the current condition of the road. The views of Nicoya Peninsula, Lake Arenal, and Arenal Volcano reward those willing to bump around a bit. Note, too, that you don't really save much time—on a good day it takes about 2½ hours as opposed to the 3 hours required via Cañas and Río Lagarto on the highway.

By car from the Fortuna area, it's at least three hours by bumpy road around Lake Arenal; some tour companies provide the trip via minibus and boat (called "Taxi-Boat-Taxi" or "Jeep-Boat-Jeep") for about $30 one way. Gray Line has daily shuttle bus service between San José, La Fortuna, Arenal ($50), and Monteverde ($49). Interbus also connects San José with La Fortuna and Monteverde (each $49) daily, with connections from here to a few of the North Pacific beaches. There will be times you wish you had your own vehicle, but it's surprisingly easy to get around the Monteverde area without a car. Given the state of the roads off the main track, you'll be happy to let someone else do the driving. However, if you do arrive by rental car, the road up the mountain from Santa Elena is paved as far as the gas station near the entrance to the Hotel Belmar. Taxis are plentiful; it's easy to call one from your hotel, and restaurants are happy to summon a cab to take you back to your hotel after

dinner. Taxis also congregate in front of the church on the main street in Santa Elena. Many tour companies will pick you up from your hotel and bring you back at the end of the day, either free or for a small fee.

ESSENTIALS

BANK/ATM Banco Nacional. ✉ *50 m north of Catholic church, and 50 m east of first corner, next to Orchid Garden, Santa Elena* ☎ *2645–5610.*

MEDICAL CLINIC Clínica Monteverde. ✉ *150 m south of soccer field, Santa Elena* ☎ *2645–5076.*

PHARMACY Farmacia Vitosi. ✉ *Across from Chamber of Tourism, Santa Elena* ☎ *2645–5004.*

POST OFFICE Correos. ✉ *50 m south of Herpetarium Adventures Monteverde, Santa Elena* ☎ *2202–2900.*

TOURIST INFORMATION Chamber of Tourism Monteverde. ✉ *Across from Súper Compro supermarket, Santa Elena* ☎ *2645–6565* ⊕ *www.exploremonteverde.com.*

Sights

The Bat Jungle

ZOO | FAMILY | Butterflies, frogs, and snakes have their own Monteverde-area exhibits, and bats get equal time with guided tours that provide insight into the life of one of the planet's most misunderstood mammals. Admission includes a 45-minute guided tour through a small exhibit and glass enclosure housing nearly 100 live bats. You can watch them fly, eat, and even give birth. Reservations are recommended. ✉ *Across from Tramonti restaurant, Monteverde* ☎ *2645–9999* ⊕ *www.batjungle.com* 🎟 *$15 for guided tour, $7 self-guided.*

Butterfly Garden (Jardín de Mariposas)

ZOO | FAMILY | Thirty species of butterflies flit about in four enclosed botanical gardens. Morning visits are best, since

the butterflies are most active early in the day. Your entrance ticket (cash only) includes an hour-long guided tour under tin roofs, meaning you won't get wet on rainy days. Be sure to visit the nonprofit gift shop benefiting the local community. ⊠ *Near Monteverde Inn, Monteverde* ✛ *Take right-hand turnoff 4 km (2½ miles) past Santa Elena on road to Monteverde, continue for 2 km (1 mile)* ☎ *2645–5512* ⊕ *www.monteverdebutterflygarden.com* ✉ *$17.*

Cafe Monteverde Coffee Tour

FARM/RANCH | Bite your tongue before requesting Costa Rica's ubiquitous Café Britt up here. Export-quality Café Monteverde is the local, sustainably grown product, and the tour lets you see the process up close from start to finish from the area's Turín plantation, 3 km (2 miles) north of Santa Elena, where the plants are grown in the shade; transport to the *beneficio,* the processing mill where the beans are washed and dried; and finally to the roaster. Reservations are required, and pickup from area hotels is available. They also operate the Monteverde Coffee Center (coffee shop) in town next to CASEM. ⊠ *Monteverde* ☎ *2645–7550* ⊕ *www.cafedemonteverde.com* ✉ *$35.*

Children's Eternal Rain Forest (*Bosque Eterno de los Niños*)

NATURE PRESERVE | FAMILY | The 54,000-acre rain forest dwarfs the Monteverde and Santa Elena reserves. It began life as a school project in Sweden among children interested in saving a piece of the rain forest, and blossomed into a fund-raising effort among students from 44 countries. The reserve's **Bajo del Tigre trail** makes for a gentle self-guided 3½-km (2-mile) hike through secondary forest. Along the trail are 27 stations at which to stop and learn about the reserve, many with lessons geared toward kids. A separate guided twilight walk ($23) begins at 5:30 pm and lasts two hours, affording the chance to see the nocturnal side of the cloud forest;

reservations are required. Much of the rest of the reserve is not open to the public, but the Monteverde Conservation League offers stays at San Gerardo and Poco Sol, two remote field stations within the forest. The $59 packages include dormitory accommodation and meals. ⊠ *100 m south of CASEM, Monteverde* ☎ *2645–5200* ⊕ *acmcr.org* ✉ *From $13.*

Curi Cancha Reserve

FOREST | FAMILY | There's no shortage of nature walks in Monteverde, but this newer, less crowded reserve—with more than 6½ km (4 miles) of trails progressing through different types of forests, fields, and gardens filled with hummingbird feeders—is one of the best. You'll get the chance to see fauna like the elusive quetzal, motmots, owls and other birds, plus sloths and snakes, as well as flora like mammoth trees, bromeliads, epiphytes, and orchids. Trails are wide and in great shape; there are bathroom facilities and benches for taking a rest, and the reserve is totally handicap accessible, with carts for folks who need them. We recommend a guide—you'll see much, much more that way. ⊠ *300 m west of the cheese factory, Monteverde* ☎ *2645–6915* ⊕ *reservacuricancha.com* ✉ *$15.*

Don Juan Coffee Tour

FACTORY | Small groups are the hallmark of these tours that last about two hours and let you see the coffee process from start to finish at the plantation of Don Juan Cruz, one of the original settlers in the area. You can also learn about chocolate and sugarcane. Transportation can be arranged from all Monteverde-area lodgings. To get a taste without the tour, you can visit their café and gift store next to the post office in Santa Elena. ⊠ *2 km (1 mile) northwest of soccer field, Monteverde* ☎ *2645–7100* ⊕ *www.donjuancoffeetour.com* ✉ *$35.*

A leisurely stroll across a suspension bridge in Monteverde

★ El Trapiche

FACTORY | Two-hour tours departing at 10 am and 3 pm guide you from the bean to the cup at this coffee plantation and old-fashioned *trapiche* (sugarcane mill) where you can sample liquor, java, and other locally made products. The hands-on tour includes a ride on an oxcart and some sweet treats made from homegrown coffee beans, sugarcane, and cacao. ⊠ *Hwy. 606, 2 km (1 mile) northwest of Santa Elena, Santa Elena* ☎ *2645–7650* ⊕ *www. eltrapichetour.com* 🖅 *$35.*

Herpetarium Adventures Monteverde

ZOO | FAMILY | If you or your kids love creepy, crawly, slithery things, head here. Operated by Sky Adventures, this herpetarium holds more than 50 species of reptiles and amphibians, such as native frogs, toads, turtles, lizards, and snakes in terrariums. Some of the more impressive species are the colorful poison arrow frog, the Jesus Christ lizard, snapping turtles, tarantulas, and the red-eyed tree frog. Animals are most active around 6 pm. Admission includes guided tours in English or Spanish. ⊠ *Across from Plaza Monteverde, Monteverde* ☎ *2645–6002, 844/468–6759 in U.S.* ⊕ *www.skyadventures.travel/herpetarium* 🖅 *$16.*

★ Monteverde Cloud Forest Biological Reserve (*Reserva Biológica Bosque Nuboso de Monteverde*)

NATURE PRESERVE | One of Costa Rica's best-kept reserves has 13 km (8 miles) of well-marked trails, lush vegetation, and a cool, damp climate. The collision of moist winds with the Continental Divide here creates a constant mist whose particles provide nutrients for plants growing at the upper layers of the forest. Giant trees are enshrouded in a cascade of orchids, bromeliads, mosses, and ferns, and in those patches where sunlight penetrates, brilliantly colored flowers flourish. The sheer size of everything, especially the leaves of the trees, is striking. No less astounding is the variety: more than 3,000 plant species, 500 species of birds, 500 types of butterflies, and 130 different mammals have so far been cataloged at Monteverde. A damp and exotic mixture of shades, smells, and sounds, the cloud forest is also famous for its population of resplendent quetzals, which can be spotted feeding on the *aguacatillo* (similar to avocado) trees; best viewing times are early mornings from January until September, and especially during the mating season of April and May. Other forest-dwelling inhabitants include hummingbirds and multicolor frogs.

For those who don't have a lucky eye, a short-stay aquarium is in the field station; captive amphibians stay here just a week before being released back into the wild. Although the reserve limits visitors to 250 people at a time, Monteverde is one of the country's most popular destinations. We do hear complaints (and agree with them) that the reserve gets too crowded with visitors at times. Early visitors have the best chance at spotting wildlife in the protected reserve.

Allow a generous slice of time for leisurely hiking to see the forest's flora and fauna; longer hikes are made possible by some strategically placed overnight refuges along the way. At the gift shop you can buy self-guide pamphlets and books; a map is provided when you pay the entrance fee. You can navigate the reserve on your own, but the 2½-hour guided Natural History Walk (7:30 am, 11:30 am, and 1:30 pm) is invaluable for getting the most out of your visit. You may also take advantage of two-hour guided night tours starting each evening at 5:45 (reservations required). The reserve provides transport from area hotels for an extra $5. Guided walking bird-watching tours up to the reserve leave from the park entrance daily at 7:30, 11:30, and 1:30 for groups of four to six people. Advance reservations are required.

If you'd like to stay in the reserve itself, you'll find six rooms of lodging at the site's La Casona. Rates of $81 per person include three meals. ⊠ *10 km (6 miles) south of Santa Elena, Monteverde* ☎ *2645–5122* ⊕ *cloudforestmonteverde. com* ✉ *From $22.*

Monteverde Ecological Sanctuary

NATURE PRESERVE | This family-run, 52-acre wildlife refuge is laced with four trails and houses birds, sloths, agoutis, and coatimundis. They focus on small group tours, including a coffee tour, cooking classes, and day hikes, where you'll come upon two waterfalls and a coffee plantation. If you can't make it all the way up to the Monteverde Reserve for the day hike, there's a two-hour guided twilight walk that begins each evening at 5:30 and 7:30. Reservations are required. ⊠ *Turnoff to Jardín de Mariposas, off main road just south of Santa Elena, Monteverde* ☎ *2645–5869* ⊕ *www.santuarioecologico.com* ✉ *From $12.*

Orchid Garden (*Jardín de Orquídeas*)
GARDEN | More than 460 species of orchids, one of which is the world's smallest, are on display. Admission includes a 30-minute tour. ⊠ *150 m south of Banco Nacional, Santa Elena* ☎ *2645–5308* ⊕ *www.monteverdeorchidgarden.net* ✉ *$14.*

Santa Elena Cloud Forest Reserve (*Reserva Bosque Nuboso Santa Elena*)
NATURE PRESERVE | Several conservation areas near Monteverde are attractive day-trip destinations, especially when the Monteverde Reserve is too busy. The 765-acre Santa Elena Reserve just west of Monteverde is a project of the Santa Elena high school, and has a series of trails of varying length and difficulty that can be walked alone or with a guide on tours that depart daily at 7:30, 9:15, and 11:30 am, and 1 pm. The 1½-km (1-mile) Youth Challenge trail takes about 45 minutes to negotiate and includes an observation platform with views that extend as far as the Arenal Volcano—that is, if the clouds clear. If you're feeling hardy, try the 5-km (3-mile) Caño Negro trail. There's a shuttle service to the reserve with fixed departures and returns; reservations are required, and the cost is $3 each way. ⊠ *6 km (4 miles) north of Santa Elena, Monteverde* ☎ *2645–5390* ⊕ *www.reservasantaelena.org* ✉ *From $16.*

🍴 Restaurants

Café Caburé

$$ | MODERN ARGENTINE | This restaurant/bakery/chocolateria is one of only a few in Costa Rica that grinds its own cocoa beans. Start with a meal in the open-air restaurant serving savory empanadas, mole dishes, and chipotle wraps with a creamy secret sauce before getting to the sweet stuff, like ganache with blackberry sauce, chocolate-passion-fruit mousse, and exquisite chocolate truffles. **Known for:** vegetarian options; curried chicken and mango salad; tours of adjoining chocolate factory. $ *Average main: $13 ⊠ Paseo de Stella Tourist Center in Old Monteverde, near the Bat Jungle, Monteverde ☎ 2645–5020 ⊕ www.cabure.net ☾ Closed Sun.*

★ Celajes

$$$ | COSTA RICAN | In the wood-polished dining room of Hotel Belmar, this elegant restaurant, whose name means "sunset clouds," is indeed the best place to admire the stunning views, with soft jazz and artisanal cocktails that set the tone for the farm-to-table menu. Start with the gorgeous cheese platter or the refreshing grilled-watermelon salad before moving on to the divine chicken stuffed with goat cheese, prosciutto, and spinach, and bathed in a white-wine-and-passion-fruit sauce. **Known for:** local organic ingredients from the Belmar family ranch; filet mignon with coffee glaze; homemade pastas. $ *Average main: $22 ⊠ Hotel Belmar, 4 km (2½ miles) north of town, adjacent to Monteverde Cloud Forest, Monteverde ☎ 2645–5201, 866/978–6424 from U.S. and Canada ⊕ www.hotelbelmar.net.*

Monteverde Beer House

$$ | MIDDLE EASTERN | Middle Eastern food and craft beer are rarities in Monteverde, but this bold combination has filled a void in the local culinary scene. An open kitchen serves a simple menu of kebabs, falafel, hummus, feta salads, and pita sandwiches. **Known for:** chocolate stout; mix-and-match Middle Eastern menu; live music on Saturday night. $ *Average main: $12 ⊠ Across from Super Compro, 50 m from Santa Elena bus station, Santa Elena ☎ 2645–6943 ⊕ www.facebook.com/monteverdebeerhouse.*

Morpho's

$$ | COSTA RICAN | With its rain-forest murals, glass patios, and tree-stump tables, you're never far from nature in this pleasant restaurant. Parsley potatoes, and creative sauces like pineapple curry, blue cheese, or bay-leaf-and-garlic sauce (a take on chimichurri) infuse the menu of flavorful chicken, pork, beef, or fish dishes. **Known for:** friendly service; fresh salads; peanut butter pie. $ *Average main: $15 ⊠ 50 m east of Banco Nacional, Santa Elena ☎ 2645–7373.*

★ Orchid Coffee Shop

(Cafe Las Orquideas)

$$ | BAKERY | An astonishing level of culinary perfection comes out of this A-frame shack serving breakfast, lunch, and early dinner. The menu is enormous, with crepes, pancakes, granola, and French toast alongside tomato soup, veggie panini, 25 types of coffee, and fresh smoothies made with homemade yogurt and local ingredients like pineapple, cucumber, carrot, and basil. **Known for:** espresso mocha made with hot chocolate, whiskey, and mint; neighboring Orchid Garden; careful attention to detail in preparation. $ *Average main: $10 ⊠ Next to Orchid Garden, 150 m south of Banco Nacional, Santa Elena ☎ 2645–6850 ⊕ www.orchidcoffeecr.com.*

Sofía

$$$ | LATIN AMERICAN | Waiters in crisp black aprons scurry attentively around the three dining rooms here, serving a wide variety of dishes. Start with yuca croquettes filled with local provolone, followed by mouthwatering favorites like shrimp in mango-coconut curry or chicken served with a guava reduction. **Known for:** nice views of valley below;

extensive cocktail selection; chile relleno.
$ *Average main: $20* ⊠ *Turnoff to Jardín de Mariposas, off main road between Santa Elena and Monteverde, Monteverde* ☎ *2645–7017.*

Stella's Bakery

$ | **CAFÉ** | This local institution is a good place to get an early-morning fix before heading to the Monteverde Cloud Forest. Pastries, rolls, muffins, natural juices, and coffee are standard breakfast fare, and light sandwiches, soups, and quiches are on offer at lunch. **Known for:** terrific pastries; homemade lasagna; local art. $ *Average main: $8* ⊠ *Across from CASEM, Monteverde* ☎ *2645–5560.*

Taco Taco

$ | **MEXICAN FUSION** | This always-busy casual eatery is a great place to stop for tacos, burritos, and other Tex-Mex fare, which you can eat in the dining room or outside on the patio. The meat is slow-cooked and flavorful, but fish and veggie options abound as well. **Known for:** Baja tacos with tempura-battered fresh avocado; pork carnitas; extensive beer list. $ *Average main: $6* ⊠ *Southeast of Banco Nacional in El Corazon de Santa Elena, Santa Elena* ☎ *2645–7900* ⊕ *tacotaco.net.*

Tramonti

$$ | **ITALIAN** | This glass-walled restaurant is warm and inviting, with dangling fairy lights, hardwood floors, candles dripping onto old wine bottles, and chefs tossing dough high overhead beside a wood-fired oven. The *pulpo* (octopus) and beef carpaccio are ultrathin, a perfect accompaniment for the pizzas that come piled high with toppings like asparagus, mushrooms, ricotta, and Gorgonzola. **Known for:** homemade rolls; eggplant ravioli; romantic atmosphere. $ *Average main: $14* ⊠ *3 km (2 miles) from Monteverde Cloud Forest, across from Bat Jungle, Monteverde* ☎ *2645–6120* ⊕ *www.tramonticr.com.*

Hotels

Most hotels in Monteverde don't have air-conditioning or heaters in the rooms, so you might have to crack a window or grab an extra blanket. It also helps to pack accordingly. Since Monteverde caters to wildlife enthusiasts and bird-watchers, most hotels serve breakfast from 6 to 9, with checkout at 10 am. If you're not an early riser, be sure to request a wake-up call so that you don't miss breakfast.

Arco Iris Lodge

$$ | **HOTEL** | You're almost in the center of town, but you'd never know it at this tranquil spot set on 4 acres of birding trails, where cozy cabins range from rustic to plush and come with porches. **Pros:** attentive owner and staff; terrific breakfast; centrally located. **Cons:** extra charge for breakfast; not all rooms have Wi-Fi; front rooms get a bit of street noise. $ *Rooms from: $91* ⊠ *50 m south of Banco Nacional, Santa Elena* ☎ *2645–5067* ⊕ *www.arcoirislodge.com* ⇌ *21 units* ⏇ *No meals.*

Casa Batsú

$$ | **B&B/INN** | This charming B&B is owned and operated by a lovely Costa Rican family that takes pride in every detail, from the homemade breakfasts and manicured gardens to the spotless rooms and warm hospitality. **Pros:** outstanding breakfasts; gracious hosts; excellent value. **Cons:** often books up well in advance; thin walls. $ *Rooms from: $99* ⊠ *Hwy. 606, 1½ km (1 mile) south of Santa Elena, 100 m northeast from El Tubu Gas Station, Monteverde* ☎ *2645–7004, 303/800–8826 in North America* ⊕ *www.casabatsu.org* ⇌ *5 rooms* ⏇ *Free Breakfast.*

El Establo Mountain Hotel

$$$ | **HOTEL** | The area's largest hotel gets high marks for its huge suites, plush decor, a long list of amenities, and many activities. **Pros:** spacious rooms; many activities; great views. **Cons:** massive

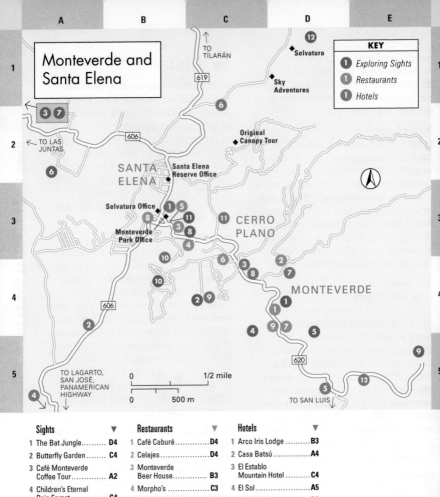

Monteverde and Santa Elena

grounds require shuttle van to navigate; no heaters; Wi-Fi doesn't reach all rooms. $ *Rooms from: $180* ✉ *3½ km (2 miles) northwest of Monteverde, Monteverde* ☎ *2645–5110* ⊕ *www.elestablo.com* ⤳ *155 rooms* ❏ *No meals.*

El Sol

$$ | **HOTEL** | A charming family tends to guests at this peaceful, bohemian Shangri-la just 10 minutes down the mountain from—and a noticeable few degrees warmer than—Santa Elena. **Pros:** great views; whimsically decorated cabins; same rates year-round. **Cons:** need a car to get here; cash only; Wi-Fi in common areas only. $ *Rooms from: $135* ✉ *5 km (3 miles) southwest of Santa Elena in La Lindora, Monteverde* ☎ *2645–5838* ▭ *No credit cards* ⤳ *4 cabins* ❏ *No meals.*

Fonda Vela

$$$ | **HOTEL** | Steep-roofed chalets have large bedrooms with wood floors and huge windows; some have views of the wooded grounds, and others, of the far-off Gulf of Nicoya. **Pros:** secluded location close to reserve; large rooms; indoor pool. **Cons:** far from town; rough road to get here; restaurant closed in low season. $ *Rooms from: $153* ✉ *1½ km (1 mile) northwest of Monteverde Reserve entrance, Monteverde* ☎ *2645–5125* ⊕ *www.fondavela.com* ⤳ *38 rooms* ❏ *No meals.*

★ Hidden Canopy Treehouses

$$$$ | **B&B/INN** | Nestled among 13½ acres of rolling hills nearly 3 km (2 miles) from town, five luxury tree houses have wraparound decks, driftwood headboards, tree-stump nightstands, waterfall showers, and skylight ceilings, ultimately fading the line between nature and decor. **Pros:** great happy hour at sunset; huge film library and board games for guests; exceptional breakfast; rooms have dehumidifiers. **Cons:** two- or three-night minimum stay depending on season; patchy Wi-Fi in rooms; no kids under 14; checkout at 10 am. $ *Rooms from: $299*

✉ *300 m east of crossroad to Los Nubes, before Sky Adventures Park, Santa Elena* ☎ *2645–5447* ⊕ *www.hiddencanopy. com* ⊘ *Closed Sept. 15–Dec. 1* ⤳ *7 units* ❏ *Free Breakfast.*

★ Hotel Belmar

$$$ | **HOTEL** | Inspired by the owners' years in Austria, two spacious chalets built into a hillside command expansive views of the Gulf of Nicoya and the hilly peninsula, and contain elegant, airy, and downright regal rooms—all with balconies, minibars, polished woods, and plush white duvets. **Pros:** excellent restaurant; free in-room coffee delivery; beautifully maintained; eco-friendly. **Cons:** far from town; steep walk if on foot; breakfast not included in rate. $ *Rooms from: $209* ✉ *4 km (2½ miles) north of Monteverde, Monteverde* ☎ *2645–5201* ⊕ *www.hotelbelmar.net* ⤳ *25 rooms* ❏ *No meals.*

Los Pinos

$$ | **HOTEL** | **FAMILY** | This 18-acre private reserve contains 16 cozy cabins with fully equipped kitchens in which you can prepare meals with produce from the hotel's hydroponic vegetable garden. **Pros:** free vegetables from on-site garden; excellent value; spacious cabins that are good for families or groups. **Cons:** some cabins are slightly dated; no restaurant or meals; steep hike to some cabins. $ *Rooms from: $95* ✉ *200 m east of Cerro Plano School, Montezuma* ☎ *2645–5252* ⊕ *www.lospinos.net* ⤳ *16 cabins* ❏ *No meals.*

Monteverde Inn

$$ | **HOTEL** | The basic rooms here have stunning views of the Gulf of Nicoya as well as hardwood floors, firm beds, and powerful, hot showers—and are a great budget option. **Pros:** good rock-bottom budget value; good views; hearty breakfasts. **Cons:** spartan rooms; cash only; rough road to hotel. $ *Rooms from: $80* ✉ *100 m south of Butterfly Garden, Monteverde* ☎ *2645–5156* ⊕ *www.monteverdeinncr.com* ▭ *No credit cards* ⤳ *14 rooms* ❏ *No meals.*

Monteverde Lodge and Gardens

$$ | HOTEL | Reminiscent of a ski lodge, this longtime favorite has extremely comfortable rooms with vaulted ceilings and great views with rates often packaged with a long list of nature activities. **Pros:** rustic luxury; attentive service; private dinners in the butterfly garden; great hiking trails. **Cons:** ground-floor rooms can be noisy; rooms have poor lighting; breakfast ends at 8:30. $ *Rooms from: $136* ⊠ *After Hotel Poco a Poco, 500 m to lodge entrance on right, Santa Elena* ☎ *2645–5057* ⊕ *www.monteverdelodge. com* ⮑ *28 rooms* ⦿ *Free Breakfast.*

Senda Monteverde Hotel

$$$$ | B&B/INN | Situated on three acres with private nature trails, these completely updated casita duplexes with large windows, separate bedrooms, porches, and luxe linens are lovely, but it's the top-notch service that sets Senda apart. **Pros:** spacious, bright, newly renovated casitas; exemplary service and welcome; impressive grounds. **Cons:** chilly in the evenings; mix of styles lacks aesthetic harmony; furniture less luxurious than price would reflect. $ *Rooms from: $280* ⊠ *North of the BCR in Cerro Plano, Monteverde* ☎ *4001–6349, 866/380–4032 from U.S.* ⊕ *www.sendamonteverde.com* ⮑ *24 casitas* ⦿ *Free Breakfast.*

Trapp Family Hotel

$$ | HOTEL | The closest lodge to the Monteverde reserve (but 6 km [4 miles] from the town center) has enormous rooms, with wood-paneled walls and ceilings, marvelously crafted wood furniture, balconies, and lovely views from most. **Pros:** spacious rooms; same rates year-round; closest lodging to reserve entrance. **Cons:** 6½ km (4 miles) from town; rough road to get here; no a/c, fans, or screens on windows; spotty Wi-Fi in rooms. $ *Rooms from: $130* ⊠ *Main road from Monteverde Cloud Forest, Monteverde* ☎ *2645–5858* ⊕ *www. trapphotelmonteverde.com* ⮑ *26 rooms* ⦿ *Free Breakfast.*

Nightlife

"Wild nightlife" takes on its own peculiar meaning here. You can still get up close with nature after the sun has gone down. Several of the reserves have guided evening walks—advance reservations and separate admission are required—and the Frog Pond of Monteverde, the Herpetarium, and the Bat Jungle keep evening hours. Beyond that, you'll probably while away the evening in a restaurant or your hotel dining room chatting with fellow travelers. Monteverde is an early-to-bed, early-to-rise kind of place—some hotels end breakfast as early as 8:30, so it's best not to oversleep.

Shopping

Cooperativa de Artesanía de Santa Elena y Monteverde (*CASEM*)

BOOKS/STATIONERY | This artisans' cooperative is made up of 45 people, mostly women, who sell locally made crafts. The prices are higher than they are at most other places, but the high quality and the knowledge that you are contributing to the livelihood of the community justifies paying a bit more. The attached restaurant serves typical Costa Rican dishes. ⊠ *Next to El Bosque Lodge, Monteverde* ☎ *2645–5190* ⊕ *casemcoop.blogspot. com.*

Dicoma

GIFTS/SOUVENIRS | Although the strip mall doesn't provide the most picturesque setting, inside you'll find lovely souvenirs and other Costa Rican made items that you won't see at the typical tourist traps. The store features handmade leather purses, beautiful and affordable jewelry, totes, art, scarves, and home goods. ⊠ *Centro Comercial, Monteverde* ☎ *2645–6832* ⊕ *www.tiendadicoma.com.*

Hummingbird Gallery

ART GALLERIES | Standouts among the books, jewelry, T-shirts, and Costa Rican coffee on display here are photographs by local nature specialists Michael and Patricia Fogden. This is a great place to emulate their efforts: you can capture an image of a hummingbird in action as hundreds flutter around the feeders. No flash photography is allowed. ⊠ *Outside entrance to Monteverde Cloud Forest, Monteverde* ☎ *2645–5030* ⊕ *www.facebook.com/ monteverdehummingbirdgallery.*

Monteverde Art House

ART GALLERIES | This lovely art gallery offers local paintings, sculptures, photography, pottery, and jewelry. The wooden artwork is amazing, and some of it is displayed inside a unique gazebo. ⊠ *100 m north of Cerro Plano School, Monteverde* ☎ *2645–5275* ⊕ *www.monteverdearthouse.com.*

Monteverde Wholefoods (*Coopesanta Elena*)

BOOKS/STATIONERY | This small local store carries organic goods and is the distributor for the area's gourmet Monteverde coffee and accoutrements. ⊠ *Next to CASEM, Monteverde* ☎ *2645–5927.*

🏃 Activities

Hiking through the cloud forest is beautiful, but if you'd like to see birds and animals and learn about the history and the flora and fauna of Monteverde, your best bet is to get a naturalist guide. Enthusiastic and passionate about where they call home and highly educated about the environment, these guides will show you so much more than you would ever see on your own.

HANGING BRIDGES, TRAMS, AND CANOPY TOURS

Original Canopy Tour

TOUR—SPORTS | FAMILY | The first company to offer zipline tours in Costa Rica has set up 12 platforms in the canopy. Included is an optional Tarzan swing and tree rappel. Tours last about 2½ hours and begin at 7:30, 10:30, and 2:30. ☎ *2291–4465 in*

San José for reservations, 305/433–2241 in U.S. ⊕ *www.canopytour.com* 🎫 *$45.*

Rafael Elizondo Nature Tours

GUIDED TOURS | You'll feel the enthusiasm of these passionate and knowledgeable English-speaking guides with years of experience. Share in the wonder of the biodiversity and beauty of the birds, mammals, and plants on a nature tour. ⊠ *Monteverde* ☎ *8838–8145* ⊕ *rafaelelizondo.com.*

★ Selvatura

SPORTS—SIGHT | FAMILY | If your time in Monteverde is limited, consider spending it at Selvatura, a kind of nature-themed adventure park—complete with a canopy tour and hanging bridges—just outside the Santa Elena Reserve. A 100-bird hummingbird garden, an enclosed 20-species *mariposario* (butterfly garden), a *herpetario* (frog and reptile house), and insect exhibition sit near the visitor center. The only zipline tour built entirely inside the Monteverde Cloud Forest has 12 lines and 18 platforms, with an optional Tarzan swing at the end to round out the excursion. The Tree Top Walkway takes you to heights ranging from 36 feet up to 180 feet on a 3-km (2-mile) walk. These are some of the longest and strongest bridges in the country and run through the same canopy terrain as the zipline tour, which sometimes makes for a not-so-quiet walk.

You can choose from numerous mix-and-match packages, depending on which activities interest you, or take it all in, with lunch included, for $121. Most visitors get by for much less, given that one day isn't enough for all there is to do here. ⊠ *Office across from church in town; Selvatura park 7 km (4 miles) northwest of Banco Nacional, Santa Elena* ✛ *Next to San Gerardo Cloud Forest Reserve* ☎ *4001–7899, 800/771–1803 in North America* ⊕ *www.selvatura.com* 🎫 *From $35.*

Sky Adventures

TOUR—SPORTS | FAMILY | Here's a tram/zipline/hanging-bridges entertainment complex all in one. A tram takes you on a 1½-km-long (1-mile-long) gondola ride through the rain-forest canopy. You can descend via the tram, or along a series of six hanging bridges, at heights of up to 138 feet, connected from tree to tree. Your third descent option is 3 km (2 miles) of ziplines through the cloud-forest canopy. Imposing towers, used as support, mar the landscape somewhat. The site's Arboreal Tree Climbing Park takes you on an eight-tree climbing circuit (33 to 60 feet) courtesy of hand-hold straps that do no damage. Sky Adventures also operates the herpetarium in town across from Plaza Monteverde. ⊠ *4 km (2½ miles) northeast of town on road toward Santa Elena Reserve, Santa Elena* ☎ *2645–6384 office, 844/468–6759 in North America* ⊕ *www.skyadventures.travel* ☎ *From $23.*

HORSEBACK RIDING

The ride from Monteverde to La Fortuna can be dangerous with outfitters that take inexperienced riders along steep trails. Desafío should be your only choice for getting from Monteverde to La Fortuna on horseback. ■TIP→ **During rainy season (July–December), book horseback trips in the morning, since rains usually begin around 2 pm.**

Caballeriza El Rodeo

HORSEBACK RIDING | Escorted 1½-hour horseback-riding tours ($30) with Caballeriza El Rodeo are on a private farm. Excursions are for everyone from beginner to experienced riders. A two-hour sunset tour ($35) begins at 3:30 pm. ⊠ *West entrance of town of Santa Elena, Santa Elena* ☎ *2645–5764* ☎ *$5.*

Monteverde Tours

HORSEBACK RIDING | This long-established company leads horseback tours between Monteverde and Arenal Volcano. You travel by car and boat, with a three-hour horseback ride on a flat trail along the lakeshore. Farms for resting the animals are at each end. This arrangement is infinitely more humane for the horses (and you) than the muddy, treacherous mountain trails used by dozens of other individuals who'll offer to take you to Arenal. ⊠ *Across from Super Compro supermarket, Santa Elena* ☎ *2645–5874, 855/811–0522 in North America* ⊕ *www.monteverdetours.com* ☎ *$85.*

Sabine's Smiling Horses

HORSEBACK RIDING | Owner Sabine—who speaks English, French, German, and Spanish—offers two-hour treks starting at $50. In addition to the regular waterfall and canyon tours, excursions at full moon are also offered once a month. Experienced riders can make reservations to go on longer, faster rides. ⊠ *1 km (½ mile) west of the cemetery, Santa Elena* ☎ *8385–2424* ⊕ *www.horseback-riding-tour.com* ☎ *From $50.*

Tenorio Volcano and the Río Celeste

Tenorio Volcano National Park is 109 km (68 miles, 3½ hrs) northwest of Monteverde Cloud Forest Biological Reserve and 92 km (57 miles, 2 hrs) northeast of Palo Verde National Park.

Legend says that when God was painting the sky he dipped the paintbrush into the Río Celeste, giving it its otherworldly cerulean hue. We now know it's the sulfur from the volcano that turns the water turquoise, but nevertheless the

---

Ants on Parade

Tread carefully when you see a tiny green parade on the ground before you. It's a troop of leaf-cutter ants carrying compost material to an underground nest.

wow factor remains. Tenorio Volcano National Park is one of the newest and most underrated parks in Costa Rica. It has easy hiking trails through primary and secondary rain forest to one of the most beautiful rivers in Costa Rica, not to mention an exquisite waterfall.

Planning

GETTING HERE AND AROUND

The best way to get to the river and park is to drive your own rental, as no buses run directly to the national park. That may change since this "local secret" has been discovered and is becoming more popular by the day, but for now, you have to take a bus to Upala, then catch a taxi to the national park. You could also hire a private shuttle. From Arenal, the 30 miles (47 km) is a pleasant 1½-hour drive to the Río Celeste. Leaving La Fortuna, head east on Route 142 for a short distance, then turn left on Route 4. Follow signs to Upala, where you'll begin to see signs for the Parque Nacional Volcan Tenorio and Río Celeste.

Driving from San José will be a roundabout no matter which route you drive, and will take a little under 4 hours. It's easiest to take the Interamerican Highway (Route 1 on a map) to Cañas, where you'll see a turnoff onto Route 6 toward Bijagua.

At the entrance to the park you'll see a secure parking lot with a guard. Parking costs $3.50 (2,000 colones). Never leave valuables in the car.

Sights

★ Tenorio Volcano National Park

NATIONAL/STATE PARK | Better known for its aquamarine river and waterfall than its namesake volcano, this park is one of the lesser known but most stunning parks in Costa Rica. The hike is not terribly arduous, but there are a lot of steps. The first part of the hike, about 1½ kilometers (1 mile), features a trail with well-maintained steps down to a breathtaking waterfall. At this point, you may choose to head back up the same way you came, especially if you have young children or have reached your limit. More adventurous hikers can go back up the steps and continue to a lookout point, the Laguna Azul (Blue Lagoon), and bubbling hot springs. The trail has some hanging bridges, and at the end, you can see the two rivers converging, as if by magic, creating an azure color. Head back the same way you came; the round trip is 6 km (3½ miles). Plan for around four hours of hiking. Swimming is prohibited inside the national park, but there are public entrances outside the park. One is about 1 km (½ mile) past the entrance, or you can pay $4 for access at Cabinas Piuri. Make sure you arrive before 2 pm, when the park stops allowing visitors. The trail can get very muddy, so don't go in flip-flops. If you don't have hiking shoes, there are rubber boots to rent at the park entrance. ✉ *Arenal Volcano National Park* ☎ *2206–5369*.

Hotels

★ La Carolina Lodge

$$$ | **ALL-INCLUSIVE** | **FAMILY** | Hark back to a simpler time as you relax in a rocking chair next to a stone fireplace, sip ever-available coffee, and listen to the river flow past at this rustic lodge, but don't think the lack of electricity and Wi-Fi means you will be deprived; it's quite the opposite. **Pros:** beautiful setting on a farm next to the river; chance to unplug and get away from it all; family-style meals. **Cons:** limited electricity and Wi-Fi only in office; rustic cabins; staff has very limited English. [$] *Rooms from: $180* ✉ *San Miguel, Bijagua de Upala, Caño Negro National Wildlife Refuge* ☎ *2466–6393, 843/343–4201 from U.S.* 🌐 *lacarolinalodge.com* 🛏 *12 units* 🍴 *All-inclusive.*

Río Celeste Hideaway

$$$ | B&B/INN | Set in the rain forest, these marvelous, secluded casitas have elegant furnishings, sizable bathrooms with private garden showers, and terraces that entice you to spend time in nature. **Pros:** spacious, well-appointed casitas in the rain forest; terrific pool and hot tubs; close to Tenorio Volcano National Park and hike to Río Celeste. **Cons:** restaurant is expensive with limited menu; far from other restaurants; pool can get chilly. $ Rooms from: $175 ⊠ 1 km (½ mile) southeast of Tenorio Volcano, Alajuela ☎ 2206–4000, 954/234–2372 from U.S. ⊕ www.riocelestehideaway.com ⇘ 26 casitas ⦵ Free Breakfast.

Caño Negro National Wildlife Refuge

100 km (60 miles, 2 hrs) north of La Fortuna.

If you're seeking a national park experience without the crowds, Caño Negro should be on your list; its excellent birding and wildlife viewing still have an "undiscovered" feel. Long a favorite among fishing enthusiasts and bird-watchers, this remote area is off the beaten track and may be difficult to get to if your time in Costa Rica is short. You can cross into Nicaragua, via Los Chiles, but there are almost no roads in this part of southern Nicaragua, making access to the rest of the country nearly impossible. The border crossing at Peñas Blancas, near the North Pacific coast, is far more user-friendly.

GETTING HERE AND AROUND

The highway from La Fortuna to Los Chiles, the gateway to the Caño Negro National Wildlife Refuge, is one of the best maintained in the northern lowlands. You can catch public buses in San José at Terminal 7-10 twice a day for a trip of about five hours to Los Chiles, with many stops. Public buses also operate between La Fortuna and Los Chiles. If they have room, many tour companies will allow you to ride along on their shuttles for around $30. If you're not staying way up here, an organized tour of the reserve from La Fortuna is the way most visitors get to and from.

⊙ Sights

★ Caño Negro National Wildlife Refuge

(Refugio Nacional de Vida Silvestre Caño Negro)

NATURE PRESERVE | It's a shame that Caño Negro doesn't grab the same amount of attention in wildlife-viewing circles as other destinations in Costa Rica. Due to the recent saturation of visitors at Tortuguero National Park to the east, however, Caño Negro is starting to gain recognition among bird-watchers and nature lovers for its isolation, diversity, and abundant wildlife. As a feeding ground for both resident and migratory birds, the refuge is home to more than 350 bird species, 310 plants, and at least 160 species of mammals. The reserve is a splendid place to watch waterfowl and resident exotic animals, including cougars, jaguars, and several species of monkeys. It's also one of the best places to see a basilisk, more commonly known as the "Jesus Christ Lizard" because of its ability to run on water. Comprising the vast wetland sanctuary is a web of channels and lagoons ideal for exploring by boat, and even more so by canoe to reach remote lowlands, swamps, and seasonal floodplains. If you're not staying at one of the two lodges up here, the refuge is easily visited as a day trip from La Fortuna. Note that most Arenal-area tour operators do not actually enter the refuge (to avoid paying the $5 per person entrance fee). Tour companies often claim that the areas surrounding the park are equally spectacular, but this is not the case. Although you're likely to see wildlife on the outskirts of the refuge, you won't see a fraction of what you encounter inside the park, which lacks the parade of tour boats disturbing the habitat. For the best tour of the refuge, book through resident guide Jimmy Gutierrez at Natural Lodge Caño Negro. There are no public facilities in the park, which consists mostly of wetlands fed by the Frio River and best explored only by boat. Bring a camera, binoculars, and plenty of bug spray. *For more information, see highlighted listing in this chapter.* ✉ *Off Hwy. 35, 180 km (112 miles) north of La Fortuna* ☎ *2471–1580* 🌐 *www.sinac.go.cr* 🎫 *$5; fishing license $30.*

Natural Lodge Caño Negro
GUIDED TOURS | Unlike the La Fortuna–based tour operators visiting the area, Natural Lodge Caño Negro offers excursions that actually take place inside the reserve rather than along its outskirts. Resident guide Jimmy Gutierrez is an expert on local wildlife and can arrange motorized boat tours or excursions by canoe to reach remote areas not accessible by motorboat. A two-hour wetlands tour departs at 8 am and 2 pm and costs $48. Sportfishing, day hikes, and night tours are also available. Rates do not include the $5 park entrance fee. ✉ *250 m west of the school* ☎ *2471–1426, 8352–6555* 🌐 *www.canonegrolodge.com* 🎫 *From $40.*

Hotels

Hotel de Campo
$$ | HOTEL | Under the shade of tropical fruit trees, white bungalows of high-quality wood each contain two bright, sparkling rooms with terra-cotta tile floors and front patios that open onto a central swimming pool. **Pros:** secluded location; close to reserve; tons of wildlife. **Cons:** need a car to get here and road is very rough; food slightly overpriced; small pool. [$] *Rooms from: $95* ✉ *Caño Negro village, 100 m past grocery* ☎ *2471–1012* 🌐 *www.hoteldecampo.com* 💳 *No credit cards* 🛏 *14 rooms, 7 bungalows* 🍴 *Free Breakfast.*

Natural Lodge Caño Negro
$$ | HOTEL | It might come as a surprise to find such attractive and comfortable rooms, with nice appointments and high ceilings, in so remote a place, but the lack of pretense and laid-back atmosphere fit right into the surroundings on the east side of the reserve. **Pros:** secluded location; close to reserve; excellent boat tour; great for bird-watching. **Cons:** need a car to get here; no Wi-Fi in the rooms; rough and bumpy road. [$] *Rooms from: $130* ✉ *Caño Negro village, 250 m west of school* ☎ *2471–1426, 8352–6555* 🌐 *www.canonegrolodge.com* 🛏 *42 rooms* 🍴 *Free Breakfast.*

Chapter 7

GUANACASTE

Updated by
Rachel White

⦿ Sights	⍟ Restaurants	⨳ Hotels	⊖ Shopping	⛾ Nightlife
★★★☆☆	★★★★★	★★★★☆	★★★☆☆	★★★★★

WELCOME TO GUANACASTE

TOP REASONS TO GO

★ **Beaches:** White sand, black sand, palm-fringed strands, beaches for swimming, partying, surfing, and sunbathing—the sheer variety of Guanacaste's beaches can't be beat.

★ **Big wind:** From November to May, the trade winds whip across Northern Guanacaste with a velocity and consistency that make the Bahía Salinas a world-class windsurfing and kitesurfing destination.

★ **Endangered nature:** Guanacaste's varied national parks protect some of Central America's last remaining patches of tropical dry forest, a distinctive ecosystem where you might spot magpie jays or howler monkeys in the branches of a gumbo-limbo tree.

★ **Scuba diving:** Forget the pretty tropical fish. Sharks, rays, sea turtles, and moray eels are the large-scale attractions for divers here.

★ **Surfing:** Offshore winds, warm water, and hollow barrels make for epic waves at more than a dozen Guanacaste beaches.

1 Bahía Salinas. Haven for kitesurfers with mostly pristine, undeveloped beaches.

2 Playa Bahía Junquillal. Bordered by Bahía Junquillal National Wildlife Refuge.

3 Santa Rosa National Park. Forests and beaches combine for untouched beauty.

4 Guanacaste National Park. A biological corridor and migratory passage with hiking trails.

5 Rincón de la Vieja National Park. Wildlife, rivers, waterfalls, and mudbaths are the tip of the volcano.

6 Liberia. The capital of Guanacaste has an international airport and many shopping centers.

7 Papagayo Peninsula. Remote paradise with a bevy of all-inclusive luxury hotels.

8 Playa Hermosa. Wide, curved beach with warm waters.

9 Playas del Coco. Messy, noisy, and colorful, with lots of dive shops and lively nightlife.

10 Playa Ocotal. Quiet and serene; a welcome respite from its noisy neighbor.

11 Las Catalinas. Car-free village with utopian beaches and mountain biking trails.

12 Playa Pan de Azúcar. An almost deserted strand of tropical beach.

13 Playa Potrero. Community with a church, school, and supermarket.

14 Playa Flamingo. Boating and swimming wonderland.

15 Brasilito and Playa Conchal. Brasilito is cluttered and noisy, a lively contrast to the gated Playa Conchal to the south.

16 Playa Grande. Wide, beautiful, pristine, and one of the best surfing beaches. Its Las Baulas National Marine Park protects sea turtles.

17 Tamarindo. Funky beach town full of surfers and the best restaurants on the coast.

18 Playa Langosta. Tranquil, elegant community with an unsullied beach.

19 Playa Avellanas. Lovely spot for anyone who likes sea and sand.

20 Playa Negra. A laid-back surfer community.

21 Playa Junquillal. Serene, uncrowded beaches and hardly a building in sight.

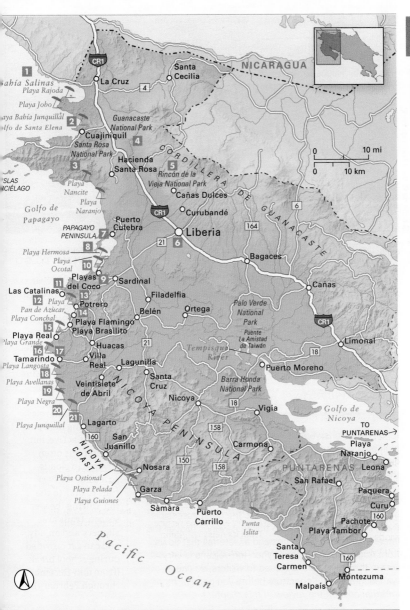

NICARAGUA

1
ahía Salinas
Playa Rajoda
Playa Jobo
aya Bahía Junquillal
olfo de Santa Elena
2
Cuajiniquil
Santa Rosa
National Park
3
SLAS
CIÉLAGO
Playa
Nancite
Golfo de
Papagayo
Playa
Naranjo
PAPAGAYO
PENINSULA **7**
Playa Hermosa **8**
Playa
Ocotal **10**
11
Las Catalinas
12 Playa
Pan de Azúcar
Playa Conchal
15
Playa Real
Playa Grande
16
Tamarindo **17**
Playa Langosta
18
Playa Avellanas
19
Playa Negra
20
21
Playa Junquillal
NICOYA
COAST
Playa Ostional
Playa Pelada
Playa Guiones

CR1
La Cruz
Santa
Cecilia
4
Guanacaste
National Park
4
Hacienda
Santa Rosa
5
Rincón de la
Vieja National Park
Cañas Dulces
Curubandé
CR1
Puerto
Culebra
Liberia
21
6
Playas **9**
del Coco
Sardinal
Filadelfia
13
Potrero
14
Belén
Ortega
Playa Flamingo
Playa Brasilito
Huacas
21
Villa
Real
Lagunilla
Tempisque River
Veintisiete
de Abril
Santa
Cruz
Nicoya
NICOYA PENINSULA
Lagarto
160
San
Juanillo
158
Nosara
150
158
Garza
Sàmara
Puerto
Carrillo

CORDILLERA DE GUANACASTE

6
164
Bagaces
Palo Verde
National Park
Puente
La Amistad
de Taiwán
Barra Honda
National Park
18
Vigia
Cañas
CR1
Limonal
18
Puerto Moreno
Golfo de
Nicoya
TO
PUNTARENAS→
Playa
Naranjo
PUNTARENAS
Leona
San Rafael
Carmona
Paquera
Curu
160
Pachote
Playa Tambor
Punta
Islita
Santa
Teresa
Carmen
160
Montezuma
Malpaís

0   10 mi
0   10 km

Pacific Ocean

RINCÓN DE LA VIEJA NATIONAL PARK

Rincón de la Vieja National Park is Costa Rica's mini-Yellowstone, with volcanic hot springs and bubbling mud pools, refreshing waterfalls, and cool forest trails. Often shrouded in clouds, the currently active volcano dominates the landscape northwest of Liberia, rising above the sunbaked plains.

It has two windswept peaks, Santa María, at 6,323 feet high on the east slope, and Rincón de la Vieja at 6,254 feet on the west. The latter slope has an active crater that hardy hikers can climb to when the trail is open. It's usually closed in the wet season, and when the crater is too active. Fumaroles on its lower slope constantly let off steam. Las Pailas entrance has the most accessible trails, including an easy loop trail that wends past all the interesting volcanic features and a waterfall that flows from August to November. When the volcano is very active, the entire park is closed to visitors, so check with lodges or tour operators before you go. *(For more information, see the review in this chapter.)*

BEST TIME TO GO

Good times to visit are January through May, during the dry season. December and January can be very windy, but that means temperatures stay cooler for hiking. May to November— the green season—is when the fumaroles and boiling mud pots are most active, but the crater is often covered in clouds, so it's not the best time to hike to the top. During the wet season, trails are slippery and muddy, and can get crowded during school break (from mid-December through February).

BEST WAYS TO EXPLORE

BIRD-WATCHING

Wherever you walk in this park, you are bound to hear the three-note song of the long-tailed manakin. It sounds something like "Toledo," and that's what the locals call this bird. Along with their lavish, long tail feathers, the males are famous for their cooperative courting dance: two pals leap back and forth over each other, but only the senior male gets any girl who falls for this act. The hard-to-spot rock wren lives closer to the top of the volcano. Birding is excellent most of the year here except for December and January when the weather is dry and often too windy.

HIKING

The only way to explore the park trails is on foot, along well-marked paths that range from easy loops to longer, more demanding climbs. The ranger station at Las Pailas entrance provides maps of the park trails and restrooms before you set off. The easiest hike is Las Pailas loop, which starts just past the ranger station; it takes about two hours to hike. If you want to venture farther afield, follow the signs for La Cangreja trail. After passing through dense, cool forest, you'll emerge through an avenue of giant agave plants into an open, windy meadow. Your reward is the cool waterfall and swimming hole at the end of the trail.

ON HORSEBACK

Saddle up to explore the lower slopes of the volcano, just outside the park borders. Local ranches and lodges organize daylong trail rides to waterfalls and sulfur springs. Your nose will tell you when you are approaching the springs—it's the distinctive rotten-egg smell of sulfur.

Mud-bathing in Rincón de la Vieja National Park

TOP REASONS TO GO

WILDLIFE

Here you can find more than 300 species of birds, plus mammals such as white-tailed deer, coyotes, howler and capuchin monkeys, armadillos, and the occasional harlequin snake (not poisonous).

CLIMBING TO THE CRATER

The hike to the crater summit is the most demanding but also the most dramatic. The trail climbs 8 km (5 miles) through shaded forest, then up a sunbaked, treeless slope to the windswept crater, where temperatures plummet. Be sure to check in at the ranger station before attempting this hike; the trail may be closed when the volcano is active.

GEOLOGICAL WONDERS

Three-kilometer (2-mile) Las Pailas loop trail showcases the park's famous geothermal features. Along the trail you'll see fumaroles with steam hissing out of ground vents, a *volcancito* (baby volcano), and boiling mud fields.

SANTA ROSA NATIONAL PARK

Surfing in Santa Rosa National Park

Renowned for its wildlife, Santa Rosa National Park, part of the larger Guanacaste Conservation Area, protects the largest swath of extant lowland dry forest in Central America, about 91,000 acres. *Dry* is the operative word here, with less than 59 inches of rainfall a year in some parts of the park.

If you station yourself near watering holes in the dry season (January to April) you may spot deer, coyotes, coatis, and armadillos. The park also has the world's only fully protected nesting beach for olive ridley sea turtles. Treetop inhabitants include spider, capuchin, and howler monkeys, as well as hundreds of bird species. The deciduous forest here includes giant kapok, guanacaste, and mahogany, as well as calabash, acacia, and gumbo-limbo trees with their distinctive peeling bark. The park is also of historical significance to Costa Rica because it was here, in 1856, that an army of Costa Rican volunteers decisively defeated an invading force of mercenaries.

BEST TIME TO GO

Dry season is the best time to visit if you want to see wildlife. The vegetation is sparse, making for easy observation. It's also the best time to drive to the park's beaches. In the rainy season, trails can become mud baths, excluding the Indio Desnudo Trail, which is fine year-round.

FUN FACT

Moving from sparse, sunlit secondary forest into the park's shady primary forest areas, you can experience an instant temperature drop of as much as 5°C (9°F).

BEST WAYS TO EXPLORE

GETTING AROUND

Only the first 12 km (7 miles) of the park's roads are accessible by vehicles. The rest of the park's 20 km (12 miles) of hiking trails have been significantly improved. It's easy to drive to La Casona headquarters along a paved road and pick up a short loop hiking trail, but beyond that point you need a 4WD vehicle.

A HISTORICAL TOUR

Costa Rica doesn't have many historical sites—relics of its past have mostly been destroyed by earthquakes and volcanic eruptions. So La Casona, the symbolic birthplace of Costa Rica's nationhood, is a particularly revered site. Most Costa Ricans come to Santa Rosa on a historical pilgrimage. Imagine the nation's horror when the place was burned to the ground in a fire purposely set in 2001 by disgruntled poachers who had been fined by park rangers. The government, schoolchildren, and private businesses came to the rescue, raising the money to restore the historic hacienda and replace the exhibits of antique farm tools and historical photos.

TURTLE-WATCHING

Thousands of olive ridley sea turtles emerge from the sea every year, from July to December, to dig nests and deposit eggs on the park's protected beaches at Playa Nancite and Playa Naranjo. Pacific green sea turtles and the huge leatherbacks also clamber ashore, but in much smaller numbers. If you're a hardy outdoors type, you can hike the 12 km (8 miles) to Playa Naranjo and pitch your tent near the beach. Unlike most other turtle-nesting beaches with organized tours, this is a natural spectacle you'll get to witness far from any crowds. Playa Nancite is a totally protected beach and thus off-limits to tourists.

The wild coastline near Santa Rosa National Park

7

Guanacaste **SANTA ROSA NATIONAL PARK**

TOP REASONS TO GO

EXPLORE THE FOREST

The short (about 1-km [½-mile]) Casona nature-trail loop, which starts from the park headquarters, is a great way to get a sampling of dry tropical forest and to spot wildlife. Look for signs leading to the Indio Desnudo (Naked Indian) path, named after the local word for gumbo-limbo trees.

SERIOUS SURFING

Off Playa Naranjo lies the famous Witch's Rock, a towering rock formation famous for its surfing breaks. If you're interested in checking it out but don't feel like walking for miles, take a boat from Playas del Coco, Playa Hermosa, or Playa Tamarindo.

WILDLIFE-WATCHING

Wildlife is easy to spot here thanks to the low-density foliage of this tropical dry forest. Scan the treetops and keep an eye out for spider, white-faced capuchin, and howler monkeys. If you're lucky, you might even spot an ocelot.

Reliably sunny, dry weather brings planeloads of sun-starved Northerners to the North Pacific area of Costa Rica every winter, and a windswept coastline makes Guanacaste popular with surfers eager to relive the legendary "Endless Summer" of the sport's early years.

Ever since the 1966 cult-classic film put Costa Rica on the map, surfers and travelers alike have flocked to the beaches where waves peel, hammocks sway, and monkeys and iguanas clamber in treetops. It's easy to understand why many who come to visit return year after year or even devise a plan to stay; Guanacaste casts its spell the moment you enter the rain forest or hit the coast. From the luxury resorts and cattle ranches to the fishing villages and surf towns, the region serves up everything from high-rise resorts to utter isolation with a side of sustainable living. An abundance of marine life and stellar diving spots also lure fishers and underwater aficionados. Add in some stunningly scenic national parks and a range of thrilling outdoor adventures, and you have all the ingredients that make this region an all-around top spot to experience Costa Rica's charms. Although most tourists head here for the dry "high" season, it's even more beautiful—and cheaper, cooler, and less crowded—in the "green" or low season, April to December.

MAJOR REGIONS

Guanacaste Province—a vast swath of land in northwestern Costa Rica—is bordered by the Pacific Ocean to the west and the looming Cordillera de Guanacaste volcanic mountain range to the east.

Far Northern Guanacaste. Dry, hot Far Northern Guanacaste is traditionally ranching country, but it does include the impressive wildernesses of Santa Rosa and Rincón de la Vieja national parks, the latter of which holds one of Costa Rica's most active volcanoes. Liberia, the capital of Guanacaste Province, is the closest town to Costa Rica's second-largest airport. Farther to the north is Bahía Salinas, second only to Lake Arenal for wind- and kitesurfing.

Guanacaste Pacific Coast. The number and variety of beaches along the northern border of the Nicoya Peninsula, from the Papagayo Peninsula to Tamarindo and down to Playa Junquillal, make it a top tourist destination. Each beach has its specialty, be it surfing, fishing, diving, or just plain relaxing. Hotels and restaurants are in generous supply.

Planning

When to Go

HIGH SEASON: MID-DECEMBER TO APRIL

This is the driest region of the country, with only 65 inches of average annual rainfall. It's also the hottest region, with average temperatures around 30°C to

35°C (86°F to 95°F) in high season. It's no wonder that winter-weary Northerners come here for guaranteed sunshine and heat. The beaches and trails can get packed during these drier months, especially mid-December to February, when school is out in Costa Rica. January can be quite breezy, especially along the coast, thanks to the annual Papagayo winds. February through April are the driest months: skies are clear, but the heat is intense and the landscape is brown and parched. Fishing and scuba diving are at their best during this period, though.

LOW SEASON: MAY THROUGH OCTOBER

Major downpours are frequent in the afternoon during the rainy season, which brings lower prices, fewer crowds, and a lush green landscape. But mornings are usually fresh and clear. Unpaved beach roads can become quite muddy, making travel difficult and some roads impassable.

SHOULDER SEASON: NOVEMBER TO MID-DECEMBER

This is the best time to visit, when the rains have abated, the landscape is lush, and the evening air is cool. Hotels and restaurants are prepped for the impending tourist influx, and staff are fresh and eager to please. Except for the popular U.S. Thanksgiving week, you can usually get a deal. High-season rates begin mid-December.

PLANNING YOUR TIME

Visiting this region for 10 days to two weeks will introduce you to its wonders and give you a real taste of the North Pacific. Schedule plenty of beach time for lounging, sunbathing, surfing, diving, and snorkeling. Logistically, you also need to take into consideration slow travel over bumpy roads. A beach like Tamarindo with lots of restaurants and nightlife can keep you entertained for a week or more, whereas a more solitary beach might merit only a couple of days. Also plan to visit some protected areas to enjoy canopy tours, wildlife viewing, and hiking. Outdoorsy types should consider spending a few days around Rincón de la Vieja National Park for its amazing hiking, bird-watching, and horseback riding. Other parks to consider are Palo Verde National Park, Santa Rosa National Park, and Barra Honda National Park. Many North Pacific beaches are just a few hours' drive from the Arenal Volcano area, so the region can be combined with the Northern Lowlands.

Getting Here and Around

AIR

Aeropuerto Internacional Daniel Oduber Quirós (LIR) in Liberia is an international gateway to the coast, with a large, air-conditioned terminal. Tamarindo also has a small airstrip. Flying from San José is the best way to get here if you are already in the country. If your primary destination lies in Guanacaste, make sure you investigate the possibility of flying directly into Liberia instead of San José, which saves some serious hours on the road.

Many airlines have direct service between major U.S. hubs and Costa Rica's two international airports in San José and Liberia. SANSA, Aerobell, and Skyway have scheduled flights between San José, Liberia, and Tamarindo but often you need to go directly to the airline's website to schedule flights. Don't forget to factor in the exit tax, $29 by air and $7 by land, payable in U.S. dollars, colones, or credit card. Some airlines include this fee in the ticket price.

AIR CONTACTS Skyway. ☎ 877/841–8330 ⊕ www.facebook.com/SkywayCR. **Aerobell Airlines.** ☎ 4000–2030 ⊕ www.aerobell.com. **SANSA.** ☎ 877/767–2672 ⊕ flysansa.com.

BUS

You can ride in a comfortable, air-conditioned minibus with Gray Line, connecting San José, Liberia, Playa Flamingo, Playa Conchal, Playa Potrero, Playa Brasilito, Playa Hermosa, Playas del Coco, Ocotal, Tamarindo, Rincón de la Vieja, and Playa Langosta. The Gray Line bus from San José to Liberia and Tamarindo begins picking up passengers from hotels daily around 8:45 am. The return bus leaves the Tamarindo and Flamingo areas around 8:40 am and 4 pm. Interbus has door-to-door minivan shuttle service from San José to all the major beach hotels (in Papagayo, Flamingo, Tamarindo, and Coco). Fares range from $42 to $57 per person. Reserve 48 hours in advance to guarantee a seat.

BUS CONTACTS Gray Line. ☎ 2220–2126 ⊕ www.graylinecostarica.com. **Interbus.** ☎ 4100–0888 ⊕ www.interbusonline.com.

CAR

Most unpaved roads here alternate between being extremely muddy and treacherous during the rainy season and extremely dusty during the dry season. That said, it can be a real adventure exploring the coastline if you have a 4WD or a hired driver with a good, sturdy car. The major artery in this region is the Pan-American Highway (CA 1), which heads northwest from San José to Liberia, then due north to the Nicaraguan border. It's fairly well maintained, but the convoys of trucks and buses often create heavy traffic and there are few passing opportunities. To skip the hours of frustrating driving, consider flying into Liberia, whose airport provides easy access to the region. Local hotels and tour companies can help you arrange for ground transportation in many cases. In Guanacaste, it's usually safe to take pirata (pirate, or unofficial) taxis, but always negotiate the price before getting into the cab, or ask your hotel to call a reputable driver.

The northwest is accessed via the paved two-lane Pan-American Highway (CA 1), which begins at the top of Paseo Colón in San José. Take the Friendship Bridge (aka Río Tempisque Bridge) across the Tempisque River to get to the Pacific beaches south of Liberia. Once you get off the main highway, dust, mud, potholes, and other factors come into play, depending on which beach you visit. The roads to Playa Flamingo, Playa Conchal, Playa Brasilito, Tamarindo, Playa Grande, Playas del Coco, Hermosa, and Ocotal are paved all the way; every other destination may require some dirt-road maneuvering.

Restaurants

Seafood and fresh fish are tops here, followed by fast food—pizza, tacos, barbecue—to satisfy the hordes of hungry surfers and beachgoers. But there are many sophisticated restaurants, too, offering Asian-fusion, Italian, French, and international cuisine, especially in the tourist-heavy beach towns of Hermosa, Flamingo, and Tamarindo. ■ TIP→ **Many restaurants, especially tourist-oriented ones with dollar-denominated menus, do not include the 13% national sales tax plus mandatory 10%–12% service. By law, menus are required to show the total price including tax, but many owners flout this law. Be sure to ask if taxes are included; otherwise you may be surprised by a bill that's 25% higher than you expected.**

Hotels

A wide range of lodging options awaits you here, so choose wisely. If your goal is to take leisurely swims and lounge quietly on the beach with a cocktail in hand, then avoid the beaches that are renowned for surfing waves. Expensive resorts like the Four Seasons are generally well balanced with budget hotels that charge less than $75 per night.

Wherever you stay, be sure to factor in the 13% sales tax. As in all of Costa Rica, the places we recommend most highly are the small owner-operated hotels and bed-and-breakfasts that blend in with unspoiled nature and offer one-on-one attention from the staff and owners. Most hotels will be able to connect you with local tour operators and knowledgeable staff members who can help show you the best aspects of each destination, whether it's a local park with howler monkeys, a great family-run restaurant on the beach, or a thrilling canopy tour. *Hotel reviews have been shortened. For full information, visit Fodors.com.*

WHAT IT COSTS in U.S. Dollars			
$	$$	$$$	$$$$
RESTAURANTS			
under $10	$10–$15	$16–$25	over $25
HOTELS			
under $75	$75–$150	$151–$250	over $250

Tours

Horizontes Nature Tours
ADVENTURE TOURS | With a focus on nature and adventure, Horizontes has independent, private tours with your own guide and driver as well as small-group tours. Customized tours are available for bird-watchers, families, couples, yogis, and beachgoers. Average tours are six nights. ☎ *4052–5850, 888/786–8748 toll-free in U.S.* ⊕ *www.horizontes.com* 🖃 *From $1,440 per person.*

Bahía Salinas

15 km (9 miles) west of La Cruz.

The large windswept bay at the very top of Costa Rica's Pacific coast is the second-windiest area in the country, after Lake Arenal, making it great for windsurfers and kitesurfers, as well as beachgoers looking for breezy, uncrowded, pristine beaches. It also happens to be the sunniest and driest side of Costa Rica. Strong onshore breezes blow from November to May, when only experienced riders are out on the waves and the water grows steadily cooler. The south (bay) side has the strongest winds, and choppy, colder water from January to May.

In July and August the wind is more appropriate for beginner kitesurfers and windsurfers, whereas any time of year you can enjoy the area's diving and beaches. On the sheltered Golfo de Santa Elena, to the west, are two beaches that rank among the most beautiful in all of Costa Rica: Playa Rajada and Playa Jobo, although Dreams Las Mareas Resort has claimed ground at Jobo Bay. Other beaches lining the bay are Playa Copal, Playa Papaturro, and Playa Pochotes. Still, it's a far cry from the overdeveloped beaches of Guanacaste's gold coast farther to the south. Just offshore is Isla Bolaños, a national wildlife refuge with white-sand beaches and turquoise water. This famous nesting spot for birds can be seen from afar only between April and November, as landing here is not allowed.

GETTING HERE AND AROUND
From Liberia, drive 45 minutes toward La Cruz, the last town before the Peñas Blancas border crossing. From a high point in La Cruz, the road to Salinas descends both in altitude and condition. Turn left toward Bahía Salinas, the only road leading to the beaches. Signs direct you to Puerto Soley where the road splits shortly thereafter and heads right to El Jobo. Playa Copal is about 13 km (8 miles) along the same road from La Cruz. The first few kilometers of the beach road are paved, but expect a bumpy ride most of the way.

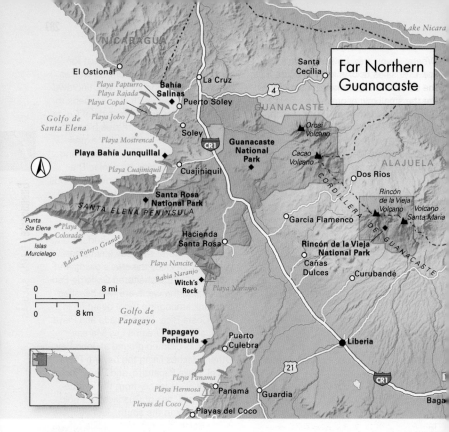

Far Northern Guanacaste

Lake Nicara

NICARAGUA

El Ostional
Playa Papturro
Playa Rajada
Playa Copal
Bahía Salinas
Puerto Soley
La Cruz
Santa Cecília
4
GUANACASTE

Golfo de Santa Elena
Playa Jobo
Playa Mostrencal
Soley
CR1
Guanacaste National Park
Orosi Volcano
Cacao Volcano
ALAJUELA

Playa Bahía Junquillal
Playa Cuajiniquil
Cuajiniquil
Dos Rios
Rincón de la Vieja Volcano
Volcano Santa Maria

SANTA ELENA PENINSULA
Santa Rosa National Park
Garcia Flamenco
CORDILLERA DE GUANACASTE

Punta Sta Elena
Playa Coloradas
Islas Murcielago
Bahía Potero Grande
Hacienda Santa Rosa
Rincón de la Vieja National Park
Cañas Dulces
Curubandé

0   8 mi
0   8 km

Playa Nancite
Bahía Naranjo
Witch's Rock
Playa Naranjo

Golfo de Papagayo

Papagayo Peninsula
Puerto Culebra
Liberia

Playa Panama
Playa Hermosa
Panamá
Guardia
21
CR1
Baga

Playas del Coco
Playas del Coco

🔱 Beaches

Playa Copal

BEACH—SIGHT | Playa Copal is a narrow, dark-beige rocky beach that is one of the main venues for kitesurfing. Winds are often gusty but consistent November to May, which is why several kite schools have set up shop nearby. A couple of kilometers to the east is Playa Papaturro, another windy beach where you'll find simple accommodations and a kitesurfing school at Blue Dream Hotel. **Amenities:** food and drink. **Best for:** solitude. ⊠ *About 2 km (1 mile) east of branch road that leads to Ecoplaya.*

Playa Jobo

BEACH—SIGHT | Dominated by the massive Dreams Las Mareas Resort, Playa Jobo is still one of the most beautiful beaches in the area. Cradled within the

sheltered cove is fine brown sand and calm water, making this beach safe for swimming. Motorized water sports are not allowed, so despite the resort's size, the bay remains relatively quiet. A few sailboats are anchored offshore. Playa Jobo is fringed with acacia trees that have sharp thorns, and there are rocks jetting on either side of the cove where many people begin a snorkel adventure (beware of sea urchins and jellyfish). This beach is a refuge to turtles and manta rays, which you might see in the shallow, clear waters. Windy days are frequent, so watch for blowing sand. At high tide, the beach is narrow. This, combined with the slight slope to the shore, has most people sunbathing by the pool or lounging in the grassy area between the sand and the resort. Although all beaches in Costa Rica are public, this strand is difficult to reach unless you're staying at

Dreams Resort. Your other options are to approach by boat or access from around the cove. **Amenities:** food and drink. **Best for:** snorkeling; sunset; swimming. ✉ *Dreams Las Mareas Resort, 3-km (2-mile) walk or drive west from Ecoplaya Beach Resort.*

Playa Rajada

BEACH—SIGHT | Gorgeous, horseshoe-shape Playa Rajada is a wide sweep of almost-white fine-grain sand that, so far, has evaded tourists. Shallow, warm waters make it perfect for swimming, and an interesting rock formation at the north end invites snorkelers. It's also a favorite beach for watching sunsets. **Amenities:** none. **Best for:** snorkeling; sunset; swimming. ✉ *5 km (3 miles) west of Ecoplaya Beach Resort or 3 km (2 miles) north of town of El Jobo.*

Hotels

Blue Dream Hotel

$ | **HOTEL** | **FAMILY** | Catering predominantly to kitesurfers, this breezy property on a steep hillside is one of the more affordable lodging options in Bahía Salinas, with suites, bungalows, rooms, and dorms just minutes from the water. **Pros:** very affordable; kitesurfing lessons; water views. **Cons:** steep climb to top rooms; not much to do outside of kitesurfing; stray animals and neglected grounds. [$] *Rooms from: $49* ✉ *60 m west of Playa Papaturro entrance* ☎ *8826–5221, 2676–1042* 🌐 *www.bluedreamhotel.com* 🛏 *16 units* 🍴 *No meals.*

★ **Cañas Castilla**

$ | **B&B/INN** | Swiss expats Guido and Agi spent their first years in Costa Rica living off the land without running water or electricity, but today their little paradise is a full-fledged farm with cows, horses, chickens, and rustic cabins for overnight guests. **Pros:** friendly owners; nature abounds; all rooms are wheelchair-accessible; delicious food. **Cons:** patchy Wi-Fi in common areas only; no phones; muddy in rainy season. [$] *Rooms from: $70* ✉ *5 km (3 miles) north from La Cruz, La Cruz* ✥ *Turn off the hwy. to right into Sonzapote after school. Follow signs 2 km east to Finca Cañas Castilla* ☎ *8381–4030 mobile* 🌐 *www.canas-castilla.com* 🛏 *6 rooms* 🍴 *No meals.*

★ **Dreams Las Mareas Costa Rica**

$$$$ | **RESORT** | **FAMILY** | As the first all-inclusive luxury resort in the Bahía Salinas area and the first hotel in Guanacaste to feature swim-up rooms, Dreams Las Mareas stands out from the AI pack with no hidden charges, no restaurant reservations, no towel cards, and no plastic wrist bands. **Pros:** lovely swim-up rooms; calm beach; designated kids' pool. **Cons:** isolated on a bumpy road; steep, vast grounds require a lot of walking; patios and bathrooms lack privacy. [$] *Rooms from: $487* ✉ *Playa Jobo, west of Bahia Salinas* ☎ *2690–2400, 866/237–3267 in U.S.* 🌐 *www.dreamsresorts.com/las-mareas* 🛏 *447 rooms* 🍴 *All-inclusive.*

The First Guanacastecos

The Chorotega tribe first settled the Guanacaste area and grew corn and fished. Chief Nicoya was the Chorotegan leader who greeted the conquistadores in 1523 and bequeathed his name to the town and peninsula.

Activities

Inshore fishing is quite good in the bay during windy months, when snapper, roosterfish, wahoo, and other fighters abound. Scuba divers might also encounter big fish from December to May, though visibility can be poor then. From May to December the snorkeling is good around the rocky points and Isla Bolaños.

TOUR OPERATORS

Costa Kite

WINDSURFING | All levels are welcome here, from first-timers who want to get their feet wet or advanced kitesurfers who are ready to jump. All instructors are certified, and they use new gear. ✉ *100 m south of Hotel Bolaños* ☎ *8907–9889* ⊕ *costakite.com* ✉ *Three-hour group lesson $90; rentals $60 per day.*

KITESURFING AND WINDSURFING

Blue Dream Kitesurfing School

WINDSURFING | Ideally situated near windy Playa Papaturro (11 km [7 miles] west of La Cruz, turn left at sign for Papaturro), this kitesurfing school is run by Nicola Bertoldi, a multilingual instructor with lots of experience; private lessons cost $45 per hour. Nine hours of beginner's kitesurfing private lessons cost $360, including equipment. But the best deals are all-inclusive packages starting at $499 that include five days of lessons, lodging, and meals at the school's Blue Dream Hotel, on a ridge with ocean views. Check their website for wind conditions and closure dates, as the school often shuts down once the breezes stop. ✉ *60 m east Playa Papaturro entrance* ☎ *8826–5221, 2676–1042* ⊕ *www.bluedreamhotel.com* ✉ *Private lessons $45 per hour.*

Playa Bahía Junquillal

26 km (16 miles) northwest of Santa Rosa National Park entrance.

This 2½-km (1½-mile), tree-fringed beach is as close as you can get to a white-sand beach in this part of Guanacaste. Not to be confused with the Playa Junquillal farther south, this beach is part of the Guanacaste Conservation Area, and is a wildlife refuge to the north of Santa Rosa.

GETTING HERE AND AROUND

From the Pan-American Highway, take the road signed for Cuajiniquil, 43 km (26 miles) northwest of Liberia and 8 km (5 miles) north of Santa Rosa National Park. Follow the paved road 14 km (8 miles) to the beach turnoff, along a dirt road for another 4 km (2½ miles). From the Bahía Salinas area, take the scenic dirt road (4WD recommended); then follow the road near Puerto Soley (signed for Cuajiniquil) 7 km (4½ miles) to the beach entrance. It's about 30 minutes from the Pan-American turnoff and one hour from Bahía Salinas.

Beaches

Bahía Junquillal (*Junquillal Bay Wildlife Refuge*)

BEACH—SIGHT | The warm, calm water makes this one of the best swimming beaches on the Golfo de Santa Elena. Stay for the day or camp out in the well-kept, shaded camping area with cold-water showers, bathrooms, grills, and picnic tables ($15 per person onetime park entrance for foreigners, plus $19 per person per night to camp). Compared with other camping areas in Costa Rica, prices are steep since this is part of the Junquillal Bay Wildlife Refuge. You can snorkel if you bring your own gear. **Amenities:** showers; toilets. **Best for:** fishing; solitude; swimming. ✉ *18 km (11 miles) west of Pan-American Hwy., Cuajiniquil turnoff* ⊕ *www.acguanacaste.ac.cr/turismo/sector-junquillal* ✉ *$15.*

Hotels

Santa Elena Lodge

$$ | **B&B/INN** | This simple family-run lodge with cozy rooms on the outskirts of Cuajiniquil provides the closest accommodations to both Playa Bahía Junquillal and Santa Rosa National Park, making it a good option for nature lovers and anyone who wants to stray from the vacationing crowds. **Pros:** friendly owners; near beach and park; clean and comfortable rooms. **Cons:** little English spoken; basic accommodations. [$] *Rooms from: $80* ✉ *10 km (6 miles) west of Pan-American Hwy., 4 km (2½ miles) east of Junquillal, Cuajiniquil* ☎ *2679–1038* 🌐 *www.facebook.com/santaelenalodge* 🛏 *8 rooms* 🍴 *Free Breakfast.*

Santa Rosa National Park

35 km (22 miles) northwest of Liberia.

Santa Rosa National Park blends forest and pristine beaches overlooking the famed surf spot Witch's Rock. North of Liberia, the park is less frequented than other national parks in Costa Rica due to the difficult terrain (especially in rainy season) and the remote location far off the beaten path. The country's first national park, it still has an untouched beauty that is evident from the chirping birds among the treetops to the white-tailed deer drinking from watering holes. There are several campsites where travelers can soak in the sounds of Santa Rosa's symphony, comprised of howler monkeys, coyotes, bats, and the occasional jaguar. The best time to experience the typical dry-forest vegetation and wildlife is during dry season when leaves are sparse and roads are accessible.

GETTING HERE AND AROUND

The turnoff for Santa Rosa National Park from the Pan-American Highway is well marked, about 30 minutes outside of Liberia. From Liberia you can hop on a bus heading north to La Cruz and get off at the park entrance, but you'll have to hike 7 km (4½ miles) in the hot sun to the Casona park headquarters from there. La Posada del Tope arranges shuttle vans from Liberia to the park entrance for $20 per person round-trip.

Sights

Santa Rosa National Park (*Parque Nacional Santa Rosa*)

NATIONAL/STATE PARK | Thanks to sparse foliage, it's not difficult to spot wildlife within Santa Rosa's tropical dry forest, especially if you're with an experienced guide. There are impressive flora and fauna, and even on a half-day visit you might see monkeys, birds, deer, and coatis hiding in the dry-forest vegetation. Santa Rosa's wealth of natural beauty is due in part to its remoteness—it isn't as busy as some of Costa Rica's other parks. Most trails are easily accessible and relatively flat. To get deep into the park, you must have a 4WD vehicle, and many roads are impassable in rainy season. The park headquarters, a historic ranch house and museum called La Casona, and a nearby camping area are 7 km (4½ miles) from the Pan-American Highway via a paved road.

From park headquarters it's 11 km (7 miles) to **Playa Naranjo,** where the famed Witch's Rock surf break is located (surfers get there by boat). The road here is rough (4WD only). **Playa Nancite**—the site of one of the world's few completely protected olive ridley turtle *arribada,* or mass nesting (permit required)—is an additional 3 miles (5 km) by footpath north of Playa Naranjo. The arribadas occur during rainy season (July to November). A permit can be obtained from the Ecotourism Office in the administrative center. The most impressive coastal views are from the Mirador Valle Naranjo and Mirador Tierras Emergidas. For bird-watching, follow the Los Platos trail about 5 km (3 miles) past the administrative center on the way to the coast. It's best to visit the park with a guide. ✉ *Km 269, Pan-American Hwy. 35 km (22 miles) north of Liberia* ☎ *2666–0623* 🌐 *www.acguanacaste.ac.cr* 🎟 *$15 park entrance; $19 camping.*

Hotels

There are basic dormitory-style lodgings and a camping area ($4) near the park's administrative center; you can also camp within Santa Rosa National Park at the very basic and remote campsites at the beaches of Naranjo and Murcielago. No more than 20 people can camp within the park at a time. Call the park headquarters (☎ 2666–5051) for information. Most people visit the park on day trips from Liberia, La Cruz, or nearby Cuajiniquil.

Tierra Madre

$$ | B&B/INN | FAMILY | Located 25 km (15½ miles) northeast of La Cruz, this remote eco-estate is made up of four hillside bungalows with stunning volcano views and a backdrop of Lake Nicaragua. **Pros:** gourmet farm-to-table meals; way off the beaten path; unique activities led by friendly and passionate owners. **Cons:** Wi-Fi in common areas only; long muddy road; lots of insects in the area. $ Rooms from: $120 ⊠ 25 km northeast of La Cruz, 5 km from nearest village of Los Andes, La Cruz ☎ 8705–4249 ⊕ www. tierramadre.co.cr ⇨ 4 bungalows ⦿ Free Breakfast ⌖ Two-night minimum stay.

Activities

HIKING

Several trails to the beaches lead off the road before it becomes impassable to vehicles. The hike to Playa Naranjo (11 km [7 miles] west of La Casona) requires good physical condition and lots of water. You can get a map of the trails at the park entrance.

Casona Nature-Trail Loop (Sendero Indio Desnudo)

HIKING/WALKING | The short (about 1-km [½-mile]) Casona nature-trail loop from the park headquarters is worth taking to get a brief sampling of the woods. Look for the handicap accesible Indio Desnudo (Naked Indian) path, named after the

local word for gumbo-limbo trees. This is one of the few trails that doesn't get overly muddy, even after a heavy rain in wet season. Carry plenty of water and insect repellent. ⊠ Santa Rosa National Park.

SURFING

Witch's Rock (Pena Bruja)

SURFING | Witch's Rock towers offshore over a near-perfect beach break off Playa Naranjo in Santa Rosa National Park. The massive boulder once howled and whistled, causing passersby to believe the rock was haunted by a witch. In reality, it was only the offshore winds billowing between the water and stone that made the eerie sound. Years of erosion have silenced the howling, but the boulder, and the name, remain. If you are interested in surfing Witch's Rock, take a boat tour from Playas del Coco, Playa Hermosa, or Playa Tamarindo, to the south. Tropic Surf offers surf trips to Witch's Rock from its shop at Four Seasons Resort Peninsula Papagayo. ⊠ Santa Rosa National Park.

Guanacaste National Park

30 km (18 miles) north of Liberia.

Sights

Guanacaste National Park

NATIONAL/STATE PARK | The 325-square-km (125-square-mile) Parque Nacional Guanacaste, bordering the east side of the Pan-American Highway 30 km (18 miles) north of Liberia, was created to preserve rain forests around Cacao Volcano (5,443 feet) and Orosi Volcano (4,879 feet), which are seasonally inhabited by migrant wildlife from Santa Rosa National Park. The connecting border of these two national parks serves as a biological corridor for birds resettling between cloud, rain, and dry forests. Popular with researchers, the park isn't quite ready for tourism yet. There are very few facilities and no well-marked trails; if you want to hike, it's best to hire a professional guide. In rainy season, roads are impassable; a 4WD vehicle is required year-round. Established under Dr. Daniel Janzen, the park is part of the Guanacaste Conservation Area, a mosaic of interdependent protected areas, parks, and refuges; the goal is to accommodate the migratory patterns of animals, from jaguars to tapirs. Much of the park's territory is cattle pasture, which is regenerating into new forest faster than predicted. Today the park has howler and capuchin monkeys, collared peccaries, white-tailed deer, pumas, sloths, coatis, bats, and more than 5,000 species of butterflies and moths. Among the 300 different birds are parakeets, hawks, cuckoos, and magpie-jays. ⊠ *35 km (22 miles) north of Liberia* ✥ *Adjacent to Santa Rosa National Park* ☎ *$15.*

Rincón de la Vieja National Park

25 km (15 miles) northeast of Liberia.

Wildlife, rivers, waterfalls, and mud baths are just the tip of the volcano when it comes to the natural wonders of Rincón de la Vieja National Park. Dominating the scenery east of the Pan-American Highway just north of bustling Liberia, the national park's 34,800 acres are home to two peaks, the most impressive being Rincón de la Vieja at 6,254 feet, which is often enveloped in clouds. Expect to see monkeys, sloths, and birds in a single day's exploration. ■ TIP→ If your vacation plans only include the Pacific Coast but you really want to visit a volcano, this is your chance. Rincón de la Vieja is a great alternative and much shorter trip than the more popular Arenal.

For lodging, take your pick from working ranches, river lodges, rustic B&Bs, and garden villas; just be sure to rent a 4WD vehicle to reach the more remote properties, especially in rainy season. To get a taste of the area, there are plenty of activities that blend nature and adventure, like horseback riding, river rafting, ziplining, and hiking on a network of trails that set off from the Santa María ranger station and wind past hot springs, mud baths, and waterfalls. Lathering up with the volcanic mud softens the skin and detoxifies the body, and it makes for a fun photo op.

GETTING HERE AND AROUND

There are two park entrances on the volcano's southern slope: the less traveled one at Hacienda Santa María on the road leading northeast from Liberia (one hour), where there is camping available; and the one at Las Pailas, past Curubandé off the Pan-American Highway. To get to Las Pailas entrance from Liberia, take the first entrance road 5 km (3 miles) northwest of Liberia off the Pan-American Highway. The turnoff is easy to miss—follow signs for Hacienda Guachipelín or the town of Curubandé. It's a 17-km (10½-mile) road, paved until the final stretch beyond Hacienda Guachipelín. Non–hotel guests must pay a small toll (about $1.50) to access the private road to the park entrance. The Santa María entrance is 25 km (15 miles) northeast of Liberia along the Colonia Blanca route, which follows the course of the Río Liberia. The turnoff from the Pan-American Highway to the hotels on the western slope of the volcano is 12 km (7 miles) northwest of Liberia, turning right at the road signed for Cañas Dulces. A 4WD vehicle is recommended for all these slow and bone-rattling rides.

◉ Sights

★ Rincón de la Vieja National Park (*Parque Nacional Volcán Rincón de la Vieja*)

NATIONAL/STATE PARK | It might be a trek to get here, but Rincón de la Vieja National Park doesn't disappoint with its multitude of natural wonders from hot springs and mud baths to refreshing waterfalls and a smoldering volcano. Dominating 140 square km (54 square miles) of the volcano's upper slopes, this tropical rain forest is usually blanketed in clouds, with a short dry transition between January and April. The park has two peaks: Santa María and the barren Rincón de la Vieja. The latter has an active crater, leading park authorities to close some trails, especially during wet season (check the status before you visit).

The wildlife here is diverse, with birds, deer, coyotes, monkeys, and armadillos. There are two main entrances: Santa María and Las Pailas; the latter is the most common place to enter the park and is closest to the trails (there's a $1.50 charge for private road use). The park does not have guides; we recommend the nature guides at Eco Explorer and Tours Your Way. Many of the attractions people visit in Rincón de la Vieja are accessible without actually entering the park, since the ranches that border it also hold significant forest and geothermal sites. (⇨ *For more information, see the highlighted listing in this chapter.*) ✉ *Rincón de la Vieja National Park* ☎ *2666–5051* 💲 *$15.*

🛏 Hotels

★ Blue River Resort

$$$ | **RESORTRESORT** | **FAMILY** | Named for the blue river that flows nearby, this property on the volcano's northern slope is worth the trek to experience the resort's hot springs, mud baths, butterfly gardens, adventure tours, and spacious rustic cabins with terrace-hammocks. **Pros:** family-friendly; great activities; nearby waterfalls. **Cons:** rough, unpaved road; limited, somewhat pricey menu; Wi-Fi in common areas only. 💲 *Rooms from: $157* ✉ *600 m west of Río Celeste Bridge* ☎ *2206–5000, 2206–5506, 954/688–3646 in U.S.* 🌐 *www.blueriverresort.com* 🛏 *25 rooms* 🍴 *Free Breakfast.*

Borinquen Mountain Resort & Spa

$$$ | **RESORT** | The spacious villas and bungalows on this 570-acre ranch are lovely, and the room rate includes access to their hot springs, mud baths, and a Costa Rican breakfast. **Pros:** attractive, well-equipped bungalows; peaceful environment; lots of outdoor activities. **Cons:** far from park entrance; 12-km (7½-mile) unpaved road; Wi-Fi only in restaurant and reception areas; occasional sound of ATVs, golf carts, and leaf blowers. 💲 *Rooms from: $194* ✉ *13 km (8 miles) northwest of Liberia on Pan-American Hwy., then 19 km (12 miles) north on dirt road toward Cañas Dulces* ☎ *2690–1900* 🌐 *www.borinquenresort.com* 🛏 *39 units* 🍴 *Free Breakfast.*

Buena Vista Lodge

$$ | **B&B/INN** | Beautiful views abound at this truly Costa Rican ecolodge, with rustic hacienda-style rooms and plenty of cultural activities. **Pros:** many activities; breathtaking views; Costa Rican culture. **Cons:** rooms may be too basic for some; patchy Wi-Fi; mediocre food. 💲 *Rooms from: $88* ✉ *Rincón de la Vieja National Park* ☎ *506/2690–1414* 🛏 *76 rooms* 🍴 *Free Breakfast.*

Hacienda Guachipelín

$$ | **HOTEL** | **FAMILY** | One of the best values in the Rincón area for hair-raising adventure and nature tours, this hotel also gets top billing for its comfortable rooms, excellent restaurant, and friendly service. **Pros:** near park entrance; lots of activities; excellent value; home-cooked Costa Rican cuisine. **Cons:** caters to large groups and day visitors; some rooms are near horse stables; $50 fee for checkout after noon. 💲 *Rooms from: $140* ✉ *17 km (10 miles) northeast of Pan-American*

Hwy., on road to Las Pailas park entrance
☎ *2666–8075, 888/730–3840 toll-free
in U.S.* ⊕ *www.guachipelin.com* ⊷ *66
rooms* ❖ *Free Breakfast.*

Activities

TOUR OPERATORS
★ **Buena Vista Lodge & Adventure**
HORSEBACK RIDING | An hour's drive west
of the park, this lodge lies on a large
ranch where visitors enjoy horseback
riding, waterfall hikes, a canopy tour,
hanging bridges, and hot springs. Tours
are $20 to $50 per person; a combination
tour that lasts six to seven hours costs
$85, including lunch. ⊠ *Western slope
of volcano, 10 km (6 miles) north of
Cañas Dulces, near Borinquen Mountain
Resort* ☎ *2690–1414 in Liberia* ⊕ *www.
buenavistalodgecr.com* ⊷ *From $20.*

Eco Explorer
GUIDED TOURS | Ranked among the top
guides in Costa Rica, Carlos Luis Jiménez
of Eco Explorer offers birding, nature, and
adventure tours to national parks in the
Liberia and Papagayo areas. Day tours
to Rincón de la Vieja, Santa Rosa, and
Palo Verde must be reserved 48 hours in
advance; they begin at 5:30 or 7:30 am
and last until 3 or 5 pm, depending on
the package. ⊠ *Rincón de la Vieja National Park* ☎ *8927–9630* ⊷ *From $100.*

★ **Hacienda Guachipelín Adventure Tours**
HORSEBACK RIDING | This experienced
outfitter has the most exciting tours in
the area, including horseback riding,
river tubing, hot springs and mud baths,
guided waterfall hikes, and hikes on
the slopes of the national park volcano
(from $25 to $62). The popular canopy
tour includes rock climbing, rappelling,
ziplines, suspension bridges, and a Tarzan
swing. The one-day, all-you-can-do adventure pass, including lunch, is a great deal.
⊠ *Road to Rincón de la Vieja National
Park* ☎ *2690–2900, 888/730–3840 toll-
free in U.S.* ⊕ *www.guachipelin.com*
⊷ *From $25.*

Sensoria
ECOTOURISM | If you want to experience
the area's natural attractions without all
the adrenaline-pumping activities, Sensoria has peaceful jungle trails, waterfalls,
pools, and an observation tower. The
entrance fee includes lunch and a guided
three-hour hike during which you'll visit
vibrant blue waterfalls, hot springs, and
natural pools. Bring a change of clothes,
bug spray, and water shoes. The hiking
tour begins daily at 9:30 am. Tours are by
reservation only, and no children under six
are allowed. ⊠ *Rincón de la Vieja National
Park* ⊕ *From Pan-American Hwy., turn
right toward Quebrada Grande. Turn left
toward Dos Ríos. Left at high school and
continue toward Buenos Aires de Upala.
Turn right at sign for "AyA." Follow signs
for Sensoria and continue 3.7 km (2.3
miles) to entrance* ☎ *506/2288–6229*
⊕ *www.sensoria.cr* ⊷ *$120.*

Tours Your Way
TOUR—SPORTS | Playas del Coco–based
Mainor Lara Bustos guides tours to
Rincón de la Vieja or Palo Verde for $120,
including transportation, entrance fees,
lunch, and snacks. Ask about family
discounts. ⊠ *Rincón de la Vieja National
Park* ☎ *8820–1829* ⊕ *www.tours-your-
way.com.*

HIKING
Nearly all the lodges and outfitters in the
area offer guided hikes through the park
to the fumaroles, hot springs, waterfalls,
and (when possible) to the summit or the
edge of the active crater.

If you're doing a self-guided hike, stop for
trail maps and hiking information at the
park stations at both entrance gates. To
give yourself enough time to complete
the longer hikes, make sure you start out
between 7 and 9 am.

La Cangreja Waterfall Loop
HIKING/WALKING | A popular hike out of
Las Pailas is the four-hour 10-km (6-mile)
Cangreja Waterfall loop, passing through
beautiful primary forests and windswept

savannas. The *catarata* (waterfall) has a cool swimming hole below; the surrounding rocks have pockets of hot springs. Check with park rangers to make sure this trail is open. Entry closes at noon; the trail is closed Saturday, Sunday, and Monday. ⊠ *Rincón de la Vieja National Park* ⊕ *www.acguanacaste.ac.cr*.

Loop Through the Park (Las Pailas)

HIKING/WALKING | A less strenuous option than the trail to the summit is the fascinating 3-km (2-mile) loop through the park, which takes about two hours to complete, starting at Las Pailas entrance. Along the well-marked trail you'll see fumaroles exuding steam, a *volcancito* (little volcano), and Las Pailas, the boiling mud fields named after pots used for boiling down sugarcane. From the mud pots, a spur trail leads 5 km (3 miles) to a series of hot springs. If you tread softly in the nearby forest, you may spot animals such as howler, capuchin, and spider monkeys, as well as raccoonlike coatis looking for handouts. Remember the cardinal rule of wildlife encounters: don't feed the animals. The park is closed Saturday through Monday. ⊠ *Rincón de la Vieja National Park.*

HORSEBACK RIDING

Borinquen Mountain Resort & Spa

HORSEBACK RIDING | A day package here begins with a horseback ride and a 90-minute canopy tour, followed by lunch and free time to soak in the hotel's hot springs and relax in the natural steam bath. ⊠ *12 km (7½ miles) northwest of Liberia on the Pan-American Hwy., then 23 km (14 miles) north on the dirt road that passes Cañas Dulces* ☎ *2690–1900* ⊕ *www.borinquenresort.com* ✉ *From $80.*

Buena Vista Lodge & Adventure

HORSEBACK RIDING | This lodge and tour operator has horseback trips to hot springs and waterfalls. If not everyone in your party is a horse lover, tractor transport ($35) is available to the hot springs as well. ⊠ *Western slope of volcano, 10 km (6 miles) north of Cañas Dulces, near*

Borinquen Mountain Resort ⊕ *www.buenavistalodgecr.com* ✉ *From $40.*

Hacienda Guachipelín

HORSEBACK RIDING | This is the premier working ranch in the area, with more than 100 well-bred and well-trained horses, and miles of trails to three waterfalls, tropical dry forest, and hot springs. In addition to horseback tours, the Hacienda also offers a cowboy-for-a-day tour that includes harnessing your horse, rounding up cattle, and milking a cow. ⊠ *Hacienda Guachipelín* ☎ *2690–2900, 888/730–3840 toll-free in U.S. or Canada* ⊕ *www.guachipelin.com* ✉ *horseback tours from $29; cowboy-for-a-day tour $50.*

Liberia

214 km (133 miles, 4–5 hrs) northwest of San José.

Once a dusty cattle-market town, Liberia has galloped toward modernization, becoming the commercial, as well as the administrative, capital of Guanacaste. There are still a few vestiges of its colonial past on quieter side streets. But Liberia has virtually become one big shopping mall, complete with fast-food restaurants and a multiplex theater. Walk a couple of blocks south of the main street along Calle Real, though, and you can still find some of the whitewashed adobe houses for which Liberia was nicknamed the "White City," as well as some grand town houses that recall the city's glory days. A few have been restored and are now hotels and cafés. Liberia today is essentially a good place to have a meal and make a bank stop at any one of a dozen banks, including Scotiabank, Citibank, and HSBC. Liberia can also serve as a base for day trips to Santa Rosa and Rincón de la Vieja national parks. Keep in mind that Liberia is the hottest city in Costa Rica, getting up to 115°F (46°C) in April. The drive from San José takes between four and five hours, so it makes

Did You Know?

In the geothermal areas around Rincón de la Vieja, you'll find mud pots (pools of bubbling mud), fumaroles (holes that emit steam and gases), and hot springs.

sense to fly directly into Liberia if you're going only to the North Pacific. It's easy to rent a car near the airport.

GETTING HERE AND AROUND

From San José, follow the Pan-American Highway west past the Puntarenas exit, then north past Cañas to Liberia. The road is paved but under construction in places. It's a heavily traveled truck and bus route, and there are miles and miles where it is impossible to pass, but many drivers try, making this a dangerous road. South of Liberia, the road is being widened, so expect delays. Hourly direct buses leave San José for Liberia each day, and there are half a dozen daily flights, so it might be worth busing or flying to Liberia and renting a car from here. International flights into Liberia are available through Alaska Airlines, American, Delta, JetBlue, Southwest, Sun Country, and United.

The *avenidas* (avenues) officially run east–west, whereas the *calles* (streets) run north–south. Liberia is not too big to walk easily, but there are always taxis lined up around the pleasant central park.

RENTAL CARS Alamo. ✉ *2 km (1 mile) northeast of Liberia airport* ☎ *2668–1111, 800/522–9696 in U.S.*. **Budget.** ✉ *1 km (½ mile) east of Liberia airport* ☎ *2436–2061*. **Enterprise.** ✉ *2 km (1 mile) northeast of Liberia airport* ☎ *2668–1819* 🌐 *www.enterprise.com*. **Hertz.** ✉ *Hwy. 21, 3 km (2 miles) east of airport* ☎ *2668–1179* 🌐 *hertzrentacarcostarica.com*. **Vamos Rent-A-Car.** ✉ *5 km (3 miles) east of Liberia Airport on Hwy. 21* ☎ *4000–0557, 800/601–8806 from U.S., 213/261–8586 text from the U.S.* 🌐 *www.vamosrenta-car.com*.

ESSENTIALS

BANK/ATM Banco de Costa Rica. ✉ *C. Ctl., Avda. 1, diagonally across from central park* ☎ *2666–9002*.

HOSPITAL Liberia Hospital. (*San Rafael Arcangel Medical Center*) ✉ *North end of town* ✥ *100 m east, 25 m south from Ascención Esquivel School* ☎ *2666–1717*.

PHARMACY Farmacia Lux. ✉ *Avda. 25 de Julio, in front of Super Compro, 100 m west of the park* ☎ *2665–1002*.

POST OFFICE Correo. ✉ *300 m west of hwy., 200 m north of Avda. Ctl., near Banco Nacional* ☎ *2666–1649*.

En Route

Yes, that is a life-size dinosaur standing beside the highway 20 minutes north of Puntarenas. It is one of 26 lifelike models of extinct and endangered animals arranged along a 1½-km (1-mile) forest trail at **Parque MegaFauna Monteverde** (✉ *Pan-American Hwy.* ☎ *2638–8193*). Along with the spectacular models outdoors, an impressive insect museum can be explored for a $5 entrance fee. The park is open daily 8 am to 5 pm. If you're just passing, you can still stop and take a photo of your kids in front of the baby dinosaur hatching out of a giant egg.

🍴 Restaurants

★ Café Liberia

$$$ | **FRENCH** | Step back 150 years into one of Liberia's grandest mansions, complete with an original ceiling painting of cupids, doves, and garlands of flowers. Creative takes on tropical ingredients, all with a French twist, make this the most sophisticated restaurant in town. **Known for:** Wagyu beef burger; mouthwatering ceviche; organic coffee and delectable crepes. [$] *Average main: $16* ✉ *C. Real Antigua, 125 m south of central park* ☎ *2665–1660* 🌐 *cafe-liberia.negocio.site* ⏲ *Closed Sun. No lunch Mon.*

The Green House

$$$ | **ECLECTIC** | This modern glass building seems almost out of place on the road connecting Liberia to the coast. Filling a void in healthy cuisine, the restaurant serves wraps, salads, sushi, and sandwiches such as organic chicken with fresh basil. **Known for:** tasty bruschetta brought to every table; a variety of vegetarian options; fresh juices. $ *Average main: $20* ⊠ *Hwy. 21, on road to airport in front of Pájaro Azul, 2 km (1 mile) from Liberia intersection* ☎ *2665–5037, 2665–8901* ⊗ *Closed Sun.*

Restaurante Café Europa (*Panaderia Alemana*)

$$$ | **GERMAN** | **FAMILY** | The aroma of baking bread is irresistible as you pass this German bakery, just south of the Liberia airport, whose baked goods are delivered all over the peninsula. The display case is filled with tempting strudels, Bundt cakes, and flaky fruit pastries. **Known for:** apple strudel and other tempting bakery desserts; savory scallops; beer garden with a playground for the kids. $ *Average main: $16* ⊠ *5 km (3 miles) west of Liberia airport* ☎ *2668–1081* ⊕ *www. panaleman.com.*

Hotels

Hilton Garden Inn Liberia Airport

$$ | **HOTEL** | Comfortable and convenient, especially if you're catching an early-morning flight or you need a break from driving before heading south to the beach, this five-story contemporary Hilton has all the mod cons, including Wi-Fi, HDTVs, microwaves, and refrigerators. **Pros:** kids under 12 stay free; excellent amenities; free shuttle to and from airport. **Cons:** no shaded parking area; service is inconsistent; some airplane noise. $ *Rooms from: $132* ⊠ *Across from Liberia International Airport on main hwy.* ☎ *2690–8888* ⊕ *www.liberiaairport. hgi.com* ⇆ *169 rooms* ⦿ *No meals.*

Papagayo Peninsula

47 km (29 miles) west of Liberia.

The Papagayo Peninsula, a crooked finger of land cradling the west side of Bahía Culebra (Snake Bay), enjoys guaranteed sun from January to April, making it a prime site for all-inclusive hotels catering to snowbirds escaping North American winters. Five large hotels are already situated around Papagayo Bay, and others are slated to be built here, all part of a government-sponsored development program modeled after Cancún. Just before the entrance to Andaz Resort is the impressive Marina Papagayo, where luxury yachts and sailboats dock. Although the hotels are reminiscent of their Caribbean counterparts, the beaches are distinctly Costa Rican, with brown sand and aquamarine water that grows cool from January to April. Isolation is the name of the game here, which means that getting out of the man-made "paradise" to explore anything off-property often entails a pricey tour.

High season here coincides with dry season, when the heat is intense and the landscape becomes brown and brittle. In the rainy season (August to December), the landscape is greener and lusher. The sparkling water and spectacular sunsets are beautiful year-round.

GETTING HERE AND AROUND

All hotels here have airport pickup. To get to the Four Seasons from the Liberia airport (the hotel refuses to put up directional signs in order to protect its privacy), drive 10 km (6 miles) south of Guardia, over the Río Tempisque Bridge, then take the turn on the right signed for Andaz Peninsula Papagayo Resort. Follow this road about 20 km (12 miles) to its end at the entrance to the resort. For Casa Conde Hotel, El Mangroove, and Secrets Papagayo, take the road toward Playa Panama.

Beaches

Playa Panama

BEACH—SIGHT | **FAMILY** | On the southern end of Culebra Bay, this calm beach with black sand stretches 2 km (1 mile), and is frequented by guests staying at nearby El Mangroove resort and Casa Conde Beachfront Hotel. Devoid of rocks and waves, the water is virtually flat, making this a popular spot for stand-up paddleboarding, kayaking, and swimming. There's a wooden shack next to El Mangroove offering overpriced water activities and equipment. Local vendors stand beachside, selling everything from sarongs to snow cones. With a minimum of six people, you can organize a snorkeling tour on a boat to the outer bay. There isn't much shade on the sand, but a grassy area between the resorts and the beach is lined with swaying palms and mesquite trees. A path meanders from one end of the bay to the other, meaning you can stroll without getting too much sun. There's guarded parking ($1 tip) between the two hotels. **Amenities:** food and drink; water sports. **Best for:** kayaking; swimming; walking. ✉ *Playa Panama, at Culebra Bay, in front of El Mangroove.*

Restaurants

Makoko

$$$ | **INTERNATIONAL** | At El Mangroove's trendy poolside restaurant, guests can dine with a glimpse of the ocean or head indoors to the more formal dining room enclosed in glass. Most ingredients are locally grown, and nearly every item on the menu is organic, including the grass-fed beef. **Known for:** seared scallops; Worcestershire-glazed short ribs slow-cooked for 24 hours; extensive wine list. [$] *Average main: $22* ✉ *At intersection near Hilton Resort, Playa Arenilla* ☎ *4701–0000* 🌐 *www.elmangroove.net* 🕓 *No lunch.*

Hotels

Andaz Costa Rica Resort at Peninsula Papagayo

$$$$ | **RESORT** | Earth tones and natural details prevail in this Hyatt property created by architect Ronald Zürcher, who utilized indigenous woods, sugarcane, and bamboo in the design of the rooms, each contemporary and bright with ocean views. **Pros:** friendly staff; free Kids' Club; design reflects natural surroundings. **Cons:** pricey meals; rooms have dim lighting; small and rocky beach. [$] *Rooms from: $525* ✉ *Peninsula Papagayo, next to Four Seasons Resort* ☎ *2690–1234* 🌐 *www.andazpapagayo.com* 🛏 *153 rooms* 🍴 *No meals.*

Casa Conde Beachfront Hotel

$$$$ | **HOTEL** | **FAMILY** | Spread over verdant grounds just behind relatively pristine Playa Panama, this all-inclusive property has an excellent location with bay views, balmy breezes, and a huge swimming pool. **Pros:** spacious rooms; immaculate grounds; close to beach. **Cons:** early check-ins cost $25 per person; rooms near pool can be noisy; no activities. [$] *Rooms from: $400* ✉ *Playa Panama, 3 km (2 miles) north of Playa Hermosa* ☎ *2586–7300 San José office, 2672–1008* 🌐 *www.grupocasaconde.com* 🛏 *50 rooms* 🍴 *All-inclusive.*

El Mangroove

$$$$ | **HOTEL** | Barefoot luxury abounds at this hip boutique hotel where an airy courtyard leads to a 45-meter pool lined with beach bungalows and modern rooms. **Pros:** 24-hour room service; nice gym and spa; gorgeous rain showers; all-inclusive plan available. **Cons:** poolside cabana costs $150 per day; only two rooms have ocean views; mosquitoes in common areas; staff lack attention to detail. [$] *Rooms from: $563* ✉ *Bahia Papagayo, at Playa Panama, at intersection before Hilton Resort, Playa Arenilla* ☎ *4701–0000* 🌐 *www.elmangroove.net* 🛏 *85 rooms* 🍴 *No meals.*

★ **Four Seasons Resort Costa Rica**
$$$$ | RESORT | With an indulgent spa, restaurants, and retail boutiques, Four Seasons is one of the most luxurious hotels in Costa Rica, but it's the unparalleled service and secluded location between two golden-sand beaches that make this resort one of a kind. **Pros:** impeccable service; lovely beach; surf trips to Witch's Rock. **Cons:** breakfast not included; 30 minutes from main road; expensive. [$] *Rooms from: $1,350* ✉ *25 km (15 miles) west of Guardia* ✥ *Follow signs to Andaz Resort and continue to end of road* ☎ *2696–0000, 800/332–3442 in U.S and Canada* 🌐 *www.fourseasons.com/costarica* ⛳ *$240 for 18 holes* 🛏 *159 units* 🍴 *No meals.*

Activities

CANOPY TOUR

Witch's Rock Canopy Tour
ZIP LINING | Taking advantage of one of the few remaining patches of dry tropical forest on the Papagayo Peninsula, Witch's Rock Canopy Tour gives you your money's worth: 24 platforms, with a thrilling 1,485-foot cable zip between two of them; three hanging bridges; a waterfall in rainy season; and hiking trails. The 1½-hour tour is $85 per person; includes transportation from area hotels. ✉ *On road to Four Seasons Resort, 17 km (10 miles) west of DYI Center on main hwy. from Liberia* ☎ *2696–7101, 2696–7103* 🌐 *www.witchsrockcanopy.com* 🎫 *From $75.*

GOLF

Four Seasons Golf Course at Peninsula Papagayo
GOLF | Teeing off from one of the highest points on the Peninsula, this 18-hole, par-72 championship course was designed by Arnold Palmer and has breathtaking views on every play. Surrounded by ocean and forest, you're likely to encounter howler and white-faced monkeys during your game. Several holes are perched on cliffs backed by ocean, like hole 17 with spectacular views from both the tee and the green. Increasing the challenge are tough drops from the tees and small greens. Signature hole 6 demands skill; it's a long 446-yard par 4 with a tee shot that plays 200 feet downhill to a valley. In addition to the award-winning course, there's a driving range, a sand-bunker practice area, putting and chipping greens, and a pro shop. Tee times are offered from 7 am to 4 pm. You can rent clubs for $85 ✉ *Four Seasons Resort Costa Rica* ✥ *26 km (16 miles) north of Liberia, follow signs to Andaz Resort* ☎ *2696–0000* 🌐 *www.fourseasons.com/costarica* 🎫 *$300 morning for outside guests, $175 afternoon* ⛳ *18 holes, 6800 yards, par 72* ⏲ *Closed Mon.*

SURFING

Tropic Surf
SURFING | No one mixes surfing and luxury better than this highly professional outfitter, offering lessons ($110) and half-day excursions ($350) to Witch's Rock and Ollies Point aboard their fleet of boats. Their quiver is top-notch, ranging from shortboards to stand-up paddleboards. Trained instructors are on hand for all levels, delivering water and sunscreen while you surf. In addition to their location at Four Seasons Resort Peninsula Papagayo, they have more than 20 destinations worldwide. ✉ *Four Seasons Peninsula Papagayo* 🌐 *www.tropicsurf.net* 🎫 *From $110.*

Playa Hermosa

27 km (17 miles) southwest of Liberia airport.

Beautiful Playa Hermosa, once a laid-back fishing community, has grown exponentially with condominiums and villas covering the scrubby hills overlooking the wide, curved beach. Warm, swimmable water, prime dive sites, choice fishing grounds, and sunset views of the Papagayo Peninsula are all reasons why Canadian and American expatriates are buying condos here. In the early morning, though, Playa Hermosa is still the kind of place where the beach is the town's main thoroughfare, filled with joggers, people walking their dogs, and families out for a stroll. Not to be confused with the mainland surfers' beach of the same name south of Jacó, this Playa Hermosa has long been occupied by small hotels, restaurants, and homes along the length of the beach, so the newer hotel behemoths and other developments are forced to set up shop off the beach or up on the surrounding hillsides.

GETTING HERE AND AROUND

Heading south from Liberia along Highway 21, take the turnoff in Comunidad signed for Playa Hermosa and Playas del Coco. Playa Hermosa is about 15 km (9 miles) northwest. The paved road forks after the small town of Sardinal, the right fork heading into Hermosa and the left leading to Playas del Coco. Local directions usually refer to the first and second entrance roads to the beach, the first entrance being the southern one. There is no through-beachfront road, so you have to approach the beach from either of these two roads. Transportes La Pampa buses leave from Liberia for Playa Hermosa daily starting at 4:30, 4:40, 4:50 am (to get workers to their hotel jobs), then at 7:30 and 11:30 am and 1, 3:30, and 5:30 pm. The trip takes about 1½ hours. A taxi from Playa Hermosa to Playas del Coco costs about $15 and takes about 15 minutes.

ESSENTIALS

Playa Hermosa has a large supermarket, Luperón, on the main road, between the first and second beach entrances, open daily 7 am to 8:30 pm, where you can stock up on just about everything you need—food, wine, liquor, toiletries, and fresh-baked bread.

Beaches

Playa Hermosa

BEACH—SIGHT | Not to be confused with the surfers' beach near Jacó by the same name, Playa Hermosa's 2-km-long (1-mile-long) crescent of dark-gray volcanic sand attracts heat, making the early morning or late afternoon the best time to visit (with the latter providing spectacular sunsets). The beach fronts a line of shade trees, so there's a welcome respite from the heat of the sun. The crystal-clear water—it's a Blue Flag beach—is usually calm, with no strong currents and with comfortable temperatures of 23°C to 27°C (74°F to 80°F). For offshore diving, there's an average visibility of 20 feet, and rock reefs that attract large schools of fish, sea turtles, sharks, manta rays, and moray eels. Sea views are as picturesque as they get, with bobbing fishing boats, jagged profiles of coastline, rocky outcroppings, and at night the twinkling lights of the Four Seasons Resort across the bay. At the beach's north end, low tide creates wide, rock-lined tidal pools. Food and drinks are available at Hotel El Velero. **Amenities:** food and drink; water sports. **Best for:** swimming; walking. ⊠ *Playa Hermosa.*

Restaurants

Aqua Sport

$$ | PERUVIAN | There's not much "aqua sport" going on at this Peruvian beach-front restaurant, unless you count drinking margaritas in a hammock. It's the kind of place you drop by on day one, and find yourself coming back to for the remainder of your vacation—blame the setting of Adirondack chairs lining the beach combined with fresh fish like grilled snapper served with shoestring fries. **Known for:** delectable fish tacos; cheerful location on the beach with a tree swing for the littles; Tato burger—juicy beef patty with bacon, cream cheese, and whiskey. $ *Average main: $14* ⊠ *2nd entrance to Playa Hermosa, at beach* ☎ *2672–0151.*

Ginger Restaurant Bar

$$$ | **TAPAS** | This tapas restaurant, featuring Asian and Mediterranean flavors, is in a modern glass-and-steel tree house that's cantilevered on the side of a hill and includes a spacious deck. Delectable appetizer-size offerings include seared pepper-crusted tuna atop pickled ginger slaw, or panfried sea bass fillets with a divine ginger-and-mandarin-orange butter sauce. **Known for:** spring rolls; pavlova; small plates, tapas-size dishes to share. Ⓢ *Average main: $18* ✉ *Main hwy., south of Hotel Condovac* ☎ *2672–0041* ⊕ *www.gingercostarica.com* ⊗ *Closed Mon. No lunch.*

 ## Hotels

Hotel & Villas Huetares

$$ | **HOTEL** | **FAMILY** | The best bargain in town, this long-established family hotel offers two-bedroom garden villas surrounding a central pool, as well as a two-story annex with 16 spacious rooms. **Pros:** close to beach; good kitchens; beautiful grounds and pool. **Cons:** lots of noise from kids, especially on weekends; no hot water unless you specifically request it; weak Wi-Fi signal. Ⓢ *Rooms from: $80* ✉ *2nd entrance road to Playa Hermosa, 100 m (1 block) in from the main hwy.* ☎ *2672–0052* ⊕ *huetarescr.com* ⤳ *40 rooms* ⏀ *Free Breakfast.*

★ Hotel Bosque del Mar Playa Hermosa

$$$ | **HOTEL** | This beachfront hotel on the southern end of Playa Hermosa features luxurious rooms and suites on a beautiful, spacious property shaded by century-old vine-draped trees. **Pros:** superb garden and beachfront location; beautiful restaurant; all rooms have terraces. **Cons:** some rooms near the pool are dark; mosquitoes; expensive for the area. Ⓢ *Rooms from: $226* ✉ *End of 1st entrance to Playa Hermosa* ☎ *2672–0046* ⊕ *www.hotelplayahermosa.com* ⤳ *33 units* ⏀ *No meals.*

Villa del Sueño

$$ | **HOTEL** | Although the handsome garden restaurant is the main attraction at this elegant hotel, the spacious rooms and well-equipped villas are quite comfortable, too, and the hotel is about a block from the beach. **Pros:** excellent restaurant; good value; updated rooms. **Cons:** not on the beach; can be noisy when there's live music; mosquitoes. Ⓢ *Rooms from: $115* ✉ *1st entrance to Playa Hermosa, 500 m west of main hwy.* ☎ *2672–0026* ⊕ *www.villadelsueno.com* ⤳ *44 units* ⏀ *No meals.*

 ## Nightlife

Hotel El Velero

THEMED ENTERTAINMENT | This lively beachfront hotel hosts beach barbecues on Wednesday and Saturday nights, and Taco Tuesday (half-off tacos). The crowd is thirtyish and up. ✉ *2nd entrance to Playa Hermosa, then 100 m north of Aqua Sport on beach road* ☎ *2672–1017* ⊕ *www.facebook.com/HotelElVeleroPlayaHermosa.*

Villa del Sueño

MUSIC CLUBS | In high season, Villa del Sueño hosts live music on Friday and Sunday nights, as well as occasional concerts featuring top national bands and performers. ✉ *1st entrance to Playa Hermosa, 500 m west of main hwy.* ☎ *2672–0026* ⊕ *www.villadelsueno.com.*

 ## Activities

BOATING AND FISHING

The fishing at Playa Hermosa is mostly close to the shores, and yields edible fish like dorado (mahimahi), snapper, amberjack, tuna, and wahoo. Roosterfish, marlin, and sailfish are all catch-and-release. Some local restaurants are happy to cook your catch for you. You can rent a boat or snorkel with **North Pacific Tours.** Most Hermosa-based snorkeling companies

Continued on page 289

Choosing a Beach

From pulverized volcanic rock and steady waves to soft white sand and idyllic settings, all of the beaches along the Nicoya Peninsula's coast have their own distinct merits. Playa Tamarindo has a restaurant so close to the ocean the surf spray salts your food; playas Hermosa and Sámara are family-friendly spots with swimmable waters; and playas Langosta and Pelada are made for contemplative walks.

GUANACASTE PACIFIC COAST

Playa Tamarindo

❶ Popular luxury resorts line the beaches of the **Papagayo Peninsula**.

❷ **Playa Hermosa** is one of the few Costa Rican beaches with calm, crystal-clear waters.

❸ Diving and fishing are the name of the game at **Playas del Coco** and its lively beach town.

❹ **Playa Ocotal** is a quiet black-sand beach with great views, diving, and good snorkeling.

❺ **Playa Pan de Azúcar** is practically deserted once you get there.

❻ **Playa Potrero** is the jumping-off point for diving trips to the Catalina Islands.

❼ Busy white-sand **Playa Flamingo** is ideal for swimming and sunning.

❽ Shells sprinkle the sand at chilled-out **Playa Conchal**, near a small fishing village.

❾ Lively **Tamarindo** is a hyped-up surfing and water-sports beach with wild nightlife.

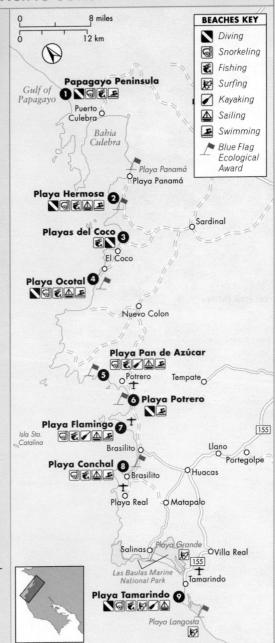

GUANACASTE AND NORTHERN NICOYA PENINSULA

(top) Playa Avellanas (bottom) Sunset at Sámara

❶ Playa Langosta is great for walks up its estuary and watching dramatic sunsets.

❷ Playa Avellanas is a perfect spot to relax with a cold drink between surf sessions.

❸ Playa Negra has some of Costa Rica's best surfing waves.

❹ Peaceful and difficult to reach, **Playa Junquillal** is all about relaxation.

❺ Hemmed in by rocks, **Playa Pelada** is staked out by territorial Tico surfers.

❻ Long, clean **Playa Guiones** is backed by dense jungle.

❼ Sámara's gentle waters make it perfect for kayakers, swimmers, and novice surfers.

❽ Perhaps the most beautiful beach in the country, **Playa Carrillo** fronts an idyllic half-moon bay.

❾ Rocky **Punta Islita** has interesting tidal pools to explore.

SOUTHERN NICOYA PENINSULA

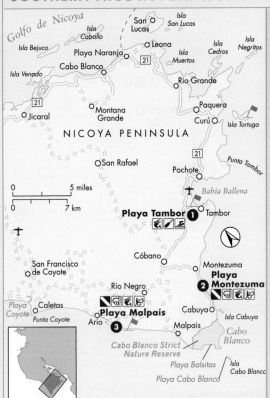

Golfo de Nicoya

Isla Caballo
San Lucas
Isla San Lucas
Isla Bejuco
Leona
Isla Cedros
Isla Negritos
Playa Naranjo
Isla Muertos
Cabo Blanco
Rio Grande
Isla Venado
Montana Grande
Paquera
Jicaral
Curú
Isla Tortuga

NICOYA PENINSULA

San Rafael
Pochote
Punta Tambor

0   5 miles
0   7 km

Bahía Ballena

Playa Tambor ❶ Tambor

San Francisco de Coyote
Cóbano
Montezuma
Playa Montezuma ❷

Rio Negro
Playa Coyote
Caletas
Punta Coyote
Playa Malpaís ❸
Ario
Cabuya
Isla Cabuya
Malpais
Cabo Blanco

Cabo Blanco Strict Nature Reserve

Playa Balsitas
Isla Cabo Blanco
Playa Cabo Blanco

(top) Montezuma (bottom) Surfing at Malpaís

❶ Crescent-shaped, shallow **Playa Tambor** is flanked by an all-inclusive resort and a fishing village.

❷ **Montezuma's** off-beat town is as much a draw as its bayside beach.

❸ Some of the largest surfing waves in Costa Rica are at **Malpaís**.

MAKING THE BEST OF YOUR BEACH VACATION

■ Tamarindo, Nosara, and Sámara are good for beginning surfers. Playas Grande, Avellanas, and Negra are best left to those with experience; other surfing waters are somewhere in between.

■ Tamarindo, Nosara, Sámara, and Tambor are beaches with air service to San José.

■ The beach road connecting most Nicoya Peninsula beaches is hard to stomach any time of year, and virtually impassable during the August through December rains. Take easier inland routes instead.

■ Riptides are seriously dangerous and hardly any Costa Rican beaches have lifeguards; get information from your hotel about where to swim safely.

head to nearby spots where you may see turtles, eagle rays, eels, parrotfish, snapper, puffer fish, and angelfish. Start out early when waters are calm.

Charlie's Adventure

BOATING | This tour company organizes ATV tours and fishing trips as well as the seven-hour Aqua Combo boat tours of Hermosa Bay, which includes snorkeling, bottom fishing, and a beach barbecue lunch ($90, including drinks). There's also a sunset boat tour. ⊠ *Panama Beach* ☎ *8842–9219, 2697–0594 (24 hrs)* ⊕ *www.facebook.com/CharliesAdventureTravel* ✉ *From $50.*

Papagayo Gulf Sport Fishing–North Pacific Tours

BOATING | Based in Playa Hermosa, this reliable outfitter has private and customized charters for fishing, surfing, and snorkeling tours aboard a 28-foot center-console panga. They run various fishing tours in the area. ⊠ *Playa Hermosa* ☎ *8398–8129* ⊕ *www.northpacifictours.com* ✉ *Tours from $60; half-day fishing excursion $400.*

Playas del Coco

25 km (16 miles) southwest of Liberia airport, 10 km (6 miles) south of Playa Hermosa.

Noisy, colorful, and interesting, Playas del Coco has the best souvenir shopping, the most dive shops, and the liveliest nightlife and barhopping on this part of the coast. It's still a working fishing port, with a port captain's office, a fish market, and an ice factory for keeping the catch of the day fresh—not for cooling margaritas, although many are enjoyed here. The beach has a beautiful boardwalk with palm trees, benches, and cold showers. Coco has had an explosion of condominium and villa projects, along with new commercial development, including the upscale Pacifico Village shopping center at the entrance to town. This center

boasts a flagship AutoMercado, the country's top grocery chain, as well as a bank, pharmacy, restaurants, fast-food chains, a UPS office, and a few clothing boutiques. Fresh seafood, myriad souvenir shops, and plenty of bars have always drawn tourists here, but Playas del Coco also has a high concentration of tour operators offering diving, fishing, and surfing excursions at remote breaks such as Ollie's Point and Witch's Rock. Because Coco is mere minutes from Playa Hermosa, however, you can just as easily enjoy those sports while staying at that more pleasant beach. If you like to shop and party, Coco's slightly raucous ambience is appealing.

GETTING HERE AND AROUND

The easy drive from the Liberia airport to Playas del Coco takes about 30 minutes. The paved highway turns into a grand, divided boulevard as you enter town; it ends at the beach. If you don't have a car, the best way to get here from Playa Hermosa is in a taxi, for about $20 one way.

ESSENTIALS

BANKS/ATMS BAC San José. ⊠ *At Pacifico Village, next to AutoMercado.* **Banco Nacional.** ⊠ *At entrance to town on main road, across street from Hard Rock Cafe.*

PHARMACY Farmacia Azul. ⊠ *7 Plaza Colonial* ☎ *2670–0339* ⊕ *www.farmaciaazul.com.*

POST OFFICE Correo. ⊠ *At entrance to town on main road* ✛ *100 m south of Hotel Flor de Itabo.*

 Restaurants

Citron

$$$ | **ECLECTIC** | It might not be beachfront, but this snazzy restaurant has an upscale vibe with hardwood floors, white brick walls, and a wine bar shaking up divine watermelon martinis. For more ambience, grab a table on the outside deck where dishes like salmon risotto, poached sea bass, and shrimp sautéed in coconut milk are served. **Known for:** creamy risotto dishes; lovely deck; caramelized pork tenderloin. [$] *Average main: $17* ✉ *Pacifico Retail Village, Suite C #10, Rte. 151* ☎ *2670–0942* 🕓 *Closed Sun. No lunch.*

La Dolce Vita

$$ | **ITALIAN** | Two Italian brothers offer well-prepared Italian classics, as well as some interesting seafood dishes like tuna tartare and tagliolini with crab in a cream sauce. For homemade goodness, try the cappellacci with beef filling sprinkled with Parmesan. **Known for:** homemade pasta; catch of the day; beautiful courtyard setting. [$] *Average main: $14* ✉ *In El Pueblito shopping center, 350 m north along road running parallel to beach* ☎ *2670–1384.*

★ **The Lookout**

$$ | **SEAFOOD** | As if the breathtaking view high in the hills above Playas del Coco weren't enough (you may recognize it from its feature on the television series *Restaurants on the Edge*), the innovative menu at one of the few oyster bars in Costa Rica takes it a step further. Try the oysters prepared charbroiled, steamed, or fried, or order sushi alongside a divine kiwitini or watermelon mojito. **Known for:** fresh raw oysters, delivered Wednesday; tuna poke bowl; 17 Monkey Head Brewing company beers on tap. [$] *Average main: $10* ✉ *Rooftop of Chantel Suites, up hill in Vista Marina* ☎ *4033–7588* 🌐 *www.thelookoutcoco.com* 🕓 *Closed Mon.*

Hotels

Chantel Suites

$$ | **HOTEL** | On a hilltop, this vacation rental property has vibrant Mediterranean-style rooms, apartments, and a luxurious two-bedroom penthouse—all with ocean views. **Pros:** breathtaking views; great rates; amazing rooftop restaurant. **Cons:** because it's a vacation rental there are no hotel amenities (no front desk, extra fee for daily cleaning); three-night minimum stay; 5-minute drive to Coco Beach, 10 minutes to Ocotal Beach. [$] *Rooms from: $89* ✉ *Playas del Coco* ✣ *At entrance to Playas del Coco, turn left at anchor, follow signs to hotel* ☎ *2670–0389* 🛏 *11 rooms* 🍴 *No meals.*

La Puerta del Sol

$$ | **HOTEL** | Facing a formal garden with sculpted shrubs and a lovely pool, this tranquil enclosure just two blocks from the beach has airy, Mediterranean-style guest rooms splashed with tropical colors. **Pros:** intimate; comfortable; new bar and restaurant. **Cons:** a few cats prowling the garden; hard beds; rooms lack charm. [$] *Rooms from: $115* ✉ *180 m to right (north) off main road to town* ☎ *2670–0195* 🌐 *lapuertadelsolhotel.com* 🛏 *9 rooms* 🍴 *Free Breakfast.*

★ **Villa Buena Onda**

$$$$ | **HOTEL** | Tucked away in the quiet hills of Playas del Coco, this adults-only hotel whose name translates to "good vibe" delivers luxury, service, and elegance. **Pros:** impeccable service; organic meals; complimentary shuttle to beach clubs. **Cons:** usually full; only top-floor rooms have ocean views; not family-friendly (no kids under 16). [$] *Rooms from: $650* ✉ *Playas del Coco* ✣ *At entrance to Coco, turn left before old anchor, stay right (straight) at fork, left before bridge, continue to top of hill, villa is on left* ☎ *4031–7707, 800/414–0159 in U.S. or Canada* 🌐 *www.villabuenaonda.com* 🛏 *8 rooms* 🍴 *All-inclusive.*

Nightlife

Coconutz

BARS/PUBS | Local expats meet up at this popular sports bar and grill, which has an all-day happy hour from 9 to 7, TVs for *Monday Night Football*, a full range of bar food, craft beer, and live music most nights. Tuesday features karaoke at 7:30. There's also free Wi-Fi, but don't expect to be able to focus on work over the noise. ✉ *Main road, across from El Coco Casino* ☎ *2670–1982* ⊕ *coconutzbar.com.*

 # Activities

BOATING

Marlin Del Rey

BOATING | With operations in Tamarindo and Playas del Coco, Marlin Del Rey offers sailing tours on their 65-foot catamaran. Trips will take you to quiet white-sand beaches and include snorkeling, lunch, and an open bar. Sunset tours depart at 1:30 pm. ✉ *Main street* ☎ *2653–1212, 877/827–8275 in U.S.* ⊕ *www.marlindelrey.com* 🛏 *$85 per person.*

DIVING AND SNORKELING

Half a dozen dive shops populate this small town. The standard price for a two-tank dive is $85; Catalina Island dives are $115. This coast doesn't have the coral reefs or the clear visibility of the Caribbean coast, but it does have a lot of plankton (hence the lower visibility) that feeds legions of fish, some of them really, really big. Manta rays and sharks (white-tipped, nurse, and bull varieties) are among the stars of the undersea show. It takes about 20 to 45 minutes to reach most dive sites.

Deep Blue Diving Adventures

SCUBA DIVING | This organization has daily scuba-diving trips to the top dive spots in the Papagayo Gulf and Catalina Islands. They also do open-water certification. ✉ *Corner of Chorrera and Cangrejo* ☎ *2670–1004* ⊕ *www.deepblue-diving.com* 🛏 *From $105.*

★ Rich Coast Diving

SCUBA DIVING | This longtime operator has enthusiastic guides and is the only PADI five-star CDC facility with the Green Star Award in Costa Rica. It offers daily fun dives, PADI courses, and local snorkeling trips. ✉ *Main street, near intersection with road to Playa Ocotal, near Medical Center* ☎ *2670–0176* ⊕ *www.richcoastdiving.com* 🛏 *From $85 without equipment.*

Sirenas Diving Costa Rica

SCUBA DIVING | With more than 20 years of experience, this dive operation has a full range of scuba activities, from beginner training to open-water PADI certification. Multitank dives are organized at more than 20 sites. Guides and trainers are very good, and their safety standards have the DAN (Divers Alert Network) seal of approval. Diving trips are personalized and private, with no more than six people. Prices range from $150 for two-tank morning dives to $975 for the PADI open-water certification course, with discounts for more than one person. Courses are offered from their PADI dive boat in Playas del Coco, and there's no physical office, so reservations are essential. They also offer combo tours with any combination of fishing, surfing, diving, and snorkeling. ✉ *Playas del Coco* ☎ *8721–8055, 8387–4710* ⊕ *www.sirenasdivingcostarica.com* 🛏 *From $150.*

Summer Salt Dive Center

SCUBA DIVING | This longstanding small dive center is especially good for beginners, but great for every level. They focus on safety and fun in diving and snorkeling. ✉ *Main street, 100 m south of the park* ☎ *2670–0308* ⊕ *www.summer-salt.com* 🛏 *From $80, plus $25 for equipment.*

FISHING

Fishing charter boats go out 24 to 64 km (15 to 40 miles) seeking yellowfin tuna, mahimahi, grouper, and red snapper close in, and sailfish, marlin, and roosterfish offshore (beyond 64 km [40 miles]).

Blue Marlin Sportfishing

FISHING | This downtown fishing-charter office has eight boats to choose from, ranging from a 30-foot boat for close-in fishing ($430 for a half day) to larger boats that go out to sea for a full day offshore ($1,750). Prices are for four to five fishers. ✉ *Main street, south of police station* ☎ *6002–0720* 🛏 *From $430.*

GOLF
Vista Ridge Golf & Country Club

GOLF | Formerly Papagayo Golf & Country Club, this 18-hole, par-72 course is affordable and just 10 minutes from Playas del Coco. You can play the whole course for $65, including a golf cart and a cooler with ice and water (and clubs if you need them), but don't expect the Four Seasons. The greens are small and slow once the afternoon winds kick in, with some challenging holes toward the back tees. Long drives through the rain forest mean you'll encounter plenty of wildlife while you play. Signature Hole 18 (par 3) drives 171 yards directly through the towering trees. The first tee time is at 7:30, and the last is at 1 pm. There's a country club, driving range, putting green, swimming pool, and a Sunday tournament that starts at 8 am ($50, includes breakfast). ⊠ *10 km (6 miles) southeast of Playas del Coco* ☎ *2697–0169* ⌨ *$65 for 18 holes* ⅄ *18 holes, 6028 yards, par 72* ⊙ *Closed Fri.*

SURFING
Witch's Rock and Ollie's Point

SURFING | These legendary surfing spots are no more than an hour's boat ride away from Playas del Coco off the coast of Santa Rosa National Park. You can surf as long as you pay the $15 park entrance fee. You can sign up for a surfing trip with any beach-town tour operator, but local authorities allow excursions to Witch's Rock and Ollie's Point to originate only from the main dock at Playas del Coco, in boats owned by local boat owners, in order to curb overcrowding and undue environmental stress. The 40-minute boat trip to Witch's Rock costs about $250, or $350 to surf both Witch's Rock and Ollie's Point, which is located an additional 20 minutes north. For those prices, your boat captain will spend the day waiting aboard while you surf. Luxury surf excursions to both breaks are also available through Tropic Surf, based at the Four Seasons Resort on Peninsula Papagayo. ⊠ *Playas del Coco.*

Playa Ocotal

3 km (2 miles) south of Playas del Coco.

Just a few minutes south of Playas del Coco, this beach couldn't be more different than its rapidly developing neighbor. Quiet and serene, there is little commercial development, aside from a couple of beachfront restaurants. A large resort hotel dominates the beach, and private condominium complexes and luxurious villas pile up on the steep hills overlooking the ocean.

GETTING HERE AND AROUND

The drive is 10 minutes from Playas del Coco on a paved road to the gated entrance of Playa Ocotal. The road winds through a heavily populated Tico residential area, so be on the lookout, especially at night, for bicyclists without lights, children playing, or dogs, cows, and horses on the road. There are no buses from Playas del Coco to Ocotal, but it's about $6 by taxi.

Sights

The Monkey Farm

FARM/RANCH | Despite the name, you're likely to see more goats, ducks, chickens, pigs, and other farm animals than you are monkeys. At this volunteer-run operation, animals are rescued, rehabilitated, and released back into the wild. At any given time, you might see reptiles, raccoons, and (usually) a monkey or two that are being treated for injuries. Keep in mind this is not a zoo, nor is it a tourist trap, meaning that animals roam free and the sanctuary survives on a donation basis. The sustainable farm has an impressive aquaponics setup and offers horseback-riding tours—$45 per hour in the jungle or $60 per two hours on the beach. ⊠ *On road from Playas del Coco to Ocotal, ½ mile from Playa Ocotal, Ocotal* ☎ *8853–0165* ⊕ *www.themonkey-farm.org* ⌨ *Donation suggested.*

Beaches

Playa Ocotal

BEACH—SIGHT | One of the most dramatic beaches in the country, this serene crescent of black-sand beach ringed by rocky cliffs contrasts nicely with the sparkling, clean turquoise water. It's only ½ km (¼ mile) long, but the views stretch for miles and include nearby offshore islands and the jagged profile of the Santa Elena Peninsula 34 km (21 miles) away. This is prime fishing, diving, and relaxing territory. Right at the entrance to the Gulf of Papagayo, it's a good place for sportfishing enthusiasts to hole up between excursions. There's good diving at Las Corridas, just 1 km (½ mile) away, and excellent snorkeling in nearby coves and islands, as well as around the rocks at the east end of the beach. **Amenities:** food and drink. **Best for:** snorkeling. ✉ *10-min drive south of Playas del Coco, Ocotal.*

 Hotels

Hotel M&M Casa Blanca

$$ | B&B/INN | If you want to be close to Playas del Coco but still have some solitude, you can't beat this Victorian-style bed-and-breakfast enveloped in a hillside bower of tropical plantings. **Pros:** romantic; quiet location; use of outdoor kitchen. **Cons:** smallish, aging rooms; noisy parrots; chilly pool. $ *Rooms from: $135* ✉ *Near Father Rooster, 150 m from beach, Ocotal* ☎ 2670–0448 🛏 *14 rooms* ⦿ *Free Breakfast.*

 Nightlife

Father Rooster

BARS/PUBS | The best place to enjoy a quiet sunset margarita—or make that a "rooster-rita"—is at this laid-back bar and restaurant on the beach. You can relax on the wooden deck, or at the tables right on the sand, and enjoy a romantic dinner featuring fresh fish and Tex-Mex favorites. Portions here are huge, and there's free Wi-Fi, a pool table, a big-screen TV, and occasional live music to keep you entertained. It's open 11 to 10, though it does close for private parties so you may want to call ahead. Guests from the Four Seasons often anchor here for a drink before sailing back to Peninsula Papagayo. ✉ *100 m west of El Ocotal Beach Resort, 3 km (2 miles) south of Playas del Coco, Ocotal* ☎ 2670–1246 ⊕ *www.fatherrooster.com.*

 Activities

DIVING AND SNORKELING

The rocky outcrop at the north end of the beach near Los Almendros is good for close-to-shore snorkeling.

Rocket Frog Divers

SCUBA DIVING | Rocket Frog promises a faster boat out to the dive site, leaving more time for diving. They offer local trips around Papagayo ($85), trips to Catalina Island ($135), and, depending on the season, they go to the Bat Islands, where you may see bull sharks ($165). You dive with knowledgeable guides—some with backgrounds in marine biology—for a unique perspective, and are likely to see rays, eels, tropical fish, and turtles. There are scuba courses for novices through instructors. ✉ *Hotel Colono Beach, 50 m west of Supercompro, Playas del Coco* ☎ 2670–1589 ⊕ *www.scuba-dive-costa-rica.com* 🤿 *From $85.*

Las Catalinas

Take a stroll through the car-free pedestrian village of Las Catalinas, and though it may feel contradictory to walk through the new streets and feel like you've gone back in time—perhaps to a European village—that's where the magic begins. Let the kids play on the Tarzan rope swings while you lounge under the trees and take in views of Paya Danta, lounge in a hammock, or mosey to the surf shop for

Did You Know?

Magnificent beaches and a dramatically sculpted shoreline are southern Guanacaste's trademarks. Here you'll find no short-age of wildlife-watching opportunities. Be sure to check out the tide pools that form on the rocky headlands at each end of Playa Ocotal.

gelato, shave ice, or some of that famous Costa Rican coffee. Feeling ambitious? Bike on some of the 22 km (13 miles) of trails through the forest.

GETTING HERE AND AROUND

From the Liberia airport, take a right out of the airport and, after 10 km (6 miles), head right toward Huacas. After passing through Brasilito, you will reach Potrero. Go around the soccer field and turn right. Follow the "Las Catalinas" signs. Ecotrans offers shared rides and transfers to Las Catalinas. It's best to stock up on groceries and cash in Potrero—there's not much here in the way of markets.

Beaches

Playa Danta

BEACH—SIGHT | Surfers will need to go elsewhere to find their waves; this natural beach, dotted with shade trees and with the Limonada restaurant a stone's throw away, has a low swell, which makes it great for kids, swimming, stand-up paddleboarding, and snorkeling. For those seeking something more remote, a quick hike north through the forest gets you to secluded Playa Dantita, your own private oasis. **Amenities:** food and drink. **Best for:** swimming. ✉ *Las Catalinas.*

Restaurants

★ Limonada

$$ | LATIN AMERICAN | Friendly staff are at your service while you kick back on cushioned sectional seating or long wooden tables with your toes in the sand. The menu offers a fresh and creative take on Costa Rican food—don't miss the homemade guacamole, served with homemade tortilla chips, fresh veggies, and tostones. **Known for:** unhurried, mellow atmosphere where kids can play while adults relax; ceviche; jalapeño margaritas. [$] *Average main: $12* ✉ *Sugar Beach Rd., Playa Danta, Las Catalinas* ☎ *2654–4600.*

Sentido Norte

$$$ | COSTA RICAN | Come for the ocean views, stay for the bounty of Costa Rican cuisine. The chef here uses local favorites like chayote and hearts of palm, as well as the usual mahimahi and tuna, in innovative and delicious ways. **Known for:** spectacular views; sea-to-table ingredients; infinity pool. [$] *Average main: $19* ✉ *Las Catalinas* ☎ *2103–1200* 🌐 *www.sentidonorterestaurant.com.*

Hotels

★ Casa Chameleon

$$$$ | HOTEL | Tucked into the hillside with jaw-dropping panoramic views of the beach and the forest, this luxury hotel with a modern Balinese feel offers private and secluded villas for couples who want to unwind and take it easy. **Pros:** private saltwater plunge pool in every room; excellent restaurant; true barefoot elegance. **Cons:** not directly on the beach; adults only; no TVs. [$] *Rooms from: $680* ✉ *Playa Danta, just before you drive into Las Catalinas, Las Catalinas* ☎ *2103–1200* 🌐 *www.casachameleonhotels.com/las-catalinas* 🛏 *16 rooms* 🍴 *Free Breakfast.*

Activities

Pura Vida Ride

BICYCLING | When it comes to bicycling in Costa Rica, many people ride the roads and take their lives into their own hands. Las Catalinas aims to change that with 22 km (13 miles) of mountain-biking trails and a large selection of mountain bikes to rent (prices start at $45 per hour). They also offer stand-up paddleboards for the relatively calm bay. ✉ *Las Catalinas at Playa Danta, Las Catalinas* ☎ *2654–6137* 🌐 *www.puravidaride.com* 🎟 *$45 per hr.*

Playa Pan de Azúcar

8 km (5 miles) north of Playa Flamingo.

Playa Pan de Azúcar literally means "Sugar Bread Beach," though most locals call it simply Playa Azúcar (Sugar Beach). With only two built-up properties, the entire stretch of beach feels practically deserted and very private—qualities that can be hard to find in this area. Sweet, indeed.

GETTING HERE AND AROUND

Getting to the beach area of Playa Pan de Azúcar is a snap because the road is paved and well marked. From Liberia Airport, head toward the Belén intersection. Turn right toward Huacas, following the signs to Flamingo and Potrero. After passing through Brasilito, veer right toward Potrero and Playa Pan de Azúcar. Don't be lured by the "shortcut" that passes through the mountains from Sardinal to Flamingo. It might actually take longer, and you'll need a 4WD vehicle and GPS if you want to drive (dry season only) this 16-km (11-mile) route that locals call the "Monkey Trail." The first part of the road is graded, but rapidly deteriorates as it travels over river crossings, through jungle, and down rocky terrain. Even some Ticos get lost on this route, so if you take it, keep asking for directions along the way. The only buses to Playa Pan de Azúcar are from Playa Flamingo for $6 or from the Santa Cruz terminal, departing five times daily for $4; a taxi from Playa Flamingo costs about $20.

Beaches

Playa Pan de Azúcar

BEACH—SIGHT | A seemingly endless stretch of soft, light-color sand, this Blue Flag beach is the idyllic paradise people picture in their tropical dreams. There is only one property on the entire beach, the Hotel Sugar Beach, offering parking, restrooms, and a restaurant open to the public except during private events. The north end of the beach has some good snorkeling when the sea is calm—usually around low tide—and swimming out from the middle of the beach is relatively safe. Watch out for a few rocks on both sides of the cove, and if the swell is big, children and weak swimmers shouldn't go in past their waist. This beach is frequented by Ticos on weekends, but it is still relatively peaceful compared with neighboring beaches. Playa Penca, a short walk south along the beach, can be a good swimming beach as well. A large part of the attraction here is the forest that hems the beach, where you may see howler monkeys, black iguanas, magpie jays, trogons, and dozens of other bird species. **Amenities:** food and drink; parking (no fee); toilets. **Best for:** solitude; swimming. ⊠ *Potrero.*

Hotels

⭐ Hotel Sugar Beach

$$ | **RESORT** | The theme of this secluded, ultracomfortable hotel with a shimmering infinity pool and thin, curving beach is harmony with nature, but it's the friendly staff and outstanding service that keep this property ahead of the pack. **Pros:** spacious one- and two-bedroom suites; natural setting; kids under 12 stay free. **Cons:** waves and rocks can make the ocean dangerous for kids; small pool; Wi-Fi in common areas only. ⓢ *Rooms from: $132* ⊠ *8 km (5 miles) north of Playa Flamingo, Potrero* ☎ *2654–4242* ⊕ *www.sugar-beach.com* ⤴ *26 units* ⓞⓘ *Free Breakfast.*

🏃 Activities

Most of the operators who work out of Flamingo can pick up guests at the Hotel Sugar Beach for diving, sportfishing, sailing, horseback riding, and other excursions.

Playa Potrero

4 km (2½ miles) north of Flamingo.

A typical small town with a school, church, and supermarket arranged around a soccer field, Potrero is not very scenic. The main attraction is the long beach on the curve of Flamingo Bay and the smattering of small hotels and restaurants lining the road to town.

GETTING HERE AND AROUND

Just before crossing the bridge at the entrance to Flamingo, take the right fork signed for Playa Potrero. The road follows the shoreline. Local buses run from Flamingo to Potrero, but it's so close that you're better off taking a taxi.

ESSENTIALS

An ATM is available at the Flor de Pacifico center near Ristorante Marco Polo, on the east side of Potrero. For groceries, there's Super Wendy across from Hotel Isolina and a small convenience store called Super Potrero next to Bar Las Brisas.

Beaches

Playa Potrero

BEACH—SIGHT | Stretching 4 km (2½ miles), this relatively undeveloped wide, brown-sand beach, across Potrero Bay from built-up Flamingo, catches ocean breezes and spectacular sunsets, which you can watch while bobbing in the warm, swimmable water. The pelican-patrolled beach is anchored at one end by the small Tico community of Potrero and at the other end by the Flamingo skyline. Although large houses and condominium developments have sprung up on any hill with a view, at beach level there is only one unimposing hotel and some low-lying private houses set well back from the beach; beachgoers never feel hemmed in or crowded, thanks to the local folks who keep the beach clean and deserving of Blue Flag status. The best area for swimming is midway between Flamingo and Potrero town, near the Bahía del Sol Hotel. About 10 km (6 miles) offshore lie the Catalina Islands, a barrier-island draw for divers and snorkelers; dive boats based in Flamingo can get there in 10 minutes. **Amenities:** food and drink. **Best for:** sunset; swimming; walking. ✉ *Potrero.*

Restaurants

The Beach House

$$ | **AMERICANAMERICAN** | On the road connecting Potrero and Flamingo, this beachfront restaurant welcomes travelers with cheerful decor and witty signs like "Trespassers will be *offered a* shot." Water laps just a few feet from your table, and there's a pier out back, making this a popular lunch spot for American classics like hamburgers, chicken sandwiches, BLTs, and fried shrimp. The tasty sangrias and margaritas are sure to keep you dazed during sunset. **Known for:** onion ring tower; breathtaking sunsets; volcano dessert to share. [$] *Average main: $15* ✉ *800 m north of Banco Nacional, Potrero* ✥ *North end of Playa Flamingo on way to Potrero* ☎ *2654–6203* 🌐 *www.beachhousecr.com.*

★ **Costa Rica Sailing Center**

$$ | **COSTA RICAN** | **FAMILY** | Relax beachside at the most laid-back yacht club you'll ever visit. There are bonfires after dark, live music, and sometimes an event like a chili cookoff or beer fest; plus, the kids can play in the pool while you enjoy a craft beer and good food. **Known for:** cold drinks; sunset views; sailing lessons and boat rentals. [$] *Average main: $14* ✉ *South of Hotel Bahía del Sol Surfside, Potrero* ☎ *2654–6056* 🌐 *www.facebook.com/costaricasailingcenter.*

The Shack

$$ | **AMERICAN** | A popular spot with expats who come for the cold beers, burritos, burgers, and *pura vida* vibe, The Shack successfully blends a Tico menu

with American and British favorites. Grab a seat under the tin roof and try the fresh fish-and-chips, heaping nachos, cheeseburgers, or the famous chili dogs. **Known for:** tantalizing breakfast choices; nachos to share; friendly owner and welcoming atmosphere. $ *Average main: $10* ✉ *200 m west of El Castillo, Potrero* ☎ *2654–6038* ⊗ *Closed Mon.*

Hotels

★ Bahía del Sol

$$$ | RESORT | FAMILY | Snagging the best spot on the beach, Bahía del Sol has a gorgeous beachfront pool and comfortable rooms built around a garden of tropical shrubs and towering trees. **Pros:** on the beach; lovely grounds; excellent restaurant; friendly, first-rate service. **Cons:** front terraces are not very private; hotel closed during October; some rooms need updates. $ *Rooms from: $205* ✉ *South end of Potrero Beach, Potrero* ☎ *2654–4671* ⊕ *www.bahiadelsolhotel.com* ⊗ *Closed Oct.* ⤳ *28 rooms* ⏺ *Free Breakfast.*

Hotel Isolina

$$ | HOTEL | This small hotel complex, a little island (*isolina*) of palm trees shading two pools, has basic and clean rooms with some of the best rates in the area. **Pros:** all rooms face the pool; affordable; secure parking; clean rooms. **Cons:** loud a/c; breakfast not included for rooms with kitchenettes; dated rooms need upgrades; Wi-Fi near reception only. $ *Rooms from: $122* ✉ *100 m north of Restaurant La Perla, on beach road, Potrero* ☎ *2654–4333* ⊕ *www.isolinabeach.com* ⤳ *34 units* ⏺ *Free Breakfast.*

Nightlife

Cerveceria Independiente

BREWPUBS/BEER GARDENS | In a land of Imperial, it's nice to find good beer. The friendly staff at this independent brewery serve up a tasty variety of stouts, IPAs, sours, lagers, and even root beer. They're conveniently located next to a beer garden of sorts, an outdoor food court with lots of options from burgers to pizza. Take a load off and sip a cold flight. ✉ *Ruta 911, 200 m east of Costa Rica Sailing Center, Potrero* ⊕ *Next to Panache Sailing* ☎ *506/8464–0935* ⊕ *www.independiente.cr.*

Perlas

BARS/PUBS | Expats come for the microbrews, the satellite TV tuned to football, a game of Ping-Pong or pool, and the live music. Although the bar brings the people in, it's the food that keeps them there—braised oxtail, pork ribs, tuna poke, and burgers seem to justify another round. If you stay long enough, you'll find that the sweet homemade cheesecake goes surprising well with a bitter IPA. ✉ *C. Principal, Avda. 3, near the Shack, Potrero* ☎ *2654–4500.*

Activities

DIVING

Catalina Islands

SCUBA DIVING | The Catalina Islands are a major destination for dive operations based all along the coast. These barrier islands are remarkable for their diversity and appeal to different levels of divers. On one side, the islands have 20- to 30-foot drops, great for beginners. The other side has deeper drops of 60 to 80 feet, better suited to more experienced divers. Among the 25 dive sites, the top are **Dirty Rock, Elephant Rock, Big Catalina,** and **Cupcake**. From January to March, when the water is colder, you are almost guaranteed manta ray sightings at these spots. Cownose and devil rays are also spotted here in large schools, as well as bull and white-tipped sharks, several types of eels, and an array of reef fish. Dive operators from Playa Hermosa south to Tamarindo offer trips to these islands. Reserve through your hotel, or directly through a dive shop. The islands are a 30-minute boat trip from Potrero Bay. ✉ *Potrero.*

Playa Flamingo

80 km (50 miles) southwest of Liberia.

One of the first northern beaches to experience overdevelopment—a fact immortalized in the concrete towers that straggle up the hill above the bay—Flamingo still has some hidden charms. Perhaps most famous for its large sport-fishing fleet, Flamingo's marina with over 200 docking spots for yachts gives the beach energy.

GETTING HERE AND AROUND

To get to Playa Flamingo from Liberia, drive 45 km (28 miles) south to Belén and then 35 km (22 miles) west on a good, paved road. The trip takes just over an hour. If you're coming from the Playas del Coco and Ocotal area, you can take a 16-km (10-mile) shortcut, called the "Monkey Trail," starting near Sardinal and emerging at Potrero. It's then 4 km (2½ miles) south to Flamingo. Attempt this only in dry season in a 4WD vehicle with GPS, because there are a few river crossings. The drive from San José takes 4½ hours, and costs about $230 per five-passenger van. You can also take a van from Liberia, a 50-minute scenic drive for around $80 per van. Ecotrans has transportation between Liberia airport and Playa Flamingo for $25 per person. (⇨ *See Bus in Travel Smart Costa Rica.*)

CONTACTS Ecotrans. ☎ *2654–5151, 954/353–6737 in U.S.* ⊕ *www.ecotrans-costarica.com.*

ESSENTIALS

BANK/ATM Banco de Costa Rica. ⊠ *On the main road to Playa Flamingo, at intersection of road to Playa Potrero, across from Hotel Flamingo Marina Resort, Flamingo* ☎ *2654–4984.*

PHARMACY Farmacia Playa Flamingo. ⊠ *La Plaza Flamingo, beside Marie's Restaurant at entrance to town, Flamingo* ☎ *2654–5524.*

Beaches

Playa Flamingo

BEACH—SIGHT | Hidden away to the southwest of the town, Flamingo Beach is picture-perfect, with almost-white sand sloping into a relatively calm sea, and buttonwood trees separating it from the road. This beach is great for swimming, with a fine-sand bottom and no strong currents, though there are a few submerged rocks in front of the Margaritaville Beach Resort, so you should swim a bit farther south. There's sometimes a bit of surf—if the waves are big, keep your eye on little paddlers. There is minimal shade along the beach's 1-km-long (½-mile-long) stretch, but Margaritaville's 5 O'Clock Somewhere Bar will deliver cocktails and serve food on the beach, or there is the Coco Loco restaurant on the south end. To find the beach, go straight as you enter town, and instead of going up the hill, turn left after the Maragaritaville Beach Resort. **Amenities:** food and drink. **Best for:** swimming; walking. ⊠ *Southwest of town, in front of Flamingo Beach Resort, Flamingo.*

 Restaurants

Angelina's

$$$ | **ITALIAN** | Guanacaste-inspired and locally sourced, the cuisine here pays tribute to the owner's Italian roots with dishes like lobster tail served with homemade black pasta. This restaurant is one of the area's more upscale places to dine, with marble tables, parchment lamps, and driftwood-integrated decor under an open-air patio. **Known for:** homemade thin-crust pizza; wide-ranging wine list; juicy steaks aged in custom Himalayan salt chamber. **$** *Average main: $18* ⊠ *Plaza Commercial, 2nd fl., Flamingo* ☎ *2654–4839* ⊕ *www.angelinasplayaflamingo.com* ☼ *No lunch.*

Coco Loco

$$ | SEAFOOD | The "crazy coconut" is one of the few places where you can dine with your toes in the sand while watching the sunset without anything separating you from the water. Start with the fried calamari or mixed ceviche, and move on to mains like the blackened swordfish wrap, the sesame-crusted yellowfin tuna taco, or the slow-cooked ribs with pineapple barbecue sauce. **Known for:** tuna tacos; exquisite sunsets; signature drink served in a fresh coconut. $ *Average main: $10* ✉ *On Playa Flamingo, 650 m south of Flamingo Beach Resort, Flamingo* ☎ *2654–6242* ⊕ *www.cocolococostarica.com.*

Marie's Restaurant

$$ | SEAFOOD | A Flamingo institution serving beachgoers and locals for more than three decades, this popular restaurant has an array of sandwiches and salads, as well as reliably fresh seafood in large portions at reasonable prices. Settle in at one of the wooden tables beneath the ceiling fans and massive thatch roof for a traditional Costa Rican ceviche, avocado stuffed with shrimp, or heart of palm and *pejivalle* (palm fruit). **Known for:** breakfasts and smoothies; kebabs featuring fish, chicken and shrimp; whole red snapper. $ *Average main: $15* ✉ *Plaza commercial center, near north end of beach, Flamingo* ☎ *2654–4136* ⊕ *www.mariesrestaurantcostarica.com.*

★ The Surf Box

$ | AMERICAN | Pop into this charming spot with "California cool" and cozy up in the corner booth, where the clean white walls set a backdrop for rainbow-hued books and surf-themed wall decor. Outside, be prepared to share the *pura vida* vibe and maybe a table—it's communal seating, and it gets busy during brunch with treats like homemade bagels with egg and avocado and rich ricotta pancakes. **Known for:** acai bowls bursting with healthy goodness like fruit, chia, and homemade granola; innovative smoothies with eco-friendly metal straws; Miami-inspired Cuban sandwich. $ *Average main: $9* ✉ *25 m south of Banco Nacional, Flamingo* ☎ *8437–7128* ⊙ *No dinner Sun.*

Hotels

Hotel Guanacaste Lodge

$$ | HOTEL | On the outskirts of Flamingo, a short drive from the beach, this Tico-run lodge offers basic accommodations for a fraction of what the town's big hotels charge. **Pros:** affordable; nice pool; large rooms. **Cons:** unattractive from the outside; no in-room phones or safes; simple furnishings with few amenities. $ *Rooms from: $100* ✉ *200 m south of Potrero-Flamingo crossroads, Flamingo* ☎ *2654–4494* ⊕ *www.guanacastelodge.com* ⤴ *10 rooms* ⦿| *Free Breakfast.*

Margaritaville Beach Resort

$$$ | RESORT | FAMILY | With a prime spot on the beach and a mammoth pool with swim-up bar to lounge around, this Jimmy Buffet–themed hotel is eager to please. **Pros:** updated rooms and suites; plenty of activities to keep kids busy; friendly staff. **Cons:** food is just okay; nice but not luxurious; some rooms have view of parking lot. $ *Rooms from: $230* ✉ *Playa Flamingo Santa Cruz, Flamingo* ☎ *2654–4444* ⊕ *www.margaritaville-beachresortcostarica.com* ⤴ *120 rooms* ⦿| *All-inclusive.*

Nightlife

Mariner Inn Bar

BARS/PUBS | This formerly boisterous bar has gotten an upgrade in service and a new, friendlier feel. ✉ *Bottom of hill, entering Flamingo, Flamingo* ☎ *2654–4081* ⊕ *www.marinerinn.com.*

🏃 Activities

BOATING

Lazy Lizard Catamaran Sailing Adventures

BOATING | Laze away a morning or afternoon sailing or sunbathing on either a 34- or 38-foot catamaran. You can swim or snorkel during the four-hour tour, starting at 8:30 am (minimum of eight people) and 2 pm. Included in the price is transportation from your hotel, snorkeling equipment, kayaks, drinks, and food. ✉ *Flamingo Marina, Flamingo* ☎ *2654–5900* ⊕ *www.lazylizardsailing. com* 🎫 *From $85.*

DIVING AND SNORKELING

Flamingo offers the quickest access to the Catalina Islands, visible from its beach, where big schools of fish, manta rays, and other sea creatures gather. Coastal reefs to the north are visited on day trips that combine snorkeling with time on undeveloped beaches. Most diving excursions to Catalina Islands depart from Potrero Bay.

Aquacenter Diving

SCUBA DIVING | Based in the Flamingo Marina Resort, this dive shop runs two-tank dives at the Catalina Islands ($100, including gear rental) and snorkeling trips ($65, including equipment), as well as offering a full range of PADI certification courses. ✉ *Flamingo Marina Resort, Flamingo* ☎ *8877–7420* ⊕ *www.aquacenter-diving.com* 🎫 *From $65.*

FISHING

There are plenty of sportfishing boats bobbing in Flamingo Bay from which to choose. Larger boats have moved to moorings in the Papagayo Marina near the Andaz Resort. In December the wind picks up, and many of the smaller, 31-foot-and-under boats head to calmer water farther south. But the wind brings cold water and abundant baitfish, which attract marlin (blue, black, and striped), Pacific sailfish, yellowfin tuna, wahoo, mahimahi, grouper, and red snapper.

The Guanacaste Tree 👁

Massive and wide spreading, with tiny leaflets and dark brown, earlike seedpods, the guanacaste tree is common through this region and is Costa Rica's national tree.

January to April is consequently prime catch-and-release season for billfish.

Brasilito and Playa Conchal

8 km (5 miles) south of Flamingo.

A small, scruffy fishing village just 1 km (½ mile) north of Playa Conchal, Brasilito has a jumble of houses huddled around its main square, which doubles as the soccer field. It's cluttered, noisy, and totally tico—a lively contrast to the controlled sophistication of the gated Playa Conchal resort and residential development less than a mile south. Fishing boats moor just off a wide beach, and there's a range of seafood restaurants, from inexpensive *marisquerías* to a few notable establishments taking pride in organic and locally sourced ingredients.

GETTING HERE AND AROUND

The drive south to Brasilito from Flamingo is 10 minutes on a paved highway. Brasilito is just 1 km (½ mile) north of the entrance to the massive Westin Golf Resort & Spa and private Reserva Conchal housing development, which blocks the main road access to Playa Conchal. To reach Playa Conchal without driving through the guard-posted resort, turn left at the end of the town square in Brasilito and follow the dirt road across a stretch of beach and over a steep hill; the beach stretch is impassable at high tide.

The reclusive zebra moray eel likes to hide its entire body in rock or coral holes.

Buses run from Flamingo to Brasilito three times daily, at 7:30 and 11:30 am and 2:30 pm. A taxi from Flamingo is about $10.

ESSENTIALS

The closest bank and ATM are in Flamingo.

PHARMACY Farmacia El Cruce. ⊠ *Crossroads at Huacas, Playa Conchal* ☏ *2653–8787.*

Beaches

Playa Brasilito

BEACH—SIGHT | Fishing boats moor just off this wide beach, about 3 km (2 miles) long with golden sand flecked with pebbles and a few rocks. The surf is a little stronger here than at Flamingo Beach, but the shallow, sandy bottom keeps it swimmable. There is one hotel almost on the beach, the quirky Hotel Brasilito with an attached restaurant called The Spot. The sea is cleaner off nearby Playa Conchal, which is also more attractive. **Amenities:** food and drink. **Best**

for: snorkeling; walking. ⊠ *Playa Brasilito, Playa Conchal.*

Playa Conchal

BEACH—SIGHT | Named for the bits of broken shells that cover its base of fine white sand (the Spanish word for shell is *concha*), lovely Playa Conchal is an idyllic strand sloping steeply into aquamarine water and lined with trees. As its Blue Flag attests, it's clean and invites safe swimming. Although it's dominated by the sprawling Westin Playa Conchal, you don't need to stay at that all-inclusive resort to enjoy Conchal, since it's a short beach walk (or drive at low tide in a four-wheel-drive vehicle) south from Brasilito. The point that defines Conchal's northern end is hemmed by a lava-rock reef that is a popular snorkeling area—locals rent equipment on the beach. Waves can be powerful at times, so keep an eye on little ones. Despite the availability of shell jewelry, remember that shell collecting is not officially permitted on Costa Rican beaches. **Amenities:** food and drink. **Best for:** snorkeling; swimming; walking. ⊠ *Playa Conchal.*

Restaurants

Gracia Mar Vista

$$$ | MODERN AMERICAN | FAMILY | Tucked into the hills of the gated Mar Vista community, this open-air restaurant comes complete with dazzling ocean views, infinity pools for guests to enjoy, and a made-from-scratch farm- and sea-to-table menu. Chef and owner Frankie Becker cooks up fresh seafood, but vegetarians are in luck too, because the crispy cauliflower and hummus platter are mouthwatering. **Known for:** lobster bisque; Cajun barbecue shrimp; amazing views. $ *Average main: $17* ⊠ *Mar Vista, 1 km (½ mile) north of the old bomb, Brasilito* ☎ *6110–1687* ⊕ *www.gracia-marvista.com.*

Papaya

$$ | ECLECTIC | Grab a table at the second-floor lounge overlooking the pool while the kitchen cooks up fresh seafood delivered daily by local fisherman. Dinner reservations are recommended, so call ahead to try the coconut shrimp, sesame-crusted tuna, or Thai curry. **Known for:** guacamole and homemade chips; wide array of vegetarian meals; fresh fruit juices (also used in cocktails). $ *Average main: $15* ⊠ *Conchal Hotel, 200 m south of bridge, Brasilito* ☎ *2654–9125* ⊕ *www.conchalcr.com* ⊗ *Closed Wed.*

★ Patagonia Del Mar

$$$ | ASIAN FUSION | This open-air Argentinian grill has a lovely ambience, great views of the beach across the street, and even better steak and seafood. Lounge poolside with a cocktail and sushi or sample their good wine selection with some shrimp tempura while the kids play on the swings. **Known for:** melt-in-your-mouth beef tenderloin with jalapeño sauce; fresh seafood poke bowls; beautiful pool. $ *Average main: $21* ⊠ *100 m north of puente brasilito, Brasilito* ☎ *8800–0005* ⊕ *patagoniadelmar.business.site.*

Hotels

★ Conchal Hotel

$$ | HOTEL | It may not be on the beach, but this quaint boutique hotel is certainly a diamond in the rough in rustic Brasilito, with breezy rooms framing an attractive pool-centered courtyard and a second-story restaurant with wholesome cuisine. **Pros:** B&B feel; outstanding restaurant; friendly owners. **Cons:** some street noise; 15-minute walk to the beach; hotel often full. $ *Rooms from: $99* ⊠ *200 m south of bridge, Brasilito* ☎ *2654–9125, 347/298–9356 in U.S.* ⊕ *www.conchalcr.com* ⊄ *13 rooms* ⦿ *Free Breakfast.*

Hotel Brasilito

$$ | HOTEL | Budget travelers who don't need amenities will love this rustic two-story wooden hotel's affordable price and seafront location, if not its no-frills but adequate A-frame rooms. **Pros:** inexpensive; beachfront; good restaurant. **Cons:** boxy rooms, some without TVs, a/c, or phones; can be noisy; rooms need upgrading. $ *Rooms from: $89* ⊠ *Between soccer field and beach, Brasilito* ☎ *2654–4237* ⊕ *www.brasilito.com* ⊄ *18 rooms* ⦿ *No meals.*

W Costa Rica–Reserva Conchal

$$$$ | RESORT | Incorporating Costa Rican culture at every turn, this convivial, unique member of the W chain leaves no detail overlooked, from the "forest" of guanacaste trees at the pool and restaurant, to the "pineapple" elevator tower. **Pros:** fun and lively atmosphere; Costa Rica–inspired architecture and decor; beautiful white sand beach. **Cons:** no breakfast included; long walk to get anywhere; somewhat pricey. $ *Rooms from: $350* ⊠ *Reserva Conchal Cabo Villas, Playa Conchal* ☎ *2654–3600* ⊄ *150 rooms* ⦿ *No meals.*

7

Guanacaste BRASILITO AND PLAYA CONCHAL

The Westin Golf Resort & Spa, Playa Conchal

$$$$ | **RESORT** | **FAMILY** | So vast that guests ride around in biodiesel shuttles, this all-inclusive Starwood property is set on 2,400 acres with nearly every vacation wish granted, from lagoon-style pools and a picture-perfect beach to eight restaurants and a championship golf course. **Pros:** saltwater pools; abundant activities; beach access. **Cons:** no food and drink service on the beach; only three rooms have ocean views; easy to get lost. $ *Rooms from: $540* ✉ *Entrance less than 1 km (½ mile) south of Brasilito, Playa Conchal* ☎ *2654–3500* ⊕ *www. starwoodhotels.com/westin* ⤳ *404 units* ❍ *All-inclusive.*

 Activities

GOLF

Reserva Conchal Golf Course

GOLF | One of the best golf courses in a country not known for golf, this 18-hole, par-71 course designed by Robert Trent Jones Jr. is perfectly maintained and reserved for guests of the Westin Golf Resort & Spa, who can try out their swing for $150, cart included; renting clubs costs an extra $60. The well-laid-out course has wide fairways and beautiful views including a couple of holes overlooking the water. Holes 16, 17, and 18 pose a challenge, with downhill tee shots and a drive that lands close to the water. Allow extra time to observe the wildlife, including howler monkeys, lizards, coatis, and birds. ✉ *The Westin Resort & Spa, Playa Conchal, entrance, less than 1 km (½ mile) south of Brasilito, Playa Conchal* ☎ *2654–3500* ⊕ *www.reservaconchal. com* ▱ *$160 for 18 holes* ⛳ *18 holes, 6956 yards, par 71.*

Playa Grande

21 km (13 miles) north of Tamarindo.

Down the (long, paved) road from Tamarindo, but only five minutes by boat across a tidal estuary, lies beautiful, pristine Playa Grande. By day, it's one of the best surfing beaches in the country, and by night it's a nesting beach for the increasingly rare giant leatherback sea turtle. The beach has thus far escaped the overdevelopment of nearby Tamarindo, and is consequently lined with thick vegetation instead of hotels and strip malls. But Playa Grande isn't immune to development; developers have sold hundreds of lots, and there are at least 75 finished houses. The ongoing battle to protect the beach continues. The good thing is that the homes are 200 meters from the beach, thanks to a legislated buffer zone and a decree that no lights can be visible from the beach, to avoid disturbing the turtles. A few hotels and restaurants make this a pleasant, tranquil alternative to Tamarindo. And if you want to go shopping or barhopping, Tamarindo is only a 2-minute boat ride away.

GETTING HERE AND AROUND

The road from Tamarindo is paved for the duration of the 30-minute drive. The gated community of Palm Beach Estates, where most hotels are, is about 2 km (1 mile) south of the main Playa Grande entrance on a potholed dirt road. Alternatively, you can take a small boat across the Tamarindo Estuary for about $3 per person and walk 30 minutes along the beach to the main surf break. A lesser-known break is just a 10-minute walk; boats travel (8–4:30) between the guide kiosk at the north end of Tamarindo and Hotel Bula Bula in Playa Grande. Otherwise, a taxi from Tamarindo to Playa Grande will cost about $30 one way.

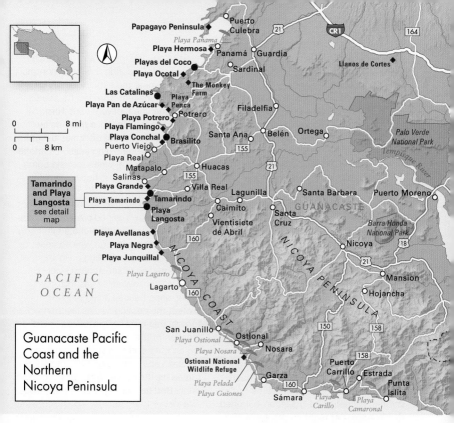

Guanacaste Pacific Coast and the Northern Nicoya Peninsula

◉ Sights

⭐ **Las Baulas National Marine Park** (*Parque Nacional Marino Las Baulas*)
NATIONAL/STATE PARK | Encompassing more than 1,000 acres of beach, mangrove swamps, and estuary, and more than 54,000 acres of ocean, this wide expanse of sand and sea will make you feel small, in the best way possible. *Baula* is the Spanish word for leatherback sea turtles, who have been nesting here for thousands of years. While their numbers continue to decline, guides still lead night hikes here between October and May to see Leatherback and Olive Ridley sea turtles lay their eggs. You can also spot scores of native birds like brown-footed boobies and pelicans, kayak through the mangroves and estuary, or learn to surf on some of the best waves in the country. There are no hotels or restaurants on the beach thanks to government regulation preventing development, but there is a taco stand and a ranger station open from 8 am to 4 pm at the entrance to the beach. Be sure to bring water and sunscreen, and your own shade. The park closes to the public at 6 pm and 5 pm during turtle nesting season. ⊠ *500 m south of Escuela de Playa Grande 933* ☎ *2653–0470* ⊕ *www.sinac.go.cr.*

Nesting Giant Leatherback Turtles
NATURE PRESERVE | Playa Grande used to host the world's largest visitation of nesting giant leatherback turtles, but the number of turtles has fallen drastically in the past 20 years, from a high of 1,504 in 1989 to less than 40 currently. This loss is due to long-line commercial fishing boats that trap turtles in their nets, causing the turtles to drown, along with poaching of

turtle eggs and loss of habitat. The beach is still strictly off-limits 6 pm to 6 am from October 20 to February 15, during the peak nesting season. You can visit only as part of a guided tour with a park ranger, from the headquarters for Las Baulas National Marine Park, 100 meters east of Hotel Las Tortugas. If you are lucky, spotters will find a nesting turtle. At their signal, you'll walk down the beach as silently as you can, where in the darkness you'll witness the remarkable sight of a 500-pound creature digging a hole in the sand large enough to deposit up to 100 golf-ball-size eggs. About 60 days later, the sight of hundreds of hatchlings scrambling toward open water in the early morning is equally impressive. Turtle-watching takes place around high tide, which can be shortly after sunset, or in the early morning. Plan on spending one to six hours at the ranger station waiting for a turtle to come up, during which you can watch a video on the turtles in English (the guides speak mostly Spanish). You are charged only if a turtle sighting is confirmed. Visitation is limited to 60 people per night (in groups of 15 max) and unregistered visitors are not allowed. Reservations should be made one week in advance either by phone or at Las Baulas National Park headquarters at Playa Grande. ✉ *100 m east of main beach entrance* ☎ *2653–0470* 🎟 *$25, includes guided tour.*

Beaches

Playa Grande

BEACH—SIGHT | In addition to being a paradise for surfers and sunbathers, the narrow woodsy patch that lines this wide, pristine Blue Flag beach holds howler monkeys and an array of birds, and the mangrove estuary on the north end of the beach has crocodiles. Because it's a protected area, the beach is unspoiled by buildings and natural beauty abounds. There is not a lot of shade. Be aware that the surf is a little heavy for safe swimming, and there's an abundance of mosquitoes during the rainy months, especially near the estuary, so bring plenty of repellent. The beach's shores and waters are part of Parque Nacional Marino Las Baulas. Admission is free during daylight hours but off-limits at night during the turtle-nesting season (October 20 to February 15), when tourists come on guided turtle tours, hoping to catch the increasingly rare sight of a leatherback turtle building a nest and depositing eggs. The beach gained protected status in part because a surfer who arrived here more than 30 years ago was so upset by the widespread turtle-egg poaching that he adopted a conservationist's agenda. Louis Wilson, owner of Las Tortugas Hotel, spearheaded a campaign to protect the nesting *baulas* (leatherback turtles) that eventually resulted in the creation of the national park. When walking on the beach, be sure to avoid the dry sand above the high tide line where turtles lay their eggs. **Amenities:** food and drink. **Best for:** surfing; walking. ✉ *Playa Grande.*

Restaurants

Bistro Cantarana

$$ | **INTERNATIONAL** | You can usually count on creative, au courant dinners at this upscale, pricey second-story restaurant in the trees. The menu changes depending on availability of local ingredients, but there's usually seafood and daring dishes like sting ray, sesame-crusted tuna, octopus salad, and shrimp brochette with coconut sauce. **Known for:** fresh seafood like tuna poke bowl and fish tacos; Thursday tapas night with tasty small plates to share; homemade tortillas and sauces. [$] *Average main: $13* ✉ *Hotel Cantarana, Palm Beach Estates, 2 km (1 mile) east of park headquarters* ☎ *2653–0486* 🌐 *www.hotel-cantarana.com* 🕒 *Closed Oct. No lunch.*

Costa Rica's shores are visited by the green turtle, the olive ridley (above), the hawksbill, the loggerhead, and the leatherback turtle.

Upstairs at the RipJack Inn

$$$ | **SEAFOOD** | Chow down at this casual place a block from the beach, or party at the extensive bar, which occupies about a third of the restaurant. Portions are large, so pace yourself—especially if you order the popular barbecue ribs with mashed potatoes. **Known for:** hot garlic shrimp; friendly atmosphere where everyone knows you; yummy breakfast sandwiches. [$] *Average main: $18* ✉ *RipJack Inn, 100 m south of park headquarters* ☎ *2653–1636* 🌐 *www.ripjackinn.com.*

Hotels

Hotel Bula Bula

$$ | **HOTEL** | At the eastern edge of the estuary in the Palm Beach Estates gated community, this pleasant hotel (the name means "Happy Happy") has its own landing for ferrying guests and restaurant patrons the 1 km (½ mile) to and from Tamarindo. **Pros:** friendly; water taxi to Tamarindo; lots of amenities. **Cons:** rooms small for price; 10-minute walk from beach; mosquitoes. [$] *Rooms from: $135* ✉ *Palm Beach Estates, 3 km (2 miles) east of Playa Grande* ☎ *2653–0975, 877/658–2880 in U.S.* 🌐 *www.facebook.com/HotelBulaBulaCostaRica* 🛏 *10 rooms* 🍴 *Free Breakfast.*

Hotel Las Tortugas

$$ | **B&B/INN** | With a prime location on the beach, this place is perfect for surfers, nature lovers, and sun worshippers with a range of budgets. **Pros:** on the beach; friendly owners; good value. **Cons:** busy location; spotty service at times; rooms lack amenities. [$] *Rooms from: $125* ✉ *Entrance to Leatherback Marine National Park, 33 km (20 miles) north of Tamarindo* ☎ *2653–0423* 🌐 *www.lastortugashotel.com* 🛏 *37 units* 🍴 *No meals.*

Activities

TIP→ Unless you are a strong swimmer attached to a surfboard, don't go in any deeper than your waist here. There is calmer water for snorkeling about a 30-minute walk north of Las Tortugas, at a black-sand beach called Playa Carbón. All Playa Grande and Tamarindo hotels can arrange guided boat tours of the estuary for around $25 per person. You may see crocodiles, monkeys, herons, kingfishers, and an array of other birdlife; go either early in the morning or late in the afternoon, and bring insect repellent.

SURFING

Playa Grande is renowned for having one of the most consistent surf breaks in the country. Only experienced surfers should attempt riding this beach break, which often features big barrels and offshore winds. The waves are best at high tide, especially around a full moon.

Hotel Bula Bula

SURFING | You can arrange to rent both long- and shortboards for $15 to $25 a day at this surfer-friendly hotel. ⊠ *Palm Beach Estates, 2 km (1 mile) east of Playa Grande* ☎ *2653–0975* ⊕ *www.facebook.com/HotelBulaBulaCostaRica.*

Hotel Las Tortugas

SURFING | The hotel rents boards for $15 to $20 a day and offers surfing lessons at their beachfront Caribbean-style snack bar. ⊠ *Playa Grande* ☎ *2653–0423* ⊕ *www.lastortugashotel.com.*

YOGA

Yoga at RipJack Inn

AEROBICS/YOGA | RipJack Inn has its own yoga shala where classes are held daily. Check the website for times. The cost is $15 and yoga mats are provided. ⊠ *100 m south of Hotel Las Tortugas, at RipJack Inn* ☎ *2653–1636* ⊕ *www.ripjackinn.com* 🗪 *$15.*

Tamarindo

82 km (51 miles) southwest of Liberia.

Once a funky beach town full of surfers and local fishermen, Tamarindo is now a pricey, hyped-up hive of commercial development and real estate speculation, happily accompanied by a dizzying variety

of shops, bars, and hotels, and probably the best selection of restaurants of any beach town on the Pacific coast. There's a shopping center at the entrance to town with an upscale AutoMercado supermarket and ATM. On the downside, the congested two-lane beach road through Tamarindo comes to a halt at times throughout the day, especially when delivery trucks stop in front of shops and restaurants, while drivers inch past the flashing hazards and distracted pedestrians. Strip malls, billboards, and high-rise condominiums clutter the rest of the main street and obscure views of the still-magnificent beach. Beyond the chaos of Diria Grand Boulevard (the commercial center), the main road bends toward Playa Langosta and gains some composure and tranquillity (other than the potholes).

Tamarindo serves as a popular base for surfing at the nearby Playas Grande, Langosta, Avellanas, and Negra. There are plenty of outdoor options in addition to surfing, among them diving, sportfishing, wildlife-watching, and canopy tours. You can also play 18 rounds at the nearby Hacienda Pinilla golf course, or simply stroll the beach and sunbathe. There have been reports of car break-ins that occur minutes after you leave your vehicle. Most upscale hotels and inns have their own security and gated parking. Once you're on the beach, almost all the negatives disappear (just keep an eye on your belongings).

GETTING HERE AND AROUND

Both Nature Air and SANSA fly to Tamarindo from San José. By car from Liberia, travel south on the highway to the turnoff for Belén, then head west and turn left at the Huacas crossroads to Tamarindo, passing through the small village of Villareal. The drive from Liberia to Tamarindo takes just over one hour. There are no direct bus connections between Playa Grande or Playa Avellanas and Tamarindo. A taxi or a shuttle van is the way to go from nearby towns if you don't have wheels.

TAXIS Juan Carlos Taxi. ☎ *8636–6358.*

SHUTTLES Tamarindo Shuttle. ☎ *2653–4444, 2653–2626* 🌐 *www.tamarindoshuttle.com.*

RENTAL CARS Alamo. ✉ *On main road, diagonal from Tamarindo Diria hotel* ☎ *2653–0727.* **Budget.** ✉ *Next to hotel Mar Rey, Main road* ☎ *2654–0756.* **Economy.** ✉ *Main road entering Tamarindo, across from Witch's Rock Surf Camp* ☎ *2653–0728.* **Hertz.** ✉ *100 m east of Hotel Pasatiempo* ☎ *2653–1358.*

ESSENTIALS

BANK/ATM Banco Nacional. ✉ *Across from Arco Iris Hotel* ☎ *2653–0366.*

HOSPITALS Beachside Clinic. ✉ *200 m west of Huacas cruce, Brasilito* ✣ *About 20 mins out of town on road to Brasilito* ☎ *2653–9911* 🌐 *beachsideclinicсr.com.*

PHARMACY Farmacia Tamarindo. ✉ *Main road into town, diagonally across from Best Western Tamarindo Villas* ☎ *2653–0210.*

POST OFFICE Correo. ✉ *Across from airport on main road between Villareal and Tamarindo* ☎ *2653–0676.*

Beaches

Playa Tamarindo

BEACH—SIGHT | Wide and flat, the sand here is packed hard enough for easy walking and jogging, but swimming and surfing have become questionable since the town lost its Blue Flag status (because of overdevelopment and the total absence of water treatment). The water quality is especially poor during the rainy months, when you'll want to do your swimming and surfing at nearby Playa Langosta or Playa Grande. Despite this, surfing is still the main attraction here, and there's a young crowd that parties hard after a day riding the waves. Witch's Rock Surf Shop has showers, toilets, surfboard rental, a swimming pool, and a restaurant where you can watch the surfers over a cold beer. Strong currents at the north end of the beach get a lot of swimmers into trouble, especially when they try to cross the estuary without a surfboard. Steer clear of the estuary, where there have been crocodile sightings. There's street parking and a public dirt lot in front of El Vaquero Brewpub. **Amenities:** food and drink; parking; showers; toilets. **Best for:** partiers; surfing; walking. ✉ *Tamarindo.*

Restaurants

Bamboo Sushi Club

$$ | SUSHI | As soon as you cross the bamboo bridge, you'll be instantly transported from a strip mall to a zen garden. And what better place to eat fish than right next to the ocean? **Known for:** fresh-off-the-boat sushi; frozen passion-fruit mojitos; spicy edamame. [$] *Average main: $10* ✉ *20 m after Diria Hotel on Main St.* ☎ *2653–4519.*

Dragonfly Bar & Grill

$$$ | ECLECTIC | Paper lanterns suspended over wooden tables and polished concrete floors bring rustic elegance to this A-frame restaurant supported by tree-trunk columns. The place has been a favorite for years and remains trendy with international fusion dishes like buddha bowls or seared yellowfin tuna with wasabi aioli. **Known for:** live music on Saturday; wood-fired grill; laid-back charm. [$] *Average main: $17* ✉ *100 m past turnoff for Langosta Beach road, then left 50 m, behind Hotel Pasatiempo, past Pizzeria La Baula* ☎ *2653–1506* 🌐 *www.dragonflybarandgrill.com* 🕑 *No lunch.*

★ La Bodega

$ | CAFÉ | Linger as long as you'd like for breakfast or lunch on the open-air deck, where you'll be served fresh, local, and organic food. Daily specials are served on heaping salads or sandwiches on homemade bread. **Known for:** homemade

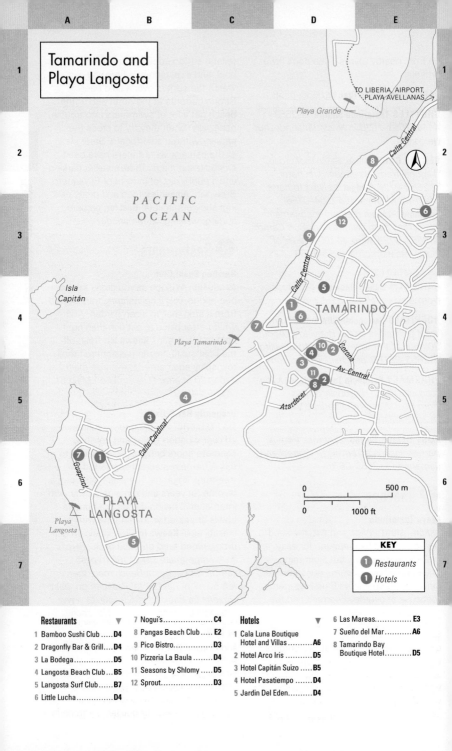

Tamarindo and Playa Langosta

A   B   C   D   E

1

2

3

4

5

6

7

TO LIBERIA, AIRPORT, PLAYA AVELLANAS

Playa Grande

PACIFIC OCEAN

Isla Capitán

Calle Central

TAMARINDO

Playa Tamarindo

Corona

Av. Central

Atardecer

Calle Cardinal

Guapinol

PLAYA LANGOSTA

Playa Langosta

0   500 m
0   1000 ft

KEY

Restaurants

Hotels

Restaurants ▼

1 Bamboo Sushi Club **D4**
2 Dragonfly Bar & Grill ... **D4**
3 La Bodega **D5**
4 Langosta Beach Club ... **B5**
5 Langosta Surf Club **B7**
6 Little Lucha **D4**

7 Nogui's **C4**
8 Pangas Beach Club **E2**
9 Pico Bistro **D3**
10 Pizzeria La Baula **D4**
11 Seasons by Shlomy **D5**
12 Sprout **D3**

Hotels ▼

1 Cala Luna Boutique
Hotel and Villas **A6**
2 Hotel Arco Iris **D5**
3 Hotel Capitán Suizo **B5**
4 Hotel Pasatiempo **D4**
5 Jardin Del Eden **D4**

6 Las Mareas **E3**
7 Sueño del Mar **A6**
8 Tamarindo Bay
Boutique Hotel **D5**

baked goods like banana bread and brownies; breakfast sandwiches; hibiscus lemonade. $ *Average main: $9* ⊠ *In the Hotel Nahua, diagonal from Banco Nacional* ☎ *8395–6184* ⊕ *www.facebook. com/LaBodegaCR* ⊗ *No dinner.*

Little Lucha

$ | MEXICAN | Decorated with figurines and images of Mexican wrestlers, with a VW bus for the bar, this restaurant serves authentic Mexico City street tacos. Feel the taco love with a platter: the *cochinita pibil,* which features pork shoulder slow-cooked in banana leaves and seasoned to citrus perfection, the veggie (not just for vegetarians) with mushrooms, onions, roasted peppers, and garlic, and the classic beer-battered fish taco topped with white sauce and a few drops of hot sauce. **Known for:** Taco Tuesday (all tacos $2); tequila cocktails and Mexican beers; colorful punk-rock atmosphere. $ *Average main: $6* ⊠ *20 m north of Super Compro, diagonal from skate park* ☎ *8829–1480* ⊗ *Closed Sun.*

Nogui's

$$$ | SEAFOOD | Pleasing a loyal legion of local fans since 1974, Nogui's offers a hearty Costa Rican menu and an ocean view. It is one of Tamarindo's best places to watch the sunset while the kids play on the beach, with a full seafood menu and various meat dishes, washed down with a local tamarind margarita. **Known for:** legendary selection of pies like pineapple, chocolate, and coconut cream; colorful Adirondack chairs on the beach; breakfast. $ *Average main: $16* ⊠ *South side of Tamarindo Circle, on beach* ☎ *2653–0029* ⊕ *www.noguistamarindo. com* ⊗ *Closed Wed.*

★ Pangas Beach Club

$$$ | FRENCH FUSION | You can't get any closer to the water than at this outdoor beach garden, where rustic tables are shaded by enormous ficus trees draped with wicker lamps. Classic French cuisine with Costa Rican flavors include dishes like fresh seafood with fruit reductions

and organic meats seared on hot lava stones. **Known for:** Sunday brunch; lovely setting on the beach; lamb seared on hot lava stones. $ *Average main: $25* ⊠ *500 m southwest of Automercado* ☎ *2653– 0024* ⊕ *pangasbeachclubcr.com.*

Pico Bistro

$ | AMERICAN | Cool off inside or relax outside on the deck at this little gem on the beach, the perfect spot to replenish the reserves with some healthy food or a good cup of coffee while you watch surfers ride the waves. Pico has the best Wi-Fi in town, so if you must look at your computer on your vacation, do it from here. **Known for:** fresh salads and Buddha bowls; brunch; unimpeded beach views. $ *Average main: $9* ⊠ *Calle Central* ☎ *8841–5338* ⊕ *pico-bistro-tamarindo. business.site.*

Pizzeria La Baula

$$ | PIZZA | FAMILY | Wildly popular, this casually chic, alfresco pizzeria on a quiet side street has plenty of cars parked outside most nights, with patrons inside feasting on the consistently delicious thin-crust pizzas. Families are especially fond of La Baula (the Costa Rican name for the leatherback turtle) because of its reasonable prices, noisy buzz, and adjacent playground and picniclike dining area. **Known for:** prosciutto, arugula, and Parmesan pizza; great place for large groups; open-air dining in a lighthearted atmosphere. $ *Average main: $15* ⊠ *Next door to Dragonfly Bar & Grill, 100 m north of Hotel Pasatiempo, behind Banco Nacional* ☎ *2653–1450* ⊗ *No lunch.*

★ Seasons by Shlomy

$$$ | MEDITERRANEAN | At his intimate, poolside restaurant in the casually chic Hotel Arco Iris, innovative Israeli-born and Cordon Bleu–trained chef Shlomy Koren transforms fresh local ingredients into sophisticated Mediterranean-fusion dishes you would pay a small fortune for on the Riviera. The alluring smell of sautéed garlic teases the senses for

what's ahead: salty soft focaccia with chicken liver pâté, perhaps a rare fillet or red snapper with sun-dried tomatoes, finished with white-chocolate mousse with strawberries. **Known for:** seared tuna; seafood pasta; consistently delicious meals. $ *Average main: $19* ⊠ *Hotel Arco Iris, uphill from turnoff to Playa Langosta road* ☎ *8368–6983* ⊕ *www.seasonstamarindo. com* ⊟ *No credit cards* ⊗ *Closed Sun. No lunch.*

Sprout

$$ | **CAFÉ** | The simple but spot-on menu, especially good for those with food sensitivities, features fresh, local, and organic ingredients in sandwiches, salads, and smoothies blended with fruits and vegetables so delightful that you'll forget they're good for you. Sink your teeth into top picks like the blackened mahimahi sandwich with mango-habanero mayo on toasted ciabatta or the piled-high hamburger on homemade brioche. **Known for:** scrumptious salads and sandwiches; pork sliders; fish tacos. $ *Average main: $10* ⊠ *Entrance to Tamarindo, across from Witch's Rock Surf Camp* ☎ *2653–2374* ⊗ *Closed Sun.*

 Hotels

Hotel Arco Iris

$$ | **HOTEL** | With eight ultraspacious, deluxe rooms with two queen beds, and five beautiful bungalows boasting high, sloping cane ceilings, handsome contemporary furniture, and sleek marble bathrooms, there's something for everyone on this chic compound, half a block off one of Tamarindo's main drags. **Pros:** transportation service and concierge; boutique feel; great restaurant. **Cons:** not a lot of privacy in bungalows; no water views; small pool. $ *Rooms from: $130* ⊠ *Follow signs past turnoff to Playa Langosta and go up hill to right* ☎ *2653–0330* ⊕ *www.hotelarcoiris.com* ⊅ *13 units* ⦿⎮ *Free Breakfast.*

Hotel Pasatiempo

$$ | **HOTEL** | **FAMILY** | This pretty collection of bungalows built around a tropical garden is clean, comfortable, and well priced, making this laid-back spot a great option for moderate budgets and families. **Pros:** affordable; gorgeous pool and garden; 10% discount when booking directly through hotel. **Cons:** seven-minute walk to beach; rooms close to the bar can be noisy; some mosquitoes. $ *Rooms from: $94* ⊠ *100 m southeast of high-rise Pacific Park condo at turnoff for Playa Langosta Rd.* ☎ *2653–0096, 2653–4701* ⊕ *www.hotelpasatiempo. com* ⊅ *22 rooms* ⦿⎮ *Free Breakfast.*

Jardin Del Eden

$$$$ | **HOTEL** | An oasis with luxurious rooms, this adults-only boutique hotel just off the main street feels a million miles away. **Pros:** exquisite gardens; poolside organic restaurant; beachside garden across the street. **Cons:** hotel isn't directly on the beach; a lot of steps to some rooms; not all rooms are the same high quality. $ *Rooms from: $295* ⊠ *Tamarindo Beach* ☎ *2653–0137* ⊕ *www. jardindeleden.com* ⊅ *46 rooms* ⦿⎮ *Free Breakfast.*

Las Mareas

$$$$ | **RENTAL** | If space, privacy, luxury, and location are your priorities, then these 2,800-square-foot vacation rentals are your best option, with Balinese decor and all the comforts of home. **Pros:** ideal for large groups; five-minute walk to central Tamarindo; high-end amenities. **Cons:** no meals; one-week minimum stay during holidays; maid service every other day. $ *Rooms from: $460* ⊠ *Across from Las Pangas Beach Club, at entrance to Tamarindo* ☎ *2653–1561, 8832–5773* ⊅ *6 villas* ⦿⎮ *No meals.*

★ Tamarindo Bay Boutique Hotel

$$ | **HOTEL** | This boutique hotel built from recycled materials is inspired by the owners' travels to Southeast Asia and has nine contemporary rooms overlooking a pool-centered courtyard. **Pros:**

outstanding breakfasts; huge rooms; immaculate and peaceful property; UV-treated pool. **Cons:** no ocean views; ground-floor rooms get some noise from above; no kids under 18. $ *Rooms from: $140* ✉ *100 m south of Banco Nacional, next to Hotel Arco Iris* ☎ *2653–2692, 8706–9470* ⊕ *www.tamarindobayhotel. com* ↻ *9 rooms* ❍❶ *Free Breakfast.*

Nightlife

Tamarindo is one of the few places outside San José and Jacó where the nightlife really jumps. Although party-hearty hot spots come and go with the tides, Tamarindo does have some perennially popular nightspots, along with a couple of low-key options.

Crazy Monkey Bar
DANCE CLUBS | Popular with the surfing crowd, Crazy Monkey Bar features live salsa music, a fire show, and DJs that attract locals who really know how to move—and a crowd of appreciative onlookers. Friday night is ladies' night. ✉ *Best Western Tamarindo Vista Villas, main road entering Tamarindo, across from Witch's Rock Surf Camp* ☎ *2653–0114* ✉ *$5 cover.*

El Vaquero Bar
BREWPUBS/BEER GARDENS | After a sunset surf session, pull up a bar stool in the sand and enjoy a craft beer made at the neighboring Volcano Brewing Company. Happy hour is from 5 to 7, and there's live music Friday and weekend nights. If you've worked up an appetite, try the chicken wings, jalapeño poppers, hamburgers, and nachos. This is the best place to watch the surfers over a cold one. ✉ *In front of Economy Rental Car, next to Witch's Rock Surf Camp* ☎ *2653–1238* ⊕ *www.witchsrocksurfcamp.com/ el-vaquero-brewpub.*

Sharky's
BARS/PUBS | This is the biggest, most popular sports bar in town, with huge TV screens showing up to six games at once. After the game, both floors play extremely loud music for dancing. There's live music on Monday, karaoke on Tuesday, and ladies' night Saturday. If sports aren't your thing, the bar food is amazingly good. The action starts at 11:30 am and goes to 2:30 am. ✉ *Avda. Ctl., across from Plaza Tamarindo* ☎ *2653–4705* ⊕ *www.sharkysbars.com.*

Shopping

Most stores lining the main road along Diria Grand Boulevard sell the same souvenirs. It's hard to leave town without at least one sarong or T-shirt in your suitcase. There are a few upscale clothing and jewelry shops as well, and some worthy farmers' markets.

Azul Profundo Boutique
CLOTHING | The theme of this Tamarindo boutique is "Don't worry, be hippy," with a collection of upscale beachwear and jewelry ranging from tie-dyed sundresses and OM pendants to pura vida earrings and wool belts. They also have beach bags, hats, and bikinis. Here you can find nicer clothes for men and women; head next door to Azul Profundo Kids for the little ones. ✉ *Local #1 Centro Comercial Plaza* ☎ *2653–0395* ⊕ *www.azulprofundoboutique.com.*

Buena Nena
CLOTHING | If you've bought too many souvenirs on your trip, stop in this funky boutique to pick up one of their handmade bags—they have a glorious selection of cool patterns and sizes. If you haven't bought enough souvenirs, stop in to pick something out from their selection of well-made dresses, hats, and jewelry. ✉ *Store #1 Hotel Zullymar, on road to rotunda* ☎ *2653–1991.*

Tamarindo Farmers' Market
OUTDOOR/FLEA/GREEN MARKETS | On Saturday from 8 am to 4 pm, the farmers' market behind the skate park is bustling. Stop by for some fresh organic fruits and veggies, homemade kombucha, or

baked goods. ⊠ *Next to Green Papaya restaurant and behind Oneida Park, Playa Tamarindo* ☎ *8779–8800* ⊕ *www.facebook.com/Market.Tamarindo.*

Tamarindo Night Market
OUTDOOR/FLEA/GREEN MARKETS | On Thursday evenings from 6 to 9 pm, join in the buzzing crowd to sample food and cocktails from around the world, buy jewelry, and listen to live music. ⊠ *In the parking lot up the road from Hotel Pasatiempo* ☎ *6051–6634.*

Activities

BOATING
Rocky Isla El Capitán, just offshore, is a close-in kayaking destination, full of sand-dollar shells. Exploring the tidal estuaries north and south of town is best done in a kayak at high tide, when you can travel farther up the temporary rivers. Arrange kayaking trips through your hotel. A number of boats offer sunset trips that allow you to snorkel, and provide food and beverages.

Blue Dolphin Sailing
BOATING | FAMILY | Set sail on a 40-foot catamaran for an afternoon of sunning, snorkeling, and kayaking aboard the *Blue Dolphin.* The boat departs at 1 pm from the beach next to El Chiringuito Restaurant and returns around sunset. It's $85 per person, including a light meal and open bar. During high season there's also a morning tour, from 8 am to noon, for $70 (including snorkel gear and fishing poles). The boat is also available for private tours. ⊠ *Tamarindo* ☎ *8842–3204, 855/842–3204 toll-free* ⊕ *www.bluedolphinsailing.com* 🕮 *From $70.*

Iguana Surf
BOATING | This longtime surf shop, with an office across from the beach, organizes jungle boat tours of the Tamarindo Estuary and offers a full roster of local tours, including snorkeling. ⊠ *Across from beach, 100 m north of El Diriá Hotel* ☎ *2653–0613* ⊕ *www.iguanasurf.net* 🕮 *From $50.*

Marlin del Rey Sailing Tours
BOATING | This custom-built, 66-foot catamaran, with a large, comfortable main saloon, takes you on a day tour ($75, minimum 15 people) that includes snorkeling, an open bar, lunch, and snacks. It leaves at 8 am. The sunset tour departs at 1:30 pm ($85, no minimum), with time to snorkel, walk along a deserted beach, and enjoy the open bar and a gourmet feast, complete with homemade chocolate-chip cookies. ⊠ *Plaza Esmeralda, next to Subway* ☎ *2653–1212, 877/827–8275 in U.S.* ⊕ *www.marlindelrey.com* 🕮 *From $75.*

FISHING
Go Fish Costa Rica
FISHING | Steve and Liisa specialize in custom-made fishing trips for everyone from serious sport-fishermen to families out for fun, matching you with the best boat and captain for your experience level. On inshore fishing trips, you'll likely catch roosterfish, snapper, and grouper. On deepwater trips you'll go for tuna, mahimahi, and wahoo; marlin and sailfish will get live released. ⊠ *Langosta Beach* ⊹ *Boats usually depart from beach near Chiringuito Restaurant* ⊕ *gofishcr.com* 🕮 *Half day from $425.*

Rhino Charger Sportfishing
FISHING | With more than 30 years of sportfishing experience, this U.S.-owned and-operated company has a well-maintained 31-foot *Island Hopper,* the only boat in the Tamarindo fleet equipped with a fly bridge. There are always two English-speaking crew members onboard, with enough room for up to seven anglers per trip. Charters cost $750 for a half day and $1,100 for a full day. Rates include fishing gear, snacks, and beverages. ⊠ *Tamarindo Bay* ☎ *506/8310–0003 cell, 772/905–2941 in U.S.* ⊕ *www.rhinocharger.com* 🕮 *From $750.*

SURFING
Costa Rica Surf Club
SURFING | Owners Diego and Sabrina go out of their way to share their love

of surfing with everyone that walks through the doors. From the novice to the advanced surfer, everyone will enjoy the waves with individual ($55) or group lessons ($35). They also have a large collection of surfboards if you'd like to rent. ✉ *Main street across from beach in Sunrise Commercial Center* ☎ *2653–0130* ⊕ *www.facebook.com/crscsurfshop* ✆ *From $35.*

Iguana Surf

SURFING | FAMILY | Right across from the beach, this popular surf shop rents surfboards ($20 per day) and boogie boards and offers group lessons four times a day ($45, for ages three and up), as well as private lessons ($80). It's open 8 to 6 daily. ✉ *Across from beach, 100 m north of Tamarindo Diria hotel* ☎ *2653–0091* ⊕ *www.iguanasurf.net* ✆ *From $20.*

Witch's Rock Surf Camp

SURFING | This hip, popular hotel, restaurant, and surf school is surfer central in Tamarindo, with a large surf shop and all the latest gear and board rentals. Surf lessons ($85) include all-day board rental, in-water training, and a surf seminar, such as a shaping tutorial with Robert August of *Endless Summer* fame. Courses for intermediate and advanced surfers are also on offer. If you're just looking to rent a board, this is the place—they have the most solid quiver in town. The shop is right on the beach, just steps from the best surf breaks. ✉ *North end of beach, main road in Tamarindo, across from Economy Rent a Car* ☎ *2653–1238, 888/318–7873 toll-free in U.S. and Canada* ⊕ *www.witchsrocksurfcamp.com* ✆ *From $85.*

TOURS

Black Stallion Surf Saloon

SPECIAL-INTEREST | FAMILY | This "Costa Rican cowboy saloon with a surfer twist" is a full-day experience that starts with ziplining, horseback riding, and ATV tours, and ends with a barbecue feast of smoked meats like ribs, pork, chorizo,

ranch chicken, and grilled vegetables. Homegrown bananas, mangoes, and citrus are used to infuse cocktails and make dressings and sauces for the farm-to-table dishes. Even vegetarians rave about the endless options of all-you-can-eat grilled fruits, vegetables, and salads. The rustic ranch dining room is intimate and memorable, and the remote location just outside of Tamarindo means you're likely to get a spectacular star show. ✉ *The Black Stallion Hills Ranch* ⊹ *10-min drive from Tamarindo* ☎ *8869–9765* ⊕ *www. blackstallionhills.com* ✆ *Dinner at 7 pm from $45* ⌂ *Reservations essential.*

TURTLE-WATCHING TOURS

ACOTAM

WILDLIFE-WATCHING | FAMILY | ACOTAM, a local conservation association, conducts turtle-viewing tours in Las Baulas National Marine Park in Playa Grande with local guides for $35, including park entrance fee. The group picks you up at your hotel and briefs you at their headquarters on the estuary that separates Tamarindo and Playa Grande. An open boat then takes you across the estuary, where you wait at the park station until a turtle has been spotted. With so few leatherback turtles nesting, you are more likely to see green sea turtles instead. The leatherback nesting season is from mid-October to mid-February. You can see the green sea turtles through April. They also offer covered-boat mangrove tours along the Tamarindo River year-round for $25 per person (minimum two people). ✉ *Tamarindo* ☎ *2653–1687* ✎ *guiaslocalestama@gmail.com* ✆ *From $25.*

Playa Langosta

2 km (1 mile) south of Tamarindo.

A chic bedroom community of Tamarindo, just five minutes away by car, Playa Langosta is tranquil and elegant. It has not totally escaped development, but most of

Continued on page 322

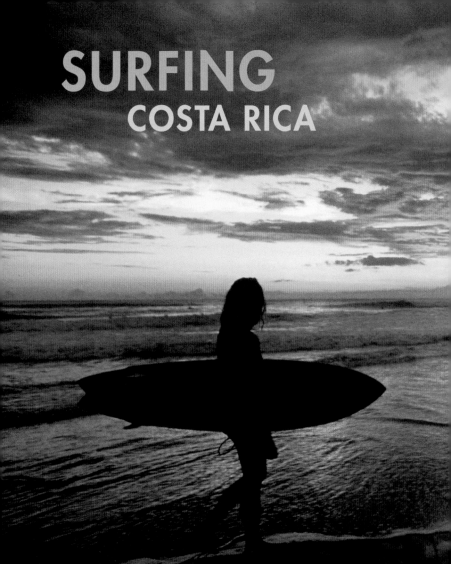

SURFING
COSTA RICA

Costa Rica's big surfing community, consistent waves, and not-too-crowded beaches make surfing accessible to anyone who is curious enough to give it a whirl; surf schools, board rentals, and beachside lessons are plentiful. At the most popular beaches, surf tourism is a regular part of the scene. Many instructors are able to bridge generational divides, giving lessons tailored for anyone from tots to retirees. First-timers would be wise to start at a begin-

by Leland Baxter-Neal

Costa Ricans are known for their laid-back attitude, and this usually translates into a welcoming vibe in the water. Of course, as the waves get more
intense, and the surfers more serious, the unspoken rules get stricter, so
beginners are advised to stay close to the shore. A good instructor should
help keep you out of the way anywhere you go, and if you're on your own,
just steer clear of the hot shots until you know the local protocol.

COSTA RICA'S SURF FINDER

THE PACIFIC COAST

For those new to surfing, destinations on the Pacific coast are more welcoming in a number of ways. There are more beaches, hotels, bars, and surf schools than in the Caribbean, and the waves are friendlier. Access to the Northern and Central Pacific coast is also made easy by (sometimes) paved and well-marked roads. As you head southward down the coast, the route becomes untamed. The remoteness of the Osa Peninsula has guarded a couple of world-class breaks surrounded by some of the country's most untouched jungle.

WHEN TO GO: Waves are most consistent from December through April. As you move southward down the coast, the breaks are best from May to November.

THE CARIBBEAN

Costa Rica's truncated Caribbean has comparatively few beaches and they draw only the most dedicated surf seekers. The laidback culture of that coast seems a perfect match for the surfer vibe. Among the Caribbean waves is perhaps Costa Rica's most famous: Puerto Viejo's Salsa Brava.

WHEN TO GO: Best conditions January through April.

TYPES OF BREAKS

BEACH BREAK: The best type for beginners. Waves break over sandbars and the seafloor. Jacó, Hermosa, and Sámara are all beach breaks.

POINT BREAK: Created as waves hit a point jutting into the ocean. With the right conditions, this can create very consistent waves. Pavones is a point break.

REEF BREAK: Waves break as they hit a reef. It can create great (but dangerous) surf. There's a good chance of getting smashed and scraped over extremely sharp coral or rocks. Salsa Brava, in Puerto Viejo, is a reef break.

PACIFIC

❶ Tamarindo: Very popular with all levels of surfers. It is most famous for its reef breaks like Ollie's Point, Playa Negra (south), and Witch's Rock (north), made famous by the film *Endless Summer*. Nice waves are formed at a point break called Pico Pequeño and at the river mouth called El Estero at the beach's north end.

❷ Playa Guiones: If not the best surf in the vicinity of Nosara, it's the best beach break for beginners and longboarders, second only to Sámara. Lots of long, fun rights and lefts.

❸ Sámara: Protected, mellow beach breaks where the greatest danger is that the waves are too small. Great for beginners and close to lots of breaks like Playa Camaronal for more advanced surfers.

❹ Malpaís: A variety of beach breaks plus a point break that's good when waves get big. Good for beginners and advanced surfers, but hard to reach.

❺ Jacó: Unless the surf gets too big, the consistent beach breaks produce forgiving waves that are good to begin and advance on. The

Tamarindo

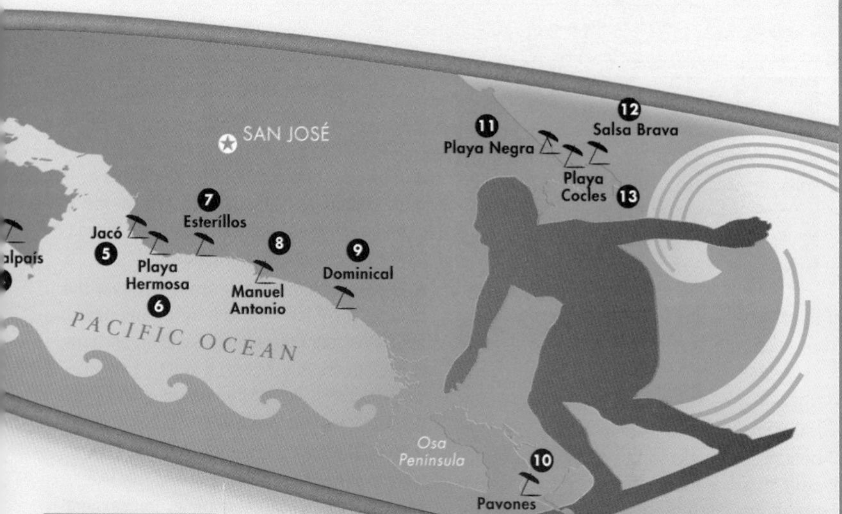
SAN JOSÉ
[11] Playa Negra
[12] Salsa Brava
Playa Cocles [13]
[7] Esterillos
Jacó [5]
Playa Hermosa [6]
[8] Manuel Antonio
[9] Dominical
PACIFIC OCEAN
Osa Peninsula
[10] Pavones

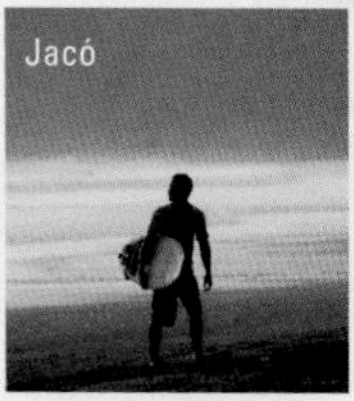
Jacó

south end is best for beginners.

[6] Playa Hermosa: A steep beach break just south of Jacó with some of the country's best waves and surfers. Waves can get big, mean, and thunderously heavy.

[7] Esterillos: Divided into three beaches, going north to south: Oeste, Centro, and Este. A beautiful stretch of coast, uncrowded to the point of desolation. The surf and currents can be tough for beginners, and Este and Centro have waves much like Hermosa. Oeste has a variety of beach breaks with softer, friendlier waves.

[8] Manuel Antonio: Just outside the national park you'll find a variety of beach breaks. Playitas, at the park's north end, is perhaps the most consistent. This spot only gets good at hightide, about three hours per day. September through December it's ususally flat.

[9] Dominical: At the foot of beautiful, forested coastal mountains. A long set of beach breaks that are fun and great for advanced levels. When waves get too big, head south to Dominicalito. This wave is fast, hollow, and powerful.

[10] Pavones: Legendary, remote, and surrounded by rain forest, Pavones is said to be one of the world's longest, left-breaking waves, with a perfect ride lasting nearly three minutes. But with fickle conditions and a tough drive to get here, it's best for the very experienced.

CARIBBEAN

[11] Playa Negra: A largely undiscovered but quality reef break for all skill levels. Be careful at low tide when rocks are exposed.

[12] Salsa Brava: When the conditions are right, this is arguably Costa Rica's best and most powerful wave; it's placed right over a shallow coral reef. For advanced surfers only.

[13] Playa Cocles: Plenty of beach breaks to pick from, good for all levels. But beware the currents or you'll drift out to sea.

SURF SCHOOL TIPS

Surf lesson

Surfing is for the young and the young at heart. At many of Costa Rica's top surf beaches, a wide range of ages and skill sets can be found bobbing together in the water. With the right board and some good instructions, just about anybody can stand up and have some fun in the waves. We strongly recommend taking a lesson or two, but be sure to take them from an actual surf school (there's one on just about every beach) rather than from the eager kid who approaches you with a board. Trained instructors will be much better at adapting their lesson plans to different skill levels, ages, and body types.

If you're a first-timer, there are a few things you need to know before getting in the water.

■ **Pick your beach carefully.** Sámara is a good choice, as is Jacó or Tamarindo. You want beach breaks and small, gentle waves. Make sure to ask about rip tides.

■ **Expect introductory lessons to cover the basics.** You'll learn how to lie on the board, paddle out, duck the incoming waves, and how to pop up on your board. If you're a natural, you'll be able to hop up and stay standing in the white wash of the wave after it breaks.

■ **Have realistic expectations.** Even if you have experience in other board sports, like snowboarding or skateboarding, don't expect to be surfing on the face of the wave or tucking into barrels on your first day. It literally takes years before you can reach that level.

■ **Choose the right gear.** If you're a beginner, start on a longboard, preferably made of foam (aka, "soft top surfboard"). Be sure to wear a rashguard or a wet suit to help protect your chest and stomach from getting scraped or stung by jellyfish. Hydrate, and apply sunscreen.

SURF SLANG (or, how not to sound like a kook)

Barrel: The area created when a wave breaks onto itself in a curl, creating a surfable tube that's the surfer's nirvana. Also called the "green room."

Drop in: To stand up and drop down the face of a wave. Also used when one surfer cuts another off: "Hey, don't drop in on that guy!"

Duck dive: A maneuver where the surfer first pushes his or her board underwater and then dives with it, ducking under waves that have already broken or are about to break. It's difficult with a longboard (⇨ see Turtle roll).

Goofy foot: Having a right-foot-forward stance on the surfboard. The opposite is known as "regular."

Close out: When a wave or a section of a wave breaks all at once, rather than breaking steadily in one direction. A frustrating situation for surfers, giving them nowhere to go as the wave comes crashing down.

Ding: A hole, dent, crack, or other damage to a board.

Grom: A young surfer, usually under 15, who "RIPs" (is amazing).

Kook: Someone (usually a beginner) trying to pass as a surfer.

Outside: The area farther out from where waves are most regularly breaking. Surfers line up here to catch waves.

Stick: A surfboard.

Turtle roll: A maneuver where the surfer rolls over on the surfboard, going underwater and holding the board upside down. Used by longboarders and beginners to keep from being swept back toward shore by breaking waves.

BOARD SHAPES

Longboard: Lengthier (about 2.5–3 m/ 9–10.5 feet), wider, thicker, and more buoyant than the often-miniscule shortboards. Offers more flotation and speedier paddling, which makes it easier to get into waves. Great for beginners and those with relaxed surf styles. Skill level: Beginner to Intermediate.

Funboard: A little shorter than the longboard with a slightly more acute nose and blunt tail, the Funboard combines the best attributes of the longboards with some similar characteristics of the shorter boards. Good for beginners or surfers looking for a board more maneuverable and faster than a longboard. Skill level: Beginner to Intermediate.

Fishboard: A stumpy, blunt-nosed, twin-finned board that features a "V" tail (giving it a "fish" like look, hence the name) and is fast and maneuverable. Good for catching small, steep slow waves and pulling tricks. At one point this was the world's best-selling surfboard. Skill level: Intermediate to Expert.

Shortboard: Shortboards came on the scene in 1967–70 when the average board length dropped from 9'6" to 6'6" (2.9 m to 2 m) and changed the wave riding styles in the surf world forever. This board is a short, light, high-performance stick that is designed for carving the wave with a high amount of maneuverability. These boards need a fast steep wave, completely different than a longboard break, which tends to be slower with shallower wave faces. Skill level: Expert.

Beginner   Expert

Fish

Funboards

Shortboards

Longboards

Shallow wave faces, easiest surfing   Steeper wave faces, difficult surfing

Just a mile south of Tamarindo, Playa Langosta is a chic community with an unsullied beach.

the low-rise buildings on the northern half are tucked behind the mangrove trees, so you can enjoy an unsullied dramatic beachscape, with surf crashing against rocky outcroppings. A few high-rise condominiums have invaded the area, but they are mostly set back. Past Playa Langosta Beach Club are a handful of hotels and B&Bs that outshine properties in neighboring Tamarindo.

GETTING HERE AND AROUND

The municipality is still working on paving the dirt road from Tamarindo to Langosta, so there are some smooth sections and some filled with potholes. A few side roads are still dirt, so to keep down the dust, the road is periodically spread with an industrial molasses mixture, which accounts for the stickiness and the lovely smell of cookies in the air. You can walk along the beach, at low tide, all the way from Tamarindo Beach, but be careful not to get caught on the headland rocks as the tide comes in. Most hotels offer pickup in Tamarindo for car-free visitors.

As an alternative you can take a taxi or rent a bicycle for the short trip.

 Beaches

Playa Langosta

BEACH—SIGHT | This Blue Flag beach is actually two beaches: To the north is an upscale residential area where every foot of beachfront has been built up; the beach here is rather narrow, since the coast is lined with rocks, and the light-gray sand is coarse. To the south, the beach is a pristine, protected annex of Las Baulas National Marine Park, where the occasional leatherback turtle nests at night and beachcombers and surfers roam by day. The dividing point is the San Francisco Estuary, the mouth of which is a knee-high wade at low tide, and a deep river with dangerous currents around high tide. The beach here is wider and less rocky, and it's where surfers find the best surf breaks. If you walk up the river at low tide, you may see snowy egrets, baby blue herons, tail-bobbing spotted sandpipers, and, if your eyes are sharp, tiny white-lored gnatcatchers, endemic to these parts. The rockier parts of the beach are excellent for spotting seabirds, including American oystercatchers, and playing in the tide pools. Amenities are available at Playa Langosta Beach Club. **Amenities:** food and drink; toilets. **Best for:** sunset; surfing; walking. ⊠ *Playa Langosta.*

🍴 Restaurants

Langosta Beach Club

$$$ | FRENCH | This beach club–restaurant–lounge–jazz club is the most romantic and sophisticated dining spot on the beach. By day, you can lounge by the pool or surf between bites of ceviche, panini, burgers, or mussels with fries; by night, you'll find tables set with white linens and candles arranged under swaying palms around two glowing pools. **Known for:** beach club atmosphere—stay for the day; ahi tuna almost too beautiful to eat, topped with arugula and caviar on a tower of thin and crispy potatoes; good wine list and light, refreshing Argentine wines by the glass. $ *Average main: $25* ⊠ *Langosta Beach road, 200 m north of Capitán Suizo* ☎ *2653–1127* ⊕ *www. langostabeachclub.com* ☞ *Beach club day pass $25.*

★ **Langosta Surf Club**

$ | DELI | If you want to feel at home on vacation, head to this family-friendly neighborhood sports bar featuring in-house roasted deli meats, local artisanal products, and famous homemade pickles. The breakfast panini and smoothie will keep you going all morning at the beach; or choose dine-in or take out lunches like big turkey sandwiches with a side of pineapple slaw or the delightful pear Gorgonzola salad. **Known for:** fun atmosphere with lots to do; huge deli sandwiches; healthy, fresh ingredients. $ *Average main: $8* ⊠ *Langosta Beach* ☎ *8332–9339* ☾ *Closed Sun.*

🛏 Hotels

★ **Cala Luna Boutique Hotel and Villas**

$$$ | RESORT | FAMILY | For your own "cove of the moon" with casual luxury, Cala Luna is the place in Langosta. **Pros:** yoga classes; gorgeous gardens; complimentary sunset cocktails. **Cons:** five-minute walk to the beach; rocky beach; mediocre restaurant. $ *Rooms from: $215* ⊠ *Cala Luna Boutique Hotel and Villas* ☎ *2653–0214* ⊕ *calaluna.com* ☞ *49 units* ⦿ *Free Breakfast.*

★ **Hotel Capitán Suizo**

$$$$ | HOTEL | Nature, tranquility, luxury, and an unbeatably beautiful beach setting make this environmentally conscious boutique hotel the most elegant choice in town. **Pros:** secluded beachfront hotel; excellent restaurant; lovely gardens and pool. **Cons:** not all rooms are beachfront; pricey; no TVs. $ *Rooms from: $295* ⊠ *Right side of Playa Langosta road, half-way between Tamarindo and Langosta* ☎ *2653–0075* ⊕ *www.hotelcapitansuizo. com* ☾ *Usually closed for maintenance between Sept. and Oct.* ☞ *35 units* ⦿ *Free Breakfast.*

Sueño del Mar

$$$ | B&B/INN | The name of this beachfront bed-and-breakfast means "Dream of the Sea," and the front gate opens into a dreamy world of intimate gardens, patios, and hand-painted tiles. **Pros:** intimate; well-appointed; amazing breakfast; great beachfront. **Cons:** tiny pool; lack of privacy in small rooms; pricey. $ *Rooms from: $210* ⊠ *130 m south of Capitán Suizo, veer right for 45 m, then right again for about 90 m to entrance gate, across from back of Cala Luna Hotel* ☎ *2653–0284* ⊕ *www.sueno-del-mar.com* ☞ *6 units* ⦿ *Free Breakfast.*

Nightlife

Playa Langosta Beach Club

PIANO BARS/LOUNGES | Sink into a comfortable chair at this chic poolside lounge on Playa Langosta to watch the sunset over the Pacific and listen to jazz under the stars (Tuesday 7 to 9 pm), or treat your ears to some Brazilian music on Friday. ✉ *Tamarindo–Playa Langosta road, 200 m north of Hotel Capitán Suizo.*

Activities

Tour operators in Tamarindo, just a few miles north, offer activities in the Playa Langosta area.

Playa Avellanas

17 km (11 miles) south of Tamarindo.

Traditionally a far cry from its northern neighbor's boom of real estate development, Avellanas has seen Tamarindo escapees slowly encroaching on it for years, building private houses and a smattering of small hotels. As you bump along the dusty, rough beach road, most of the cars you pass have surfboards on top. But nonsurfers are welcome, as Avellanas (pronounced *ah-vey-YA-nas*) is a lovely spot for anyone who just likes sea and sand.

GETTING HERE AND AROUND

You have to drive inland from Tamarindo to Villareal, where you turn right for the 13-km (8-mile) trip down a bumpy road to reach Playa Avellanas. It takes about 20 minutes. There are rivers to cross in rainy season, when you may want to drive via Paraíso and Playa Negra. All of the roads in the gated community of Hacienda Pinilla are paved.

SHUTTLES Tamarindo Shuttle. ☎ *2653–4444* 🌐 *www.tamarindoshuttle.com.*

Beaches

Playa Avellanas

BEACH—SIGHT | This beach's main claims to fame are surfing and hanging around at Lola's, a sexy beach restaurant-bar. Wide and sandy at the main access point, the beach itself is beautiful, with a line of palms and beach almonds for shade. Rocky outcroppings and a small river mouth mark its southern end, and a mangrove swamp lies behind its northern half. Its Blue Flag designation means the water is clean, but you shouldn't go in deeper than your waist when the waves are big, because of rip currents. That's when the surfers take over. Jellyfish can be a problem, so you might want to wear a rash guard. Unfortunately, security is an issue here, as at most Costa Rican beaches; posted signs warn visitors not to leave anything of value in parked cars or unattended on the beach. There is guarded parking at the beach entrance near Lola's; be sure to have small bills to tip the attendant when you leave. If you are staying in the gated resort community of Hacienda Pinilla, it's better to park in the private lot and enter from its beach club. **Amenities:** food and drink; parking (no fee). **Best for:** surfing; walking. ✉ *Playa Avellanas.*

Restaurants

★ **Lola's**

$$ | **VEGETARIAN** | This hip beach café has exactly the kind of ambience one comes to Costa Rica for, with tables scattered along the beach amid palm and almond trees, hammocks swinging in the wind, palm fronds rustling, and surfers riding the glistening waves in front. Seating, or more precisely, lolling, is on reclining, African-style hardwood chairs, or at shaded tables. **Known for:** Ave and Ana the pigs, their mascots; great spot to camp out for the day; flatbread pizza, fresh-fruit smoothies, and organic meats. [$] *Average main: $11*

✉ *At main entrance to Playa Avellanas*
☎ *2652–9097* ⊕ *www.lolascostarica.info*
☉ *Closed Mon. No dinner.*

Hotels

Cabinas Las Olas

$$ | **B&B/INN** | **FAMILY** | Frequented mainly by surfers, this is a good option for anyone seeking easy beach access, relative solitude, and comfortable, if not fancy, lodging. **Pros:** near beach; surf shop with board rental and lessons; secluded. **Cons:** mosquitoes a problem in rainy season; simple rooms; patchy Wi-Fi. $ *Rooms from: $100* ✉ *1 km (½ mile) before Avellanas, on right* ☎ *2652–9315* ⊕ *www. cabinaslasolas.com* ☉ *Closed Oct.* ⇝ *10 rooms* ⚹ *Free Breakfast.*

JW Marriott Guanacaste Resort & Spa

$$$$ | **RESORT** | In the gated community of Hacienda Pinilla, this luxury resort is centered around a 25,000-square-foot infinity pool that merges with a short stretch of beach in the west, making every sunset a major event. **Pros:** luxurious; largest infinity pool in Central America; equestrian center. **Cons:** very pricey; beach is rocky; ground-level rooms facing walkways get outside noise. $ *Rooms from: $500* ✉ *In Hacienda Pinilla Beach resort and residential community* ⊕ *www.marriott.com/ sjojw* ⇝ *310 rooms* ⚹ *No meals.*

⭐ Los Altos de Eros Luxury Inn & Spa

$$$$ | **HOTEL** | This intimate adults-only inn is the place to be for honeymooning couples with enough money left over after the wedding to pamper themselves, or for stressed-out high achievers in need of some serious relaxation therapy. **Pros:** secluded location; excellent service, including the outstanding spa; complimentary transportation for hotel guests to Tamarindo and Avellanas 6:30–8:30. **Cons:** scheduled mealtimes; no kids under 18; difficult to find. $ *Rooms from: $330* ✉ *14 km (8½ miles) southeast of Tamarindo, Cañafistula* ☎ *8850–4203* ⊕ *www.losaltosdeeros.com* ⇝ *6 rooms* ⚹ *Free Breakfast.*

A Surf Classic

Americans—surfer Americans, at least—got their first look at Playa Negra in 1994's *The Endless Summer II*, a film by legendary surf documentarian Bruce Brown.

🏃 Activities

SURFING

Locals claim there are eight breaks here when the swell is big, which means Avellanas doesn't suffer the kind of overcrowding as the breaks at Playas Negra and Langosta. Tamarindo-based surf schools can arrange day trips here.

Cabinas Las Olas

SURFING | You can rent boards at Cabinas Las Olas for $20 a day. ✉ *Main road, on right* ☎ *2652–9315.*

Playa Negra

3 km (2 miles) south of Playa Avellanas.

Surfer culture is apparent here in the wave of beach-shack surfer camps along the road that leads to the rocky strand of beach. But Playa Negra is growing up fast, with some interesting cafés and restaurants popping up to cater to beachgoers and residents of an upscale residential development called Rancho Playa Negra.

GETTING HERE AND AROUND

From Playa Avellanas, continue south 10 minutes on the rough beach road to Playa Negra. If it's rainy season and the road is too rough, you can approach along a slightly more civilized route from Santa Cruz. Drive 27 km (16½ miles) west, via Veintisiete de Abril, to Paraíso, then follow signs for Playa Negra for 4 km (2½ miles). Taxis are the easiest way to get around if you don't have a car; they cost about $40 from Tamarindo.

Beaches

Playa Negra

BEACH—SIGHT | Contrary to the name, the beach is not black, but rather beige with dark streaks. This is primarily a surfer's beach, so it's not great for swimming because it tends to have fast hollow waves and is lined with rocks. There is one calm, short stretch of clear sand to the south of the Playa Negra Hotel, and at low tide a large tidal pool forms there. The spindly buttonwood trees that edge the beach provide sparse shade. The dirt road to Playa Negra is always bumpy and muddy during rainy season, so drive with caution. Food and drink are served at Playa Negra Hotel's *palapa* restaurant on the beach. **Amenities:** food and drink; parking (no fee). **Best for:** surfing; walking. ✉ *Playa Negra.*

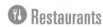

Restaurants

Café Playa Negra

$$ | **PERUVIAN** | This surf café features such Peruvian specialties as ceviche and *causa* (cold mashed potatoes studded with shrimp and tuna chunks). The menu also includes mahimahi prepared five different ways, and a few familiar favorites like hamburgers and BLTs. **Known for:** ceviche and sushi; pisco sour cocktails; beautiful presentation. $ *Average main: $12* ✉ *Main street* ☎ *2652–9351* 🌐 *www.cafeplayanegra.com* 🕒 *Closed Tues. and Oct.*

Kon-Tiki

$$ | **ITALIAN** | A favorite local hangout, this rustic pizzeria has an outdoor clay oven and an open kitchen. There are 14 types of pizza, like the house special with goat cheese, pesto, and caramelized onions. **Known for:** amazing crispy crust; busy atmosphere; sangria. $ *Average main: $14* ✉ *700 m after soccer field at Los Pargos* ☎ *2652–9117* 🌐 *www.facebook.com/kontikiplayanegra/* 🕒 *Closed Mon. No lunch.*

★ **Restaurant Deevena**

$$$ | **FRENCH FUSION** | An unexpected outpost of divine French cuisine, this oasis of elegance overlooks a sparkling blue pool edged by lush palms, while lounge chairs shaded by orange umbrellas tempt diners to stay overnight (six stylish rooms are available). Lunch and dinner feature lots of local seafood, produce, and goat cheese from the chef's nearby farm. **Known for:** tantalizing pasta, steak, and seafood prepared in a French style; volcano dessert with chocolate lava; fresh catch of the day. $ *Average main: $24* ✉ *25 m off main road that runs through Playa Negra; watch for Villa Deevena sign* ☎ *2653–2328* 🌐 *www.villadeevena.com* 🕒 *Closed Mon. and Sept.–Oct.*

Hotels

Hotel Playa Negra

$$ | **HOTEL** | Pastel-color, round cabinas are sprinkled across sunny lawns strewn with tropical plants at this gorgeous oceanfront place with a huge round pool. **Pros:** in front of reef break; comfortable accommodation; family suites available. **Cons:** not a great swimming beach; rocky road to hotel; some rooms lack a/c and Wi-Fi. $ *Rooms from: $120* ✉ *4 km (2½ miles) northwest of Paraíso on dirt road (watch signs for Playa Negra), then follow signs carefully at forks in road; or 10 mins south of Playa Avellanas on beach road* ☎ *2652–9134* 🌐 *playanegra.com* 🕒 *Restaurant closed Sept. and Oct.* 🛏 *17 units* 🍴 *No meals.*

Villa Deevena

$$ | **HOTEL** | Although most travelers visit this out-of-the-way spot for its famed French restaurant by the same name, Deevena is equally gaining renown for its hospitable staff and elegant rooms that surround a pool. **Pros:** excellent restaurant; saltwater pool; family-run business. **Cons:** outdoor showers attract bugs; not on the beach; breakfast not included. $ *Rooms from: $110* ✉ *25 m off main road that runs through Playa Negra;*

watch for Villa Deevena sign ☎ *2653–2328* ⊕ *www.villadeevena.com* ☉ *Closed Sept. and Oct.* ⊷ *6 rooms* ❑ *No meals.*

Activities

SURFING

Surfers dig the waves here, which are almost all rights, with beautifully shaped barrels. It's a spectacular, but treacherous, rock-reef break for experienced surfers only. There's also a small beach break to the south of the rocks where neophytes can cut their teeth. Both breaks can be ridden from mid- to high tide.

Hotel Playa Negra

SURFING | The point break is right in front of the only beachfront hotel, which can arrange surfing classes ($40 per hour for a private lesson) and rent boards ($20 per day). ⊠ *4 km (2½ miles) northwest of Paraíso on dirt road, then follow signs carefully at forks in road; or 10 mins south of Playa Avellanas on rough beach road* ☎ *2652–9298* ⊕ *playanegra.com* ⊡ *From $40.*

Playa Junquillal

4 km (2½ miles) south of Paraíso, 34 km (22 miles) southwest of Santa Cruz.

Seekers of oceanfront tranquility need look no further than Junquillal (pronounced *hoon-key-YALL*), a beach town as far away from the crowd as you can get on a decent road. A surprisingly cosmopolitan mélange of expats has settled in this out-of-the-way area. There's a supermarket at the entrance to an upscale housing development, but Junquillal is still barely on the tourist map; consequently its few hotels offer some of the best deals on the North Pacific coast. Avoid visiting between September and November, when hotels close, beaches are empty, and Junquillal virtually turns into a ghost town.

GETTING HERE AND AROUND

In rainy season, the 4-km-long (2½-mile-long) beach road from Playa Negra to Playa Junquillal is sometimes not passable. The alternative is driving down from Santa Cruz one hour on a road that's paved most of the way. The Castillos bus company runs a bus to Junquillal from the central market in Santa Cruz four times a day (at 5 and 10 am, and 2:30 and 5:30 pm); the trip takes about 40 minutes. A taxi from Santa Cruz or Tamarindo costs about $50; from the Liberia airport, $95 to $100.

ESSENTIALS

The closest town for most services is Santa Cruz, 34 km (22 miles) northeast.

Beaches

Playa Junquillal

BEACH—SIGHT | **FAMILY** | This wide swath of light-brown sand stretches over 3 km (2 miles), with coconut palms lining much of it and hardly a building in sight. Two species of sea turtle nest here, and a group of young people collect and protect their eggs, releasing the baby turtles after sunset. The surf is a little strong, so watch children carefully. There's a kids' playground right at the beach, and a funky little restaurant with concrete tables amid the palms. At low tide, it's a perfect beach for taking long, romantic strolls or for exploring active tide pools. Surfers head here to ride the beach break near Junquillal's northern end because it rarely gets crowded. **Amenities:** food and drink. **Best for:** surfing; walking. ⊠ *Playa Junquillal.*

Hotels

★ Guacamaya Lodge

$$ | **HOTEL** | **FAMILY** | Spread across a breezy hill with expansive views above the treetops of the surrounding forest and the sea, the Guacamaya is a real find, with affordable, spacious cabinas surrounding a generous-size pool, lawn, and tropical plants. **Pros:** excellent value; clean; friendly. **Cons:** hilly five-minute walk to the beach; meals and taxes not included in rate; some rooms may need updating. [$] *Rooms from: $75* ✉ *275 m east of Playa Junquillal* ☎ *2658–8431* 🌐 *www.guacamayalodge.com* 🕒 *Closed Sept. and Oct.* 🛏 *12 units* 🍴 *No meals.*

Mundo Milo Eco Lodge

$$ | **B&B/INN** | This hidden ecolodge with a kidney-shape pool is made up of five bungalows themed after Africa, Persia, and Mexico. **Pros:** 300 meters from the beach; great value; delicious food at restaurant. **Cons:** ecolodge equals natural, so there may be some bugs; closed September and October; bumpy road. [$] *Rooms from: $77* ✉ *C. Mundo Milo, 300 m from beach* ☎ *2658–7010* 🌐 *www.mundomilo.com* 💳 *No credit cards* 🕒 *Closed Sept. and Oct.* 🛏 *6 units* 🍴 *Free Breakfast.*

Chapter 8

THE NICOYA PENINSULA

8

Updated by
Rachel White

 Sights
★★★★☆

 Restaurants
★★★☆☆

 Hotels
★★★★☆

 Shopping
★★★☆☆

 Nightlife
★★★★☆

WELCOME TO THE NICOYA PENINSULA

TOP REASONS TO GO

★ **Beaches:** Whether you enjoy hidden coves or popular spots to share a sunset with new friends, there is a beach for you here.

★ **Flora and Fauna:** From sea turtles and howler monkeys to caves and deciduous forest, nature abounds.

★ **Laid-back vibes:** Life moves a little slower here, so expect to linger over dinners and endless beach days. It's the *pura vida* everyone keeps talking about.

★ **Yoga:** Now a major wellness destination, the Nicoya Peninsula has yoga on seemingly every corner (and monkeys leaning in to watch your savasana).

★ **Surfing:** There are gentle beach breaks and overhead swells and barrels; the consistent waves of the Nicoya Peninsula are ideal for experts and newbies alike.

Lively beach towns dot the coast of the Nicoya Peninsula from Nosara down to Playa Tambor, at the southern tip. In the south, communities are small and quiet, with a funky, European vibe. National parks Palo Verde and Barra Honda are the main attractions in the interior of the peninsula. The former is a prime bird-watching park; the latter has caves and waterfalls to explore.

1 Nosara. Despite its growth, this surf and yoga haven retains its sleepy, offbeat feel.

2 Sámara. Popular beach bars and an array of restaurants make this a lovely little international beach community.

3 Playa Carrillo. Long, reef-protected crescent beach backed by swaying coconut palms and sheltering cliffs.

4 Punta Islita. One of the few places aside from the capital with art, Punta Islita also has a beautiful rocky beach and a tiny tuft of land that becomes an island at high tide.

5 Palo Verde National Park. A hot, dry deciduous forest that is decidedly not lush, but is home to deer, monkeys, peccaries, lizards, and thousands of waterfowl.

6 Barra Honda National Park. A massive peak with hiking trails leading to dazzling vistas and beneath which lurks an labyrinth of caves to be explored.

7 Curú National Wildlife Refuge. This private refuge has some of the best wildlife viewing opportunities on the Nicoya Peninsula, a pristine beach, and cool bioluminescent kayaking tours.

8 Playa Tambor Area. One of the lesser developed group of beaches and towns on the peninsula, perfect for solitary relaxing and soaking up the sun.

9 Isla Tortuga. A lavish and impressive, if somewhat crowded, island oasis; a quick boat ride away from Playa Tambor or Montezuma.

10 Montezuma. An artsy, eccentric beach community beautifully positioned on a sandy bay that has avoided overdevelopment.

11 Malpaís and Santa Teresa. Small-town surfers' paradise with a stretch of hotels, restaurants, and shopping centers lining a sometimes sandy and sometimes rocky beach filled with wave seekers.

PALO VERDE NATIONAL PARK

Horseback riding in Palo Verde

One of the best wildlife- and bird-watching parks in the country, Palo Verde extends over 198 square km (76 square miles) of dry deciduous forest, bordered on the west by the wide Tempisque River.

With fairly flat terrain and less density than a rain forest, wildlife is often easier to spot here. Frequent sightings include monkeys, coatis, peccaries, lizards, and snakes. Keep an eye out for the harlequin snake. It's nonpoisonous but its coloring mimics the deadly coral snake.

The park contains seasonal wetlands at the end of the rainy season that provide a temporary home for migratory and resident aquatic birds, including herons, wood storks, jabirus, and flamingo-like roseate spoonbills. Crocodiles can be spotted in the waters of the Tempisque River year-round, and storks nest on islands at the mouth of the river where it empties into the Gulf of Nicoya. Trails are well marked, but the weather here can be very hot and windy. Mosquitoes, especially in the marshy areas, are rampant during the wet season (May–December). *(For more information, see the review in this chapter.)*

BEST TIME TO GO

The best time of year to visit is at the beginning of the dry season, especially in January and February, when the seasonal wetlands are shrinking and birds and wildlife are concentrated around smaller ponds. During the month of April, the wetlands are completely dry.

FUN FACT

The park is named after the light-green palo verde bush, also known as the Jerusalem thorn. Even when it loses its leaves, this tree can still photosynthesize through its trunk.

BEST WAYS TO EXPLORE

BIRD-WATCHING

The greatest number of wildlife species you're likely to see here are birds, close to 300 recorded species. Many of them are aquatic birds drawn to the park's vast marshes and seasonal wetlands. The most sought-after aquatic bird is the jabiru stork, a huge white bird with a red neck and long black bill. You may well spot it soaring overhead—it's hard to miss. Palo Verde and surrounding areas are the most important breeding sites for this species.

PARK STRATEGIES

Unlike many of the other national parks, you can drive 7 km (4½ miles) of fairly rough road from the park entrance to the Organization for Tropical Studies (OTS) research station, where most of the trailheads begin. From that point, the best way to see the park is on foot. Plan to spend a couple of nights in the dormitory-style park lodge so that you can get an early-morning start. You'll want to get out early because this is a very, very hot area. Hike open areas in the cooler mornings and then choose shaded forest trails for hikes later in the day. Make sure you have a good sun hat, too.

RIVER CRUISE

A river does run through the park, so a delightful and less strenuous wildlife-viewing option is to cruise down the Tempisque River on a chartered boat with a guide who'll do the spotting for you. Without a boat, you are limited to observing the marshy areas and riverbanks from a long distance. Be sure the boat you choose has a bilingual naturalist on board who knows the English names of birds and animals. River cruises are by reservation only, which can be arranged through the OTS research station.

Wildlife abounds in Palo Verde.

TOP REASONS TO GO

BIRDS, BIRDS, BIRDS

Even if you're not used to looking at birds, you'll be impressed by the waves of migratory waterbirds that use this park as a way station on their routes. Think of the 2001 documentary *Winged Migration* and you'll have an idea of the number of birds that flock here.

LOTS OF WILD ANIMALS

Hiking the forest trails is hot work, especially in the dry season. But the wildlife viewing here makes it worthwhile. Watch for monkeys, peccaries, spiny tailed iguanas, and coatis. Take plenty of water, and use insect repellent or wear long sleeves and pants.

OUTDOOR ADVENTURES

The Organization for Tropical Studies has a number of activities to choose from, including guided nature walks, mountain biking, boat tours, and even an occasional nighttime tour. The park service offers bunk-bed lodging without air-conditioning.

On this quirky peninsula south of Tamarindo, you'll find the interesting anomaly of a trendy restaurant or upscale hotel plunked at the end of a tortuous dirt road. The key to enjoying the Nicoya Peninsula is to pick your spot—happening beach town or off-the-beaten-path seclusion.

The parks and wildlife refuges in and around the Río Tempisque are prime places to hike, explore caves, and spot birds and other wildlife. And there's a smattering of culture, too, in the town of Nicoya, with its colonial-era church, and in Guaitil, with pottery made in the pre-Columbian Chorotega tradition.

The town of Nicoya is the commercial and political hub of the northern Nicoya Peninsula. By road, Nicoya provides the best access to Sámara, Nosara, and points south and north, and is linked by a smooth, well-paved road to the northern Nicoya beach towns.

The southern tip of the Nicoya Peninsula is one of Costa Rica's less developed regions, where some of the country's most gorgeous beaches, rain forests, waterfalls, and tidal pools lie at the end of some of its worst roads. Within the region are quiet, well-preserved parks where you can explore pristine forests or travel by boat or sea kayak to idyllic islands for bird-watching or snorkeling. Other outdoor options include horseback riding, gliding through the treetops on a canopy tour, or surfing on some of the country's most consistent waves. In the laid-back beach towns of Montezuma, Santa Teresa, and Malpaís, an international cast of surfers, nature lovers, yoga enthusiasts, holistic new-agers, and expatriate massage therapists live out their dreams in paradise.

Planning

When to Go

HIGH SEASON: MID-DECEMBER TO APRIL
The driest and hottest time of the year, with average temperatures hovering between 86°F and 95°F, this is the time to come if you're looking to soak up some sun with nary a raindrop in sight. The beaches and parks are the busiest this time of year, especially when school is out for Costa Ricans, mid-December to February. With the new year in January come the Papagayo winds, bringing lots of gusts, especially along the coast. These breezes usually die down by mid-February. This is the best period for snorkeling, whale-watching, and fishing. The landscape isn't at its most resplendent during this time—much of the green gives way to brown.

LOW SEASON: MAY THROUGH OCTOBER

Although the mornings are usually clear, pretty much every afternoon during low (rainy) season brings showers. These rains are accompanied by smaller crowds, lush green landscapes, and more affordable accommodations. Some roads become impassable during this time, making alternate (longer) routes neccessary.

SHOULDER SEASON: NOVEMBER TO MID-DECEMBER

Shoulder season, verdant and lush, is the best time to visit the Nicoya Peninsula. Smaller crowds and reasonable temperatures make getting around more pleasant, while hotels and restaurants are ready for guests.

PLANNING YOUR TIME

Each little beach town on the peninsula has its own flavor, so it's nice to be able to stay in more than one place. With that said, the roads here are tough going, so schedule driving time into your plans. "As the crow flies" is rare here, so expect bumpy, winding dirt roads. Plan to spend at least a week on the peninsula. Split your time between beach activities like surf lessons, snorkeling, and turtle and whale watching, in addition to land explorations of the caves and other parks. Whatever you do, don't forget to lounge.

Getting Here and Around

AIR

Aeropuerto Internacional Daniel Oduber Quirós (LIR) in Liberia is an international gateway to the coast, with a large, air-conditioned terminal. Tamarindo, Nosara, Playa Sámara, and Punta Islita also have small airstrips. Flying from San José to these airports is the best way to get here if you are already in the country. If your primary destination lies in Nicoya, make sure you investigate the possibility of flying directly into Liberia instead of San José, which saves some serious hours on the road.

Many airlines have direct service from major hubs to Costa Rica's two international airports in San José and Liberia. SANSA and Aerobell have scheduled flights between San José and Liberia, as well as destinations on the Nicoya Peninsula. Don't forget to factor in the exit tax, $29 by air and $7 by land, payable in U.S. dollars, colones, or by credit card. Some airlines include this fee in the ticket price.

CAR

You will want to rent a four-wheel-drive vehicle to drive around the peninsula. Waze is the best driving app in Costa Rica—download it before you come for updated road conditions and accurate driving directions. The roads get muddy and full of potholes during rainy season, and they can be dusty and bumpy in the dry season. Depending on whether you look at this as an adventure or an agony, you will either love the trip or wish you had flown the national airlines. Highway 150, which runs from Nicoya to Sámara is smooth sailing all the way. The same applies to Route 21 from Liberia to the southern Nicoya Peninsula. Route 160 to reach Montezuma and Malpaís takes you a bit off the beaten path, with some gravel, dirt, and river crossings, where it's easy to get stuck in the mud when conditions are wet. The road from Tamarindo south to Nosara has some major river crossings and is not advised during rainy season.

FERRY

If you're headed to the southern Nicoya Peninsula (Curú, Tambor, Montezuma, Malpaís, or Santa Teresa), the ferry ride from Puntarenas to Paquera across the Gulf of Nicoya is not only the fastest route, it's also the most scenic, with great views of the mountainous coast and islands.

Restaurants

The varied and wonderful restaurants of the peninsula, many with tables in the sand, ocean waves in the background, and twinkling lights strung overhead, rival any in Costa Rica. In many of the areas where more Europeans have settled, like Sámara and Malpaís, you will find French and Italian restaurants with homemade pasta and from-scratch sauces. Don't rule out the healthy fare at wellness destinations—dishes are often innovative and enticing.

■ TIP→ **Many restaurants, especially tourist-oriented ones with dollar-denominated menus, do not include the 13% national sales tax plus mandatory 10%–12% service. By law, menus are required to show the total price including tax, but many owners flout this law. Be sure to ask if taxes are included; otherwise you may be surprised by a bill that's 25% higher than you expected.**

Hotels

The hotels on the Nicoya Peninsula range from boutiques perched on mountainsides to cabinas in the jungle where you can wake up to howler monkeys to all-inclusive beach resorts. No matter your choice, you will always get the best hospitality from the eager-to-please independently owned lodging. Hotel owners are generally folks who have come here and fallen in love with the place, so they can usually give you the best tips on hidden waterfalls, good-natured guides, and where to spot the monkeys. *Hotel reviews have been shortened. For full information, visit Fodors.com.*

WHAT IT COSTS in U.S. Dollars			
$	**$$**	**$$$**	**$$$$**
RESTAURANTS			
under $10	$10–$15	$16–$25	over $25
HOTELS			
under $75	$75–$150	$151–$250	over $250

Tours

Horizontes Nature Tours

ADVENTURE TOURS | With a focus on nature and adventure, Horizontes has independent, private tours with your own guide and driver as well as small-group tours. Customized tours are available for bird-watchers, families, couples, yogis, and beachgoers. Average tours are six nights. ☎ 4052–5850, 888/786–8748 toll-free in U.S. ⊕ www.horizontes.com ✉ From $1,440 per person.

Nosara

28 km (17 miles) southwest of Nicoya.

One of the last beach communities for people who want to get away from it all, Nosara's attractions are the wild stretches of side-by-side beaches called Pelada and Guiones, with surfing waves and miles of sand on which to stroll, and the tropical dry forest that covers much of the hinterland. While it is becoming one of the most popular destinations in Costa Rica, it somehow manages to feel as if you've discovered your own tropical paradise (nice, after you finally arrive from the bumpy, dusty dirt road). Regulations here limit development to low-rise buildings 600 feet from the beach, where they are thankfully screened by trees. Americans and Europeans, with a large Swiss contingent, are building at an increasingly rapid pace. There still appears to be an aesthetic sense here that is totally lacking in Guanacaste's Tamarindo, despite a plethora of trendy juice bars, fast-food taco stands, and souvenir stalls cropping up at the beach entrances. Offsetting the fast-food wave are the two organic farmers' markets in town, Sunday 9 to 2 and Tuesday starting at 8 am, in the Esquinas Skate Park next to the police station. Hotel owners and community members are participating in a reforestation project along the beachfront to create a lusher biological corridor and the results are beautifully evident already. The town of Nosara itself is inland and not very attractive, but it does have essential services, as well as the airplane landing strip. Almost all the tourist action is at the beaches.

For years, most travelers headed here for the surf. The wide range of surf schools and waves varying from beginner to expert levels make Nosara one of the best places to learn to surf. Along with surfing, the Nosara Yoga Institute, which offers instructor training and daily classes for all levels, is a major draw for health-conscious visitors. Healthy food options, spas, and exercise classes abound. You'll see lots of yoga practitioners on the beaches around sunrise and sunset.

Bird-watchers and other nature enthusiasts can explore the tropical dry forest on hiking trails, on horseback, or by floating up the tree-lined Nosara River in a kayak, guide boat, or paddleboard. The last leg of the access road to Nosara, from either direction, is still abysmal, and the labyrinth of woodsy roads around the beaches and hard-to-read signs make it easy to get lost, which is why most hotels here provide local maps for their guests. Don't get in your car without one—especially at night. For local news and tourist information, pick up a free copy of the excellent monthly bilingual newspaper *The Voice of Guanacaste* (⊕ *www.vozdeguanacaste. com*).

GETTING HERE AND AROUND

From Liberia, it's about a three-hour drive to Playa Guiones, the beach in Nosara. Take Route 21 south all the way to Nicoya. While on a map the beach drive may look more desirable, in practice, it is infinitely longer and dustier. From Nicoya drive south, almost to Sámara, but take the very first road sign for Nosara, 1 km (½ mile) south of the big gas station before Sámara. This high road is rough for about 8 km (5 miles), but there are bridges over all the river crossings. When you join up with the beach road near Garza, you still have a very bumpy 10 km (6 miles) to go. The roads into Nosara are in really bad shape, so a 4WD vehicle is definitely recommended. Budget about one hour for the trip from Nicoya. On the bright side, the main road above the beaches has finally been paved, cutting down on the choking dust in dry season. But all the dirt side roads to the beaches are still either dust bowls or mired in mud. The more remote the area, the more likely that someone will stop to help you change a tire or tow you out of a river. Usually, Good Samaritans won't accept any payment and are more trustworthy than those who offer to "help" in the States.

Coming from San José, you can fly directly to the town of Nosara on daily scheduled SANSA and Aerobell flights, or take an air-conditioned shuttle van from San José. To book flights you need to go directly to the airline's website. Major rent-a-car companies have offices in Playa Guiones.

RENTAL CARS Alamo/National. ✉ *Playa Guiones road next to Café de Paris* ☎ *2682–0894.* **Economy.** ✉ *Below Marlin Bill's Restaurant, at intersection of main road and Playa Guiones road* ☎ *2682–1146.*

AIRLINES Aerobell Airlines. ✉ *Nosara Airport* ☎ *4000–2030* ⊕ *www.aerobell. com.* **Sansa Airlines.** ✉ *Nosara Airport* ☎ *2290–4100* ⊕ *flysansa.com.*

ESSENTIALS
BANKS/ATMS Banco de Costa Rica.
✉ *Next to Servicentro Nosara gas station, main road* ☎ *2682–5232.* **Banco Popular.** ✉ *Main St., next door to Café de Paris, Playa Guiones* ☎ *2682–0011.*

HOSPITAL Centro Médico Nosara. ✉ *Next door to Mandala shop, 100 m west of Café de Paris, on road to Playa Guiones* ☎ *2682–1212.*

PHARMACY Farmacia Nosara. ✉ *In town, on right side of airstrip* ☎ *2682–5149.*

POST OFFICE Correo. ✉ *Next to soccer field in town* ☎ *2682–0100* ⊕ *correos. go.cr.*

 Sights

⭐ **Ostional National Wildlife Refuge** (*Refugio Nacional de Fauna Silvestre Ostional*)
NATURE PRESERVE | FAMILY | This wildlife refuge protects one of Costa Rica's major nesting beaches for olive ridley turtles. If you get to go when the turtles are hatching, it is a magical experience. Locals have formed an association to run the reserve on a cooperative basis, and during the first 36 hours of the *arribadas* (mass nesting) they are allowed to harvest the eggs, on the premise that eggs laid during this time would likely be destroyed by subsequent waves of mother turtles. Though turtles nest here year-round, the largest arribadas, with thousands of turtles nesting over the course of several nights, occur from July to December; smaller arribadas take place between January and May. They usually occur around high tide, the week of a new moon. It's best to go very early in the morning, at sunrise. People in Nosara can tell you when an arribada has begun, or check the Facebook page *Asociacion de Guias Locales de Ostional (AGLO) Costa Rica.* To avoid overcrowding on the beach, visitors must join a guide-led tour of the nesting and hatching areas for $10 per person. Stop at the kiosk at the entrance to the beach to arrange a tour,

or at the Association of Guides office, 25 meters south of the beach entrance on the main road, next to Cabinas Ostional. A new bridge over the Río Montaña has made access easier from Nosara, but it's sometimes difficult to get to from the north during rainy season (May to mid-December). ✉ *7 km (4½ miles) north of Nosara* ☎ *2682–0428* 🖾 *$10.*

 Beaches

⭐ **Playa Guiones**
BEACH—SIGHT | This beach is one of the natural wonders of Costa Rica: a wide expanse of light-brown sand, sandwiched between rolling surf and green sea-grape vines starting at the high-tide mark and backed by rejuvenating secondary forest. With some of the most consistent surf on the Pacific coast, Playa Guiones attracts a lot of surfboard-toting visitors, but the always-breezy beach is also a haven for sun lovers, beachcombers, and anyone who wants to connect with nature. The only building in sight is the bizarre Hotel Nosara, which was originally the only choice for lodging in town but is now one of many. Otherwise, this glorious Blue Flag beach has 7 km (4½ miles) of hard-packed sand, great for jogging, riding bikes, and saluting the sun. Because there's a 10-foot tide, the beach is expansive at low tide but rather narrow at high tide, when waves usually create strong currents that can make the sea dangerous for nonsurfers. Most hotels post tide charts. Guiones is at the south end of the Nosara agglomeration, with three public accesses. The easiest one to find is about 300 meters past the Harmony Hotel, beyond the parked ATVs and souvenir stalls. **Amenities:** none. **Best for:** surfing; walking. ✉ *Playa Guiones.*

Playa Pelada
BEACH—SIGHT | North along the shore, Playa Guiones segues seamlessly into crescent-shape Playa Pelada, where the water is a little calmer and just as clean, also designated a Blue Flag beach. There

are tide pools to explore and a blowhole that sends water shooting up when the surf is big. Lots of trees provide shade. This is the locals' favorite vantage point for watching sunsets—great photo ops, with beached fishing boats adding color and interest to the foreground. Olga's Beach Club bar is nothing fancy, but it's a good place for a cool beer and fried red snapper. More upscale and romantic are the cushioned settees in front of La Luna Bar & Grill, on a slight rise overlooking the beach. **Amenities:** food and drink. **Best for:** sunset; surfing; swimming. ⊠ *Playa Pelada.*

🍴 Restaurants

Café de Paris
$$ | ECLECTIC | FAMILY | Vestiges of the original Swiss-French owners linger on at this bakery and alfresco eatery, open for breakfast and lunch. In addition to hearty sandwiches, the café serves burgers and salads. **Known for:** lunch with a dip in the pool; bakery goodies like baguettes, tarts, and pastries; coffee and espresso. $ *Average main: $12* ⊠ *Main road, at Playa Guiones entrance* ☎ *2682–1036* ☾ *Café closed Sun. No dinner.*

Destiny Café & Restaurant
$$ | AMERICAN | A feast for the senses, this plant-filled haven has coffee, smoothies, and food that look lovely and taste delicious. Whether you order the impeccably presented "Eggs Nest" (sous vide eggs in a nest of crispy, fried sweet potatoes) or the art-topped green matcha latte, having an enjoyable meal here is practically kismet. **Known for:** fresh salads, poke bowls, and brunch food like truffle avo toast; outdoor garden setting; thirst quenchers like the blue majik (spirulina) smoothie. $ *Average main: $12* ⊠ *Playa Guiones Norte, The Courtyard of The Living Hotel* ☎ *8708–0129* ⊕ *www. facebook.com/Destinynosara.cr.*

★ El Chivo Cantina
$$ | MEXICAN | FAMILY | With an atmosphere as fun and funky as the *luchadora* (Mexican wrestler) legend for which it's named, everyone will have a great time and an even better meal at this Mexican cantina. A large garden strung with lights beckons to families, and the long bar is a great place to try some churros after your meal. **Known for:** gorgeous garden with kids' playground; Taco Tuesday specials; jalapeño margaritas. $ *Average main: $15* ⊠ *Road to Playa Pelada* ☎ *2682–0887* ⊕ *www.elchivo.co.*

Il Peperoni
$$ | ITALIAN | FAMILY | Head to this spot for the biggest pizzas in town in a large, roofed-over garden near Playa Pelada. The house pizza is thin crust with carrots, broccoli, olives, red peppers, onions, mushrooms, ham, and pepperoni. **Known for:** wood-fired brick-oven pizzas; spicy dipping oil; family-friendly setting. $ *Average main: $15* ⊠ *Across from Condominios Las Flores, road to Playa Pelada* ☎ *2682–0545.*

★ La Luna Bar & Grill
$$$ | MEDITERRANEAN | FAMILY | Dawn to dusk, this casually chic restaurant overlooking Playa Pelada is the most scenic place to have breakfast, lunch, cocktails, or dinner, with tables spilling out of the interior onto a wide, covered terrace and onto the sand. The menu is mostly Mediterranean, ranging from Moroccan-spiced or limoncello-marinated fish of the day, to beef or fish carpaccio and brick oven–fired pizzas. **Known for:** crispy-crust pizza; Mediterranean platter with hummus and tzatziki; spectacular sunsets. $ *Average main: $16* ⊠ *Playa Pelada, overlooking beach* ☎ *2682–0122.*

Marlin Bill's
$$ | AMERICAN | FAMILY | Carnivores can sink their teeth into a 22-ounce bone-in, rib-eye steak or 16-ounce pork chops in American-size portions at this open-air restaurant with a great sunset view. Lighter choices include grilled fish and

salads, eggplant Parmesan, homemade spinach-and-ricotta ravioli in marinara sauce, and delicious "dorado fingers" (battered fish-fillet strips served with tartar sauce). **Known for:** craft beer on tap; key lime pie; margaritas and rum-based drinks. $ *Average main: $14* ⊠ *Hilltop above main road, near Coconut Harry's Surf Shop* ☎ 2682–0458 ⊙ *Closed Sun.*

Robin's Cafe & Ice Cream

$ | **VEGETARIAN** | **FAMILY** | Robin's is famous for homemade ice cream in an array of tempting flavors—the Mayan Chocolate is a standout—along with refreshing tropical-fruit sorbets. This casual patio café also serves breakfast all day and lunch and dinner options like overstuffed veggie quesadillas, pad thai rolls, and yummy vegan veggie burgers. **Known for:** tasty sandwiches on home-baked bread; gluten-free options; fudgy brownies. $ *Average main: $9* ⊠ *Road to Playa Guiones, 25 m west of Banco Popular* ☎ 2682–0617 ⊟ *No credit cards* ⊙ *No dinner.*

 Hotels

★ The Bodhi Tree Yoga Resort

$$ | **RESORT** | With three pools, a spa, and luxurious rooms, there's more to this resort than just yoga. **Pros:** lush grounds and beautiful rooms; first-rate yoga classes; range of accommodations for every budget. **Cons:** lots of stairs; not right on beach; dormitory-style rooms lack privacy. $ *Rooms from: $95* ⊠ *Bodhi Street* ☎ 2682-0256 ⊕ *bodhitreeyogaresort.com* ☝ 42 rooms ⦿ Free Breakfast; All-inclusive.

Casa Romántica Hotel

$$ | **B&B/INN** | Calm, tranquil, and close to the beach, this hotel's name (Romantic House) says it all: the Spanish colonial–style house has an upstairs veranda and a graceful arcade with views of a crystal-blue kidney-shape pool surrounded by a glorious tropical garden. **Pros:** very close to beach; good restaurant;

good value. **Cons:** rooms comfortable but not spectacular; usually quiet but children can make the pool area noisy at times; often full. $ *Rooms from: $110* ⊠ *200 m southwest of Gilded Iguana* ☎ 2682–0272 ⊕ *www.casa-romantica.net* ☝ 13 units ⦿ Free Breakfast.

The Gilded Iguana Surf Hotel

$$$ | **HOTEL** | **FAMILY** | This lively hotel-bar-restaurant has been a Nosara fixture for more than 25 years and has a chic, modern aesthetic. **Pros:** upscale and modern; fun and lively swimming area; directly across from surf breaks, with surf club. **Cons:** slow service at restaurant; outdoor showers lack privacy; can feel crowded. $ *Rooms from: $179* ⊠ *Playa Guiones* ☎ 2682–0259 ⊕ *www.thegildediguana.com* ☝ 29 rooms ⦿ Free Breakfast.

★ The Harmony Hotel

$$$$ | **B&B/INN** | This ultracool, holistic retreat gets top marks for both comfort and sustainability, thanks to American owners who are surfers that believe comfort, quiet, and thinking ecologically are more appealing than partying. **Pros:** on beach; excellent food; aromatic, eco-friendly toiletries and natural repellent; one free yoga class per guest per stay. **Cons:** pricey; not overly kid-friendly but babies welcome; standard rooms are smallish. $ *Rooms from: $450* ⊠ *From Café de Paris, take road almost all the way to Playa Guiones, look for sign leading to tree-shaded parking lot on right* ☎ 2682–4114, 2682–1073 ⊕ *www.harmonynosara.com* ☝ 24 rooms ⦿ Free Breakfast.

★ Hotel Lagarta Lodge

$$$$ | **B&B/INN** | A birders' and nature-lovers' Valhalla, this magnificent nature lodge on a promontory has amazing views of the forest, river, and coast north of Nosara. **Pros:** amazing views and grounds; close to nature; sustainable. **Cons:** not on the beach; some steps to rooms; steep, rough road to get here. $ *Rooms from: $277* ⊠ *Top of hill at*

north end of Nosara ☎ 2682–0035 ⊕ www.lagartalodge.com ➳ 26 suites ⊙ No meals.

★ Luna Azul

$$$ | **B&B/INN** | Sequestered in the green hills above Playa Ostional, 8 km (5 miles) north of Nosara, tranquil, tasteful Luna Azul is full of clever design and healthful attributes, surrounded by a private nature reserve abounding with birds and wildlife. **Pros:** isolated in a picturesque environment; good restaurant; luxurious rooms; excellent breakfast; free Wi-Fi. **Cons:** getting here involves some rough roads; restaurant prices do not include tax and service; not near the beach. $ Rooms from: $170 ⊠ 1 km (½ mile) north of Ostional, 8 km (5 miles) north of Nosara ☎ 8821–0075, 2682–1400 ⊕ www.hotellunaazul.com ➳ 5 bungalows ⊙ Free Breakfast.

★ Olas Verdes Hotel

$$$$ | **HOTEL** | **FAMILY** | A private path through native jungle gets you to the beach at this welcoming hotel, which has a surf school and organic restaurant on-site. **Pros:** exemplary service; spacious rooms; highly rated surf school on-site and close to beach. **Cons:** small pool; rooms facing pool lack privacy; not in the center of the "action" in town (but a complimentary bike ride away). $ Rooms from: $265 ⊠ Playa Guiones ⊹ 500 m west and 300 m south of Café de Paris ☎ 2682–0608 ⊕ www.olasverdeshotel. com ➳ 17 suites ⊙ Free Breakfast.

Tierra Magnifica

$$ | **B&B/INN** | Perched on the mountainside with breathtaking ocean views, Tierra Maginifica has all the attentiveness and personalization of a boutique hotel and all the amenities of a resort. **Pros:** panoramic views; great restaurant that caters to personal needs; chic, clean minimalist aesthetic. **Cons:** not all rooms are same quality; some precipitous cliffs may not be suitable for young children; some people may not like the owners' pet dogs. $ Rooms from: $120 ⊠ Proyecto

Americano Las Huacas, Lote EE90 ☎ 2682–0270, 800/409–4760 from U.S. ⊕ www.tierramagnifica.com ➳ 9 rooms ⊙ Free Breakfast.

Nightlife

The Gilded Iguana

MUSIC CLUBS | Live acoustic music on Sunday night draws a big crowd. ⊠ Playa Guiones ☎ 2682–0259.

Olga's

BARS/PUBS | Sunset is the main event in the evening on Playa Pelada, and both locals and tourists gather to watch it here at this beach shack and bar with the best view. Olga's also serves an excellent fried whole red snapper. ⊠ End of the road to Playa Pelada.

Restaurante La Luna

CAFES—NIGHTLIFE | Sip an exotic tropical cocktail or munch on hummus and pita bread while watching the sun set at this lovely Mediterranean restaurant and bar, which has settees and rattan chairs set out on the sand, as well as seats in the chic new indoor lounge. You'll most likely need a reservation for sunset. ⊠ Beachfront, Playa Pelada ☎ 2682–0122.

Tropicana Discobar

BARS/PUBS | The popular Tropicana is where the Latin dance action is on Friday and Saturday nights, from 9:30 pm to 2:30 am, for locals who love to dance and visitors who want to salsa, too. ⊠ Downtown Nosara, beside the soccer field ☎ 2682–0140.

Shopping

Arte Guay

CRAFTS | This is the place to find the largest selection of local crafts and every imaginable souvenir, plus beachwear and sun hats. ⊠ Just past Café de Paris on road to Playa Guiones, right-hand side ☎ 2682–1406.

Love Nosara Store

GIFTS/SOUVENIRS | The owner and designer of this trendy open-air boutique invites you to take a piece of Nosara with you. All the high-quality items they sell are designed in house and consciously crafted in Costa Rica from fair-trade materials. Find T-shirts, beachwear, hats, bags, jewelry, and more. ⊠ *West of Cafe Paris.*

Mandala

SPECIALTY STORES | Yoga fans will swoon over the pretty yoga tops here, made of feather-light Peruvian pima cotton. There are also yoga pants and cool beachwear of the shop's own design. There's a selection of Birkenstock sandals, too. An array of aromatherapy potions makes the shop a pleasant place to be, along with the air-conditioning. Look for the large Buddha posed in front of the shop; open 9 to 5 daily. ⊠ *Playa Guiones road, beside Alamo car rental* ☎ *2682–1431.*

The Silver Tree

JEWELRY/ACCESSORIES | This elegant jewelry store is a cut above the usual souvenir shop, with beautiful handmade pieces from local artists as well as sophisticated resort wear. There are also unusual, high-quality handcrafted gifts, art, and one-of-a-kind curios, locally made and from around the world. ⊠ *2nd fl. in mini-mall beside Café de Paris, on Playa Guiones road* ☎ *2682–1422.*

Activities

TOUR OPERATORS

Experience Nosara

TOUR—SPORTS | For in-depth insights into the natural world, join a bilingual naturalist on a three-hour kayak or stand-up paddleboard tour along the Río Nosara ($65 per person), or on a leisurely hike to a hidden waterfall with swimming holes ($65 per person). Out on the ocean, the company offers surfing, and on the calmer side, two-hour stand-up paddleboard lessons and 2½- to 3-hour tours ($100); plus a five-hour snorkeling tour at Playa Juanillo, including coconut water and fruit ($75, minimum four people). ⊠ *Nosara* ☎ *8705–2010* ⊕ *www.experience-nosara. com.*

BIRD-WATCHING

Experience Nosara

BIRD WATCHING | Bilingual naturalist and ornithologist Allan Azofeifa leads serious birders on bird-watching tours, with an early-morning expedition on foot in the Nosara Biological Reserve or a kayak paddle upriver to catch sight of some of the 270 species recorded here. ⊠ *Nosara* ☎ *8705–2010* ⊕ *www.experience-nosara. com* 🔾 *$65, minimum two people.*

FISHING

Fishing Nosara

TOUR—SPORTS | This outfit can hook you up with local English-speaking captains who can take you fishing for 2½ hours, a half day, or full day, on boats ranging from 20 to 31 feet. The shop sells rods, lures, fishing shirts, hats, and souvenir T-shirts. ⊠ *In Paradise Rentals office on main road to Playa Guiones, Playa Guiones* ☎ *2682–0606* ⊕ *www.fishing-nosara.com* 🔾 *From $200 for 2½ hours to $900 for a full day on the largest, best-equipped boat.*

SPAS

Tica Massage

SPA/BEAUTY | Relaxing massages, facials, and salt glows in a jungle setting ($65 per hour) are available by appointment at Tica Massage. They accept cash only. ⊠ *Across from Harmony Hotel, Playa Guiones* ☎ *2682–0096* ⊕ *www.ticamassage. com.*

SURFING

Nosara has been called the best place in the world to learn how to surf, so if you've always wanted to try it, this is the place. Surf shops and surf schools are proliferating to satisfy the growing demand. Guiones is the perfect beginners' beach, with no rocks to worry about. Local surf instructors say that the waves here are so consistent that there's no week throughout the year when you won't be able to surf. Every year, the Costa Rica National Surfing Circuit comes here for surf trials.

Coconut Harry's Surf Shop

SURFING | This Nosara surfing institution on the main road has a store full of surfing gear, along with a new taco bar. Most of the surfing action has shifted to a convenient beach location 100 meters from the main Playa Guiones beach entrance. You'll find board rentals ($20 per day), gear, lessons ($55 for 1½ hours, board included, for a group of three; a private lesson is $75), and board storage. ⊠ Main road, across from Café de Paris ☎ 2682–1852 main road shop, 8602–1852 beach location ⊕ www.coconutharrys.com.

Nosara Surf Shop

SURFING | This large surf shop offers group lessons ($65 for 1½ hours), rents boards by the day ($15 to $20), and has lots of gear for sale, too. It also rents ATVs ($65 for the day). ⊠ 500 m west of Café de Paris, on road to Playa Guiones ☎ 2682–0186 ⊕ www.nosarasurfshop.com.

Safari Surf School

SURFING | This popular beachfront school, owned by a veteran surfer from Hawaii, is certified by the International Surfing Association. There are special packages for women, as well as a kids' surf camp. Most students come on package deals that include transportation and lodging at the school's brand-new Olas Verdes surfer lodge, with 17 spacious suites, an alfresco restaurant, and a swimming pool. A short trail through the woods leads straight to the beach and surfing breaks. You can also pay as you learn, $55 for a 1½-hour group lesson or $75 for a private lesson, surfboard included. ⊠ Olas Verdes, Guiones beach road, 300 m south of Harbor Reef Hotel, Playa Guiones ☎ 2682–0113 ⊕ www.safarisurfschool.com.

YOGA

★ Bodhi Tree Yoga Resort

AEROBICS/YOGA | Up to seven yoga classes are offered daily here, as well as spinning and Pilates. Stop into one of the juice bars after your class for a healthy treat. A free shuttle zips around town hourly, so you can hop on from your hotel and they will give you a ride back as well. ⊠ Bodhi St. ☎ 2682–0256 ⊕ bodhitreeyogaresort.com ⊠ From $10 for most classes, $20 for aerial yoga.

Harmony Hotel Healing Center

AEROBICS/YOGA | Close to Playa Guiones, the Harmony Hotel holds yoga classes daily. It also has a wide selection of New Age therapeutic massages and a full range of herbal spa services. ⊠ Playa Guiones road, near beach entrance ☎ 2682–4114 ⊕ www.harmonynosara.com ⊠ $15 per session.

Sámara

36 km (23 miles) southwest of Nicoya, 26 km (16 miles) south of Nosara.

Sámara has miles of palm-shaded beach, safe swimming water, and an abundance of budget accommodations and seafront restaurants, making it especially popular with budget travelers, both Tico and foreign. This can be a lively place on weekends, with beach bars and handicraft vendors setting up on the main drag. A sandy roadway with the occasional car runs alongside the coconut palms and Indian almond trees that line the beach, so be sure to look both ways when you move between the surf and the town. Like nearby Nosara, Sámara is becoming more nature- and health-conscious.

GETTING HERE AND AROUND

The drive from Nicoya to Sámara is one of the most scenic in Costa Rica, passing through rolling hills and green vistas before descending to the wide, south-facing bay hemmed by palm-lined sand. The road is paved all the way and takes about an hour. ■ **TIP→ Potholes are spreading, so drivers need to keep their eyes on the road instead of the beautiful views.** A rough beach road from Nosara is passable in dry season (it's more direct, but takes just as long); do not attempt this road when it rains. To get from Nosara to Sámara via the paved road, drive south 5 km (3 miles) past Garza. At the T in the road, ignore the road toward Sámara (the beach road) and take the road to the left, toward Nicoya. This will take you uphill to merge with the main Nicoya–Sámara highway. There are daily bus routes to Samara from San José ($8) and Nicoya ($2.50). For the latest bus schedule, look online at 🌐 *www.samara-beach.com.*

RENTAL CARS Alamo. ✉ *Main road into town, beside Hotel Samara Beach* ☎ *2656–0958.*

ESSENTIALS

BANKS/ATMS Banco de Costa Rica. ✉ *North side of soccer field, Downtown* ☎ *2656–2112.* **Banco Nacional.** ✉ *50 m west of Catholic church* ☎ *2656–0089.*

HOSPITAL Medical Center. ✉ *160 m east of Supermarket Palí Sámara* ☎ *2656–0992.*

PHARMACY Farmacia Sámara. ✉ *Main road at entrance to Sámara, next door to Miniplaza Patio Colonial* ☎ *2215–6093.*

POST OFFICE Correo. ✉ *Beside church, across from soccer field* 🌐 *correos.go.cr.*

Beaches

Playa Sámara

BEACH—SIGHT | This is the perfect hangout beach, with plenty of shade, bars, and seafront restaurants to take refuge in from the sun. Devoid of rip currents or big waves, it's also perfect for families with children. Its wide sweep of light-gray sand is framed by two forest-covered hills jutting out at either end. The waves break out on a reef that lines the entrance of the cove several hundred yards offshore, which keeps the water calm enough for safe swimming and leaves enough surf to have fun in. The reef holds plenty of marine attractions for diving and snorkeling excursions. Isla Chora, at the south end of the bay, provides a sheltered area that is especially popular with kayakers and snorkelers—it even has a tiny beach at lower tides. After years of hard work to clean up the beach, Sámara Beach now sports a Blue Flag. Those seeking solitude should head to the beach's western or eastern ends. **Amenities:** food and drink; water sports. **Best for:** snorkeling; surfing; swimming.

🍴 Restaurants

BoutiCafe Bohemia

$ | **CAFÉ** | **FAMILY** | Take a beach break and stop at this funky open-air café for a smoothie or espresso, and stay for a panini or avocado toast—just make sure to get here before the freshly baked bread runs out. The seats may be unconventional (think swings and couches) but the food is pure delight. **Known for:** spicy panini; "Bohemian" smoothie; strong coffee. [$] *Average main: $8* ✉ *In front of Sámara Natural Center* ☎ *8468–8007.*

Di Mare Di Vino

$$ | **ITALIAN** | **FAMILY** | An ample selection of good Italian food, including crispy pizzas, decadent pastas, generous salads, and a lengthy Italian wine list (available by the glass, too), makes this sidewalk trattoria a good spot for lunch or dinner. Tuna carpaccio is a lighter option, or try the *insalata caprese,* with fresh basil. **Known for:** poolside dining; seafood; tiramisu. [$] *Average main: $14* ✉ *Hotel Giada lobby, main road, 150 m north of beach* ☎ *2656–0848.*

El Lagarto Steakhouse and Seafood

$$$ | **BARBECUE** | El Lagarto serves up fresh, local seafood and high-quality meat, grilled to perfection on a massive, open-air, wood-fired barbecue. Sink your teeth into juicy tenderloin, lamb chops,

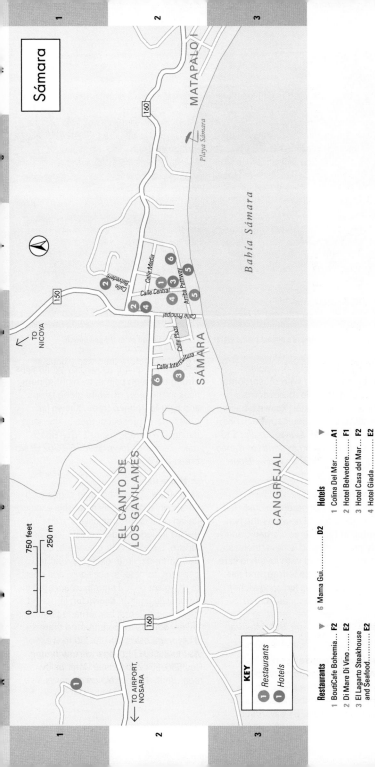

Sámara

Restaurants ▶

1 BoutiCafe Bohemia... **F2**
2 Di Mare Di Vino **E2**
3 El Lagarto Steakhouse
  and Seafood........... **E2**
4 El Tigre Verde **E2**
5 Gusto Beach
  Creativo................ **E2**
6 Mama Gui............. **D2**

Hotels ▶

1 Colina Del Mar....... **A1**
2 Hotel Belvedere....... **F1**
3 Hotel Casa del Mar... **F2**
4 Hotel Giada............ **E2**
5 Sámara Tree
  House Inn.............. **F2**
6 Villas Kalimba **F2**

MATAPALO

Playa Sámara

Bahía Sámara

SÁMARA

EL CANTO DE
LOS GAVILANES

CANGREJAL

TO
NICOYA

TO AIRPORT,
NOSARA

Calle Belvedere
Calle Media
Calle Central
Calle Principal
Arriba Pathway
Calle Plaza
Calle InterCultura

750 feet

250 m

150

160

Beginning surfers love Sámara's almost placid water and its undeveloped palm-fringed beach.

mahimahi, prawns, tuna, mussels, chicken breast stuffed with mushrooms and cheese, portobello mushrooms, or a whole grilled lobster. **Known for:** banana splits; dry-rubbed baby back ribs; specialty cocktails. [$] *Average main: $18* ✉ *200 m west and 150 m south of Banco Nacional* ☎ *2656–0750* 🌐 *www.ellagartobbq.com* 🕓 *No lunch.*

★ El Tigre Verde

$ | **INTERNATIONAL** | Unceremoniously set within the food court known as the Natural Center, El Tigre Verde's organic and uniquely prepared food is nevertheless outstanding. Prepared with love and care, it's all gluten-free, lactose-free, and has no added sugar. **Known for:** sandwiches made on plantain patacones "bread"; their original green juice; amazing ceviche. [$] *Average main: $9* ✉ *Natural Center* ☎ *6221–0776* 🕓 *No dinner.*

★ Gusto Beach Creativo

$$$ | **ITALIAN** | A romantic setting, ocean breezes, and a creative Italian menu make this the one of the most popular restaurants in Sámara. By day, rustic wooden tables are shaded by white sails strung between palms; by night, diners bask in the glow of white globe lamps and light-festooned trees. **Known for:** tuna tartare; prosecco; toes-in-the-sand dining. [$] *Average main: $16* ✉ *Beach road, center of town* ☎ *2656–0252* 💳 *No credit cards.*

★ Mama Gui

$$ | **ITALIAN** | Elegant design aligns with ultrasophisticated cuisine at this exciting Italian restaurant. Tropical-inspired dishes include tender corvina (sea bass) tartare, blended with pineapple, coriander, almonds, lime, ginger, sweet red peppers, tomatoes, scallions, and pear, or the giant grilled shrimp, marinated in limoncello liqueur. **Known for:** imported Italian ingredients; homemade pasta and savory sauces; deconstructed tiramisu. [$] *Average main: $14* ✉ *250 m west of Catholic church, before narrow bridge* ☎ *2656–2347* 🕓 *Closed Wed. in low season, Sept.–Nov.* 💳 *No credit cards.*

Hotels

Colina Del Mar
$$ | **B&B/INN** | Tucked into the jungle-covered hills with impressive views over two beaches, this relaxing haven's 10 rooms have beautiful balconies from which to watch the wildlife. **Pros:** good place to get away from it all; super hospitality; best views in town. **Cons:** not walking distance to town (it's a five-minute drive); basic rooms; rough road to reach hotel. [$] *Rooms from: $140* ✉ *West of the Cangrejal intersection* ☎ *2656–0609* 🌐 *colinadelmarcr.com* 🛏 *10 rooms* 🍴 *Free Breakfast.*

Hotel Belvedere
$$ | **B&B/INN** | After a day on the beach, it's refreshing to retreat to this small hotel buried in a dense, cool garden on a breezy hill overlooking Sámara. **Pros:** affordable; clean; quiet. **Cons:** 10-minute walk down to beach and a bit longer climbing back up the hill; breakfast not included; Wi-Fi can be spotty. [$] *Rooms from: $85* ✉ *Sámara* ✥ *Entering Sámara, go 100 m left at 1st cross street* ☎ *2656–0213* 🛏 *22 units* 🍴 *No meals.*

Hotel Casa del Mar
$ | **B&B/INN** | Facing the beach, this small, pleasant, well-tended hotel is one of Sámara's best values. **Pros:** close to beach; easy on the wallet; free Wi-Fi. **Cons:** not right on the beach; no swimming pool; some noise from road; six rooms have a shared bathroom. [$] *Rooms from: $65* ✉ *Main beach strip, 45 m east of school* ☎ *2656–0264* 🌐 *www.casadelmarsamara.net* 🛏 *17 rooms* 🍴 *Free Breakfast.*

Hotel Giada
$ | **B&B/INN** | This eco-conscious hotel in the heart of town has two small swimming pools surrounded by greenery and brilliant bougainvillea. **Pros:** affordable; friendly; hair dryers in rooms. **Cons:** not right on the beach; smallish rooms; street noise can affect some rooms. [$] *Rooms from: $67* ✉ *Main strip, 250 m north of beach* ☎ *2656–0132* 🌐 *www.hotelgiada.net* 🛏 *24 rooms* 🍴 *Free Breakfast.*

Sámara Tree House Inn
$$$ | **B&B/INN** | One of the few hotels right on the beach, this small inn has lofty, breezy bungalows with air-conditioned bedrooms perfect for folks who love the open air and looking down on the beach action. **Pros:** right on the beach; small and cozy; short walk to restaurants and shops. **Cons:** neighboring bars and restaurants can be noisy; very small pool; beach bungalows with no screens can get buggy. [$] *Rooms from: $192* ✉ *Beach road, across from supermarket* ☎ *2656–0733* 🌐 *www.samaratreehouse.com* 🛏 *6 units* 🍴 *Free Breakfast.*

Villas Kalimba
$$$ | **RENTAL** | You may never want to leave this tranquil oasis of luxury villas hidden behind scrolled white-and-orange walls, where the architecture is Mexican but the style is all Italian. **Pros:** spacious villas; all the comforts of home; lovely garden. **Cons:** not right on beach; some noise from beach road. [$] *Rooms from: $175* ✉ *200 m east of Sámara Police Station, along beach road* ☎ *2656–0929* 🌐 *www.villaskalimba.com* 🛏 *10 units* 🍴 *No meals.*

Nightlife

Lo Que Hay Bar & Taquería
MUSIC CLUBS | Live music plays some nights at this friendly bar right on the beach with free Wi-Fi. If you stayed up all night, this place also serves breakfast starting at 7 am. ✉ *Beach road, across from Sámara Organics Market Café* ☎ *2656–0811.*

Micro Bar
BREWPUBS/BEER GARDENS | This tiny boîte of a bar is the coolest place in town, with an Escher-inspired tile floor and hip lighting. Bellying up to the bar is a pleasure; in fact, practically the entire space is given over to a handsome bar

with an old-fashioned bar rail to lean on. A cool soundtrack accompanies your beer tasting. You can try a sample of any of the 24 Costa Rican craft microbrews on tap for $1. Once you find your favorite, a 12-ounce cold brew costs around $4. A few high tables spill out onto the street, surrounded by groups of happy beer drinkers. ⊠ *Beach road, across from Sámara Tree House Inn* ☎ *8539–1805.*

Shopping

Souvenir stands are set up along the main street and the entrance to the beach, along with the inevitable hand-made-jewelry stalls. Most shops here have pretty much the same beachwear and souvenirs for sale.

CoCo Tales
JEWELRY/ACCESSORIES | Delicate coconut carvings and sophisticated, one-of-a-kind jewelry made with polished amber, turquoise, and orange spondylus shells are the specialty of Carlos, a skilled local artisan. You'll find him in his workshop, 9 to 7:30 daily, on Sámara's main street into town. Carlos and his wife, Simon, also make lovely papier-mâché globe lamps, along with a range of coconut-oil soaps and lotions. ⊠ *In front of Cabinas Arenas, Main street into town* ☎ *8807–7056* ⊕ *isamara.co/cocotales/index.htm.*

Sámara Organics Market
LOCAL SPECIALTIES | More than a market for a wide range of gluten-free, dairy-alternative, and organic foods, this spacious, pleasant shop sells imported olive oils and other gastronomic treats—rare in these parts. There's also a selection of artisan-made objets d'art. You can sit in one of the lounge chairs here and sip an espresso, a just-pressed exotic fruit drink, or a healthy, organic potion. Vegetable dips and spreads are packaged to go, along with organic brownies, cookies, and cakes. ⊠ *On beach road, across from Sporting Club Gusto Beach* ⊕ *www.samaraorganics.com.*

Activities

TOUR OPERATORS
Sámara is known more for gentle water sports such as snorkeling, kayaking, and paddleboarding than for surfing, although the calmer waters provide a good place for beginners, so surf schools have multiplied fast. There are also two high-flying adventures here: a zipline tour and ultralight flights and flying lessons. ATV tours, tearing along dirt roads, are popular with travelers who are particularly fond of dust (or mud, according to the season). For a quieter, closer contact with nature, there's a new guided hike in a private forest reserve. For information on area activities, visit the informative website (⊕ *www.samarainfocenter.com*) or drop into their office at the entrance to Lo Que Hay Taquerìa, on the beach road. You'll find brochures, maps, and friendly advice.

Carrillo Tours Eco Adventures
TOUR—SPORTS | Horseback riding, river and sea kayaking, dolphin-watching, fishing, snorkeling, and trips to Palo Verde, Arenal, and Monteverde national parks can all be booked here. This long-established local tour company also provides daily shuttle service to the Liberia airport at 8:30 am ($50 per person, minimum two people) and to Tamarindo for the same price. ⊠ *200 m west of Banco Nacional* ☎ *2656–0606* ⊕ *www.carrilloadventures.com* ⊇ *From $35.*

Octopus Tours
BOAT TOURS | **FAMILY** | This Costa Rican–owned boat tour company puts an emphasis on respecting animals and the ocean. Morning dolphin tours begin with pickup at your hotel and are hosted by an experienced, passionate guide. You'll snorkel around the reefs of Playa Carrillo to end your trip. They almost always see dolphins, and you may spot whales, sea turtles, and manta rays as well. Prices include water, juice, beer, and pineapple. ⊠ *Playa Carrillo* ☎ *8638–2320.*

8

Samara Adventure Company

TOUR—SPORTS | This tour operator offers an array of local tours, including kayaking, dolphin-watching, and mountain-bike tours, as well as paddleboarding and tours in Monteverde and Arenal national parks. It also arranges transportation by private shuttle to other parts of the country. ⊠ *Main street, beside Hotel Giada* ☎ *2656–0920* ⊕ *www.samaraadventures. com* ⊠ *From $50.*

Sámara Trails

HIKING/WALKING | Take a 2½-hour hike with a bilingual naturalist guide through a mango plantation and into a private reserve to experience the tropical dry forest and its denizens—howler monkeys, trogons, and motmots, among them. There's a daily morning tour at 7 am, or earlier if you want to see more birds, and another at 3 pm. Transportation from Sámara is included; book at Sámara Adventure Tours in town. ⊠ *Werner Sauter Biological Reserve, 3 km (2 miles) northeast of Sámara* ☎ *2656–0920, 800/726–8120 toll-free in U.S.* ⊠ *$40 for 2½-hour hike.*

CANOPY TOURS

Wing Nuts Canopy Tour

TOUR—SPORTS | FAMILY | Named after a famous surfer, this three-hour, 10-platform zipline tour flies through a patch of tropical forest just south of town, with ocean views from some of the platforms. It's small but just right for younger or timid children, and they have special tot-size harnesses for kids as young as three years old. Canopy tours take off at 8, 9, noon, and 1 pm; reserve by phone. ⊠ *In hills above Sámara, Office 1 km (½ mile) east of downtown Sámara* ☎ *2656–0153* ⊕ *www.wingnutscanopy.com* ⊠ *$60.*

KAYAKING

Samara Adventure Company and Carrillo Adventures organize kayaking tours, on both ocean and river, in plastic sit-on-top kayaks.

C&C Surf School

KAYAKING | You can rent boards or take lessons at this established surf school, which also runs three-hour guided kayak snorkeling tours on the Río Tigre and out to Isla Chora and the nearby reef ($40, including gear and a fruit snack). ⊠ *On beach next to Tree House Inn* ☎ *8817–2203.*

Ticos Surf School

KAYAKING | This beachfront surf school also has stand-up paddleboards and kayaks to rent. Kayaking tours through the mangroves or on the ocean are $45 per person; 1½-hour paddleboard lessons (also $45) include an extra hour of practice time. ⊠ *On beach* ☎ *8457–0132.*

SURFING

The surf is relatively gentle at Sámara, so it's a good place for beginners to learn to get up on a board. The challenging waves for more experienced surfers are farther south, at Playa Camaronal, which has both left and right breaks.

C&C Surf School

SURFING | The most experienced beachfront surf school offers lessons from beginner up ($60 per 90-minute private lesson, including five-day board rental; $40 for two or more beginners) with certified instructors, and a huge selection of boards for rent ($4 per hour; $10 per day or $15 for 24 hours). ⊠ *On beach next to Gusto Beach Creativo* ☎ *8817–2203, 8457–0132.*

ULTRALIGHT FLIGHTS

Fly With Us–Ultralight Tours

FLYING/SKYDIVING/SOARING | Take off for a thrilling ride over Sámara on an ultralight flight in an open gyrocopter ($120 cash for 20-minute tour, $160 for 30 minutes.) Pilot Jörg also gives flying lessons. ⊠ *Playa Buena Vista, 6 km (4 miles) northwest of Sámara* ☎ *8330–3923* ⊕ *flywithus. aero.*

Playa Carrillo

7 km (4½ miles) southeast of Sámara.

With its long, reef-protected crescent beach backed by an elegant line of swaying coconut palms and sheltering cliffs, Playa Carrillo (interchangeably called Puerto Carrillo) is a candidate for the most picturesque beach in Costa Rica. A smooth, paved boulevard runs along the beach, with sparkling turquoise waters on the sea side and a hedge of scarlet bougainvillea on the land side. The main landmark here is the Hotel Guanamar, high above the south end of the beach. Unfortunately, the former private fishing club and previously grand hotel has been bought and sold so often that its charm has faded. But its bar still has the best view. A massive new hotel, called Nammbú, with dozens of villas, is being built on the hill overlooking the beach on the south side, so Playa Carrillo may be more populated in future.

GETTING HERE AND AROUND

It's an easy 15-minute drive south on the smooth, paved road from Sámara. If you're not staying at a hotel in Carrillo, you'll have to park your car either in a sunbaked concrete lot halfway along the beach or on the grassy median at the south end of the beach. You can also take a taxi from Sámara or hop on the local bus.

ESSENTIALS

Sámara is the closest town for banks and other services.

👁 Sights

La Selva Wild Animal Refuge & Zoo

ZOO | FAMILY | This modest collection of mostly rescued small animals offers a great chance to see them up close in chest-high corrals under the shade of trees and shrubs. The Italian owners are a little eccentric, and the place is not terribly well kept. There are plenty of usually hard-to-see nocturnal animals, so the best time to visit is just before sunset, when the roly-poly armadillos and big-eyed kinkajous are starting to stir. There are also skunks, spotted pacas, raccoons, bats, and scarier species like boas, poison dart frogs, caimans, and crocodiles. A bromeliad and orchid collection is artistically arranged around the zoo. If you come early in the day (the best time to see the day animals in action) your ticket is also good for a return early-evening visit. It's pricey, but the ticket price helps to buy food for the animals. Crocodile feeding time is every Tuesday and Friday at 5 pm. ✉ *Look for signed road on left, just after crossing bridge at south end of beach, Carrillo* ☎ *2656–2236* 🌐 *$20.*

🏖 Beaches

⭐ Playa Carrillo

BEACH—SIGHT | Unmarred by a single building at beach level, this picture-perfect pristine white strand is ideal for swimming, snorkeling, strolling, and lounging—just remember not to sit under a loaded coconut palm. Signs posted by the municipality announce that the only entry "fee" is: make no fires, and take your garbage away with you. There are some concrete tables and benches, but they get snapped up quickly. This is a popular beach with locals, and it gets quite busy on weekends. The only commercial activity is a hand-wheeled cart selling fruit ices. ⚠ **Sometimes crocodiles hang out at the river mouths at both ends of the beach, so keep a lookout and wade or swim only in the middle of the beach. Amenities:** none. **Best for:** snorkeling; swimming; walking. ✉ *Carrillo.*

🍴 Restaurants

El Colibrí Steakhouse

$$$ | ARGENTINE | FAMILY | Sink your chops into steak (rib eye, New York, or T-bone) grilled on an open fire and served

Idyllic Playa Carrillo is perfect for swimming, snorkeling, or just sunning.

Argentine-style with garlicky chimichurri sauce at this family-run, pleasant rancho restaurant. Other specialties include grilled chorizo sausages or Milanesa, the classic Argentine breaded steak, served with french fries. **Known for:** mouthwatering steaks cooked to perfection; mussels with white wine sauce; Argentine wines. $ *Average main: $18* ✉ *From main beach road, turn left at soccer field, then left again, Carrillo* ☎ *2656–0656* ⊕ *www. cabinaselcolibri.com* ☾ *Closed Mon. June–Nov. No lunch.*

 Activities

FISHING

From January to April, the boats moored off the beach take anglers on fishing expeditions for catch-and-release marlin and sailfishing, as well as good-eating dorado, yellowfin tuna, and wahoo.

Kingfisher Sportfishing

FISHING | Captain Rick Ruhlow, a U.S. Coast Guard–licensed skipper with years of experience fishing Costa Rican waters, takes up to five anglers out on *Kingfisher,* a fully equipped 31-foot Palm Beach fishing boat; it's the only boat that stays full-time in Carrillo from November to September. A full day's fishing offshore costs $1,250; inshore $900. ✉ *Carrillo* ☎ *8834–7125, 2656–0091* ⊕ *www.costaricabillfishing.com.*

Punta Islita

16 km (11 miles) south of Playa Carrillo in dry season, 30 km (21 miles) south of Carrillo by alternative mountain route in rainy season.

Punta Islita is named for a tiny tuft of land that becomes an island at high tide. It's synonymous in Costa Rica with Hotel Punta Islita, one of the country's most exclusive, luxurious, and gorgeous resorts, popular with honeymooners and romantics of any age. Just about everything in Punta Islita—from outdoor activities to food—revolves around, and is available through, this resort. Just uphill from the beach, the small village of Punta Islita is an artistic work in progress, thanks to a community art project led by a few renowned Costa Rican artists who have turned almost all the buildings into galleries, workshops, or works of art themselves.

GETTING HERE AND AROUND

Thanks to the bridge over the Río Oro, it's a quick, 30-minute trip south of Playa Carrillo. A 4WD vehicle is recommended since the dirt road on the other side of the bridge is hilly and rough. Most well-heeled guests fly into the hotel's private airstrip.

Sights

Museo Islita

MUSEUM VILLAGE | This open-air contemporary art museum—the only one in the country—is a treasure trove of art displayed in a gallery and throughout the entire village. Supported by Hotel Punta Islita, visiting resident artists have inspired local villagers to create colorful murals and mosaics ornamenting public spaces and buildings, even beautifying the recycling center and trees in the village plaza. The museum building showcases one-of-a-kind textile prints, folk-art paintings on wood, jewelry, and objets d'art made from recycled materials, all for sale. ✉ *Punta Islita* ☎ *2656–2039.*

Beaches

★ **Punta Islita**

BEACH—SIGHT | The curved beach here is rocky but good for walking, especially at low tide when tidal pools form in the volcanic rock. Sunsets are gorgeous, but despite its Blue Flag designation, this is not a great swimming beach. Be sure to take a stroll through the small village up from the beach, which is a memorable experience. Outdoor activities, food, and drinks are all available through the beachside resort. **Amenities:** food and drink. **Best for:** sunset; walking. ✉ *Punta Islita.*

Restaurants

Los Cocos Beach Club

$$ | **LATIN AMERICAN** | The hammocks, palapas, pool, and beach here are open to the public, so take a dip, grab some beach food, and take in a sunset, all the while trying to spot some red macaws. **Known for:** ubiquitous seafood, particularly whole red snapper; patacones; brick-oven pizza. [$] *Average main: $14* ✉ *Islita Beach* ☎ *2231–6122.*

Hotels

★ **Hotel Punta Islita**

$$$$ | **RESORT** | Overlooking the ocean from a forested ridge, this secluded and sublime hotel is luxury incarnate, with villas, casitas, suites, and spacious rooms sprinkled around the bougainvillea-bedecked hillside, and all activities, including horseback riding, ziplining, and sea-turtle spotting, included in the rate. **Pros:** gorgeous views; ultraluxurious rooms; top-notch service. **Cons:** isolated; distant, rocky beach; very pricey. [$] *Rooms from: $293* ✉ *16 km (11 miles) south of Playa Carrillo* ☎ *2565–3500 in San José, 2656–2020 hotel, 866/446–4053 toll-free in U.S.* 🌐 *www.hotelpuntaislita.com* 🛏 *56 units* 🍴 *Free Breakfast.*

Palo Verde National Park

52 km (32 miles) south of Liberia.

Definitely not most people's idea of a lush, tropical jungle, Palo Verde National Park's deciduous forest is hot, but also very dry and an ideal habitat for easy-to-spot monkeys, deer, peccaries, and lizards. Seasonal wetlands the size of lakes attract waterfowl by the thousands, as well as the photographers who come to shoot the grand avian spectacle.

GETTING HERE AND AROUND

To get to Palo Verde from Liberia, drive south along the Pan-American Highway to Bagaces, then turn right at the small, easy-to-miss sign for Palo Verde, along a rough dirt road for 28 km (17 miles). Count on an hour to drive the distance from the main highway to the park entrance; it's a very bumpy road. You'll have to pay the $12 park entrance fee to get to the Organization for Tropical Studies station. The OTS station is about 7 km (4½ miles) beyond the park entrance; the park headquarters is less than 1 km (½ mile) farther. The gatekeeper takes lunch from noon to 1 pm. The drive from Liberia should take a total of about 1½ hours.

⊙ Sights

Las Pumas Rescue Shelter (*Centro de Rescate Las Pumas*)

NATURE PRESERVE | Sad but true, one of the few places left in the country where you are guaranteed to see large wild cats, including a jaguar, is this animal rescue center. The small enclosures also hold jaguarundis, pumas, margays, and ocelots. The shelter houses other species, including otters, grissons, white-faced and spider monkeys, and scarlet macaws, all native to the area. Some animals and birds are rehabilitated and released into the wild. The larger cats are probably here for life, as it's dangerous for them to be released. Donations to the nonprofit foundation, founded in 2003 by a Swiss conservationist, are welcomed. ⊠ *4½ km (3 miles) north of Cañas on main hwy.* ☎ *2669–6044, 2669–6019 for reservations* ⊕ *www.centrorescatelaspumas.org* ⊿ *$12.*

Llanos de Cortés

BODY OF WATER | Just 3 km (2 miles) north of the Palo Verde road at Bagaces, take the dirt road signed for Llanos de Cortés to get to this hidden waterfall less than 2 km (1 mile) off the highway. About ½ km (¼ mile) along the dirt road you'll see on your right a large rock with "Cataratas" scrawled on it. Follow this bumpy road about 1.3 km (0.8 mile) to its end and then clamber down a steep path to the pool at the bottom of a spectacular, wide 50-foot waterfall. This is a great place for a picnic; avoid weekends if you can when it's often crowded and noisy. Don't leave anything of value in your car. ⊠ *Off Pan-American Hwy., Bagaces* ⊿ *$7* ☞ *Restrooms.*

★ Palo Verde National Park (*Parque Nacional Palo Verde*)

NATIONAL/STATE PARK | Because this dry deciduous forest is less dense than a rain forest, it's much easier to spot the fauna along the hiking trails, including white-tailed deer, coatis, collared peccaries, and monkeys. This park's 198 square km (76 square miles) of terrain is fairly flat—the maximum elevation is 879 feet. The west boundary of the park is bordered by the Río Tempisque, where crocodiles ply the waters year-round. The park also holds Costa Rica's highest concentration of waterfowl, the most common the black-bellied whistling duck and the blue-winged teal, with close to 30,000 during dry season. Although not as common, other waterfowl spotted here are the fulvous whistling duck, the glossy ibis, the pinnated bittern, the least bittern, the snail kite, and the very rare masked duck. Other birds endemic to the north-west, which you may find in the park's dry-forest habitat, are streaked-back orioles, banded wrens, and black-headed trogons. In the wet season, the river and the park's vast seasonal wetlands host huge numbers of migratory and resident aquatic birds, including herons, wood storks, jabirus (giant storks), and elegant flamingo-like roseate spoonbills. There is a raised platform near the OTS research station, about 8 km (5 miles) past the park entrance, with a panoramic view over a marsh filled with ducks and jacanas. A narrow metal ladder leads to the top of the old tower, big enough for just two people at the top. For a good look at hundreds of waterfowl, there's also a long boardwalk jutting out over the wetlands. It's almost always hot and humid in these lowlands—March is the hottest month—so be prepared with water, a hat, and insect repellent. Hostel-type lodging in rustic dormitory facilities with bunk beds and shared bathrooms ($13), and family-style meals for overnight guests only ($7 breakfast; $9 for lunch or dinner) can be arranged through the park headquarters. ⇨ *For more information, see the highlighted listing in this chapter.* ✉ *29 km (18 miles) southwest of Bagaces* ☎ *2206–5965* 🎫 *$12.*

Restaurants

★ Tres Hermanas Bar-B-Q & Grill

$$$ | BARBECUE | FAMILY | This roadside grill is home to the country's best barbecued pork and beef, slow roasted for 16 to 18 hours over a wood fire and served with dynamite barbecue sauce. Sides go beyond coleslaw or fries to include lentils stewed with bacon and onions. **Known for:** barbecue ribs; Costa Rican–style chicharrones; playground to keep the kids busy. [$] *Average main: $16* ✉ *Pan-American Hwy., in Limonal, at turnoff for Puente La Amistad and Nicoya* ☎ *2662–8584.*

Hotels

La Ensenada Lodge

$ | B&B/INN | Part of a national wildlife refuge, this is the most comfortable and affordable base for bird-watching, crocodile spotting, and nature appreciation on this side of the Río Tempisque. **Pros:** wildlife; interesting setting; good value. **Cons:** very simple rooms; large tour groups at times; no air-conditioning. [$] *Rooms from: $66* ✉ *Take signed turnoff at Km 155 of Pan-America Hwy. and drive along gravel road, about 13 km (8 miles) southwest to lodge* ☎ *2289–6655 office in San José, 2661–4090 lodge* 🌐 *www.laensenada.net* 💳 *No credit cards* 🛏 *25 cabin rooms* 🍴 *No meals.*

Rancho Humo Estancia

$$ | B&B/INN | The most comfortable way to experience the birds and wildlife of the Tempisque wetlands is to roost at this eco-boutique hotel, a luxurious version of a traditional hacienda, set in a private reserve directly across from Palo Verde National Park. **Pros:** wetlands setting; incredible bird-watching; most luxurious hotel in the area. **Cons:** meager portions at meals; dusty gravel road for 26 km (16 miles). [$] *Rooms from: $121* ✉ *Pozo de Agua, 26 km (16 miles) north of Quebrada Honda, on east side of Puente de la Amistad, Nicoya* ☎ *2105–5400* 🌐 *www.ranchohumo.com* 🛏 *3 rooms, 5 junior suites, 2 family suites* 🍴 *Free Breakfast.*

Activities

TOUR OPERATORS

Organization for Tropical Studies

BIRD WATCHING | This nonprofit scientific consortium of universities offers overnight packages with a guided walk, excellent family-style meals, and lodging in very basic, no-frills rooms with bunk beds, overhead fans, and private bathrooms ($93 per person). Although the accommodations are spartan, staying here is the only way to set off on a 6 am birding tour (the park gates don't open till 8). The biological research station overlooks the Palo Verde wetlands, and expert naturalist guides can arrange a boat tour ($45 plus guide fee) along wetlands lining both sides of the Río Tempisque, as well as long hikes on the park trails. Call at least a day ahead to arrange the boat tour. Bring binoculars and cameras. Guides can direct you to a perennial nest where jabirus are in residence with their chicks, January through February. Guests still have to pay the $12 entrance fee per person to the national park. ✉ *7 km (4½ miles) past park entrance* ☎ *2524–0607* 🌐 *www.threepaths.co.cr.*

BIRD-WATCHING

The best bird-watching in Palo Verde is on the wetlands in front of the Organization for Tropical Studies (OTS) biological station. The OTS has expert guides who can help you see and identify the varied birds in the area ($80 private tour; $48 per person for two or more), but if you have good binoculars and a bird book, you can identify plenty of species on your own. A boat excursion to Isla Pájaros south of the Río Tempisque is particularly interesting for birders. Toward the end of rainy season this 6-acre island near Puerto Moreno is an exciting place to see hundreds of nesting wood storks, cormorants, and anhingas. You can get close enough to see chicks being fed in nests.

■ TIP→ The best time to go is very early in the morning, to avoid heat and to guarantee the most bird sightings.

Aventuras Arenal

BIRD WATCHING | This adventure-tour company specializes in ecological tours and has guides with good eyes who usually know the English names for birds. The river safari and Llanos de Cortés waterfall combo is $99 per person. The river safari chugs slowly up the Río Tempisque ($55, including juice and lunch). ⊠ *Palo Verde National Park* ☎ *2479–9133* ⊕ *www. aventurasarenal.com.*

RIVER RAFTING

Safaris Corobici

WILDLIFE-WATCHING | **FAMILY** | This small, local company specializes in three-hour float trips down the Río Corobicí ($40; $52 with lunch) to see birds, bats, crocs, iguanas, and more. They put in (and end) near its office location, near Km 192 on the Pan-American Highway. It also offers an early-morning bird-watching float tour ($52 with lunch) and a half-day float, with lunch in its Cocobolo restaurant afterward ($65). Boats are launched from 7 to 3:30 daily. There are also gentle float trips that connect with the Tenorio River ($60 including lunch). The office is right at the entrance to Las Pumas Rescue Shelter.

⊠ *Km 192 on main hwy. to Liberia, 4½ km (3 miles) north of Cañas, Cañas* ☎ *2669–6191* ⊕ *nicoya.com.*

Barra Honda National Park

100 km (62 miles) south of Liberia, 13 km (8 miles) west of Río Tempisque Bridge.

You can't miss this park's massive peak, once thought to be a volcano. Within that mountain, however, is an intricate network of caves to be explored, and hiking trails on its slopes lead to scenic cascades and views over the Gulf of Nicoya.

GETTING HERE AND AROUND

From the Río Tempisque Bridge, drive west along a paved highway. Then follow a dirt road (signed off the highway) for 10 km (6 miles) to the park entrance. If you don't have a car, there is a bus that departs from the town of Nicoya at 7:30 am, Monday through Saturday. You can also take a taxi from Nicoya to the park entrance or go with one of many tour companies in beach towns on the Nicoya Peninsula.

Sights

Barra Honda National Park (*Parque Nacional Barra Honda*)
NATIONAL/STATE PARK | **FAMILY** | A mecca for speleologists, the caves beneath the 1,184-foot **Barra Honda Peak** were created millions of years ago by erosion after the ridge emerged from the sea. You can explore the resulting calcium carbonate formations on a guided tour, and perhaps catch sight of some of the abundant underground animal life, including bats, birds, blindfish, salamanders, and snails. The caves are spread around almost 23 square km (9 square miles), but many of them remain unexplored.

Every day starting at 8 am, local guides take groups 58 feet down ladders into **Terciopelo Cave,** which shelters unusual formations shaped (they say) like fried eggs, popcorn, and shark's teeth. You must wear a harness with a rope attached for safety. The tour costs $29 per person (minimum of two) including equipment rental, guide, and entrance fee. Kids under 10 are not allowed into this cave, but they can visit the kid-size La Cuevita cavern ($5), which also has interesting stalagmites. Both cave visits include interpretive nature hikes. The caves are not open during the wet season for fear of flooding.

Those with a fear of heights, or claustrophobia, may want to skip the cave tour, but Barra Honda still has plenty to offer, thanks to its extensive forests and abundant wildlife. You can climb the 3-km (2-mile) Los Laureles trail (the same trail that leads to Terciopelo Cave) to Barra Honda's summit, where you'll have sweeping views over the surrounding countryside and islet-filled Gulf of Nicoya. Wildlife you may spot on Barra Honda's trails include howler and white-faced monkeys, skunks, coatis, deer, parakeets, hawks, dozens of other bird species, and iguanas. It's a good idea to hire a local guide from the **Asociación de Guías Ecologistas.** The park has camping facilities ($2 per night), and the ranger station, open 8 am to dusk, has potable water and restrooms. There are also a couple of basic cabins to rent ($30). ⊠ *13 km (8 miles) west of Río Tempisque Bridge* ☎ *2659–1551* ▨ *$12 (cash only).*

Curú National Wildlife Refuge

7 km (4½ miles) south of Paquera, 1½ to 2 hrs southwest of Puntarenas by ferry.

With miles of trails through forest and mangrove swamp, this uncrowded private refuge is most famous for its pristine beach, perfectly sited for swimming, snorkeling, and easy kayaking to nearby Tortuga Island. The land was once owned by the Pacific Lumber Company, which logged the area's rosewood, cedar, and mahogany trees. Thanks to its protected status, the area is now home to more than 230 species of birds, 78 species of mammals, and 500 species of plants.

GETTING HERE AND AROUND
From the town of Paquera it's a short drive to Curú National Wildlife Refuge. You can also take a bus bound for Cóbano; just ask the driver to drop you off at the entrance to the refugio.

Curú National Wildlife Refuge (*Refugio Nacional de Vida Silvestre Curú*)
NATURE PRESERVE | **FAMILY** | Established by former farmer and logger-turned-conservationist Frederico Schutt in 1933, this 106-hectare (262-acre) refuge is named after the indigenous word for the spiky-barked *pochote* trees that flourish here. The reserve is home to hordes of phantom crabs on the beach, howler and white-faced capuchin monkeys in the trees, red brocket deer grazing in open fields, and plenty of hummingbirds, kingfishers, woodpeckers, trogons, and manakins (including the bird-watcher's coveted long-tailed manakin). The refuge, classified as a Blue Flag project, is working on building an artificial reef. Visitors can stay in very basic beachfront cabins with solar power ($30 per person, including entrance fee); meals are $10 each. Call ahead to arrange for lodging or horseback rides ($15 for one hour; $25 for three-hour tour). Kayaking tours and early-morning bird-watching walks are organized by Turismo Curú. The entrance fee to the reserve is $13. ⊠ *7 km (4½ miles) south of Paquera on road to Cóbano, left side of road, Paquera* ☎ *2641–0100* ⊕ *www.curuwildliferefuge.com* ▨ *$13.*

Activities

TOUR OPERATORS

Seascape Kayak Tours

KAYAKING | From November to May, experienced Canadian guide Bruce Smith leads half- and full-day kayak excursions in Ballena Bay, leaving from Curú and Playa Tambor ($85 to $165, minimum two people). Smith also leads three- and five-day kayaking tours and goes to Tortuguero National Park and Golfo Dulce. ✉ *Curú National Wildlife Refuge, Paquera* ☎ *8314–8605, 866/747–1884 toll-free* ⊕ *www.seascapekayaktours. com* ⛵ *From $85.*

Turismo Curú

TOUR—SPORTS | Guided 90-minute nature walks of the Curú Wildlife Refuge are a specialty of this tour operator ($15, plus $12 admission to refuge). The company also offers inexpensive kayaking trips to nearby Isla Tortuga, including snorkeling; a half-day tour is $67, full day $127, and the refuge admission fee. A bioluminescence tour ($50) allows you to kayak to Quesera Beach and view the otherworldly underwater phenomena after enjoying sunset. You can rent kayaks by the hour ($10 single, $15 double). All tours require a minimum of two people. For large groups, there is boat transportation from Puntarenas directly to Curú. The tour operator has an office in Paquera and a dive shop on-site at the refuge, with tanks, tours, and diving lessons. A two-tank dive, including boat to Isla Tortuga, gear, and cool drinks, is $102 for certified divers; a Discovery tour for noncertified divers is also $102, including 30 minutes of instruction and one tank. You can do a 2½-hour bioluminescence tour at night by boat, snorkeling with the glowing sea creatures for $35, plus a $12 admission fee. ✉ *Main road, across from Esso station, Paquera* ☎ *2641–0004, 2641–0688* ⊕ *www.turismocuru.com* ⛵ *$12.*

Playa Tambor Area

27 km (17 miles) south of Paquera.

Much of the vast Bahía Ballena shoreline is taken up by a massive all-inclusive hotel and an adjoining private residential development and golf course. But to the south, near the actual village of Tambor, visitors can explore the barely developed Playa Tambor, a beautiful flat beach with nothing more than a volleyball net, a few concrete tables set under shade trees, and one beach shack serving pizza. This beach was never developed as much as Montezuma or Malpaís, making it a better destination for those who want to get away from the crowds. It can serve as a convenient base for fishing excursions, bird-watching, horseback-riding trips, and day trips to Curú National Wildlife Refuge and Isla Tortuga.

GETTING HERE AND AROUND

You can fly directly to Tambor (TMU) from San José on SANSA and Nature Air. Taxis meet every flight and can take you to a nearby hotel ($15), to Montezuma ($50), or to Malpaís ($60).

🛏 Hotels

Tambor Tropical

$$$ | B&B/INN | Centered on the scenic sweep of placid Bahía Tambor with its warm, shallow water, intimate Tambor Tropical offers "beds with a view" in spacious suites, along with sportfishing, a turtle hatchery, horseback riding, bird-watching, and just lolling in a hammock by the pretty, blue-tile pool. **Pros:** spacious suites; tranquil, beautiful setting; easy access. **Cons:** no kids under 16; continental, not full, breakfast included. 💲 *Rooms from: $232* ✉ *From Tambor main street, turn left at beach, Tambor* ☎ *2683–0011, 866/890–2537 in U.S.* ⊕ *www.tambortropical.com* ⤴ *12 suites* ❢❙ *Free Breakfast.*

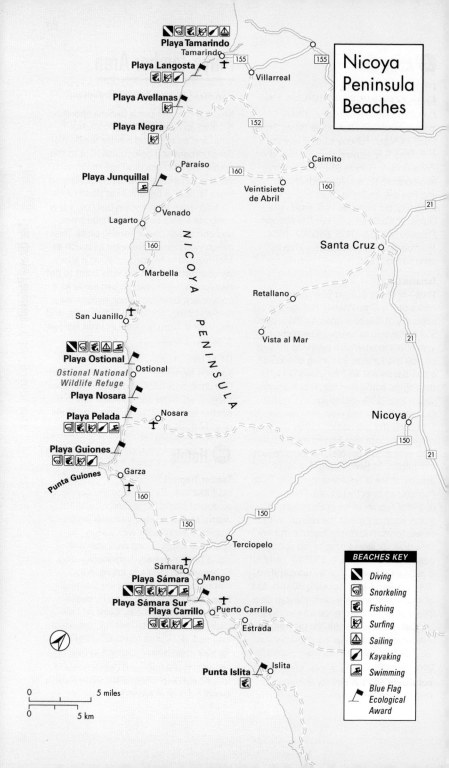

Nicoya Peninsula Beaches

Playa Tamarindo
Tamarindo

155

Villarreal

Playa Langosta

Playa Avellanas

Playa Negra

Paraíso

Playa Junquillal

Venado

Lagarto

160

Marbella

San Juanillo

Playa Ostional
Ostional National Wildlife Refuge
Ostional

Playa Nosara

Playa Pelada
Nosara

Playa Guiones

Punta Guiones
Garza

160

155

152

Caimito

160

Veintisiete
de Abril

160

21

Santa Cruz

Retallano

Vista al Mar

21

Nicoya

150

21

150

Terciopelo

150

Sámara

Playa Sámara
Mango

Playa Sámara Sur
Playa Carrillo
Puerto Carrillo

Estrada

Punta Islita
Islita

0   5 miles
0   5 km

BEACHES KEY

- ◣ *Diving*
- ◲ *Snorkeling*
- 🎣 *Fishing*
- 🏄 *Surfing*
- ⧖ *Sailing*
- ⬙ *Kayaking*
- 🏊 *Swimming*
- ⚑ *Blue Flag Ecological Award*

★ Tango Mar Resort

$$$ | RESORT | FAMILY | Set on stunning, palm-fringed Playa Quizales and backed by 15 acres of exuberant gardens and a 9-hole executive golf course, this comfortable, contemporary resort has a wide range of luxurious lodging options that appeal to families and couples of every age, including honeymooners. **Pros:** gorgeous setting; friendly service and attention to detail; lots of activity options. **Cons:** quiet evenings; large groups on occasion; stairs to climb to villas and some rooms. [$] *Rooms from: $230* ✉ *Playa Quizales, 3 km (2 miles) south of Tambor, Tambor* ☎ *2683–0001, 800/297–4420 in North America* 🌐 *www.tangomar.com* 🛏 *38 rooms* 🍴 *Free Breakfast.*

Activities

Unlike other beach towns, tiny Tambor doesn't have tour operators on every corner or rental shops of any kind—not even for a basic bike. The receptionist at your hotel can set up tours of the area's diverse natural attractions.

FISHING

In the open sea off the Gulf of Nicoya, sailfish, marlin, tuna, mahimahi, and wahoo are in abundance from November to March. Local fishermen in small boats are your best guides to finding fish in the gulf, including snapper, sea bass, and jacks, almost year-round. Prices for fishing range from $375 for half-day trips to $900 for full-day excursions.

HIKING

An easy and quick excursion from Tambor is the 1-km (½-mile) hike south of town to the secluded beach of Palo de Jesús. From the town's dock, follow the road south until it becomes a shady trail that winds its way over rocks and sand around Punta Piedra Amarilla. The trees along the way resound with squawks of parakeets and the throaty utterings of male howler monkeys.

HORSEBACK RIDING

The Tango Mar Resort has its own stables and offers horseback tours that can take you down trails through the rain forest or down to the beach to see an array of wildlife. Set off early in the morning or late in the afternoon, when it's cooler and you're more likely to see birds and animals. Tours range from $40 for a two-hour ride on hotel property to $60 for a longer ride to Montezuma, along the beach.

Isla Tortuga

90 mins by boat from Puntarenas.

Soft white sand and casually leaning palms fringe this island of tropical dry forest off the southern coast of the Nicoya Peninsula. Sounds heavenly? It would be if there weren't quite so many people. Tours from Jacó, Herradura, San José, Puntarenas, and Montezuma take boatfuls of visitors to drink from coconuts and snorkel around a large rock. On the boat ride from Playa Tambor or Montezuma you might spot passing dolphins. Though state owned, the island is leased and inhabited by a Costa Rican family. It makes for an easy day trip out to sea, costing $20 to $109, depending on the duration and departure point.

GETTING HERE AND AROUND

Every tour operator in Playa Tambor and Montezuma offers trips to Isla Tortuga, one of the area's biggest attractions, or you can kayak from the nearby Curú National Wildlife Refuge. Admission to the island is $7 (included in tour prices).

Beaches

Isla Tortuga

ISLAND | FAMILY | This idyllic, unpopulated island has a white-sand beach fronting clear turquoise water, where you'll see a good number of colorful fish, though in the company of many tourists, arriving in

Isla Tortuga, just off the coast near Curú National Wildlife Refuge

many boats of all sizes; try to avoid the weekends if you can. A 40-minute hiking trail (small fee) wanders past monkey ladders, strangler figs, bromeliads, orchids, and the fruit-bearing *guanábana* (soursop) and *marañón* (cashew) trees up to a lookout point with amazing vistas. **Amenities:** food and drink; toilets; water sports. **Best for:** snorkeling; swimming. ✉ *Isla Tortuga* 🕮 *$7.*

Activities

KAYAKING

★ **Calypso Cruises Island Tours**

BOATING | FAMILY | This company pioneered excursions in the Gulf of Nicoya in 1975 with tours aboard a luxury catamaran yacht to Isla Tortuga. You can depart from San José, Manuel Antonio, or anywhere in between. A typical itinerary includes a tico breakfast en route to the port, snorkeling, banana boat rides, and five hours on the island, with a first-class lunch served with chilled white wine—all for about $150. If you're in Puntarenas, the Calypso Cruises dock has an air-conditioned, elegant restaurant, the Shrimp Shack, serving excellent lunches. ✉ *Isla Tortuga* 🕾 *2256–2727, 855/855–1975 in North America* ⊕ *www. calypsocruises.com* 🕮 *From $150.*

Turismo Curú

KAYAKING | FAMILY | This tour operator arranges motorboat tours to the island, leaving from Curú Wildlife Refuge at 9 am and spending one hour on a less-frequented beach on one of the Morteros Islands, and two hours on the beach at Tortuga, plus snorkeling ($55 per person, including snorkeling gear, lunch, and entrance fee to Curú). Tortuga Island is only 3 km (2 miles) off the beach of Curú, so experienced kayakers can paddle there ($65 per person). You can also take a boat tour to Tortuga and spend an hour kayaking around the island ($55). ✉ *Main road, across from Esso station, Paquera* 🕾 *2641–0004* ⊕ *www.turismocuru.com* 🕮 *From $55.*

Montezuma

7 km (4½ miles) southeast of Cóbano, 45 km (28 miles) south of Paquera, 18 km (11 miles) south of Tambor.

Beautifully positioned on a sandy bay, Montezuma is hemmed in by a precipitous wooded shoreline that has prevented the overdevelopment that has affected so many other beach towns. Its small, funky town center is a pastel cluster of New Age health-food cafés, trendy beachwear shops, jaunty tour kiosks, lively open-air bars and restaurants and, at last count, three ice-cream shops, two selling Italian gelato. Most hotels are clustered in or around the town's center, but the best ones are on the coast to the north and south, where the loudest revelers are the howler monkeys in the nearby forest. The beaches north of town, especially Playa Grande, are lovely.

Montezuma has been on the international vagabond circuit for years, attracting backpackers and alternative-lifestyle types. Yoga is a main attraction, with a wide range of classes, and the town is becoming more of a cultural draw, with a low-key film festival of shorts and documentaries, and an occasional poetry festival. At night, the center of town often fills up with tattooed travelers and artisans who entertain each other and passersby. When college students are on break, the place can be a zoo. People used to jokingly refer to the town as "Monte-fuma" (*fuma* means "smoke" in Spanish—get it?) but, for better or for worse, Montezuma is being tamed and becoming more civilized and attractive, with plenty of grown-up lodging and dining options to choose from.

North and south of the town center have always been quiet, and the attractions here include swaths of tropical dry forest, waterfalls, and beautiful virgin beaches that stretch across one national park and two nature preserves. One especially good walk (about two hours) or horseback ride leads to a small waterfall called El Chorro that pours into the sea, where there is a small tidal pool at lower tides.

GETTING HERE AND AROUND

Most people get here via the ferry from Puntarenas to Paquera, which is an hour's drive from Montezuma, with a bumpy dirt-road stretch from Cóbano to Montezuma. The quickest way to get here, however, is to fly to nearby Tambor. One of the taxis waiting at the airstrip will take you to Montezuma for $50, about a 1½-hour drive. There are also one-hour water taxis ($40) that travel every morning between Jacó and Montezuma, departing from Montezuma at 9:30 am and Jacó at 10:45 am. There are no banks in town; the closest bank is in Cóbano. There is an ATM on the beach road in Montezuma, but it's not the most secure or reliable place to withdraw money.

ESSENTIALS

BANK/ATM Banco Nacional. ✉ *Main road, Cóbano* ☎ *2212–2000.*

🍴 Restaurants

★ Clandestina

$ | **LATIN AMERICAN** | **FAMILY** | This cozy and charming café perched on the mountainside and decorated with colorful garlands fluttering in the wind has a mixed Mexican and Costa Rican menu. Their slow-cooked pork is tasty, but they're vegetarian-friendly, too. **Known for:** tacos; butterfly garden on-site; Inca Maracuyá, a passion-fruit-and-habanero-infused vodka cocktail. [$] *Average main: $9* ✉ *Calle Montezuma-Delicias* ☎ *8315–8003.*

Cocolores

$$$ | **ECLECTIC** | Follow the glow of multicolor lanterns to this dinner-only, open-air eatery within sight and sound of the ocean. The simple wooden tables are on a patio bordered with gardens or, during the drier months, practically on the beach. **Known for:** ceviche;

Lovely beaches, yoga, and New Age cafés are the main attractions in Montezuma.

mouthwatering coconut curry; unique oceanfront atmosphere. ⓢ *Average main: $16 ☒ Behind Hotel Pargo Feliz, on beach road ☎ 2642–0348 ▭ No credit cards ⊙ Closed Mon. and last 2 wks of Oct. No lunch.*

El Sano Banano Restaurant

$$ | **VEGETARIAN** | Montezuma's first natural-food restaurant is named after the chewy dried bananas made by the owners, who also own the upscale Ylang Ylang resort on the beach. This popular eatery serves the best vegetarian fare in town, including scrambled tofu for breakfast and excellent wraps, salads, fajitas, and spring rolls, with plenty of vegan and gluten-free options. **Known for:** fresh patacones (smashed and fried plantains); great people-watching; super breakfasts. ⓢ *Average main: $12 ☒ Main road ☎ 2642–0638 ⊕ elsanobanano.com.*

Ice Dream

$ | **ITALIAN** | Literally, the coolest place in town is this blissfully air-conditioned ice-cream parlor with an array of refreshing Italian gelato flavors, cool fruit

smoothies, and milk shakes. It's airy and bright, with large windows looking onto the main street and an outdoor terrace. **Known for:** a variety of gelatos to cool you off; good selection of paninis; Lavazza coffee. ⓢ *Average main: $6 ☒ Southeast corner of main street and beach road ☎ 2642–0160 ▭ No credit cards.*

★ Playa de los Artistas

$$$ | **ITALIAN** | Arty driftwood tables and sculpted chairs scattered along the rocky beach and an inventive Mediterranean menu have made this one of the most scenic, as well as one of the best, restaurants in the country for more than 20 years. The eclectic menu changes daily and features local seafood, lamb, beef, and even duck. **Known for:** spectacular beach setting; homemade ravioli; funky found-art decor. ⓢ *Average main: $20 ☒ 275 m south of town, near Los Mangos Hotel ☎ 2642–0920 ⊙ Closed Sun. No lunch weekdays; no dinner Sat.*

★ Ylang Ylang Restaurant

$$$ | VEGETARIAN | One of Montezuma's most scenic and sophisticated restaurants, Ylang Ylang is nestled between the beach and the jungle, offering views of waves crashing against the rocks. The lunch menu lists a selection of sushi, salads, wraps, and sandwiches with various vegan, gluten-free, and raw dishes. **Known for:** remote location; fresh flavorful sushi; blackened tuna. $ *Average main: $18* ⊠ *On beach, ½ km (¼ mile) north of town, at Ylang Ylang Beach Resort* ☎ *2642–0636* ⊕ *www.ylangylangbeachresort.com.*

 Hotels

Hotel El Jardín

$$ | HOTEL | Spread across a hill a few blocks from the beach, this hotel has refreshed rooms and villas with ocean, pool, and garden views. **Pros:** central location; good value; spacious rooms. **Cons:** a few rooms catch a bit of noise from bars in town; steep paths to climb; no breakfast. $ *Rooms from: $85* ⊠ *West end of main road* ☎ *2642–0074* ⤴ *16 rooms* ◉ *No meals.*

Hotel Los Mangos

$$ | HOTEL | The rhythmic sounds of the nearby ocean make these affordable octagonal wood bungalows spread across a shady, green mango grove the perfect place to practice yoga or just relax. **Pros:** great pool; lots of wildlife; yoga. **Cons:** road noise; could use updating; no a/c. $ *Rooms from: $90* ⊠ *Near entrance to waterfall trail, ½ km (¼ mile) south of town* ☎ *2642–0384* ⊕ *www.hotellosmangos.com* ⤴ *19 rooms* ◉ *No meals.*

Sano Banano Beachside Hotel

$$ | B&B/INN | If quiet and cool is what you are seeking, these comfortable, tastefully decorated rooms above the popular restaurant of the same name are air-conditioned and soundproofed—and they are a bargain. **Pros:** budget-friendly; Ylang Ylang Beach Resort privileges; excellent restaurant. **Cons:** most guest rooms lack windows; can feel a little claustrophobic; lacks some things like hair dryer and TV. $ *Rooms from: $75* ⊠ *Main road* ☎ *2642–0636* ⊕ *elsanobanano.com* ⤴ *12 rooms* ◉ *Free Breakfast.*

★ Ylang Ylang Beach Resort

$$$ | RESORT | Secluded and serene, this gorgeous tropical resort with a holistic slant sits in an exuberant garden, nestled between the sea and a lush forest. **Pros:** gorgeous, natural setting; great restaurant; excellent service. **Cons:** ocean-view tent cabins offer limited privacy; 15-minute walk to town along beach; spotty Wi-Fi. $ *Rooms from: $198* ⊠ *700 m north of school in Montezuma* ☎ *2642–0636, 888/795–8494 in North America* ⊕ *www.ylangylangbeachresort.com* ⤴ *21 units* ◉ *Free Breakfast.*

 Nightlife

Montezuma's nightlife is focused on a handful of bars where locals and out-of-towners mix, a refreshing change from larger beach towns. A few venues boasting live music have recently appeared on the scene, including El Sano Banano and Ylang Ylang Beach Resort, where guest musicians and bands perform. Streetside artisans selling their creations often animate the area with drumming and dancing that draw passersby to stop and dance, too.

Cafe Restaurant Organico

CAFES—NIGHTLIFE | There's live music almost every night and open-mic night on Monday at this Italian-owned hot spot. The fun gets started around 7:30 and goes late into the night if enough performers show up. Cool down with a bowl of excellent, chili-spiced, chocolate Italian gelato while you watch the show. ⊠ *Across from Cocolores, on beach road* ☎ *2642–1322.*

Chico's Bar

BARS/PUBS | Music blasts from the dark, uninviting entrance, but farther back is a brighter, spacious deck with pool tables and dancing. Directly behind is an open-air beach bar with a more laid-back atmosphere and a breezy ocean view. You're likely to see fire dancers in the street out front. ⊠ *On beach road, where main street through Montezuma ends* ☎ *2642–0578.*

Restaurante Moctezuma

BARS/PUBS | You can't get any closer to the beach than at this breezy, casual bar, which serves the cheapest beers in town. At night, candles and moonlight illuminate the tables in the sand. ⊠ *1st fl., Hotel Moctezuma* ☎ *2642–1522.*

Shopping

Beachwear, banana paper, wooden crafts, and indigenous pottery are some of what you find in colorful shops in the town's center. During the dry season, traveling artisans from around the world unfold their streetside tables just before the sun begins to set; candles light up the handmade leather-and-seed jewelry, dream catchers, and knit tops.

Galeria La Floresta

CRAFTS | Visit this outdoor gallery to see a display of fantastical, stunning lamps and sconces made from driftwood, bamboo, and shells. Swiss artist Claudia Bassaeur makes unique and beautiful lamp shades with marbled, handmade paper imported from Santa Fe, New Mexico. She also makes extraordinary jewelry, using found "treasure." Call ahead to make an appointment. The gallery is on the main road in Cabuya, on the way to Cabo Blanco Absolute Nature Reserve. ⊠ *7 km (4½ miles) south of Montezuma on road to Cabuya, 200 m past Hotel Celaje* ☎ *2642–1211, 8836–6876.*

Chorotegan Pottery

In the country village of Guaitil, 24 km (15 miles) north of Nicoya, artists—most of them women—have revived a vanishing tradition by producing clay pottery handmade in the manner of indigenous Chorotegans. The town square is a soccer field, and almost every house facing it has a pottery shop out front and a round, wood-fired kiln in back. Pottery designs range from traditional Costa Rican to inspired Cubist abstractions. Prices range from $12 to $300; most are around $30.

🏃 Activities

In Montezuma it seems that every other storefront is occupied by a tour operator. In spite of the multitude of signs advertising "Tourist Information," none are officially sanctioned by the Costa Rican tourist office.

TOUR OPERATORS

Cocozuma Traveller

TOUR—SPORTS | Montezuma's oldest and most experienced tour company offers horseback riding to a beachfront waterfall ($40), a full-day snorkeling trip to Isla Tortuga with lunch ($50), and various sportfishing options ($250–$800). ⊠ *Main road, next to El Sano Banano* ☎ *2642–1011* 🚌 *From $40.*

Zuma Tours

TOUR—SPORTS | If you want to get out on the water, this reliable agency organizes snorkeling tours to Tortuga Island ($65), sportfishing trips from three to eight hours, and surf lessons. There are tours of Curu Wildlife Refuge and the Montezuma Waterfall Canopy. They also offer ATV rentals and transport by shuttle van, and taxi boats ($45) between Jacó and Montezuma (a much faster trip than by land). ✉ *Main street, south of El Sano Banano Hotel* ☎ *2642–0024* ⊕ *www.zumatours. net* ✆ *From $45.*

HIKING

Hiking is one of the best ways to explore Montezuma's natural treasures, including beaches, lush coastline, jungles, and waterfalls. There are plenty of options around town or in nearby parks and reserves. Just over a bridge, 10 minutes south of town, a slippery path patrolled by howler monkeys leads upstream to two waterfalls and a fun swimming hole. If you value your life, don't jump or dive from the waterfalls. Guides from any tour operator in town can escort you, but save your money. This one you can do on your own. The path is very crowded on weekends, especially in January and around Easter.

El Chorro

HIKING/WALKING | To reach the beachfront waterfall called El Chorro, head left from the main beach access and hike about two hours to the north of town along the sand and through the woods behind the rocky points. The trip takes you across seven adjacent beaches, on one of which there is a small store where you can buy soft drinks. Leave as early in the morning as possible to beat the heat, and bring water and good sunblock. El Chorro can also be reached on a horseback tour organized by any of the local tour operators. ✉ *Montezuma.*

J. C.'s Journeys

BIRD WATCHING | In pursuit of nature, bilingual certified guide Juan Carlos Aguirre leads three-hour bird-watching tours starting at 5:30 am ($60 per person, minimum two people) including breakfast; a local cultural tour where you'll visit with a rural farmer and learn about sustainable farming; and two-hour nocturnal tours, complete with a night-vision scope to help you spot creatures along a forest stream ($30 per person, minimum of two). You can also hire Juan Carlos for a private birding tour. ✉ *Montezuma* ☎ *8975–8832* ⊕ *www.jcsjourneys.com.*

Malpaís and Santa Teresa

12 km (7½ miles) southwest of Cóbano, 52 km (33 miles) south of Paquera.

Once frequented mostly by diehard surfers in search of some of the country's largest waves and by naturalists en route to the nearby Cabo Blanco Absolute Nature Preserve, this area is now a 10-km (6-mile) stretch of hotels, restaurants, and shopping centers strung along a mostly dirt road that is choked with dust in the dry season and awash in mud the rest of the year. Despite the congestion, the string of beaches and consistent surf still draw a multitude of surfers. Health-oriented spas, organic restaurants, and yoga classes are also attracting a very international, young crowd, from Europe, Australia, and North America.

Coming from Cóbano, the road alternates between paved and dirt sections until it reaches an intersection, known locally as El Cruce, marked by a cluster of shopping centers, banks, restaurants, and hotel signs. To the left is the partially paved route to relatively tranquil Malpaís, and to the right is the road to Santa Teresa, which has a few paved sections but is mostly a rutted, narrow dirt road clogged with trucks, ATVs, bicycles, and pedestrians. Playa Carmen, straight ahead, is the area's best place for surfing, though swimmers will want to be careful of rip currents. Malpaís and Santa Teresa are so close that locals disagree on where one begins and the other ends. You could travel up the road parallel to the ocean that connects them and not realize you've moved from one town to the other.

GETTING HERE AND AROUND

From Paquera it's an hour's drive to Malpaís via Cóbano. After Cóbano, the road is partially paved. There are some bumpy dirt sections, which can become quite muddy in the rainy season, so a 4WD vehicle is your best bet. There is a direct bus from San José, leaving at 6 am and 2 pm to Santa Teresa, crossing with the ferry from Puntarenas (Transportes Hermanos Rodríguez ☎ 2642–0219). The trip takes about six hours and costs about $15, including ferry fare. Taxis waiting at Tambor's airstrip will take up to four people to Malpaís for $45–$50.

SHUTTLES Tropical Tours Shuttles. ✉ *50 m north of El Cruce, Malpais* ☎ *2640–1900* ⊕ *www.tropicaltourshuttles.com.*

TAXI Taxi. ☎ *8360–8166.*

ESSENTIALS

BANK/ATM Banco Nacional. ✉ *Centro Comercial Playa Carmen, At crossroads, Malpais* ☎ *2640–0640.*

MEDICAL CENTER Lifeguard Urgent Medical Centre. ✉ *At crossroads, around corner from BCR bank, Malpais* ☎ *4001–9867 ext 12/2220–0911* ⊕ *lifeguardcostarica.com.*

PHARMACY Farmacia Amiga. ✉ *Centro Comercial Playa Carmen, at crossroads, Malpais* ☎ *2640–0463.*

Sights

★ **Cabo Blanco Absolute Nature Preserve**
(*Reserva Natural Absoluta Cabo Blanco*)
NATURE PRESERVE | Conquistadores named this area Cabo Blanco on account of its white earth and cliffs, but it was a more benevolent pair of foreigners—Swede Nicolas Wessberg and his Danish wife, Karen Mogensen, arriving here in the 1950s—who made it a preserve. Appalled by the first clear-cut in the Cabo Blanco area in 1960, the pioneering couple launched an international appeal to save the forest. In time their efforts led not only to the creation of

the 12-square-km (4½-square-mile) reserve but also to the founding of Costa Rica's national park service, the National Conservation Areas System (SINAC). Wessberg was murdered on the Osa Peninsula in 1975 while researching the area's potential as a national park. A reserve just outside Montezuma was named in his honor. A reserve has also been created to honor his wife, who dedicated her life to conservation after her husband's death.

Informative natural-history captions dot the trails in the Cabo Blanco forest. Look for the sapodilla trees, which produce a white latex used to make gum; you can often see V-shape scars where the trees have been cut to allow the latex to run into containers placed at the base. Wessberg cataloged a full array of animals here: porcupine, hog-nosed skunk, spotted skunk, gray fox, anteater, cougar, and jaguar. Resident birds include brown pelicans, white-throated magpies, toucans, cattle egrets, green herons, parrots, and blue-crowned motmots. A fairly strenuous 10-km (6-mile) round-trip hike, which takes about two hours in each direction, follows a trail from the reserve entrance to **Playa Cabo Blanco.** The beach is magnificent, with hundreds of pelicans flying in formation and paddling in the calm waters offshore—you can wade right in and join them. Off the tip of the cape is the 7,511-square-foot **Isla Cabo Blanco,** with pelicans, frigate birds, brown boobies, and an abandoned lighthouse. As a strict reserve, Cabo Blanco is open only five days a week. It has restrooms, picnic tables at the entrance, and a visitor center with information panels on park history and biological diversity, but no other tourist facilities, and overnight camping is not permitted. Most visitors come with their own guide. This is one of the hottest parks in the country, so be sure to bring lots of water with you. ⚠ **An official sign at the entrance warns people with cardiovascular problems NOT to walk the strenuous trail to Cabo Blanco**

Playa Santa Teresa, on the southern tip of the Nicoya Peninsula

beach. ✉ *10 km (6 miles) southwest of Montezuma via Cabuya, Montezuma* ☎ *2642–0093, 2642–0312* ⊕ *www. costarica-nationalparks.com/caboblanco-absolutenaturalreserve.html* ✉ *$12.*

 Beaches

Playa Carmen

BEACHES | This Blue Flag beach, sometimes referred to as El Carmen, is just a stone's throw from the commercial development along the beach road, so it tends to attract more people. There's a parking lot and palm trees for shade. The waves offer excellent surfing for all levels, with dozens of beach breaks scattered along the wide, sandy strand. The sea grows rough and dirty during the May-to-December rainy season, with frequent swells that sometimes make it impossible to get out on a surfboard. Swimmers need to be careful of rip currents. Lifeguards are on duty year-round on weekends, from 9 am to sunset; more days during holiday periods.

Amenities: food and drink. **Best for:** surfing. ✉ *Playa Carmen, Santa Teresa.*

Playa Malpaís

BEACHES | South of the bustle of Playas Carmen and Santa Teresa, this Blue Flag beach is quieter and rockier, with interesting volcanic formations. The tougher surfing here was the original attraction that drew surfers from around the world, with a challenging break over a rock platform. Swimming is not advised, but the dramatic scenery is unbeatable. **Amenities:** food and drink. **Best for:** surfing; sunset. ✉ *Malpais, Malpais.*

Playa Santa Teresa

BEACHES | Playa Carmen seamlessly segues into Playa Santa Teresa, about 1 km (½ mile) to the north. This flat, sandy Blue Flag beach is edged by forest and punctuated with rocky sections and tide pools at low tide. It's usually a calmer option for surfers, but swimmers need to take care, especially since there are no lifeguards here. The farther north you go, the less crowded the beach is. Beachfront hotels include Trópico Latino,

Latitude 10, Florblanca and Pranamar; Rancho Itauna provides food and entertainment facing the beach. **Amenities:** none. **Best for:** surfing; walking. ✉ *Santa Teresa, Santa Teresa.*

🍴 Restaurants

Koji's Restaurant
$$$ | **SUSHI** | North of Santa Teresa, this trendy sushi place off a dusty dirt road is one of the most popular restaurants in the area. Fabulous sushi, sashimi, and tempura are carefully crafted, and there's a daily blackboard menu featuring hand rolls and wraps. **Known for:** Koji roll made with shrimp tempura, avocado, cucumber, spicy tuna, and special sauce; locally sourced seafood, fruits, and vegetables; cash only. [$] *Average main: $18* ✉ *200 m north of Pranamar, near Playa Hermosa, Santa Teresa* ☎ *2640–0815* 🌐 *kojisrestaurant.com* 🕒 *Closed Mon. No lunch.*

★ **Nectar**
$$$ | **SEAFOOD** | Fresh seafood is the specialty at this poolside alfresco restaurant, with inventive daily specials that focus on the day's catch prepared with Asian and Mediterranean flavors. After 3:30, the dedicated sushi chef produces such treats as panko-crusted prawn roll with ahi tuna, mango, and avocado. **Known for:** fresh sushi; sea view and tropical foliage; organic and local produce. [$] *Average main: $25* ✉ *Resort Florblanca, 2 km (1 mile) north of soccer field, Malpais* ☎ *2640–0232.*

★ **Product C Playa Carmen**
$ | **SEAFOOD** | For the freshest, tastiest, and most affordable seafood in town, make a beeline to this fish market and restaurant that also features the most entertaining chefs. A trio of cheerful Canadian expats shucks, slices, grills, and prepares fresh local oysters, sashimi, grilled fish fillets doused in ginger and sesame dressing, savory fish cakes, and refreshing ceviche. **Known for:** "candied" tuna with pineapple glaze; Friday-night live music; ice-cold craft beer. [$] *Average main: $9* ✉ *Centro Commercial Playa Carmen, at Cruce, behind Farmacia Amiga, Santa Teresa* ☎ *2640–1026* 🕒 *Closed weekends. No dinner.*

Restaurante Al Chile Viola
$$ | **MODERN ITALIAN** | Sit yourself down amidst a sea of chili-pepper-red tabletops, chandeliers, hangings, and funky objets d'art for an Italian meal like you have never tasted before. Chef Emiliano from Florence will challenge your taste buds with imaginative dishes using authentic Italian ingredients like traditional homemade pastas including beef lasagna, eggplant Parmesan, and osso buco alla Romana. **Known for:** creative homemade pastas; sea bass with grilled vegetables; bull testicle ravioli. [$] *Average main: $14* ✉ *200 m north of Super La Hacienda, on main road, Santa Teresa* ☎ *2640–0433* 🕒 *Closed Sun., and Sept. and Oct. No lunch.*

🛏 Hotels

Blue Jay Lodge
$ | **B&B/INN** | Perched along a forested mountainside, these wooden cabins feel like tree houses; you'll hear howler monkeys and an array of birdsong from your bed. **Pros:** natural setting; good value; nice respite from lowland heat and dust, since road in front is paved. **Cons:** steep terrain; most bungalows don't have air-conditioning. [$] *Rooms from: $73* ✉ *From El Cruce, 800 m south toward Malpaís, Santa Teresa* ☎ *2640–0089* 🌐 *www.bluejaylodgecostarica.com* 🛏 *14 cabins* 🍽 *Free Breakfast.*

★ **Casa MarBella**
$$ | **HOTEL** | **FAMILY** | It is indeed a picture-perfect view of the "beautiful sea" that you find at this lovely casa, nestled into the side of a hill. **Pros:** owners who feel like old friends; infinity pool; large three-bedroom option perfect for families. **Cons:** steep, bumpy climb up the road; suites are on the smaller side;

some rooms lack privacy. $ Rooms from: $88 ⊠ 125 m east and 25 m north of Super Ronny's, Santa Teresa ☎ 2640–0749 ⊕ www.facebook.com/casamarbellahotel ⇆ 12 rooms ❮O❯ No meals.

⭐ Florblanca

$$$$ | **RESORT** | Named for the white flowers of the frangipani trees growing between the restaurant and the beach, this ultraluxurious resort is dedicated to relaxation and rejuvenation. **Pros:** gorgeous villas and grounds; friendly; great yoga classes; no kids under age 6. **Cons:** very expensive; on rocky stretch of beach; insects sometimes a problem. $ Rooms from: $600 ⊠ 2 km (1 mile) north of soccer field, Santa Teresa ☎ 2640–0232, 800/685–1031 toll-free in North America ⊕ www.florblanca.com ⇆ 11 rooms ❮O❯ No meals.

Hotel Tropico Latino

$$$ | **HOTEL** | **FAMILY** | This beachfront hotel has everything: a spectacular beach with major surf break; a trendy restaurant with ocean views; a round, palm-fringed pool; bungalows and rooms sprinkled throughout a mature garden; twice-daily yoga sessions on the beach; and a full-service spa. **Pros:** great location on beach; large pool; lush gardens. **Cons:** cheaper rooms are dark and close to dusty, noisy road; not quiet—more of a buzz with lots of people coming and going. $ Rooms from: $160 ⊠ 700 m north of crossroads, Santa Teresa ☎ 2640–0062 ⊕ www.hoteltropicolatino.com ⇆ 31 units ❮O❯ No meals.

Pranamar Oceanfront Villas & Yoga Retreat

$$$$ | **B&B/INN** | You don't have to be on a yoga retreat to appreciate this nirvana of design, artistry, and natural beauty in a serene setting. **Pros:** gorgeous garden and beach setting; excellent restaurant; warm, friendly service and daily complimentary yoga classes. **Cons:** noisy children may not suit the serenity here; bumpy dirt road to get here. $ Rooms from: $275 ⊠ Playa Hermosa, 5 km (3 miles) north of Cruce in Playa Carmen, Santa Teresa ☎ 2640–0852 ⊕ www.pranamarvillas.com ⇆ 10 units ❮O❯ Free Breakfast.

Ritmo Tropical

$$ | **HOTEL** | **FAMILY** | Tranquil, comfortable, and nicely priced, this small hotel and spa a short walk from the beach is consistently the best deal in Malpaís. **Pros:** very clean rooms; economical; lively restaurant; quiet. **Cons:** a bit of a walk to town, but on a paved road. $ Rooms from: $80 ⊠ 100 m south of El Cruce on road toward Malpaís, Malpais ☎ 2640–0174 ⊕ hotelritmotropical.com ⇆ 11 units ❮O❯ No meals.

Nightlife

Ranchos Itauna

MUSIC CLUBS | This beachfront restaurant-lounge in Santa Teresa is a fixture on the nightlife scene, with "Sunset Sessions" Tuesday and Saturday, featuring international live and DJ music, from 4 to 11 pm. Bonfires and torch-fire shows add to the excitement. The crowd is a mix of locals and tourists. ⊠ 100 m north of Super Costa, Santa Teresa ☎ 2640–0095 ⊕ www.ranchos-itauna.com.

Shopping

Local 31

JEWELRY/ACCESSORIES | For a truly unique souvenir, have designer Esteban del Monserrat create a custom ring, necklace, or pair of earrings with natural gemstones. The ready-made designs by this well-traveled jewelry maker are stunning, made of chunky, beaten silver reminiscent of sunken Spanish treasure. ⊠ Centro Commercial Playa Carmen, at Cruce, Santa Teresa ☎ 8388–8015.

Pranamar

JEWELRY/ACCESSORIES | At the far-north end of Santa Teresa, the gift shop in this yoga-centered retreat sells exquisite jewelry from Bali, Guatemala, and local Costa Rican artisans. Delicate filigree silver armlets, headbands, and bracelets are made with freshwater pearls, abalone, amethyst, and other semiprecious stones. ⊠ *Pranamar Oceanfront Villas & Yoga Retreat, north end of Playa Santa Teresa, Malpais* ☎ *2640–0852* ⊕ *www.pranamarvillas.com.*

 Activities

TOUR OPERATORS

Tropical Tours

TOUR—SPORTS | This outfitter can set you up with a horseback-riding jaunt ($45), or a day trip to Isla Tortuga ($70). ⊠ *50 m north of El Cruce, Malpais* ☎ *2640–1900* ⊕ *www.tropicaltourshuttles.com* 🖃 *From $40.*

CANOPY TOURS

Canopy del Pacífico Malpaís

ZIP LINING | The only canopy tour in the area has an 11-platform adventure with ocean views that takes about an hour and a half ($55). Transportation to the zipline, near the entrance of Cabo Blanco Absolute Nature Reserve, is $10 round-trip. ⊠ *Near entrance to Cabo Blanco Absolute Nature Reserve, Malpais* ☎ *2640–0360* ⊕ *www.canopymalpais.com* 🖃 *From $55.*

SURFING

From November to May, the Malpaís area has some of Costa Rica's most consistent surf, as well as clear skies and winds that create idyllic conditions.

Kina Surf Shop

SURFING | This shop stands out among the dozens of surf shops scattered along the beach road for its surfing expertise and wide range of boards and accessories. If you're a first-time surfer, they can fit you with the correct board from their stock of more than 60 different shapes and sizes. Surf lessons for all levels cost $60 (minimum two people) for about two hours, including board for the rest of the day and a rash guard. ⊠ *Plaza Solar, in front of Brunelas, main street, Santa Teresa* ☎ *2640–0627* ⊕ *www.facebook.com/kinasurfshop* 🖃 *From $60.*

MANUEL ANTONIO AND THE CENTRAL PACIFIC COAST

Updated by
Rachel White

◉ Sights	🍴 Restaurants	🛏 Hotels	🛍 Shopping	🍸 Nightlife
★★★★★	★★★★☆	★★★★★	★★★☆☆	★★★★☆

WELCOME TO MANUEL ANTONIO AND THE CENTRAL PACIFIC COAST

TOP REASONS TO GO

★ **Adventure sports:** Snorkel among colorful fish, get muddy on mountain adventures, and zip through treetops near Jacó and Manuel Antonio.

★ **Fishing:** Deep-sea fishing at Quepos, Jacó, or Herradura gives a chance to hook a sailfish, marlin, wahoo, or yellowfin tuna.

★ **Nature and wildlife:** Explore the seaside forest and see sloths, iguanas, agoutis, monkeys, and 350 species of birds at Manuel Antonio National Park.

★ **Sunsets:** Whether you view it from the beach or while sipping hilltop cocktails in Manuel Antonio, this region has some of the country's best venues for watching the sunset.

★ **Surfing:** This is Costa Rica's surf central. Jacó, Playa Hermosa, Esterillos, and Manuel Antonio beckon surfers, from beginners to pros.

Most of the Central Pacific is mountainous, and beach towns are backed by forested peaks. Humid evergreen forests, oil-palm plantations, and cattle pastures blanket the land. The coastal highway connects all towns from Tárcoles to the southern Pacific. The hub town of Jacó makes a good base for visiting surrounding beaches and wildlife areas. Farther south are neighboring Quepos and Manuel Antonio, Costa Rica's most popular destination, followed by smaller towns barely touched by tourism.

1 Tárcoles. This small town is famous for its crocodiles. You can get a peek at the huge reptiles as they lounge on the riverbanks or take a river tour.

2 Punta Leona. Past Tárcoles on the Central Pacific Coast, Punta Leona is worth a trip if your ideal stay is an upscale villa in the lush rain forest with killer views and access to a private beach.

3 Playa Herradura. Just north of Jacó, this beautiful coastal town named for its horseshoe-shaped beach is known for its marina, golf course, and sportfishing.

4 Jacó. Famous for nightlife and surfing, this lively, popular destination is the most developed beach town in Costa Rica and offers something for both beach lovers and adventure seekers.

5 Playa Hermosa. Not to be confused with the beach of the same name in Guanacaste, this surf town south of Jacó has ample outdoor activities, including turtle tours and surfing lessons.

6 Esterillos Este. This under-the-radar gem has some great beachfront boutique hotels.

7 Quepos. The gateway town to Manuel Antonio is good for stocking up on supplies, visiting the area's nature reserve, and taking canopy tours.

8 Manuel Antonio. One of the most popular spots in Costa Rica is home to the wildlife-rich, beach-lined Manuel Antonio National Park and a nice selection of restaurants and hotels.

MANUEL ANTONIO NATIONAL PARK

Manuel Antonio National Park

At only 7 square km (3 square miles), Manuel Antonio National Park—Costa Rica's smallest park—has impressive natural attractions: wildlife, rain forest, white-sand beaches, and rocky coves with abundant marine life.

The forest is dominated by massive ficus, silk-cotton trees, black-and-white Guapinols, and Panama trees as well as guacimo colorado, bully tree, cedar, and ceniza-ro. It's home to both two- and three-toed sloths, green and black iguanas, agoutis (similar to the guinea pig, but with longer legs), raccoons, coatis, three species of monkey, and more than 350 species of birds.

The well-maintained trails are short, mostly paved—and heavily traveled. Make no mistake about it: this is no undiscovered wilderness. In fact, Manuel Antonio is Costa Rica's most visited attraction. There are 5 km (3 miles) of coastline, and it's one of the few parks where you can combine nature walks with swimming off idyllic beaches. There's no commercial beach development, so the beaches are picture-perfect. *(For more information see the review in this chapter.)*

BEST TIME TO GO

Visit any day and any month but October, when it's very wet. Although it rains in September, you're likely to have the park to yourself, and showers usually don't kick in until early afternoon. Keep in mind that the park is closed on Monday.

FUN FACT

The park's territory is too small to support all of its monkeys, so forested corridors and suspended bridges have been built to allow them to come and go.

BEST WAYS TO EXPLORE

HIKING

Don your hiking shoes and set off on Sloth Trail, the main route that leads to Manuel Antonio beach. The coral reef here makes it a good spot for snorkeling. A second trail leads to Playa Espadilla Sur. These two stunning beaches lie on either side of a *tombolo,* a sandy strip that connects the mainland to rocky Punta Catedral, which used to be an island thousands of years ago. Farther east, where fewer visitors venture, Playa Escondido is rocky and secluded. Trails from the entrance to Punta Catedral and Playa Escondido are in excellent shape. Trails farther east are progressively rougher due to the steep terrain. Sturdy walking sandals are good enough for most of the trails, but light hiking boots or closed shoes will help you avoid nasty encounters with biting ants.

WILDLIFE-WATCHING

Manuel Antonio is famous for its monkeys, especially the noisy white-faced monkeys that pester tourists at the beach. A troop of rare squirrel monkeys also lives here, one of the few places in the country where you can still find them. These tiny monkeys—*mono titi* in Spanish—are endangered. Catching sight of them is a real wildlife coup. The smallest of Costa Rica's four monkey species, these little guys have squirrel-like bushy tails, but they use them only for balance—they can't swing from them.

Watch, too, for less active creatures, such as the more-or-less stationary sloth, especially along the park's Sloth Trail. They sleep much of the day, curled up high in the trees. Look for clumps of green and brown and watch carefully to see if they move. You'll see many more animals and birds with a guide than without one. Hire an official guide at the park entrance.

TOP REASONS TO GO

BEACHES
There are gorgeous beaches with no commercial clutter or noise, but you need to bring your own snorkeling gear, snacks, and drinks. Only sandwiches, fruit, and nonalcoholic beverages are allowed in the park. There are toilet facilities and cold-water, open-air showers.

MONKEYS
Along with the ubiquitous capuchin monkeys performing for visitors on the beaches, you'll also find howler monkeys (*congos*) draped over tree branches in the forest, and more rarely, the endangered squirrel monkey.

PELICANS
Just off Playa Espadilla, you can swim out to some rocks and tread water while pelicans dive for fish.

VIEWS
For a fabulous coastal view, take the path that leads up to Punta Catedral's rocky hill, draped with thick jungle. You'll pass a lookout point with a view out at the Pacific and the park's islets.

An iguana sunbathes in Manuel Antonio.

The Central Pacific region of Costa Rica is a long swath of gorgeous land, encompassing sublime coastline dotted with national parks and palm-lined beaches, and inland stretches of ranches, coffee plantations, small villages, and forested mountains. There's a reason this is a popular place to visit: the region has a lot of *pura vida* to offer.

If you're a first-timer to Costa Rica, this region is all about Manuel Antonio and the acclaimed national park of the same name. (Manuel Antonio and the Arenal Volcano in the Northern Lowlands make the classic "get your feet wet" visit to Costa Rica.) For Costa Ricans, the Central Pacific often means Jacó, the closest beach town to San José, and an odd mix of burgeoning condo developments, nightclubs, hotels, and surf shops. But you need not limit yourself to these two anchors: Herradura, Playas Hermosa, Esterillos, and Bejuco along this stretch of coast offer a little more solitude, although development is slowly creeping up here, too.

The region is easily accessible by way of the San José–Caldera Highway CR27, which connects to the Southern Coastal Highway CR34.

MAJOR REGIONS

From Tárcoles to Quepos along Costa Rica's **Central Pacific Coast,** you'll find patches of undeveloped jungle, small surf towns, and some of the country's most accessible beaches. The proximity of these strands to San José leads Costa Ricans and foreigners alike to pop down for quick weekend beach vacations. Surfers have good reason to head for the consistent waves of Playas Jacó and Hermosa, and anglers and golfers should consider Playa Herradura for its golf courses and ocean access. You might find Herradura and Jacó overrated and overdeveloped, but the latter is a good option if you're looking for shopping, surfing, and nightlife.

South of the beach communities and surf stops along the Central Pacific coast are the towns of Quepos and **Manuel Antonio,** as well as the popular Manuel Antonio National Park. Unless you're stocking up on supplies or making a bank run, it's better to bypass Quepos, a former banana port and now a somewhat run-down fishing town. Most travelers head straight to Manuel Antonio, where boutique hotels and luxury resorts are perched on beachside cliffs or frame the national park. Between surf lessons, canopy tours, exploring the national park, and relaxing on the beach, it's easy to fall in love with this quaint town where the jungle meets the shore. Equally impressive is the town's reputation for sustainability practices, from green hotels to organic cuisine. Although some consider Manuel Antonio overdeveloped, nobody can deny its spectacular natural beauty.

Planning

When to Go

HIGH SEASON: DECEMBER TO APRIL

Dry season means high season here. Your payback for braving the crowds is nearly ideal weather. Expect warm, sunny days and pleasant evenings. If, however, you're not big on heat, March and April may feel stiflingly hot. Lots of visitors push hotel prices up and crowd the beaches, especially on dry-season weekends. Weekdays offer a slight respite from the crowds. During Holy Week and the last week of December, rooms are even harder to come by. If you're in the area during high season and want to visit one of the parks, especially Manuel Antonio, get an early start and arrive by 7 am.

LOW SEASON: SEPTEMBER TO NOVEMBER

This is the wettest of the rainy season, when showers become frequent and prolonged. The landmass and wind patterns that cause hurricane activity off the Caribbean coast create significant rain in the Central Pacific. Nature-themed activities usually go on rain or shine, but beach-lazing plans may well go awry. Keep in mind that some smaller hotels and restaurants actually close for several weeks during low season.

SHOULDER SEASON: MAY TO AUGUST

The rains begin in mid-May, but the first half of the wet season sees warm, mostly sunny days with lighter afternoon showers. It's easy to plan around them, and the precipitation keeps everything lush and green. Midyear school vacations fall in early July, with Costa Rican families flocking to the beach, especially Jacó and Manuel Antonio.

Planning Your Time

A week gives you enough time to visit several beaches on the central coast and still explore the wildlife of Manuel Antonio National Park. Adventure seekers might want to set aside a day for a surf lesson, forest hike, or canopy tour. The perfect balance is three days in scenic Manuel Antonio, two days at a secluded beach near Tárcoles or Playa Bejuco, and a couple of days for surfing and action close to bustling Jacó.

Getting Here and Around

AIR

The 20-minute flight between San José and Quepos, on Skyway, or SANSA, can save you the three-hour drive and costs between $65 and $85 one way. From San José, all airlines have daily flights to Quepos departing between 8 and 3.

SANSA Airlines. ⊠ *Juan Santamaría International Airport (SJO), Alajuela* ☎ *2290–4100* ⊕ *www.flysansa.com.* **Skyway.** ⊠ *Juan Santamaría International Airport (SJO), Alajuela* ☎ *4002–3816, 888/524–9396 from U.S.* ⊕ *www.facebook.com/SkywayCR.*

BUS

Public buses to and within this entire region are punctual and economical, and local shuttles from San José can drop you off at your hotel's doorstep. Public buses leave San José almost hourly between 6 am and 7:30 pm and take four hours to reach Quepos. From here you have to take local transportation to your hotel in Manuel Antonio. Gray Line and Interbus are more direct, with hotel pickup in San José and Quepos or Manuel Antonio. Both companies offer a morning and afternoon trip for around $57 one way.

BUS CONTACTS Gray Line. ☎ *2220–2126, 800/719–3905 toll-free from U.S. and Canada* ⊕ *www.graylinecostarica.com.*

Interbus. ☎ 4100–0888 ⊕ www.interbusonline.com.

CAR

Highway 27 connects San José to the Pacific port of Caldera, near Puntarenas. This 77-km (46-mile) toll road eliminates a winding drive through the mountains and puts the coast just one hour from the capital. Costa Ricans call the modern road the Carretera a Caldera (Caldera Highway). Before the coast, an exit to the two-lane paved coastal highway, or Costanera, leads southeast to Tárcoles, Herradura, Jacó, Hermosa, Esterillos, Bejuco, and Quepos. An asphalt road winds its way over the hill between Quepos and Manuel Antonio National Park—plan on about 1½ hours to drive to Jacó and 2½ hours to Quepos.

Tours

King Tours

ADVENTURE TOURS | A roster of tours includes trips to renowned attractions like Manuel Antonio National Park, as well as crocodile boat adventures, whale watching, deep-sea and coastal fishing trips, horseback rides to waterfalls, and canopy tours. The company can also book tours to destinations elsewhere in the country, such as Poás and Arenal volcanoes, Monteverde Cloud Forest, and Isla Tortuga. ⊠ Main road into Playa Herradura, in front of Los Sueños, Herradura ☎ 8819–1920, 800/213–7091 in North America ⊕ www.kingtours.com ⊠ From $85.

Team CRT

ADVENTURE TOURS | The many services include a variety of Central Pacific tours, such as a canopy tour near Manuel Antonio, kayaking, and rafting. ☎ 2508–5000, 888/236–4447 in North America ⊕ www.costarica4u.com ⊠ Kayaking $69; canopy tour $75; rafting and national park tour $98.

BIRD-WATCHING GUIDES

Birding Costa Rica

GUIDED TOURS | For a Manuel Antonio–area day trip, Johann Fernandez will pick you up early and take you to two spots to see toucans, tanagers, flycatchers, herons, spoonbills, kingfishers, and more. You can see 50–100 species on this full-day tour. He also does longer tours in which you go across the country. ⊠ Manuel Antonio ☎ 8825–6323 ⊕ costaricanbirder.com ⊠ $195 for groups up to 4.

Restaurants

You'll find the liveliest dining mix in the country outside San José here, especially in Manuel Antonio. The crowd of international visitors has brought international restaurants ranging from Japanese to Italian, but as you'd expect in a coastal region, seafood still reigns here. For traditional Costa Rican cuisine, your best bet is a roadside *soda* where locals gather for their daily *casado* (rice, beans, plantains, and an entrée of chicken, beef, or fish). Your final bill will include a 13% sales tax and a 10%–12% service charge.

Hotels

The Central Pacific has a good mix of high-quality resorts, eco-lodges, rental villas, boutique hotels, and *cabinas* (usually low-cost, freestanding cabins with more amenities than a standard room). You'll also find some of the country's priciest lodgings. As a rule, prices drop 20% to 30% during the rainy season. Hotel rooms are taxed at the national rate of 13%. Reserve as far in advance as possible during the busy dry season, especially on weekends. Near Manuel Antonio National Park, the cliffside hotels with ocean views are the more activity-rich, attractive, and expensive places to stay. *Hotel reviews have been shortened. For full information, visit Fodors.com.*

WHAT IT COSTS in U.S. Dollars			
$	$$	$$$	$$$$
RESTAURANTS			
under $10	$10–$15	$16–$25	over $25
HOTELS			
under $75	$75–$150	$151–$250	over $250

Tárcoles

90 km (54 miles) southwest of San José.

Crocodile boat tours on the Río Tárcoles are this small town's claim to fame. You don't actually have to drive to Tárcoles to do the tour; operators can pick you up in Herradura or Jacó. Budget (or time-conscious) travelers may want to simply stop near Río Tárcoles bridge where dozens of crocodiles gather on the banks. It's easy to snap a few photos from the top of the bridge, but be sure to lock your car and watch for oncoming traffic and Tourist Police, who make this a regular ticketing location for speedy drivers. The muddy river has gained a reputation as the country's dirtiest, thanks to San José's inadequate sewage system, but it amazingly remains an impressive refuge for wildlife. A huge diversity of birds results from a combination of transitional forest and the river, which houses crocodiles, herons, storks, spoonbills, and other waterbirds. This is also one of the few areas in the country where you can see scarlet macaws, which you may spot on a boat tour or while hiking in a private reserve nearby. If you have the time, drive 12 km (8 miles) south of the Río Tárcoles bridge and take a dip in the pools of Catarata Manantial de Agua Viva. As the highest waterfall in Costa Rica, these freshwater cascades are located 4 km (2½ miles) past Hotel Villa Lapas.

GETTING HERE AND AROUND

By car, head west from San José on Highway 27 to Orotina and follow the signs to Herradura, Jacó, and Quepos. After crossing the bridge over the Río Tárcoles, look for the entrance to the town of Tárcoles on the right. On the left is the dirt road that leads to the Hotel Villa Lapas and the waterfall reserve. Any bus traveling to Jacó can drop you off at the entrance to Tárcoles. Let the driver know in advance.

 ## Activities

BOAT TOURS

On the two-hour riverboat tours through the mangrove forest and Tárcoles River, you might see massive crocodiles, Jesus lizards, iguanas, and some of roughly 50 colorful bird species, including the roseate spoonbill and boat-billed heron. Tours reach the river's mouth, providing nice sea views, especially at sunset. ■**TIP**→ **Around noon is the best time to spot crocs sunbathing; bird enthusiasts prefer afternoon rides to catch scarlet macaws. During the rainy season (May to November), the river may grow too rough for boats in the afternoon.**

Crocodile Man Tour

TOUR—SPORTS | Small scars on the hands of the two brothers who run the company are the result of the tour's most original (and optional) attraction: feeding fish to the crocs. The boats are small enough to slide up alongside the mangroves for a closer look. Transportation is provided from nearby beaches (at an added cost), but not from San José. Daily tours take place every two hours from 8 to 4. They also offer a bird-watching tour at 6 am. ✉ *Main road into Tárcoles* ☎ *2637–0771* ⊕ *crocodilemantour.com* 💲 *$35.*

HIKING

Catarata Manantial de Agua Viva

BODY OF WATER | This is Costa Rica's tallest waterfall, cascading 600 feet into freshwater pools where you can cool off after a strenuous 3-km (2-mile) hike to the river basin. You're not likely to see other tourists here—it's not one of the more well-known waterfalls. This trek is not suitable for children, the elderly, or those with health conditions. Wear proper shoes as rocks can be sharp and slippery. ⊠ *On dirt road 4 km (2½ miles) past Hotel Villa Lapas* ✢ *Look for a sign reading "cascada".* ☎ *8831–2980* ⌦ *$20.*

Hotels

Hotel Villa Lapas
$$ | **RESORT** | **FAMILY** | Within a tranquil rain-forest preserve, the stucco rooms here are nothing special, but are a great escape for nature lovers with their white tile floors, hardwood ceilings, and large baths. **Pros:** surrounded by forest; lots of activities; birds. **Cons:** rooms sometimes musty; property is a bit tired looking; often busy with tour groups. $ *Rooms from: $79* ⊠ *Off Costanera, 3 km (2 miles) after bridge over Río Tárcoles, turn left on dirt road for 600 m* ☎ *2637–0232* ⊕ *www.villalapas.com* ⊰ *67 rooms* ⦿ *Free Breakfast.*

Punta Leona

13 km (8 miles) south of Tárcoles.

Past Tárcoles, the first sizable beach town of the Central Pacific coast is Playa Herradura. In between, the road passes tiny Playa La Pita, then heads inland where it crosses the entrance to Punta Leona, a vast hotel and residential complex. The road then winds its way up a steep hill, atop which is the entrance to the luxury hotel Villa Caletas. On the other side of that ridge is the bay and beach of Herradura.

Beaches

Playa La Pita
BEACH—SIGHT | About a kilometer (½ mile) south after the entrance to Tárcoles, the Costanera passes this small beach that provides your first glimpse of the Pacific if you're coming down from San José or the Central Valley. The beach is rocky, and its proximity to the crocodile-infested Río Tárcoles makes the water murky and dangerous for swimming, but it's a nice spot to stop and admire the ocean and birds. **Amenities:** food and drink. **Best for:** sunset; walking. ⊠ *Tárcoles.*

Restaurants

Mirador Restaurant
$$$$ | **ECLECTIC** | White tablecloths, glass walls, and yellow-and-blue-checkered curtains contribute to the sophisticated but not overly stuffy atmosphere of this hotel dining room. Appetizers range from the traditional escargots to a shrimp-and-lobster bisque, and entrées include beef tenderloin with chimichurri, jumbo shrimp sautéed with white wine and passion fruit, and roasted duck with truffle oil. **Known for:** extensive wine list; creamy risotto; stunning sunset views. $ *Average main: $50* ⊠ *Villa Caletas hotel, off coastal hwy., 3 km (2 miles) south of Punta Leona, Tárcoles* ☎ *2630–3000* ⊕ *hotelvillacaletas.com* ⊘ *No lunch.*

Hotels

★ Villa Caletas
$$$ | **RESORT** | Perched 1,200 feet above the sea on a promontory south of Punta Leona, the elegant rooms sequestered in the jungle have jaw-dropping views of the surrounding foliage and sea below. **Pros:** gorgeous views; secluded setting; on-site spa. **Cons:** some rooms are musty; lots of stairs; 20-minute drive to nearest beach. $ *Rooms from: $200* ⊠ *Off coastal hwy., 3 km (2 miles) south of Punta Leona, on right, Tárcoles*

Diving the Deep at Cocos Island

Rated one of the top diving destinations in the world, Isla del Coco is uninhabited and remote (32 hours by boat), and its waters are teeming with marine life. It's no place for beginners, but serious divers enjoy 100-foot visibility and the underwater equivalent of a big-game park. Scalloped hammerheads, white-tipped reef sharks, Galápagos sharks, bottlenose dolphins, billfish, and manta rays mix with huge schools of brilliantly colored fish.

Encompassing about 22½ square km (9 square miles), Isla del Coco is one of the largest uninhabited islands on Earth. Its isolation has led to the evolution of dozens of endemic plant and animal species. The rocky topography is draped in rain forest and cloud forest and includes more than 200 waterfalls. Because of Isla del Coco's distance from shore (484 km [300 miles]) and its craggy topography, few visitors to Costa Rica—and even fewer Costa Ricans—have set foot on the island.

Costa Rica annexed Coco in 1869, and it became a national park in 1978. Today only extremely high-priced specialty cruise ships, park rangers, volunteers, and scientists visit this place. The dry season (December to April) brings calmer seas and is the best time to see silky sharks. During the rainy season large schools of hammerheads can be seen, but the ocean is rougher.

Two boats, *Okeanos Aggressor* and *Undersea Hunter*, offer regular 8- to 10-day dive cruises from Puntarenas that include three days of travel time on the open ocean and cost roughly $5,000 to $6,000, depending on the boat and dates.

☎ 2630–3000, 2257–3653 *in San José* ⊕ *hotelvillacaletas.com* 🛏 *52 units* 🍽 *Free Breakfast.*

Playa Herradura

20 km (12 miles) south of Tárcoles.

Just north of bustling Jacó, this small beach town, named for its horseshoe-shape bay, is made up of hotels, a golf course, and a marina. Once a sleepy fishing village, it has transformed into one of the country's fastest-developing areas. The entrance to town is marked by a shopping complex complete with fast-food chains and a surf shop. A paved road connecting the coastal highway to the beach dead-ends at the sand where three seafood shacks line the shores; the best is the more upscale El Pelicano.

Golfers and sportfishing fans alike are drawn to the pristine beauty of Playa Herradura, and the placid waters tend to keep surfers farther down the coast, where waves are abundant. It's an attractive alternative to Jacó if you'd like to be driving distance to the hustle and bustle but in a more tranquil spot.

GETTING HERE AND AROUND
By car, head 20 minutes straight down the Pacific Highway. The town's entrance is on the right-hand side, where a long paved road leads to the beach. Follow the signs to the Marriott.

 ## Beaches

Playa Herradura
BEACH—SIGHT | If sportfishing, boating, and golfing are your priorities, this is a good option. If you're looking for

seclusion, a beautiful beach, or a bargain, keep driving. Rocky Playa Herradura is a poor representative of Costa Rica's breathtaking beaches, although its tranquil waters make it considerably safer for swimming and stand-up paddleboarding than most central and southern Pacific beaches. It gets its name from the Spanish word for "horseshoe," referring to the shape of the deep bay in which it lies. Playa Herradura's safety factor, coupled with the fact that it's the closest beach to San José, has turned it into a popular weekend getaway for Josefinos, who compete for shade beneath the sparse palms and Indian almond trees that line the beach. On the north end is Los Sueños, which includes a large marina, shopping center, hundreds of condos, a golf course, and a massive Marriott hotel. This is the sportfishing capital of Costa Rica, so expect plenty of boats anchored offshore. The rough black sand makes the water look somewhat dark and dirty at times. **Amenities:** food and drink; toilets; water sports. **Best for:** swimming. ✉ *Near Los Suenos Marriott, 4 km (2½ miles) north of Jacó, Herradura.*

 Restaurants

Restaurante El Pelícano
$$$ | SEAFOOD | It may not look like much at first glance, but this open-air restaurant across the street from the beach serves some dishes you'd be hard-pressed to find in other casual beach-town places. Request one of the outdoor tables under the bamboo dome and dine on dishes like fish croquettes in a lemon sauce, grilled tuna in mango sauce, and clams au gratin. **Known for:** "formal" beachfront dining; deep-fried whole red snapper; tagliata: lobster, octopus, jumbo shrimp, and mahimahi complete with tableside fire show. $ *Average main: $20* ✉ *Turn left at end of main road into Playa Herradura, Herradura* ☎ *2637–8910* ⊕ *elpelicanorestaurante.com.*

 Hotels

Los Sueños Marriott Ocean and Golf Resort
$$$ | RESORT | FAMILY | This mammoth multimillion-dollar resort in a palatial colonial-style building has a gorgeous view of Herradura Bay and combines modern amenities with traditional Central American decorative motifs, such as barrel-tile roofing and hand-painted tiles. **Pros:** good base for excursions; kids' club with activities throughout the day; swimming pool the size of a soccer field. **Cons:** expensive; so-so rooms and service; beach can be dirty. $ *Rooms from: $190* ✉ *1 km (½ mile) west of road to Jacó from San José, follow signs at entrance of road to Playa Herradura, Herradura* ☎ *2630–9000, 888/236–2427 in North America, 2298–0000 in San José* ⊕ *www.marriott.com* ⤳ *201 rooms* ❍❘ *No meals.*

🏃 Activities

Few activities are available directly in Playa Herradura, but most of the area's diverse outfitters can pick you up at your hotel for activities near Jacó and Playa Hermosa. Your hotel's reception desk is often a good source of information.

FISHING
Maverick Sportfishing
FISHING | One of the area's oldest and most reputable sportfishing outfitters offers trips to fishing grounds just an hour offshore in calm waters. As the only authorized charter operator in Los Sueños, tours leave the marina at 7 am and return at 4 pm. Also available are half-day fishing trips, sunset cruises, and boat trips to Tortuga Island. ✉ *Los Sueños Marina, at charter dock at Playa Herradura, Herradura* ☎ *2637–8516, 337/205–0665 in North America* ⊕ *www.costaricadreams.com* ☎ *From $1,500 half day for up to 4 people.*

GOLF

La Iguana Golf Club

GOLF | Designed by Ted Robinson, this course at Los Sueños Marriott is cradled between rain forest and ocean, allowing you to play alongside local wildlife like macaws, iguanas, and monkeys (known to steal the ball when you're not looking). The championship course is long, narrow, and well manicured, and there's a putting green, driving range, and PGA-qualified golf instructors. Overlooking the 18th hole is a restaurant where you can take a break and admire the scenery. Marriott members get a discount on the greens fees; otherwise expect a pricey game of golf and expensive restaurant and pro shop. ⊠ Los Sueños Marriott, 1 km (½ mile) west of Herradura entrance, Herradura ☎ 2630–9151 ⊕ www.golflaiguana. com ⊵ 18 holes from $195 ⅄. 18 holes, 6698 yards, par 72.

Jacó

7 km (4 miles) south of Playa Herradura, 114 km (70 miles) southwest of San José.

Its proximity to San José has made Jacó the most developed beach town in Costa Rica. Nature lovers and solitude seekers may want to skip this rather seedy but bustling town. While in the past, Jacó has been known mostly for its nightlife, surf scene, and prostitution, recent efforts to make it a more family-friendly destination include parks, playgrounds, and kid-friendly restaurants. More than 80 hotels and cabinas back its long, gray-sand beach, and the mix of restaurants, shops, and bars lining Avenida Pastor Díaz (the town's main drag) give it a cluttered appearance devoid of any greenery. Any real Costa Rican–ness evaporated years ago; U.S. chain hotels, casinos, restaurants, and a new shopping center have invaded the area, and you can pretty much find anything you need, from law offices and dental clinics to tattoo parlors and appliance stores. In recent years, several expats have opened a handful of cheerful cafés, restaurants, and hotels on side streets, offering a splash of color to the grungy town. Jacó does provide everything in terms of tours and outdoor activities, and makes a convenient hub for exploring neighboring beaches and attractions. Theft can be a problem here.

GETTING HERE AND AROUND

The drive from San José takes less than two hours; take Highway 27 west of San José beyond Orotina, and then take the exit to Jacó and Quepos. The exit, on the right after Herradura, is well marked. There's a gas station at the second entrance to town close to Club del Mar. Buses leave from San José's Terminal 7-10 station seven times daily, with an extra run on weekends.

RENTAL CARS Alamo. ⊠ Avda. Pastor Díaz, 50 m south of Subway ☎ 2643–1752 ⊕ www.alamocostarica.com. **Budget.** ⊠ Avda. Pastor Díaz, 100 m South of Supermarket Mas X Menos ☎ 2643–2665 ⊕ www.budget.co.cr. **Economy.** ⊠ Avda. Pastor Díaz, 100 m south of Best Western ☎ 2643–1719 ⊕ www.economyrentacar.com. **Hertz.** ⊠ Plaza Coral 20 ⊹ Next to MegaSuper ☎ 2643–1802 ⊕ www.hertzcostarica.com.

TAXIS Taxi services. ☎ 2643–2020, 2643–2121, 2643–3030.

ESSENTIALS

BANKS/ATMS BAC San José. ⊠ Centro Comercial II Galeone ☎ 2295–9797. **Banco Nacional.** ⊠ Avda. Pastor Díaz ☎ 2643–3621 ⊕ www.bncr.fi.cr.

HOSPITAL Clínica De Jacó. ⊠ In front of Plaza de Deportes ☎ 2643–1767.

PHARMACIES Farmacia Jacó. ⊠ Plaza El Jardín, Avda. Pastor Díaz, across from Mas X Menos supermarket ☎ 2643–3205. **Farmacia La Económica.** ⊠ Avda. Pastor Díaz, across from Banco Nacional ☎ 2643–6544.

Did You Know?

Jacó's gray-sand beach is a great place to surf and soak up the sun.

POST OFFICE Correos. ⊠ *Avda. Pastor Díaz, across from the municipality and Transit Police* ☎ *2643–2175.*

 Beaches

Playa Jacó

BEACH—SIGHT | This long, palm-lined beach west of town is a pleasant enough spot in the morning but can burn the soles of your feet on a sunny afternoon. Though the gray sand and beachside construction make this spot less attractive than most other Costa Rican beaches, it's a good place to soak up the sun or enjoy a sunset. The beach is popular with surfers for the consistency of its waves, but when the surf is up, swimmers should beware of dangerous rip currents. Smaller waves make this beach ideal for surf lessons or longboarders. Bigger waves are found 5 km (3 miles) south at Playa Hermosa (a blue flag beach). During the rainy months the ocean here is not very clean. The stretch near Jacó Laguna Resort is less crowded and their tiki bar is a great spot to grab a cocktail at sunset. **Amenities:** food and drink; toilets (at local restaurants and hotels). **Best for:** sunsets; surfing. ⊠ *Jacó.*

Restaurants

★ Amancio's Pizza Pasta and Drinks

$$ | ITALIAN | Taste the passion that the chef and owner has for the simple things in life: fresh ingredients, made-from-scratch bread and pasta, and sauces that simmer all day. Grab some calzones to take to the beach, or dine in on the Italian plate, an overflowing platter of house-cured salami and other meats, along with olives and cheeses straight from Italy. **Known for:** pizza; family atmosphere; lobster fettuccine. $ *Average main: $15* ⊠ *Centro Comercial El Jardín* ☎ *6021–8455.*

Graffiti Restro Cafe and Wine Bar

$$ | ECLECTIC | The gritty-gourmet concept of this upscale Jacó hot spot plays with the senses with a menu that features fresh, locally grown ingredients. Check the blackboard for specials—whatever has inspired the chef that day—and wash it down with a signature lemongrass martini. **Known for:** cacao-and-coffee-rubbed beef tenderloin; tuna tower; live music on Wednesday and Friday. $ *Average main: $15* ⊠ *Jacó Walk Open Air Shopping Plaza* ☎ *2643–1708* ⊕ *graffitirestro.com* ☾ *No lunch.*

Green Room

$$ | CAFÉ | Bordered by a white picket fence, this charming café serves meals prepared with organic ingredients delivered daily by local farmers. The ever-changing chalkboard menu usually features home-ground burgers with fresh-baked buns or seared ahi on buckwheat noodles with roasted vegetables. **Known for:** barbecue ribs; live entertainment every night; lavender honey cocktail, with honey whiskey, muddled blueberries, and a lavender reduction. $ *Average main: $10* ⊠ *Corner of Avda. Pastor Díaz and C. Cocal* ☎ *2643–4425* ⊕ *greenroomjaco.com.*

Ohana Sushi Tapas Bar

$$ | ASIAN FUSION | Don't worry about getting dressed up for this unfussy sushi fusion restaurant, built from a colorful shipping container, found driftwood, and recycled pallets. The food is made with as much innovation, creativity, and care, blending flavors perfectly in popular sushi, salads, and Asian-fusion meat dishes. **Known for:** consistently fresh, delicious sushi; yaki sticks (grilled skewers with tenderloin, fish, seafood, or chicken); vegan and gluten-free options. $ *Average main: $13* ⊠ *Calle El Hicaco, 50 m before beach* ☎ *2643–2226* ⊕ *ohana-sushi-tapas-y-bar.business.site* ☾ *Closed Wed.*

PuddleFish Brewery

$$ | MODERN AMERICAN | FAMILY | This brewery tasting room serves tasty American-style pub grub. Sit in the modern outdoor area under the shade, or belly up to the bar inside and try a beer flight to go along with your burger or sandwich. **Known for:** flavorful craft beers; tuna steak sandwich; Sunday brunch with bottomless mimosas. $ *Average main: $12* ✉ *Jacó Walk Open Air Shopping Center* ☎ *2643–1659* ⊕ *puddlefishbrewery.com.*

Hotels

Club del Mar

$$$ | RESORT | FAMILY | At the second entrance to Jacó on the beach's southern end, one of the town's better lodgings includes green-and-cream-hue rooms with private teak balconies and spacious one- and two-bedroom condos. **Pros:** beautiful beachfront location; washer and dryer; friendly, helpful staff. **Cons:** some highway noise reaches back to condos; hard mattresses; no bathtubs in standard rooms. $ *Rooms from: $160* ✉ *Costanera, 300 m south of El Arroyo gas station* ☎ *2643–3194, 866/978–5669 in North America* ⊕ *www.clubdelmarcostarica. com* ⇴ *33 units* �‖ *Free Breakfast.*

DoceLunas

$$$ | HOTEL | The spacious, teak-furnished rooms at "Twelve Moons" are a couple of miles from the sea and sand, and noise, set amid 5 acres of lawns shaded by tropical trees and luxuriant gardens with a mountainous green backdrop. **Pros:** more secluded than other Jacó lodgings; terrific restaurant; beautiful grounds. **Cons:** 10-minute walk to beach; some rooms are rather dark; some rooms need updating. $ *Rooms from: $170* ✉ *On coastal hwy. from San José, pass 1st entrance to Jacó; take dirt road on left with signs for DoceLunas at main entrance to Quebrada Seca* ☎ *2643–2211* ⊕ *www.docelunas.com* ⇴ *20 rooms* �‖ *Free Breakfast.*

Hotel Mar de Luz

$$ | HOTEL | FAMILY | A few blocks from the beach, this family-focused property boasts three swimming pools, equipped kitchens, and comfortable rooms of varying size and style. **Pros:** attentive owner; solar-powered property; close to the beach. **Cons:** some rooms are musty with lukewarm water; bathrooms need renovation; thin walls. $ *Rooms from: $129* ✉ *C. Mar de Luz, behind Subway, east of Avda. Pastor Díaz* ☎ *2643–3000* ⊕ *www.mardeluz.com* ⇴ *29 rooms* �‖ *Free Breakfast.*

★ Hotel Pumilio

$$$$ | HOTEL | FAMILY | A peaceful retreat just five minutes outside bustling Jacó, this all-suites hotel is surrounded by lush rain forest and has tastefully decorated rooms with fully equipped kitchens and patios overlooking the pool, mountains, and gardens. **Pros:** quiet location; beautiful and clean rooms; excellent staff. **Cons:** far from beach; restaurant serves breakfast only; very firm beds. $ *Rooms from: $273* ✉ *From Herradura's stoplight 2 km (1 mile) on Rte. 34 south, 1 km (½ mile) to left* ☎ *2643–5678, 800/410–8018 in U.S.* ⊕ *www.hotelpumilio.com* ⇴ *10 rooms* �‖ *Free Breakfast.*

Jacó Laguna Resort

$$ | HOTEL | On the quiet southern end of Jacó beach, this property is clean and comfortable and just far enough from town to offer a peaceful night of sleep. **Pros:** in low season, guests are generously upgraded; great tiki bar; ideal location. **Cons:** hallway noise; weak Wi-Fi signal in some rooms; mattresses lack support. $ *Rooms from: $133* ✉ *Corner of C. Madrigal and Avda. Pastor Díaz* ☎ *2643–3362, 215/942–5135 in U.S.* ⊕ *www. jacolagunaresort.com* ⇴ *26 rooms* �‖ *No meals.*

Nightlife

Whereas other beach towns may have a bar or two, Jacó has an avenue full of them, with enough variety for many different tastes. After-dinner spots range from restaurants perfect for a quiet drink to loud bars with pool tables and dance

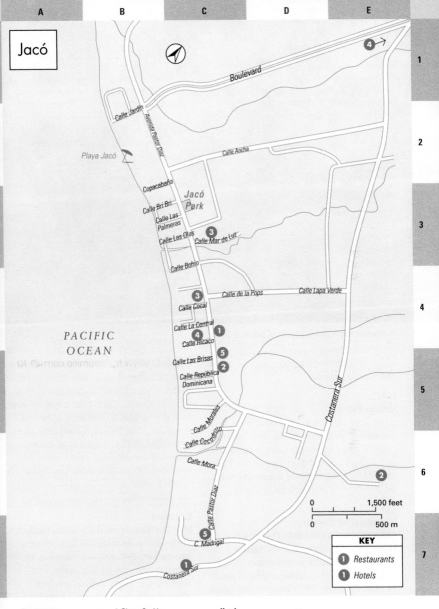

	A	B	C	D	E

Jacó

Boulevard

Calle Jardín

Avenida Pastor Díaz

Playa Jacó

Calle Ancha

Copacabaña

Jacó Park

Calle Bri Bri

Calle Las Palmeras

Calle Las Olas

Calle Mar de Luz

Calle Bohío

Calle de la Pops

Calle Lapa Verde

PACIFIC OCEAN

Calle Cocal

Calle La Central

Calle Hicaco

Calle Las Brisas

Calle República Dominicana

Costanera Sur

Calle Morales

Calle Cocodrillo

Calle Mora

Calle Pastor Díaz

C. Madrigal

Costanera Sur

0   1,500 feet

0   500 m

KEY

1 Restaurants

1 Hotels

Restaurants ▼

1 Amancio's Pizza Pasta and Drinks **C4**

2 Graffiti Restro Cafe and Wine Bar **C5**

3 Green Room **C4**

4 Ohana Sushi Tapas Bar **C4**

5 PuddleFish Brewery **C5**

Hotels ▼

1 Club del Mar.............. **C7**

2 DoceLunas **E6**

3 Hotel Mar de Luz......... **C3**

4 Hotel Pumilio **E1**

5 Jacó Laguna Resort..... **C7**

A beautiful heron perched near the beach at Jacó

clubs. You can even try your luck at one of the town's casinos.

BARS
Orange Pub
BARS/PUBS | This is a good choice for a cocktail, after-dinner drinks, or a late-night meal. It has a big bar in back, pool tables, and DJs and dancing on weekends. ⊠ *Avda. Pastor Díaz, north of Il Galeone mall, across from C. Bohio* ☎ *8318–7206.*

LIVE MUSIC
★ PuddleFish Brewery
BREWPUBS/BEER GARDENS | This colorful bistro has live music several days of the week and handcrafted brews made in-house. ⊠ *C. Copacabana, 250 m south of Best Western, 20 m west of Bar Isaga* ☎ *2643–2724.*

Shopping

Souvenir shops with mostly the same mass-produced merchandise are crowded one after the other along the main street in the center of town. Most of the goods, like wooden crafts and seed jewelry, are run-of-the-mill souvenir fare, but a few shops have more unusual items. If you plan on buying any surf-related products, this is your place, as even surf wax is hard to come by once you leave Jacó. Jacó Walk, a shopping area with retail stores, restaurants, entertainment venues, cultural exhibits, and business offices all in one open space, is worth a visit.

CRAFTS
Cocobolo
CRAFTS | Named for the tropical hardwood of the cocobolo tree, this large shop is jam-packed with wooden handicrafts hanging from the ceiling, walls, and shelves. It's much of what you find in other stores, but with more tasteful items and a richer variety. In addition to wood carvings, they sell clothing, hammocks, jewelry, and locally made crafts. ⊠ *Avda. Pastor Díaz, 300 m north of Banco Nacional, next to Jass Surf Shop* ☎ *2643–3486.*

FOOD AND CANDY

Fruity Monkey Poop / Costa Rica Coffee Experience

FOOD/CANDY | For locally grown coffee and reasonably priced artisan crafts, this place offers the best shopping in Jacó. They serve marvelous iced coffees, natural iced teas, and fresh-roasted coffee. Be sure to try a sample of their chocolate, pineapple licorice, and "Fruity Monkey Poop" (actually just candied nuts). ⊠ *Avda. Pastor Díaz, across from Banco Nacional and Mas X Menos market* ☎ *2643–6197.*

SPORTING GOODS

Cartón

SPORTING GOODS | Cartón sells new and used boards and shapes for some of Costa Rica's top surfers. It's not only the shape, but also the artwork that makes Cartón's boards so extraordinary. Boards can be shipped internationally for around $80. Their two-hour surf lessons are held just past the surf shop at Madrigal Beach. They also offer surf tours. ⊠ *C. Madrigal, near gas station* ☎ *2643–3762 7210–9799* ⊕ *www.cartonsurfboards.com.*

Jass Surf Shop

SPORTING GOODS | As Jacó's first surf shop, this well-stocked store has a good variety of surf gear at decent prices. They sell new and used surfboards and stand-up paddleboards, and will buy back your board at the end of your trip for half the purchase price. Two-hour surf lessons cost $45. ⊠ *Avda. Pastor Díaz, next to La Perla, 200 m north of Banco Nacional* ☎ *2643–3850.*

🏃 Activities

TOUR OPERATORS

You don't have to physically step into any tour office, because everyone from a reception desk attendant to a boutique salesperson can book you a local adventure. Almost every tour can pick you up at your hotel's doorstep. ■TIP→ **Keep in**

Riptides

Riptides (or rip currents), common in Jacó and Manuel Antonio's Playa Espadilla, are dangerous and have led to many deaths over the years. If you get caught in one, don't panic and don't try to swim against it as paddling to shore will simply expend your energy. Riptides are generally less than 100 feet wide, so simply swim parallel to shore until you feel the power dissipate. Once you are out of the current, swim back to the beach. The best policy is not to go in deeper than your waist when the waves loom large, and never swim alone.

mind that part of your price tag includes the salesperson's commission, so if you hear higher or lower prices from two different people, it's likely a reflection of a shift in the commission. You can try negotiating a better deal directly from the outfitter.

Adventure Tours

TOUR—SPORTS | Although this company is best known for having the safest ATV tours with the longest routes, we recommend their eco-friendly adventures like canopy tours, whitewater rafting, kayaking, and canyoning. ⊠ *Avda. Pastor Díaz, in center of Playa Jacó, behind Subway* ☎ *2643–5720, 800/761–7250 in North America* ⊕ *www.adventuretourscostarica.com* 🎟 *From $59.*

Gray Line Costa Rica

TOUR—SPORTS | Specializing in transportation services, Gray Line also arranges day trips from Jacó to Arenal and Poás volcanoes, Manuel Antonio National Park, Sarchí, Isla Tortuga, and raft trips on the Savegre River. ⊠ *Best Western Jacó Beach Resort* ☎ *2643–3231 in Jacó, 800/719–3905 in U.S.* ⊕ *www.graylinecostarica.com* 🎟 *Sightseeing from $59; rafting from $99.*

CANOPY TOURS

★ Rainforest Adventures

TOUR—SPORTS | A modified ski lift offers easy access to the tropical transitional forest, with eight-seat gondolas that float through the treetops within a 222-acre private nature reserve. The company has guided tours that explain aspects of the local ecology, sustainability programs, as well as a variety of eco-adventures. There is also a small serpentarium, a butterfly garden, a bat sanctuary, and a medicinal plant garden. A "Tranopy" tour combines the tram with a 10-cable zipline tour. A top attraction is a 164-foot waterfall climbing tour that includes ziplines, forest trekking, and a free fall. The International Ecotourism Society named Rainforest Adventures one of the most sustainable theme parks in the world. It is also considered to be one of the safest due to their double cables, chest harnesses, platform railings, certified guides, braking system, and high-tech equipment inspected annually. ✉ *3 km (2 miles) west of Jacó* ☎ *2224–5961, 866/759–8726 in North America* ✉ *From $65.*

HORSEBACK RIDING

■ **TIP→ When selecting a horseback-riding company, make sure the horses look healthy, cared for, and well fed, since some local outfitters place profits over the welfare of the horses.**

Discovery Horseback Tours

HORSEBACK RIDING | During these 2½-hour trail rides on healthy horses, you'll spend some time in the rain forest and also stop at a small waterfall where you can take a dip. The jungle spa will get you dirty at some mud baths, and another tour takes you on a sunset ride on the beach. For experienced riders only, the Bird's Eye View is a 2½-hour challenging ride through rivers and rain forest. Tours start at 8:30 and 2:30 weekdays, and only at 8:30 on Saturday. ✉ *Jacó* ☎ *8838–7550* ⊕ *www.horseridecostarica.com* ✉ *From $90 (cash only).*

KAYAKING AND CANOEING

Kayak Jacó

CANOEING/ROWING/SKULLING | **FAMILY** | Looking for waters calmer than those at Jacó Beach? Kayak Jacó takes you to secluded beaches for sea-kayaking tours and Hawaiian-style outrigger canoe trips that are appropriate for everyone in the family, from children to grandparents. The half-day tours include snorkeling (conditions permitting) at secluded beaches. A 2½-hour night tour starts at sunset and ends with s'mores and a bonfire on the beach. You can also charter a private sailboat. ✉ *Playa Agujas* ☎ *2643–1233* ⊕ *www.kayakjaco.com* ✉ *From $65. Transportation to/from your hotel $25.*

SURFING

Jacó has several beach breaks, all of which are best around high tide. Surfboard-toting tourists abound in Jacó, but you don't need to be an expert to enjoy the surf, as waves are often small enough for beginners, especially around low tide. Abundant surf shops rent boards and give lessons, usually closer to the south end of the beach where most surf schools set up camp. Prices range from $50 to $60 for two hours and usually include a board and transportation. If you plan to spend more than a week surfing, it might be cheaper to buy a used board and sell it back at the standard half price before you leave. Otherwise, you'll be paying airline transportation fees around $150 one way, and most likely your board will arrive damaged despite your bubble-wrapping efforts. For rental, Jacó has plenty of surf shops with solid quivers, with cheaper boards starting at $10 an hour. If you don't have much experience, don't go out when the waves are really big—Jacó sometimes gets very powerful swells, which result in dangerous rip currents. During the rainy season, waves are more consistent than in the dry months, when Jacó sometimes lacks surf.

School of the World

SURFING | Prefer your vacations with a side of knowledge? This unique camp-type school offers something for everyone. During a one-week stay you can do a course in photography, yoga, different levels of Spanish, surfing, and any combination thereof. Shared or private lodging includes private bathroom, air-conditioning, Wi-Fi, and fully equipped kitchen. ✉ *Off Avda. Pastor Díaz, 300 m east of POPS* ✛ *Turn left after Condominiums Nasua, 50 m on left* ☎ *2643–2462, 305/517–7689 in U.S.* ⊕ *www.schooloftheworld.org* ✉ *From $543 for a week.*

Tortuga Surf School

SURFING | Private surf lessons with Tortuga include board rental, water, fruit, and ISA-certified instructors (International Surfing Association). They also offer 7-, 14-, or 22-day Surf and Stay camps that combine lodging, lessons, and local excursions. ✉ *Hotel Perico Azul, C. Santana and Avda. Pastor Díaz* ☎ *8847–6289* ⊕ *www.tortugasurfcamp.com* ✉ *From $50 (cash only).*

SWIMMING

The big waves and dangerous rip currents that make surfing so popular here can make swimming dangerous. Lifeguards are on duty only at specific spots and only sporadically. If the ocean is rough, stay on the beach—dozens of swimmers have drowned here over the years.

When the ocean is calm, especially around low tide, you can swim just about anywhere along Playa Jacó. The sea is always calmer near the beach's northern and southern ends, but the ocean bottom is littered with rocks there, as it is in front of the small rivers that flow into the sea near the middle of this beach.

Playa Hermosa

5 km (3 miles) south of Jacó, 113 km (70 miles) southwest of San José.

On the other side of the rocky ridge that forms the southern edge of Playa Jacó is Playa Hermosa, a swath of dark-gray sand and driftwood stretching southeast as far as the eye can see, with consistent waves for surfers. For nonsurfers, outdoor options include horseback and canopy tours in the nearby forested hills, but all of these can be done from other beaches. As for the town itself, there's really not much, which is part of the attraction for travelers who want to escape Jacó's crowds and concrete towers. Most of the restaurants, bars, and hotels have cropped up one after the other on a thin stretch separating the highway and the beach. From June to December, olive ridley turtles nest on the beach at night, especially when there's not much moonlight. ■TIP➜ **Note: there is a second Playa Hermosa on the Guanacaste Pacific coast.**

GETTING HERE AND AROUND

If you have a car, take the coastal highway 5 km (3 miles) past Jacó. You'll see the cluster of businesses on the right. If you don't have your own transportation, take a taxi from Jacó or a local bus toward Quepos.

 ## Beaches

Playa Hermosa

BEACH—SIGHT | Despite its name, "Beautiful Beach" is hardly spectacular. The southern half of the wide beach lacks palm trees or other shade-providing greenery; its sand is scorching-hot in the afternoon; and frequent rip currents make it unsafe to swim when there are waves. But board riders find beauty in its consistent, hollow surf breaks. Beginner surfers should stick to Jacó since waves here are powerful and punchy, and will close out on big days. The beach's northern end is popular because it often has waves when other spots are flat, and the ocean is cleaner than at Jacó, except after heavy rains when there is floating debris. There is also plenty of forest covering the hills, and scarlet macaws sometimes gather in the Indian almond trees near the end of the beach. Amenities are all at the Backyard Bar. **Amenities:** food and drink; showers; toilets. **Best for:** sunset; surfing. ✉ *Playa Hermosa.*

🍴 Restaurants

The Backyard Bar

$$ | **ECLECTIC** | Playa Hermosa's original nightlife spot has a wooden deck in back overlooking the beach that is great for lunch and sunset, mostly because of the pleasant sea breezes and view of the surfers. The usual bar food—Tex-Mex standards and burgers—is complemented by fresh seafood, including ceviche, grilled tuna, lobster, and jumbo shrimp. **Known for:** surfing contest every Friday and Saturday; buffalo wings; breakfast. [$] *Average main: $11* ✉ *Costanera, southern end of town, next to the Backyard Hotel* ☎ *2643–7011* 🌐 *www.backyardhotel.com.*

🛏 Hotels

The Backyard Hotel

$$ | **HOTEL** | Surfers are the main clientele in these nice rooms with high ceilings, clay-tile floors, and sliding-glass doors that open onto semiprivate balconies and terraces, most of which have good views of Playa Hermosa. **Pros:** steps from the surf; gated parking; friendly staff. **Cons:** noise from bar next door; bland breakfast; thin sheets and towels. [$] *Rooms from: $140* ✉ *Costanera, southern end of town* ☎ *2643–7011* 🌐 *www.backyardhotel.com* 🛏 *8 rooms* 🍽 *Free Breakfast.*

Not that Playa Hermosa

"*¡Ojo!*" as they say. Watch out: Costa Rica has two Playa Hermosas. Don't confuse this one with the larger, more developed beach of the same name on the Guanacaste Pacific coast. Each has its fans, but the Central Pacific's Playa Hermosa is better known to Costa Ricans and to surfers.

Surf Inn

$$ | **B&B/INN** | Right in front of Hermosa's beach break, a mural of tall palms and peeling waves marks the entrance to this well-priced inn, which offers small apartments and studios. **Pros:** surfers' paradise; almost half-price in low season; kitchens in rooms. **Cons:** noise from neighboring bar; studios are dark; two-night minimum stay on weekends and holidays. [$] *Rooms from: $120* ✉ *Costanera, next to Backyard Hotel, 200 m south of soccer field* 🌐 *www.surfinnhermosa.com* 🛏 *6 units* 🍽 *No meals.*

🏃 Activities

You can arrange activities throughout the Central Pacific from Playa Hermosa. Most tour operators and outfitters include transportation in their prices. *For more options, see Activities in Jacó, above, or consult your hotel's reception.*

NATURE AND WILDLIFE TOURS

Playa Hermosa Turtle Tours

TOUR—SPORTS | Raúl Fernández takes small groups to look for nesting sea turtles on Playa Hermosa between July and December, as part of a government project to collect the eggs and raise them in a hatchery. The best months to spot nesting turtles are September through November. Tour times vary depending on the tide; he can provide transportation from hotels in Jacó. Part of the money collected goes to the local school. ✉ *Hotel Las Olas* 🕾 *8817–0385* 💲 *Tour $45.*

SURFING

Most people who bed down at Playa Hermosa are here for the same reason—the waves that break just a shell's toss away. There are a half dozen breaks scattered along the beach's northern end, and the surf is always best around high tide. Hermosa's conditions change rapidly, depending on the tides, wind, and swell activity. Because it is a beach break, though, the waves here often close out, especially when the surf is more than 8 feet. If you don't have much experience, don't go out when the waves are really big—Hermosa sometimes gets very powerful swells, which result in dangerous rip currents. If you're a beginner, don't go out at all. Surf instructors in Hermosa take their students to Jacó, an easier place to learn the sport. If you need to rent a board, some hotels have their own quiver and will allow you to rent by the hour ($10).

Nika Surfboards

SURFING | For all your surfing needs, Nika has ding repair, surf lessons, and boards for rent or sale. ✉ *Costanera, 4 km (2½ miles) south of Hermosa on road to Esterillos* 🕾 *2643–2871* ⊕ *www.nikasurfboards.com* 💲 *2-hr lessons $50.*

Esterillos Este

20 km (12 miles) southeast of Playa Hermosa, 3 km (2 miles) northwest of Playa Bejuco.

Just 20 minutes southeast of Jacó, Playa Esterillos is divided into three sections; Este (East), Central, and Oeste (West). While Esterillos Oeste and Central are inhabited by locals, the undeveloped area of Esterillos Este is where you'll find several boutique hotels capitalizing on the seclusion and beachfront location.

Head-high waves break year-round, making it one of the most consistent surf spots in Costa Rica. At low tide, the dark stretch of sand is unbelievably wide, inviting beachcombers for a leisurely stroll. Almond trees and swaying palms frame the shoreline, and you can walk for miles without seeing another soul. If you want to get away from it all, the isolation and "best-kept secret" feel make Esterillos Este the perfect escape.

GETTING HERE AND AROUND

From Playa Hermosa, head 20 km (12 miles) south on the coastal highway (Costanera). Pass Esterillos Oeste and Esterillos Central before turning right onto the dirt road labeled Esterillos Este. Continue ½ km (¼ mile) to the beach road and follow the signs in either direction to your hotel.

ESSENTIALS

The nearest medical facilities are at the hospital in Parrita, 15 minutes south on the coastal highway. Construction is under way for a shopping center outside of Esterillos Este past Playa Bejuco: a grocery store, gym, and several shops are open, and other services including an ATM are in the works. Supplies are also available at the Mini Super in Playa Bejuco or at the Super Sol in Esterillos Oeste. Other services can be found north in Jacó or south in Parrita.

🏖 Beaches

Playa Esterillos

BEACH—SIGHT | Serious surfers from Jacó and Playa Hermosa head to Playa Esterillos to ditch the crowds when waves are pumping. This isolated beach break dishes up hollow barrels, and gets more swell than neighboring surf spots. It works best at high tide with a south or southwest swell direction, but beginners will want to stay clear of the pounding waves. Lessons ($60) and board rental ($20) can be organized through Encantada Ocean Cottages, but if you're a novice

Did You Know?

With their strong swells, beaches like Jacó and Playa Hermosa are a surfer's paradise.

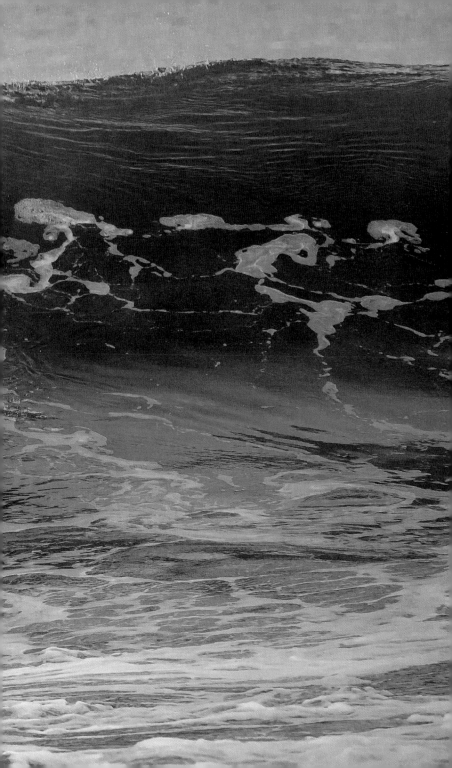

surfer, it's best to stick to the inside whitewash with supervision. At low tide, this dark beach looks like a chocolate field, perfect for beachcombing or an afternoon stroll. You can walk for miles without seeing another set of prints in the sand. Other than a couple sodas in Esterillos Oeste, there are no beach amenities, and those within local hotels are exclusively for guests. Just offshore in Esterillos Oeste is a mermaid statue that you can walk to at low tide. If you drive here, don't leave any valuables in the car. **Amenities:** parking (roadside; no fee). **Best for:** solitude; surfing. ⊠ *Playa Esterillos, Costanera Sur, 20 mins south of Playa Jacó, Esterillos Este.*

 Hotels

Alma Del Pacifico Beach Hotel & Spa
$$$$ | HOTEL | Combining Costa Rica's vibrant architecture with modern design, this tranquil property offers spacious rooms and colorful beach bungalows with indoor-outdoor rain showers and private gardens. **Pros:** very private; spacious rooms; creative and colorful design. **Cons:** wild beach, far from town; hard mattresses; simple breakfast. Ⓢ *Rooms from: $283* ⊠ *3 km (2 miles) north of Playa Bejuco, next to Encantada Cottages, Esterillos Este* ☎ *2778–7070, 303/459–7939 in North America* ⊕ *www. almadelpacificohotel.com* ↪ *20 rooms* ⊺Ⓞ⊺ *Free Breakfast.*

★ Encantada Ocean Cottages
$$ | HOTEL | FAMILY | Framing a blue-tiled pool are freestanding cottages with thoughtful and creative touches like luxurious bedding atop artsy bed frames (made from repurposed pallets), colorful throws, polished cement floors, and lofts with twin beds. **Pros:** peaceful location with 24-hour security; surf lessons and board rental available along with daily yoga classes; comfy beds. **Cons:** smaller breakfast; often full; no shower curtains. Ⓢ *Rooms from: $145* ⊠ *Next to Alma Del Pacifico Beach Hotel, Esterillos Este*

☎ *2778–7048, 855/580–0006 in North America* ⊕ *www.facebook.com/encanta-dacr* ↪ *7 units* ⊺Ⓞ⊺ *Free Breakfast.*

 Activities

HORSEBACK RIDING
The Riding Adventure
HORSEBACK RIDING | Beach riding is the specialty here. Trips set out from a cattle ranch 20 minutes south of Jacó and include a stop at a waterfall for swimming or trail walking. Tours take place twice daily and include a stop at the Pelican restaurant for lunch. Transportation from your hotel can be arranged for $10, or you can start at the meeting point for beach tours next to Monterey Del Mar Hotel in Esterillos Este. ⊠ *Monterey Del Mar Hotel, Esterillos Este* ☎ *8834–8687, 6080–0501* ⊕ *www.theridingadventure. com* ↪ *From $55.*

Quepos

23 km (14 miles) south of Parrita, 174 km (108 miles) southwest of San José.

This hot and dusty town is the gateway to Manuel Antonio, and also serves as the area's hub for banks, supermarkets, and other services. Because nearby Manuel Antonio is so much more attractive, there is little reason to stay here, but many people stop for dinner, for a night on the town, or to go sportfishing. Quepos's name stems from the indigenous tribe that inhabited the area until the Spanish conquest wiped them out. For centuries the town of Quepos barely existed, until the 1930s, when the United Fruit Company built a banana port and populated the area with workers from other parts of Central America. The town thrived for nearly two decades, until Panama disease decimated the banana plantations in the late 1940s. The fruit company then switched to less lucrative African oil palms, and the area declined. Only since the 1980s have tourism revenues lifted the town out of its slump, a renaissance owed to the beauty of the nearby beaches and nature reserves. Forests around Quepos were destroyed nearly a century ago, but the massive Talamanca Mountain Range, some 10 km (6 miles) to the east, holds one of the largest expanses of wilderness in Central America.

GETTING HERE AND AROUND

The drive from San José to Quepos is less than three hours. Follow the directions for Jacó and continue south another 40 minutes. Buses from San José's Tracopa bus station (Avenida 5, Calles 14–16) drop you off in downtown Quepos. SANSA and Nature Air run multiple flights per day, 20 minutes one way, between San José and Quepos (XQP), as well as direct flights between Quepos and Palmar Sur in the Southern Pacific and La Fortuna in the Northern Lowlands.

RENTAL CARS Alamo. ⊠ *Downtown, next to Pali supermarket* ☎ *2242–7733, 2777–3344, 800/462–5266 in U.S.* **Hertz.** ⊠ *75 m south of the Catholic church* ☎ *2777–3365, 888/437–8927 in North America* ⊕ *hertzrentacarcostarica.com.*

TAXIS Taxi services. ☎ *2777–3080, 2777–1207.*

ESSENTIALS

BANKS/ATMS BAC San José. ⊠ *Avda. Central* ☎ *2777–0781.* **Banco Nacional.** ⊠ *Calle 2, 50 m west and 100 m north of bus station* ☎ *2777–0113.*

MEDICAL ASSISTANCE Centro Medico Quepos. ⊠ *Rancho Grande de Quepos* ☎ *2777–1727.* **Farmacia La Económica.** ⊠ *Main road, in front of market at La Galeria Comercial* ☎ *2777–2130, 2777–3213.*

POST OFFICE Correos. ⊠ *Avda. Central, next to soccer field* ☎ *2777–1471.*

TOURIST INFORMATION Instituto Costarricense de Turismo. ⊠ *25 m east of docks* ☎ *2299–5800, 2777–4221 in Quepos, 866/267–8274 in North America* ⊕ *www. visitcostarica.com.*

Sights

Rainforest Spices / Villa Vanilla

FARM/RANCH | Thirty minutes north of Quepos, this spice plantation produces vanilla, cinnamon, cocoa, pepper, allspice, turmeric, and a variety of exotic fruits, essential oils, and medicinal plants. Half-day tours include a visit to the harvesting warehouse, a walk through the fields, and a tasting of Ceylon cinnamon and chocolate gourmet treats prepared by the in-house pastry chef. If you get hooked on the vanilla-bean cheesecake, the cardamom ice cream, or the cinnamon tea, you can stock up on organic spices at the shop on your way out. Tastings and transportation from the Quepos–Manuel Antonio area are included in the tour price. ⊠ *16 km (10 miles) east of Quepos* ⊹ *Take paved road toward hospital and airport, at gas station intersection, continue east. After 6 km (4 miles), pass through Naranjito and continue 1 km (½ mile) to "Y" intersection. Stay left, continue 5 km (3 miles) to Villa Vanilla on left* ☎ *2779–1155, 8839–2721* ⊕ *www. rainforestspices.com* ⊠ *$40 cash only.*

Rainmaker Conservation Project

NATURE PRESERVE | This private nature reserve is spread over Fila Chota, a lower ridge of the Talamanca Range 22 km (13 miles) northeast of Quepos, and protects more than 1,500 acres of lush and precipitous forest, with river-walk or canopy-bridge routes to follow in the lower section. The reserve is home to many of Costa Rica's endangered species, and you may spot birds here that you won't find in Manuel Antonio. You are likely to see scarlet macaws and toucans, due to a repopulation of the species in the Quepos Biological Corridor. Their long-time resident sloth "Charlie Rainmaker" helps educate guests about rain-forest conservation. The reserve encompasses five ecozones and represents 75% of the species found in Costa Rica. It isn't as good a place to see animals as the national park, but Rainmaker's forest is different—lusher and more precipitous—and the view from its bridges is impressive. Guided tours are available from Manuel Antonio, or you can stop and take a self-guided tour on your way to or from Quepos. The park also offers an early-morning bird-watching tour and a night reptiles-and-amphibians hike. The restaurant serves lunch ($8), and there's an on-site microbrewery that utilizes Rainmaker's mountain waters. It's best to visit Rainmaker in the morning, since—true to its name—it often pours in the afternoon. ✉ *22 km (13 miles) northeast of Quepos* ☎ *8588–2586, 540/349–9848 in U.S., 8960–3836 park cell* 🌐 *www.rainmakercostarica.org* 🎟 *From $20 (cash only).*

🍴 Restaurants

Runaway Grill

$$$ | **SEAFOOD** | This favorite with sportfishermen ("You hook 'em, we cook 'em") is the town's best place for seafood, serving everything from shrimp scampi to fresh tuna with mushrooms to bouillabaisse and paella. Their location, overlooking the marina, offers the best view in town. **Known for:** fresh tuna and ceviche; free marina shuttle service to local hotels; kids' menu. [$] *Average main: $20* ✉ *Marina Pez Vela* ☎ *2519–9095* 🌐 *www.runawaygrill.com.*

🏃 Activities

There's a tour operator or travel agency on every block in Quepos that can sell you any of about a dozen tours, but some outfitters give discounts if you book directly through them. The dry season is the best time to explore the area's rain forests. If you're here during the rains, do tours first thing in the morning.

CANOPY TOURS

★ **Canopy Safari**

TOUR—SPORTS | **FAMILY** | There are many zipline tours in the area that take you flying through the treetops, but Canopy Safari has earned a reputation for long and fast-paced rides. The company's privately owned forest is about a 30-minute car ride from Quepos, and the tour includes gliding down 11 ziplines, a Tarzan swing, two rappel lines, and a visit to the on-site butterfly garden and serpentarium. Tours take place at 7 and 10 and include either breakfast or lunch. They also offer rafting tours. ✉ *Office downtown, next to Poder Judicial* ☎ *2777–0100, 888/765–8475 in North America* 🌐 *www.canopysafari.com* 🎟 *Tour $85.*

FISHING

Quepos is one of the best points of departure for deep-sea fishing in southwestern Costa Rica. The best months for hooking a marlin are from October to February and in May and June, whereas sailfish are abundant from November to May and are caught year-round. From May to October you're more likely to catch yellowfin tuna, roosterfish, mahimahi, and snapper. Sailfish and marlin are always catch-and-release.

Bluefin Sportfishing and Tours

FISHING | A fleet of 27-, 29-, and 33-foot boats is used for catch-and-release sportfishing, conventional fishing, and fly-fishing. ✉ *Downtown, next to Adobe Rent-A-Car and across from soccer field* ☎ *2777–0000, 2777–2222* 🌐 *www.bluefinsportfishing.com* 🎟 *Full-day charters from $845.*

Costa Mar Fishing

FISHING | The largest fleet in Quepos has eight boats ranging from 26 to 60 feet and consequently has a wide range of rates. ✉ *Entrance to Quepos, next to Café Milagro* ☎ *2777–0593* 🌐 *www.costamarfishing.com* 🎟 *Full-day charters from $850.*

KAYAKING AND RAFTING

Iguana Tours

KAYAKING | Guides show off the area's natural beauty on white-water rafting trips on the Naranjo (Class III–IV) and

Local guides lead hikes in the hills outside of Quepos.

Savegre (Class II–III) rivers and kayak adventures at sea or in a mangrove estuary. They also offer bird-watching, horseback riding, dolphin-watch catamaran trips, and canopy tours. ✉ *Downtown Quepos, across from soccer field* ☎ *2777–2052* ⊕ *www.iguanatours.com* 💳 *From $65.*

Manuel Antonio

3 km (2 miles) south of Quepos, 179 km (111 miles) southwest of San José.

You need merely reach the top of the forested ridge on which many of Manuel Antonio's hotels are perched to understand why it is one of Costa Rica's most popular destinations. That sweeping view of beaches, jungle, and shimmering Pacific dotted with rocky islets confirms its reputation. Unlike the tropical forests in other parts of the country, Manuel Antonio's humid tropical forest remains green year-round. The town itself is spread out across a hilly and curving 5-km (3-mile) road that originates in Quepos and dead-ends at the entrance to Manuel Antonio National Park. Along this main road, near the top of the hill, or on Punta Quepos are the area's most luxurious hotels and fine-dining restaurants, surrounded by rain forest with amazing views of the beaches and offshore islands. The only problem with staying in one of those hotels is that you'll need to drive or take public transportation to and from the main beach and national park, about 10 minutes away. More hotel and restaurant options are available at the bottom of the hill, within walking distance of the beach, but they lack the sweeping view.

GETTING HERE AND AROUND

Manuel Antonio is a 15-minute drive over the hill from Quepos and 25 minutes from the Quepos airport. Between Aerobel Airlines, SANSA and Skyway, a flight from San José and Quepos (XQP) will be easy to find. Flying time is 20 minutes. There are also direct flights between Quepos and La Fortuna and Quepos and Liberia. Buses depart from

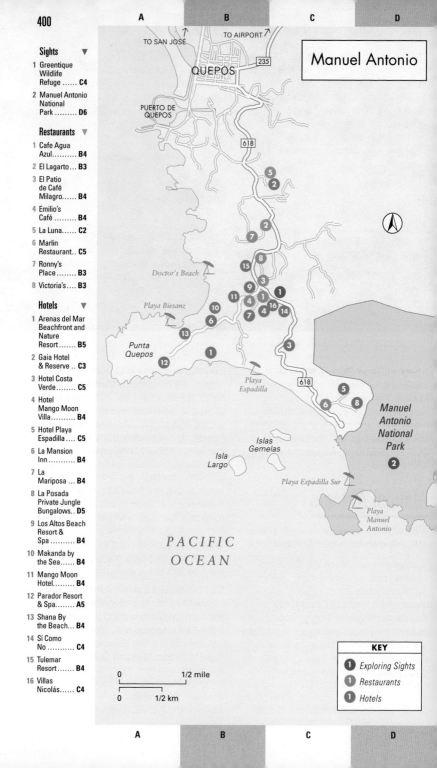

Manuel Antonio

TO SAN JOSÉ

TO AIRPORT

QUEPOS

PUERTO DE QUEPOS

235

618

Doctor's Beach

Playa Biesanz

Punta Quepos

618

Playa Espadilla

Islas Gemelas

Isla Largo

Playa Espadilla Sur

Manuel Antonio National Park

Playa Manuel Antonio

PACIFIC OCEAN

0 ___ 1/2 mile
0 ___ 1/2 km

KEY

1 *Exploring Sights*

1 *Restaurants*

1 *Hotels*

San José's Tracopa bus station (Avenida 5, Calles 14–16) for Manuel Antonio four times a day, at 6 am, noon, and 6 and 7:30 pm, traveling the opposite direction at 6 and 9:30 am, noon, and 5 pm. They pick up and drop off passengers in front of hotels on the main Quepos–Manuel Antonio road. Shuttle services Gray Line and Interbus offer hotel-to-hotel service to and from San José, Jacó, Monteverde, Arenal, and major North Pacific beaches. The trip from San José takes about 2½ hours by car or 3½ hours by bus. A local public bus makes the 20-minute trip from Quepos to Manuel Antonio every half hour from 7 to 7, then hourly until 10 pm.

RENTAL CARS Economy. ✉ *Next to Banco Promérica, across from Salsipuedes* ☎ *2777–5353.*

TAXIS Taxi Services. ☎ *2777–1207.*

ESSENTIALS

BANK/ATM Banco Promérica. ✉ *Main road, at top of hill, between Economy Rent a Car and Cafe Milagro* ☎ *2505–7000.*

Sights

Greentique Wildlife Refuge
NATURE PRESERVE | FAMILY | This park (previously named Manuel Antonio Nature Park and Fincas Naturales Wildlife Refuge) is operated by Hotel Sí Como No. A former teak plantation has been reforested to allow native trees to spring back among the not-so-native ones. A footpath winds through part of the 20-acre tropical forest, and naturalist guides do a good job of explaining the local ecology and identifying birds. The reserve is home to three kinds of monkey, as well as iguanas, motmots, toucans, tanagers, and seed-chomping rodents called agoutis. Two-hour guided walks are given throughout the day, plus a nighttime jungle trek that departs at 5:30 pm. Unfortunately, you can't explore the reserve at your own pace, but you

can book a day tour of the jungle trails, butterfly house, botanical garden, and amphibian lagoon with a guide for $35. ✉ *Main road Km 4; entrance across from Sí Como No Hotel,* ☎ *2777–0777* ⊕ *www.sicomono.com* ✆ *Guided tours from $15.*

★ Manuel Antonio National Park (*Parque Nacional Manuel Antonio*)
NATURE PRESERVE | FAMILY | Costa Rica's smallest park packs in an assortment of natural attractions, from wildlife sheltered by rain forest to rocky coves teeming with marine life. Meandering trails framed by guácimo colorado, mangrove, and silk-cotton trees serve as refuge to sloths, iguanas, agoutis, coatis, raccoons, monkeys, and birds. This is one of the country's best places to see squirrel monkeys and white-faced capuchin monkeys. The great diversity of wildlife is easily spotted from the well-maintained trails, and because the animals are so used to humans, you're likely to see them up close, especially near groups of tourists eating lunch at the beach. Security guards now inspect bags at the park entrance as new restrictions allow visitors to bring only fruit, sandwiches, and nonalcoholic beverages. The mass amounts of junk food stolen and consumed by wildlife has led to serious health problems for the animals. As tempting as it may be, do not feed the wildlife.

Just beyond the entrance, the park's main trail leads to Playa Manuel Antonio, with white sand and submerged volcanic rock great for snorkeling. A second trail winds through the rain forest and spills onto Playa Espadilla Sur, the park's longest beach, which is often less crowded due to rough waters. Farther east, Playa Escondido (Hidden Beach) is rocky and secluded, but not open to the public due to safety precautions; however, you can view it from afar.

Despite its size, Manuel Antonio is Costa Rica's most-visited national park before Poás Volcano. A few tips to make the most of a visit:

Park entrance tickets are sold exclusively at Coopealianza offices in Quepos and Manuel Antonio, one of which is located 50 meters before the park entrance. Tickets are valid for one year from date of purchase, for a single visit. Hire a private guide with ICT certification issued by the Costa Rica Tourism Board.

Arrive as early as possible—between 7 and 8 am is the best time to see animals (and it's cooler, too).

Beware of manzanillo trees (indicated by warning signs)—their leaves, bark, and applelike fruit secrete a gooey substance that irritates the skin.

⚠ It's common for noncertified guides to approach tourists and offer their services. Even if you ask to see identification, they might show only a Costa Rican ID or a driver's license. Make sure that you hire only a guide that has a badge reading "ICT" with a valid expiration date. Noncertified guides often charge as much as ICT-approved guides, but tours last only an hour to 90 minutes (as opposed to three hours), and you won't see a fraction of the wildlife you might with an experienced guide.

⇨ For more information, see the highlighted listing in this chapter. ✉ Manuel Antonio ☎ 2777–5185 ✒ $16.

Beaches

When the surf is up, riptides are a dangerous problem on Playa Espadilla, Manuel Antonio's main beach, which runs parallel to the road near the park's entrance. ■ TIP→ Never leave your valuables unattended while you're swimming.

Playa Biesanz
BEACH—SIGHT | For a less turbulent swim and smaller crowds than at other Manuel Antonio beaches, head to this quiet beach within a sheltered cove. There are a few tide pools near a cluster of rocks and, during low tide, you can see fragments of turtle traps dating back to AD 900, when the area was inhabited by the indigenous Quepoa people. You can rent snorkeling gear for $10 and kayaks for $30. Prepare to pay $1–$2 to the unofficial parking attendant who monitors cars. Bring your own food, drinks, and bug spray since there are no amenities and a few mosquitoes on the jungle trail. You're likely to see monkeys and butterflies on the trail connecting the road to the sand. **Amenities:** none. **Best for:** snorkeling; solitude. ✉ Near Hotel Parador.

Playa Espadilla
BEACH—SIGHT | As the road approaches Manuel Antonio National Park, it skirts the lovely, forest-lined beach of Playa Espadilla, which stretches for more than 2 km (1 mile) north from the rocky crag that marks the park's border to the base of the ridge that holds most of the hotels. One of the most popular beaches in Costa Rica, it fills up with sunbathers, surfers, volleyball players, strand strollers, and sand-castle architects on dry-season weekends and holidays. For most of the year, it is surprisingly quiet, especially at the northern end below Arenas del Mar. Even on the busiest days it is long enough to provide an escape from the crowd, which tends to gather around the restaurants and lounge chairs near its southern end. Though many people often swim and surf here, beware of rough seas and deadly rip currents. There are usually lifeguards on duty closest to the park. If you plan on surfing on the north end, beware of the rocks lurking just below the break closest to the cliffs. You can access this isolated section of Playa Espadilla by way of a 1-km (½-mile) dirt road near Arenas del Mar. There's free parking on the sand, accessible by four-wheel-drive vehicles only. **Amenities:** food and drink. **Best for:** surfing; walking. ✉ Manuel Antonio.

Playa Manuel Antonio

BEACH—SIGHT | The town's safest swimming area is sheltered Playa Manuel Antonio, the second beach in the national park. Its white sand makes it attractive for lounging around, and the warm, clean water is good for snorkeling. There are plenty of palm trees where you can find shade on this wide stretch of sand, and just outside the park are vendors selling fresh coconut water and lychees. Keep watch over your food as raccoons and monkeys are known to steal lunches while people are swimming. Huge mounds of lava rock shelter this cove on both sides of the rugged coastline. Several shacks just outside the park rent beach chairs for about $15 a day. Beaches inside the national park do not have lifeguards or food vendors, unlike those near the entrance. **Amenities:** parking; showers; toilets. **Best for:** snorkeling; swimming; walking. ✉ *6 km (4 miles) south of Quepos; near park entrance.*

Restaurants

Cafe Agua Azul

$$$ | SEAFOOD | Follow your nose to this simple second-floor room offering breathtaking views by day and a deliciously inventive selection of seafood by night. The lunch menu is strong on salads and sandwiches, but the dinner options include some of the best entrées in town, like seared tuna over a tequila-and-lime cucumber salad, calamari sautéed with capers and olives, and coconut-crusted mahimahi. **Known for:** blackened fish sandwich; seafood pasta with a Parmesan cream tomato sauce; burger and fries. [$] *Average main: $18* ✉ *Main road, above Villas del Parque office, 2nd fl.* ☎ *2777–5280* 🕓 *Closed Wed. and Oct.*

El Lagarto

$$$$ | STEAKHOUSE | Meat lovers can get their fix at this local grill, where sizzling cuts are seared on a wood-fire grill and served on chopping blocks. A palapa bar serves powerful margaritas and daiquiris, but it's the grass-fed beef from neighboring La Fortuna that you'll want to try. **Known for:** killer sunset views; grass-fed beef served with baked potato; grilled seafood. [$] *Average main: $30* ✉ *200 m north of the soccer field* ☎ *2777–6932* 🌐 *www.ellagartobbq.com* 🕓 *No lunch.*

El Patio de Café Milagro

$$$ | CAFÉ | This cozy café is the only place in town that serves its own fresh-roasted coffee, with an eclectic menu serving inventive dishes like chilled avocado soup, mango chayote salad, roasted pork with sautéed papaya, and dorado with Caribbean salsa. The breakfast burritos, baked goods, and variety of sandwiches make this a top breakfast and lunch spot. **Known for:** fresh roasted coffee; live music (usually acoustic) every night 8–10; craft beer on tap. [$] *Average main: $17* ✉ *Main road to park, across from Los Altos* ☎ *2777–2272* 🌐 *elpatiodecafemilagro.com.*

★ **Emilio's Café**

$$ | MEDITERRANEAN | While it doesn't look like much from the outside, just inside the doors of this popular café you'll find sweeping views, organic cuisine, and a bohemian vibe that sets the stage for all kinds of good eats (and drinks). Breakfast offerings include eggs Benedict,

In the Thick of It

There's more rain forest on private land than in Manuel Antonio National Park, which means it's not unusual to see many of the animals the park is famous for from the balcony of your hotel room or from your breakfast table. It also means that local landowners play an important role in conserving the area's flora and fauna.

You can hike to white-sand beaches in Manuel Antonio National Park—just one of the reasons it is so popular.

waffles, or delectable French toast, while sesame-crusted tuna, falafel pita, or one of the vegetable sandwiches served with homemade pesto or salsa picante are available for lunch or dinner. **Known for:** a wide range of delectable homemade desserts; a Mediterranean spin on classics like ceviche and poke; excellent coffee. [$] *Average main: $12* ✉ *40 m before Hotel Mariposa* ☎ *2777–6807* 🕒 *Closed Tues.*

★ La Luna

$$$$ | INTERNATIONAL | It's hard to know what's more impressive—the view or the cuisine at this restaurant without walls, where the sun melts into the Pacific and La Luna (the moon) takes center stage. Innovative starters range from Gorgonzola-and-tomato tarts to honey-garlic calamari. **Known for:** fine dining tasting menu with wine pairing; ginger-and-panko-crusted tuna; happy hour with tapas and cocktails. [$] *Average main: $35* ✉ *Gaia Hotel, Km 2.7 Carretera Quepos* ☎ *2777–9797* 🌐 *www.gaiahr.com.*

Marlin Restaurant

$$$ | COSTA RICAN | The outdoor tables are pretty much always full, owing to a location on Manuel Antonio's busiest corner, across the street from the beach near the national park entrance. This is a convenient place to grab breakfast after an early-morning hike—maybe banana pancakes or a *típico,* with eggs and *gallo pinto* (black beans and rice). **Known for:** casado (typical Costa Rican food); fresh fish; nachos. [$] *Average main: $17* ✉ *Main road, south of hill, on corner across from bus stop and beach* ☎ *2777–1134.*

Ronny's Place

$$ | COSTA RICAN | A spectacular sunset view comes with friendly, attentive service and a small but tempting menu that includes such typical tico dishes as *sopa negra* (black-bean soup), ceviche, shrimp and fish on a skewer, and filet mignon wrapped with bacon and topped with a mushroom sauce. Up a long dirt road, this is the best place in town to soak in the ocean views—especially when accompanied by a glass of their famous white-wine-and-vodka sangria. **Known for:** piña coladas served in pineapples; seafood platters with whole red snapper; coconut crusted jumbo shrimp. [$] *Average main: $15* ✉ *1 km (½ mile) west of main road, down dirt road across from Amigos del Río* ☎ *2777–5120* 🌐 *www.ronnysplace.com* 🕓 *Closed Oct. 1–15.*

Victoria's

$$$ | **ITALIAN** | This Italian eatery is the perfect place to stop for brick oven pizza or homemade pastas. Thin and crispy top picks include New York style with pepperoni, sausage, and ham, or pesto-chicken pizza with toasted walnuts and caramelized onions. **Known for:** homemade meatballs; live music Saturday; banana flambé. [$] *Average main: $24* ✉ *Across from Pacifico Colonial Condominiums, next to Kapi Kapi* ☎ *2777–5143* 🌐 *www.victoriasgourmet.com* 🕓 *No lunch.*

🛏 Hotels

Arenas del Mar Beachfront and Nature Resort

$$$$ | **RESORT** | On hillsides sloping down to two pristine, almost-deserted beaches, chic and elegant rooms are decorated with gorgeous natural fabrics and local art and have huge private terraces with comfortable outdoor seating. **Pros:** best of both worlds: luxury and eco-consciousness; best beach access in Manuel Antonio; wonderful bird-watching and wildlife viewing; beach with surf lessons and lifeguard. **Cons:** very steep paths and stairs; humidity can leave bathrooms somewhat musty; pricey. [$] *Rooms from: $550* ✉ *El Parador road at far west end of Playa Espadilla* ☎ *2104–0589, 888/240–0280 in U.S.* 🌐 *www.arenasdelmar.com* 🛏 *48 rooms* 🍴 *Free Breakfast.*

Gaia Hotel & Reserve

$$$$ | **HOTEL** | **FAMILY** | On 13 acres of private reserve, this boutique hotel is contemporary and very chic, with rooms rendered in slate, hardwood, and rattan with Italian fittings. **Pros:** outstanding service; free shuttle to beach and town; best spa in Manuel Antonio. **Cons:** children over 13 only; rooftop pools are shallow and impractical; 3 km (2 miles) from the beach. [$] *Rooms from: $330* ✉ *Km 2.7 Carretera Quepos, near Plaza Yara* ☎ *2777–9797, 800/226–2515 in U.S.* 🌐 *www.gaiahr.com* 🛏 *21 units* 🍴 *Free Breakfast.*

Hotel Costa Verde

$$ | **RESORT** | **FAMILY** | Their motto, "still more monkeys than people" is not an understatement, as you're likely to see howler and white-faced monkeys on the forest trails surrounding these varied accommodations (including a couple converted from airplanes). **Pros:** great ocean views; wildlife; daily yoga. **Cons:** most efficiencies suffer road noise; 1½ km (1 mile) from the beach; service inconsistent. [$] *Rooms from: $149* ✉ *Road to national park, on south side of hill, on left* ☎ *2777–0584, 866/854–7958 in North America* 🌐 *www.costaverde.com* 🛏 *70 rooms* 🍴 *No meals.*

Hotel Mango Moon Villa

$$$ | **HOTEL** | The rooms vary in size and amenities, but the intimate atmosphere and hospitable staff make you feel as if you're staying with a friend rather than at a hotel. **Pros:** nice view; tranquil area; friendly staff. **Cons:** thin curtains and weak a/c; not much privacy; some rooms dark and dated. [$] *Rooms from: $160* ✉ *Between La Mariposa and Makanda* ☎ *2777–5323* 🌐 *www.mangomoonvilla.com* 🛏 *10 rooms* 🍴 *Free Breakfast.*

Hotel Playa Espadilla

$$$ | **HOTEL** | **FAMILY** | Simple but spacious mint-green and cream rooms are a short walk from the beach and are surrounded by green lawns bordered on two sides by the tall trees of Manuel Antonio National Park. **Pros:** surrounded by forest; close to beach and national park; guests can use amenities at sister property Cabinas Espadilla. **Cons:** service inconsistent; showers often lack hot water; basic

The Pacific coast is backed by mangrove, rain, transitional, and tropical dry forests.

rooms. $ *Rooms from: $220* ✉ *150 m on side road from Marlin Restaurant, 1st left, 300 m before park entrance* ☎ *2777–0903* ⊕ *www.espadilla.com* ⬐ *16 rooms* ⦿ *Free Breakfast.*

La Mansion Inn

$$$ | **B&B/INN** | White silk curtains, black onyx flooring, and classical music welcome you to the reception area of this boutique hotel, where rooms have ocean views, white tile floors, balconies, and a mixed bag of styles. **Pros:** excellent views; unique bar; free shuttle to Manuel Antonio National Park. **Cons:** steep driveway with limited parking; hodgepodge of styles; no children under 12. $ *Rooms from: $180* ✉ *1 km (½ mile) west of La Mariposa, next to Hotel Makanda* ☎ *2777–3489, 800/360–2071 in U.S.* ⊕ *www.lamansioninn.com* ⬐ *24 rooms* ⦿ *Free Breakfast.*

La Mariposa

$$$ | **RESORT** | The best view in town—a sweeping panorama of verdant hills, the aquamarine ocean, and offshore islands—is the claim to fame for this array of spacious rooms tucked between the jungle and gardens ablaze with colorful flowers. **Pros:** gorgeous views; free shuttle to the beach; infinity pool. **Cons:** 2 km (1 mile) from beach; some ocean-view balconies lack privacy; sections of hotel slightly dated. $ *Rooms from: $200* ✉ *West of main road, right after Barba Roja, across from Mango Moon Hotel* ☎ *2777–0355, 800/572–6440 in U.S.* ⊕ *www.lamariposa.com* ⬐ *62 rooms* ⦿ *Free Breakfast.*

★ La Posada Private Jungle Bungalows

$$ | **RESORT** | This cluster of distinctive A-frame bungalows, nestled on the edge of the national park and also just a short walk from the beach, is as close as you'll get to sleeping in the park. **Pros:** good value; near beach and park; friendly staff. **Cons:** chaotic outside the hotel during park hours; small pool; rooms slightly dated. $ *Rooms from: $140* ✉ *250 m up side road from Marlin Restaurant, at park entrance* ☎ *2777–1446* ⊕ *www.laposada-jungle.com* ⬐ *12 units* ⦿ *Free Breakfast.*

Los Altos Beach Resort & Spa

$$$$ | **RESORT** | **FAMILY** | These three- and four-bedroom Balinese-inspired luxury condo suites boast 2,500 square feet of living space with industrial kitchens, slate floors, granite counters, rich hardwoods, and rattan furnishings. **Pros:** great views; cooking classes available; ideal for families; enormous rooms. **Cons:** higher-level suites cost more; $150 charge per room over two guests; only high-rise in Manuel Antonio (a bit of an eyesore). $ *Rooms from: $450* ✉ *Km 4 on road to Manuel Antonio National Park, across from Café Milagro* ☎ *2777–8888, 888/803–1332 in U.S.* ⊕ *losaltosresort.com* ⬙ *28 condos* ⦿ *Free Breakfast.*

Makanda by the Sea

$$$$ | **RESORT** | These bright, spacious white-and-cream villas are among the area's most tasteful (and expensive) accommodations, and the hypnotic views of the jungle-framed Pacific Ocean make this secluded rain-forest retreat worth every penny. **Pros:** tranquil; rooms recently remodeled; ocean views. **Cons:** 15-minute hike to the beach; no children under 16; spotty Wi-Fi; slippery steps. $ *Rooms from: $400* ✉ *1 km (½ mile) west of La Mariposa* ☎ *2777–0442, 888/625–2632 in North America* ⊕ *www.makanda.com* ⬙ *27 units* ⦿ *Free Breakfast.*

Parador Resort & Spa

$$$$ | **RESORT** | Terra-cotta floors, steamer trunks, marble statues, bronzed knights, and elaborate antiques create a high-end Spanish colonial style at this beachfront resort perched on the end of a secluded peninsula. **Pros:** outstanding service; tranquil location; free shuttle to national park. **Cons:** pricey food; 15-minute drive to Manuel Antonio National Park; not ideal setting for kids. $ *Rooms from: $283* ✉ *End of peninsula at Biesanz Beach* ☎ *2777–1414* ⊕ *www.hotelparador.com* ⬙ *122 rooms* ⦿ *Free Breakfast.*

Shana By The Beach

$$$ | **RESORT** | With some of the best service in Manuel Antonio and updated rooms, Shana By the Beach is a lovely option with jungle- or ocean-view balconies in every room. **Pros:** attentive service; relaxing spa; sleek design. **Cons:** not oceanfront; weak Wi-Fi signal in some rooms; steep driveway. $ *Rooms from: $225* ✉ *Road to Quepos, 300 m downhill from La Mansión Inn* ☎ *2777–7373* ⊕ *www.shanahotel.com* ⬙ *56 rooms* ⦿ *Free Breakfast.*

Sí Como No

$$$$ | **RESORT** | **FAMILY** | This sustainable resort with its own wildlife refuge sits atop one of the most idyllic hillsides in Manuel Antonio. **Pros:** neighboring wildlife refuge; nice views; good restaurants. **Cons:** 3 km (2 miles) from beach; standard rooms overpriced; a few suites too close to road. $ *Rooms from: $279* ✉ *Road to park, just after Villas Nicolás, right-hand side* ☎ *2777–0777, 888/742–6667 in North America* ⊕ *www.sicomo-no.com* ⬙ *58 units* ⦿ *Free Breakfast.*

★ Tulemar Resort

$$$$ | **HOTEL** | Tucked inside the peaceful 33-acre gated Tulemar Gardens, circular glass villas perched on jungle hillsides are connected by paved trails that meander past four swimming pools and spill onto the beach. **Pros:** accommodating staff; exceptional design; within private gated reserve surrounded by wildlife. **Cons:** some units don't have ocean views; not wheelchair accessible; condo-hotel means some services are lacking. $ *Rooms from: $295* ✉ *Tulemar Gardens, next to Los Altos Beach Resort* ☎ *2777–0580, 800/518–0831 in North America* ⊕ *www.tulemarresort.com* ⬙ *35 units* ⦿ *No meals.*

Villas Nicolás

$$$ | **HOTEL** | On a hillside about 3 km (2 miles) from the beach, these terraced, privately owned Mediterranean-style villas have impressive views and offer

one and two bedrooms, kitchens, and (in most) large balconies with hammocks. **Pros:** good location; most rooms have great views; grounds are well maintained. **Cons:** some units need updating; fee to use beach towels; a bit of hike to the beach; no TVs. $ *Rooms from: $160* ✉ *Road to park, across from Hotel Byblos* 📞 *2777–0481* ⊕ *www.villasnicolas.com* 🛏 *19 rooms* 🍽 *Free Breakfast.*

Nightlife

BARS
Barba Roja
BARS/PUBS | As one of Manuel Antonio's first restaurants, this is still one of the best places to go for sunset cocktail hour, live music, and local beers on tap. ✉ *Main road, 100 m before Cafe Milagro* 📞 *2777–0331* ⊕ *www.barbarojarestaurant.com.*

DANCE CLUBS
Karma Lounge
DANCE CLUBS | Considered the LGBTQ+-friendly lounge bar of Manuel Antonio, this club has dancing, live DJs, and happy hour from 8 to 10. ✉ *Below Victoria's Restaurant, next to Kapi Kapi* 📞 *2777–7230* 💰 *$4 cover.*

MUSIC CLUBS
Victoria's
MUSIC CLUBS | This upscale Italian restaurant is also a popular nightspot, with great wine and a romantic atmosphere. ✉ *Main road, across from Pacifico Colonial Condominiums, next to Kapi Kapi* 📞 *2777–5143* ⊕ *www.victoriasgourmet.com.*

Shopping

There's no shortage of shopping in this town. The beach near the entrance to the park is lined with a sea of vendors who sell T-shirts, hats, and colorful beach wraps. More-authentic handicrafts are sold at night by artisans positioned along the sidewalk in central Manuel Antonio.

Regalame
ART GALLERIES | This appealing art gallery is a showplace for paintings, drawings, pottery, woodwork, and jewelry by area artists. ✉ *Next to Sí Como No Hotel* 📞 *2777–0777.*

Activities

TOUR OPERATORS
Manuel Antonio's list of outdoor activities is almost endless. Tours generally range from $40 to $100 per person and can be booked through your hotel's reception desk or directly through the outfitter. During the rainy season, some outdoor options might lose their appeal, but clouds usually let loose in the afternoon, so take advantage of sunny mornings. Most nature-themed activities go on rain or shine.

Jade Tours
PERSONAL GUIDES | The certified and knowledgeable guides at Jade Tours will turn your park trek through the National Park into an entertaining biology class, as they point out camouflaged wildlife in the treetops. Try the mangrove night tour for a spooky learning adventure. Their team has more than a decade of experience and will help you snap all those picture-perfect images of Costa Rica's flora and fauna through their high-powered scope. Included in the rate are transportation, park entrance, and eco-friendly snacks. ✉ *Manuel Antonio* 📞 *2777–0932, 8632–8760* ⊕ *www.costaricajadetours. com* 💰 *$49.*

★ Johan Chaves Nature and Birding Tours
PERSONAL GUIDES | Raised in Manuel Antonio, Johan Chaves provides three-hour guided tours of the national park that start bright and early at 7:30. Johan's true passion for wildlife and nature make him one of the most sought-after guides in the region, so reserve (by email) well in advance. In addition to being an expert birder, he is extremely knowledgeable about animal behavior and Costa Rica's

wildlife around every turn. Bring water, sunscreen, walking shoes, bug spray, a camera, and swimsuit if you plan to linger at the beach following the tour. The fee includes park entrance and transportation to and from your hotel. ⊠ *Manuel Antonio* ☎ *2779–1189, 8850–4419 mobile* ⊕ *manuelantoniobirdwatching.com* 🖃 *$46 cash only.*

CANOPY TOURS

El Santuario Canopy Adventure Tour

ZIP LINING | Just 20 minutes from Manuel Antonio National Park, this canopy tour boasts the longest single zipline in Central America, extending nearly 1½ km (1 mile) over the treetops. Tours include 14 platforms, 3 towers, 6 bridges, 3 nature walks, and 1 double-belay rappel. The company has double-anchored ziplines with built-in braking systems. Transportation and lunch are included in the tour fee. ⊠ *Manuel Antonio* ☎ *2777–6908, 877/914–0002 in U.S.* ⊕ *www.elsantuariocanopyadventure.com* 🖃 *Tour $75.*

Tití Canopy Tour

TOUR—SPORTS | You'll find a relatively slow-paced zipline tour here—a rarity in Costa Rica—on 10 cables through a forest reserve that is contiguous with the national park. On the last platform there are dual lines, so you can race. Lunch is included. Also available is a night zipline tour, lighting your way by headlamp. Guides go above and beyond to make you feel comfortable and safe and will help you spot animals. ⊠ *Costanera Hwy., 150 m south of Quepos Hospital* ☎ *2777–3130* ⊕ *www.titicanopytour.com* 🖃 *$60.*

HIKING

Highly visited Manuel Antonio National Park is the obvious place to go, but you can also gain a rich appreciation of the local forests' greenery and wildlife in private reserves like Greentique Wildlife Refuge and Rainmaker. ■TIP➔ **Bring binoculars!**

HORSEBACK RIDING

Brisas del Nara

HORSEBACK RIDING | This outfitter takes riders of all ages and levels through the protected Cerro Nara mountain zone, 8 km (5 miles) from Manuel Antonio, and ends with a swim in a natural pool at the foot of a 300-foot waterfall. Full-day tours include three hours on horseback, along with breakfast and lunch; the ride on the half-day tour lasts two hours. For those who want a little less trot in their tour, they have a safari-truck option that visits many of the same attractions. ⊠ *Manuel Antonio* ☎ *2779–1235* 🖃 *From $65.*

KAYAKING

Iguana Tours

KAYAKING | Half-day sea-kayaking trips from Quepos to snorkel at Playa Biesanz in Manuel Antonio National Park require some experience when the seas are high. On a mellower paddle through the mangrove estuary of Isla Damas you might see monkeys, sloths, and various birds. If you'd like to kick back and relax, try the catamaran. White-water rafting tours are also available. Lunch is included. ⊠ *Downtown Quepos, across from Catholic church, Quepos* ☎ *2777–2052, 506/8706–9584 WhatsApp* ⊕ *www.iguanatours.com* 🖃 *From $65.*

SNORKELING AND DIVING

The islands that dot the sea in front of Manuel Antonio are surrounded by volcanic rock reefs with small coral formations. They attract schools of snapper, jacks, barracudas, rays, sea turtles, moray eels, and other marine life.

Oceans Unlimited

SCUBA DIVING | This PADI 5-star career development center offers all-day diving excursions to Caño Island, local dives, and PADI-certification courses; rental equipment is included. A half-day, two-tank dive for certified divers at Manuel Antonio is $109. Note that tours leave from Quepos. ⊠ *Marina Pez Vela, Quepos* ☎ *2519–9544* ⊕ *www.scubadivingcostarica.com* 🖃 *From $109; Caño Island day trip $175.*

SURFING

Manuel Antonio Surf School (*MASS*)

SURFING | Beginner surfers are in good hands with this reputable surf school that guarantees every student will get up on a wave by the end of the session. They teach the mechanics of surfing, wave theory, and offer lessons for all levels at several breaks in Manuel Antonio, Isla Damas, and Dominical. Three-hour group lesson fees include transportation, gear, snacks, and certified instruction. Half-day tours to Damas Island include lunch. If just one lesson isn't enough, they have a surf retreat five minutes outside Dominical. Solo surfers traveling without boards can rent from their solid quiver. ⊠ *C. Principal, across from Pajaro Azul* ☏ *2777–4842* ⊕ *www.manuelantoniosurfschool.com* ✉ *Lessons from $70, tours from $100, rentals from $10.*

WHITE-WATER RAFTING

The three white-water rivers in this area have limited seasons, when the rains from August to October raise them to their perfect peak. The **Naranjo River** offers a short but exciting run, with Class III–V rapids calling for some experience (April–December only). The **Parrita River** provides a relatively mellow (Class II–III) white-water route, but it's only navigable in two-person inflatable duckies. The **Savegre River** has two navigable stretches: a Class II–III lower section that's a mellow trip perfect for neophytes, and a more rambunctious upper section of Class III–IV rapids. It flows past patches of rain forest that are usually navigable year-round, and it's also good for fly-fishing.

Amigos del Río (*ADR*)

WHITE-WATER RAFTING | Catering to all levels of adrenaline junkies, Amigos del Río has six-hour rafting trips on the Savegre River (Class III rapids), four-hour trips on the Naranjo River (Class III–IV), and five-hour trips on the El Chorro section of the Naranjo River (Class IV–V). Included in the rate are breakfast, lunch, transportation, equipment, and bilingual guides. Tours depart at 7 and 11:30 am daily. The Naranjo River tour runs May to December, El Chorro runs from January to April, and Savegre trip is available year-round. ⊠ *2 km (1 mile) on main road to Manuel Antonio National Park, 100 m past Hotel Gaia* ☏ *2777–0082, 877/393–8332 in North America* ⊕ *www.amigosdelrio.net* ✉ *From $79.*

H2O Adventures

WHITE-WATER RAFTING | The Manuel Antonio franchise for Ríos Tropicales, the biggest rafting outfitter in the country, runs kayaking excursions and rafting trips on the Naranjo River, departing daily at 8 and 1 from Quepos. For something less turbulent, they have a rafting trip down the Savegre River at 8 and 1 suitable for ages 5 to 70. Transportation and lunch are included. ⊠ *250 m east from Catholic church, Quepos* ☏ *2777–4092, 506/8959–8989 WhatsApp, 888/532–3298 in U.S.* ⊕ *www.h2ocr.com* ✉ *From $77.*

Chapter 10

THE OSA PENINSULA AND THE SOUTH PACIFIC

Updated by
Rachel White

⊙ Sights	🍴 Restaurants	🛏 Hotels	🛍 Shopping	🍸 Nightlife
★★★★★	★★☆☆☆	★★★★☆	★☆☆☆☆	★☆☆☆☆

WELCOME TO THE OSA PENINSULA AND THE SOUTH PACIFIC

TOP REASONS TO GO

★ **Bird-watching:** Spot beauties such as the scarlet macaw and resplendent quetzal.

★ **Enormous Corcovado National Park:** The last refuge of endangered jaguars and tapirs.

★ **Kayaking:** Head to the Golfo Dulce or along the jungly channels of the Sierpe or Colorado River.

★ **Mountain hikes:** Hiking paths here range from easy daytime treks around luxurious lodges to Costa Rica's toughest: 12,532-foot Cerro Chirripó.

★ **Wild places to stay:** Relax in the country's top eco-lodges, rustic thatch-roof beach bungalows, and cozy mountain cabins.

1 Zona de Los Santos. Beautiful, mountainous coffee region.

2 San Gerardo de Dota. Top nature destination with great hiking trails.

3 San Isidro de El General. Bustling market town and the gateway to Chirripó National Park.

4 San Gerardo de Rivas. Wild, scenic place for bird-watching, hiking, and Chirripó National Park.

5 San Vito. Agricultural market town with Italian flair.

6 Dominical. A lively surfer haven next to lush forest.

7 Ballena National Marine Park. 10 km (6 miles) of pristine beaches and a chance to watch dolphins and migrating whales.

8 Golfito. The eastern Golfo Dulce draws anglers and kayakers.

9 Playa Zancudo. Slow-paced beach town with good sportfishing.

10 Playa Pavones. Surfing town with bird-watching nearby.

11 Puerto Jiménez. Frontierlike town and gateway to Corcovado National Park.

San Gerardo de Dota

Division

CR2

San Isidro de El General

SAN JOSÉ

Dominical

Ballena National Marine Park

12 Corcovado National Park. 1,153 square km (445 square miles) of rain forest straight out of a David Attenborough nature documentary.

13 Cabo Matapalo. Rain forest meets the sea at the southern tip of the Osa Peninsula.

14 Carate. Remote, black volcanic-sand beach that feels like the end of the road.

15 Drake Bay. Adventure-filled destination great for hiking, snorkeling, and boat rides.

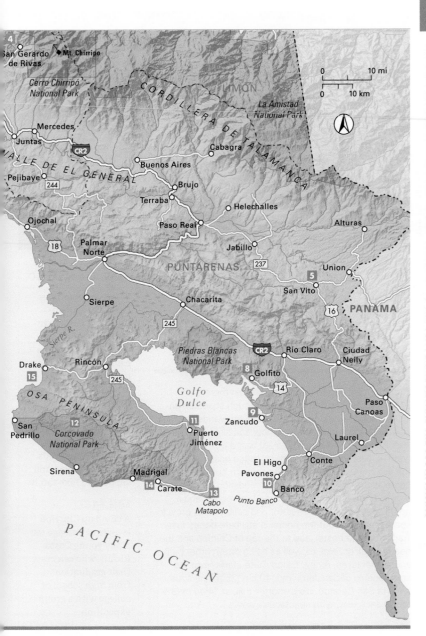

San Gerardo de Rivas — **4**

Mt. Chirripó

Cerro Chirripó National Park

Mercedes

Juntas

CR2

VALLE DE EL GENERAL

Pejibaye

244

CORDILLERA DE TALAMANCA

LIMÓN

La Amistad National Park

0   10 mi
0   10 km

Cabagra

Buenos Aires

Brujo

Terraba

Helechalles

Paso Real

Alturas

Ojochal

Palmar Norte

18

Jabillo

PUNTARENAS

237

Union

Sierpe

Chacarita

San Vito

5

245

16

PANAMA

Piedras Blancas National Park

CR2

Río Claro

Ciudad Neily

Drake

15

Rincón

245

8 Golfito

14

Paso Canoas

OSA PENINSULA

12

11

Puerto Jiménez

Zancudo

9

Conte

Laurel

San Pedrillo

Corcovado National Park

Golfo Dulce

El Higo

Pavones

10

Banco

Sirena

Madrigal

14

Carate

13

Cabo Matapolo

Punto Banco

PACIFIC OCEAN

CHIRRIPÓ NATIONAL PARK

Chirripó National Park

Chirripó National Park is all about hiking. The ascent up Mt. Chirripó, the highest mountain in Costa Rica, is the most popular, challenging, and exclusive hike in the country.

From the trailhead to the peak, you gain more than 8,000 feet of elevation, climbing through shaded highland forest, then out into the wide-open, windswept wilds of the *páramo,* scrubby moorland similar to the high Andes. It's a 48-km (30-mile) round trip, and you need at least three days to climb to the base, explore the summits, and descend. The modern but chilly stone hostel is the only available accommodation, with small rooms of four bunks each, shared bathrooms, and a no-frills restaurant. A generator and solar panels provide some electricity, but the hostel is still bare-bones rustic. Trails from the hostel lead to the top of Chirripó and the nearby peak of Terbi, as well as half a dozen other peaks and glacier lakes. A new hiking route starts from the small pueblo of San Jerónimo, 40 km (25 miles) southwest of San Gerardo. It's a shorter trail, at 14½ km (9½ miles) each way, with spectacular views.

BEST TIME TO GO

Between sometimes freezing temperatures and more than 150 inches of rain a year, timing is of the essence here. The best months are in the dry season (January–May). The park is open all year, but during much of October, and all of November and December, the trails are often too wet and slippery to hike safely.

FUN FACT

A climb up Chirripó is a rite of passage for many young Costa Ricans, who celebrate their graduation from high school or college with a group expedition.

BEST WAYS TO EXPLORE

HIKING

There's no getting around it: the only way to explore this park is on foot. And the only way is up. It's a tough climb to Mt. Chirripó's base camp—6 to 10 hours from the official park entrance, depending on your physical condition—so most hikers head out of San Gerardo de Rivas before the first light of day. You can hire porters to lug your gear up and down for you, so at least you can travel relatively light.

People who live in Costa Rica train seriously for this hike, so be sure you are in good enough shape to make the climb. Smart hikers also factor in a couple of days in the San Gerardo de Rivas area to acclimate to the high altitude before setting out. The hike down is no picnic, either: your knees and ankles will be stretched to their limits. But it's an adventure every step of the way—and the bragging rights are worth it.

MOUNTAIN HIGHS

The base-camp hostel at Los Crestones is at 11,152 feet above sea level, so you still have some hiking ahead of you if you want to summit the surrounding peaks. Take your pick: Chirripó at 12,532 feet; Ventisqueros at 12,467 feet; Cerro Terbi at 12,336; and, for the fainter of heart, Mt. Uran at 11,811 feet.

BIRD-WATCHING

Although your eyes will mostly be on the scenery, there are some highland species of birds that thrive in this chilly mountain air. Watch for the volcano junco, a sparrowlike bird with a pink beak and a yellow eye ring. Only two hummingbirds venture up this high—the fiery-throated hummingbird, which lives up to its name; and the volcano hummingbird, which is the country's smallest bird.

Planning to hike in Chirripó? Prepare for high altitudes.

TOP REASONS TO GO

YOU DID IT!
The sheer sense of accomplishment at completing this tough hike is the number-one reason to take on this challenge. You need to be in very good shape.

OCEAN VIEWS
On rare, perfectly clear days, the top of Chirripó is one of the few places in the country where you can see both the Pacific and Atlantic oceans.

TOP OF THE WORLD
The exhilaration of sitting on top of the world, with only sky, mountain peaks, and heath as far as the eye can see, motivates most visitors to withstand the physical challenges and the spartan conditions in the hostel.

UNIQUE ENVIRONMENT
A climb up Chirripó gives visitors a unique chance to experience extreme changes in habitat, from pastureland through rain forest and oak forest to bleak, scrubby *páramo* (a high-elevation ecosystem).

BALLENA NATIONAL MARINE PARK

A whale breaches in Ballena National Marine Park.

Great snorkeling, whale-watching, and beachcombing draw visitors and locals to Ballena National Marine Park, which protects four relatively tranquil beaches as well as a mangrove estuary, a remnant coral reef, and a vast swath of ocean.

Playa Uvita, fronting the small town of Bahía Ballena, is the longest, widest, and most visited beach, and the embarkation point for snorkeling, fishing, and whale-watching tours. Restaurants and cabinas line the nearby main street of the town. Playa Colonia, the most easily accessible beach, has safe swimming and a view of rocky islands. Playa Ballena, south of Playa Colonia, is a lovely strand backed by lush vegetation. Finally, tiny Playa Piñuela is the prettiest of the park beaches, in a deep cove that serves as the local port. It's also the narrowest beach, with a pebbled slope down to the sand. Along with the tropical fish you'll see while snorkeling, you may be lucky enough to see humpback whales and dolphins. *(For more information, see the review in this chapter.)*

BEST TIME TO GO

December to April is the best time for guaranteed sunny beach weather, as well as for sightings of humpback whales with their young. The whales also roam these waters in late July through late October. Bottlenose dolphins abound in March and April.

FUN FACT

Playa Uvita features a *tombolo*, a long swath of sand connecting a former island to the coast. At low tide, the exposed brown sandbar resembles a whale's tail.

BEST WAYS TO EXPLORE

BEACHCOMBING

The park's beaches are ideal to explore on foot, especially Playa Uvita, which has the longest and widest stretch of sand. Visitors and locals flock here in the late afternoon to catch spectacular sunsets. Don't forget your camera! At low tide, you can walk out onto the Whale's Tail sandbar. During the day, you'll see moving shells everywhere—hermit crabs of every size are constantly scuttling around. Although it all looks idyllic—and it mostly is—don't leave valuables unattended on the beach.

CAMPING

If you brought a tent, pitch it here. Camping on the beach is allowed at Playas Ballena, Colonia, and Piñuela. You can't beat the price, as camping is included in the park admission. Every beach has *sanitarios* (basic toilets) and cold-water showers. But bring your own drinking water. Costa Ricans are avid (and often noisy) campers, so try to avoid busy weekends and school holidays.

IN AND ON THE WATER

Swimming here is relatively safe, but check with the park ranger or your hotel about the best swimming spots. Watch for the *banda amarilla* (yellow ribbon) signs that indicate dangerous currents. Whale- and dolphin-watching excursions are also a fun option—bottlenose dolphins are most often spotted, but humpback whales, especially mothers with babes, are the stars of the show. If you want to be the captain of your boat, sea kayaks are a popular way to explore the park's mangroves and river estuaries. Playa Ventanas, just south of the park's official border, has tidal rock caves you can kayak through.

Playa Uvita's wide beach is uncrowded.

TOP REASONS TO GO

ALONE TIME

If solitude is what you're after, the park's beaches are relatively uncrowded, except on weekends and school holidays when locals come to camp and relax. Neither Playa Colonia nor Playa Piñuela sees a lot of traffic, so you can have them virtually to yourself almost anytime. Just don't hang out after dark.

BEACHES

Miles of wide, sandy beach backed by palm trees and distant green mountain ridges make this one of the most scenic and accessible coastlines in the country. Playa Uvita and Playa Ballena, with their warm, swimmable waters and soft sand, attract the most beachgoers.

WHALES AND DOLPHINS

Catching sight of a mother humpback whale with her young swimming alongside is a thrill you won't soon forget. And watching dolphins cavorting around your boat is the best entertainment on water.

CORCOVADO NATIONAL PARK

Corcovado National Park

For those who crave untamed wilderness, Corcovado National Park is the experience of a lifetime. Covering one-third of the Osa Peninsula, the park is blanketed primarily by rain forest and holds Central America's largest remaining tract of lowland Pacific rain forest.

The remoteness of Corcovado and the difficult access to its interior make it one of the country's most pristine parks—barely disturbed by human presence—where massive, vine-tangled primary-forest trees tower over the trails, and birds and wildlife abound. Your chances of spotting endangered species are better here than anywhere else in the country, although it still takes a combination of luck and determination. The rarest and most sought-after sightings are the jaguar and Baird's tapir. Corcovado also has the largest population of scarlet macaws in the country. Bordering the park are some of Costa Rica's most luxurious eco-friendly jungle lodges and retreats. *(For more information, see the review in this chapter.)*

BEST TIME TO GO

Dry season (January–May) is the best time to visit, but it's also the most popular. With only a limited number of camping spots available, it's crucial to reserve well in advance if you want to stay overnight in the park. New rules require that you are accompanied by a certified guide. June through August will be wetter, but may also be a little cooler. The long-distance trails are virtually impassable from September to December, when most visitors arrive in boats.

BEST WAYS TO EXPLORE

BIRD-WATCHING AND WILDLIFE

The holy grail of wildlife spotting here is a jaguar or a Baird's tapir. You may be one of the lucky few to see one of these rare, elusive animals. In the meantime, you can content yourself with coatis, peccaries, and agoutis on the ground and, in the trees, some endemic species of birds you will see only in this part of the country: Baird's trogon, riverside wren, and black-cheeked ant-tanager, to name a few.

GETTING HERE AND AROUND

The easiest way to visit the park is on a guided day trip by boat to the San Pedrillo station, organized by a lodge or tour company in Drake Bay, Sierpe, or Uvita. The well-heeled can fly in on an expensive charter plane to the Sirena airfield. But no matter how you arrive, the only way to explore is on foot. There are no roads, only hiking trails. If you have a backpack, strong legs, a certified guide, and a reservation for a tent site you can enter the park on foot at three staffed ranger stations and spend up to five days deep in the wilds.

HIKING

There are two main hiking routes to Corcovado. When you're planning your itinerary, keep in mind that the hike between any two ranger stations takes at least a day. The hike from La Leona to Sirena is about 16 km (10 miles) and requires crossing a wide river mouth and a stretch of beach best negotiated at low tide. Some people plan this hike before dawn to avoid the blistering sun. The 25-km (15½-mile) route from Los Patos to Sirena is the coolest trail, through forest all the way.

TOP REASONS TO GO

FLORA AND FAUNA

The sheer diversity of flora and fauna and the chance to see wildlife completely in the wild are the main draws here. The number of cataloged species, to date, includes 500 trees, 150 orchids, 375 birds, 124 mammals, 123 butterflies, 71 reptiles, 46 amphibians, and more than 8,000 insects.

OFF THE BEATEN TRACK

Day visitors get to taste the thrill of being completely off the beaten track, in an untamed natural world. But for campers at La Sirena and San Pedrillo stations, the chance to spend days roaming miles of trails without hearing a single man-made sound is a rare treat.

TEST YOUR LIMITS

The physical challenges of hiking in high humidity and living basically, along with the psychological challenge of being completely out of touch with "the real world," can be rewarding.

71 reptile species live in Corcovado National Park.

Visitors go south to heed the call of the wild. The jewels in the South Pacific crown are the idyllic Golfo Dulce and the wild Osa Peninsula, brimming with wildlife and natural adventures. There is no place like it, especially when you travel off the grid, far from the sounds of modern civilization. With miles of undulating Pacific coastline, there is rarely a crowded beach. Up in the highlands, the hiking and bird-watching are unsurpassed.

The South Pacific encompasses everything south of San José, down to the border with Panama, and all the territory west of the Talamanca Mountains, sloping down to the Pacific coast. Adventures abound in this rugged region. On land, hiking, bird-watching, horseback riding, and wildlife viewing are the main activities, along with some thrilling tree-climbing, ziplining, and waterfall-rappelling opportunities. On the water, there's surfing, snorkeling, diving, fishing, sea kayaking, and whale- and dolphin-watching, as well as swimming and beachcombing.

What makes many of these activities special is that, given the wildness of the locations, the focus is more on nature than on entertainment. No matter what you're doing, you'll come across interesting flora and fauna and natural phenomena. Another key to what sets this area apart is the large number of trained naturalist guides. Most eco-lodges have resident guides who know not only where to find the birds and wildlife, but also how to interpret the hidden workings of the natural world around you.

The hiking in the south is simply spectacular, so don't leave home without your hiking boots. The most challenging hike in the country is Chirripó Mountain, a 6- to 10-hour haul up to the national-park hostel, a base camp for exploring surrounding peaks. Dramatic but less challenging hikes include the well-maintained, wide trails in the cool high-altitude forests of the Savegre Valley; the dramatic Coastal Path south of Drake; and forest trails to waterfalls and swimming holes in the Golfo Dulce, Osa Peninsula, and around Dominical.

MAJOR REGIONS
The most remote part of Costa Rica, the South Pacific encompasses the southern half of Puntarenas Province and La Amistad International Biosphere. The region

descends from mountainous forests just an hour south of San José to the humid Golfo Dulce and the richly forested Osa Peninsula, six to eight hours from the capital by car.

Famous for spectacular mountain vistas, high-altitude coffee farms, cloud-forest eco-lodges, and challenging mountain hikes, the **Central Highlands** of Cerro de la Muerte are less than an hour south of San José, climbing up the Pan-American Highway.

The **Valle de El General** (the General's Valley) area encompasses vast expanses of highland wilderness on the upper slopes of the Talamanca mountains and the high-altitude páramo of Chirripó National Park, as well as prosperous agricultural communities amid vast, sunbaked fields of pineapple and sugarcane. It is bounded to the north and west by the central highlands of the massive Cordillera de Talamanca and to the south by La Amistad International Park.

On the other side of a mountain ridge, just a scenic hour-long drive west of San Isidro de El General, you reach the sunny southern Pacific coast, with its miles of beaches for surfing, strolling, kayaking, and snorkeling. In addition to surfer haven **Dominical, Ballena National Marine Park** alone encompasses almost 10 km (6 miles) of protected beaches. Scattered along the coast are small communities with increasing numbers of international residents and interesting restaurants and lodging options.

One of only three tropical fjords in the world, the **Golfo Dulce** has 600-foot-deep waters in the center of a usually placid gulf where you can watch dolphins swim and humpback whales feed. At Chacarita, 33 km (20 miles) south of Palmar Sur, the southern coast assumes a split personality. Heading west, you reach the Osa Peninsula and, eventually, the Pacific Ocean and the wildest region of Costa Rica. Continuing due south brings you to the Golfo Dulce, which means "Sweet Gulf," reflecting the usually tranquil waters. This gulf creates two shorelines: an eastern shore that is accessible only by boat above Golfito, and a western shore, which is the eastern side of the Osa Peninsula. South of Golfito the coast fronts the Pacific Ocean once again (rather than the calm gulf), with wilder beaches that beckon surfers and nature lovers.

You'll find the country's most breathtaking scenery and most abundant wildlife on the **Osa Peninsula,** a third of which is protected by Corcovado National Park. And complementing the peninsula's lush forests and pristine beaches is the surrounding sea, with great fishing, snorkeling, diving, and some surfing. There are two sides to the Osa: the gentler Golfo Dulce side, much of it accessible by car, albeit along rough roads; and the much wilder and dramatic Pacific side, which is accessible only by boat, by plane, or by hiking a sublimely beautiful coastal trail.

Planning

When to Go

PEAK SEASON: JANUARY TO APRIL

The dry season has the most reliably sunny weather. But be aware that the climate swings wildly in the south, from bracing mountain air to steamy coastal humidity. In the mountains it's normally around 24°C (75°F) during the day and 10°C (50°F) at night. Temperatures can fall close to freezing on the upper slopes of Cerro de la Muerte and elsewhere, so be sure to pack warm layers. Temperatures in coastal areas are usually 24°C–32°C (76°F–90°F), but it's the humidity that does you in.

OFF-SEASON: SEPTEMBER TO DECEMBER

The rainy season can be very wet indeed, especially September through November. The wet season is longest in the Osa Peninsula, where showers usually last through January. Roads sometimes flood and many lodges close in the rainiest months (October and November). Elsewhere during the long rainy season, mornings tend to be brilliant and sunny, with refreshing rain starting in mid-afternoon. Many lodges offer discounted "green season" rates. Often, there is a two- or three-week period of dry weather with brilliant sunshine in late June into July, a mini-summer called *el veranillo*.

SHOULDER SEASON: EARLY DECEMBER AND APRIL TO MAY

Early December, when the landscape is lush and green after months of rain and crowds of tourists have yet to arrive, can be delightful in most of the Southern Zone. April into May is another good time to visit, when crowds have thinned out and the rains are just starting to freshen up the landscape.

Planning Your Time

You need at least a week to truly experience any part of the Osa Peninsula. Even if you fly, ground transportation to your lodge may be painfully slow, so plan two days for travel alone. It's best to choose one base and take day trips from there. In three weeks, you can experience the entire region, including mountains, beaches, and the Osa Peninsula.

If you are driving south, keep in mind that Cerro de la Muerte is often covered with fog in the afternoon, so plan to cross the mountains in the morning. This mountain road has been much improved, but it's safer—not to mention more scenic—to drive it in dry, clear weather. More and more visitors take the coastal highway these days, but they miss out on the dramatic mountain vistas.

Don't try to cover too much ground on a set schedule. It is simply impossible to overestimate how long it takes to drive a certain route or make transportation connections in this part of the country, especially during rainy season, when flooding and landslides can close roads and bad weather can delay flights. But remember, getting there is part of the adventure.

Getting Here and Around

AIR

Three of Costa Rica's domestic airlines—SANSA, Skyway, and Aerobell—all have direct flights from San José to Puerto Jiménez, Drake Bay, and Golfito. They all fly small planes that hold 14 to 19 passengers. Be aware that Aerobell flies out of Tobias Bolaños airport north of Pavas, about a 20-minute taxi ride from SJO.

BUS

Bus fares from San José average about $10, depending on distance and number of stops. The best way to get around the region's roads is by bus—let someone else do the driving. Bus fares are cheap, and you'll meet the locals. But the going is generally slow, departures are often very early in the morning, and schedules change so frequently that you'll want to confirm the day before you travel.

Based in Dominical, Monkey Ride has shuttle-van services in each direction between San José and the Dominical/Uvita/Ojochal area starting at $52 per person.

BUS CONTACT Monkey Ride. ✉ *Main street, Pueblo del Río, Dominical* ☎ *2787–0454, 8651–9090.*

CAR

Driving in the southern reaches of the South Pacific can be rough, especially in rainy season. If you decide to drive, make sure your vehicle has 4WD, high clearance, and a spare tire. Give yourself lots of daylight time to get to where you're going (the sun sets around 5:30). You can also fly to Golfito or the Osa Peninsula and rent a 4WD vehicle. The Southern Zone was the very last part of Costa Rica to be settled, and the first road from San José to San Isidro wasn't begun until the 1950s.

Health and Safety

You are more likely to suffer from dehydration than any other health issue. Carry plenty of water wherever you go, wear a hat, and use sturdy hiking boots and long pants when hiking trails where biting insects may strike or the occasional snake might be sleeping in the sun. Do not leave any valuables in your car or your room—always put them in the safe provided by your hotel or lodge.

Money Matters

ATMs are sprouting up everywhere in the Southern Zone. The places you won't find a bank are remote communities, for example the beaches south of Golfito on the mainland, or in Drake Bay and lodges south of Puerto Jiménez.

Restaurants

Count on finding lots of fresh fish and tropical fruits on the menu, whether at a roadside *soda* (casual eatery) serving *comida típica* (typical food) or a sophisticated restaurant in Dominical or Ojochal. Up in the mountains, don't miss out on eating fresh, farmed trout. The food at most remote eco-lodges is excellent.

Hotels

Expect reasonable comfort in unbelievably wild settings. Most accommodations are in small hotels, lodges, and cabins run by hands-on owners, many of them foreigners who fell in love with the country during a vacation here and stayed. Generally speaking, the farther south and more remote the lodge, the more expensive it is. Bad roads (causing supply problems) and lack of electricity and communications make hotel-keeping costly, especially in the Osa Peninsula and Golfo Dulce, where a fresh egg can cost up to a dollar. When comparing per-person prices, take into account that most of these places include meals, transport, guides, and unique locations.

The country's premier eco-lodges are almost all in the Southern Zone, ranging from simple tents to sophisticated lodges. But keep in mind that if you yearn to be close to nature, you have to be prepared for encounters of the natural kind in your shower or bedroom. Keep a flashlight handy for nighttime trips to the bathroom and always wear shoes. *Hotel reviews have been shortened. For full information, visit Fodors.com.*

WHAT IT COSTS in U.S. Dollars			
$	**$$**	**$$$**	**$$$$**
RESTAURANTS			
under $10	$10–$15	$16–$25	over $25
HOTELS			
under $75	$75–$150	$151–$250	over $250

Tours

Costa Rica Expeditions

ECOTOURISM | The most experienced ecotourist outfit in Costa Rica specializes in customizing countrywide nature tours led by expert, bilingual, local naturalist guides. ☎ 2521–6099 ⊕ *www.costaricaexpeditions.com* ✉ *From $1500 per person for a 7-day trip.*

Horizontes Nature Tours

ECOTOURISM | This expert ecotourist company arranges small-group and custom tours with naturalist guides and ornithologists, including nature-photography tours. They can also offer guided day trips to Corcovado National Park, cultural tours in Puerto Jiménez, or volunteer opportunities with a sea turtle rescue organization. ☎ 2222–2022, 888/786–8748 toll-free in U.S. ⊕ www.horizontes.com ✉ From $1500.

Traveling with Kids

The Southern Zone is like Outward Bound for families, where kids and parents can face challenges (such as no TVs or video games!) and have fun together. Plunge the family into real-life adventures with added educational value. You might inspire a future herpetologist or marine biologist among your progeny.

Go horseback riding to waterfalls and swimming holes. Steal into the night with infrared flashlights to scout out frogs and other fascinating, nocturnal creepy-crawlies. Paddle a kayak in a calm gulf where dolphins play. Rappel down a waterfall, climb inside a hollow tree, or zipline through the canopy.

The more remote areas of the south are ideal for kids ages seven and up. Babies and all their paraphernalia are hard to handle here, and toddlers are tough to keep off the ground where biting insects and snakes live.

Visitor Information

There aren't many official tourist offices in the south. The Dominical Information Center is a great source for everything from bus schedules to maps to tour arrangements. There is also a hard-to-find, official government tourist office in Río Claro, en route to Golfito. Always ask for recommendations from your hosts. Lodge and hotel owners know their turf and they want happy guests, so they are unlikely to steer you astray.

Zona de Los Santos

Santa María de Dota is 65 km (40 miles) south of San José.

Empalme, at Km 51 of the Pan-American Highway, marks the turnoff for Santa María de Dota, the first of the picturesque coffee-growing towns, named after saints, that dot this mountainous area known as the Zona de Los Santos (Zone of the Saints). The route itself is about 24 km (15 miles) long.

GETTING HERE AND AROUND

From San José, drive southeast on the paved Pan-American Highway, heading toward Cartago, then follow the signs south for San Isidro de El General. The two-lane road climbs steeply, and there are almost no safe places to pass heavy trucks and slow vehicles, but the views are worth it. Make an early start, because the road is often enveloped in mist and rain in the afternoon. It typically takes about 90 minutes to reach Km 51, where you turn right at Empalme to reach Santa María de Dota, 14 km (8½ miles) along a wide, curving, paved road.

Sights

Ruta de Los Santos (*Route of the Saints*)
SCENIC DRIVE | The scenic road that winds through the high-altitude valleys from Empalme to San Pablo de León is appropriately called the Ruta de Los Santos—the towns it passes are named after saints. It's nicely paved to facilitate shipping the coffee produced in the region. On the 30-minute drive from Empalme to San Pablo de León Cortés, you travel through misty valleys ringed by precipitous mountain slopes terraced with lush, green coffee plants. The 24-km (15-mile) route also captures the essence of a fast-disappearing traditional tico way of life built around agriculture. Stately churches anchor bustling towns full of prosperous, neat houses with pretty gardens and a

few vintage 1970s Toyota Land Cruiser trucks parked in the driveways.

Restaurants

Café de Los Santos

$ | **CAFÉ** | This pretty café, within sight of the town's majestic church in San Marcos de Tarrazú, showcases the area's high-altitude *arabica* Tarrazú coffee, the "celestial drink" for which this zone is famous. **Known for:** 30 specialty coffee drinks; homemade sweet and savory pastries; vintage photos of oxcarts and coffee harvests. $ *Average main: $5* ✉ *6 km (4 miles) west of Santa María de Dota, 200 m east of church, San Marcos de Tarrazú* ☎ *2546–7881* ⊘ *Closed Sun.*

Mutute Café Boutique Tarrazú

$ | **COSTA RICAN** | A giant, colorful *chorreador,* the traditional wooden stand for making coffee with a socklike filter, marks the spot for this tiny but sophisticated café, a showplace for the award-winning, high-altitude coffee from the nearby Tarrazú coffee region. Watch barista Monserrath Navarros expertly concoct flavorful espresso and cappuccino, complete with artistic swirls in the milk foam. **Known for:** homemade fig cake; handsome packages of coffee to buy; easy parking. $ *Average main: $5* ✉ *Empalme, Km 51, Pan-American Hwy.* ☎ *2571–2323* ▭ *No credit cards.*

Hotels

Toucanet Lodge

$$ | **B&B/INN** | **FAMILY** | For serenity and mountain greenery, you can't beat this lodge in a secluded valley with panoramic views and the opportunity to see hummingbirds and some of the 200-plus highland species on the lodge's list, including the resplendent quetzal. **Pros:** fresh mountain air; seclusion and tranquility; excellent birding trails. **Cons:** simple furnishings; bumpy dirt-road access; some steps to climb to cabins. $ *Rooms from: $84* ✉ *Hwy. 315, 7 km (4½ miles)*

east of Santa María de Dota, Copey ⊹ *To get here from Pan-American Hwy., turn at sign for Copey and follow scenic dirt road 8 km (5 miles)* ☎ *2541–3045* ⊕ *www.toucanetlodge.com* ⤴ *8 rooms* ¶◐¶ *Free Breakfast.*

⬤ Shopping

Coopedota Santa Maria

FOOD/CANDY | The best place to buy local coffee is where 800 farmers bring their raw coffee beans to be roasted and packed into jute bags at the first carbon-neutral coffee producer in the world. You can buy three dozen different coffee beverages and export-quality coffee at the café shop for about $8 per pound (about half the price you'll pay at the airport). Choose between light or dark roast and *en grano* (whole bean) or *molido* (ground). A variety of tours are offered ($32 to $41), covering everything from processing to tasting to the cooperative's innovative recycling. Check out the website for details of tours or email to make reservations. ✉ *C. Ctl., Santa María de Dota* ☎ *2541–2827 for coffee tour, 2541–0102 café* ⊕ *www.coopedota.com.*

San Gerardo de Dota

89 km (55 miles) southeast of San José, 52 km (32 miles) south of Santa María de Dota.

Cloud forests, invigorating mountain air, well-maintained hiking trails, and excellent bird-watching make San Gerardo de Dota one of Costa Rica's premier nature destinations. The tiny hamlet is in the narrow Savegre River valley, 9 km (5½ miles) down a twisting, partially paved track that descends abruptly to the west from the Pan-American Highway. The peaceful surroundings look more like the Rocky Mountains than Central America, but hike down the waterfall trail and the vegetation quickly turns tropical again. Beyond hiking and bird-watching, activities include horseback riding and ziplining.

GETTING HERE AND AROUND

The drive from San José takes about three hours, and from Santa María de Dota about an hour. At Km 80 on the Pan-American Highway, turn down the dirt road signed "San Gerardo de Dota." It's a harrowing, twisting road with signs warning drivers to gear down and go slow. Some newly paved sections help ease the steepest curves. Tourist vans often stop along the road when the guides spot birds; grab your binoculars and discreetly join them!

The Resplendent Quetzal

The forest around San Gerardo de Dota is renowned for resplendent quetzals, considered by many to be the most beautiful bird in the Western world. Male quetzals in full breeding plumage have metallic green feathers, crimson stomachs, helmetlike crests, and extravagantly long tail feathers. Early morning during the March–May nesting season is the best time to spot them, but a program to plant aguacatillo trees, the birds' favorite food source, means they are seen most of the year.

🍴 Restaurants

Kahawa

$ | **COSTA RICAN** | Perched on the boulder-strewn bank of the rushing Savegre River, this handsome blond-wood-and-stone rancho specializes in serving up fresh trout in myriad ways at riverside tables, perfect for bird-watching. If you're not a fan of fish, try the *kuku tamu*, a chicken breast sandwich with *chiverre* (black seed squash) preserve, red onion, fresh cheese, mustard, and arugula. **Known for:** fried trout tacos; trout fillet with coconut sauce; homemade desserts. [$] *Average main: $9* ✉ *San Gerardo de Dota, San Gerardo* ✥ *From Pan-American Hwy. at Km 80, about 8 km (5 miles) down steep road to San Gerardo de Dota* ☎ *2740–1081* 🌐 *kahawa.co* 🕒 *Dinner by reservation only for six people or more.*

🛏 Hotels

★ **Dantica Lodge and Gallery**

$$$ | **B&B/INN** | High style at high altitude, this avant-garde lodge clinging to the side of a mountain has unbeatable valley views, great bird-watching, luxury accommodations, a sophisticated restaurant, and the top ecological sustainability rating. **Pros:** whirlpool bathtubs; top-notch Latin American craft gallery; excellent restaurant. **Cons:** steep, narrow trails to forest casitas; some casitas close to road; high altitude. [$] *Rooms from: $159* ✉ *Road to San Gerardo de Dota, 4 km (2 miles) west of Pan-American Hwy., San Gerardo* ☎ *2740–1067* 🌐 *www.dantica.com* 🔑 *12 rooms* 🍽 *Free Breakfast.*

Paraíso Quetzal Lodge

$$ | **B&B/INN** | A paradise for resplendent quetzals, this rustic but comfortable lodge is amid cloud-enshrouded mountains and valleys with 16 km (10 miles) of hiking and birding trails through ancient oak forests dripping with moss and epiphytes. **Pros:** cozy, heated cabins with modern bathrooms; nature photographer's outdoor studio; excellent espresso. **Cons:** very simple food; steep paths to some cabins; very cold nights. [$] *Rooms from: $83* ✉ *Km 70, Pan-American Hwy., Cerro de la Muerte* ☎ *2200–0241, 8810–0234* 🌐 *www.quetzalsparadise.com* 🔑 *14 rooms* 🍽 *No meals.*

★ **Savegre Hotel, Natural Reserve & Spa**

$$$ | **B&B/INN** | Famous for miles of bird-watching trails and expert guides, this lodge has comfortable, spacious rooms with two double beds and modern

A male white-throated mountain-gem hummingbird in a defense posture; Río Savegre, San Gerardo de Dota

bathrooms, some with bathtubs, set in colorful, bird-attracting gardens. **Pros:** room heaters; convivial fireplace lounge; pleasant riverside spa. **Cons:** steep trails and high altitude may tax some visitors; many meals are uninspired buffets; many tour groups. [$] *Rooms from: $165* ✉ *C. San Gerardo, Km 80, Pan-American Hwy., San Gerardo* ✣ *Take very steep road for 9 km (5½ miles) to hotel entrance, a bridge over Río Savegre* ☎ *2740–1028* 🌐 *www.savegre.com* 🛏 *50 rooms* 🍴 *Free Breakfast.*

Trogón Lodge

$$$ | **B&B/INN** | **FAMILY** | Set in a riotous garden filled with fuchsias, hydrangeas, and hummingbirds, Trogón Lodge is more picturesque hideaway than hiking-heavy destination. **Pros:** picturesque garden and river setting; convivial public areas; small but excellent gift shop. **Cons:** steep, short trails that end at road; shared verandas; can be noisy with families. [$] *Rooms from: $154* ✉ *San Gerardo de Dota, San Gerardo* ✣ *At Km 80 on Pan-American Hwy., follow very steep, partially paved road down 7½ km (4½ miles)* ☎ *2740–1051 lodge, 2293–8181 for reservations only* 🌐 *www.trogonlodge.com* 🛏 *23 rooms* 🍴 *Free Breakfast.*

Activities

BIRD-WATCHING

Although you can see many birds from your cabin porch and viewing platform, most bird-watching requires hiking, some of it along steep paths made extra challenging by the high altitude (from 7,000 to 10,000 feet above sea level). Come fit and armed with binoculars and layers of warm clothing. The early mornings are brisk up here, but you'll warm up quickly with the sun and the exertion of walking.

★ **Savegre Hotel, Natural Reserve & Spa**

BIRD WATCHING | With the best bird guides in the area, including veteran birder Marino Chacon ($90 for a half day), this hotel organizes the best highland birding and hiking tours in the oak forests and surrounding mountains. For nature photographers, the Batsú Garden ($20) is an outdoor studio with battery-charging facilities for cameras and computers, perched on a hillside garden overlooking a bird-friendly orchard. ⊠ *Savegre Hotel, Natural Reserve & Spa, Km 80, Pan-American Hwy., San Gerardo* ☎ *2740–1028* ⊕ *www.savegre.com.*

Tropical Feathers

BIRD WATCHING | Guided by Noel and Carlos Ureña, an expert birder with 20 years of experience, Tropical Feathers offers multiday bird-watching packages and arranges customized tours, including wildlife-photography tours, in the San Isidro de El General and Dominical area, as well as the entire country. Half-day birding tours start at $100 for two people; $150 including transportation. Check the website for excellent photos and bird lore. ☎ *8382–1148* ⊕ *www.costaricabirdingtours.com.*

HIKING

Some of the best hiking in the country is in this valley.

Savegre Hotel, Natural Reserve & Spa

HIKING/WALKING | This world-renowned bird-watching hotel runs a daylong, guided, natural-history hike that starts with a drive up to the *páramo* (high-altitude ecosystem) of Cerro de la Muerte. The trail descends through oak forest into the valley. Miles of prime bird-watching and hiking trails wind through the private forest reserve. Night temperatures on the slopes of Cerro de la Muerte can approach freezing. Pack accordingly for cold mornings. ⊠ *Savegre Hotel, Natural Reserve & Spa, C. San Gerardo, San Gerardo* ☎ *2740–1028* ⊕ *www.savegre.com* ⊠ *$165 for one to four birders, plus $55 per person for transportation.*

San Isidro de El General

54 km (34 miles) south of San Gerardo de Dota.

Although San Isidro de El General has no major attractions, the bustling market town is a good place to have lunch, get cash at one of the many ATMs, or fill your tank—the main highway into town is lined with service stations, some operating 24 hours. Advice to map readers: there are other San Isidros in Costa Rica, but this is the only San Isidro de El General. Just to confuse matters more, this town also goes by the name Peréz Zeledón. The town is the jumping-off point for hiking the scenic highlands around San Gerardo de Rivas, and climbing the country's highest peak, Mt. Chirripó. There's also excellent bird-watching in nearby nature reserves, including the original homestead, now a museum, of famed ornithologist Alexander Skutch.

GETTING HERE AND AROUND

The Pan-American Highway takes you straight into San Isidro de El General. It's 129 km (80 miles) south of San José and about 1½ hours' drive south of the San Gerardo de Dota highway exit. Truck traffic can be heavy and painfully slow. For folks in a hurry, there's a daily 35-minute SANSA flight from San José to the San Isidro airstrip, leaving San José at 7:55 am and returning at 8:40 am. Buses to Dominical leave from the San Isidro de El General bus terminal, southeast of the cathedral, near the Pan-American Highway. Buses bound for San Gerardo de Rivas, the starting point of the trail into Chirripó National Park, depart from San Isidro de El General at 5:30 am from the central park and at 2 pm from a stop at the central market.

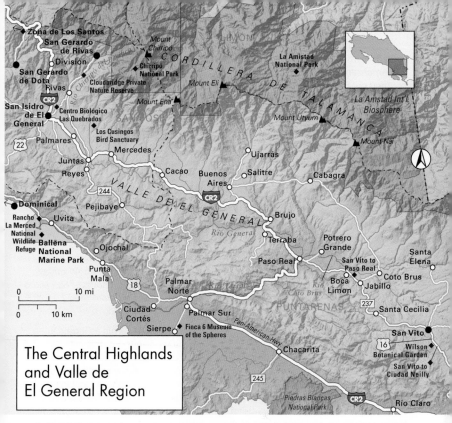

ESSENTIALS

BANKS/ATMS ATH Coopealianza. ⊠ *South side of central park beside Hotel Chirripó, San Isidro* ☎ *4800–2000.* **Banco Nacional.** ⊠ *North side of central park, San Isidro* ☎ *2212–2000.*

HOSPITAL Hospital Escalante Pradilla. ⊠ *Off main street, east of municipal stadium, San Isidro* ☎ *2785–0700.*

PHARMACY Farmacia Santa Marta. ⊠ *Northwest of central park, across from cultural center, San Isidro* ☎ *2771–4506.*

POST OFFICE Correo. ⊠ *From southeast corner of central park, 1 block south, San Isidro.*

VISITOR INFORMATION Selva Mar. ⊠ *South of central park, San Isidro* ☎ *2771–4582* ⊕ *www.selvamar.com.*

⊙ Sights

Centro Biológico Las Quebradas (*Las Quebradas Biological Center*)

NATURE PRESERVE | FAMILY | In a lush valley 7 km (4½ miles) northeast of San Isidro de El General, this community-managed nature reserve protects 1,853 acres of dense forest in which elegant tree ferns grow in the shadows of massive trees, and colorful tanagers and euphonias flit about the foliage. Five kilometers (3 miles) of trails wind uphill through the forest and along the Río Quebradas, which supplies water to San Isidro de El General and surrounding communities. There's also an easily accessible sensory garden, with plants to smell and taste, and a butterfly garden. To get here from the Pan-American Highway, head 7 km (4½ miles) northeast at the sign for Las Quebradas. The reserve is 2 km (1 mile) north of town on an unpaved road. ✉ *Off Pan-American Hwy., 7 km (4½ miles) northeast of San Isidro de El General, Quebradas* ☎ *2771–4131* 🌐 *www.fudebiol.com* 🎟 *$4.*

Los Cusingos Bird Sanctuary

HOUSE | This property contains birding trails and the house of the late Dr. Alexander Skutch, the region's preeminent ornithologist and coauthor of *A Guide to the Birds of Costa Rica,* the birders' ultimate companion. His 190-acre estate, an island of forest amid a sea of new farms and housing developments, is now run by the nonprofit Centro Científico Tropical (Tropical Science Center), which has improved 2 km (1 mile) of trails and maintains the simple house where Dr. Skutch lived—without electricity—from 1941 until his death in 2004, just a week shy of his 100th birthday. Room by room, the moldy books, piles of journals, vintage typewriter, and humble bedrooms and kitchen speak to Skutch's lifelong philosophy of simplicity. Among the 200 or so bird species that still visit the property are *cusingos* or fiery-billed araçaris—colorful, small members of the toucan family, for which the property is named—and mixed tanager flocks. The sanctuary is a half-hour's drive southeast of San Isidro de El General in the town of Quizarrá. Just show up, or call ahead if you want a guided tour. ✉ *15 km (10 miles) southeast of San Isidro de El General, Quizarrá* ✥ *South on Pan-American Hwy., cross bridge over Río General and watch for small, blue Riserva Biológica sign on left, take that turn, through town of Peñas Blancas, past cemetery and watch for sign on right for Quizzará and Los Cusingos* ☎ *2738–2070* 🌐 *www.costarica.com/attractions/los-cusingos-bird-sanctuary* 🎟 *$10.*

🍴 Restaurants

El Trapiche de Nayo

$ | **COSTA RICAN** | **FAMILY** | The panoramic valley view is worth a stop at this rustic roadside restaurant that serves the kind of food Ticos eat at *turnos* (village fund-raising festivals), including *gallos,* thick tortillas cooked on a wood stove, which you stuff with cooked hearts of palm, root vegetables, or chicken in salsa. Some Saturdays, raw sugarcane is pressed in an antique mill and boiled in huge iron cauldrons. **Known for:** mondongo (tripe soup); decent restrooms; homemade molasses-flavored fudge. [$] *Average main: $9* ✉ *Pan-American Hwy., 6 km (4 miles) north of San Isidro de El General, San Isidro* ☎ *2771–7267.*

Kafe de la Casa

$ | **COSTA RICAN** | As hip as it gets in downtown San Isidro, this café serves excellent cappuccino and homemade muffins or an all-day breakfast in a funky, retro-rustic atmosphere combining 1950s diner and tico country. There's also a full menu of meat and chicken dishes. **Known for:** monster plate of bocas (snacks) to share; healthy yogurt smoothies; cultural happenings. [$] *Average main: $9* ✉ *C. 4, Avda. 3, behind MUSOC bus station, San Isidro* ☎ *2770–4816* ⏲ *Closed Sun.*

🛏 Hotels

Hotel Los Crestones

$ | **HOTEL** | Flowering hedges make this pleasant and affordable motel feel homey, even though it's near the sometimes-noisy stadium (the quietest rooms are Nos. 18 to 21). **Pros:** affordable prices; close to downtown; secure parking and easy wheelchair access. **Cons:** noisy rooms at the front; some rooms lack a/c; breakfast not included. [$] *Rooms from: $65* ✉ *Road to Dominical, southwest side of stadium, San Isidro* ☎ *2770–1200* 🌐 *www.hotelloscrestones.com* 🛏 *27 rooms* 🍽 *No meals.*

⚡ Activities

HIKING

The major tourist draw is climbing Mt. Chirripó (the highest peak is about 12,532 feet) in Chirripó National Park. There is a limit of 52 hikers in the park on any one day.

All lodging, food, and porter arrangements are now made by a local cooperative, **Consorcio Aguas Eternas** ⊕ *www. chirripo.org* ☎ *2742–5097.*

A new system is in place to make reservations easier and hiking safer, with tour packages that include lodging before the hike, porters, guides, and accommodation in the park hut. *See Hotel de Montaña El Pelícano for details.* Alternatively, opt for a different hike in the surrounding area.

San Gerardo de Rivas

20 km (12½ miles) northeast of San Isidro.

Chirripó National Park is the main reason to venture to San Gerardo de Rivas, but if you aren't up for the physically challenging adventure of hiking up Chirripó it's still a wildly scenic place, reminiscent of the Himalayas, to spend a day or two. Spread over steep terrain at the end of the narrow valley of the boulder-strewn Río Chirripó, San Gerardo de Rivas has cool mountain air, excellent bird-watching, invigorating hiking trails, and ethereal views.

GETTING HERE AND AROUND

The good news is that most of the winding road from San Isidro de El General to San Gerardo de Rivas is paved. There are a few gravel patches and some steep, narrow stretches, however, so 4WD is recommended. Buses run twice a day from San Isidro.

👁 Sights

Chirripó National Park (*Parque Nacional Chirripó*)
NATURE PRESERVE | The main attraction of this national park is Mt. Chirripó, the highest mountain in Costa Rica and a mecca for both hikers and serious summiteers. It's a 48-km (30-mile) round-trip hike, with an elevation gain of 6,890 feet to reach the hostel, and another 1,000 feet to reach the summit. You need to be very fit and acclimatize before setting out. The round trip usually takes three days: one day to climb to the hostel, one day to explore the surrounding summits, and one day to descend.

With the number of hikers limited to 52 per day on the San Gerardo route, and only 15 hikers per week from the new San Jerónimo trail, it's becoming an ever more exclusive experience to hike here. Lodging at the summit hut is set at $35 per night. Though the hostel is slightly more comfortable than it used to be, keep in mind that it is still fairly basic, with bunk beds and no hot water for showers. It's chilly at the top, so be sure to pack lots of layers. The maximum stay at the hostel is three days, two nights. Lodging and food service in the simple restaurant are arranged by Consorcio Aguas Eternas, which also can provide all the gear you need, from pillows, towels, and sleeping bags to porters to haul them. Depending on which of the various meal packages and local lodging before and after the hike you choose, prices for a hike start at about $250 per person. Porter fees are set at about $4 per kilo, and charged each way. The easiest way to arrange a hike is through one of the hotels that belong to the consortium, such as Hotel de Montaña El Pelícano, which can arrange all the details, from park reservation to lodging, food, and gear. ⊠ *Consorcio Aguas Eternas, Main street, south side of soccer field, San Gerardo* ☎ *2742–5200, 2742–5097* ✏ *infochirriposervicios@gmail.com* 💲 *$18 per* *day park fee; $36 per day for lodging in park, plus food* 🕒 *Closed 2 wks in Nov.*

Cloudbridge Private Nature Reserve

NATURE PRESERVE | FAMILY | This private nature reserve staffed by volunteers and a senior biologist has an easy trail to a waterfall, plus almost 12 km (8 miles) of river and ridge trails, including one trail that utilizes 4 km (2½ miles) of the Chirripó National Park trail. It's a pleasant alternative for hikers who aren't up to the challenge of Chirripó or haven't reserved a spot far in advance. You can take a guided 3½ hour tour past two waterfalls and learn about the flora and fauna of the cloud forest for $35. There's also an art gallery featuring nature paintings by artist Linda Moskalyk, and accommodations in four fully equipped houses (starting at $70, two-night minimum). Volunteers often occupy the simple rental cabins, so check the website for availability. There's no admission fee to hike in the reserve, but donations are requested. ✉ *2½ km (1 mile) northeast of San Gerardo de Rivas, San Gerardo* 🌐 *www.cloudbridge.org* 🎟 *By donation.*

Hotels

Hotel de Montaña El Pelícano

$ | B&B/INN | On a precipitous ridge, this modest wooden lodge is an affordable and comfortable launching pad for a hike up Chirripó, or a pleasant spot to relax and breathe in fresh mountain air and scenery and watch birds. **Pros:** official Chirripó hike operator; one-of-a-kind folk art museum; affordable. **Cons:** smallish rooms in main lodge; very steep drive to hotel; friendly but slow service. [$] *Rooms from: $72* ✉ *Main road, south of Chirripó National Park office, San Gerardo* ☎ *2742–5050* 🌐 *hotelpelicano.com* 🛏 *13 rooms* 🍴 *Free Breakfast.*

Río Chirripó Retreat

$$$ | B&B/INN | FAMILY | In one of the most beautiful mountain settings imaginable, this yoga-centric riverside lodge, reminiscent of a Himalayan temple, is pure pleasure, from the lush flower gardens to the sophisticated room design to the open-air yoga studio within sound of the rushing river. **Pros:** enchanting riverside setting; excellent breakfasts loaded with fresh fruits; room balconies with river views. **Cons:** no sit-down lunch; yoga groups may dominate; smallish double rooms. [$] *Rooms from: $168* ✉ *San Gerardo de Rivas* ☎ *2742–5109* 🌐 *www.riochirripo.com* 🛏 *10 rooms* 🍴 *Free Breakfast.*

Shopping

★ **Samaritan Xocolata**

FOOD/CANDY | The sign says "Fine, Organic Artisan Chocolate," but all you need to know is that this chocolate is delicious. You can buy chocolate to-go, including turtle-shape chocolates filled with caramel and nuts, bonbons filled with ginger citrus or pistachio with Himalayan pink salt, beautifully gift-wrapped 70% dark chocolate, or truffles (including vegan-friendly rosemary-walnut and nondairy mixed-berry, so no one has any dietary excuse to resist). Sit down in the patio chocolate lounge and sip thick hot chocolate or devour a frozen banana encased in thick dark chocolate. If you're in the area for a while, you can book a 2½-hour chocolate workshop to learn how it's all made ($25, minimum of two people; two days' notice required). ✉ *Canaan de Rivas on main road to Chirripó, 75 m north of Catholic church and soccer field, San Gerardo* ✥ *2½ km (1½ miles) south of San Gerardo de Rivas* ☎ *8820–7095* 🌐 *www.samaritanxocolata.com.*

Activities

Costa Rica Trekking Adventures

HIKING/WALKING | Selva Mar runs tours around San Gerardo de Rivas, and will coordinate and guide a trip to Chirripó. For a four-day, three-night climb including basic lodging and all meals, it's $440 for

Gesneriaceae flowers at the Wilson Botanical Garden in San Vito

one person or a hefty discount for two or more. ⊠ *San Gerardo* ☎ *2771–4582* ⊕ *chirripo.com.*

San Vito

110 km (68 miles) southeast of San Isidro, 61 km (38 miles) northeast of Golfito.

Except for the tropical greenery, the rolling hills around the bustling hilltop town of San Vito could be mistaken for a Tuscan landscape. The town actually owes its 1952 founding to 200 Italian families who converted forest into coffee, fruit, and cattle farms. A remnant of the Italian flavor lingers on in the statue dedicated to the *pioneros* standing proudly in the middle of town. San Vito today is a bustling agricultural market town, the center of the Coto Brus coffee region. Many coffee pickers are from the Guaymí indigenous group, who live in a large reserve nearby and also over the border in Panama. They're easy to recognize by the women's colorfully embroidered, long cotton dresses.

GETTING HERE AND AROUND

If you're driving south from San Isidro, your best route is along the wide, smooth Pan-American Highway via Buenos Aires to Paso Real, about 70 km (43 miles). Then take the scenic high road to San Vito, 40 km (25 miles) farther along. This road is paved and it's the most direct and prettiest route. Another route, which many buses take, is via Ciudad Neily, about 35 km (22 miles) northeast of Golfito, and then 24 km (15 miles) of winding steep road up to San Vito, at almost 3,280 feet above sea level. There are direct buses from San José four times a day, and buses from San Isidro twice a day.

ESSENTIALS

Most of the banks in town have cash machines that accept foreign cards.

BANKS/ATMS ATH Coopealianza. ⊠ *Center of town, 200 m east of Catholic church and north of hospital* ☎ *2773–3763.*

Banco Nacional. ✉ *Across from south side of central park* ☎ *2212–2000.*

HOSPITAL Hospital San Vito. ✉ *South of town, on road to Wilson Botanical Garden* ☎ *2773–3103.*

PHARMACY Farmacia Assisi. ✉ *Center of town, main street* ☎ *2773–5580.*

POST OFFICE Correo. ✉ *Far north end of town, beside police station* ☎ *2773–3130.*

Sights

★ Wilson Botanical Garden

GARDEN | A must-see for gardeners and bird-watchers, the world-renowned Wilson Botanical Garden is enchanting even for those who are neither. Paths through the extensive grounds are lined with exotic plants and shaded by avenues of palm trees and 50-foot-high bamboo stalks. In 1961, U.S. landscapers Robert and Catherine Wilson bought 30 acres of coffee plantation and started planting tropical species, including palms, orchids, bromeliads, and heliconias. Today the property extends over 635 acres, and the gardens hold around 2,000 native and more than 3,000 exotic species. The palm collection—more than 700 species—is the second largest in the world. Fantastically shaped and colored bromeliads, which usually live in the tops of trees, have been brought down to the ground in impressive mass plantings, providing one of many photo opportunities. Guided walks are conducted at 7:30 am and 1:30 pm.

The garden was transferred to the Organization for Tropical Studies in 1973, and in 1983 it became part of Amistad Biosphere Reserve. Under the name Las Cruces Biological Station, Wilson functions mainly as a research and educational center, so there is a constant supply of expert botanists and biologists to take visitors on natural-history tours in the garden and the adjoining forest trails. Birders can hike to the new canopy tower in the forest, funded by the local San Vito Birding Club, to get up to eye level with birds in the treetops. Twice a month, members of the San Vito Bird Club lead free birding tours of the garden, complete with binoculars and field guides to share. Check 🌐 *www.sanvitobirdclub.org* for the bird-walk schedule. If you spend a night at the garden lodge, you have the garden all to yourself in the late afternoon and early morning, when wildlife is most active. Guests also have access to the Río Java trail, where monkeys abound. ✉ *Road to Ciudad Neily, 6 km (4 miles) south of San Vito* ☎ *2773–4004* 🌐 *tropicalstudies.org* 🎟 *From $10 with no guide; guided tour $30 per person.*

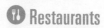

Restaurants

Pizzería Liliana

$$ | **ITALIAN** | **FAMILY** | At the classiest restaurant in town you can treat yourself to authentic pizza made from all-natural ingredients, or dig into the macaroni *sanviteña* style: with white sauce, ham, and mushrooms. The classics are here as well, and they're all homemade—lasagna, cannelloni, and ravioli—as well as hearty chicken and meat dishes. **Known for:** macaroni sanviteña with ham and mushrooms; plato mixto: half portion of lasagna with a quarter roast chicken; one of the few places open late. [$] *Average main: $11* ✉ *West of central square, up short hill* ☎ *2773–3080.*

Hotels

Casa Botania B&B

$$ | **B&B/INN** | **FAMILY** | Comfortable rooms with sweeping views of forest and mountains, birding trails, and bountiful buffet breakfasts are the highlights at this delightful, small hilltop B&B. **Pros:** amiable hosts; scenic garden setting; birding and photography tours. **Cons:** close to road and traffic noise (but not much at night); big but friendly dog;

En Route

San Vito to Ciudad Neily The 33-km (21-mile), recently paved road from San Vito to Ciudad Neily is twisting and spectacular, with views over the Coto Colorado plain to the Golfo Dulce and Osa Peninsula beyond. You can stop halfway at **Mirador La Torre** to enjoy excellent fruit *naturales* (fruit juice) and the view from their counter stools. Watch out for some tricky curves where there are no guardrails. ✉ *San Vito.*

San Vito to Paso Real The paved, scenic road from San Vito to Paso Real travels along a high ridge with sweeping valley views on either side. Halfway between Boca Limón and Las Vueltas, stop to enjoy a *refresco* and the views at open-air **Restaurante La Carreta.** As the road descends, the wide valley of El General River opens up before you, planted with miles of spiky pineapples and tall sugarcane. Few passing opportunities require a lot of patience, especially in the valley if you find yourself caught in a slow-moving convoy of trucks hauling pineapple and sugarcane. ✉ *San Vito.*

slightly cramped dining terrace. [$] *Rooms from: $75* ✉ *Road to Wilson Botanical Garden, 5 km (3 miles) south of San Vito* ☎ *2773–4217, 8711–3008* 🌐 *www.casabotania.com* 🛏 *5 rooms* 🍴 *Free Breakfast.*

Cascata del Bosco Hotel, Restaurant & Bar
$$ | **B&B/INN** | Just 656 feet from the entrance to Wilson Botanical Garden, this collection of four totally private, round bungalows, set amid gardens and forest teeming with birds, is designed for nature-lovers. **Pros:** close to Wilson Botanical Garden; attractive cabins; affordable. **Cons:** no phones in rooms; not a lot of parking; bar can be noisy on weekends. [$] *Rooms from: $75* ✉ *200 m from entrance to Wilson Botanical Garden, Las Cruces* ☎ *2773–3208* 🌐 *www.cascatadelbosco.com* 🛏 *4 rooms* 🍴 *Free Breakfast.*

★ **Wilson Botanical Garden**
$$$ | **B&B/INN** | The best features of the dozen comfortable rooms here, in three modern buildings built of glass, steel, and wood, are the private balconies cantilevered over a forested ravine, perfect for bird-watching. **Pros:** 24-hour access to botanical garden and nature trails; excellent birding and wildlife viewing; chance to meet researchers. **Cons:** family-style meals served on a strict schedule; modest rooms; possible noise from adjoining terraces. [$] *Rooms from: $180* ✉ *Las Cruces Biological Station, Road to Ciudad Neily, 6 km (4 miles) south of San Vito* ☎ *2524–0607 Organization for Tropical Studies office in San José, 2773–4004 Wilson Botanical Garden reception* 🌐 *tropicalstudies.org/portfolio/las-cruces-research-station* 🛏 *12 rooms* 🍴 *All-inclusive.*

Shopping

Finca Cántaros
CRAFTS | In a vintage farmhouse between San Vito and Wilson Botanical Garden, Finca Cántaros sells crafts by indigenous artisans from near and far, including charming calabash gourds painted by Maleku artists, and colorful *molas* (appliqué work) made by Kuna women from the San Blas Islands in Panama. The owner's own mixed-media prints celebrate tropical nature with watercolor, colored pencil, and hand-carved rubber blocks used as printing stamps. You can also find a great selection of colorful,

high-glaze ceramics from San José artists, as well as Sibú artisanal chocolates. Profits help support the adjacent free lending library. Behind the shop lies a 17.3-acre private nature reserve ($6), where you can walk the bird-filled forest trails around a lake, explore an indigenous archaeological site, or park a camper van overnight ($10). ⊠ *Linda Vista, Road to Ciudad Neily, 3 km (2 miles) south of San Vito* ☎ *2773–3760* ⊕ *www.fincacantaros.com.*

Dominical

34 km (21 miles) southwest of San Isidro, 40 km (25 miles) south of Quepos.

Sleepy fishing village–turned–surfer town, Dominical has undergone a lively makeover, with a paved beach road, new restaurants and shops, a farmers' market on Friday morning, and an artisans' fiesta with live music the first Saturday night of the month. As more and more luxury villas pop up all over the hillsides above the beaches, you're likely to find the private jet set rubbing elbows with the bohemian set. It's still a major surfing destination, attracting surfers of all ages, with a lively restaurant and nightlife scene. Favorite local hangouts come and go, so don't hesitate to try something new.

Dominical's real magic lies beyond the town, in the surrounding terrestrial and marine wonders: the rain forest grows right up to the beach in some places, and the ocean offers world-class surfing.

Much of the lush forest that covers the steep hillsides above the beaches is protected within private nature reserves. Several of these reserves, such as Hacienda Barú, protect significant tracts of the rain forest.

GETTING HERE AND AROUND
The paved road west over the mountains and down to Dominical is scenic at its best and fog-shrouded at its worst.

There are lots of curves and a few dicey landslide areas, so take your time and enjoy the scenery along the hour-long drive from San Isidro de El General. From Quepos, the paved Costanera Highway makes for an easy half-hour drive to Dominical, although you do have to contend with huge transport trucks barreling along. Buses from San Isidro de El General leave six times a day, three times a day from Quepos. If you want to avoid driving altogether, Monkey Ride has air-conditioned vans with room for six to eight passengers that make trips to and from San José (starting at $49). There's an ATM in the Pueblo del Río center; if you need a full-service bank, the nearest is in Uvita.

RENTAL CARS Solid Car Rental. ⊠ *Hwy. 34, Uvita* ⊹ *Across the street from the Sandias de Colonia grocery store* ☎ *2442–6000, 800/390–7065 in the U.S.* ⊕ *www.solidcarrental.com.*

ESSENTIALS
TOUR COMPANIES Costa Rica Dive and Surf. ⊠ *Main street, 20 m south of church* ☎ *2743–8679, 2787–0362 Dominical office* ⊕ *www.costaricadiveandsurf.com.* **Dominical Surf Adventures.** ⊠ *Main street, across from Pueblo del Río* ☎ *8897–9540, 2787–0431* ⊕ *www.dominicalsurfadventures.com.* **Pineapple Kayak Tours.** ⊠ *Main street* ⊹ *Beside police station* ☎ *8873–3283* ⊕ *www.pineapplekayaktours.com.*

VISITOR INFORMATION Dominical Information. ⊠ *Pueblo del Río, Main street* ☎ *2787–0454, 323/285–8832 in the U.S.* ⊕ *www.dominicalinformation.com.*

Sights

★ Hacienda Barú
NATURE PRESERVE | FAMILY | This leading ecotourism and conservation wildlife refuge offers spectacular bird-watching tours and excellent naturalist-led hikes (starting at $34), a thrilling Flight of the Toucan canopy tour ($49), a chance to

spend the night in the jungle ($149), or self-guided walks along forest and mangrove trails ($15). The refuge also manages a turtle-protection project and nature-education program in the local school. You can stay at two- and three-bedroom cabins or in poolside rooms—or just come for the day. ⊠ *Costanera Hwy., 3 km (2 miles) north of Dominical* ☎ *2787–0003, 888/583–5980 in the U.S.* ⊕ *www.haciendabaru.com* ☜ *From $15.*

★ Nauyaca Waterfalls

BODY OF WATER | FAMILY | This massive double cascade, the longer one tumbling down 150 feet, is one of the most spectacular sights in Costa Rica. The falls (aka Barú River Falls) are on private property, so the only ways to reach them are on horseback, hiking, or riding in an open truck. ⊠ *Hwy. to San Isidro de El General, 10 km (7 miles) northeast of Dominical* ⊹ *On the road to Platanillo* ⊕ *www.cataratasnauyaca.com* ☜ *$10 to hike.*

Parque Reptilandia

ZOO | FAMILY | With more than 300 specimens, this impressive collection includes snakes, lizards, frogs, turtles, and other reptilian creatures, housed in visitor-friendly terrariums and large enclosures. Stars of the exhibit are a Komodo dragon, Gila monsters, a very large anaconda, and a 150-pound African spur-thighed tortoise that likes to be petted. Kids love the maternity ward showcasing newborn snakes. More mature snakes live under a retractable roof that lets in sun and rain. Although snakes are generally more active in sunlight, this is still a great rainy-day activity. Guided night tours can also be arranged to watch nocturnal animals. If you're not squeamish, snake-feeding day is Friday, spread out from 10 am to 3 pm. ⊠ *Road to San Isidro, 11 km (7 miles) east of Dominical* ☎ *2787–0343* ⊕ *www.crreptiles.com* ☜ *$12.*

Poza Azul

BODY OF WATER | FAMILY | Hidden in a forest above Dominicalito Beach, this waterfall is considerably smaller than Nauyaca Waterfalls, but it has a lovely swimming hole at its base. Off the main highway, turn left past the Dominicalito soccer field and through a stream; follow the road straight uphill for about 984 feet to where the road widens. (If the stream is too high to cross, go back to the highway and drive south to the next left turn, where there's a bus stop, and go through a small village, over the new bridge, then turn right up the mountain for 984 feet.) You can park here and climb down the steps to the swimming hole at the base of a waterfall. The pool is often populated by local kids when school is out and by surfers late in the afternoon. Pay strict attention to the posted sign that warns not to leave anything of value in your parked car. Avoid holiday times and weekends, when there are often large crowds. ⊠ *Dominical.*

Beaches

Playa Dominical

BEACH—SIGHT | Long and flat, Playa Dominical is good for beachcombing among all the flotsam and jetsam that the surf washes up onto the brown sand. There's shade and parking under palm trees along the new brick-paved road that parallels the beach. The water is relatively clean and local businesses make sure things look tidy. Photo opportunities abound here, with buff surfers riding the waves and vendors' clotheslines of colorful sarongs flapping in the sea breeze. Tortilla Flats restaurant is practically on the beach. Huge waves and dangerous rip currents make it primarily a surfing beach. In high season, flags mark off a relatively safe area for swimming, under the watchful gaze of a professional lifeguard. **Amenities:** food and drink; lifeguards; parking (no fee). **Best for:** surfing; walking. ⊠ *Dominical.*

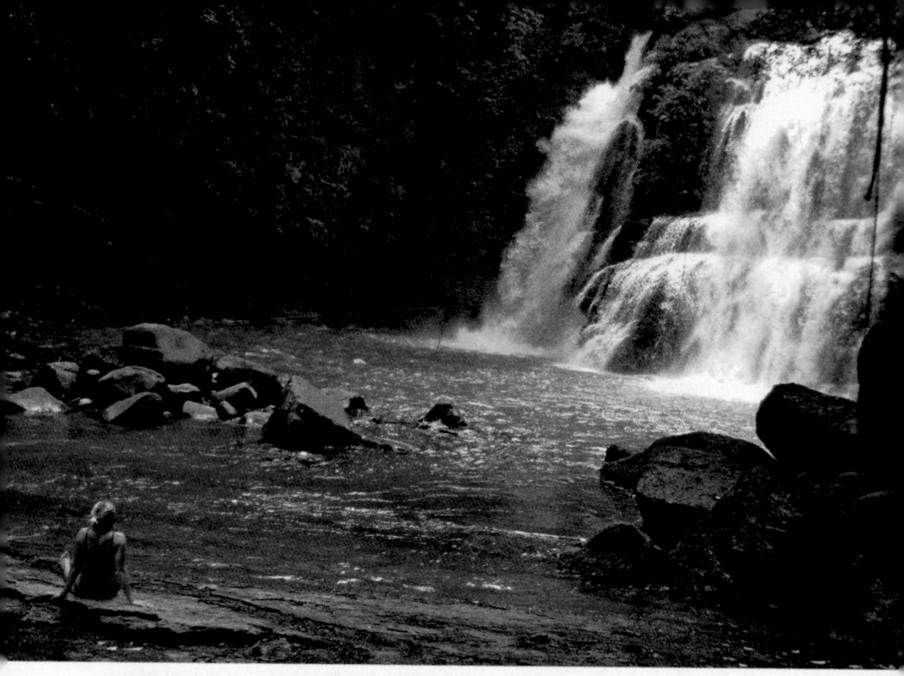

Nauyaca waterfalls is a three-tier waterfall and well worth the visit.

Playa Dominicalito

BEACH—SIGHT | About 1 km (½ mile) south of Playa Dominical, this wide beach is usually calmer and more suited to boogie boarding and beginner surfers. There are hidden rocks near the shore, so the best time to swim is at low tide. This is one of the best walking beaches, with lots of shade under tall palms and beach almond trees early in the morning. The sun sets behind a huge rocky outcropping topped with tiny palm trees, an ideal shot for photographers. There is an unofficial campground running parallel to the beach, which is popular with locals, especially during Easter, Christmas, and school holidays. **Amenities**: parking (no fee). **Best for:** solitude; sunset; walking. ✉ *Dominical.*

🍴 Restaurants

Cafe Mono Congo

$ | **VEGETARIAN** | Pull up a counter stool or sit at a table on the popular riverside terrace at this friendly café with creative vegetarian and gluten-free dishes, organic juices, local and imported craft beers on tap, kombuchas, and herbal teas. Desserts are not only gluten-free, they are addictive: the chocolate papaya pie combines dark chocolate with papaya to make a rich mousse filling for a date, almond, and coconut crust. **Known for:** smashed avocados on toasted gluten-free bagel with goat cheese; chocolate papaya gluten-free pie; excellent organic coffee. [$] *Average main: $8* ✉ *Pueblo del Río, Main St.* ☎ *8485–5523, 6312–8766 WhatsApp, for ordering* 🌐 *cafemonocongo.com.*

El Pescado Loco

$ | **SEAFOOD** | Beer-battered onion rings, fresh hand-cut fries, and fried pickles have taken Dominical by storm at this laid-back alfresco kiosk in the Pueblo del Río complex on the riverfront. The fish tacos are outstanding—crispy beer-battered fish fillets accompanied by guacamole, red cabbage, and a spicy sauce are folded into a thin soft tortilla. **Known for:** outstanding fish tacos; great fries; gluten-free tortillas. [$] *Average* main: $8 ⊠ *Pueblo del Río, Main street* ☎ *8303–9042* ▭ *No credit cards.*

Gate One Charter Restaurant

$$ | ECLECTIC | FAMILY | This alfresco restaurant tucked beside a bona fide Boeing 727 (minus the engine) delivers generous portions of upscale pastas, succulent meats, and tasty fish and seafood, including Peruvian-style ceviches. During the day kids can frolic in the swimming pool and adults can order spicy tropical chicken wings in the plane's cocktail bar. **Known for:** red snapper in a mushroom cream sauce; spicy chicken wings; karaoke and live-music evenings. $ *Average main: $13 ⊠ 1½ km (1 mile) northeast of Dominical, on road from San Isidro de El General* ☎ *506/2787–0172.*

La Parcela

$$ | COSTA RICAN | Picture a dream location: a high headland jutting out into the sea with vistas up and down the coast, and throw in a breeze-swept terrace, polished service, a boat-shape bar, and some fine seaside cuisine, and you are at La Parcela. Sunsets here are spectacular, and shrimp and lobster dishes are pricey but excellent. **Known for:** beer-battered fish served with crunchy carrot salad; fried calamari; decadent chocolate mud pie. $ *Average main: $15 ⊠ 4 km (2½ miles) south of Dominical, off Costanera Hwy.* ☎ *2787–0016* ⊕ *www.laparcelacr. com.*

Maracatù

$$ | VEGETARIAN | Who says vegetarian food has to be boring? From spicy pad thai with tofu to crunchy falafel served with brown rice and organic salad, this hip restaurant can make vegetarians ecstatic and even the most committed carnivore happy. **Known for:** fish tacos; spicy pad thai; popular bar with music in evenings. $ *Average main: $12 ⊠ Main street, across from soccer field* ☎ *2787– 0091* ☉ *No lunch.*

Phat Noodle

$ | INDONESIAN | Spice up your day with skewers of Indonesian satays and generous bowls of peanutty pad thai and red or green curry at this hip open-air caravansary under a high corrugated-metal green roof. The kitchen, in a gaily painted converted bus, turns out portions large enough to share. **Known for:** pork ribs with pineapple and tamarind sauce; pad thai; spicy tropical cocktails. $ *Average main: $9 ⊠ Main street, across the street from Pueblo del Río* ☎ *2787–0017.*

¿Por Qué No?

$$$ | ECLECTIC | The most romantic restaurant in Dominical, this pretty, garden-terrace spot sparkles with fairy lights and offers a view of sky and sea and seating close enough for diners to hear waves crashing on the rocks below. The menu is upscale and sophisticated and focused on local seafood and wood-fired pizzas with unconventional ingredients. **Known for:** red snapper in an almond crust; coconut vegetable curry; romantic sunset cocktail deck. $ *Average main: $20 ⊠ Costa Paraiso Hotel, off Costanera Hwy.* ⊹ *2 km (1½ miles) south of Dominical* ☎ *2787–0340* ☉ *Closed Mon.*

Restaurant Su Raza

$ | COSTA RICAN | Among the handful of sodas in town serving typical Costa Rican food, this one is notable for its affordably priced whole fish and hearty portions of seafood served on a breezy veranda. Stick to the *desayuno típico* for breakfast, with traditional rice and beans and eggs, starting at 7 am. **Known for:** pleasant alfresco terrace; hearty breakfast; inexpensive. $ *Average main: $8 ⊠ Main street* ☎ *2787–0105* ▭ *No credit cards.*

Dominical Sushi

$$ | JAPANESE | With a view over the Barú estuary, this open-air Japanese restaurant serves local seafood in all the usual rolls and sashimi, with some tropical twists, plus imported Sapporo beer, sake, or green tea to drink. Dark bamboo furniture, Japanese lanterns, and colored and colored globes set the modern, minimalist scene, while smooth, jazzy music mix sets a cool mood. **Known for:** tico shrimp roll with mango; ahi poke salad with raw tuna; cool jazz soundtrack. [$] *Average main: $12* ✉ *Pueblo del Río, Main street* ☎ *8826–7946* ⏲ *No dinner Fri.; no lunch Sat.*

Tortilla Flats

$$ | **SOUTHWESTERN** | This perennially popular and casual surfer hangout is right across from Dominical Beach, which you can spy through a fringe of palm trees. Favorite menu items are the fresh-baked baguette sandwiches stuffed with interesting combinations and the excellent margaritas and flavored daiquiris, usually downed at the huge U-shape bar. **Known for:** baguette chicken-and-avocado sandwich; fish tacos; live bands some evenings. [$] *Average main: $13* ✉ *Across from Dominical Beach* ☎ *2787–0033.*

Hotels

Lodgings in the lowlands of Dominical and the area a little to the north are closer to the beach, but tend to be hot and muggy and not as comfortable as the more luxurious, private, and breezy places up in the hills above Dominicalito, to the south.

Coconut Grove Oceanfront Cottages

$$ | **RENTAL** | **FAMILY** | Practically on the beach, this well-maintained cluster of equipped cabins and beach houses is ideal for travelers who want to fend for themselves, turn off the air-conditioning at night, and fall asleep to the sound of the ocean. **Pros:** best location in town (right on beach); close enough to feel cool ocean breezes; free Wi-Fi. **Cons:** furnishings are simple and a little tired; guests must love animals; very steep driveway. [$] *Rooms from: $95* ✉ *Dominicalito Beach, Km 147, Costanera Hwy., 3 km (2 miles) south of Dominical* ☎ *2787–0130* 🌐 *www.coconutgrovecr.com* 💳 *No credit cards* 🛏 *5 rooms* 🍴 *No meals.*

Cuna del Angel Hotel and Spa

$$$ | **B&B/INN** | With an excellent restaurant, a lush garden, a pretty infinity pool, and exceptional service, this elegant hotel is a heavenly spot for those who like to indulge themselves. **Pros:** delightful decor; excellent restaurant; friendly, professional service in hotel. **Cons:** ground-level rooms lack privacy; water pressure is sometimes low; steep steps to Jungle Rooms and restaurant. [$] *Rooms from: $226* ✉ *Costanera Hwy., Puertocito, 9 km (5 miles) south of Dominical* ☎ *2787–4343* 🌐 *www.cunadelangel.com* 🛏 *22 rooms* 🍴 *Free Breakfast.*

★ **Hacienda Barú National Wildlife Refuge and Ecolodge**

$$ | **B&B/INN** | **FAMILY** | This wildly family-friendly, comfortable eco-lodge makes a great base for exploring vast tracts of surrounding forest (both primary and secondary), plus there are mangroves, a beach with nesting turtles, a netted-in butterfly garden, and a charming orchid garden—and 366 bird species. **Pros:** prime wildlife viewing; excellent guides; great value. **Cons:** older cabins are not fancy; no a/c (but rooms are well ventilated with ceiling and wall fans); pool is in full sun (wear sunscreen!). [$] *Rooms from: $129* ✉ *Off Costanera Hwy., 3 km (2 miles) north Dominical* ☎ *2787–0003* 🌐 *www.haciendabaru.com* 🛏 *12 rooms* 🍴 *Free Breakfast.*

Roca Verde

$$ | **B&B/INN** | Small and friendly, this is the only hotel with direct beach access in the area, so it's popular with surfers, anglers, and beach lovers, as well as locals who come here on Friday night for a live music mix of classic rock, bluegrass, and jazzy blues. **Pros:** right on the beach; friendly bar; reasonably priced. **Cons:** can be noisy on Friday night; no phones or TV reception in rooms; cash only. [$] *Rooms from: $145* ✉ *Off Costanera Sur Hwy., on Dominical Beach, 1 km (½ mile) south of*

Dominical ☎ 2787–0036 🌐 rocaverde.net ▭ No credit cards 🛏 9 rooms 🍴 Free Breakfast.

Villas Alturas

$$$ | B&B/INN | One of the best lodging deals on this coast, these seven, no-frills villas are in a sublime, lofty setting, with a large swimming pool and a huge terrace overlooking a million-dollar view of the Pacific. **Pros:** excellent value; fabulous views; wildlife refuge on-site. **Cons:** long, steep drive requiring 4WD; long way down to beach and activities; sparsely furnished villas. [$] *Rooms from: $220* ✉ *Off Costanera Hwy., 7 km (4½ miles) south of Dominical, 800 m up steep hill* ☎ *2200–5440* 🌐 *www.villasalturas.com* 🛏 *7 rooms* 🍴 *Free Breakfast.*

Villas Río Mar

$ | HOTEL | FAMILY | This upscale yet very affordable resort hotel, with two pools, spa, and tennis courts is upriver from Dominical beach on exquisitely landscaped grounds filled with orchids, bougainvillea, and hibiscus. **Pros:** huge pool; lovely grounds; excellent restaurant. **Cons:** children can be noisy in pool; 15-minute walk to the main beach; rate does not include tax. [$] *Rooms from: $71* ✉ *Off main hwy. into town, 1 km (½ mile) west of Dominical* ☎ *2787–0052* 🌐 *www.villasriomar.com* 🛏 *52 rooms* 🍴 *Free Breakfast.*

Nightlife

During the high season, Dominical hops at night, and when the surfers have fled to find bigger waves, there are enough locals around to keep some fun events afloat.

Fuego Brew Co.

BREWPUBS/BEER GARDENS | With an on-site, full-scale brewery below and a rancho restaurant above, this hip brewpub with live music many nights has become the liveliest nightspot in town. Belly up to the long bar, relax in a quieter lounge area, or take a table overlooking the garden and the Barú River estuary. Above-average bar food and pizza accompany the many beers on tap; you can order a flight of five ales to taste, then order your favorite. It's open till 10:30. ✉ *Off main street, next door to yoga center* ☎ *8992–9559* 🌐 *www.fuegobrew.com.*

Roca Verde

MUSIC CLUBS | FAMILY | Friday nights year-round feature a local bluesy rock band electrifying the happy, upbeat crowd, which consists of a mix of local families, expats, and tourists. Guest artists often join the band. ✉ *Roca Verde, 1 km (½ mile) south of Dominical* ☎ *2787–0036.*

Shopping

Mama Toucan's Natural & Organic Foods

FOOD/CANDY | Colorful and comfortably air-conditioned, this whole-foods store is a treat to browse in. Along with the fresh organic vegetables, there is a wide selection of gluten-free foods, including bagels and breads, and a deli with ready-to-eat vegan and gluten-free snacks and sandwiches. The ice cream, sorbet, and gelato made with coconut milk are delicious whether you are a vegan or an omnivore. The shop also carries hard-to-find, imported specialty foods, spices, and excellent local chocolates. It's open from 8:30 to 7:30 daily. ✉ *Pueblo del Río, Main St.* ☎ *8433–4235.*

Activities

HORSEBACK RIDING

Don Lulo

HORSEBACK RIDING | FAMILY | Horseback-riding tours to Nauyaca Waterfalls depart Monday to Saturday at 8 am from Don Lulo's stables. The tour ($85) includes a light breakfast and lunch at the family homestead near the falls. You can swim in the cool pool beneath the falls, so bring a bathing suit and sunscreen. There is a river to cross, but otherwise the 12-km (7½-mile) ride is easy. You can also ride in an open truck ($32) or hike in on your own ($10). Be sure to reserve a day in advance. In rainy season, raincoats are provided. ⊠ *Road to San Isidro, 10 km (6 miles) northeast of Dominical* ☎ *2787–0541, 2787–0542* ⊕ *www.nauyacawaterfallscostarica.com.*

SURFING

The surfing is great in Dominical, thanks to the runoff from the Barú River mouth, which constantly changes the ocean bottom and creates well-shaped waves big enough to keep intermediate and advanced surfers challenged. The best surfing is near the river mouth, and the best time is two hours before or after high tide, to avoid the notorious riptides.

Dominical Surf Adventures

ADVENTURE TOURS | One-on-one, two-hour surfing lessons are $60; group lessons are $50 per person. All lessons include transportation, surfboard, rash guard, fruit, and soft drinks. Board rental starts at $10 per day. ⊠ *Main street, across from mercadito* ☎ *2787–0431, 8897–9540* ⊕ *www.dominicalsurfadventures.com.*

Dominical Surf Lessons

SURFING | Owned and operated by Costa Rican surf champion Debbie Zec, this surf school holds lessons at several local breaks and can take surfers to nearby Playa Dominical between Quepos and Uvita. Their standard ratio is two students per instructor, and they offer two-hour courses from beginner to advanced. Rates include equipment and drinking water. ⊠ *Dominical* ☎ *8673–9543* 🍴 *From $60.*

Ballena National Marine Park

20 km (12 miles) southeast of Dominical.

Named for the whales (*ballenas,* in Spanish) that seasonally migrate here, this park protects marine life in miles of ocean, as well as 10 km (6 miles) of coastline, incorporating four separate beaches, each with its own character. Opportunities abound for fishing, whale- and dolphin-watching tours, kayaking, camping, beachcombing, and swimming. Sunsets here are unbeatable.

GETTING HERE AND AROUND

The park area includes the communities of Uvita, Bahía Ballena, and Ojochal, all easily accessible off the Costanera, a wide, paved highway now officially called Carretera Nacional Pacifica Fernández. As soon as you get off the highway, however, the roads are often bumpy and dusty. Alternatively, take a taxi or bus from Dominical. Eight buses leave Dominical, starting at 4:45 am until 5:30 pm daily, and there are longer-haul buses that pass along the Costanera and can drop you off in Uvita. Each of the park's four sectors, open 7 to 4, has a small ranger station where you pay your $6 admission.

ESSENTIALS

HOSPITAL Dome Plaza Medical Services. ⊠ *Dome Plaza, 50 m south of bridge, Uvita* ☎ *2743–8595 doctor, 2743–8418 dentist, 2743–8558 pharmacy.*

VISITOR INFORMATION Uvita Information Center. ⊠ *On Costanera Hwy., across from BM Supermarket, Uvita* ☎ *8843–7142, 2743–8889* ⊕ *www.uvita.info.*

◉ Sights

★ Ballena National Marine Park (Parque Nacional Marino Ballena)

BEACH—SIGHT | FAMILY | Named for the whales who use this area as a nursery, the park has four separate Blue Flag beaches stretching for about 10 km (6 miles) and encompasses a mangrove estuary, a remnant coral reef, and more than 12,350 acres of ocean, home to tropical fish, dolphins, and humpback whales. Playa Uvita is the most popular sector of the park, with the longest stretch of beach and shallow waters calm enough for kids. Restaurants line the road to the Playa Uvita park entrance, but there are no food concessions within the park. Access to each of the four beaches—from north to south, Uvita, Colonia, Ballena, and Piñuela—is off the Costanera Highway. Although the official park offices are open 7 am to 4 pm, visitors can stay on longer, especially to view sunsets or camp. ⊠ *Entrance at Playa Uvita, about 20 km (12 miles) south of Dominical, Uvita* ☎ *2743–8236* ⌐ *$6.*

Finca 6 Museum of the Spheres

ARCHAEOLOGICAL SITE | About an hour from Uvita, you can learn about the mystery of Costa Rica's pre-Columbian spheres—massive, perfectly round stones uncovered in the 1930s—in this archaeological museum, built on a recently designated UNESCO World Heritage Site near Sierpe, the port for boats to Drake Bay. Dating from 800 to 1500 AD, these carefully arranged spheres of varying sizes cover acres of land, popping up miles from the source of the rock used to carve them. Anthropologists speculate they may have served as agricultural calendars or as ceremonial sites similar to Stonehenge. All of the theories are outlined, in English and Spanish, along with displays of period pottery, sculpture, and other artifacts in a light and airy new museum, a branch of San José's National Museum. Much of the museum is outdoors, to view archeological sites and see the spheres in situ. The sun is hot, so come early and bring along a hat and a water bottle. Squirrel monkeys and birds inhabit the wooded areas along the trails, so it's a good idea to carry binoculars and cameras, too. If you are on your way to the Osa Peninsula, by car or boat, don't miss this opportunity to encounter a surviving vestige of indigenous culture. ⊠ *8 km (5 miles) west of turnoff from Costanera to Palmar Sur, on road to Sierpe; look for Finca 6 sign on left, just before small bridge ✛ 45 km (28 miles) south of Uvita, on Costanera Hwy., to turnoff for Palmar Sur, then follow signs to airport and Sierpe* ☎ *2100–6000* ⊕ *www.museocostarica. go.cr* ⌐ *$6* ⊘ *Closed Mon.*

Oro Verde Private Nature Reserve

NATURE PRESERVE | You'll find excellent bird-watching and hiking in this nature preserve, uphill from the Costanera. Family-run, the property has well-groomed trails through a majestic, primary forest reserve. Early-morning, three-hour birding tours start at 6 ($40) and end with a hearty home-cooked breakfast. In the afternoon, you can set out for a three-hour birding walk. For a totally different perspective on wildlife, join the naturalist-guided night tour, from 6 to 9 pm. The best way to book is through the Uvita Information Center. ⊠ *Km 159, Costanera Hwy., 3 km (2 miles) uphill from Rancho La Merced, Uvita* ☎ *2743–8889, 8843–8833.*

Rancho La Merced National Wildlife Refuge

FARM/RANCH | FAMILY | Ride the range on a 1,250-acre property combining forest and pasture ($55) or gallop along the beach at sunset on horseback ($60). Explore the forest on a nature hike ($40) or go bird-watching ($55) with an excellent guide. Riding tours also include a guide and helmets, and kid-size saddles are available. All tours begin at the pleasant reception center, where you can freshen up in clean, modern restrooms. For $6 you can explore the 10 km (6 miles) of hiking trails on your own with a trail map that includes a wildlife picture guide. There's also a night tour with a naturalist guide ($40). ⊠ *Km 159, Costanera Hwy., north of Uvita, Uvita*

An iguana on Playa Uvita

☎ *2743–8032, 8861–5147* ⊕ *www.rancho-lamerced.com* ✉ *From $40.*

Uvita Market

MARKET | From 8 am to noon on Saturday, the place to be is this combination farmers' market and weekly gathering place for locals. About 20 vendors show up to sell organic produce, chocolate, homemade cheeses and hot sauces, fresh fish, baked goods, jams, and frozen gourmet dinners and soups to take home. You can also feast on ready-to-eat breakfast burritos, tamales, cakes, cookies, and the freshest, best doughnuts in the country, made right on the spot. Artists sell painted masks, colorful textiles, and beautiful wildlife photographs. Every third Saturday there's a garage-sale table, too. This is a great place to meet English-speaking locals as they meet and greet. Some weeks, there's live music by local bands. You'll find the market just off the Costanera Highway, across from the Banco de Costa Rica and down a short side road. Just look for all the parked cars. ✉ *Off Costanera Hwy., across from Banco de Costa Rica, Uvita.*

Beaches

Playa Ballena

BEACH—SIGHT | This lovely strand is backed by lush vegetation and is fairly easy to get to from the main highway, along a short, bumpy dirt road. Gas and charcoal barbecues are permitted here, so locals often have barbecues on weekends. There's free parking close to the beach. **Amenities:** showers; toilets. **Best for:** swimming; walking. ✉ *Ballena National Marine Park, 4 km (2½ miles) south of Playa Colonia access road, off Costanera Hwy., Ojochal* ✉ *$6.*

Playa Colonia

BEACH—SIGHT | This beach is safe for swimming and has a view of rocky islands, which you can visit by kayak. The access road is a well-graded dirt road. There is a sandy break for surfing, with gentle waves for beginners. In high season, vendors sell cold drinks and souvenirs at the beach entrance. It's the only beach where cars can park practically on the beach, and camping is included in the admission price.

Amenities: food and drink; showers; toilets. **Best for:** swimming. ⊠ *Ballena National Marine Park, 2 km (1¼ miles) south of Playa Uvita along Costanera Hwy., Ballena Marine National Park* 🖃 *$6.*

Playa Piñuela

BEACH—SIGHT | Nestled in a deep cove with views of small islands, tiny Playa Piñuela is the prettiest, and many times the most private, of the Ballena National Marine Park beaches. It's not always the best beach for swimming at high tide, however, since the shore is strewn with large stones and the waves can be a little rough. At low tide, the smooth, sandy beach emerges. The access road is very bumpy but also short. **Amenities:** showers; toilets. **Best for:** walking. ⊠ *Ballena National Marine Park, 3 km (2 miles) south of Playa Colonia, off Costanera Hwy., Ojochal* ✛ *Turn off Costanera just past Km 172 marker* 🖃 *$6.*

★ Playa Uvita

BEACH—SIGHT | At the northern end of Ballena National Marine Park, wide, palm-fringed Playa Uvita stretches out along a *tombolo* (a long swath of sand) connecting a former island to the coast. At low tide, you can walk out to the famous "whale tail," where you'll get magnificent views of the hills and jungles of Uvita (and maybe spot a macaw). This is the most popular beach, especially on weekends, with shallow waters for swimming. On weekdays you may have it almost to yourself. It's also the launching spot for boat tours and the favorite vantage point for spectacular sunsets. There is no parking at the beach, but there are private parking lots along the road leading to the park entrance, charging $4 a day. **Amenities:** food and drink; showers; toilets. **Best for:** sunset; swimming; walking. ⊠ *Ballena National Marine Park, Uvita* 🖃 *$6.*

Playa Ventanas

BEACH—SIGHT | This scenic beach has interesting tidal caves, popular for sea kayaking. Coconut palms edge the beach, which is sometimes pebbly, with quite a dramatic surf, especially at high tide when the waves break against huge offshore rock formations. The ocean views are rivaled by the vistas of green, forested mountains rising up behind the beach. You can camp here and use very basic toilets and cold-water showers. There's a new access road to the beach and a guarded parking area ($3 for the day). But it is advisable to not leave anything of value in your car. **Amenities:** parking (fee); showers; toilets. **Best for:** walking. ⊠ *Ballena National Marine Park, 1½ km (1 mile) south of Playa Piñuela, off Costanera Hwy., Ojochal.*

🍴 Restaurants

The Bamboo Room

$$ | MODERN CANADIAN | Bamboo decks the walls at this hilltop restaurant with a spectacular view of land and sea, but it's the upscale menu that grabs one's attention due to its innovative takes on fish, shrimp, chicken, and out-of-the-ordinary bar food. Crunchy, panko-crispy shrimp make appearances in salads, burgers, and on their own, while crispy beer-battered cauliflower tacos, a creamy mushroom alfredo pasta, and a vegan coconut curry will keep vegetarians happy. **Known for:** BamBOOM! salad with panko-crisp shrimp; sampler platter with wings, shrimp, jalapeño poppers, onion wedges; nightly live music. 🖫 *Average main: $13* ⊠ *Alma Hotel, C. Perezoso, Ojochal* ☎ *2786–5295* ⌚ *Closed Sun.–Tues.*

★ Citrus Restaurante + Tapas

$$$ | ECLECTIC | Tangy, tart, and refreshing, this ultrasophisticated restaurant lives up to its name, both in its daring decor and inventive fusion menu spanning the globe from the Far East, across the Mediterranean to chef Marcella Marciano's culinary homeland, France. The menu careens from classic French escargots and *moules marinières* to Japanese wasabi-spiced shrimp, to Indian chicken curry. **Known for:** seafood platter in lemon-garlic sauce; choco-choco flourless cake; chic and romantic setting.

Did You Know?

Just outside of Ballena
National Marine Park,
Uvita is the longest,
widest, and most visited
beach in the area.

$ *Average main: $20* ✉ *Plaza Tangara main road in Ojochal, Ojochal* ☎ *2786–5175, 8304–1717* ⊗ *Closed Sun.*

★ Exotica Restaurant

$$$ | FRENCH | Fabulous French cuisine with tropical accents served on an intimate alfresco patio in the tiny French-Canadian enclave of Ojochal keeps this romantic restaurant at the top of locals' list of go-to special-occasion restaurants. The menu, culled from France's colonial past, delights, as does the warm and friendly service. **Known for:** chili-spiced flourless chocolate cake; spicy Vietnamese chicken soup; reasonably priced international wine list. $ *Average main: $20* ✉ *Main road into Ojochal, off Costanera Hwy., Ojochal* ☎ *2786–5050* ⊗ *Closed Sun.; Sept.–Oct.; and Mon. May–Aug. No lunch.*

Pancito Café

$ | FRENCH | Besides crusty baguettes, buttery croissants, and divine pastries to go, this French bakery near the entrance to Ojochal serves hearty breakfast omelets, gluten-free fare, and light lunches of fish soup, sandwiches, quiches, crepes, salads, and mussels with French fries. Customers perch on high stools at tables and counters in this casual thatch-roof café. **Known for:** moules frites (mussels with French fries); salade niçoise; pork rillettes. $ *Average main: $8* ✉ *Plaza de Los Delfines, off Costanera Hwy. at entrance to Ojochal, Ojochal* ☎ *506/2786–5774, 8729–4115* ▭ *No credit cards* ⊗ *Closed Sun. No dinner.*

★ Sabor Español

$$$ | SPANISH | Authentic paella, made with nutty, saffron-infused Spanish rice and the freshest seafood, is the main reason to wend your way along a rutted dirt road behind Playa Ballena to this jungle outpost of Catalan cuisine. The smallish, open-air rancho is nothing fancy, with wooden chairs and tables and a few potted palms, but it fills up fast. **Known for:** whiskey-flambéed shrimp; garlicky marinated mushrooms; sangria by the pitcher. $ *Average main: $17* ✉ *1 km (½ mile)*

south of Uvita BM Supermercado along Costanera, Bahía Ballena ✛ *Turn right at Cabinas Gato sign; look for left-turn Sabor Español sign onto dirt road running parallel to Playa Ballena* ☎ *2743–8312, 8768–9160* ▭ *No credit cards* ⊗ *Closed Mon. and Sept. 15–Dec. 15. No lunch.*

Tilapias El Pavón

$ | COSTA RICAN | FAMILY | To enjoy an authentically tico day in the country, follow a winding river road about 20 minutes up to this family-run tilapia fish farm in the tiny hamlet of Vergel, where you catch your own tilapia on the way. The cooks at the open-air wooden restaurant overlooking the scenic fishponds will fry up your fish in 10 minutes, presenting it whole or filleted, with rice, salad, yuca, and excellent *patacones* (fried, mashed plantains), plus a pitcher of refreshing fruit naturale, a feast for less than $10. **Known for:** fried, breaded, or grilled fresh tilapia; crisp fried plantain patacones; fishponds set in gardens. $ *Average main: $9* ✉ *3 km (2 miles) south of Ojochal, then just before bridge in Punta Mala, follow dirt road 4 km (2½ miles) uphill to tiny hamlet of Vergel, Punta Mala* ☎ *2200–4721* ▭ *No credit cards.*

Villa Leonor

$$ | COSTA RICAN | FAMILY | No worries if you can't decide between lunch or the beach, because you can get both at this cheerful, casual restaurant and beach club, complete with swimming pool and showers. Just steps from Playa Ballena, Villa Leonor allows you to stroll down to the beach between courses or chill out with ice-cold beer while the kids play in the pool. Typical *casados* are a bargain, with fish or chicken and lots of sides. **Known for:** Sunday barbecue brunch; swim-up bar; fruit smoothies. $ *Average main: $13* ✉ *Between Km 170 and 171 on Costanera, Bahía Ballena* ✛ *1 km (½ mile) south of road to Hotel Cristal Ballena, turn right on road signed Villa Leonor* ☎ *2786–5380* ▭ *No credit cards* ⊗ *Closed mid-May–mid-June.*

Coffee and Quick Bites

Sibu Coffee & Chocolate

$ | **CAFÉ** | It's not always easy to find a great cup of coffee around Uvita, but the espresso here, brewed using organic coffee beans from the high-altitude Dota region, is excellent and ready by 7:15 am. Pair it with a homemade pastry for a heavenly morning. **Known for:** best macchiato in the area; chocolate-and-almond cake; freshly roasted coffee beans to buy. [$] *Average main: $9* ✉ *Across from BM supermercado in center of Uvita, Uvita* ☎ *2743–8674.*

Hotels

Cristal Ballena Boutique Hotel & Spa

$$$ | **B&B/INN** | **FAMILY** | High on a hillside with spectacular ocean views framed by giant traveler's palm trees, this Austrian-owned hotel is a luxurious base for exploring the area. **Pros:** wonderful swimming pool for serious swimmers and loungers; great ocean, mountain, and sky views; luxurious rooms. **Cons:** stairs to manage between rooms and restaurant; steep walk down to beach; a little away from the center of town. [$] *Rooms from: $225* ✉ *Costanera Hwy., 7 km (4 miles) south of Uvita, Uvita* ☎ *2786–5354* 🌐 *www.cristal-ballena.com* 🛏 *21 rooms* 🍴 *Free Breakfast.*

El Castillo

$$$$ | **B&B/INN** | With one of the most spectacular ocean views on the Costa Ballena, this modern "castle" is a luxury boutique hotel with seven ultrachic guest quarters with private terraces. **Pros:** million-dollar view; luxury accommodation; scenic pool with room to swim laps. **Cons:** some noise from trucks on nearby Costanera; stairs to ocean-view rooms and guest deck; overpriced restaurant. [$] *Rooms from: $289* ✉ *C. Perezoso, off Costanera Hwy., Ojochal* ✣ *500 m south of Ojochal* ☎ *2786–5543 hotel, 214/329–9866 in U.S.* 🌐 *www.elcastillocr.com* 🛏 *7 rooms* 🍴 *Free Breakfast.*

★ **Kurá**

$$$$ | **B&B/INN** | Stunning contemporary design, high-tech comforts, and a lofty location overlooking the Pacific combine to set a whole new standard of luxury at this adults-only property. **Pros:** the ultimate in contemporary design and comfort; excellent restaurant; no children under 16. **Cons:** the ultimate in price (but worth the splurge); a long, steep drive down to the beach; isolation, for good or bad. [$] *Rooms from: $850* ✉ *1 km (½ mile) above Uvita, to parking lot; hotel transport up to Kurá, Bahía Ballena* ☎ *8521–3407, 800/728–0466 toll-free U.S.* 🌐 *www.kuracostarica.com* ⏲ *Closed Oct.* 🛏 *8 rooms* 🍴 *Free Breakfast.*

La Cusinga Eco-Lodge

$$$ | **B&B/INN** | **FAMILY** | Along with one of the best sunset views along the coast, this comfortable eco-lodge on a high cliff bordering Ballena National Marine Park has spacious, airy cabins and a forest trail to a pristine beach. **Pros:** magnificent views; forest and beach access; pleasant restaurant. **Cons:** steep path between cabins and lodge; remote. [$] *Rooms from: $219* ✉ *Between Km 166 and 167 on Costanera Hwy., south of Dominical, Bahía Ballena* ☎ *2770–2549 reservation office, 8318–8598 lodge* 🌐 *www.lacusingalodge.com* 🛏 *9 rooms* 🍴 *Free Breakfast.*

Rancho Pacifico

$$$$ | **B&B/INN** | Nestled into the mountainside overlooking the Pacific, these private, spacious, one-, two-, and three-bedroom villas and suites are the ultimate getaway. **Pros:** private and romantic adults-only atmosphere; jungle setting and gorgeous views; great restaurant. **Cons:** steep roads require 4WD to get here; isolated; some rooms don't have a/c (but not really neccessary at these elevations). [$] *Rooms from: $495* ✉ *1 Rancho Pacifico Rd., Uvita* ☎ *8715–7397* 🌐 *ranchopacifico.com* 🛏 *7 units* 🍴 *Free Breakfast.*

Rio Tico Safari Lodge

$$ | **B&B/INN** | **FAMILY** | You may feel as though you're on a luxury safari when you step inside one of these spacious South African tents perched on sturdy wooden platforms cantilevered over a rushing mountain river. **Pros:** gorgeous natural setting; luxury tents; helpful hosts. **Cons:** steps to climb up and down from main lodge to tents; no a/c; no dinner restaurant. $ *Rooms from: $81* ⊠ *3 km (2 miles) south of Ojochal on Costanera, turn off just before bridge in Punta Mala near Km 179, 4 km (2½ miles) up winding dirt road to Vergel de Punta Mala, Punta Mala* ☎ *8996–7935, 4000–0680* ⊕ *www.riotico.com* ⇨ *12 rooms* ⦿ *Free Breakfast.*

★ Vista Celestial

$$$$ | **HOTEL** | These modern 1,000 square-foot villas, on the rain-forested peak overlooking Costa Ballena and the "whale tail," feel lavish and luxurious; each has indoor and outdoor showers and large soaking tub, private terraces with infinity plunge pool, posh beds, and heavenly views. **Pros:** stunning views in a wild setting; spacious cabinas with all the amenities; beautiful common area with lounge, pool, and jacuzzi. **Cons:** trekking up the mountain can be tough—you need 4WD; pricey; there are some steps from the restaurant to villas (but they will give you a ride). $ *Rooms from: $475* ⊠ *2 km northeast of the Catarata de Uvita, Uvita* ☎ *8523–0627* ⊕ *www.vistacelestial.com* ⇨ *5 villas* ⦿ *Free Breakfast.*

Yaba Chigui Lodge

$$ | **B&B/INN** | You'll be charmed by this boutique eco-lodge at jungle's edge, a modern representation of indigenous dwellings. **Pros:** Costa Rican hospitality; delicious breakfasts; eco-conscious. **Cons:** thin walls; not on beach; only four cabinas. $ *Rooms from: $140* ⊠ *1.6 km after C. Papagayo, Ojochal* ☎ *2786–5120* ⊕ *yabachigui.com* ⇨ *4 cabinas* ⦿ *Free Breakfast.*

Nightlife

The Bamboo Room

CABARET | Ojochal has a whole new lease on nightlife with live music at sunset, Wednesday through Saturday, at the Bamboo Room in the Alma Hotel. You could see owner/musician John on the piano, or Ken Nickell, a song writer, singer, and story teller. On Friday, catch Raphael Stey and Jeff Olson with their variety show. Local and visiting musicians including notable blues bands from the States fill in the rest of the week. ⊠ *Alma Hotel, C. Perezoso, Ojochal* ☎ *2786–5295* ⊕ *almacr.com/the-bamboo-room.*

Activities

DIVING AND SNORKELING

The best spot for snorkeling in the park is at the north end of Playa Ballena, near the whale's tail.

Bahía Aventuras

BOAT TOURS | Bilingual guides lead half-day tours in covered boats that combine whale- and dolphin-watching with snorkeling for $90. Whale season begins at the end of December and runs until March and July to October. A boat tour of the Terraba Sierpe Mangrove costs $85. If you want to try your luck, you can fish from a 23-foot boat designed and built locally; a half day for up to four people costs $570, and a full day for a group of up to eight people around Caño Island costs $995. There is a pleasant waiting room at the tour office, with clean, accessible bathrooms and parking. ⊠ *Bahía Ballena* ☎ *2743–8362, 8846–6576* ⊕ *www.bahiaaventuras.com.*

Dolphin Tours of Bahía Ballena

FISHING | This tried-and-true tour company takes a minimum of two people on four-hour boat tours that combine dolphin- and whale-watching with snorkeling, a visit to ocean caverns, and a rocky island bird sanctuary for $80 per person. All-day fishing trips for snook and red snapper cost $950 for up to four anglers. ☎ *2743–8013, 8825–4031* ⊕ *www.dolphintourcostarica.com.*

ZIPLINING
Osa Canopy Tour

ZIP LINING | Ziplines are a dime a dozen in Costa Rica, but this one gets rave reviews. With 11 platforms and more than 3 km (2 miles) of cable, you will certainly get your money's worth. For the really adventurous, there are also two rappelling stations (one 30 feet high, the other 90 feet) and a Tarzan swing. Count on flying through the forest, 100 feet high at times, for two to three hours, all for $75 per person; $50 for kids under 13. There is a discount if you pay cash. The maximum weight for a zipliner is 230 pounds. Call ahead to reserve three days in advance. ⊠ *Ticket office at Km 196, Costanera Hwy., south of Uvita, Bahía Ballena* ☎ *2788–7555, 8884–1237* ⊕ *www.osacanopytour.com.*

Golfito

130 km (81 miles) south of Uvita, 339 km (212 miles) southeast of San José.

Overlooking a small gulf (hence its name) and hemmed in by a steep bank of forest, Golfito has a scenic location. Lodges supply kayaks for paddling the gulf's warm, salty, and crystal-clear waters. When the sun sets behind the rolling silhouette of the Osa Peninsula, you can sometimes spot phosphorescent fish jumping. Fishing, both commercial and for sport, is the main activity here, with lively marinas providing slips to visiting yachts and charter fishing boats.

Golfito was once a thriving banana port—United Fruit arrived in 1938—with elegant housing and lush landscaping for its plantation managers. After United Fruit pulled out in 1985, Golfito slipped into a state of poverty and neglect. The town itself consists of a pleasant, lushly landscaped older residential section and a long strip of scruffy commercial buildings. Visiting U.S. Coast Guard ships dock here, and small cruise ships moor in the harbor. The Costa Rica Coast Guard Academy is also here.

GETTING HERE AND AROUND

From San José the trip used to take eight hours, along paved roads crossing over often-foggy mountains. But with the new toll road from San José, connecting to the paved Costanera Highway, travel time has been cut to five hours. Your best bet, especially if you are visiting a lodge on the gulf, is to fly to Golfito, which takes only about an hour. Direct buses from San José leave twice daily, at 7 am and 3:30 pm, following the longer mountain route; the 6:30 am bus from San José uses the faster Costanera route.

Taxis and boats take you wherever you need to go in and around Golfito. You can hire taxi boats at the city dock in Golfito (about $90 round-trip, often negotiable, to go to area lodges or across the Golfo Dulce to Puerto Jiménez). The only way to reach the remote Golfo Dulce lodges above Golfito is by boat. Early morning is the best time, when the water in the gulf is at its calmest. Most lodges include the boat transport in their rates.

A long-planned marina is now in place, with slips and a fuel dock, as well as a bait and tackle shop and upscale restaurant, with hopes for a hotel and more shops in the future.

For tour, lodging, and general tourist information, check out ⊕ *www.golfitocostarica.com*, a website managed by longtime Golfito residents.

TAXI Taxi service. ⊠ *Taxi stand beside gas station in center of town, near municipal dock* ☎ *2775–2020.*

ESSENTIALS

BANKS/ATMS ATH Coopealianza. ⊠ *North end of town, across from hospital* ☎ *2775–0025.* **Banco Nacional.** ⊠ *South of hospital on main road through Golfito* ☎ *2212–2000.*

The view of Golfo Dulce from the road to Puerto Jiménez

HOSPITAL Hospital de Golfito Manuel Mora Valverde. ✉ *400 meters north of the Catholic church, near Deposito* ☎ *2775–7800.*

PHARMACY Farmacia Golfito.
✉ *Main street, across from city park* ☎ *2775–2442.*

POST OFFICE Correo. ✉ *Off main road, south of central park* ☎ *2775–1911.*

VISITOR INFORMATION Land Sea Services. ✉ *Next to Banana Bay Marina* ☎ *8886–9360* ⊕ *www.golfitocostarica. com.*

 Sights

American Zone
NEIGHBORHOOD | The northwestern end of town is the so-called American Zone, full of handsome wooden houses where the expatriate managers of United Fruit lived amid flowering trees imported from all over the world. Many of these vintage houses, built of durable Honduran hardwoods, are now being spruced up. Eccentric garden features, such as a restored railway car, make the neighborhood worth a stroll. If you're on foot, there's also excellent birding in and around the gardens. ✉ *Golfito.*

Piedras Blancas National Park (*Parque Nacional Piedras Blancas*)
NATIONAL/STATE PARK | There is some good birding in the dense forest here, which is also an important wildlife corridor connecting to Corcovado National Park. Follow the main road northwest through the American Zone and past the airstrip and a housing project. The place where a dirt road heads into the rain forest is great for bird-watching. There are no marked trails actually in the park; the best birding is along the road. ✉ *Adjacent to Golfito National Wildlife Refuge.*

 Restaurants

Banana Bay
$$ | **AMERICAN** | For consistently good American-style food, you can't beat this marina restaurant with a view of

expensive yachts and sportfishing boats. Locals complain that the prices are high, but portions are hefty and include generous salads, sizzling hamburgers, excellent chicken fajitas, and a delicious grilled dorado sandwich with a mountain of fries. **Known for:** McBilge breakfast sandwich; grilled fish sandwich; free Wi-Fi. $ *Average main: $13* ⊠ *Main street, south of town dock* ☎ *2775–0383.*

Restaurante Mar y Luna

$$ | **SEAFOOD** | This pleasant terrace restaurant jutting out over the water has the best harbor view in Golfito, along with jaunty nautical decor and the coolest breezes in town. The seafood-heavy line-up includes grilled whole fish served in a variety of ways, including Caribbean style with coconut milk and a side of *patacones* (fried, mashed plantain). **Known for:** fish tacos; seafood soup with coconut milk; harbor view. $ *Average main: $15* ⊠ *South end of main street, north of Hotel Las Gaviotas* ☎ *2775–0192.*

 ## Hotels

The atmosphere of the in-town hotels differs dramatically from that of the lodges in the delightfully remote east coast of the Golfo Dulce. The latter is a world of jungle and blue water, birds and fish, and desert-island beaches, with lodges accessible only by boat from either Golfito or Puerto Jiménez.

Casa Roland Marina Resort

$$ | **HOTEL** | Everything at this luxury resort—designed like an art deco ocean liner incongruously dry-docked in Golfito's American Zone—is first-class, and guests stroll among gleaming hardwoods, polished brass, and stained glass. **Pros:** style and luxury; excellent service; resort facilities for bargain price. **Cons:** dark hallways and low ceilings on lower floor; often deserted and too quiet with few guests; a/c is sometimes too cold. $ *Rooms from: $120* ⊠ *American Zone* ☎ *2775–3405* ⊕ *www.casarolandgolfito. com* ➫ *57 rooms* ○⃝ *Free Breakfast.*

Esquinas Rainforest Lodge

$$$$ | **B&B/INN** | **FAMILY** | This well-managed eco-lodge in a 35-acre nature preserve bordering Piedras Blancas National Park is run by Austrians who have successfully instilled some sense of Teutonic order in the jungle (which might be why more than 80% of the guests are from Germany and Austria). **Pros:** top-notch trails and wildlife-viewing opportunities in unique natural setting; excellent meals; freshwater pool. **Cons:** no a/c and it can get hot here; some trails are challenging, and you need to be steady on your feet; lodge is geared to nature lovers who aren't looking for luxury. $ *Rooms from: $300* ⊠ *Near village of La Gamba, 5 km (3 miles) west of Villa Briceño turnoff* ☎ *2741–8001* ⊕ *www.esquinaslodge.com* ➫ *18 rooms* ○⃝ *All-inclusive.*

★ Playa Cativo Lodge

$$$$ | **B&B/INN** | Planted between the tranquil Golfo Dulce and tropical forest, this luxury eco-lodge brilliantly fuses high design, luxe comfort, and gastronomic flights of fancy in two restaurants with an eco-consciousness dictated by its castaway location accessible only by boat. **Pros:** castaway seclusion; high-style bathrooms with vintage tiles; two innovative restaurants. **Cons:** stairs to upper suites, but views are worth it; not as much privacy in main lodge; no a/c. $ *Rooms from: $570* ⊠ *Playa Cativo* ☎ *506/2775–6262* ⊕ *www.playacativo. com* ➫ *5 rooms* ○⃝ *All-inclusive.*

★ Playa Nicuesa Rainforest Lodge

$$$$ | **RESORT** | Hands down, this is the best eco-lodge on the gulf, combining comfortable, upscale accommodations and great food with an emphasis on adventure on both land and sea. **Pros:** everything you need to have an active vacation; excellent food and service; rate includes boat transport. **Cons:** no a/c; some insects outside the mosquito netting at night; pebbly beach. $ *Rooms*

from: $510 ⊠ Golfo Dulce, accessible only by boat from Golfito or Puerto Jiménez ☎ 2258–8250 in San José, 2222–0704 in San José, 866/504–8116 in U.S. toll-free ⊕ www.nicuesalodge. com ⊘ Closed Oct.–Nov. 15 ⇆ 10 rooms ⍟ All-inclusive.

Nightlife

Happy hour is popular in Golfito. The bar at Banana Bay Marina is hopping every day from 5 to 7, when drinks are half price. The lively bar at Samoa del Sur has a mix of Ticos and foreigners, mostly of the hard-drinking fishermen type. On Friday night there's karaoke and dance music at the huge, high-tech disco-bar by the pool at the Casa Roland Marine Resort.

Fish Hook Marina & Lodge

BARS/PUBS | The curved, polished-wood bar at this marina is cooled by breezes off Golfito Bay. It's a pleasant place to meet locals, tell fish tales, and sit and watch the sunset over the bay. Happy-hour drink specials on local beers and national-brand cocktails are offered from 4 to 8 pm. *⊠ Main street, south of Banana Bay ☎ 2775–1624 ⊕ www.fish-hook-marina. com.*

Activities

FISHING

The open ocean holds plenty of sailfish, marlin, and roosterfish during the dry months, as well as mahimahi, tuna, and wahoo during the rainy season; there's excellent bottom fishing any time of year. Captains are in constant radio contact with one another and tend to share fish finds.

Banana Bay Marina

FISHING | This marina houses a fleet of four charter fishing boats, fitted with tournament-quality tackle and skippered by English-speaking, world-record-holding captains. A day's fishing averages $660

for up to three people and $780 for up to four fishers. Food and beverage included. *⊠ Golfito ☎ 2775–0255, 2775–0003 ⊕ www.bananabaymarinagolfito.com.*

Playa Zancudo

51 km (32 miles) south of Golfito.

Life here is laid-back and casual, centering on walking the beach, fishing, kayaking, paddleboarding, swimming, and hanging out at the local bars and restaurants. Zancudo has a good surf break at the south end of the beach, but it pales in comparison with Playa Pavones a little to the south. Swimming is especially good two hours before or after high tide, especially at the calmer north end of the beach. The water is always warm.

If you get tired of playing in the surf and sand, you can arrange a boat trip to the nearby mangrove estuary to see birds and crocodiles. Zancudo is also home to one of the area's best sportfishing operations, headquartered at the Zancudo Lodge.

GETTING HERE AND AROUND

The road from Golfito is fully paved for the first 11 km (7 miles), but after the turnoff at El Rodeo, you'll encounter some rough patches. A bridge has finally replaced the ancient cable ferry, making the trip a little shorter, but count on 1½ hours to get here. Instead of driving, you can hire a boat at the municipal dock in Golfito for the 25-minute ride ($60 for two) or take a cheaper *collectivo* (communal) boat that leaves from Golfito's Samoa del Sur Hotel twice a week; check the schedule at the hotel because it varies throughout the year. A taxi ride from Golfito to Zancudo costs about $85, so the boat is a bargain.

Getting around Playa Zancudo doesn't take much, since there's really only one long, dusty road parallel to the beach. You can rent a bike at Cabinas Sol y Mar or Tres Amigos Supermercado, both on the main road in Zancudo, for about $10 per day.

There is water-taxi service to Golfito ($60 for up to three passengers; $20 each extra) and Puerto Jiménez ($80, up to three people) from Cabinas Los Cocos.

WATER TAXI Cabinas Los Cocos. ⊠ *Beach road, Zancudo* ☎ *2776–0012.*

Beaches

Playa Zancudo
BEACH—SIGHT | For laid-back beaching involving hammocks strung between palms and nothing more demanding than watching the sunset, you can't beat Playa Zancudo, with its miles of wide, flat beach and romantic views of the Osa Peninsula across the Golfo Dulce. The water is amazingly warm for swimming and except for local holiday times, this beach is pretty much deserted. It isn't picture-perfect: the 10 km (6 miles) of dark, volcanic sand is sometimes strewn with flotsam and jetsam. But there's a constant breeze and a thick cushion of palm and almond trees between the beach and the dirt road running parallel. Away from the beach breezes, be prepared for biting *zancudos* (no-see-ums). **Amenities:** food and drink. **Best for:** sunset; swimming; walking. ⊠ *Zancudo.*

Restaurants

Coloso del Mar Restaurant
$ | **SEAFOOD** | Fabulous fish cakes, tasty fish burritos, and a savory fillet of sea bass with a smoky jalapeño cream sauce are a few of the delights at this screened-in-porch restaurant in a bright-yellow clapboard cottage on the beach. Chicken or fish curry is popular with the locals. **Known for:** fish cakes and creamy mashed potatoes; banana pancakes; service with a smile. $ *Average main: $9* ⊠ *Main road, 200 m north of Soda Tranquilo,* *Zancudo* ☎ *2776–0050* ⊕ *www.colos-odelmar.com* ⊗ *No lunch.*

Restaurant Sol y Mar
$ | **ECLECTIC** | On a porch with a palm-fringed beach view, this thatch-roof restaurant is open year-round and has an eclectic menu ranging from spicy quesadillas and burritos to fresh fish. There's a touch of Thai here, too; one of the most popular dishes is mahimahi in a coconut-curry sauce. **Known for:** barbecue specials twice a week; homemade desserts; huge breakfasts. $ *Average main: $9* ⊠ *Cabinas Sol y Mar, Main road, south of Cabinas Los Cocos, Zancudo* ☎ *2776–0014.*

🛏 Hotels

Cabinas Los Cocos
$$ | **RENTAL** | This secluded cluster of self-catering cabins right on the beach, under palm trees swaying in the breeze, is designed for people who want to kick back and enjoy the beach. **Pros:** like having your own beach house on an idyllic beach; friendly host helps you get the most out of your stay; Wi-Fi in cabins. **Cons:** no a/c, but there are ceiling fans and ocean breezes; no phone in cabins; no TV. $ *Rooms from: $79* ⊠ *Beach road, north of Cabinas Sol y Mar, Zancudo* ☎ *2776–0012* ⊕ *www.loscocos.com* ⇨ *4 rooms* ⏁ *No meals.*

Cabinas Sol y Mar
$ | **B&B/INN** | Just as the name implies, Cabinas Sol y Mar have plenty of sun and sea, as well as a beach fringed by coconut palms and apricot-color wooden cabinas with porches where you can take in the spectacular views of the Osa Peninsula year-round. **Pros:** beach location; bargain price; lively restaurant and bar. **Cons:** no a/c; bare-bones furniture; no-frills bathrooms. $ *Rooms from: $56* ⊠ *Main road, south of Cabinas Los Cocos, Zancudo* ☎ *2776–0014* ⊕ *www. zancudo.com* ⇨ *6 rooms* ⏁ *No meals.*

★ The Zancudo Lodge

$$$$ | **ALL-INCLUSIVE** | The carefully groomed grounds of this top-notch, luxury beachfront resort are a riot of tropical foliage and flowers, shaded by massive mango trees. **Pros:** luxurious hotel; excellent fishing boats and captains; a/c, rare in these parts. **Cons:** pricey for the area; very quiet evenings because fishers go to bed early in order to rise at 5 am; boisterous groups. $ *Rooms from: $295* ⊠ *Main road, northern end of town, Zancudo* ☎ *2776–0008, 800/854–8791 in U.S. toll-free* ⊕ *www.zancudolodge.com* ⊘ *Closed July–Oct.* ⊅ *15 rooms* ⦿| *Free Breakfast.*

Activities

FISHING

If you've got your own gear, you can do some good shore fishing from the beach or the mouth of the mangrove estuary, or hire a local boat to take you out into the gulf. The main edible catches are yellowfin tuna, snapper, and snook; catch-and-release fish include marlin, roosterfish, and swordfish.

The Zancudo Lodge

FISHING | This luxury lodge runs the biggest charter operation in the area, with 16 boats ranging in length from 28 to 36 feet, including two TwinVee catamarans and two state-of-the-art Contender 32ST. During high season, fishing packages are $985 per day for up to four anglers. ⊠ *Main road, north end of town, Zancudo* ☎ *2776–0008* ⊕ *www.zancudolodge.com.*

KAYAKING

The kayaking is great at the beach and along the nearby Río Coto Colorado, lined with mangroves. You can also test your balance on a paddleboard over ocean waves or on the river.

Cabinas Los Cocos

KAYAKING | The popular tour ($60 per person, minimum three passengers) takes you for a 1½-hour motorboat ride up the Coto Colorado River, then a magical two-hour kayak tour along a jungly mangrove channel and a relaxing paddle, moving downstream with the current, back to the river mouth. Captain Susan can identify the birds you'll see along the way. The lodge also rents user-friendly sit-on-top kayaks with backrests for $5 per hour, and paddleboards (with instruction) at $20 for two hours. ⊠ *Beach road, north of Cabinas Sol y Mar, Zancudo* ☎ *2776–0012.*

Playa Pavones

53 km (33 miles) south of Golfito.

Surfing is the main draw here, especially from April to September when the waves are most reliable. But the dramatic scenery, looking across the Golfo Dulce to the Osa Peninsula, along with a very laid-back vibe, make it a popular destination year-round. The area is not heavily developed but there are some excellent restaurants in town, and nearby Tiskita Jungle Lodge is a birder's paradise.

GETTING HERE AND AROUND

There's no avoiding the bumpy road from Golfito to Conte, where the road forks north to Zancudo and south to Pavones. But the dirt road to Pavones is usually well graded. A public bus leaves from Golfito twice a day, and the trip takes about two hours. A taxi from the airstrip in Golfito costs upward of $80.

TAXIS 4X4 Taxi Service. ☎ *8874–9325.*

Beaches

Playa Pavones

BEACH—SIGHT | Driving along remote Playa Pavones, one of the most scenic beaches in Costa Rica, you catch glimpses through the palms of brilliant blue water, white surf crashing against black rocks, and the soft silhouette of the Osa Peninsula. This area at the southern edge of the mouth of Golfo Dulce attracts serious surfers, but also has pristine black-sand beaches and virgin rain forest. The coast is very rocky, so it's important to ask locals before surfing or swimming. One of the best places to swim is in the Río Claro, under the bridge or at the river mouth (dry season only). The town of Pavones itself is a helter-skelter collection of guesthouses and sodas a few blocks from the beach. **Amenities:** food and drink. **Best for:** surfing; swimming; walking. ✉ *Pavones.*

Restaurants

Café de la Suerte

$ | **VEGETARIAN** | Fortunately for food lovers, the "Good Luck Café" serves truly astonishing vegetarian food, along with intriguing exotic juices and thick fruit smoothies. The homemade yogurt is a revelation: light, almost fluffy, and full of flavor, served over a cornucopia of fruits, sprinkled with the café's own granola, and mixed into refreshing fruit-flavored lassis. **Known for:** creamy quiches; vegetarian lasagna; delectable brownies. [$] *Average main: $8* ✉ *Main street, next to soccer field, Pavones* ☎ *2776–2388* 💳 *No credit cards* 🕓 *Closed Oct., Nov., and Sun. Aug.–Mar. No dinner most nights.*

Ristorante Italiano La Bruschetta

$$ | **ITALIAN** | **FAMILY** | This kitschy Italian spot within earshot of the surf serves savory bruschetta and 16 varieties of the town's most authentic pizza: crispy, with a thin crust, Neapolitan-style. The four-seasons pizza is a triumph, with thin, spicy pepperoni, flavorful ham, olives, eggplant, peppers, onion, and zucchini. **Known for:** knockout gnocchi; tiramisu; funky, fun atmosphere. [$] *Average main: $15* ✉ *Main road between Pavones and Punto Banco, north of La Ponderosa Beach and Jungle Resort, Pavones* ☎ *2776–2174* 💳 *No credit cards.*

Hotels

★ La Ponderosa Beach and Jungle Resort

$$ | **B&B/INN** | The world-famous Playa Pavones surf break is a 10-minute walk from La Ponderosa, the area's only beach resort and several cuts above the usual surfer hangout, with accommodations verging on luxurious. **Pros:** great value; close to beach and town; magnificent garden and forest trails. **Cons:** tends to attract a younger crowd; mosquitoes love the garden when there's no breeze; dirt road access. [$] *Rooms from: $115* ✉ *Road between Pavones and Punta Banco, on beach, Pavones* ☎ *2776–2076, 954/771–9166 in U.S.* 🌐 *www.laponderosapavones.com* 🛏 *8 rooms* 🍴 *All-inclusive.*

★ Tiskita Jungle Lodge

$$$$ | **ALL-INCLUSIVE** | This last-outpost eco-lodge, near the border with Panama, is a draw for bird-watchers as well as nature lovers, yoga enthusiasts, and adventurers who want to really get away from it all in relative comfort and at an affordable, all-inclusive price. **Pros:** unrivaled wildlife viewing and birding; splendid natural isolation; friendly, knowledgeable owners. **Cons:** some steep walks to cabins in forest; no a/c; not a lot of privacy in joined double and triple cabins, which share verandas. [$] *Rooms from: $285* ✉ *On road between Pavones and Punta Banco, 6 km (4 miles) south of Playa Pavones, Pavones* ☎ *2296–8125* 🌐 *www.tiskita.com* 🕓 *Closed May–Nov. except to groups of 8 or more* 🛏 *17 rooms* 🍴 *All-inclusive* ☞ *All-inclusive package includes all meals, 2 guided tours.*

Activities

SURFING

Pavones is famous for one of the longest waves in the world, thanks to the mouth of the Río Claro. The most consistent waves are from April to September, and that's when the surfing crowd heads down here from the Central Pacific beaches. But even at the crest of its surfing season, Pavones is tranquility central compared with the surfing hot spots farther north.

Clear River Sports & Adventures

SURFING | Down by the beach, this outfit rents surfboards from $15 per day. Bicycles rent for $10 per day, with discounts for longer rentals. There's Wi-Fi access, a library, and rooms for surfers for $15 per person per night. This outfit also arranges local tours. ✉ *Main street, north of soccer field, Pavones* ☎ *8629–2508* ⊕ *www. pavonesclearriver.com.*

Sea Kings Surf Shop

SURFING | You can buy top-of-the-line surfboards and other gear here, along with heavy-duty sunscreen, board wax, and the latest in surfer wear. You can also rent surfboards for $15 per day and boogie boards for $10. ✉ *Main street, near Café de la Suerte, Pavones* ☎ *2776–2015* ⊕ *www.facebook.com/ SeaKingsSurfShop.*

Puerto Jiménez

130 km (86 miles) west of Golfito, 364 km (226 miles) from San José.

You might not guess it from the rickety bicycles and ancient pickup trucks parked on the main street, but Puerto Jiménez is the largest town on the Osa Peninsula and the main gateway to the rest of the peninsula and to Corcovado National Park. This one-iguana town has a certain frontier charm, with an interesting, funky edge provided by eco-lodge owners and backpacking nature lovers. A bayside promenade has added a touch of civility, with benches where you can sit and admire the gulf views. At night, elegant street lamps light your way to the restaurants along the waterfront.

This is the last civilized outpost on the peninsula. Heading south, you fall off the grid. Cell service is spotty, so make

your phone calls, send your email, get cash, and stock up on supplies here. Be prepared for the humidity and mosquitoes—Puerto Jiménez has plenty of both.

If you need a refreshing dip, head southeast of the airport to Playa Platanares, where there is a long stretch of beach with swimmable, warm water. At low tide, you can also walk out onto a narrow, pebbly beach beside the town dock.

The main reason to come to Puerto Jiménez is to spend a night before or after visiting Corcovado National Park, because the town has the best access to the park's two main trailheads and an airstrip with flights from San José. It's also the base for the *colectivo* to Carate.

GETTING HERE AND AROUND

Because the drive is long, most visitors fly to Puerto Jiménez from San José. Driving from Golfito is a little easier these days thanks to the paved road all the way from Rincón to Puerto Jiménez; even the formerly potholed road between Chacarita and Rincón has been paved. A faster option from Golfito is the motorboat launches, which make the trip in 45 minutes for only $6, leaving Golfito at 7:30, 10, 11:30, 1, and 3:15. Going in the opposite direction, the fast launches to Golfito leave Puerto Jiménez at 6, 8:45, 11:30, 2, and 4:15. The schedule changes frequently, so check before you head to the dock. Be sure to arrive 15 minutes early, because the boats often depart as soon as they are full. You can also hire a private taxi at the city dock in Golfito for about $100, which can drop you off in Puerto Jiménez or at your lodging.

A *colectivo* taxi—actually an open truck with bench seats—leaves Puerto Jiménez daily at 6 am and 1:30 pm for Cabo Matapalo and Carate. At $9 it's the cheapest way to travel, but the trip is along a bumpy road and is not recommended in rainy season (May through December). It leaves from a stop 656 feet west of the Super 96.

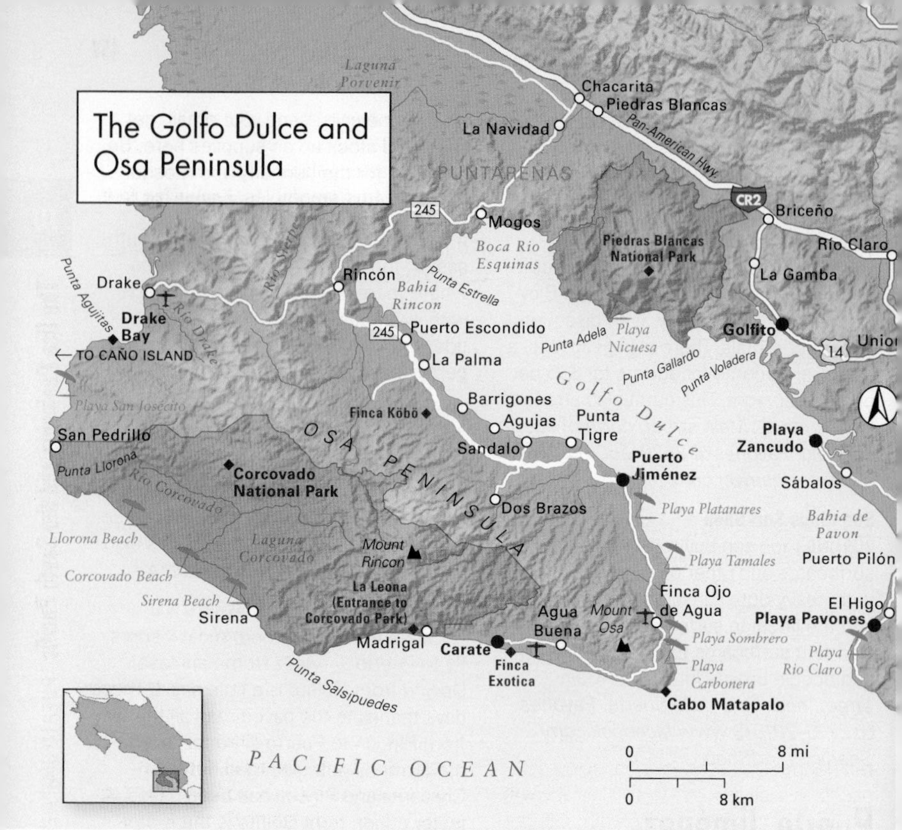
The Golfo Dulce and Osa Peninsula
Laguna Porvenir
Chacarita
Piedras Blancas
Pan-American Hwy.
La Navidad
PUNTARENAS
CR2
Briceño
Río Claro
245
Mogos
Boca Rio Esquinas
Piedras Blancas National Park
La Gamba
Rio Sierpe
Punta Agujitas
Drake
Rincón
Bahia Rincon
Punta Estrella
Golfito
Drake Bay
Río Drake
245
Puerto Escondido
Punta Adela
Playa Nicuesa
14
Union
← TO CAÑO ISLAND
La Palma
Punta Gallardo
Punta Voladera
Playa San Josecito
Golfo Dulce
Barrigones
Finca Köbö
Agujas
Punta Tigre
Playa Zancudo
San Pedrillo
OSA PENINSULA
Sandalo
Puerto Jiménez
Punta Llorona
Corcovado National Park
Río Corcovado
Sábalos
Dos Brazos
Playa Platanares
Bahia de Pavon
Llorona Beach
Laguna Corcovado
Mount Rincon
Playa Tamales
Puerto Pilón
Corcovado Beach
La Leona (Entrance to Corcovado Park)
Finca Ojo de Agua
El Higo
Sirena Beach
Agua Buena
Mount Osa
Playa Pavones
Sirena
Madrigal
Carate
Playa Sombrero
Playa Rio Claro
Finca Exotica
Playa Carbonera
Punta Salsipuedes
Cabo Matapalo
PACIFIC OCEAN
0
8 mi
0
8 km

Once you arrive in Puerto Jiménez, you can get around on foot or bicycle.

RENTAL CARS Alamo. ✉ *Airport St.* ☎ *2735–5175* 🌐 *alamocostarica.com.*

ESSENTIALS

The new, air-conditioned, modern Barrantes pharmacy also has doctors' offices and a dentist, by appointment.

BANK/ATM Banco Nacional. ✉ *Main street, 1 block north of Corcovado BM Supermarket* ☎ *2735–5020.*

PHARMACY Barrantes Farmacia. ✉ *Main street, next door to Banco de Costa Rica, diagonally across from Banco Nacional* ☎ *2735–5507.*

POST OFFICE Correo. ✉ *Main street, west side of soccer field* ☎ *2735–5045.*

URGENT CARE Centro Clínico Dras. Barrantes y Asociados. ✉ *One block east of Route 245* ☎ *2735–5507.*

VISITOR INFORMATION National Parks Service Headquarters. ✉ *Road running north, parallel to airstrip* ☎ *2735–5036.*

🍴 Restaurants

Corcovado Marisquería, Restaurante y Bar
$$ | **SEAFOOD** | If you want to enjoy a little local atmosphere, join the anglers, families, and backpackers at this tiny restaurant that has spilled over into a large waterfront garden. You can spend $9 for a plate of grilled fish or $36 on lobster. **Known for:** grilled fresh fish; lobsters when available; gulf view and breezes. [$] *Average main: $14* ✉ *On waterfront, east of city dock* ☎ *2735–5659, 8898–2656.*

Il Giardino

$$ | **ITALIAN** | Northern Italian–inspired cooking, in the form of tasty risotto, homemade pasta, and excellent salads is on offer at this popular garden spot. The best feature of this restaurant is its waterfront location, where you can sit on the terrace and take advantage of the views and fresh breezes off the gulf. **Known for:** barbecue; pastas and salads; breezy views. [$] *Average main: $15* ✉ *Waterfront promenade, near public dock* ☎ *2735–5129* 🌐 *www.ilgiardinoitalianrestaurant.com.*

★ **Pearl of the Osa**

$$ | **ECLECTIC** | Head to this casually chic, open-air beachfront restaurant for the most upscale and memorable dining, with a dazzling, postcard-perfect beach view and the most sophisticated menu in the Puerto Jiménez area. Standouts on the tantalizing menu include a four-soup sampler: black bean with egg, avocado, and cilantro; warm carrot ginger with red-pepper coulis; and a cold, spicy gazpacho as well as a green version. **Known for:** soup sampler; spicy grilled mahimahi; vegetarian choices. [$] *Average main: $15* ✉ *Iguana Lodge grounds, Playa Platanares, 5 km (3 miles) south of airstrip* ☎ *8848–0752* 🌐 *www.iguanalodge.com.*

PizzaMail.It

$ | **ITALIAN** | This cheerful, family-run café comes with an authentic pedigree: the Colovattis are from Trieste, and the pizza is simply the best in the area. The crust is toasty crisp on the outside and chewy inside, topped with high-quality fixings and sauce made fresh every day. **Known for:** fabulous pizza and calzones; authentic Italian pastas; cheerful atmosphere. [$] *Average main: $9* ✉ *Main street, across from soccer field* ☎ *2735–5483* ⏲ *Closed Tues. and Sept.–Nov. No lunch.*

Restaurante Carolina

$ | **COSTA RICAN** | This simple alfresco restaurant in the heart of Puerto Jiménez is the most likely spot to meet locals and run into just about every visitor in town, making it a good place to pick up information. It serves decent comida típica, salads, pasta, reliably fresh seafood, and excellent fruit smoothies. **Known for:** fruit shakes; good meeting place; comida típica. [$] *Average main: $8* ✉ *Main street* ☎ *2735–5185.*

Hotels

Playa Platanares is only about 6 km (4 miles) outside Puerto Jiménez, but lodgings there have a different feeling from those in town because they are on a lovely and quiet beach. Bosque del Río Tigre is also outside town, but inland, in a forested area beside a river, on the northeastern edge of Corcovado Park.

★ **Bosque del Río Tigre Lodge**

$$$$ | **B&B/INN** | You can't get any closer to nature than this off-the-grid lodge, famous for its excellent birding and hiking trails, wedged between forest and the banks of the Río Tigre. **Pros:** a birder's paradise; great hiking trails; fabulous food. **Cons:** shared bathroom and outdoor showers; limited electricity; must love living very close to nature. [$] *Rooms from: $344* ✉ *Riverside, in Dos Brazos de Río Tigre, 12 km (7½ miles) northwest of Puerto Jiménez, Dos Brazos del Tigre* ✣ *Turn off main hwy. at sign for Dos Brazos and follow dirt road to village and beyond, to river* ☎ *8705–3729 text messages only* 🌐 *www.bosquedelriotigre.com* ⏲ *Closed May, Sept., and Oct.* 🛏 *5 rooms* 🍴 *All-inclusive.*

★ **Danta Corcovado Lodge**

$$ | **B&B/INN** | **FAMILY** | Follow the giant tapir-footprint signs to this extraordinary, rustic lodge, reminiscent of an Adirondacks camp but with oversize, whimsical wood furniture, all within hiking distance of the western edge of Corcovado National Park. **Pros:** proximity to Corcovado National Park; comfortable rusticity; unique design. **Cons:** no a/c; close encounters of the insect kind in cabins; restaurant a little pricey. [$] *Rooms from:*

Did You Know?

There are more than 80 species of reef fish in Costa Rica.

$110 ✉ *Road from La Palma to Guadalupe, 3 km (2 miles) northwest of La Palma, La Palma* ☎ *2735–1111* 🌐 *www.dantalodge.com* 🛏 *9 rooms* 🍴 *Free Breakfast.*

★ **Iguana Lodge**

$$$ | **B&B/INN** | If a long stretch of deserted beach is your idea of heaven, check out this idyllic lodge with two-story cabins set in an exquisite botanical garden. **Pros:** tranquil tropical setting; complimentary kayaks; breakfast and dinner included in casita rooms. **Cons:** no a/c; club rooms are small and can be noisy; be prepared to get friendly with an insect or two. [$] *Rooms from: $214* ✉ *Playa Platanares, 5 km (3 miles) south of airport* ☎ *8848–0752* 🌐 *www.iguanalodge.com* 🛏 *13 rooms* 🍴 *Free Breakfast.*

Nightlife

Pearl of the Osa

MUSIC CLUBS | With pulsing salsa music pumped out by a DJ, this beachfront bar is a lively place to go on Friday night, starting at 7. There's a mix of ages, and the music is loud and a lot of fun. Tuesday night there's a barbecue with tiki torches, a bonfire, and tables right on the beach. Come at 5:30 to watch the sunset; it's a good idea to reserve ahead. ✉ *Playa Platanares, next to Iguana Lodge* ☎ *8848–0752.*

Activities

TOUR OPERATOR

Osa Tropical

TOUR—SPORTS | Isabel Esquivel runs the best general tour operation on the peninsula. Whatever travel question you ask the locals, they will usually reply "Ask Isabel," whether it's help with arranging flights, ground transportation, hotel rooms, rental houses, guided tours, or car rentals. ✉ *Main street, across from Banco Nacional* ☎ *2735–5722, 2735–5062* 🌐 *www.osa-tropical.com.*

BIRD-WATCHING

The birding around the Osa Peninsula is world renowned, with more than 400 species. Regional species include Baird's trogon, yellow-billed cotinga, whistling wren, black-cheeked ant-tanager, the glorious turquoise cotinga, and, of course, the brilliant, impossible-to-miss scarlet macaws, which make frequent visits to the almond trees around town and all along the coast.

★ **Bosque del Río Tigre Lodge**

BIRD WATCHING | The area's best English-speaking birding guides are at Bosque del Río Tigre Lodge, just west of Puerto Jiménez, in prime birding habitat, with river, forest, and open areas. A three-hour morning bird walk starts at 5:30 am; it does not include transportation to lodge, but it does include coffee and banana bread beforehand and a hearty breakfast afterward. ✉ *12 km (7½ miles) northwest of Puerto Jiménez, at end of dirt road and across shallow river, Dos Brazos del Tigre* 🌐 *www.bosquedelriotigre.com* 🎟 *$63 per person for three-hour bird walk.*

Rincón

BIRD WATCHING | One of the best spots on the peninsula to spot a rare and highly endangered yellow-billed cotinga is along the north side of the bridge over the river at Rincón. Scan the forested hills above the road. Turquoise cotingas are also spotted here. Make sure to get there before 7 am for the best birding. ✉ *Main road, 40 km (25 miles) north of Puerto Jiménez, Rincón.*

BOATING

Cabinas Jiménez Adventure Boat Tour

SNORKELING | If you just want to get out onto the water, Captain John offers five-hour tours on a covered boat. You can explore the gulf, look for dolphins, do some snorkeling, or try plane boarding. Snacks, fruit, and soft drinks are included ($65 per person, minimum six people). The boat sails at 7:30 am. ✉ *Cabinas*

Jiménez, On waterfront ☎ *2735–5090* ⊕ *www.cabinasjimenez.com.*

FISHING

Puerto Jiménez is a major fishing destination, with plenty of billfish, tuna, snapper, and snook, almost all year, with the exception of June and July, when things slow down. The best offshore fishing is between December and April. Charter captains follow the fish up and down the Pacific coast, so ask at your hotel for their recommendation of the best fishing boats currently in town.

Tropic Fins Adventures

FISHING | Head out onto the Golfo Dulce or the open ocean on a sportfishing adventure aboard a custom-built 28-foot Ocean Runner, equipped with all the latest fishing equipment, a full cooler, plenty of snacks, and a healthy lunch. Captain Cory Craig, a transplanted Canadian, has been fishing these waters for more than a decade. The boat comfortably accommodates four anglers. Half-day excursions are $650; full-day trips, which can last up to nine hours, depending on how the fish are biting, are $950. Or, if you only have two people in your party, try your luck on the smaller SeaPro 21-foot bay boat for inshore fishing only for $550 half day and $750 full day. Package tours include flight from San José, plus lodging, meals, and fishing. ⊠ *Playa Platanares* ☎ *8834–6079* ⊕ *www.tropic-fins.com.*

HIKING

★ Osa Aventura

HIKING/WALKING | Many hiking guides have come on the scene since Corcovado made guides compulsory. But this long-standing company has been specializing in multiday hiking adventures into the park for more than 20 years. Mike Boston, an ebullient tropical biologist, is the most experienced and most knowledgeable guide in the area. Hikers stay in way-off-the-beaten-track rustic lodges en route to Corcovado National Park. Boston also employs bilingual biologists

to lead hikes and conduct scientific research projects in which visitors can sometimes participate. ⊠ *Puerto Jiménez* ☎ *2735–5670, 8372–6135* ⊕ *www.osaaventura.com* ✉ *$552 for guided hike with two nights in the park, all meals and equipment, for two hikers.*

Osa Wild

HIKING/WALKING | The focus here is on sustainable tourism, including horseback-riding treks, nighttime insect tours, kayak tours, visits to local farms, and low-impact, low-cost biologist-guided tours into Corcovado National Park. A three-day, two-night hike into the park for two averages $389 per person and includes transportation, guide, entrance fees, accommodation in tents, and all the necessary camping gear. Reserve at least a month ahead. You can rent bikes here for $10 per day. ⊠ *Main street, north of Banco Nacional, across from gas station* ☎ *2735–5848* ⊕ *www.osawildtravel.com.*

Tigre Sector

HIKING/WALKING | If you have a sturdy vehicle, it's just a 30-minute drive west to the village of Dos Brazos and the Tigre Sector of Corcovado Park. This is the newest official park entrance, with a brand-new ranger station and a community tourist center offering guided day hikes, horseback rides, and bird-watching. Few hikers come to this pristine part of the park because it's more difficult to access, which means you'll likely have it to yourself. But you must be accompanied by a certified guide, available in Dos Brazos. ⊠ *Dos Brazos de Río Tigre, Off main hwy. between Rincón and Puerto Jiménez* ☎ *8691–4545* ⊕ *www.dosbrazosderiotigre.com.*

KAYAKING

Puerto Jiménez is a good base for sea-kayaking trips on the calm Golfo Dulce and for exploring the nearby mangrove rivers and estuaries.

Beach views at Drake Bay on the Osa Peninsula

Aventuras Tropicales Golfo Dulce

KAYAKING | Alberto Robleto has amassed an impressive fleet of kayaks with excellent safety equipment for snorkeling, dolphin-watching, and bird-watching tours. The most popular tours are the three-hour mangrove tour and the sunset kayaking tour on the gulf, when dolphins are often jumping (each tour $50). There's also an evening kayaking tour, from 4:30 to 7:30, to watch the sunset and witness the bioluminescence phenomenon, offered eight days before and after a new moon. ⊠ *Road to Playa Platanares, southeast of airport* ☎ *2735–5195* ⊕ *www.aventurastropicales.com.*

Corcovado National Park

The crown jewel of the country's national park system, Corcovado is the ultimate in off-the-grid adventure. The only way to see it is on foot, with a certified naturalist guide to interpret the incredible biodiversity that has made this park the most rewarding and challenging natural experience in the country.

GETTING HERE AND AROUND

The easiest way to visit remote Corcovado National Park is by boat from Drake Bay or on foot from Carate. A 20-minute boat trip from Drake Bay gets you to the San Pedrillo entrance. The boat trip from Drake Bay to Sirena takes 45 minutes to one hour. From Carate airfield, where the road and therefore taxis from Puerto Jiménez stop, it's about a 45-minute walk along the beach to La Leona park entrance. You also can access the park for guided day tours from Corcovado el Tigre (⊕ *www.corcovadoeltigre.com*) or from the Los Patos entrance near La Palma.

You can hire a private taxi in Puerto Jiménez ($90) to take you to Carate, pay $15 per person for a shared taxi or, the cheapest option, hop on the colectivo pickup truck for $9. Since all visitors must be accompanied by a guide, transportation to the park is usually included in the cost of an overnight package tour.

Sights

Corcovado National Park (*Parque Nacional Corcovado*)

NATIONAL/STATE PARK | This is the last and largest outpost of virgin lowland rain forest in Central America, and it's teeming with wildlife. Visitors who tread softly along the park's trails may glimpse howler, spider, and squirrel monkeys, coatimundis, peccaries (wild pigs), poison dart frogs, scarlet macaws, and, very rarely, jaguars and tapirs.

Most first-time visitors to Corcovado come on a daylong boat tour from Drake Bay or hike in from Carate, Los Patos, or Dos Brazos del Río Tigre. But to get to the most pristine, wildlife-rich areas, you need to walk, and that means a minimum of three days: one day to walk in, one day to walk out, and at least one day inside the park. Park policy requires every visitor to be accompanied by a certified naturalist guide. Whichever guide or tour company you hire can make the park reservation and pay the park entrance fees for you in Puerto Jiménez. All accommodation and food within the park are now provided by a local community consortium called **ADI Corcovado** (*reservaciones@adicorcovado.org*).

The daily limit on the number of overnight visitors at the Sirena station is 70, bunking down in platform tents with all meals and bedding provided. No outside food is allowed. There's also camping ($4) at the San Pedrillo sector, but without meals or bedding. Ranger stations are officially open from 7 am to 4 pm daily, but you can walk in almost any time with a certified guide, as long as you have reserved and paid in advance. For safety reasons, there is no longer any night walking permitted into or out of the park. ⇨ *For more information, see the highlighted listing in this chapter.* ✉ *Corcovado National Park, Carate* ⊕ *www.sinac.go.cr* ✆ *$15 per day.*

Hotels

Meals and lodging at Sirena station are now organized by ADI Corcovado, a community organization that has greatly improved everything from platform tents to meals to bathrooms. All reservations have to be arranged and paid for in advance by emailing *reservaciones@adicorcovado.org*.

Camping is your only option inside the national park. You must reserve camping and prepared meals well in advance since there's room for only 70 campers at La Sirena. Excellent meals served in the Sirena station cost $20 for breakfast, $25 for lunch or dinner (children half price). Meal times are 6–8 am for breakfast, noon–1 for lunch, and 6–7 for dinner. Accommodation is in bunkbeds on a covered platform, with bedding included, $30 per night. You cannot prepare any food in the park, but you can bring in trail mix and snacks. There's a shop at Sirena where you can buy snacks and bottled water. Camping at San Pedrillo, with your own gear and no meals, is $4 per night. The maximum stay in the park is four nights and five days. Guides are mandatory; therefore, the guide making all the arrangements is usually included in a guided package tour.

Activities

If your reason for coming to the Osa Peninsula is Corcovado National Park, choose a lodge that has resident naturalist guides. On the Drake Bay and gulf sides of the park, all the lodges arrange guided trips into Corcovado, most with their own guides. Tour operators in Puerto Jiménez and Drake Bay also run guided trips in the park.

HIKING

Corcovado has 13 ecosystems within its boundaries, ranging from mangroves and swamps to lowland rain forest. The park also has more forest giants (trees that stand 165 to 264 feet high) than anywhere in Central America.

There are two main hiking routes to Corcovado. One begins near La Palma, at Los Patos entrance. The other is a beach trail—an easy, if hot, 3½-km (2¼-mile), 45-minute shore walk from Carate to La Leona entrance, followed by a 16-km (10-mile) walk to La Sirena. You can hike from Drake Bay to San Pedrillo; it's 14 km (8½ miles) and you need to pay attention to tides and some rocky sections. You can also take a boat to the San Pedrillo station and hike the trails there, as well as camp. There are two other, less-traveled official entrances to the park with ranger stations: Los Planes, inland from Drake Bay, and a new entrance at El Tigre, west of Puerto Jiménez.

Hiking is always tough in the tropical heat, but the forest route from Los Patos is cooler than the beach hike to La Leona. Although it is possible to hike La Leona at high tide, it's more difficult because you have to walk on a slope rather than the flat part of the beach. The hike between any two stations takes all day.

The hike from La Leona to Sirena requires crossing one big river mouth and a stretch of beach that can be crossed only at low tide. Some guides do it very early in the morning, just before sunrise, to avoid the blistering heat along the beach.

The hike from Los Patos to Sirena is shady all the way; it's 25 km (about 14 miles) and takes about eight hours. Bring plenty of water along. The Sirena ranger station and El Tigre sector have great trails that can easily fill a couple of days.

Swimming on the beach near Sirena is not advised because of rip currents and bull sharks. Also steer clear of the brackish Río Sirena, home to crocs, bull sharks, and snakes. The only advisable swimming area is the Río Claro.

Cabo Matapalo

21 km (14 miles) south of Puerto Jiménez.

The southern tip of the Osa Peninsula, where virgin rain forest meets the sea at a rocky point, retains the kind of natural beauty that people travel halfway across the world to experience. From its ridges you can look out on the blue Golfo Dulce and the Pacific Ocean, sometimes spotting whales in the distance. The forest is tall and dense, with the highest and most diverse tree species in the country, usually draped with thick lianas.

The name Matapalo refers to the strangler fig, which germinates in the branches of other trees and extends its roots downward, eventually smothering the supporting tree by blocking the sunlight. Flocks of brilliant scarlet macaws and troops of monkeys are the other draws here.

GETTING HERE AND AROUND

If you drive one hour south from Puerto Jiménez, be prepared for a bumpy ride and a couple of river crossings. During the height of rainy season, in October and November, cars are sometimes washed out along rivers to the ocean. Most hotels arrange transportation in 4WD taxis or their own trucks. The cheapest—and the roughest—way to travel is by colectivo ($10), which leaves Puerto Jiménez at 6 am and 1 pm. Buses do not serve Cabo Matapalo.

🍴 Restaurants

Martina's Bar & Restaurant

$$ | CONTEMPORARY | Formerly known as Bar Buena Esperanza, as the road sign still says, this is the coolest, liveliest—and only!—upscale bar-restaurant on the road from Puerto Jiménez to Carate. It would still be the best even if there were others, thanks to a short but scrumptious menu featuring contemporary versions

The view from the deck of the Toucan cabina at Bosque del Cabo

of local fish, pork, chicken, and salads. **Known for:** grilled sesame tuna with Thai coleslaw; panko-encrusted mahimahi with tropical fruit salsa; gnocchi with fresh vegetable sauce, Parmesan, and arugula salad. $ *Average main: $15* ⊠ *On road to Carate, just before Río Carbonera crossing, in Matapalo* ☉ *Closed wk before Easter.*

🛏 Hotels

Blue Osa Yoga Retreat & Spa
$$$$ | B&B/INN | Brilliant blue sky, sparkling blue sea, and bright blue decor make this upscale, beachfront eco-resort and yoga center a true blue heaven, for a rather rarefied price. **Pros:** yoga classes and private instruction; gorgeous beach setting; comfortable rooms. **Cons:** check when group yoga retreats are scheduled if yoga isn't your thing; remote location; no a/c. $ *Rooms from: $398* ⊠ *Playa Tamales, 11 km (7 miles) south of Puerto Jiménez* ☎ *No phone* ⊕ *www.blueosa.com* ⤵ *15 rooms* ❄ *All-inclusive.*

⭐ Bosque del Cabo
$$$$ | RESORT | Atop a cliff at the tip of Cabo Matapalo, this lodge has unparalleled views of the Golfo Dulce merging with the endless blue of the Pacific, as well as hundreds of acres of primary forest, home to plenty of monkeys and peccaries, as well as the occasional puma and ocelot. **Pros:** luxurious bungalows; fabulous trails and guides; congenial atmosphere among guests at cocktail hour and dinner. **Cons:** steep trail to beach and back; limited electricity supply; rates do not include $30 round-trip transfer fee per person. $ *Rooms from: $580* ⊠ *Road to Carate, 22 km (14 miles) south of Puerto Jiménez* ☎ *2735–5206, 8389–2846 at lodge* ⊕ *www.bosquedelcabo. com* ⤵ *18 units* ❄ *All-inclusive.*

⭐ El Remanso Rainforest Wildlife Lodge
$$$$ | B&B/INN | This tranquil, sophisticated retreat in a forest brimming with birds and wildlife, 400 feet above a mostly deserted beach studded with tide pools, has luxurious two-person cabinas with screened windows, king-size beds,

contemporary bathrooms with spacious showers behind curving walls, and private decks with forest and ocean views. **Pros:** gorgeous natural setting; jungle views; easy access to beach. **Cons:** no a/c; no hair dryers; steep drive down to lodge. ⓢ *Rooms from: $550* ✉ *Main road to Carate, 22 km (14 miles) south of Puerto Jiménez* ☎ *2735–5569 office, 8814–5775* ⊕ *www.elremanso.com* ⤵ *12 rooms* ⓞ *All-inclusive.*

★ Lapa Ríos

$$$$ | **ALL-INCLUSIVE** | Set in a vast, private nature reserve, with a breathtaking view from the lodge's high jungle ridge, this is the first and most spectacular eco-lodge in Costa Rica, garlanded with numerous awards for its mix of sustainability, conservation, service, and comfort. **Pros:** excellent, professional service; price includes tours and transportation and all à la carte meals; retains local flavor with friendly, well-trained staff. **Cons:** many steps to climb to most cabins; steep trail to get to beach (unless you take the shuttle service); most cabins are duplex style. ⓢ *Rooms from: $1,148* ✉ *Road to Carate, 20 km (12 miles) south of Puerto Jiménez* ☎ *2735–5130* ⊕ *www.laparios.com* ⤵ *17 rooms* ⓞ *All-inclusive.*

Activities

TOUR OPERATOR
★ Everyday Adventures

TOUR—SPORTS | Andy Pruter, an engaging, experienced outfitter, might call his company Everyday Adventures, but his trips are anything but. He will take you on guided adrenaline-pumping activities: rappelling down waterfalls ($95), climbing up a 70-foot strangler fig vine ($65), and hiking the rain forest ($50). Or you can go all out with a combination rappelling-and-climbing tour for $130. ✉ *Cabo Matapalo* ☎ *8353–8619* ⊕ *www.psychotours.com.*

SURFING

On the eastern side of Cabo Matapalo, on Pan Dulce beach, waves break over a platform that creates a perfect, very forgiving right, drawing surfers from far and wide, especially beginners.

Pollo Surf School

SURFING | Local surf expert Oldemar (aka Pollo) Fernandez offers daily lessons at Pan Dulce Beach at his Pollo Surf School. Soft-top boards and rash guards make learning a little less painful. Expect to pay $60 per person for a two-hour group lesson, or $120 for a private lesson. Pollo also offers 1½-hour stand-up paddleboard tours, starting at the beach ($55, minimum age 14). ✉ *Cabo Matapalo* ☎ *8366–6559, 8363–1481* ⊕ *www.pollo-surfschool.com.*

Carate

60 km (37 miles) west of Puerto Jiménez.

Carate is literally the end of the road. The volcanic black-sand beach stretches for more than 3 km (2 miles), with dramatically high surf that's perfect for boogie boarding and body surfing. Swimming is best and safest around low tides. The main entertainment at the beach is watching the noisy but magnificent scarlet macaws feasting on nuts in the beach almond trees that edge the shore. Though remote, lodges now have Wi-Fi and some mobile phone coverage.

GETTING HERE AND AROUND

The road from Matapalo to Carate covers 40 suspension-testing km (25 miles); there is a bridge over the Agua Buena River and the road is periodically graded and relatively smooth—but that can all change to a sea of mud with one drenching wet season. You're better off taking the colectivo from Puerto Jiménez *(see Getting Here and Around in Puerto Jiménez, above).* Or give yourself a break and fly via charter plane to Carate's small airport, which has been upgraded recently; arrange flights through your lodge. From here it's 3 km (2 miles), roughly a 40-minute walk along the beach to La Leona ranger station entrance to Corcovado National Park. In rainy season (May to December) it is sometimes impossible to cross the raging Río Carate that separates the landing strip from the beach path to the park, and you may end up stranded on either side. Parking at the store in Carate is $5 per day.

Hotels

★ Finca Exotica

$$$ | **ALL-INCLUSIVE** | A garden paradise that lives up to its name, this combination organic farm, botanical garden, and sophisticated eco-lodge is an otherworldly experience, meant to be slowly and thoughtfully absorbed over a three-night minimum stay. **Pros:** gorgeous gardens; exotically delicious food; charming hosts. **Cons:** no a/c; must enjoy being in a totally natural setting; communal dining. $ *Rooms from: $220* ✉ *Main road, east of Carate airstrip* ☎ *4070–0054, 8359–8408 WhatsApp* ⊕ *www.fincaexotica.com* ⊘ *Closed Oct.* ➩ *14 rooms* ⦿❘ *Free Breakfast.*

Lookout Inn

$$$ | **B&B/INN** | **FAMILY** | This lively barefoot inn—shoes come off at the bottom step, and steps here are plentiful—is set on a precipitous hillside with a spectacular panorama that includes a colorful garden and scarlet macaws foraging in the almond trees that line the beach. **Pros:** proximity to beach and access on foot to Corcovado Park; excellent food; party atmosphere. **Cons:** very steep climb to lodge and down to beach; cabins are quieter than lodge rooms; stairs to dining room. $ *Rooms from: $200* ✉ *Main road to Carate, east of Carate landing strip* ☎ *2735–5431* ⊕ *www.lookout-inn.com* ➩ *11 rooms* ⦿❘ *Free Breakfast.*

★ Luna Lodge

$$$$ | **B&B/INN** | Perched on a sublime mountaintop overlooking rain forest and ocean, this is the quintessential yoga retreat, though it's universally enjoyed for its remoteness and proximity to wildlife. **Pros:** scenic setting for peace, yoga, and therapeutic massages; comfortable lodging and healthful food; excellent birding. **Cons:** extremely steep road up to lodge; beach is quite a hike; large yoga groups come for retreats. $ *Rooms from: $450* ✉ *2 km (1 mile) up a steep, partially paved road from Carate* ☎ *4070–0010, 888/760–0760 in U.S. and Canada* ⊕ *www.lunalodge.com* ➩ *16 rooms* ⦿❘ *All-inclusive.*

Activities

Activities here revolve around Corcovado National Park and its environs. Hiking, horseback riding, canopy tours, and other adventures must be organized through your hotel.

Drake Bay

18 km (11 miles) north of Corcovado, 40 km (25 miles) southwest of Palmar Sur, 310 km (193 miles) south of San José.

This is castaway country, a real tropical adventure, with plenty of hiking and some rough but thrilling boat rides to get here. The rugged coast that stretches south from the mouth of the Río Sierpe to Corcovado probably doesn't look much different from what it did in Sir Francis Drake's day (1540–96), when, as legend has it, the British explorer anchored here. Small, picture-perfect beaches with surf crashing against dark volcanic rocks are backed by steaming, thick jungle. Nature lodges scattered along the coast are hemmed in by the rain forest, which is home to troops of monkeys, sloths, scarlet macaws, and hundreds of other bird species.

Boat trips are a must to explore the wild Osa Peninsula.

The cheapest accommodations in the area can be found in the town of Drake, which is spread out around the bay. A trio of upscale nature lodges—Drake Bay Wilderness Resort, Aguila de Osa Inn, and La Paloma Lodge—are clumped near the Río Agujitas on the bay's southern end. They all offer comprehensive packages, including trips to Corcovado and Caño Island. Lodges farther south, such as Copa del Arbol, Punta Marenco Lodge, and Casa Corcovado, run excursions from even wilder settings.

GETTING HERE AND AROUND

The fastest way to get to Drake Bay is to fly directly to the airstrip. You can also fly to Palmar Sur and take a taxi to Sierpe and then go on a thrilling, if bumpy, boat ride to Drake Bay. From the airport, it's a 25-minute taxi ride to Sierpe. You can pay $15–$20 per person for a seat in a communal boat. These small, open boats leave at low tide, usually 11 to 11:30 am for the one-hour trip to Drake. You need to be at the dock at least an hour early to ensure a seat. There is also boat service from Drake Bay to Sierpe, from the beach, between 7 and 7:30 am, and around 2:30 in the afternoon. Many lodges arrange boat transportation from Drake Bay or Sierpe, and captains will often stop along the way to view wildlife in the river mangroves. From Rincón you can drive to Drake on a 30-km (19-mile) sometimes-graded dirt road, but only in dry season when the rivers are low enough to cross. Getting here by bus is not easy. Buses leave Puerto Jiménez for La Palma about every two hours from 6 am to 8 pm, connecting in La Palma with buses to Drake Bay at 11:30 am and 4 pm daily, except Sunday. Buses leave Drake at 4:30 am and 1 pm heading for La Palma, to connect with buses in Rincón de Osa to either Puerto Jiménez or San José. These bus schedules often change, so be sure to check with a local source. The drive from San José to Drake is a scenic but exhausting seven hours long.

Snorkelers' Paradise

Most of uninhabited 2½-square-km (1-square-mile) **Caño Island Biological Reserve** is covered in evergreen forest that includes fig, locust, and rubber trees. The indigenous Diquis tribe used the island as a ceremonial and burial site until the Spanish arrived, and the numerous bits and pieces unearthed here have prompted archaeologists to speculate about pre-Columbian long-distance maritime trade. But virtually none of these indigenous artifacts remain. The main attraction is the ocean around the island, offering advanced scuba diving and snorkeling. The snorkeling is best around the rocky points flanking the island's main beach; if you're a certified diver, you'll want to explore Bajo del Diablo and Paraíso, where you're guaranteed to encounter thousands of good-size fish, and if you're lucky, white-tip, nurse, and trigger sharks. As of this writing, visitors are once again allowed to land on the island, to hike a trail that climbs to the island's summit. But no picnicking is allowed on the beach, and there are no toilet facilities, owing to runoff that was damaging the surrounding coral.

The only way to get to the island, 19 km (12 miles) due west of the Osa Peninsula, is by boat, arranged by your lodge or a tour company. Reserve well ahead, since tour operators have to keep to specific time limits and visitor quotas of 200 visitors per day, split between morning and afternoon. Drake Bay hotels run trips here, as do tour companies in Dominical, Uvita, and Sierpe.

Hotels

★ **Casa Corcovado Jungle Lodge**
$$$$ | **B&B/INN** | **FAMILY** | This hilltop jungle lodge has it all: exquisite bungalows in the closest location to Corcovado National Park, extensive gardens, two swimming pools, a beach, excellent tours, naturalist guides, and first-class service. **Pros:** unrivaled location adjoining national park; excellent tours, service, and facilities; reasonably priced. **Cons:** an adventure to get here: be prepared for a thrilling, wet landing; no a/c; steep road to beach. [$] *Rooms from: $915* ✉ *Northern border of Corcovado, Drake* ☎ *2256–3181, 888/896–6097 in U.S. toll-free, 2206–4611 lodge* 🌐 *www.casacorcovado.com* 🕒 *Closed Sept.–mid-Nov.* 🛏 *14 rooms* 🍴 *All-inclusive.*

★ **Copa de Arbol Beach & Rainforest Resort**
$$$$ | **RESORT** | Copa de Arbol is ultraluxurious, ultracool (comes with air-conditioning), ultra-expensive, and is idyllically situated between crashing ocean surf and dense jungle, right on the coastal path walking trail that connects Drake Bay to Corcovado. **Pros:** comfort, hotel-like luxury in the jungle; idyllic location; spacious rooms. **Cons:** accessible only by boat (with a wet landing) or on foot; boat transportation and tours not included; lots of steps to negotiate. [$] *Rooms from: $660* ✉ *Along coastal path, one beach north of Playa Caletas, Drake* ☎ *8935–1212* 🌐 *www.copadearbol.com* 🛏 *10 rooms* 🍴 *All-inclusive.*

Drake Bay Wilderness Resort
$$$$ | **B&B/INN** | **FAMILY** | Perfect for multigenerational families, this beautifully maintained resort is the best deal in Drake Bay and has the most kid-friendly

grounds, with lots of flat, open space for romping, plus a refreshing saltwater swimming pool and rocky tidal pools to explore. **Pros:** great location; excellent food; free perks (laundry service, snacks at sunset, and kayaks to borrow). **Cons:** not much privacy in the cabins with open screen windows; no a/c in open-air dining room; some cabins adjoin one another. [$] *Rooms from: $600* ✉ *Southern end of bay, at mouth of Río Agujitas, Drake* ☎ *2775–1716* 🌐 *www.drakebay.com* 🛏 *20 rooms* 🍴 *All-inclusive.*

Jinetes de Osa

$$ | **B&B/INN** | This small bayside hotel overlooking the beach and almost hidden behind flowering hedges is the most comfortable and reasonably priced place to stay in the village of Drake. **Pros:** convenient location; affordable rates; adventuresome, active clientele. **Cons:** standard rooms are smallish with no a/c; access is on foot, since the tide washes right up to the lodge steps; many steps up to hillside rooms. [$] *Rooms from: $113* ✉ *West side of bay, Drake* ☎ *8996–6161* 🛏 *19 rooms* 🍴 *Free Breakfast.*

★ La Paloma Lodge

$$$$ | **B&B/INN** | Sweeping ocean views, impeccably appointed accommodations, and lots of tropical-foliage privacy make this lodge the area's most romantic option. **Pros:** ocean views and easy access to beach; great service; interesting guests from all over the world. **Cons:** steep, long climbs to some ranchos; small pool; three-night minimum stay. [$] *Rooms from: $766* ✉ *On Drake Bay, near Drake Bay Wilderness Resort, Drake* ☎ *2239–0954 office in San José, 2775–1684 lodge* 🌐 *www.lapalomalodge.com* ⏲ *Closed Sept.–Oct.* 🛏 *11 rooms* 🍴 *All-inclusive.*

Activities

TOUR OPERATORS

Jinetes de Osa

DIVING/SNORKELING | Experienced guides run popular diving ($115 for a two-tank dive, plus $20 for gear), snorkeling ($85), and dolphin-watching ($115) tours, as well as a canopy tour ($65) with some interesting bridge transitions between platforms. ✉ *West side of bay, Drake* ☎ *8996–6161.*

★ Night Tour

WILDLIFE-WATCHING | **FAMILY** | When you're on the Osa Peninsula, the wildest nightlife is outdoors. Join entomologist Tracie Stice (also known as the Bug Lady) and herpetologist Gianfranco Gomez on their night tour of insects, bats, reptiles, and anything else creeping or crawling around at night. Tracie is a wealth of bug lore, with riveting insect stories from around the world. Top-of-the-line Petzl headlamps help you see in the dark. Tours are $45 per person. Book ahead because these nightly tours, at 5:30 and 7:30 pm, are popular. ✉ *Drake* ☎ *8701–7356* 🌐 *www.thenighttour.com.*

Reel Escape

FISHING | With its ideal location close to the offshore fish-filled Furuno banks and river mouths along the coast, this charter operation has great fishing options aboard a 35-foot CABO sportfishing boat equipped with twin 450 CAT engines. There's a full-size galley, bathroom, and shower on board, and top-of-the-line fishing gear. Bilingual Capt. Willy Atencio has fished internationally, but he has come home to his native Drake Bay. He and his mates will transport you to the boat, take you where the fish are, then clean and fillet your catch. Half-day, inshore trips accommodate up to four fishers, are aboard a 26-foot panga with a 250-horse-powered Yamaha outboard motor, and cost $450. A full-day offshore (lunch included) expedition aboard the CABO runs $1,500 for up to five fishers. ✉ *Drake Bay* ☎ *8824–3036, 855/372–5322 toll-free in U.S.* 🌐 *www.fishdrakebay.com.*

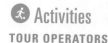

Chapter 11

TORTUGUERO AND THE CARIBBEAN COAST

11

Updated by
Jeffrey Van Fleet

 Sights
★★☆☆☆

 Restaurants
★★★★☆

 Hotels
★★★★☆

 Shopping
★★☆☆☆

 Nightlife
★★☆☆☆

WELCOME TO TORTUGUERO AND THE CARIBBEAN COAST

TOP REASONS TO GO

★ **Dolphin-watching:** Bottlenose, tucuxi, and Atlantic spotted dolphins ply the southern Caribbean coast.

★ **Food and flavors:** Leave *gallo pinto* (rice and beans) behind in favor of mouthwatering *rondón* (meat or fish stew) or *caribeño* (Caribbean) rice and beans, stewed in coconut milk.

★ **Music:** Mix reggae and calypso with your salsa. Rhythms waft in from the far-off Caribbean islands, and homegrown musicians are making names for themselves, too.

★ **Sportfishing:** World-class tarpon and snook attract serious anglers to the shores off Tortuguero National Park.

★ **Turtles:** People from around the world flock to the northern Caribbean for the annual nesting of four sea turtle species.

Costa Rica's Caribbean coast is sometimes called its Atlantic coast, so as not to confuse tourists looking for the white sand and clear blue waters of the Caribbean Islands. This Caribbean is different, with sands in shades of brown and black, waters that are rough and murky, dense jungle, heavy and frequent rain, and a laid-back approach to tourism.

1 The Sarapiquí Loop. The Sarapiquí Loop circles Braulio Carrillo National Park, rare for its easy-to-access primary rain forest.

2 Puerto Viejo de Sarapiquí. A prime spot for wildlife viewing, the lesser-known Puerto Viejo is home to nature-themed activities.

3 Tortuguero. The roadless northern Caribbean coast encompasses the coastal jungles and canals leading to and through Tortuguero National Park.

4 Cahuita. A sloth sanctuary, national park, and several beaches are big draws here.

5 Puerto Viejo de Talamanca. A hot spot for backpackers, this colorful town is home to wildlife refuges.

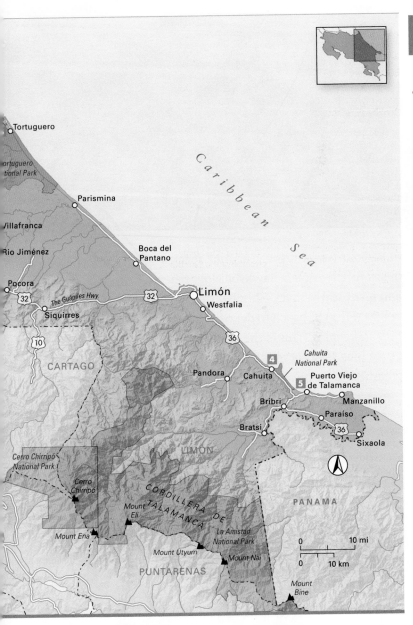

TORTUGUERO NATIONAL PARK

Tortuguero National Park

At various times of the year, four species of sea turtle—green, hawksbill, loggerhead, and giant leatherback—lumber up the 35 km (22 miles) of beach to deposit their eggs for safekeeping. This is the best place in Costa Rica to observe these magnificent creatures' nesting and hatching rituals.

In 1975 the Costa Rican government established Tortuguero National Park to protect the sea turtle population, which had been decimated after centuries of being hunted for its eggs and shells. Still, despite preservation efforts, fewer than 1% of the hatchlings will make it to adulthood.

Turtles may be the top draw here, but keep your eyes peeled for other species: tapirs, jaguars, anteaters, ocelots, howler monkeys, capuchin monkeys, three-toed sloths, collared and white-lipped peccaries, coatis, and blue morpho butterflies also populate the park. You can wander the beach when the turtles aren't nesting, but riptides make swimming dangerous, and shark rumors persist.

BEST TIME TO GO

The green turtle's July-through-October nesting season is the most popular time to visit. It rains here (a lot!) year-round, so expect to get wet no matter when you go. February through April is a tad drier.

FUN FACT

One of nature's mysteries is how turtles find their way back to the same beach where they hatched. It's thought that the sand leaves a biological imprint on the turtle hatchlings during their scurry to the sea.

BEST WAY TO EXPLORE

BIRD-WATCHING AND WILDLIFE

This is a birder's dream destination. Some of the rarer species you'll find here include the snowy cotinga, palm warbler, and yellow-tailed oriole. Waterbirds and herons abound. On a recent foray, members of the Birding Club of Costa Rica were treated to a close-up view of a wide-eyed rufescent tiger-heron chick sitting in his nest, squawking impatiently for food. You'll also see iguanas, caimans, and sloths. Bird-watching and wildlife spotting sometimes collide: while watching two beautiful agami herons feeding on a muddy bank, birders were shaken up by the sudden splash of a crocodile attacking the herons. Happily, the herons were quicker off the mark than the birders were!

BOAT RIDES

It's not quite *The African Queen,* but a boat ride along the narrow vine-draped canals here is close. Once you're off the main canal, the specially designed, narrow tour boats glide relatively quietly (using mandated electric motors) and slowly, which makes for better wildlife spotting and fewer waves that erode the lagoon banks. Another alternative is to rent a kayak and go at your own speed along the canals.

TOURS

Most visitors opt for a fully escorted tour with one of the big lodges, because you're looked after from the moment you're picked up at your San José hotel until you're dropped off a day or two or seven later. All include a couple of standard tours of the park in their package prices. It's entirely possible to stay at a smaller in-town place and make à la carte arrangements yourself.

TOP REASONS TO GO

LUXURY IN THE JUNGLE

Don't let tales of Tortuguero's isolation dissuade you from making a trip. No question: the place is remote. But the lodges up here package everything (overnight lodging, meals, tours, and, best of all, guided round-trip transportation) into one price, in true "leave the driving to them" fashion. You won't lift a finger.

PLANE OR BOAT ONLY

Whoever coined the old adage "Getting there is half the fun" might have had Tortuguero in mind. Plane and boat are the only ways to get to this no-road sector of Costa Rica. If you have the time, the fully escorted boat trips to and from the jungle give you a real Indiana Jones experience.

TURTLES

Tortuguero takes its name from the Spanish word for turtle (*tortuga*), and here you'll get the chance to observe the nesting and hatching of four species of sea turtle.

Turtle hatchlings make their way to the sea.

CAHUITA NATIONAL PARK

Cahuita National Park

In a land known for its dark-sand beaches, the coral-based white sand of Cahuita National Park (Parque Nacional Cahuita) is a real standout.

The only Costa Rican park jointly administered by the National Parks Service and a community, it starts at the southern edge of the village of Cahuita and runs pristine mile after pristine mile southward. Whereas most of the country's protected areas tender only land-based activities, this park entices you offshore as well.

Roughly parallel to the coastline, a 7-km (4-mile) trail passes through the forest to Cahuita Point. A hike of a few hours along the trail—always easiest in the dry season—lets you spot howler and white-faced capuchin monkeys, coatimundis, armadillos, and raccoons. The coastline is encircled by a 2½-square-km (1-square-mile) coral reef. The park was first created to protect this reef. You'll find superb snorkeling off Cahuita Point, but sadly, the coral reef is slowly being killed by sediment, intensified by deforestation and the erosive effects of the 1991 earthquake that hit the coast.

BEST TIME TO GO

As elsewhere on this coast, you can expect rain here no matter what the time of year. February through April and September and October are drier months, and offer the best visibility for snorkeling; they are the least desirable months if you're here to surf, however.

FUN FACT

Here is Costa Rica's only national park with two-tiered entry fees. You'll pay $5 if you enter in the village of Cahuita. The entrance at Puerto Vargas, several kilometers south of town, charges $10.

BEST WAY TO EXPLORE

BEACHING IT
The waves here are fabulous for bodysurfing along the section of beach at the Puerto Vargas entrance. This wide swath of shoreline is also great for strolling, jogging, or just basking in the Caribbean sun, but be careful of riptides along this stretch of coast. The safest swimming is in front of the camping area.

CYCLING
Cycling makes a pleasant way to see the park in the dry season. Seemingly everybody in Cahuita and Puerto Viejo de Talamanca rents bicycles. (The southern entrance to the park is close enough to Puerto Viejo that it could be your starting point, too.) The park trail gets muddy at times, and you run into logs, river estuaries, and other obstacles.

HIKING
A serious 7-km (4-mile) hiking trail runs from the park entrance at Kelly Creek all the way to Puerto Vargas. Take a bus or catch a ride to Puerto Vargas and hike back around the point in the course of a day. Remember to bring plenty of water, food, and sunscreen.

SNORKELING
Tour operators in Cahuita will bring you to a selection of prime snorkeling spots offshore. If you want to swim out on your own, the best snorkeling spot is off Punta Vargas at the south end of the park. Along with the chance to see some of the 500 or so species of tropical fish that live here, you'll see some amazing coral formations, including impressive elk horn, majestic blue stag horn, and eerie yellow brain corals. When the water is clear and warm, the snorkeling is great. But that warm water also appeals to jellyfish—if you start to feel a tingling sensation on your arms or legs, head for shore.

Look up to spot wildlife on a hike in Cahuita National Park.

TOP REASONS TO GO

EASY ACCESS
With one of its two entrances sitting in "downtown" Cahuita, access to the park is a snap. But ease of access does not mean the place is overrun with visitors. Fortunately, this is no Manuel Antonio.

LOTS OF LODGING
Closeness to Cahuita and Puerto Viejo de Talamanca and their spectrum of lodging options means you'll have no trouble finding a place to stay that fits your budget. You can even camp in the park if you're up for roughing it.

SNORKELING
Costa Rica's largest living coral reef just offshore means the snorkeling is phenomenal here. Watch for blue parrotfish and angelfish as they weave their way among equally colorful species of coral, sponges, and seaweeds. Visit during the Caribbean coast's two mini dry seasons for the best visibility.

The tourist brochures tout the country's Caribbean coast as "the other Costa Rica." Everything about this part of Costa Rica seems different: different culture, different history, different climate, and different activities. (Expect different prices, too. Your travel dollar goes further here than elsewhere in the country.) This region was long ago discovered by European adventure seekers—you're quite likely to hear Dutch, German, and Italian spoken by the visitors here— but is lesser known in North American circles.

The ethnic mix differs markedly here, as it does all along the Caribbean coast of Central America. The region was first settled by the British, and then, throughout the 19th century, by the descendants of Afro-Caribbean slaves who came to work on the banana plantations and construct the Atlantic railroad. That makes the Caribbean coast the best place in the country to find English speakers, although the language is disappearing as Spanish takes over.

It is rainier here than in other parts of Costa Rica, and the rain is distributed pretty evenly year-round without a distinct dry season—though October (when the rest of Costa Rica is getting deluged with rain) is the driest month. The region will never draw the typical fun-in-the-sun crowd that frequents the drier Pacific coast, but it does offer a year-round forested lushness and just as many activities at a more reasonable price.

MAJOR REGIONS

The Sarapiquí Loop circles Braulio Carrillo National Park, rare for its easy-to-access primary rain forest.

The **Southern Caribbean coast** stretches south from port-of-call Limón to Panama. Towns along the coast have an Afro-Caribbean vibe that echoes Jamaica—and some of them are more backpackerish than others. Beaches are fringed with forest, and waters are rough. Surfers make the trip for Salsa Brava.

Planning

When to Go

HIGH SEASON: FEBRUARY TO APRIL

Climate is the Caribbean's bugaboo and will forever prevent it from becoming the same high-powered tourist destination that the northern Pacific coast is. (Frankly, we consider that to be a blessing.) The Caribbean lacks a true dry season, though February to April could be called a "drier" season, with many sunny days and intermittent showers. Yet, despite weather patterns that differ from the rest of Costa Rica, places here charge high-season rates from December to April, just as they do elsewhere in the country. Prices skew a bit lower in the Caribbean, though, than elsewhere in Costa Rica.

LOW SEASON: MAY TO AUGUST AND DECEMBER THROUGH JANUARY

The heaviest rains (and periodic road closures) come in December and January, high season elsewhere in Costa Rica. During the rainiest months visitors are fewer. May through August sees rain, too, although not quite as much. The popularity of this part of the country among European travelers means that July and August become mini high seasons here, often with a slight increase in lodging prices. Tortuguero sets its own seasons, with higher prices the norm during the prime turtle-watching months of July through September.

SHOULDER SEASON: SEPTEMBER TO NOVEMBER

Want in on a little secret? When the rest of Costa Rica settles into the soggiest time of year, the sun comes out and the weather begins to dry up in this part of the country. The Caribbean coast makes the perfect refuge from the insufferably wet months of September and October elsewhere.

Planning Your Time

Attractions near Braulio Carrillo National Park lend themselves to day trips from San José. Tour operators also have whirlwind daylong Tortuguero trips from the capital. We recommend you avoid these—the area really deserves two or, ideally, three days. Choose a single Caribbean destination and stay put if you have just a few days; Cahuita and Puerto Viejo de Talamanca are ideal for that purpose. If you have a week, you can tackle the north and south coasts.

Getting Here and Around

AIR

SANSA flies daily from San José to the small airport in Limón (LIO) and the airstrip in Tortuguero (TTQ).

CONTACTS SANSA. ☎ *2290–4100, 877/767–2672 in North America* ⊕ *www. flysansa.com.*

BUS AND SHUTTLE

Grupo Caribeños buses, some snazzy double-deckers, connect San José's Gran Terminal del Caribe with hourly service to Guápiles, Siquirres, and Limón. Autotransportes MEPE, which has a lock on bus service to the south Caribbean coast, has a reputation for being lackadaisical but is really quite dependable. Its San José buses depart from the capital's Terminal Atlántico Norte. MEPE drivers and ticket sellers are accustomed to dealing with foreigners; even if their English is limited, they'll figure out what you want. MEPE occasionally runs extra buses to Cahuita and Puerto Viejo de Talamanca during the high season. Bus fares to this region are reasonable. From San José, expect to pay $4 to Guápiles, $7 to Limón, $11 to Cahuita, $12 to Puerto Viejo de Talamanca, and $16 to Sixaola on the Panamanian border.

If you prefer a more private form of travel, consider taking a shuttle. Comfortable air-conditioned vans of the nationwide company Interbus or the Caribbean-based Caribe Shuttle depart from San José hotels daily for Cahuita and Puerto Viejo de Talamanca. Reserve tickets ($49 one-way) at least a day in advance.

BUS CONTACTS Autotransportes MEPE.
✉ *C. 9, Avda. 12, San José* ☎ *2257–8129* ⊕ *www.mepecr.com.* **Caribe Shuttle.** ☎ *2750–0626, 800/274–6191 in North America* ⊕ *www.caribeshuttle.com.* **Grupo Caribeños.** ✉ *C. Ctl., Avda. 13, Barrio Tournón* ☎ *2222–0610* ⊕ *www. facebook.com/grupocaribenos.* **Interbus.** ☎ *4100–0888* ⊕ *www.interbusonline. com.*

CAR

With the exception of Tortuguero, this region is one of the country's most accessible. The southern coast is a three- to four-hour drive from San José, over mostly decent roads (by Costa Rican standards), and public transportation is frequent and reliable. Gas stations are plentiful between Guápiles and Limón, but their numbers dwindle to two on the southern coast between Limón and Puerto Viejo de Talamanca. The northern Caribbean coast is another story: The total absence of roads means you have to arrive by plane or boat. Most travelers go with a tour booked through one of the large Tortuguero lodges.

If you're driving here, remember that fog often covers the mountains in Braulio Carrillo National Park, north of San José, by early afternoon. Cross this area in the morning if you can. Always exercise utmost caution on the portion of highway that twists and turns through the park: You'll share the highway with large trucks. Check road conditions before you set out; occasional landslide closures through Braulio Carrillo necessitate leaving San José from the southeast, passing through Cartago, Paraíso, and Turrialba (*See The Central Valley, Chapter 5*), then rejoining the Caribbean Highway at Siquirres, a detour that adds a tiring extra 90 to 120 minutes onto your trip.

Health and Safety

All the standard tropical precautions apply when traveling in the Caribbean region. This is a very warm part of the country, so carry water, wear a hat, and use plenty of sunscreen. The undertow is dangerous along virtually the entire coast, making swimming risky. Wear mosquito repellent in low-lying coastal areas, where a few cases of dengue and chikungunya have been reported. Costa Ricans, most of whom have never been here, will caution you on safety in this region. Crime here is no worse than anywhere else in the country.

Money Matters

ATMs are becoming more common in this part of the country, although we recommend, if possible, stocking up on cash in San José. You'll find cash machines in Puerto Viejo de Sarapiquí, Guápiles, Guácimo, Siquirres, and several in Limón. Puerto Viejo de Talamanca has two; Cahuita has one. ATMs in smaller towns may run out of cash on weekends. Remember: many smaller places—there are a lot of those here in the Caribbean—do not accept credit cards.

Restaurants

The many open-air dining spots out here provide you with that ultimate tropical dining experience, with Puerto Viejo de Talamanca offering one of Costa Rica's most varied dining scenes. Think seafood, chicken, coconut, and fruits in the Caribbean. Restaurateurs take advantage of the bounty of the land and sea in this part of the country.

Hotels

The glitzy high-rise resorts of the Pacific coast are nowhere to be found in the Caribbean. The norm here is small, independent lodgings, usually family owned and operated. Fewer visitors in this region mean plenty of decent lodging at affordable prices most of the year. But tourism *is* growing, so it's risky to show up without reservations. Despite weather patterns that differ from the rest of the country, most Caribbean lodgings charge high-season rates from Christmas through Easter, just like elsewhere in Costa Rica. Many also impose another mini high season in July and August, prime vacation months for the region's predominantly European tourist clientele. Surprisingly few places here have air-conditioning, but sea breezes and ceiling fans usually provide sufficient ventilation. Smaller places frequently don't take credit cards; those that do may give discounts if you pay with cash. *Hotel reviews have been shortened. For full information, visit Fodors.com.*

WHAT IT COSTS in U.S. Dollars			
$	$$	$$$	$$$$
RESTAURANTS			
under $10	$10–$15	$16–$25	over $25
HOTELS			
under $75	$75–$150	$151–$250	over $250

Package Tours

One of Costa Rica's most remote regions is also one of its prime tourist destinations. No roads lead to Tortuguero on the northeast coast, so plane or boat are your only options. If you don't want to bother with logistics, consider booking a package tour with one of the lodges. It will include all transport from San José and back, overnights, meals, and guided tours. Prices look high at first, but considering all you get, they are quite reasonable. Other types of regional tours are also available: **Horizontes** (☎ *2222–2022* ⊕ *www.horizontes.com*) tours include naturalist guides and transport by 4WD vehicle.

The Sarapiquí Loop

The area immediately north of the San José metro area doesn't leap to mind when discussing ecotourism in Costa Rica, but it should. The Sarapiquí River gave its name to this region at the foot of the Cordillera Central mountain range. To the west is the rain forest of Braulio Carrillo National Park, and to the east are Tortuguero National Park and Barra del Colorado National Wildlife Refuge. These splendid national parks share the region with thousands of acres of farmland, including palm, banana, and pineapple plantations, as well as cattle ranching. Cheap land and rich soil brought a wave of Ticos to this area a half century ago. Until the construction of Highway 126 in 1957, which connects the area to San José, this was one of the most isolated parts of Costa Rica, with no tourism. Government homesteading projects brought many residents, who cleared massive swaths of the rain forest for cattle grazing and agriculture. Now, old-growth lowland rain forest, montane cloud forest, and wetlands exist only within the borders of the national parks and several adjoining private reserves. A growing selection of nature lodges have set up shop here, and you can enjoy their offerings 60 to 90 minutes after you leave the capital. (Just try getting to the Osa Peninsula on the southern Pacific coast in that same time.)

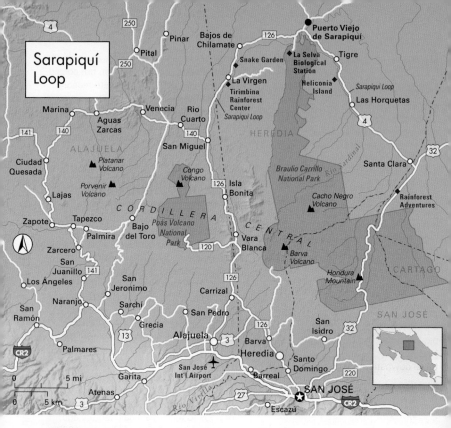

◉ Sights

★ Rainforest Adventures

NATURE PRESERVE | Just beyond the northeastern boundary of Braulio Carrillo National Park, about 15 km (9 miles) before the Caribbean-slope town of Guápiles, a 1,200-acre reserve houses a privately owned and operated engineering marvel: a series of gondolas strung together in a modified ski-lift pulley system. Each of the 21 gondolas holds five people plus a bilingual biologist-guide equipped with a walkie-talkie to request brief stops for snapping pictures. The ride covers 2½ km (1½ miles) in 80 minutes. The price includes a biologist-guided walk through the area for ground-level orientation before or after the tram ride. Several add-ons are possible, too, with frog and butterfly exhibits, a medicinal-plant garden, and a zipline canopy tour on-site, as well as a half-day birding tour. There is also on-site lodging. You can arrange a personal pickup in San José for a fee, or there are public buses (on the Guápiles line) every half hour from the Gran Terminal del Caribe in San José. Drivers know the tram as the *teleférico*. Many San José tour operators offer a day tour that combines the tram with another half-day option; combos with the Britt Coffee Tour, near Heredia, are especially popular. These folks operate a similar facility near the Central Pacific town of Jacó as well as in Panama and the Caribbean islands of Jamaica, Saint Lucia, and St. Maarten. ⊠ *Hwy. 32, 10 km (6 miles) northeast of Braulio Carrillo National Park, Braulio Carrillo National Park* ☎ *2224–5961 in San José* ⊕ *www.rainforestadventure.com* ⊠ *Tram $65, multi-activity packages $99.*

Puerto Viejo de Sarapiquí

80 km (48 miles) north of San José.

One of Costa Rica's lesser-known eco-destinations has been developing a growing selection of nature-themed activities in recent years. In the 19th century, Puerto Viejo de Sarapiquí was a thriving river port and the only link with the coastal lands straight east. Fortunes nose-dived with the construction of a full-fledged port in the town of Moín near Limón, and today Puerto Viejo has a slightly run-down air. The activities of the Nicaraguan Contras made this a danger zone in the 1980s, but now that the political situation has improved, boats once again ply the old route up the Sarapiquí River to the San Juan River on the Nicaraguan border, from where you can travel downstream to Barra del Colorado or Tortuguero. (The relationship between Costa Rica and Nicaragua could be called "icy," but that need not concern you as a visitor.) A few tour companies have Sarapiquí River tours with up to Class III rapids in the section between Chilamate and La Virgen, with plenty of wildlife to see. If you prefer to leave the driving to them, many of the lodges operate boat tours on the tamer sections of the river. Don't confuse Puerto Viejo de Sarapiquí with Puerto Viejo de Talamanca on the south Caribbean coast. Locals refer to both as simply "Puerto Viejo." We use the complete names of both towns to avoid any mix-up.

GETTING HERE AND AROUND

The Braulio Carrillo Highway runs from Calle 3 in San José and passes the Zurquí and Quebrada González sectors of Braulio Carrillo National Park. It branches at Santa Clara, north of the park, with the paved Highway 4 continuing north to Puerto Viejo de Sarapiquí. Alternatively, an older winding road connects San José with Puerto Viejo de Sarapiquí, passing through Heredia and Vara Blanca. The former route is easier, with less traffic; the latter route is more scenic but narrow, and if you are at all prone to motion sickness, the newer road is a safer bet. Heavy rains sometimes cause landslides that block the newer highway near the Zurquí Tunnel inside the park, in which case you have to go via Vara Blanca. Check conditions before you set out. Get an early start; fog begins to settle in on both routes by the middle of the afternoon. ■TIP→ **There are gas stations on the Braulio Carrillo Highway at the turnoff to Puerto Viejo de Sarapiquí, as well as just outside town. Fill the tank when you get the chance.**

Grupo Caribeños buses travel several times daily via both routes—more frequently via the newer route, though—and leave from San José's Gran Terminal del Caribe.

ESSENTIALS

BANK/ATM Banco Nacional. ☒ *Across from post office* ☎ *2766–6012* ⊕ *www.bncr.fi.cr.*

MEDICAL CLINIC Red Cross. (*Cruz Roja*) ☒ *West end of town* ☎ *2766–6901.*

PHARMACY Farmacia Alfa. ☒ *50 m northeast of Parque Central* ☎ *2766–6348.*

POST OFFICE Correos. ☒ *Across from Banco Nacional* ⊕ *correos.go.cr.*

Sights

Heliconia Island

GARDEN | Some 70 species of the heliconia, a relative of the banana, are among the collections that populate 5 acres of botanical gardens on this island in the Sarapiquí River. Expect to see ample bird and butterfly life, too. ☒ *La Chaves, 8 km (5 miles) south of Puerto Viejo de Sarapiquí* ☎ *2764–5220* ⊕ *www.heliconiaisland.com* ☒ *From $10.*

★ La Selva Biological Station

NATURE PRESERVE | FAMILY | At the confluence of the Puerto Viejo and Sarapiquí rivers, La Selva packs about 420 bird species, 460 tree species, and 500 butterfly species into just 15 square km (6 square miles). Sightings might include the spider monkey, poison dart frog, agouti, collared peccary, and dozens of other rare creatures. Extensive, well-marked trails and swing bridges, many of which are wheelchair accessible, connect habitats as varied as tropical wet forest, swamps, creeks, rivers, secondary regenerating forest, and pasture. The site is a project of the Organization for Tropical Studies (OTS), a research consortium of 63 U.S., Australian, South African, and Latin American universities, and is the oldest of three biological stations OTS operates in Costa Rica. (OTS also operates one research station in South Africa.) To see the place, take an informative three-hour morning or afternoon nature walk with one of La Selva's bilingual guides, who are among the country's best. Walks start every day at 8 am and 1:30 pm. For a completely different view of the forest, set off on a guided two-hour walk at 5:45 am or the night tour at 6 pm. If you get at least seven people together, you can enroll in the daylong Bird-Watching 101 course, which can be arranged anytime for $80 per person; if you have at least six, you can tag along with one of the resident research scientists for a half day. Young children won't feel left out either, with a very basic nature-identification course geared to them. Even with all the offerings, La Selva can custom-design excursions to suit your own special interests, too. Advance reservations are required for the dawn and night walks and any of the courses. *✥ Drive 6 km (4 miles) south from Puerto Viejo de Sarapiquí, and look for signs on west side of road. La Selva is a $12 taxi ride from Puerto Viejo de Sarapiquí ☎ 2766–6565, 2524–0607 in San José, 919/684–5774 in North America 🌐 www.tropicalstudies.org 🎫 From $40.*

Snake Garden

ZOO | FAMILY | One of a growing number of Costa Rica's serpentaria, the Snake Garden shows off some 50 species of reptiles, including all the poisonous snakes (and most of the nonpoisonous ones) found in Costa Rica, as well as pythons, anacondas, and rattlesnakes from elsewhere in North and South America. You can handle a few specimens upon request and under supervision. *✉ Centro Neotrópico Sarapiquís, La Virgen de Sarapiquí ☎ 2761–1004 🌐 www.sarapiquis.com 🎫 $33.*

Tirimbina Rainforest Center

NATURE PRESERVE | This working biological research station, 17 km (11 miles) southwest of Puerto Viejo, encompasses 750 acres of primary forest and 8 km (5 miles) of trails, some of them traversing hanging bridges at canopy level. Tours introduce you to bats, frogs, and other common but often misunderstood creatures, and show off the beauty of the forest. Reservations are recommended for all activities, and required for the bat, frog, birding, and night tours. *✉ La Virgen de Sarapiquí ☎ 4020–2900 🌐 www.tirimbina.org 🎫 From $29.*

Hotels

Hotel Gavilán

$ | HOTEL | Beautiful gardens run down to the river, and colorful tanagers and three types of toucan feast in the citrus trees on the grounds of this two-story lodge, where comfortable, terra-cotta-floor rooms are nicely accented with decorative crafts. **Pros:** lovely gardens; many activities; great for birders. **Cons:** rustic rooms; need a car to stay here; no a/c; patchy Wi-Fi. *[$] Rooms from: $60 ✉ 700 m north of Comando Atlántico (naval command) ☎ 2766–6743, 2234–9507 in San José 🌐 www.gavilanlodge.com 🛏 20 rooms 🍴 No meals.*

La Selva Biological Station Lodge

$$ | **B&B/INN** | Other lodges provide more luxury for the money, but none can match the tropical nature experience at this working biological-research station where accommodations are in dorm-style rooms with large bunk beds and lots of screened windows. **Pros:** many activities included in lodging rate; plenty of wildlife; ecology-minded staff. **Cons:** cabins are rustic; no a/c; sometimes difficult to procure overnight space. [$] *Rooms from: $130* ✉ *6 km (4 miles) south of Puerto Viejo de Sarapiquí* ☎ *2766–6565, 2524–0607 in San José, 919/684–5774 in North America* 🌐 *www.tropicalstudies.org* 🛏 *60 bunk beds in dorms, 18 cabins, 1 house* 🍴 *Free Breakfast.*

Sarapiquís Rainforest Lodge

$$ | **HOTEL** | **FAMILY** | Within the Centro Neotrópico Sarapiquís, an environmental educational center, museum, and garden, you can stay the night inside indigenous-inspired circular *palenque* (huts) with palm-thatch roofs. **Pros:** large rooms; private terraces; buffet-style restaurant. **Cons:** some rooms need updating; sometimes difficult to find space; a/c is extra. [$] *Rooms from: $110* ✉ *Centro Neotrópico Sarapiquís, La Virgen de Sarapiquí, 17 km (11 miles) southwest of Puerto Viejo* ☎ *2761–1004* 🌐 *www.sarapiquis.com* 🛏 *40 rooms* 🍴 *Free Breakfast.*

★ **Selva Verde Lodge**

$$ | **HOTEL** | Built on stilts over the Sarapiquí River on the edge of a 2-square-km (1-square-mile) private tropical rain-forest reserve, the lodge caters primarily to those seeking natural-history tours. **Pros:** ecology-minded staff; many activities; great for birders. **Cons:** popular with tour groups; sometimes difficult to find space in high season; steep walk to reach a few bungalows. [$] *Rooms from: $115* ✉ *Chilamate, 7 km (4 miles) west of Puerto Viejo de Sarapiquí* ☎ *2761–1800, 833/344–5835 in North America* 🌐 *www.selvaverde.com* 🛏 *45 units* 🍴 *Free Breakfast.*

Tirimbina Rainforest Lodge

$$ | **B&B/INN** | A variety of comfy lodge accommodations put you close to this research complex's many fun nature-themed activities. **Pros:** access to nature-themed activities; terrific rates for what's offered; rooms have a/c, a rarity in this region. **Cons:** standard rooms are a bit spartan; can be difficult to find space; caters to groups, so not a place to go if you crave privacy. [$] *Rooms from: $89* ✉ *La Virgen de Sarapiquí, 17 km (11 miles) southwest of Puerto Viejo* ☎ *4020–2900* 🌐 *www.tirimbina.org* 🛏 *18 rooms* 🍴 *Free Breakfast.*

Activities

TOUR OPERATORS

Hotel Gavilán Río Sarapiquí

TOUR—SPORTS | The hotel runs wildlife-watching and birding tours from its site on the river near Puerto Viejo de Sarapiquí. ✉ *700 m north of Comando Atlántico (naval command)* ☎ *2766–6743, 2234–9507 in San José* 🌐 *www.gavilanlodge.com* 🎟 *From $49.*

Pozo Azul

BICYCLING | This working horse ranch and dairy farm, 17 km (11 miles) southwest of Puerto Viejo, offers a variety of nature-themed excursions. The canopy tour ($58) has 12 ziplines, ranging in height from 60 to 90 feet. Horseback excursions for all experience levels take you through the area around La Virgen. A half-day tour is $58. If you're an experienced rider, check out the multiday tours, too. A guided 90-foot river canyon rappelling descent is $50. ✉ *La Virgen de Sarapiquí* ☎ *2438–2616, 877/810–6903 in North America* 🌐 *www.pozoazul.com.*

RAFTING

The Virgen del Socorro area is one of the most popular put-in points for white-water rafters, and offers both Class II and III rapids. The upper Sarapiquí River gets wilder and woolier with Class IV rapids to navigate. Trips leaving from the Chilamate

Steep hills and heavy rainfall make this country a mecca for white-water sports.

put-in are more tranquil, with mostly Class I rapids. The put-in point depends on the weather and season. Several operators lead tours on the Sarapiquí River.

Ríos Tropicales

WHITE-WATER RAFTING | You can raft the Class II–III La Virgen section of the Sarapiquí River as well as the upper river (Class IV) on day excursions from the Arenal area. ✉ *San José* ☎ *2233–6455, 866/722–8273 in North America* ⊕ *www. riostropicales.com* ✑ *From $95.*

Tortuguero

30 mins by air and 4 hrs by road and boat northeast of San José.

Some compare these dense layers of green set off by brilliantly colored flowers—a vision doubled by the jungle's reflection in mirror-smooth canals—to the Amazon. That's stretching it, but there's still an "Indiana Jones" mystique to the journey up here, especially when you get off the main canals and into the narrower lagoons. The region remains one of those Costa Rican anomalies: roadless and remote, it's nevertheless one of the country's most visited places. The tourism seasons here are defined not by the rains or lack thereof (with 200 inches of rain annually, Tortuguero is wet most of the year) but by the months of prime turtle hatching.

The stretch of beach between the Colorado and Matina rivers was first mentioned as a nesting ground for sea turtles in a 1592 Dutch chronicle. Nearly a century earlier, Christopher Columbus compared traversing the north Caribbean coast and its swimming turtles to navigating through rocks. Because the area is so isolated—there's no road here to this day—the turtles nested undisturbed for centuries. By the mid-1900s, however, the harvesting of eggs and poaching of turtles had reached such a level that these creatures faced extinction. In 1963 an executive decree regulated the hunting of turtles and the gathering of eggs, and in 1970 the government established

Tortuguero National Park; modern Tortuguero bases its economy on tourism. When the 2020 COVID-19 pandemic hit Tortuguero, the lack of tourism revenue hampered its ability to fund turtle-conservation efforts. Without that added vigilance that the community is famous for, egg poaching increased once again. Tourism dollars continue to help restore the equilibrium.

A system of canals running parallel to the shoreline provide safer access to the region than the dangerous journey up the seacoast. You can continue up the canals (natural and man-made) that begin in Moín, near Limón, and run all the way to Tortuguero. Or you can embark at various points north of Guápiles and Siquirres, as do public transportation and most of the package tours. (The lodges' minivans bring you from San José to the put-in point, where you continue your journey by boat.)

Just north of the national park of the same name, the hamlet of Tortuguero is a pleasant little place with 600 inhabitants, two churches, three bars, a handful of souvenir shops, and a small selection of inexpensive lodgings. And one more plus: there are no motor vehicles here, a refreshing change from the traffic woes that plague the rest of Costa Rica. You can also take a stroll on the 32-km (20-mile) beach, but avoid swimming here because of strong riptides and large numbers of bull sharks and barracuda.

GETTING HERE AND AROUND

It's easier than you'd think to get to remote Tortuguero. Flying is the quickest (and most expensive) option. SANSA flies daily to and from San José.

If you're staying at one of the lodges, its boat will meet you at the airstrip.

The big lodges all have packages that include transportation from and back to San José, along with lodging, meals, and tours. Guide-staffed minivans pick you up at your San José–area hotel and drive you to their own put-in site, usually somewhere north of Siquirres, where you board a covered boat for the final leg on the canals to Tortuguero. The trip entails sightseeing and animal viewing. The trip back to San José stops only for a lunch break. This is the classic "leave the driving to them" way to get to Tortuguero.

A boat from the port of Moín, near Limón, is the traditional budget method of getting to Tortuguero if you are already on the Caribbean coast. Arrive at the docks before 10 am and you should be able to find someone to take you there. The going price is $40 per person each way, and travel time is about three hours.

If you arrive in Moín in your own vehicle, JAPDEVA, Costa Rica's Atlantic port authority, operates a secure, guarded parking facility for your car while you are in Tortuguero.

It's entirely possible to make the trip independently via public transportation from San José, and it's a good option if you are staying in the village rather than at a lodge. A direct bus departs from San José's Gran Terminal del Caribe to Cariari, north of Guápiles, at 9 am. At Cariari, disembark and walk five blocks to the local terminal, where you can board an 11:30 am bus for the small crossroads of La Pavona. From here, boats leave at 1 pm to take you to Tortuguero, arriving around 3 pm. La Pavona has secure parking facilities. The charge is $10 per night. The Cariari–La Pavona–Tortuguero bus-boat service is provided by COOPETRACA or Viajes Clic-Clic for $10 one-way. They operate jointly, alternating days, and honor each other's tickets. Cariari has only spartan accommodation; La Pavona has none.

BUS AND BOAT CONTACTS COOPETRACA. ☎ 2767–7137. **Viajes Clic-Clic.** ☎ 2709–8155, 8844–0463.

■ TIP→ If you can, avoid Rubén Bananero, a company that provides bus-boat transportation from Cariari. Its aggressive agents begin to hustle you the minute you get off the bus in Cariari. They'll pressure you into buying a round-trip ticket, limiting your return options, and do everything they can to steer you toward hotels that pay them a commission. Others will also try to take you to their own dedicated "information dock" in the village, steering you toward their own guides. If you've made advance reservations for guides or hotels, be firm and say *No, gracias.*

Water taxis provide transportation from multiple points in the village to the lodges. Expect to pay about $3 to $5 per trip.

ESSENTIALS

This unstaffed kiosk with free brochures offers information on the town's history, the park, turtles, and other wildlife.

VISITOR INFORMATION Kiosk. ✉ *Town center.*

Sights

★ **Tortuguero National Park** (*Parque Nacional Tortuguero*)

NATURE PRESERVE | FAMILY | There is no better place in Costa Rica to observe sea turtles nesting, hatching, and scurrying to the ocean. The July–October nesting season for the green turtle is Tortuguero's most popular time to visit. Toss in the hawksbill, loggerhead, and leatherback—the three other species of sea turtle that nest here, although to a lesser extent—and you expand the season from February through October. You can undertake night tours only with an authorized guide, who will be the only person in your party with a light, and that will be a light with a red covering. Photography, flash or otherwise, is strictly prohibited. The sight of a mother turtle furiously digging in the sand to bury her eggs is amazing, even from several yards away, and the spectacle of a wave of hatchlings scurrying out to sea is simply magnificent. *For more information see the highlighted listing in this chapter.* ✉ *South of Tortuguero village* ☎ *2710–2929, 1192 national parks hotline in Costa Rica* 🎟 *$15.*

Beaches

Playa Tortuguero

BEACH—SIGHT | The crashing waves and misty air (it rains a lot in Tortuguero) give you the unsettling feeling that you're standing at the edge of the world. Swimming and surfing are simply not possible here—sharks are present along this stretch of coast, for one thing—but by night, depending on the season, this beach comes alive with the age-old ritual of Tortuguero's four species of sea turtles laying and burying their eggs. They then hatch and the baby turtles scurry out to sea, a spectacle that's viewable only in the company of a licensed guide. Sunbathing? People-watching? Who needs those when this is the real show? **Amenities:** none. **Best for:** solitude; sunrise; walking. ✉ *North of Tortuguero village.*

Restaurants

If you stay at one of the big lodges up here, your meals will be included in the package price, both in Tortuguero and on your way to and from. Usually *not* included in package prices are alcoholic beverages, soda, and bottled water. Ask to be sure.

If you're staying in town, you have a couple of simple, but satisfying, restaurant options.

Budda Café

$ | ITALIAN | Pizza, crepes, pastas, and fresh fish are on the menu at this small, canalside café in the center of town. Wood lattice over the windows, a thatch roof, and, not surprisingly, a Buddha statue make up the furnishings. Jazzy cha-cha or a Dean Martin ballad might be playing in the background. **Known for:** good cocktail selection; friendly service; cool canalside setting. [$] *Average main: $8* ✉ *Next to ICE Bldg.* ☎ *2709–8084* 🌐 *www.buddacafe.com* 💳 *No credit cards.*

Dorling's Bakery

$ | CAFÉ | Pizza, pasta, and sandwiches are on the menu, but this small bakery and coffee shop is also a great place to stop for breads made with banana, carrot, and *natilla* (sour cream). They'll provide sustenance for a morning of sightseeing. **Known for:** hearty, fortifying breakfasts; canal views; variety of breads. $ *Average main: $5* ⌖ *25 m north of Catholic church* ☎ *2709–8132* ▤ *No credit cards* ◔ *No dinner.*

Hotels

The big lodges here offer one- or two-night excursion packages. Given the choreography it takes to get up here, opt for a more leisurely two-night stay if you can. Rates look expensive at first glance, but prices include everything from guides, tours, meals, and snacks to minivan and boat transportation, and in some cases air travel from and back to San José. The $15 entrance fee to Tortuguero National Park may or may not be included in the package price; ask to make sure. If you calculate what you get, the price is actually quite reasonable, and the tours are undeniably great fun. Some lodges do not have phones, although all have radio contact with the outside world. All reservations must be made with their offices in San José. Be sure to travel light; you get a baggage allowance of 25 pounds, strictly enforced. There's simply no space in the boats for you to bring more. Since you're likely returning to San José at the completion of your Tortuguero tour, your hotel in the capital *might* allow you to store your bigger bags there. Ask ahead of time.

★ Casa Marbella

$ | B&B/INN | This B&B, the best of the in-town lodgings, is a real find, and the owner, Canadian-born naturalist Daryl Loth, is a virtual encyclopedia of all things Tortuguero and one of the community's biggest boosters. **Pros:** knowledgeable, enthusiastic owner; immaculate rooms;

walking distance to all village attractions. **Cons:** some pedestrian street noise; no access to lodge-package amenities; can be difficult to find availability. $ *Rooms from: $45* ⌖ *Across from Catholic church* ☎ *2709–8011* ⊕ *casamarbella.tripod.com* ▤ *No credit cards* ⇄ *11 rooms* ⦿ *Free Breakfast.*

★ Evergreen Lodge

$$$$ | RESORT | The Evergreen offers an entirely different (and intimate) concept in Tortuguero lodging: whereas other lodges have cabins arranged around a clearing, at Evergreen they penetrate deep into the forest. **Pros:** seclusion from other lodges; lush wooded setting; informative tours with knowledgeable guides. **Cons:** rustic rooms; farther from town than other lodges; quietest of area accommodation, so not a place if you look for action. $ *Rooms from: $500* ⌖ *2 km (1 mile) from Tortuguero village on Canal Penitencia* ☎ *2709–8213, 2222–6840 in San José* ⊕ *www.evergreentortuguero.com* ⇄ *55 cabins* ⦿ *All-inclusive.*

Laguna Lodge

$$$$ | RESORT | Laguna is the largest of the Tortuguero lodges, with a mix of concrete and wood buildings spread out over 12 acres of grounds on a thin sliver of land between the ocean and the first canal inland, and it hums with activity. **Pros:** many activities; unique architecture; open-air restaurant that extends over the canal. **Cons:** large numbers of guests; not for those who crave solitude; some rooms on the basic side. $ *Rooms from: $534* ⌖ *Between ocean and first canal inland* ☎ *2709–8082, 2253–1100 in San José* ⊕ *www.lagunatortuguero.com* ⇄ *110 rooms* ⦿ *All-inclusive.*

Manatus Hotel

$$$$ | RESORT | Amenities such as air-conditioning, satellite television, fitness centers, Wi-Fi, and spa treatments are typically not found in Tortuguero, but the area's most luxurious hotel has them all. **Pros:** intimate surroundings; numerous creature comforts not ordinarily found

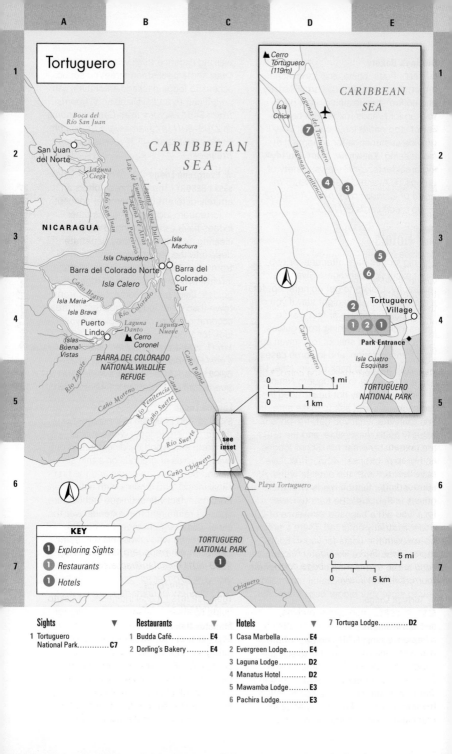

Tortuguero

Cerro Tortuguero (119m)

CARIBBEAN SEA

Isla Chica

CARIBBEAN SEA

Boca del Río San Juan

San Juan del Norte

Laguna Ciega

NICARAGUA

Isla Machura

Isla Chapudero

Barra del Colorado Norte

Isla Calero

Barra del Colorado Sur

Isla Maria

Isla Brava

Puerto Lindo

Islas Buena Vistas

Laguna Danto

Cerro Coronel

Laguna Nueve

BARRA DEL COLORADO NATIONAL WILDLIFE REFUGE

Río Zapote

Río Penitencia

Caño Suerte

Caño Moreno

Caño Palma

Río Suerte

Caño Chiquero

see inset

Tortuguero Village

Park Entrance

Isla Cuatro Esquinas

TORTUGUERO NATIONAL PARK

0 —— 1 mi
0 —— 1 km

Playa Tortuguero

TORTUGUERO NATIONAL PARK

Chiquero

0 —— 5 mi
0 —— 5 km

KEY

- ① Exploring Sights
- ① Restaurants
- ① Hotels

Sights ▼	Restaurants ▼	Hotels ▼	7 Tortuga Lodge............**D2**
1 Tortuguero National Park............**C7**	1 Budda Café...............**E4** 2 Dorling's Bakery **E4**	1 Casa Marbella ....**E4** 2 Evergreen Lodge.........**E4** 3 Laguna Lodge ....**D2** 4 Manatus Hotel ....**D2** 5 Mawamba Lodge........**E3** 6 Pachira Lodge............**E3**	

here; gourmet restaurant. **Cons:** fills up quickly in high season; degree of luxury may feel out of place in Tortuguero; quiet seclusion, so not a place to go if you seek action. [$] *Rooms from: $540* ✉ *Across river, about 1 km (½ mile) north of village* ☎ *2709–8197, 2239–7364 in San José* 🌐 *www.manatuscostarica.com* 🛏 *12 rooms* 🍴 *All-inclusive.*

Mawamba Lodge
$$$$ | RESORT | Nestled between the river and the ocean, Mawamba is the perfect place to kick back and relax, and it is also the only jungle lodge within walking distance (about 10 minutes) of town. **Pros:** many activities; walking distance to village; includes meals, guided tours, and transportation. **Cons:** rustic rooms; not for those who crave solitude; trip to beaches and sunset dinner cruise aren't included in the price. [$] *Rooms from: $508* ✉ *½ km (¼ mile) north of Tortuguero on ocean side of canal* ☎ *2709–8181, 2293–8181 in San José* 🌐 *www.mawamba.com* 🛏 *58 cabinas* 🍴 *All-inclusive.*

★ Pachira Lodge
$$$$ | RESORT | This is the prettiest of Tortuguero's lodges, but not the costliest—the owners here market competitively and keep prices reasonable. **Pros:** many activities; turtle-shape pool; beautiful surroundings. **Cons:** large numbers of guests; can be difficult to find space; not for those who crave solitude. [$] *Rooms from: $490* ✉ *Across river from Sea Turtle Conservancy* ☎ *2709–8172, 2257–2242 in San José, 800/644–7438 in North America* 🌐 *www.pachiralodge.com* 🛏 *88 rooms* 🍴 *All-inclusive.*

★ Tortuga Lodge
$$$$ | RESORT | Lush lawns, orchids, and tropical trees surround this thatch riverside lodge, renowned for its nature packages and top-notch, personalized service. **Pros:** many activities; seclusion from other lodges; top-notch guides. **Cons:** rustic rooms; this is farther from the park than most lodges in the area; two-night minimum stay. [$] *Rooms from: $592* ✉ *Across river from airstrip, 2 km (1 mile) from village* ☎ *2709–8034, 2521–6099 in San José, 800/672–8704* 🌐 *www.tortugalodge.com* 🛏 *27 rooms* 🍴 *All-inclusive.*

Did You Know?

Some people still believe turtle eggs to be an aphrodisiacal delicacy, and some bars around Costa Rica (illegally) serve them as snacks. It's a big part of the human contribution to the turtles' disappearance.

Activities

TOUR GUIDES AND OPERATORS

Tortuguero is one of those "everybody's a guide" places. Quality varies, but most guides are quite knowledgeable. If you stay at one of the lodges, guided tours are usually included in your package price (check when you book). If you hire a private guide, $15 to $20 per person per hour is the going rate, depending on the excursion, with most lasting three hours.

Daryl Loth
TOUR—SPORTS | Canadian-born naturalist Daryl Loth has a wealth of information about the area and conducts boat excursions on the canals and, with advance notice, responsible turtle-watching tours in season. ✉ *Tortuguero* ☎ *8833–0827, 2709–8011* 📧 *safari@racsa.co.cr.*

Riverboat *Francesca*
TOUR—SPORTS | Local indigenous Miskito guide Modesto Watson is legendary for his bird- and animal-spotting skills as well as for his howler-monkey imitations. The family's riverboat, *Francesca,* can take you up the canals for two-day, one-night excursions to Tortuguero for $225 to $250 per person, depending on the lodge used. As with all Tortuguero excursions, Watson offers a more leisurely three-day,

two-night trip as well. If you're interested only in seeing the canals, a four-hour tour ($85) includes lunch. Trips begin at the Caribbean port of Moín, 5 km (3 miles) northwest of Limón. ☎ 2226–0986 in San José, 810/433–1410 in North America ⊕ www.tortuguerocanals.com.

Victor Barrantes

TOUR—SPORTS | Local guide and area expert Victor Barrantes conducts hiking and boating tours around the area. ⊠ Tortuguero ☎ 2709–8055, 8928–1169 ⊕ tortugueroinfo.tripod.com.

FISHING

You have your choice of mackerel, tarpon, snook, and snapper if you fish in the ocean; snook and calba if you fish in the canals. If you opt for the latter, the National Parks Service levies a $30 license fee (you are fishing in the confines of Tortuguero National Park), good for one month. Operators include the fee in your tour price.

Eddie Brown

FISHING | With 40 years of experience, longtime area fishing expert Eddie Brown and his brother Roberto offer half-day fishing packages for $300; daylong excursions are $580. ⊠ Tortuguero ☎ 8834–2221 ⊕ www.captaineddiebrown.com.

Tortuguero Sport Fishing

FISHING | Known as "Primo" to everyone in town, Elvin Gutiérrez takes two passengers out on the ocean for two hours or more, at $80 per hour, or for a full nine-hour day ($550). Prices include boat, guide, and refreshments. ⊠ Tortuguero ☎ 2709–8115 ⊕ www.tortuguerosport-fishing.com.

TURTLE-WATCHING

If you want to watch the *deshove* (egg laying), contact your hotel or the parks office to hire a certified local guide, required on turtle-watching excursions. Note that you won't be allowed to use a camera—flash or nonflash—on the beach, and only your guide is permitted to use a flashlight (and that must be covered with red plastic), because lights can deter the turtles from nesting. Wear dark clothing if you can, and avoid loud talking. Smoking is prohibited on the tours. ■**TIP**➜ **A few unscrupulous locals will offer to take you on a turtle-watching tour outside the allowed February–November season, disturbing sensitive nesting sites in the process. If it's not the season, don't go on a turtle excursion. As the signs around town admonish: "Don't become another predator."**

Cahuita

44 km (26 miles) southeast of Limón.

Dusty Cahuita (pronounced *cah-WEE-tah*), its main street flanked by wooden-slat cabins, is a backpackers' vacation town—a hippie hangout where you can be immersed in Afro-Caribbean culture. Tucked in among the backpackers' digs are a few surprisingly nice get-away-from-it-all lodgings, and restaurants with some tasty cuisine at decent prices. After years of negative crime-related publicity, Cahuita has beefed up security and has made a well-deserved come-back on the tourist circuit. No question that nearby Puerto Viejo de Talamanca has overtaken Cahuita and become the hottest spot on the southern Caribbean coast. But as Puerto Viejo grows exponentially, Cahuita's appeal is that it remains small and manageable. It's well worth a look.

GETTING HERE AND AROUND

Autotransportes MEPE buses travel from San José's Terminal Atlántico Norte seven times a day—plan on four hours for the trip—and approximately hourly throughout the day from Limón and Puerto Viejo de Talamanca. The bus terminal here sits at the entrance to Cahuita, about four blocks from the town center. You can give yourself a wider selection of times than the six daily San José–Cahuita services: hourly Grupo Caribeños

The magnificent emerald basilisk is just one of the creatures found in Tortuguero National Park.

buses connect San José with Limón, and hourly MEPE buses connect Limón with Cahuita. The MEPE and Caribeños terminals are one block apart in Limón. Walking could be an option if you're not laden with bags and if it's still light out. Unlike MEPE vehicles, Caribeños buses are air-conditioned.

Car travel is straightforward: watch for signs in Limón and head 45 minutes south on the coastal highway. Road conditions fluctuate with the severity of the previous year's rains and with the speed at which highway crews patch the potholes (the road's blacktop surface makes it a never-ending battle). Cahuita has three entrances from the highway: the first takes you to the far north end of the Playa Negra road, near the Magellan Inn; the second, to the middle section of Playa Negra, near the Atlántida Lodge; and the third, to the tiny downtown.

The proximity of the Panamanian border means added police vigilance on the coastal highway. No matter what your mode of travel, expect a passport inspection and cursory vehicle search at a police checkpoint just north of Cahuita. If you're on public transportation, you may be required to disembark from the bus while it's searched.

NAVIGATING CAHUITA

Cahuita's tiny center is quite walkable, if dusty in the dry season and muddy in the wet season once you get off the few paved streets. It's about a 30-minute walk to the end of the Playa Negra road to Hotel La Diosa. Always take a taxi to or from Playa Negra and Playa Grande after dark. Cahuita has a couple of officially licensed red taxis, but most transportation is provided informally by private individuals. To be on the safe side, have your hotel or restaurant call a driver for you.

Bicycles are a popular means of utilitarian transportation in Cahuita. Seemingly everyone rents basic touring bikes for $20 per day, but quality varies widely—and note that no one rents helmets.

ESSENTIALS

BANK/ATM Banco de Costa Rica.
⊠ *Bus terminal at entrance to town*
☎ *2755–0401.*

PHARMACY Farmacia Quiribrí. ⊠ *Bus terminal* ☎ *2755–0505.*

POST OFFICE Correos. ⊠ *Bus terminal*
⊕ *correos.go.cr.*

Sights

Cahuita National Park (*Parque Nacional Cahuita*)

NATIONAL/STATE PARK | With rain forest extending right to the edge of a curving, utterly undeveloped 3-km (2-mile) white sand beach, this popular national park is the stuff of picture postcards. The park was created to protect the 2½-square-km (1-square-mile) coral reef that encircles the coast and offers excellent snorkeling off Cahuita Point. Trails into the rain forest reveal a wealth of wildlife. February through April and September and October are slightly drier months, and offer the best visibility for snorkeling. A nice touch to the infrastructure here is the "plastic walk," a boardwalk path made of recycled plastic. Visitors in wheelchairs can be wheeled down to the surf in the park's own chairs. The location means you'll find a great selection of in-town dining and lodging options within a few blocks of the park's northern entrance, making this one of the country's easiest protected areas to visit. Choose from two park entrances: one is in downtown Cahuita; the other is at Puerto Vargas, just off the main road, 5 km (3 miles) south of town. If you don't have a car, you can get here easily via bike or taxi. ⊠ *Southern end of Cahuita* ☎ *2755–0461 Cahuita entrance, 2755–0302 Puerto Vargas entrance, 1192 national parks hotline in Costa Rica* 🖾 *$5 at Cahuita entrance; $10 at Puerto Vargas entrance.*

★ **Sloth Sanctuary of Costa Rica**

NATURE PRESERVE | **FAMILY** | This full-fledged nature center a few miles northwest of Cahuita is well worth a stop. Many of the sloths that live on the premises are here because of illness or injury and are not on display to the public, but Buttercup, the very first of their charges, holds court in the nature-focused gift shop. She has been joined by Leno, a Bradypus male—that's one of the two sloth species found in Costa Rica—who can be found in the aquarium. A visit is a good way to learn about these little-known animals. Tours include a short canoe ride—the staff does all the paddling—to show you a sloth's natural habitat. (Numerous requests from visitors to hold or pet the sloths have to be turned down.) Your admission includes a two-hour tour (no reservations are needed) and contributes to further care and research by the good-hearted folks who operate the facility. Reservations are required for a special insider's tour that takes you behind the scenes into the sloth clinic and nursery. ⊠ *Cahuita ✛ 9 km (5 miles) northwest of Cahuita; follow signs on Río Estrella delta* ☎ *2750–0775* ⊕ *www.slothsanctuary. com* 🖾 *From $30* ☉ *Closed Mon.*

Tarantula's Way

ZOO | If you want a primer on things that creep and crawl in the night, here's the tour for you. An expert guide takes you on a two-hour walk through a jungle setting, and you'll spot ants, frogs, lizards, snakes, and, of course, tarantulas. Advance reservations are required. Group size is limited to four. No tours are given on rainy nights. ⊠ *Cahuita ✛ 300 m west of bus station at entrance to town* ☎ *8720–3253* 🖾 *$40.*

Tree of Life Wildlife Rescue Center (*El Árbol de Vida*)

NATURE PRESERVE | **FAMILY** | Capuchin and howler monkeys, peccaries, sloths, iguanas, raccoons—they're all here at this wildlife sanctuary just off the Playa Negra road. As much as possible, the

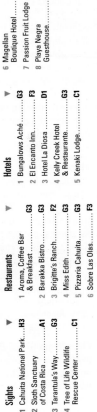

Cahuita

CARIBBEAN SEA

Playa Grande

Playa Negra

Playa Blanca

Plaza Vargas

PLAYA NEGRA

CAHUITA

Ent. Playa Negra

La Unión

Cahuita National Park

TO PUERTO VIEJO
DE TALAMANCA

TO LIMON

36

11

Tortuguero and the Caribbean Coast   CAHUITA

KEY

1 *Exploring Sights*
1 *Restaurants*
1 *Hotels*

| 0 | | 750 feet |
| 0 | | 250 m |

Sights ▶

1 Cahuita National Park....**H3**
2 Sloth Sanctuary
   of Costa Rica.............**A1**
3 Tarantula's Way............**G3**
4 Tree of Life Wildlife
   Rescue Center..............**C1**

Restaurants ▶

1 Aroma, Coffee Bar
   & Breakfast...............**G3**
2 Barakka Bistro............**G3**
3 Brigitte's Ranch..........**F2**
4 Miss Edith................**G3**
5 Pizzeria Cahuita..........**G3**
6 Sobre Las Olas............**F3**

Hotels ▶

1 Bungalows Aché...........**G3**
2 El Encanto Inn...........**F3**
3 Hotel La Diosa...........**D1**
4 Kelly Creek Hotel
   & Restaurante...........**G3**
5 Kenaki Lodge.............**C1**
6 Magellan
   Boutique Hotel..........**D1**
7 Passion Fruit Lodge......**A2**
8 Playa Negra
   Guesthouse..............**F2**

goal is to reintroduce these rescued animals back to nature, although the fragile condition of some means this will be their permanent home. Your admission for an 11 am guided tour supports the good work these folks do. As is the case in such facilities, visitors may not touch or hold the animals. ✉ *3 km (2 miles) north of town at end of Playa Negra road* ☎ *2755–0014* 🌐 *www.treeoflifecostarica.com* 🎟 *$20* 🕓 *Closed Mon., Apr.–June, Sept., and Oct.*

Beaches

Playa Blanca (*White Beach*)
BEACH—SIGHT | Costa Rica's Caribbean coast has no true white-sand beaches, but Cahuita's in-town beach is as close as it gets (*blanca* means "white" in Spanish). Right at the town entrance to the national park, you're a few steps from local eateries. The park's jungle comes right up to the beach's edge, creating one of those postcard-perfect views. The undertow can be strong here; swimmers are more likely to venture out near the center of the beach. Use caution in any case. **Amenities:** food and drink. **Best for:** sunrise; walking. ✉ *Town center.*

Playa Grande
BEACH—SIGHT | Beyond the Atlántida Lodge, Playa Negra's black sand lightens to a dark brown. Whether this constitutes a separate beach or not is open for debate, but the lodgings out here distinguish their stretch of sand as "Playa Grande." You're much farther from town here; the beach feels even more isolated. Do be careful. As with all beaches on this coast, the undertow makes swimming risky. **Amenities:** none. **Best for:** sunrise; walking. ✉ *Cahuita.*

Playa Negra (*Black Beach*)
BEACH—SIGHT | Cahuita's Playa Negra—it's not the same as the beach of the same name in Puerto Viejo de Talamanca—fronts a narrow road heading north out of the town center. Depending on the stretch of sand, it puts you a few steps from eateries. Your fellow beachgoers will likely be surfers. Remember: the waves that make for good surfing conditions cause problems for swimming. Most stretches of black-sand Playa Negra feel isolated. If there aren't visitors around, don't linger. **Amenities:** food and drink. **Best for:** sunrise; surfing; walking. ✉ *Cahuita.*

Restaurants

Aroma, Coffee Bar & Breakfast
$$ | **VEGETARIAN** | Fortify yourself for a day of sightseeing with a vegan breakfast, perhaps banana pancakes or crepes, at this semi-open-air spot. For lunch, dig into a variety of vegan burgers and salads (mango is a favorite) with fruit cheesecakes for dessert. **Known for:** great selection of smoothies; cheery owners; extensive vegan menu, a rarity in Costa Rica. [$] *Average main: $13* ✉ *Cahuita* ✣ *50 m northeast of bus station* ☎ *8808–6445* 🕓 *Closed Sun. No dinner.*

★ **Barakka Bistro**
$$$ | **ITALIAN** | An expat Italian-French couple have fused the cuisines of their respective countries into Cahuita's most stylish and cozy dining spot. Combine a ricotta cannelloni with a croque madame in bechamel sauce, or steak tartare with a variety of bruschettas. **Known for:** innovative blending of two cuisines; macadamia pesto; attentive service. [$] *Average main: $17* ✉ *Cahuita* ✣ *50 m southeast of Coco's Bar* ☎ *2755–0145* 🌐 *www.facebook.com/barakkabistrocahuita* 🕓 *Closed Mon.*

Brigitte's Ranch
$ | **CAFÉ** | Fuel up for the day's activities at this informal, open-air café on the Playa Negra road. A hearty breakfast—served until noon—of banana pancakes and fruit with honey or pineapple jam does the trick. **Known for:** hearty, fortifying breakfasts; American-style omelets; tasty gallo pinto. [$] *Average main: $7* ✉ *Playa*

Negra road, 1½ km (1 mile) from town ☎ 2755–0053 🌐 www.brigittecahuita.com 💳 No credit cards 🕒 No lunch or dinner.

Miss Edith

$ | **CARIBBEAN** | Miss Edith—women in Caribbean communities are addressed as "Miss" regardless of marital status—is revered for her flavorful Caribbean cooking, vegetarian meals, and herbal teas for whatever ails you. She dishes up food (albeit at a slower pace than you might be used to back home) at her semi-open-air restaurant on an easy-to-miss street at the north end of town. Jerk chicken and *rondón,* a fish stew, are specialties (the latter is quite labor-intensive; stop by in the afternoon to see if it will be on the menu that night). **Known for:** jerk chicken; rondón (fish stew); Jesus-themed decor. [$] *Average main: $9* ✉ *75 m east of police station* ☎ *2755–0248* 💳 *No credit cards.*

Pizzeria Cahuita

$$ | **PIZZA** | Pastas and meat entrées are on the menu, but the real draw here is the 30 varieties of thin-crust pizza whipped up and served with style by a gregarious Italian family from Ravenna. The Cuatro Quesos (four cheeses) with mozzarella, Gorgonzola, Parmesan, and fontina is the most popular. **Known for:** casual setting; friendly service; takeout. [$] *Average main: $10* ✉ *50 m east of police station* ☎ *2755–0179* 🕒 *Closed Wed. and Thurs. No lunch weekdays.*

Sobre Las Olas

$$ | **SEAFOOD** | The name means "over the waves," and this is one of the few dining spots in Cahuita perched this close to the shore. Red snapper is the house specialty, but other seafood and pasta dishes are on the menu, too, along with affordable sandwiches and lighter fare. **Known for:** good wine selection; natural fruit juices; terrific ocean views. [$] *Average main: $14* ✉ *Playa Negra road, just north of El Encanto* ☎ *2755–0109* 🕒 *Closed Tues.*

Recycle!

Unfortunately, it's difficult to recycle in most places in Costa Rica, but Cahuita and Puerto Viejo de Talamanca have made it a breeze. Separate and deposit your aluminum cans and glass and plastic beverage bottles in the *Recicaribe* barrels you'll see in either community.

Hotels

Bungalows Aché

$ | **B&B/INN** | Aché has wooden bungalows—three octagonal structures in this case—nestled amid wooded grounds that make the close-by town center seem far away. **Pros:** central location; friendly staff; bargain rates. **Cons:** small rooms; spartan decor; can be difficult to find space. [$] *Rooms from: $50* ✉ *180 m west of national park entrance* ☎ *2755–0119* 🌐 *www.bungalowsache.com* 💳 *No credit cards* 🛏 *2 bungalows* 🍴 *No meals.*

★ **El Encanto Inn**

$$ | **B&B/INN** | Cahuita doesn't get more serene than these lodgings spread out in a garden with an extensive bromeliad collection. **Pros:** friendly owners; good value for what's offered; central location without being right in the heart of things. **Cons:** not for young travelers looking for a scene; friendly dogs on-site, so not a place to go if you dislike canines; some reports of patchy Wi-Fi. [$] *Rooms from: $98* ✉ *200 m west of police station on Playa Negra road* ☎ *2755–0113* 🌐 *www.elencantocahuita.com* 🛏 *8 units* 🍴 *Free Breakfast.*

Hotel La Diosa

$$ | **HOTEL** | Brightly painted stone or wood cabins—most have air-conditioning, a rarity here—are scattered around the grounds at this place on the far north

Kayaking is a popular activity in Tortuguero.

end of Playa Grande. **Pros:** seclusion; a/c available; friendly service. **Cons:** far from sights; small rooms; a car is needed to get around. [$] *Rooms from: $90* ✉ *2 km (1 mile) north of town at end of Playa Negra road* ☎ *2755–0055, 800/854–7761 in North America* 🌐 *www.hotelladiosa.net* 🛏 *10 cabins* 🍴 *Free Breakfast.*

Kelly Creek Hotel & Restaurante

$ | **B&B/INN** | This wonderful budget option in a handsome wooden hotel sits on the creek bank across a short pedestrian bridge from the Cahuita National Park entrance. **Pros:** good value; hearty breakfasts; friendly owner. **Cons:** dark rooms; occasional, but rare, street noise; two-night minimum stay. [$] *Rooms from: $70* ✉ *Next to park entrance* ☎ *2755–0007* 🌐 *www.kellycreekhotel.com* 🛏 *4 rooms* 🍴 *No meals.*

Kenaki Lodge

$$ | **B&B/INN** | The rooms and bungalows at this serene lodge have dark hardwood floors and vaulted ceilings and are decorated with bright tropical colors. **Pros:** quiet seclusion; good value for what's offered; ample parking (a rarity here). **Cons:** far from town and sights; group events may create commotion in dining area; breakfast not included in bungalow prices. [$] *Rooms from: $104* ✉ *Playa Grande, far north end of Playa Negra road* ☎ *2755–0485* 🌐 *www.kenakilodge.com* 🛏 *6 units* 🍴 *No meals; Free Breakfast.*

Magellan Boutique Hotel

$$ | **B&B/INN** | One of Cahuita's most elegant lodgings, this group of bungalows is graced with tile-floor terraces facing a pool and gardens growing on an ancient coral reef. **Pros:** seclusion; scrumptious dinners; a/c in some rooms. **Cons:** far from sights; staff can be too business-like; friendly dogs on-site, so not a place to go if you dislike canines. [$] *Rooms from: $101* ✉ *2 km (1 mile) north of town at end of Playa Negra road* ☎ *2755–0035* 🌐 *www.magellanboutiquehotel.com* 🛏 *6 rooms* 🍴 *Free Breakfast.*

Respecting Costa Rica's Animals

Yes, sloths are adorable. But if you came to Costa Rica with dreams of holding one, think again: the experience of hugging, petting, or offering food to an animal to manipulate it for photos is unlawful (not to mention, they actually hate to be touched by an unfamiliar person). Such irresponsible actions put you at risk—these are still wild animals, after all—and harm the animal's health and viability as they mend for potential rehabilitation into the wild.

If you're visiting one of the country's many animal-rescue centers, remember that every responsible center will turn down any visitor request to hold or pet the animals. Even the workers treating the animals try to limit

tactile contact as much as possible. A few unethical sites allow visitors to touch the animals and snap pics. Do not participate.

In response to the disturbing trend of the "animal selfie" in which visitors try to hold animals or entice them with food into that "perfect" photo op, Costa Rica has even started the hashtag #StopAnimalSelfies on social media to bring a halt to this practice and encourage you to share respectful photos without holding the animals, at a safe distance. Your social-media post will be just as endearing with only the animal in the photo, and you'll know that you helped to keep them safe and healthy.

Passion Fruit Lodge

$$ | **HOTEL** | Five houses, each named for a tropical fruit, congregate on lush, secluded gardens on the highway outside of Cahuita. **Pros:** bright, cheery houses; friendly service; pool (a rarity in these parts). **Cons:** far from the beach; a car is needed to stay here; easy to miss when driving by. $ *Rooms from: $75* ⊠ *5 km (3 miles) north of town on highway* ☎ *8939–9823* ⊕ *passionfruitcolodge.com* ⤶ *5 houses* ❏*Free Breakfast.*

★ Playa Negra Guesthouse

$$ | **HOTEL** | This gracious, Québécois-owned lodging set in lush, hibiscus-strewn gardens has become a Cahuita favorite. **Pros:** stylish surroundings; attentive owners; terrific rates for what's offered. **Cons:** friendly dogs on-site, so not a place to stay if canines aren't your thing; a car is needed to get around; can be difficult to find space. $ *Rooms from: $84* ⊠ *Playa Negro road, 50 m north of soccer field* ☎ *2755–0127* ⊕ *www.playa-negra.cr* ⤶ *4 units* ❏*Free Breakfast.*

Nightlife

Aside from the local bars, Cahuita's nightlife centers on restaurants, all pleasant places to linger over dinner for the evening.

Chao's Paradise

BARS/PUBS | If you're out this way, Chao's makes for a pleasant open-air space for a beer and some seafood and fries. After dark, get here and back by taxi. ⊠ *Playa Negra road, 50 m north of soccer field* ☎ *2755–0284.*

Coco's Bar

BARS/PUBS | Lively reggae, soca, and samba blast weekend evenings from the turquoise Coco's Bar. The assemblage of dogs dozing on its veranda during the day illustrates the rhythm of local life. ⊠ *Main road* ☎ *2755–0437.*

Cocorico

CAFES—NIGHTLIFE | Italian eatery Cocorico shows movies many evenings at 7:30. ⊠ *Main road* ☎ *2755–0409.*

Reggae Bar

BARS/PUBS | As befits the name of the place, reggae music is on tap here a few evenings of the week. You're bound to hear "No Woman, No Cry" and all the other anthems. After dark, take a taxi to and from here. ⊠ *Playa Negra road, 50 m north of soccer field* ☎ *2755–0209* ⊕ *www.facebook.com/reggaebar.cahuita.*

Ricky's Bar

BARS/PUBS | Quieter than Coco's across the street (although if Coco's is hosting live music, you'll hear it from here, too), Ricky's is a good place to kick back with a beer and watch the passing parade on the main street. (The food here is nothing special, though.) It's "Ricky's" or "Rikki's," depending on which sign you look at. ⊠ *Main road.*

Activities

Cahuita is small enough that its tour operators don't focus simply on the town and nearby national park, but instead line up excursions around the region, even as far away as the Tortuguero canals to the north and Bocas del Toro, Panama, to the south.

Brigitte's Ranch

HORSEBACK RIDING | Here you can rent good bikes for $15 per day, as well as take part in half- or full-day horseback-riding excursions. ⊠ *Playa Negra road, 1½ km (1 mile) from town* ☎ *2755–0053* ⊕ *www.brigittecahuita.com* ⊠ *From $45.*

★ The Biologist from Cahuita

GUIDED TOURS | Dutch biologist and longtime resident David Geurds imparts his knowledge in a terrific selection of half-day and evening hiking tours in the area. ⊠ *Cahuita* ☎ *8997–4714* ⊕ *banani-to-tours.jimdofree.com.*

Willie's Tours

HIKING/WALKING | The town's largest tour operator can set you up with a variety of adventures, including rafting, kayaking, hiking the national park, and visiting indigenous reserves for a glimpse into traditional life. Willie's also offers tours that take you farther afield, north to Tortuguero and south to Bocas del Toro, Panama. ⊠ *Main St., 100 m north of Coco's Bar* ☎ *2755–1024* ⊕ *www.willies-tourscostarica.com* ⊠ *From $29.*

Puerto Viejo de Talamanca

16 km (10 miles) south of Cahuita.

This muddy, colorful little town is one of the hottest spots on the international budget-travel circuit, and swarms with backpackers, surfers, and New Agers. For better or for worse, though, Puerto Viejo de Talamanca has outgrown its surfer roots and you'll find plenty of more "grown-up" offerings on the road heading southeast and northwest out of town.

At the last count, some 50 nationalities were represented in this tiny community, and most are united in concern for the environment and orderly development of tourism—few want to see the place become just another Costa Rican resort community. Some locals bemoan the loss of their town's innocence, as drugs and other evils have surfaced, but this is still a fun town to visit, with a great variety of hotels, cabinas, and restaurants in every price range. Unlike some other parts of Costa Rica, no one has been priced out of the market here.

Locals shorten the name to just "Puerto Viejo" (British settlers called the area "Old Harbour") but we use the complete name to avoid confusion with the other Puerto Viejo covered in this chapter: Puerto Viejo de Sarapiquí in northern Costa Rica. (Note that you may also see this Caribbean town referred to as "Puerto Viejo de Limón.") You have access to the beach right in town, and the Salsa Brava, famed in surfers' circles for its pounding waves, is here off the coast, too.

Wildlife-watching in Cahuita National Park

The best strands of Caribbean sand are outside the village: Playa Cocles, Playa Chiquita (technically a series of beaches), and Punta Uva, all dark-sand beaches, line the road heading southeast from town. Playa Negra—not to be confused with the Playa Negra near Cahuita—is a black-sand beach northwest of town. Punta Uva, with fewer hotels and the farthest from the village, sees fewer crowds and more tranquility. Playa Negra shares that distinction, too—for now—but developers have eyed the beach as the next area for expansion.

GETTING HERE AND AROUND

The turnoff to Puerto Viejo de Talamanca is 10 km (6 miles) down the coastal highway south of Cahuita. (The highway then continues southeast to Bribri and Sixaola at the Panamanian border). The village lies another 5 km (3 miles) beyond the turnoff. The paved road passes through town and continues to Playas Cocles and Chiquita and Punta Uva all the way to the village of Manzanillo. "Periodically potholed" describes the condition of the road from the highway into town and as far as Playa Cocles. The newer paved sections beyond Cocles haven't disintegrated (yet). Autotransportes MEPE buses travel from San José's Terminal Atlántico Norte seven times a day—plan on 4½ hours for the trip—and approximately hourly throughout the day from Limón and Cahuita. The town has no actual bus terminal. If you arrive on public transportation, you disembark at a bus shelter strewn with a few beer bottles on the street fronting the beach. (It makes an awful first impression, but this is an enjoyable town, so keep your disappointment in check.) The MEPE ticket office is about a half block away. All buses from San José go into Puerto Viejo de Talamanca; most, though not all, Limón-originating buses do as well, but a couple drop you off on the highway. Check if you board in Limón. You can give yourself a wider selection of times than the six daily San José–Puerto Viejo services. Hourly Grupo Caribeños buses connect San José with Limón, and hourly MEPE buses connect Limón with Puerto

Viejo. The MEPE and Caribeños terminals are one block apart in Limón. Walking could be an option if you're not weighed down with bags and if it's still light out. Unlike MEPE vehicles, Caribeños buses are air-conditioned.

Local buses ply the 15-km (9-mile) paved road between Puerto Viejo and Manzanillo every two hours during the day. Unless your schedule meshes exactly with theirs, you're better off biking or taking a taxi to and from the far-flung beaches along the way. Most taxi service is unofficial here. To be on the safe side, have your hotel or restaurant call one for you. Taxis charge roughly $5 to Playa Negra, $7 to Playa Cocles, $10 to Playa Chiquita, $12 to Punta Uva, and $17 to Manzanillo. Indian-made "tuktuks" provide some Puerto Viejo taxi service. Picture a covered three-wheel auto rickshaw.

You can manage the town center quite easily on foot, though it is dusty in the dry season and muddy when it rains. The main street is, thankfully, paved. Everyone gets around by bike here, and seemingly everyone has one for rent (invariably without a helmet). Quality varies widely, but we recommend renting from Cabinas Grant. Expect to pay $20 per day for a good bike.

BIKE RENTALS Cabinas Grant. ⊠ *100 m south of bus stop* ☎ *2750–0292.*

ESSENTIALS

BANKS/ATMS Banco de Costa Rica. ⊠ *50 m south of bridge at entrance to town* ☎ *2750–0707* ⊕ *www.bancobcr.com.* **Banco Nacional.** ⊠ *25 m south of Correos* ⊕ *www.bncr.fi.cr.*

PHARMACY Farmacia Caribe. ⊠ *Next to Banco de Costa Rica* ☎ *2750–0698.*

POST OFFICE Correos. ⊠ *Next to Banco de Costa Rica* ⊕ *correos.go.cr.*

VISITOR INFORMATION ATEC. (*Talamancan Association of Ecotourism and Conservation*) ⊠ *Across from Restaurant Tamara* ☎ *2750–0398* ⊕ *www.ateccr.org.*

Sights

Ara Manzanillo

NATURE PRESERVE | FAMILY | An ambitious project begun three decades ago has slowly improved the survival prospects for the once-endangered great green (*Ara ambiguus*) and scarlet macaws (*Ara macao*). A daily 3 pm tour of the field station here acquaints you with the breeding and reintroduction into the wild of these colorful birds. Advance reservations are required. ⊠ *Manzanillo* ☎ *8971–1436* ⊕ *www.aramanzanillo.org* 🎟 *$20.*

Chocorart

FARM/RANCH | FAMILY | Cacao once ruled the Talamanca region, but few plantations are left these days. One friendly Swiss couple continues the tradition and shows you the workings of their chocolate plantation on their chocolate tour. Follow the little-known life cycle of this crop from cultivation to processing. There's sampling at the tour's conclusion. Call or email to reserve a tour, given weekdays at 3 pm. Since these folks are Swiss, they can tailor the commentary in German, French, or Italian, in addition to the standard English or Spanish. ⊠ *6 km (4 miles) southeast of Puerto Viejo at Playa Chiquita* ☎ *8866–7493* ⊕ *www.facebook.com/chocorart* 🎟 *$25* ⊘ *Closed weekends.*

Finca la Isla Botanical Garden (*Jardín Botánico Finca la Isla*)

GARDEN | At the Finca la Isla Botanical Garden, you can explore a working tropical-fruit, spice, and ornamental-plant farm. Sloths abound, and you might see a few poison dart frogs. A guided tour (three-person minimum, must be reserved in advance) lasts two hours and includes admission and a glass of the farm's homemade fruit juice. Tours can be arranged in advance on days outside the Friday through Monday opening hours. You get the fruit juice if you wander around on your own, too (a $1 tour book is available in English, Spanish,

French, and German). Watch the demonstration showing how cacao beans are turned into chocolate, and sample some of the product at the end of the tour. ⊠ *½ km (¼ mile) west of Puerto Viejo at Playa Negra* ☎ *8829–4929* ⊕ *www.costaricaorganicsfarm.com* 🗓 *From $6* ⊗ *Closed Tues.–Thurs.*

Gandoca-Manzanillo National Wildlife Refuge (*Refugio Nacional de Vida Silvestre Gandoca-Manzanillo*)

NATURE PRESERVE | The refuge stretches along the southeastern coast from southeast of Puerto Viejo de Talamanca to the town of Manzanillo and on to the Panamanian border. Its limits are not clearly defined. Because of weak laws governing the conservation of refuges and the rising value of coastal land in this area, Gandoca-Manzanillo is less pristine than Cahuita National Park and continues to be developed. (Development thins out the farther you get from Puerto Viejo and the closer you get to the village of Manzanillo.) However, the refuge still has plenty of rain forest, *orey* (a dark tropical wood) and *jolillo* (a species of palm) swamps, 10 km (6 miles) of beach where four species of turtle lay their eggs, and almost 3 square km (1 square mile) of *cativo* (a tropical hardwood) forest and coral reef. The Gandoca estuary is a nursery for tarpon and a wallowing spot for crocodiles and caimans. ⊠ *15 km (9 miles) southeast of Puerto Viejo de Talamanca, Gandoca-Manzanillo National Wildlife Refuge* ☎ *2750–0398 for ATEC, 1192 national parks hotline in Costa Rica* 🗓 *Free.*

Green Iguana Foundation (*Fundación Iguana Verde*)

NATURE PRESERVE | **FAMILY** | You'll no doubt see Costa Rica's ubiquitous iguanas scurrying across roads on your travels around the country. A project of the nearby Tree House Lodge acquaints you with the lives of these fascinating animals. The green iguana—one of eight species and the most common found on the Caribbean coast—grows up to 6 feet in length, with

two-thirds of that span consisting of the tail. The goal here is the breeding and raising of iguanas with their release into the wild in the adjoining Gandoca-Manzanillo Wildlife Refuge. Admission goes to support that work. ⊠ *Punta Uva* ☎ *2750–0706* ⊕ *www.iguanaverde.com* 🗓 *$15.*

★ **Jaguar Rescue Center** (*Centro de Rescate Jaguar*)

NATURE PRESERVE | **FAMILY** | Many regard a visit to the Jaguar Rescue Center as the highlight of their trip to Puerto Viejo de Talamanca. The name is a bit misleading. The original rescued animal here was an orphaned, injured jaguar cub that ultimately did not survive. His memory lives on in the facility's name, even if there are no other jaguars on-site. Primarily howler monkeys, sloths, and lots of snakes make up the charges of the capable staff here. The goal, of course, is to return the animals to the wild, but those that are too frail are assured a permanent home here. Your admission fee for the 90-minute tour (English or Spanish) helps fund the rescue work. (Tours in French, German, or Dutch can be arranged with advance notice.) Touching the animals is not permitted, for your safety as well as theirs. A two-hour tour, morning or evening, at Punta Uva lets you participate in the release of rehabilitated animals. ⊠ *3 km (2 miles) southeast of Puerto Viejo, between Playa Cocles and Playa Chiquita* ☎ *2750–0710* ⊕ *www.jaguarrescue.foundation* 🗓 *From $22* ⊗ *Closed Sun.*

 Beaches

Playa Chiquita

BEACH—SIGHT | Nothing against Puerto Viejo, but the farther you get from town, the quieter things get—to put it bluntly, the "riff-raff" factor lessens out here. The downside is that you'll find fewer visitors congregating on dark-sand Chiquita, and isolated stretches of beach can spell trouble. Stay only if you see a lot of other people around. The undertow is strong out here. Swim at your own risk,

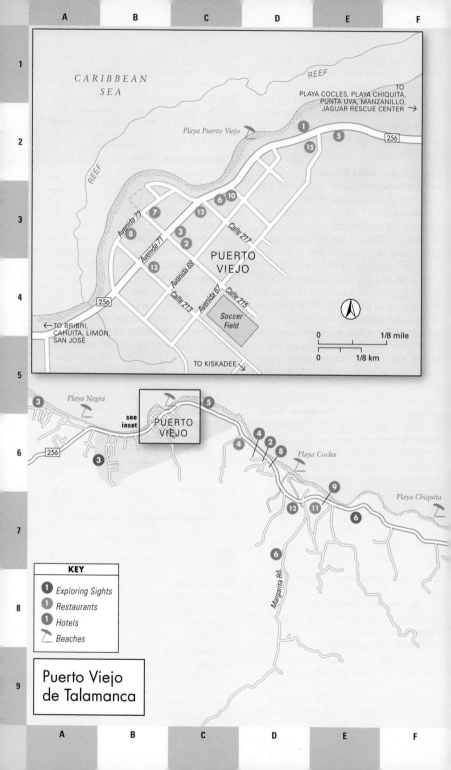

0 ——— 3,000 feet
0 ——— 1,000 m

C A R I B B E A N

S E A

Sights ▼

1 Ara Manzanillo **I8**
2 Chocorart **G7**
3 Finca la Isla Botanical
  Garden **A6**
4 Gandoca-Manzanillo National
  Wildlife Refuge **I9**
5 Green Iguana Foundation **G7**
6 Jaguar Rescue Center **E7**

Restaurants ▼

1 Amimodo **D2**
2 Bread & Choclate **C3**
3 Café Viejo **C3**
4 Caribeans **C6**
5 Cheeky Monkey **E2**
6 Chile Rojo **C3**
7 Como en Mi Casa **B3**
8 Dread Nut Coffee **B3**
9 El Refugio Grill **I7**
10 Koki Beach **C3**
11 La Pecora Nera **E7**
12 Restaurant Tamara **C3**
13 Sel & Sucre **B4**
14 Selvin's **G7**
15 Stashus Con Fusion **E2**

Hotels ▼

1 Almonds & Corals **J8**
2 Azania Bungalows **D6**
3 Banana Azul **A5**
4 Cariblue Beach & Jungle
  Resort **D6**
5 Escape Caribeño **C5**
6 Geckoes Lodge **D7**
7 Korrigan Lodge **H7**
8 La Costa de Papito **D6**
9 Le Caméléon **E7**
10 Nature Observatorio **J9**
11 Pachamama Jungle
  River Lodge **H7**
12 Physis Caribbean B&B **D7**
13 Tree House Lodge **G7**

Punta
Uva

Paraiso Rd

256

Gandoca Manzanillo
National Wildlife Refuge

G H I J

preferably in company, and don't venture out too far. **Amenities:** none. **Best for:** sunrise; surfing; walking. ✉ *6 km (4 miles) southeast of Puerto Viejo de Talamanca.*

Playa Cocles

BEACH—SIGHT | The sand gets a bit lighter and the crowd slightly more upscale—it is still Puerto Viejo, though—a couple of kilometers outside of town. Fewer vendors will pester you here than in the town itself, and it'll be mostly you and other travelers. (If there's nobody around, don't linger. There's always safety in numbers.) As with all Puerto Viejo area beaches, the undertow can be strong on Cocles. Never venture out too far. **Amenities:** food and drink. **Best for:** partiers; sunrise; surfing, walking. ✉ *Puerto Viejo de Talamanca* ✣ *2 km (1 mile) southeast of Puerto Viejo de Talamanca.*

Playa Negra (*Black Beach*)

BEACH—SIGHT | Not to be confused with Cahuita's beach of the same name, Puerto Viejo's black-sand Playa Negra lies close to town but is relatively undeveloped. That situation is expected to change in coming years, but for now you'll likely have this stretch of sand north of town to yourself. While this sounds idyllic, remember that there's always safety in numbers on beaches in this area. Be careful about going into the water; the undertow can be strong. **Amenities:** none. **Best for:** sunrise; surfing; walking. ✉ *1 km (½ mile) north of Puerto Viejo de Talamanca.*

Playa Puerto Viejo

BEACH—SIGHT | The clutter of the unnamed in-town beach epitomizes Puerto Viejo. Locals gather here. The strong undertow makes swimming risky along this stretch, but surfers delight in the consistently good waves. The upside is that you're just a few steps from the in-town restaurants. **Amenities:** food and drink. **Best for:** partiers; sunrise; surfing; walking. ✉ *In town.*

Punta Uva

BEACH—SIGHT | The area's most beautiful beach—with dark sand like all area strands—lies a long way from Puerto Viejo and offers splendid isolation from the commotion of town. *Uva* means "grape" in Spanish, and the beach gets its name from the sea-grape trees found out here. A few nearby restaurants can take care of your culinary needs. As always here, there's the undertow to contend with. Be careful and never venture too far out into the water. **Amenities:** food and drink. **Best for:** sunrise; surfing; walking. ✉ *9 km (5½ miles) south of Puerto Viejo de Talamanca.*

🍴 Restaurants

Amimodo

$$ | ITALIAN | The name translates to "my way," and the exuberant Italian owners really do it their way, combining the cuisine of their native northern Italy with Caribbean flavors. Antipasto might be classic bruschetta or *jamón de tiburón* (shark ham) with avocado dressing, and ravioli might be stuffed with tropical shrimp, pineapple, and curry, with avocado sauce on the side. **Known for:** ever-changing creative menu; tropical veranda setting; exuberant service. [$] *Average main: $14* ✉ *200 m east of Lazy Mon Beach Café (aka Stanford's)* ☎ *2750–0257.*

Bread & Chocolate

$ | CAFÉ | The takeaway line for brownies forms at the gate before this place opens at 6:30 am. Stick around, though, for a hearty breakfast of cinnamon-oatmeal pancakes, French toast, or creamy scrambled eggs, washed down with a cup of French-press coffee. **Known for:** jerk chicken; fresh-baked goods; homemade sauces. [$] *Average main: $8* ✉ *50 m south of post office* ☎ *2750–0723* 🌐 *www.breadandchocolatecr.com* 💳 *No credit cards* 🕘 *Closed Mon. and Tues. No dinner.*

Café Viejo

$$ | ITALIAN | This is the hot place to see and be seen on Puerto Viejo's main drag. The owners learned to cook at the knee of their Italian grandmother back in Rimini, and have concocted a menu, several pages long, of pizzas and handmade pastas. **Known for:** traditional Italian cooking; impressive pizza variety; place to view Puerto Viejo's passing parade. ⓢ *Average main: $12* ✉ *Across from ATEC* ☎ *2750–0817* ⊕ *www.cafeviejo. com* ⊗ *Closed Tues. No lunch.*

Cheeky Monkey

$$ | PIZZA | Flatbread pizza is the name of the game at this dining spot, which you'll see as you head out of town toward Playa Cocles. The folks here come up with some innovative combinations, such as date and gorgonzola or *camote* (a Central American sweet potato) with jalapeño and chimichurri sauce, in addition to more standard pizzas. **Known for:** inventive pizza toppings; homemade ice cream; good cocktail selection. ⓢ *Average main: $14* ✉ *Puerto Viejo de Talamanca* ✛ *300 m east of Lazy Mon Beach Café (aka Stanford's)* ☎ *2750–0530* ⊕ *www.cheekymonkeycr.com.*

Chile Rojo

$$ | THAI | Not a thing about the name or furnishings reflects its Thai and Middle Eastern offerings, but this restaurant does a brisk business. Choose from Thai grilled tuna, falafel, hummus, samosas, or sushi. **Known for:** Costa Rican twist on Asian cuisine; cool second-floor dining terrace; friendly, leisurely service. ⓢ *Average main: $12* ✉ *Across from ATEC* ☎ *2750–0421.*

Como en Mi Casa

$ | VEGETARIAN | Everything is made on-site at this small second-floor café. Start off the day with an order of vegan pancakes or ease into lunch with veggie burritos and a tomato, oregano, and olive oil bruschetta. **Known for:** fresh homemade ingredients; friendly service; many gluten-free offerings. ⓢ *Average main: $9* ✉ *100 m east of bus stop* ☎ *8674–2853* ⊕ *www.facebook.com/ comoenmicasaartcafe* ▭ *No credit cards* ⊗ *Closed Tues. No dinner.*

Dread Nut Coffee

$ | CARIBBEAN | An easy-to-miss Caribbean-style clapboard house near the bus stop makes a great place to fortify yourself for a day of sightseeing. The industrious staff here start the day with omelets and freshly baked banana bread, bagels, and pastries, and lunch gives way to a variety of sandwiches—you choose from ingredients to construct your own. **Known for:** homemade ice cream; cool tropical vibe; organic coffee. ⓢ *Average main: $6* ✉ *50 m east of bus stop* ☎ *8995–6103* ⊗ *No dinner* ▭ *No credit cards.*

★ El Refugio Grill

$$$ | ARGENTINE | This tiny rancho-style restaurant in the middle of a forest clearing is one of Costa Rica's top Argentine restaurants. The menu varies throughout the year and might consist of beef in chimichurri sauce, spinach crepes, curried shrimp, mussels in white wine, or *milanesa de corvina* (sea-bass cutlet). **Known for:** intimate and secluded forest setting; hearty Argentine menu; homemade guacamole and chips. ⓢ *Average main: $20* ✉ *Puerto Viejo de Talamanca* ☎ *2759–9007* ⊗ *Closed Wed. No lunch* ▭ *No credit cards.*

Safety

Swimming alone at the beach is never safe, and walking alone on the beach here is not safe either. The forest comes right up to the edge of many of the stretches of sand. Stick to areas where other people congregate, and you can have a safe, secure time in Puerto Viejo.

Koki Beach

$$ | **ECLECTIC** | This slightly elevated terrace restaurant with colorful furniture (and colorful characters) is a great place to watch Puerto Viejo's parade of evening passersby and the ocean waves lapping on the beach across the street. The mostly surf-and-turf menu means lots of shrimp and sea bass and lots of beef and chicken, all served on or off skewers according to your preference. **Known for:** live music; good drink selection; place to see and be seen. [$] *Average main: $13* ✉ *100 m west of Lazy Mon Beach Café (aka Stanford's)* ☎ *2750–0902* 🌐 *kokibeach.blogspot.com* ⏲ *Closed Mon. No lunch.*

★ **La Pecora Nera**

$$$ | **ITALIAN** | There's a lot more to choose from than you'll see on the sparse-looking menu at this roadside Italian restaurant. You'll be surprised at all the additional light Tuscan entrées, appetizers, and desserts the chef-owner has concocted that day. **Known for:** innovative Italian menu; exuberant owner; leisurely dining experience. [$] *Average main: $24* ✉ *3 km (2 miles) southeast of town at Playa Cocles* ☎ *2750–0490* ⏲ *Closed Mon. No lunch.*

Restaurant Tamara

$$ | **CARIBBEAN** | Puerto Viejo's first restaurant still dishes up tasty, authentic Caribbean food, like fresh fish or chicken in Caribbean sauce. In the nondescript indoor seating area, you're cooled by a fan and entertained by TV; the outdoor seating area has a palpable Jamaican motif and is a great place for people-watching. **Known for:** great people-watching; solid Caribbean menu; reggae music. [$] *Average main: $11* ✉ *Across from ATEC* ☎ *2750–0148* ⏲ *Closed Tues. May–Nov.*

Sel & Sucre

$ | **FRENCH** | The *sel* (salt) in this restaurant's name reflects the ham, chicken, spinach, goat cheese, and roasted almonds you'll find as ingredients in a huge selection of crepes. *Sucre* (sugar) shows up in the sweet versions of crepes, with the Grand Marnier a special standout. Light side salads, waffles, and cheese fondue round out the menu. **Known for:** cheese fondue; gourmet coffee; fruit smoothies. [$] *Average main: $9* ✉ *120 m south of bus stop* ☎ *2750–0636* 🌐 *www.seletsucrecr.com* 💳 *No credit cards* ⏲ *Closed Mon.*

Selvin's

$$ | **CARIBBEAN** | Blanca, the owner of this longtime standby at Punta Uva, cooks up a menu of rondón, rice and beans, lobster, shrimp, and chicken with sweet mole sauce. The cool breezes of the seaside setting could not be more pleasant. **Known for:** hearty Caribbean cooking; friendly service; irregular hours. [$] *Average main: $13* ✉ *7 km (4½ miles) southeast of town at Punta Uva* ☎ *2750–0664* 🌐 *www.selvinpuntauva.com* ⏲ *Closed Mon.–Wed.*

★ **Stashus con Fusion**

$$ | **ECLECTIC** | This restaurant epitomizes Puerto Viejo: lively, organic, popular, but confident enough not to seek trendiness. Ordering is by sauces: Thai peanut, Indonesian-Caribbean curry, Mexican chipotle, Jamaican jerk-style, or Malaysian-guayaba curry, which is served on vegetables, chicken, shrimp, or fish (marlin or tuna). **Known for:** live music; mix-and-match menu; organic offerings. [$] *Average main: $13* ✉ *200 m south of Lazy Mon Beach Café (aka Stanford's)* ☎ *2750–0530* ⏲ *Closed Wed. No lunch.*

☕ Coffee and Quick Bites

Caribeans

$ | **CAFÉ** | At first glance, this small café could use a spelling lesson, but since Caribeans deals in coffee and chocolate, the play on words is apt. Treat yourself to a latte, mocha, or coconut cappuccino, all made from organic, fair-trade coffee from the Turrialba region in the far-eastern Central Valley, and roasted here. **Known for:**

Calm waters over the reef just off Punta Uva Beach near Puerto Viejo de Talamanca

organic, fair-trade coffee; locally roasted beans; coconut cappuccino. $ *Average main: $9* ✉ *2 km (1 mile) southeast of town at Playa Cocles* ☎ *2750–0504* ⊕ *www.caribeanscr.com* ▭ *No credit cards* ☾ *Closed Tues.*

 Hotels

Almonds & Corals (*Almendros y Corales*)
$$ | **RESORT** | Hidden in a beachfront jungle within the Gandoca-Manzanillo Wildlife Refuge, Almonds & Corals features scattered bungalows raised on stilts and linked by boardwalks lighted by kerosene lamps. **Pros:** rustic comfort; lots of activities; cool jungle surroundings. **Cons:** far from sights; need a car to stay here; could use a bit of upkeep. $ *Rooms from: $130* ✉ *Near end of road to Manzanillo, Gandoca-Manzanillo National Wildlife Refuge* ☎ *2759–9056, 2271–3000 in San José* ⊕ *www.almondsandcorals.com* ⤳ *24 bungalows* †◯† *Free Breakfast.*

Azania Bungalows
$$ | **B&B/INN** | Ten thatch-roof A-frame bungalows are spread around Azania's ample gardens, and each sleeps four. **Pros:** good value; good Argentine restaurant; friendly service. **Cons:** difficult to make reservations; bungalows are dark inside; mosquito netting provided is necessary. $ *Rooms from: $105* ✉ *1½ km (1 mile) southeast of town at Playa Cocles* ☎ *2750–0540* ⊕ *www.azania-costarica.com* ⤳ *10 bungalows* †◯† *Free Breakfast.*

Banana Azul
$$ | **RESORT** | Hardwood furnishings are abundant at this gay-friendly (but by no means exclusive) hotel at the secluded far end of Playa Negra. **Pros:** friendly management and staff; seclusion (set away from hubbub of town); great ocean views. **Cons:** no kids allowed, so not an option for families; best to have a car to stay here; can be difficult to find space. $ *Rooms from: $135* ✉ *1½ km (1 mile) north of Puerto Viejo at end of Playa Negra* ☎ *2750–2035, 305/846–8220*

⊕ www.bananaazul.com ↝ 12 rooms
⫿◎⫿ Free Breakfast.

★ Cariblue Beach & Jungle Resort

$$ | HOTEL | The youthful Italian owners came here to surf years ago, stayed on, and built a lodging that combines refinement with that hip Puerto Viejo vibe in exactly the right proportions. **Pros:** friendly owners; good restaurant; a/c. **Cons:** ideal to have a car to stay here; can be difficult to make reservations; can be difficult to find a parking space. $ Rooms from: $117 ⊠ 2 km (1 mile) southeast of town at Playa Cocles ☎ 2750–0035, 305/749–5269 in North America ⊕ www.cariblue.com ↝ 43 rooms ⫿◎⫿ Free Breakfast.

Escape Caribeño

$$ | B&B/INN | The wonderfully friendly Italian owners—who treat you like family—are what make this place, with immaculate hardwood bungalows lining a pleasant garden amply populated with hummingbirds, just outside town. **Pros:** central location without being right in town; gregarious owners; friendly staff. **Cons:** some rooms are small; spartan in some places; some rooms get noise from the road. $ Rooms from: $99 ⊠ 400 m southeast of Lazy Mon Beach Café (aka Stanford's) ☎ 2750–0103 ⊕ www.escapecaribeno.com ↝ 14 bungalows ⫿◎⫿ No meals.

★ Geckoes Lodge

$$$ | B&B/INN | Impeccable service gives this place an edge among the area's handful of set-back-in-the-woods lodgings, and the Wi-Fi, private plunge pool, and barbecue that come with each house are unexpected touches in a setting such as this. **Pros:** wonderful, personalized service; lush, sumptuous surroundings; careful attention to environment. **Cons:** can be difficult to find; only two accommodations; best to have a car to stay here. $ Rooms from: $240 ⊠ 3 km (2 miles) southeast of town and 1 km (½ mile) inland at Playa Cocles ☎ 2750–0908 ⊕ www.geckoeslodge.com ↝ 2 houses ⫿◎⫿ No meals.

Korrigan Lodge

$$ | B&B/INN | Four octagonal wood bungalows are scattered around the secluded wooded property, with its wonderfully cool surroundings (no air-conditioning is needed). **Pros:** lush, green setting; attentive service; great rates for offerings. **Cons:** can be difficult to find; dogs on-site, so not a place to stay if you dislike canines; best to have a car to stay here. $ Rooms from: $115 ⊠ Punta Uva, 8 km (5 miles) south of Puerto Viejo de Talamanca ☎ 2759–9103 ⊕ www.korriganlodge.com ↝ 4 bungalows ⫿◎⫿ Free Breakfast.

La Costa de Papito

$$ | HOTEL | Papito's raised cabins extend back into the property's wooded grounds and are furnished with whimsical, bright, tropical-blue-and-zebra-stripe prints. **Pros:** good value; friendly owner; offers surfing lessons. **Cons:** need a car to stay here; some noise from bar area; can be difficult to find space. $ Rooms from: $112 ⊠ 2 km (1 mile) southeast of town at Playa Cocles ☎ 2750–0080 ⊕ www.lacostadepapito.com ↝ 13 cabins ⫿◎⫿ No meals.

Le Caméléon

$$$$ | HOTEL | This boutique hotel fronting Playa Cocles is decidedly un–Puerto Viejo in its luxury, but if you're in the mood for a splurge here on the coast, this is the spot. **Pros:** stylish luxury; attentive staff; many amenities. **Cons:** such luxury might seem out of place in Puerto Viejo; expensive; pets accepted, which may not appeal to some visitors. $ Rooms from: $275 ⊠ Playa Cocles, 200 m east of soccer field ☎ 2750–3096 ⊕ www.lecameleonhotel.com ↝ 23 rooms ⫿◎⫿ Free Breakfast.

Nature Observatorio

$$$$ | B&B/INN | If you're looking for some "Guess where we stayed!" bragging rights following your return from Costa Rica, this lodging option high in a tree provides them. **Pros:** definitely has the "wow" factor; the ultimate in seclusion; platform can sleep up to six people. **Cons:**

not for those with fear of heights; cannot come and go as you please; hoisting yourself to the platform requires physical strength. $ Rooms from: $460 ☒ South of Manzanillo village, Gandoca-Manzanillo National Wildlife Refuge ☎ 8628–2663, 647/344–5843 in North America ⊕ www. natureobservatorio.com ⌁ 1 platform ⦿ All-inclusive.

Pachamama Jungle River Lodge

$$ | **B&B/INN** | Though still within sight of the Puerto Viejo–Manzanillo road, this French-owned place delivers a get-away-from-it-all nature experience within the confines of the Gandoca-Manzanillo Wildlife Refuge at a fraction of the cost of other Costa Rican eco-lodges. **Pros:** wonderful seclusion; friendly owners; hearty breakfasts. **Cons:** far from sights; need a car to stay here; can be difficult to find. $ Rooms from: $90 ☒ 9 km (5½ miles) southeast of town at Punta Uva ☎ 6482–4685 ⊕ www.pachamamacaribe. com ▭ No credit cards ⌁ 5 units ⦿ Free Breakfast.

★ **Physis Caribbean B&B**

$$ | **B&B/INN** | If you want to experience the area's well-known vibe but have outgrown Puerto Viejo's backpacker digs, this lodging owned by a fun couple is the ticket. **Pros:** hip, knowledgeable owners; impeccable service; immaculate rooms. **Cons:** friendly dogs on-site, so not ideal if you dislike canines; one room is on the small side; may be a little too hip for some visitors. $ Rooms from: $96 ☒ 1½ km (1 mile) southeast of town at Playa Cocles ☎ 2750–0941 ⊕ www.physiscaribbean.net ⌁ 4 rooms ⦿ Free Breakfast.

Tree House Lodge

$$$ | **HOTEL** | This lodging complex among forested ground contains six large, stylish houses, all at ground level, one of which is built around a tree (that's the Tree House). **Pros:** attention to style in furnishings; romantic seclusion; unique architecture. **Cons:** far from sights; easiest to stay here if you have a car; a bit on the pricey side. $ Rooms from: $200

☒ Punta Uva ☎ 2750–0706 ⊕ www.cos-taricatreehouse.com ⌁ 6 units ⦿ Free Breakfast.

Nightlife

The distinction between dining spot and nightspot blurs as the evening progresses, as many restaurants become pleasant places to linger after dinner. You'll also find bars with live music on certain nights. The town's main drag is packed with pedestrians, bicycles, and a few cars most evenings, the block between Café Viejo and Hot Rocks getting the most action. Wander around; something is bound to entice you. Be aware that some of the strictly local hangouts get pretty rough around the edges at night. The Lazy Mon Beach Café, which everyone knows by its former name, Stanford's, is used as a landmark for finding addresses on the road heading out of town toward Playa Cocles, but it's one of those rough places. We recommend against it. ■ **TIP→ When out after dark, ask a staff member at the restaurant, bar, or club to call you a taxi when you're ready to call it an evening.**

BARS

BriBri Springs Brewery

BREWPUBS/BEER GARDENS | One of a handful of Costa Rican microbreweries has set up shop on Playa Negra and serves up eight brews, some year-round, some seasonal. Brewery tours are offered daily at 4:20 pm. ☒ Kaya's Place, 200 m north of town on Playa Negra, Cahuita ☎ 2750–0690, 802/489–0217 in North America ⊕ www.bribrispringsbrewery.com.

Hot Rocks

BARS/PUBS | A wonderful breeze wafts through this huge, semi-open-air U-shape bar just off the beach. Nights are dedicated variously to bingo, karaoke, live music, and open-mic performances. ☒ 50 m east of ATEC.

Crossing into Panama via Sixaola

Costa Rica's sleepy border post at Sixaola fronts Guabito, Panama's equally quiet border crossing, 44 km (26 miles) south of the turnoff to Puerto Viejo de Talamanca. Both are merely collections of banana-plantation stilt houses and a few stores and bars; neither has any lodging or dining options, but this is a much more low-key crossing into Panama than the busy border post at Paso Canoas on the Pan-American Highway near the Pacific coast. If you've come this far, you're likely headed to **Bocas del Toro**, the real attraction in northwestern Panama. This archipelago of 68 islands continues the Afro-Caribbean and indigenous themes seen on Costa Rica's Atlantic coast, and has opportunities for diving, snorkeling, swimming, and wildlife viewing. The larger islands are home to a growing selection of hotels and restaurants—everything from funky to fabulous. Boats at Almirante, Panama, on the mainland 36 km (22 mi) from the border, transport you to the islands.

If you decide to stay overnight in "Bocas," you'll likely base yourself on Isla Colón, the main island. You'll find the best dining and lodging selections here in Bocas Town, (Picture Puerto Viejo de Talamanca, but with paved streets and not quite so much clutter.) More secluded accommodation has sprung up in recent years on some of the outer islands, and there's something undeniably cool about bopping from island to island in one of the motorized launches that serve as the archipelago's taxi system.

Tips:

■ Locals appear to cross the border at will in both directions. You may not do so. Go through official passport formalities.

■ Costa Rican rental vehicles may not exit the country.

■ Panama is one hour later than Costa Rica. Set your watch ahead.

■ Panama uses the U.S. dollar as its currency, but calls it the balboa. No one will accept or exchange your Costa Rican colones.

Puerto Viejo Wine Bar (*Bar de Vinos*)
WINE BARS—NIGHTLIFE | The bar's pretty, semi-open-air setting with lots of greenery makes a nice place to sip wine and nosh on *tapas* (Spanish-style appetizers). ⊠ *Puerto Viejo de Talamanca* ✛ *3 km (2 mi) southeast of Puerto Viejo between Playa Cocles and Playa Chiquita* ☎ *8584–3234* ⊕ *www.puertoviejowinebar.com.*

Tasty Waves Cantina
BARS/PUBS | Tuesday is $2 taco night at the lively, sometimes rowdy, Tasty Waves Cantina. Movies get under way at 7:30 pm on Monday and occasionally

other nights of the week as well. ⊠ *Playa Cocles, 1 km (½ mile) southeast of town* ☎ *2750–0507* ⊕ *www.facebook.com/TastyWavesCantina.*

LIVE MUSIC
Stashus con Fusion
MUSIC CLUBS | You can hear live music many Saturday evenings at this organic-food restaurant. ⊠ *200 m south of Lazy Mon Beach Café (aka Stanford's)* ☎ *2750–0530.*

🎩 Shopping

Vendors set up stands at night on the beach road heading out of town toward Playa Cocles, cheap jewelry being the prime fare. But the town counts a couple of honest-to-goodness souvenir shops, too.

Feria Agrícola

OUTDOOR/FLEA/GREEN MARKETS | Puerto Viejo's Saturday-morning farmers' market is a good place to stock up on fresh fruits and veggies for that weekend beach picnic. It takes place in a building just south of the bus stop. ✉ *50 m south of bus stop* ☎ *2750–0883.*

Luluberlu

CRAFTS | Puerto Viejo's nicest shop sells a wonderful selection of local indigenous carvings—balsa and *chonta* wood are especially popular—as well as jewelry, paintings, and ceramics by 30 artists from the region. Prices run a tad higher here than other places around town, but you're assured of good quality. ✉ *200 m south and 50 m east of bus stop* ☎ *2750–0394* ⊕ *www.facebook.com/luluberlugaleria.*

Tienda del Mar

CLOTHING | Really two stores in one, Tienda del Mar sprawls around a street corner in the center of town and specializes in bright, colorful batik clothing of all sizes, as well as more run-of-the-mill T-shirts, sandals, wood carvings, and postcards. ✉ *Next to Restaurant Tamara* ☎ *2750–0762.*

Wanderlust

CLOTHING | This shop near the bus stop offers a good selection of locally made crafts and colorful clothing. ✉ *Puerto Viejo de Talamanca* ✛ *50 m southeast of bus stop* ☎ *8310–6418.*

Caution

The conditions that make the Caribbean so popular among surfers spell danger for swimmers. A few drownings occur each year. Strong riptides can pull you out to sea, even in waist-deep water, before you realize what's happening. Never swim alone in these parts—good advice anywhere.

🏃 Activities

TOUR OPERATORS

As in Cahuita, tour operators and outfitters here can set up tours and activities anywhere on the south Caribbean coast.

ATEC (*Talamancan Association of Ecotourism and Conservation*)

TOUR—SPORTS | Tours with ATEC have an environmental or cultural bent: rain-forest hikes, coral-reef snorkeling trips, fishing trips, bird-watching tours, night walks, adventure treks, dance lessons, and Afro-Caribbean or indigenous-culture walks—tours to the nearby Kekoldi indigenous reserve are especially popular. Local organizations and wildlife refuges receive 15% to 20% of ATEC's proceeds. ✉ *Across from Restaurant Tamara* ☎ *2750–0398* ⊕ *www.ateccr.org* ✉ *From $45.*

Terraventuras

TOUR—SPORTS | This well-established operator can lead you around Puerto Viejo de Talamanca and Cahuita, or take you on excursions to Tortuguero, the Gandoca-Manzanillo Wildlife Refuge, and Bocas del Toro in Panama. It also rents good-quality surfboards, bicycles, boogie boards, and snorkeling gear. ✉ *100 m south of bus stop* ☎ *2750–0750* ⊕ *www.terraventuras.com* ✉ *From $55.*

RAFTING

Exploradores Outdoors

WHITE-WATER RAFTING | Rafting excursions lie about two hours away, but one San José–based outfitter has an office here. Exploradores Outdoors is highly regarded and has one- and two-day excursions on the Pacuare River, with a pickup point here or in San José and the option to start in one place and be dropped off at the other. The outfitter also offers sea-kayaking excursions off the coast of the Gandoca-Manzanillo Wildlife Refuge. ✉ *100 m east of Lazy Mon Beach Café (aka Stanford's)* ☎ *2750–2020, 2222–6262 in San José, 646/205–0828 in North America* ⊕ *www.exploradoresoutdoors. com* 🛶 *From $59.*

SURFING

Surfing is the name of the game in Puerto Viejo, for everyone from newbies to Kelly Slaters. The best conditions are late December through March, but there's action all year. Longtime surfers compare the south Caribbean with Hawaii, but without the "who do you think you are?" attitude. There are a number of breaks here, most famously **Salsa Brava,** which translates to "wild sauce." It breaks fairly far offshore and requires maneuvering past some tricky currents and a shallow reef. Hollow and primarily right-breaking, Salsa Brava is one gnarly wave when it gets big. If it gets *too* big, or not big enough, check out the breaks at Punta Uva, Punta Cocles, or Playa Chiquita. Boogie boarders and bodysurfers can also dig the beach-break waves at various points along this tantalizingly beautiful coast.

Rocking J's

SURFING | If you've always wanted to try surfing, consider the friendly 90-minute surf school ($40) offered through Rocking Js hostel. They'll start you out with a small wave near the bus stop. A two-hour private lesson will run you $60. You can also rent equipment here. ✉ *Rockin' J's hostel, 1 km (½ mile) southeast of Lazy Mon Beach Café (aka Stanford's)* ☎ *2750–0665* ⊕ *www.rockingjs.com.*

Index

524

Photo Credits

Notes

Notes

Fodor's ESSENTIAL COSTA RICA

Publisher: Stephen Horowitz, *General Manager*

Editorial: Douglas Stallings, *Editorial Director*; Jill Fergus, Jacinta O'Halloran, Amanda Sadlowski, *Senior Editors*; Kayla Becker, Alexis Kelly, Rachael Roth, *Editors*

Design: Tina Malaney, *Director of Design and Production*; Jessica Gonzalez, *Graphic Designer*; Mariana Tabares, *Design and Production Intern*

Production: Jennifer DePrima, *Editorial Production Manager*; Elyse Rozelle, *Senior Production Editor*; Monica White, *Production Editor*

Maps: Rebecca Baer, *Senior Map Editor*; David Lindroth, Mark Stroud (Moon Street Cartography), *Cartographers*

Photography: Viviane Teles, *Senior Photo Editor;* Namrata Aggarwal, Ashok Kumar, Carl Yu, *Photo Editors;* Rebecca Rimmer, *Photo Intern*

Business and Operations: Chuck Hoover, *Chief Marketing Officer*; Robert Ames, *Group General Manager*; Devin Duckworth, *Director of Print Publishing*; Victor Bernal, *Business Analyst*

Public Relations and Marketing: Joe Ewaskiw, *Senior Director Communications and Public Relations*

Fodors.com: Jeremy Tarr, *Editorial Director;* Rachael Levitt, *Managing Editor*

Technology: Jon Atkinson, *Director of Technology;* Rudresh Teotia, *Lead Developer*; Jacob Ashpis, *Content Operations Manager*

Writers: Jeffrey Van Fleet, Rachel White

Editor: Kayla Becker

Production Editor: Monica White

3rd Edition

ISBN 978-1-64097-320-6

ISSN 2578–3068

Library of Congress Control Number 2018950371

SPECIAL SALES
This book is available at special discounts for bulk purchases for sales promotions or premiums. For more information, e-mail SpecialMarkets@fodors.com.

PRINTED IN THE UNITED STATES OF AMERICA

10 9 8 7 6 5 4 3 2 1

About Our Writers

San José–based freelance writer and pharmacist **Jeffrey Van Fleet** has spent the better part of the last two decades enjoying Costa Rica's long rainy seasons and Wisconsin's cold winters. (Most people would try to do it the other way around.) He saw his first resplendent quetzal, that bird-watcher's Holy Grail, while researching this guide. Jeff is a regular contributor to Costa Rica's English-language newspaper, *The Tico Times,* and has written for United Airlines' in-flight magazine, *Hemispheres.* He has contributed to Fodor's guides to Guatemala, Honduras, Panama, Chile, Argentina, Peru, Los Cabos & Baja, Cancun & the Riviera Maya, Mexico, Cuba, and Central and South America. For all the fun and exciting travel around Latin America that the guidebook work offers, he always appreciates coming back home to Costa Rica. He updated Experience Costa Rica, Biodiversity, San José, The Central Valley, Tortuguero and the Caribbean Coast, and Travel Smart.

Rachel White is a wanderer and writer chasing the sun from Michigan to Costa Rica. In between, she ushers her four children to as many other countries as she can. She is a contributor to Fodor's *Belize, Michigan HOME & Lifestyle,* and *parent.com.* Rachel updated the Guanacaste, Nicoya Peninsula, Manuel Antonio, Arenal, and Osa Peninsula chapters this edition.